Blumenfeld's
DICTIONARY
OF MUSICAL
THEATER

Blumenfeld's
DICTIONARY
OF MUSICAL
THEATER

OPERA, OPERETTA, MUSICAL COMEDY

ROBERT BLUMENFELD

AN IMPRINT OF HAL LEONARD CORPORATION
NEW YORK

Published in 2010 by Limelight Editions
An Imprint of Hal Leonard Corporation
7777 West Bluemound Road
Milwaukee, WI 53213

Trade Book Division Editorial Offices
19 West 21st Street, New York, NY 10010

Printed in the United States of America

Book design by UB Communications

Library of Congress Cataloging-in-Publication Data

Blumenfeld, Robert.
  Blumenfeld's dictionary of musical theater : opera, operetta, musical comedy / Robert Blumenfeld.
      p. cm.
  Includes bibliographical references and index.
  ISBN 978-0-87910-372-9
  1. Musical theater—Dictionaries. I. Title.
  ML102.M875B58 2010
  792.503—dc22
                                                2010004978

www.limelighteditions.com

To Jay Lesenger, Artistic/General Director, Chautauqua Opera;
the Staff;
my fellow Guest Artists;
and the inspiring Young Artists of the 2008
Chautauqua Opera season

Contents

Preface

What Is Musical Theater?

From their inception, theater and music have been inseparable, all over the world. Theater itself seems to have originated in religious rites and rituals, which included chanting and dance as expressions of awe and worship.

We don't really know much about performance practice in antiquity. But in Europe, music is supposed to have been an integral part of theatrical performance beginning with the ancient Greek practices of singing verse and accompanying plays with incidental music. Several ancient writers tell us that at the first Dionysia, the ancient Athenian theater festival in honor of the god Dionysus, Thespis sang his own dithyrambs with answering choral refrains. That is why he is considered the first actor: he dared to step out of the chorus to respond to it as an individual.

Dance and dance-like movement were important in stage presentations: Each kind of play had a characteristic dance, and the Chorus would have moved in rhythmic, ritualized unison, chanting at the same time: some dances were solemn and stately, some were more pantomime than dance, and some dances involved lewd miming with phallic props, as in Aristophanes' *Lysistrata*. But usually, Greek dances were done from the waist up, with standardized movements of the arms and feet, and the pelvis area as still as possible.

Most music in the theater was unaccompanied vocal melody that followed closely the rhythm and pitch accents of the verse. The Chorus sang in unison, or in octaves. There was also instrumental accompaniment as incidental music to both tragedies and comedies. It is conjectured that the authors of plays were also the composers of music for their own works.

In ancient Rome, too, music and dance were an integral part of theatrical presentations, as they continued to be in the medieval theater, which evolved from the church liturgy into secular forms. During the Renaissance, it was usual to include interpolated songs in plays, as we see in Shakespeare, and there were masques and other staged musical court entertainments throughout Europe. The late sixteenth century also saw the invention of ballet and opera, which were redefined and expanded as the centuries passed. Light opera—opera's sibling—evolved and existed alongside it.

The musical theater, the lyric theater, the lyric drama—they are all phrases for the same phenomenon. Simply defined, musical theater is drama, tragedy, or comedy with music as one of its essential, indispensable components. In the eighteenth and throughout much of the nineteenth centuries, opera was the popular music of its day. Alongside serious dramatic pieces were operas in a satirical or comic vein, like Donizetti's *L'elisir d'amore* and many of Offenbach's witty pieces. But mid-twentieth century operatic music would become more inaccessible—that is, harder to listen to—and less interesting to the public at large.

Every major European city from the eighteenth through the twentieth centuries was also a creative center of musical theater. The epicenter shifted from Rome, Naples and Venice, to Paris, London, Berlin, or Vienna at various times in history. In the twentieth century, it was the turn of the new world, with its innovative jazz styles, and the epicenter was Broadway in New York. Alongside opera, more popular forms of musical theater had developed; the music itself was very accessible and melodious, easy to listen to, appealing, sentimental, and full of lively, catchy rhythms and tunes. French, Viennese, and Berlin operettas; London comic opera, which evolved from ballad opera; and Broadway musical comedies developed and flourished. They used all the available musical idioms. Some contemporary Broadway and West End musicals are rock extravaganzas that use the most up-to-date popular idioms to tell their stories. But to whatever genre they belong, musical theater pieces can be seen as being on a continuum from the popular to the so-called highbrow.

Meant as a supplement and companion to *Blumenfeld's Dictionary of Acting and Show Business* (Limelight, 2009), this dictionary includes information about all the various genres of musical theater; thumbnail plot summaries of many well known and some more obscure works; thumbnail biographies of composers and writers; and some dance, theatrical, singing, and music terminology. Some historical and foreign terms are also included, since the lyric theater has a centuries-long, international history.

Every culture has a vast musical theater literature: There are dozens of Hungarian operetta composers, whose works have never been heard outside Hungary; scores of zarzuela composers unknown outside the Hispanophone world; Chinese operas by the thousands; a host of contemporary European musicals; and a hundred 18th-c. Italian opera composers whose works are now forgotten. One of the aims of this book is to give a sense of how much there is to learn and to know. I hope it proves useful as a research tool for the theater and music lover, student, teacher, and professional, and enjoyable to those who wish to browse between its covers for nuggets of amusing information and for discoveries that might provide much listening pleasure.

Pronunciation Guide, Abbreviations, Symbols, and General Notes

Pronunciation Guide

Vowels, Semivowels, and Diphthongs

a: like the "a" in *that*.
ah: like the "a" in *father*.
aw: like the long vowel in *law*.
ay: like the diphthong "ay" in *say*.
é: like the French vowel in *café*.
ee: like the "ee" in *meet*.
eh: like the "e" in *met*.
I: like the diphthong "I" in *I'm*.
ih: like the "i" in *bit*.
o: like the short "o" in *hot*.
ö: like the German umlauted "o," as in the name *Goethe*.
oh: like the diphthong "o" in *home*.

oo: like the "oo" in *boot*.
oo: like the "oo" in *book*.
ow: like the diphthong "ow" in *cow*.
oy: like the diphthong "oy" in *boy*.
ü: the French "u," pronounced by protruding and rounding the lips, and saying "ee"; also, the German umlauted "u."
uh: like the "e" in *the*; schwa; or the "u" in *fun*.
w: as in *wet*.
y: like the "y" in *yet*.

Consonants

b: as in *bow*.
ch: as in *church*.
d: as in *dog*.
dg: as in *edge* or *just*.
f: as in *off*.
g: as in *go*.
[g]l as in the unique Italian sound in ***Pagliacci;*** the sound is formed by gliding the back of the tongue over a lightly pronounced "g" and pronouncing "l" immediately.

h: as in *hot*.
k: as in *king*.
kh: as in German *ach*.
kh: as in German *Ich*.
ks: as in *box*.
l: as in *look*.
m: as in *my*.
n: as in *no*.
n: the nasal final "n" as in French *enfant*.
ng: as in *sing*.

p: as in *pie.*

r: the English retroflex or Italian, Portuguese, Polish, Russian, or Spanish trilled "r." An italicized r in brackets—[*r*]—indicates an r-influenced vowel; or a very lightly pronounced "r."

r: the French or German uvular "r." An italicized *r* in brackets—[*r*]—indicates an *r*-influenced vowel; or a very lightly pronounced "*r.*"

s: as in *so.*

sh: as in *shoe.*

t: as in *tea.*

th: as in *the.*

th: as in *thin.*

ts: as in *sits.*

v: as in *very.*

z: as in *zoo.*

zh: like the "s" in *pleasure.*

Abbreviations

abbrev.	abbreviation; abbreviated		Hist.	historical
adj.	adjective		i.e.	that is [Latin: id est]
adv.	adverb		lit.	literally
b.	born		mezz.	mezzo-soprano
bar.	baritone		n.	noun
BCE	before the common era		n. pl.	plural noun
Brit.	British		p.	page
c.	century		perf.	performance; performances
ca.	circa [Latin: around]		pl.	plural
CE	common era		prep.	preposition
contr.	contralto		pron.	pronunciation
cf.	compare [Latin: confer]		sop.	soprano
c.-ten.	counter-tenor		syn.	synonym(s); synonymous
def.	definition			
e.g.	for example [Latin: exempli gratia]		ten.	tenor
esp.	especially		v.	verb
et al.	and others [Latin: et alii]		v. i.	intransitive verb
etc.	and so forth [Latin: et cetera]		v. t.	transitive verb
fig.	figuratively		vol.	volume
fr.	from			

Symbols and General Notes

:   a colon after a vowel means it is lengthened.

'   following a syllable in a pronunciation indicates that it is given secondary stress

( )   parentheses enclose pronunciations, translations, dates, and voice categories for operatic roles.

[ ]   brackets enclose etymological and other information.

A syllable in CAPITAL LETTERS in a pronunciation indicates that it is given primary stress.

A word in **boldface** within an entry is a cross-reference to another entry; or distinguishes members of a family, e.g., the **Strauss family**.

An opera, operetta or musical comedy that does not have its own entry, but is discussed under the entry for its composer, is cross-referenced to the composer; e.g., **Mireille** Opera by Charles **Gounod**; **Redhead** Broadway musical by Albert **Hague**.

The following alphabetical convention has been followed: For all languages, titles are listed alphabetically by their first important word. Any initial definite or indefinite article is placed afterwards, preceded by a comma; e.g., English: **Mikado, The**; **Tree Grows in Brooklyn, A**; French: **mascotte, La**; **Roi Carotte, Le**; **étoile, L'**; **Troyens, Les**; German: **Dreimädlerhaus, Das**; **Vampyr, Der**; **Dreigroschenoper, Die**; Italian: **barbiere di Siviglia, Il**; **traviata, La**; **nozze di Figaro, Le**; **elisir d'amore, L'**; **ballo in maschera, Un**; etc.

Native rules of capitalization for titles in foreign languages are followed.

All operas, operettas, and musical comedies that have their own entries will be found alphabetized under their original titles, and cross-referenced with their English titles; e.g., **Merry Wives of Windsor, The** Operas by Otto **Nicolai** and Carl Ditters von **Dittersdorf**. See LUSTIGEN WEIBER VON WINDSOR, DIE.

Definitions include parts of speech for individual words, but not for phrases, or for titles or names of individuals. Pronunciations of foreign words and names are included, with the exception of certain extremely well known names, e.g., Hans Christian **Andersen**; Ludwig van **Beethoven**; Victor **Hugo**.

Dates of birth and death have been included, where available.

The names of famous performers, directors, and choreographers are not included among the alphabetical entries, but information on many of these artists can be found in entries regarding projects with which they are associated; e.g., Ethel Merman in *Annie Get Your Gun* and other entries; Peter Pears in entries concerning the operas of Benjamin **Britten**; Harold Prince in *Cabaret* and other entries.

Acknowledgments

First of all, I wish to give a very special acknowledgement to my wonderful friend Christopher Buck, whose friendship over the many years we have known each other has meant so much. Among those very dear friends who have contributed directly and indirectly to this book are Albert S. Bennett; Michael Mendiola and Scot Anderson; Peter Subers and Rob Bauer; Tom and Virginia Smith; Robert Perillo; Alice Spivak; noted singer and actress Gail Nelson; Christopher Layton and Ronald Hornsby; François Roulmann; Matthew Deming and Andrew Gitzy; Ian Strasfogel; Gannon McHale; Nina Koenigsberg; sound engineer Mikhail Shirokov; author Bruce Pollock; composers Lance Horne, Jorge Martin, and Mel Marvin; classical singer Jesse Cromer; opera singer Laura Bohn; Gordon Ostrowski, Assistant Dean/Opera Producer of the Manhattan School of Music; Dona D. Vaughn, noted professional performer and director, and Artistic Director of Opera Programs and Director of Undergraduate Opera Theater at the Manhattan School of Music; Jorge Parodi, Coach and Music Director, Senior Opera Theater at the Manhattan School of Music; the students I coached at the Manhattan School of Music; those friends whom I had the great pleasure of working with and befriending at the Chautauqua Opera in 2008: noted coach and conductor John Keene, noted conductor Jerome Shannon; stage manager Laine Goerner; noted stage director and choreographer William Fabris, an expert in light opera; noted pianist and opera coach Miriam Charney; opera singers Carolyn Amaradio, Jacob Smith, Clayton Hilley, Stephen Brody, Brenda Harris, Richard Bernstein, Deborah Selig, Peter Kazaras, Liz Pojanowski, Michael Krzankowski, and Vira Slywotzky; and Chautauqua's artistic/general director, Jay Lesenger. And, as always, I express my gratitude and thanks for their love and support to my wonderful family, most especially to my father, Max David Blumenfeld (1911–1994) and to my mother, Ruth Blumenfeld; my brothers, Richard Blumenfeld and Donald Blumenfeld-Jones, and Donald's wife, my wonderful sister-in-law, Corbeau; my nephew Benjamin and my niece Rebecca; my uncle, my mother's brother, Sy Korn; and to my cousin, Jonathan Blumenfeld, distinguished oboist with the Philadelphia Orchestra, who has been very helpful indeed with advice on musical terminology.

Many thanks are owed to my very knowledgeable, conscientious and helpful copy editor, Michael Portantiere. I want to thank my publisher, John Cerullo; supervising editor Carol Flannery; and my erudite, empathetic editor, Jessica Burr, who have all been terrifically supportive and helpful throughout. Lastly, I owe an incalculable debt to all the authors of the books in the bibliography, and to all the people I have worked with as an actor or dialect coach in various musical theater venues. Any errors are entirely my responsibility.

The Dictionary of
Musical Theater

A

ABBA A 1970s Swedish rock band: Agnetha Fältskog (b. 1950) (ahy NEH tah FEHL sko:yuh), Benny Andersson (b. 1946) (BEH nee AHN dehrs so:n), Björn Ulvaeus (b. 1945) (BYÖRN *OOL* VEH: *oos'*), and Anni-Frid Lyngstad (b. 1945) (AH nee FRIH:D LÜNG stahd) composed their own hit songs, which were later used as the score for the long-running Broadway musical and film *Mamma Mia!* The name ABBA is an acronym formed from the first letters of the band members' first names.

Abbott, George (1887–1995) Famed American director, actor, producer, and musical book writer; co-author of the books for *On Your Toes* (1936), *A Tree Grows in Brooklyn* (1951), *The Pajama Game* (1954), *Damn Yankees* (1955), and *Flora, the Red Menace* (1965), all of which he directed. His career spanned eighty-four years, and included the staging of *The Boys from Syracuse* (1938), for which he also wrote the book; *Pal Joey* (1940); *On the Town* (1944); *Call Me Madam* (1950); *Wonderful Town* (1953); Bock and Harnick's *Fiorello* (1959), for which he co-wrote the book with Jerome **Weidman**; and *Once Upon a Mattress* (1959).

Abraham, Paul (1892–1960) [b. Ábrahám Pál] (POWL AH b*r*ah hahm) Hungarian composer of fourteen Viennese operettas. His three greatest hits, all later filmed, were the superbly vibrant, gorgeously melodic *Viktoria und ihr Husar* (Victoria and Her Hussar) (1930) (vihk TAW*R* ee ah *oo*nt ee[*r*] hoo SAH[*R*]); the effervescent *Die Blume von Hawaii* (The Flowers of Hawaii) (1931) (dee BLOO muh fuhn hah VAH ee), with its bright, American sound; and *Ball im Savoy* (Ball at the Savoy) (1932) (BAHL ihm zah VOY), all with libretti by Alfred **Grünwald** and Fritz **Löhner**. Abraham was also a conductor, notably at the Budapest Operetta Theater, and a prolific composer of film scores. His composing style was much influenced by American **jazz**, combined with old-fashioned waltz melodies. When the Nazis came to power, his life was in danger because he was Jewish. Eventually, he fled to the U.S., returning to Europe in the mid-1950s.

abstract movement In **dance**, steps and gestures expressive of a particular mood, or simply done as beautiful patterns without any particular situational or narrative objective.

a capella; a cappella (ah' kah PEHL lah) [Italian: in the manner of the chapel, or of chapel singing] Unaccompanied; singing without instrumental accompaniment.

accent *n., v.* —*n.* **1.** The strong beginning of a musical **beat**: the stress or emphasis on a note or pitch; hence, *accentuation*: the placing of the strong musical beats in a rhythmic phrase. **2.** A musical ornament, e.g., a grace note, which gives a note a brief stress. **3.** A pattern or model of the pronunciation of a language, associated with region, social class, and historical period. —*v. t.* **4.** To stress or emphasize a musical beat. **5.** To stress or emphasize a particular syllable when speaking.

accompanied recitative Sung dialogue in opera that is underscored with orchestration meant to enhance it and to create a desired atmospheric effect.

accompaniment *n.* Music performed as background support for a dance, or for a singer or singers: *piano accompaniment*; *orchestral accompaniment*; *choral accompaniment*. Accompaniment enhances and complements the vocal or instrumental line, and adds **texture** and depth.

accompanist *n.* An instrumentalist who *accompanies*, i.e., plays along with, singers or dancers, and provides background support during auditions, rehearsals, or performances.

acid rock A type of American music that originated in the hippie drug culture of the 1960s and 1970s; named for LSD, which was called "acid." It is characterized by distorted over-amplification and heavy textures. Acid rock was usually played with a light show, and the audiences, sometimes high on drugs, swayed and gyrated to its pulsing rhythms. Vestiges of it are seen in such musical comedies as *Hair* (1968).

Acis and Galatea (A sihs and ga' luh TEE ah) **1.** Myth from Ovid's *Metamorphoses*, used as the subject of at least ten operas, including those by Jean-Baptiste **Lully** (1686) and Franz Josef **Haydn** (1762). The nymph Galatea is in love with the shepherd Acis, who is pursued by the giant Polyphemus (po' lih FEE muhs), his jealous rival. Polyphemus crushes Acis, who is turned into a spring and is mourned by Galatea while the chorus celebrates his elevation to immortality.
2. A pastoral **masque**/opera/serenata in three acts by George Frideric **Handel**; libretto by John **Gay**, based on the myth, with material taken from poets Alexander Pope (1688–1744) and John Dryden (1631–1700); 1718–1721; first complete performance, an amateur presentation, London, King's Theatre, 1731. The masque was not originally staged, but was sung from a stage fully set with **pastoral** motifs, fountains, and grottos, in which were disposed the chorus in costumes and various attitudes.

acoustics *n.* **1.** The science of sound, studying its nature, production, perception, and effects. **2.** The art and science of arranging and controlling the sound environment in a theater or other space. **3.** The audibility, nature, and quality of sound in a theater or other space. Each space is acoustically unique — e.g., a large as opposed to a small auditorium, or a church as opposed to a theater, changes how the same piece performed in each such venue is heard. Hence, the adj. *acoustic*, pertaining to sound: *the acoustic qualities of a theater*, i.e., how vibrant the resonance is, and how well sound carries.

act music *Hist.* In the late 17th and early 18th centuries, a composition played during intermission or between the acts or scenes of an opera, **semi-opera**, or other musical theater piece. An *act tune* was played at the end of each act, except the last.

adagio (ah DAH dgoh) *n., adj., adv.* [Italian: slow and stately] —*n.* **1.** The movement of a symphony, concerto, etc., played at a slow tempo, often somewhat somber in nature; also, a slow, melancholy instrumental composition, e.g., the *Adagios* of **Albinoni**. **2.** A slow dance movement; e.g., in a ballet. **3.** The first part of a ballet class, in which balance, posture, line, and positions are studied and perfected, usually at the **barre**; followed by the **allegro** part of the class. —*adj., adv.* **4.** A performance mark: at a slow tempo.

Adam, Adolphe (1803–1856) (a DOLF a DAHN) Prolific French composer of ballets, including *Giselle* (1844) (zhee ZEHL) and *Le corsaire* (1856) (luh kawr SEH:R), and of many *opéras comiques*. His most important works for the musical theater were *Le postillon de Lonjumeau* and *Si j'étais roi* (If I Were King) (1851) (see zhé teh: RWAH)

Adami, Giuseppe (1878–1946) (dgoo ZEHP peh: ah DAH mee) Italian playwright and librettist; wrote texts for Puccini's *La rondine* (1917), *Il tabarro* (1918), and *Turandot* (1926), the latter co-written with Renato Simoni.

Adamo, Mark (b. 1962) American composer of choral works and operas, among them *Little Women* (1998) and *Lysistrata or The Nude Goddess* (2005).

Adams, John (b. 1947) Innovative minimalist American opera composer who chooses contemporary events as subjects for his works, e.g., *Nixon in China* (1987) and *The Death of Klinghoffer* (1991), both with libretti by Alice Goodman (b. 1958); and *Dr. Atomic* (2005), about the making of the atomic bomb.

Adams, Lee (b. 1924) and Charles Strouse (b. 1928) Songwriting team who collaborated on Broadway musicals, including *Bye Bye Birdie* (1960); *All American* (1962), with a book by Mel **Brooks**; and *Applause* (1970). Adams wrote the lyrics, while Strouse wrote the music. Strouse is also noted as the composer of *Annie* (1977), with lyrics by Martin Charnin and a book by Thomas **Meehan**.

adaptation *n.* A musical comedy, opera, operetta, stage play, or screenplay taken from an existing source, e.g., a novel adapted for the stage or screen, such as Victor Hugo's *Les Misérables* or Sir Walter Scott's *Ivanhoe*.

added number An interpolated song or aria in a musical theater piece, e.g., the numbers done by party guests in act 2 of some productions of *Die Fledermaus*.

Adler, Richard (b. 1921) Popular American composer; collaborated with lyricist Jerry **Ross** on the successful Broadway musicals *The Pajama Game* (1954) and *Damn Yankees* (1955), co-written with George **Abbott**.

ad lib; adlib *n., v.* [Latin: *ad libitum* (ad LIH bih toom); at will] —*n.* **1.** In acting, a spontaneously improvised line or lines, or bit of stage business. **2.** In music, an improvisation built on an extant piece, e.g., a variation on a theme; a jazz **riff**. — *v. it.* **3.** To make an off-the-cuff remark or to improvise business. **4.** In music, to **vamp**; to improvise on a theme, add ornamentation, or otherwise alter musical material.

Adonis Broadway musical comedy, billed as a "burlesque nightmare"; music adapted from hit songs of the day; book by William F. Gill and Edward E. **Rice**; Bijou Theatre,1884 (603 perf.).

Talamea, a sculptress, falls in love with a statue of Adonis, who is brought to life by a goddess. Adonis becomes a playboy, but, disillusioned by humankind, begs to be restored to his original stone state.

Adriana Lecouvreur (ah' dree AH nah luh koo VRUHR) A **verismo** opera in four acts by Francesco **Cilea**; libretto by Italian nationalist Arturo Colautti (1851–1914) (ahr TOO ro: ko LOWT tee), based on a play by Eugène **Scribe** and Ernest Legouvé (1764–1812) (luh goo VÉ), drawn from the life of the 18th-century French actress Adrienne Lecouvreur (1692–1730); Teatro Lirico (teh: AH tro: LEE ree ko:), Milan, 1904.

Adriana (sop.) and the Princess Bouillon (boo YOH*N*) (mezz.) are both in love with Maurice de Saxe (mo *r*ees' duh SAHKS) (ten.) [Maurizio (mow REE tsee o:)]. The princess sends Adriana a bouquet of poisoned violets. She inhales their perfume, and dies.

afterpiece *n.* A short musical or spoken play that concludes a musical theater evening, e.g., the one-act comic operas often presented after **Gilbert and Sullivan** full-length perf. during their original runs. Their one-act operetta, ***Trial by Jury***, was originally an afterpiece that producer Richard D'Oyly Carte commissioned for the 1875 run of Offenbach's ***La Périchole***.

Africaine, L' (The African Woman) (lah f*r*ee KEH:N) [often sung in Italian as *L'Africana* (lah free KAH nah]. **Grand opera** in five acts by Giacomo **Meyerbeer**; libretto by Eugène **Scribe**; Paris Opéra, 1865.

The explorer Vasco da Gama (ten.) suffers shipwreck on the African coast. He falls in love with Selika (seh LEE kah) (mezz.), whom he takes back to Portugal along with his captive, Nelusko (neh L*OO*S ko:) (bar.). After a series of complicated plot developments, Selika sacrifices her life so that Vasco can marry Inez (ee NEHZ) (sop.), his first love.

Ahrens, Lynn American lyricist. See FLAHERTY, STEPHEN.

Aida (ah EE dah) **1.** Opera in three acts by Giuseppe **Verdi**; libretto by Antonio **Ghislanzoni**; Egypt, Cairo Opera House, 1871.

In ancient Memphis, Amneris (ahm NEH: rees) (mezz.), daughter of the Pharaoh of Egypt (bass), is betrothed to Radamès (rah' dah MEH:S) (ten.), general of the Egyptian armies. He is in love with her Ethiopian slave, Aida (sop.). Unknown to Radamès and Amneris, Aida is the daughter of King Amonasro (ah' mo: NAH sro:) (bar.), who, captured in battle, reveals that he is her father, but conceals his identity as king. During a tryst with Radamès, Aida coaxes the general to reveal secrets that Amonasro, concealed, overhears. All three are on the point of making good their escape when they are surprised by Amneris and the High Priest, Ramfis (RAHM fees) (bass), who have followed them. Radamès is arrested, but Aida and Amonasro escape. The general is condemned to death for high treason. Amneris offers to have the sentence rescinded if he will marry her, but he refuses. He descends into his tomb, which is then sealed, and discovers that Aida has hidden there. She will join him in death.

2. Broadway musical with the same plot as the opera; music by Elton **John**, lyrics by Tim **Rice**, and book by David Henry **Hwang**, Linda Woolverton, and the show's director, Robert Falls; Palace Theatre, 2000 (1852 perf.).

3. Broadway musical, *My Darlin' Aida*, using Verdi's music; book by Charles Friedman, which changed the setting to a plantation near Memphis, TN, in the first year of the American Civil War (1861); Winter Garden Theatre, 1952 (89 perf.). Aida retained her name, but some of the other characters' names were changed: Amneris became Jessica Farrow, Radamès was renamed Ray Darrow, and Pharaoh became General Farrow, owner of the plantation.

Ain't Misbehavin' Off-Broadway musical revue conceived and directed by Richard Maltby, Jr. (b. 1937); moved to Broadway: Longacre Theatre, 1978, (1618 perf.); Broadway revival: Ambassador Theatre, 1988 (184 perf.). A highly entertaining retrospective of the music of Thomas "Fats" Waller (1904–1943).

air *n.* **1.** A melody; a tune. **2.** An **aria**.
See also ARIOSO.

air dancing Performing dance steps and using gestures while suspended on cables or wires above the stage; the cables are operated by technicians; the semi-transparent wires are concealed as much as possible, and worn attached to a hidden harness; used in certain ballets or musicals, e.g., *Billy Elliot*; similar to **wire flying**.

A Kékszekállú herceg vára (Duke Bluebeard's Castle) (AH KEH:K seh' kah:' loo:' HEHR tsehg' VAH: rah') Opera in one act by celebrated Hungarian composer and ethnomusicologist Béla Bartók (1851–1945) (BEH: lah' BAHR tok'); libretto by Béla Balázs (1884–1949) (BAH lah:z'); Budapest Opera House, 1918.

The score is known for its rich, evocative, explosive, and exciting orchestration, and its compelling sensuality.

Bluebeard (bass) longs for love. His new wife, Judith (sop.), whom he brings home to his windowless castle, wants to satisfy her curiosity, and demands the keys to the castle's seven doors. Bluebeard hands them to her. When she opens them, she discovers a torture chamber, an armory, a treasury, a rose garden, a vision of the duke's estates, and a lake of tears. Blood tinges all of them, and behind the seventh door, she discovers Bluebeard's other wives, who had also been curious. She must join them, and Bluebeard is once again left to his sad musings on life and love.

Akhnaten (ahk NAH tehn) Opera in three acts by Philip **Glass**; libretto by the composer, based on a text by writer and professor Shalom Goldman; Stuttgart Staatsoper (SHTOOT gah[r]t SHTAHTS O: puh), 1984.

Akhnaten (c.-ten.) is so in love with his wife Nefertiti (neh' fuhr TEE tee) (contr.) that he institutes monogamy, and gives up his polygamous lifestyle. He also builds a temple to the new god, Aten (AH tehn). But his rule is disastrous, he and his family are destroyed, and the old customs are reinstituted.

Albert, Eugen d' (1864–1932) (OY gehn DAHL beh*r*t) German pianist and innovative late-romantic opera composer. He is best known now for his powerful verismo opera *Tiefland*.

Albert Herring Opera in three acts by Benjamin **Britten**; libretto by stage director and writer Eric Crozier (1914–1994), based on a short story by French writer Guy de Maupassant (1850–1893) (gee' duh mo: pah SAH*N*); Glyndebourne, 1947.

The villagers in a Suffolk town find themselves unable to choose a proper, virtuous young lady to be May Queen. Instead, they choose young Albert Herring (ten.), who spends his prize money on licentiousness and debauchery, much to their chagrin. But in doing so, he frees himself from the domination of his tyrannical mother (mezz.).

Albinoni, Tomaso Giovanni (1671–1751) (to: MAH zo: dgo: VAHN nee ahl bih: NO: nee) Italian composer resident in Venice; best known now for his *Adagios*, oboe concerti, and other instrumental works; composed more that fifty full-length operas. His operas include a setting of Metastasio's *Didone abbandonata* (1725).

Alceste (ahl SEHST) **1.** Opera in a prologue and five acts by Jean-Baptiste **Lully**; libretto by Philippe **Quinault**, based on ancient Greek writer Euripides' play *Alkestis* (ahl KEHS tees); Paris Opéra, 1674.

Gravely ill, King Admetus (ad MEE tuhs) (ten.) is doomed by the Apollonian oracle to die unless someone takes his place. His wife, Alceste (sop.), volunteers and is sent to Hades. Admetus recovers and cannot bear to live without her. Alcide (ahl SEED) (bar.) [Hercules] rescues her from the underworld.
2. Opera in three acts by Christoph Willibald Ritter von **Gluck**; libretto by writer and prolific librettist, Ranieri de' Calzabigi (1714–1795) (rah NYEH: ree de: kahl' tsah BEE dgee); Vienna, Burgtheater (BOO[*R*]K teh: AH tuh), 1767, revised 1776.

The preface to Alceste sets forth Gluck's philosophy that opera is true drama set to music: singers must act their roles, and not just stand about in costume.

The plot is the same as the Lully piece, with the additional episodes of Apollo (ten.) decreeing that Hercules (bar.) is a god because of his good actions in defying Pluto, and Admetus (ten.) and Alceste (sop.) being declared the perfect example of conjugal love.

Alcina (ahl CHEE nah) Opera in three acts by George Frideric **Handel**; libretto by Antonio Marchi (16?–1725) (MAHR kee), based on Ariosto's *Orlando Furioso* (ah' ree O: sto:) (o:r LAHN do foo' ree O: zo:); London, Covent Garden, 1735.

Alcina (sop.), a sorceress and ruler of an enchanted isle, rejects all suitors, and turns them into strange, abject creatures, except for Ruggiero (roo DGEH: ro:) (c.-ten.), with whom she is besotted. He has forgotten his betrothed, Bradamante (brah' dah MAHN teh:) (mezz.), who travels to seek him out, disguised as her brother, and suffers shipwreck on the isle, together with her guardian, Melisso (meh LIH:S so:) (bass). Ruggiero and Bradamante are reunited when Alcina's magic powers are destroyed. All her suitors are restored to human form.

alegrias (ah' leh GREE ahs) *n.* [Spanish: merry, agreeable, light-hearted things] Elegant, basic **flamenco** dance, with the torso held still, and featuring elaborate arm movements and flourishes; a dance in 3/4 or 6/8 tempo.

Alessandro Stradella (ah' lehs SAHN dro: strah DEHL lah) Opera in three acts by Friedrich von **Flotow**; libretto by "Wilhelm Friedrich" [Pen name of Friedrich Wilhelm Riese (*R*EE zeh) (1805–1879), German writer and translator of more than 100 Italian, French, and English plays]; Hamburg Stadttheater (SHTAHT teh: AH tuh), 1844.

The very pretty but little known score is full of lilting, romantic melodies and exciting dance music. Here is an opera worth reviving!

Alessandro Stradella (ten.) is a brilliant composer, and a rash, headstrong roisterer. He has the temerity to kidnap Leonore (leh:' o: NO: reh) (sop.) at the Venetian carnival and take her to Rome, where he is pursued by Barbarino (bahr' bah REE no:) (ten.) and Malvolino (mahl' vo: LEE no:) (bass), assassins hired by her guardian, Bassi (BAHS see) (bass). But everyone is so captivated by Stradella's music, which even the hardened murderers cannot resist, that all ends happily in love and rejoicing.

Alfano, Franco (1875–1954) (FRAH*N* ko ahl FAH no:) Italian opera composer and librettist, best known for having completed Puccini's *Turandot* after the composer's death.

See also CYRANO DE BERGERAC.

alignment *n.* **1.** In singing, the correct positioning of the body and the musculature in a relaxed, balanced posture that permits optimal airflow. See also NOBLE POSITION. **2.** In dancing, the correct positioning, posture, and stance of the body and limbs, allowing optimal freedom of movement without strain.

allegro (ahl LEH gro:) *n., adj., adv.,* [Italian: gay; ebullient; joyous; merry] —*n.* **1.** The fast movement of a symphony, concerto, etc.; usually the first movement. **2.** A fast combination of rapid dance steps, or a rapid dance movement in a ballet. **3.** The second part of a ballet class, after the **adagio**: away from the **barre**, combinations of steps, often fast and lively, are done to help develop coordination, style, and balance. —*adj., adv.* **4.** A performance mark: with a fast, lively rhythm, briskly, and in happy spirits.

Allegro Broadway musical by **Rodgers and Hammerstein**: Richard **Rodgers** (music) and Oscar **Hammerstein** (book and lyrics); Majestic Theatre, 1947 (315 perf.).

Hammerstein's own original story concerns a small-town doctor, Joe Taylor, Jr., who moves to Chicago with his wife Jennie, and develops a successful practice. She is unhappy and bored. While pushing her husband to advance in his career, she has a series of love affairs. Joe knows nothing of this, but when he learns the truth, he decides to leave her and return to his hometown, accompanied by his faithful nurse, Emily, who has been in love with him all the time.

allemande (ah luh MAH*N*D) *n*. [French n., adj.: German (feminine gender)] A dance that is presumably of German origin; popular esp. in the 18th c. as a term for a dance in 3/4 time in which couples holding each other closely did a series of turns. The term is also applied to a Renaissance processional dance, and to a movement of a baroque instrumental dance suite.

allestimento (ahl lehs' tee MEHN toh) *n*. [Italian: treatment] The plan of a new opera production.

allusion *n*. An incidental, passing reference to a work of art, person, place, etc. In an opening night review of the operetta *The Nautch Girl* (1892) by Edward **Solomon**, in which the composer had introduced themes from **Handel** in what was meant to be a witty way, George Bernard **Shaw** said that he ought to have had more respect for his own music than to remind people of Handel's whilst it was proceeding.

See also QUOTATION.

alto *n*. The lowest-pitched female singing voice, short for contralto; and the highest-pitched male voice, called a countertenor. There are also boy altos.

Amahl and the Night Visitors A Christmas opera in one act, written for television by Gian-Carlo **Menotti**; libretto by the composer; produced by NBC in 1951; it has since been produced on stage.

The three Magi (ten.; bar.; bass), on their way to see the newborn Jesus, stop at the hut of the crippled boy, Amahl (treble), and his mother (mezz.). She steals some of their gold as they are sleeping, and, when she is caught, tells them that she could not resist the temptation and wanted it for her son. The Magi allow her to keep it, since Christ is love and redemption. Amahl offers to give the infant Jesus his crutch. Suddenly, he can walk, and his mother allows him to leave with the Magi on their journey.

amor coniugale, L' (Conjugal Love) Opera by Johann Simon **Mayr**. See FIDELIO.

amore dei tre re, L' (The Love of Three Kings) (lah MO: re: de:ee TREH: REH:) Opera in three acts by Italo **Montemezzi**; libretto by Sem Benelli (1877–1949) (SEHM beh NEHL lee), based on his own play set in medieval Italy; Teatro alla Scala (teh: AH tro: ahl lah SKAH lah), Milan, 1913.

This is considered one of the great masterpieces of early 20th-c. opera, with its dramatic, brilliantly orchestrated score. Montemezzi himself conducted the opera in a 1941 recording, available on CD from Eklipse (EKR CD 9; 1992).

Princess Fiora (FYO: rah) (sop.) has been coerced into marrying Manfredo (mahn' FREH: do:) (bar.), son of blind King Archibaldo (ahr' kee BAHL do:) (bass), but she is in love with Avito (ah VEE to:) (ten.), her former fiancé. Archibaldo knows she has a lover, but does not know who, and he strangles Fiora when she refuses to tell him. He then smears her lips with poison in order to trap

10

her lover, and Avito, kissing her, dies. Manfredo, who adores her, commits suicide by kissing her. The blind old king is bereft of all he held dear.

amplification *n.* The enhancement and magnification of sound by means of mechanical equipment, e.g., a microphone plugged into an amplifier and loud-speakers. Wearing personal head or body mikes in Broadway musicals is now almost universal, whereas in the old days, singers and actors relied on their own lung power and **vocal technique**. Body mikes and head mikes are either wireless, or attached by a wire that runs from the microphone to a transmitting device or battery pack, which sends signals through a central amplifier. In most Off-Broadway or other small theaters, as well as in opera houses, actors and singers continue to rely on good projection and diction. General area miking is sometimes used; i.e., the strategic placement of microphones on a set, at the rim of the stage apron, etc.

anchoring *n.* The secure technical connection between the voice and the body, which should have a perfect **alignment** or posture so as to permit optimal airflow in vocal production, as a result of good training.

Andersen, Hans Christian (1805–1875) Danish author known for his fairy tales, many of which were adapted for operas and musicals, e.g., *Once Upon a Mattress*; *The Little Mermaid*; *Le jardin du paradis* by Alfred **Bruneau**. Andersen also wrote several opera libretti, including one adapted from Sir Walter Scott's *The Bride of Lammermoor*, years before Donizetti's *Lucia di Lammermoor*.

Anderson, Maxwell (1888–1959) American playwright known for his historical verse dramas; author of several musical comedy books, notably *Knickerbocker Holiday* and *Lost in the Stars*, both with music by Kurt **Weill**.

Andrea Chénier (ahn DREH: ah shé: NYEH:) Opera in four acts by Umberto **Giordano**; libretto by Luigi **Illica**; Teatro alla Scala, Milan, 1896.
   The plot is based on the life of the French Revolutionary poet André Chénier (1762–1794), and his love for the aristocrat Madeleine de Coigny (mah duh lehn' duh cwah NYEE). They are denounced by her former servant, Gérard (zhé *RAHR*) (bar.), now a revolutionary leader, who is in love with her. To save the poet's life, Madeleine (sop.) [Maddalena (mah dah LEH: nah)] offers herself to Gérard, but Chénier (ten.) is condemned to death, and she goes to the guillotine with him.

Anelli, Angelo (1761–1820) (ah NEH:L lee) Prolific Italian librettist who pro-vided the texts for operas by **Cimarosa**, **Mayr**, **Pacini**, and, notably, for Rossini's *L'italiana in Algeri*, and *Ser Marcantonio* by Stefano **Pavesi**.

anglaise (ah*n* GLEHZ) *n.* [French n., adj.: Englishwoman; English (feminine gender)] **1.** The French term for an 18th c. English **contredanse** in which couples lined up in rows facing each other, as opposed to the French contredanse, in which the couples were in a circle. **2.** Any English dance, or dance of English origin.

anima del filosofo, L' (**The Philosopher's Soul**) Original title for *Orfeo ed Euridice*, Franz Joseph Haydn's last, unfinished opera.

Anna Bolena (AHN nah bo: LEH: nah) Opera in two acts by Gaetano **Donizetti**; libretto by Felice **Romani**; Teatro Carcano (kahr KAH no:), Milan, 1830.

The story is based on the life of King Henry the Eighth's (1491–1547) (bass) second wife, Anne Boleyn (1501/07–1536) (sop.), at the point where Henry has fallen in love with Jane Seymour (1508–1537) (mezz.). Anne is tried for adultery and condemned to death.

Annie Broadway musical by Charles **Strouse**; lyrics by Martin Charnin; book by Thomas **Meehan**, based on the characters in Harold Gray's (1894–1968) comic strip "Little Orphan Annie"; Alvin Theatre, 1977 (2377 perf.); Broadway revival, Martin Beck Theatre, 1997 (253 perf.).

During the Great Depression, millionaire Daddy Warbucks is looking for a poor waif on whom to bestow a Christmas treat. He finds Little Orphan Annie and invites her to spend the holiday season at his mansion, to the chagrin of the surly Miss Hannigan, head of the orphanage. Annie is looking for her real parents, and Miss Hannigan's brother and his girlfriend masquerade as Annie's mother and father. Their con game is exposed, Annie's parents turn out to be dead, and Daddy Warbucks adopts Annie and her dog Sandy.

Annie Get Your Gun Broadway musical comedy by Irving **Berlin**; book and lyrics by Dorothy **Fields**, based loosely on the life of sharpshooter Annie Oakley (1860–1926); Imperial Theatre, 1946 (1147 perf.); Broadway revivals: Broadway Theatre, 1966 (78 perf.); Marquis Theatre, 1999 (1080 perf.); innumerable summer revivals; film, 1950.

The role of Annie was created by the exuberant, brassy-voiced Ethel Merman (1909–1984), who also starred in the 1966 revival.

Annie is a brilliant sharpshooter who starts out as a rough hillbilly, but develops into a sophisticated young woman. Her rival is Frank Butler, principal sharpshooter of Buffalo Bill's Wild West Show. She falls in love with him when she joins the show. On the sage advice of Sitting Bull, one of the stars of the show, she lets Frank win a shooting match, and their romance is assured.

Anseaume, Louis (1721?–1784?) (loo EE ah*n* SO:M) French librettist who provided texts for many composers, among them **Philidor** and **Grétry**; author of more than thirty **opéra comique** libretti; held managerial positions in Paris at the Opéra-Comique theater. His libretti represented a departure from the prevailing artificial style and were written in more realistic terms, with actions to be played by the performers; he also introduced ensemble pieces in which the characters expressed their individual, conflicting feelings.

Antheil, George (1900–1959) American pianist and composer, known for his *Ballet Mécanique* (bah LEH: mé kah NEEK) (1924), originally meant as a film score and later performed as a concert piece; and for the theme music to the CBS television show *The 20th Century* (1957–1970). His operas include *Transatlantic*

(1930), for which he also wrote the libretto; and *Volpone* (1953), with a libretto by Alfred Perry, based on the play by Ben Jonson (1532–1637).

anthem *n.* A sacred song, often with biblical words, similar to a **hymn**; by extension, an inspirational song meant to arouse emotion, as in national songs identified with a particular country, or such numbers as "It Was Good Enough for Grandma (But Not Good Enough for Me)" from ***Bloomer Girl***, "Climb Ev'ry Mountain" from ***The Sound of Music***, "You'll Never Walk Alone" from ***Carousel***.

antiphony *n.* Singing by two groups, or individual performers, who alternate, or sing in opposition to each other. Hence, the adj. *antiphonal*: pertaining to singing in which two groups or performers alternate.

Antony and Cleopatra Opera in three acts by Samuel **Barber**; libretto by Franco **Zeffirelli**, revised by Gian-Carlo **Menotti**, based on Shakespeare's play; Metropolitan Opera, New York, 1966.
　　The Roman general Mark Antony (bass-bar.) is passionately in love with the Egyptian queen Cleopatra (sop.), but he is forced to abandon her and marry Octavia (sop.), sister of the emperor Augustus (ten.). Mark Antony goes back to Cleopatra, whereupon Augustus launches a war against them. Antony and Cleopatra both commit suicide.

anvil *n.* A musical instrument that imitates a blacksmith's metal-forging table and hammer, themselves sometimes used as a musical instrument: the most famous examples are in ***Il trovatore***, with its celebrated "Anvil Chorus," sung by the gypsies; the **Ring cycle** opera *Das Rheingold*, in which eighteen anvils are used; and *Siegfried*, in which an anvil on stage is part of the scene. The percussion instrument consists of a metal bar that is struck with a mallet.

Anything Goes Broadway musical with music and lyrics by Cole **Porter**; book by playwriting team **Lindsay and Crouse**: Howard Lindsay, who also directed, and Russel Crouse, revised from an earlier script by P. G. **Wodehouse** and Guy **Bolton**; Alvin Theatre, 1934 (420 perf.); Off- Broadway revival, 1962 (239 perf., with interpolated numbers from other Porter hits); Lincoln Center revival, Vivian Beaumont Theatre, 1987 (784 perf.), directed by Jerry Zaks (b. 1946); many summer perf.; film, 1936, featuring Ethel Merman reprising her role as Reno, but without the full Cole Porter score.
　　This brilliant piece is vintage Porter. Among its hit numbers are "I Get a Kick Out of You," sung by Reno, first to Billy, and then to Evelyn, when she realizes he is the one; "You're the Top"; and the title song.
　　Billy Crocker has stowed away on an ocean liner carrying his beloved Hope Harcourt to Europe. Nightclub singer Reno Sweeney is sailing as well, and she is enamored of Billy. Hope's mother wants her to marry Lord Evelyn Oakleigh, but Billy and Hope end up together, and Reno and Evelyn fall in love with each other.

apache (ah PAHSH) *n.* [Fr. the French gang called the Apaches, after the Native American nation] An early 20th-c. Parisian **music hall** and **revue** dance, characterized by brutal sexuality and violent movement in fast, lively rhythms; done by a couple in which a macho man treats his underdressed female partner with simulated violence. It originated at the famous Moulin Rouge cabaret, and later became a ballroom dance, with its violence toned down.

Applause Broadway musical by Charles **Strouse**, with dance and incidental arrangements by Mel **Marvin**; book by **Comden and Green**, based on the film *All About Eve* (1950); lyrics by Lee **Adams**; Palace Theatre, 1970 (900 perf.).

As in the film, the conniving Eve Harrington worms her way into the life of star actress Margo Channing—the Bette Davis (1908–1989) role, created in the musical by film star Lauren Bacall (b. 1924)—and takes over, eventually clawing her way to the top and becoming a star herself.

appoggiatura (ahp' po:' dgah TOO rah) *n.* [Italian: something appended; something leaning against something else] **1.** A dissonant note above or below an accented note, which resolves to the correct pitch. **2.** An ornamental, i.e., grace note that occurs on the beat, temporarily replaces the main note, and then resolves to it.

appoggio (ahp PO: dgo:) *n.* [Italian: lean; support; posture] The system of muscular breath support used during singing, allowing the singer to control breathing and the flow of air from the lungs through the larynx to the resonators; the muscular balance necessary in controlling the intake and exhalation of the breath, involving the diaphragm and the abdominal and thoracic musculature. This international system of breath support is superbly described and elucidated by Richard Miller in his magisterial *Solutions for Singers: Tools for Performers and Teachers* (Oxford University Press, 2004) Cf. its opposite, **belly breathing**.

Arabella (ah' rah BEHL lah) Opera in three acts by Richard **Strauss**; libretto by Hugo von **Hofmannsthal**; Dresden Staatsoper, 1933.

The debt-ridden Graf Walder (G*R*AHF VAHL duh) (bass) [Graf: Count] seeks a rich husband for his daughter, Arabella (sop.). After romantic complications involving the officer Matteo (mah TEH: o:) (ten.), who is in love with her, but whom she rejects, Arabella eventually accepts Mandryka (mahn D*R*EE kah) (bar.), who has offered to pay her father's debts. Matteo is happy to transfer his love to her younger sister, Zdenka (ZDEHN kah) (sop.).

arabesque (a' ruh BEHSK) *n.* **1.** A fundamental ballet position in which the dancer balances on one leg while the other is stretched out behind, balanced by any number of graceful positions of the arm. **2.** In music, florid **ornamentation**; e.g., in passages that contain variations on a theme.

Arcadians, The A "Fantastic Musical Play" in three acts, with music by Lionel **Monckton** and Howard **Talbot**; libretto by Mark Ambient (1860–19?) [b. Howard Harley], A. M. Thompson (1861–1948), and Robert Courtneidge (1859–1939); lyrics by Arthur Wimperis (1874–1953); London, Shaftesbury Theatre, 1909 (809 perf.); New York, Liberty Theatre, 1910 (201 perf.).

The Arcadians, who live in the remote land of the lotus-eaters, have heard of a strange place called England. Father Time arranges for some of them to be transported in time and space to that Edwardian country through the good offices of James Smith, owner of a catering company. Eventually, the Arcadians hear the pipes of Pan calling, and return home.

Arditi, Luigi (1822–1903) (loo EE dgee ahr DEE tee) Italian conductor, violinist, and composer; lived in London for eleven years, where he conducted many opera premieres by **Verdi**, **Wagner**, **Mascagni**, and others; composed four operas, and many songs, including the famous, much recorded waltz song, *Il bacio* (The Kiss) (1864) (ih:l BAH cho:), which the celebrated Italian sop. Adelina Patti (1843–1919) (a deh LEE nah PAHT tee) used to interpolate in the Lesson Scene in *Il barbiere de Siviglia*; her 1905 recording of it is available on *The Complete Adelina Patti and Victor Maurel* (Marston CD 52011-2; 1998). Maurel (1848–1923) (mo: REHL) was an important French bar. who created Iago in *Otello* and the title role in *Falstaff* for **Verdi**; he can be heard in this album singing excerpts from them. Arditi wrote *My Reminiscences* (1896), memoirs detailing 19th-c. musical life.

Argento, Dominick (b. 1927) American opera composer, known for his combination of tonal, atonal, and twelve-tone music. His notable works include *The Boor* (1957), based on Chekhov's one-act farce, *The Masque of Angels* (1964), and *Miss Havisham's Fire* (1977), all with libretti by opera director John Olon-Scrymgeour; *Postcard from Morocco* (1971), with a libretto by John Donahue, after Robert Louis Stevenson's *A Child's Garden of Verses*; and *The Aspern Papers* (1987), with his own libretto adapted from Henry James's novel.

aria (AH ree ah) *n.* [Italian: air] A melodic set piece in an **opera**, in the form of a **solo** song expressing the character's feelings.

The principal kinds of operatic arias:

1. *Aria buffa* (BOO fah): a comic aria, e.g., Leporello's "Catalogue aria" in Mozart's ***Don Giovanni***.
2. *Aria concertante* (kon' cheh:r TAHN teh:): a dramatic set piece often preceded by a long introduction, e.g., Constanze's "Marten aller Arten" (Martyrdom of All Kinds) (MAH[R] tehn AHL uh[r] AH[R] tehn) in Mozart's *Die Entführung aus dem Serail*.
3. *Aria d'entrata* (dehn TRAH tah): a character's entrance aria, such as Papageno's "Der Vogelfänger bin ich, ja" (I Am the Bird Catcher, Yes) (deh FO: guhl FEH:NG uh[r] BIH:N ih:*kh* YAH) in Mozart's ***Die Zauberflöte***.
4. *Aria di sortita* (dee so:r TEE tah): exit aria, i.e., the aria sung just before a character's exit.
5. *Aria di bravura* (dee brah VOO rah): a highly ornamented, difficult aria meant to show off a singer's voice, as in many **bel canto** operas. Similar are the *aria d'agilità* (aria of agility) (dah dgee' lee TAH), an aria with complicated ornamentation and variations; the *aria di **portamento*** (smoothly sung aria) (dee po:r' tah MEHN to:), an unornamented aria with a broad range; and the *aria **cantabile*** (beautifully sung aria), a sad aria with light ornamentation.

15

There are many other types of arias, including arias displaying a particular feeling, e.g., the *aria infuriata* (een foo' ree AH tah), *aria agitata* (ah' dgee TAH tah), *aria di lamento* (lah MEHN to:), and *aria sentimentale* (sehn' tee mehn TAH le:). In the *aria di imitazione* (ee' mee tah tsee O: neh:), singers and orchestra imitate natural sounds, such as birdsongs, often in alternation with each other. There are also dramatic, declamatory arias, called *aria parlante* (speaking aria) (pahr LAHN teh:), and *aria di declamazione* (deh' klah mah tsee O: neh:).

See also DA CAPO ARIA; DAL SEGNO ARIA; METAPHOR ARIA; MOTTO ARIA.

aria concertante; aria di concerto (kon chehr TAHN teh:) (dee kon CHEHR to:) [Italian: concertizing; for a concert] An aria written for the concert stage, rather than for an opera.

aria del sorbetto (dehl sawr BEH:T to:) [Italian: sorbet aria] An aria sung by a supporting character, during which, in the 19th c., audience members would often leave to get refreshments; e.g., the housekeeper Berta's (BEHR tah) (mezz.) aria in act 2 of *Il barbiere di Siviglia*.

aria di baule (dee BOW leh:) [Italian: trunk or suitcase aria] In the early 19th c., a famous singer's favorite aria, packed in a suitcase, so to speak, and taken out and inserted at a convenient point in any opera he or she happened to be singing.

aria di catàlogo (dee kah TAH lo: go:) [Italian: catalogue aria] An aria that lists names, things, etc., usually sung in a fairly rapid **patter**; e.g., Leporello's "Catalogue Aria" in Mozart's *Don Giovanni*.

aria di chiesa (dee KYEH: zah) [Italian: of the church] A church aria; i.e., one sung as part of a religious service.

aria di vendetta (dee vehn DEHT tah) [Italian: vengeance aria] In 18th- and 19th-c. opera, a standard kind of number in which the character, often a villainous one, vents his or her fury and informs the audience of the deadly desire for revenge; e.g., the Queen of the Night's, "Der Hölle Rache kocht in meinem Herzen" (Hellish Vengeance Boils in My Heart) (deh: HÖL leh *R*AH kheh KOKHT ihn MI nehm HEH[*R*] tsehn), from Mozart's *Die Zauberflöte*; Dr. Bartolo's "La vendetta" (Vengeance) (lah vehn DEHT tah), from Mozart's *Le nozze di Figaro*; Don Pizzaro's "Ha! Welch' ein Augenblick" (Hah! What a Moment!) (HAH vel*kh* In OW gehn BLIH:K), from Beethoven's *Fidelio*.

Ariane et Barbe-bleue (Ariane and Bluebeard) (ah' *r*ee AHN eh: bah*r*' buh BL*OO*) Opera in three acts by Paul Dukas (1865–1935) (po:l dü KAH); libretto by Maurice **Maeterlinck**; Paris, Théâtre de l'Opéra-Comique (teh: AH t*r*uh duh lo pé *r*ah ko: MEEK), 1907.

The lush score to Dukas' only opera is involving, haunting, and almost otherworldly in its impressionistic romanticism.

Bluebeard's (bar.) sixth wife, Ariane (mezz.), wanting to discover the secret of what has happened to his other five wives, demands that he give her the silver keys to the doors in the castle. She finds his treasures hidden behind them. At first, he refuses to give her the one gold key, but finally does, and when he is away, she and the Nurse (mezz.) open the door and find a staircase. They hear the sobbing of his other wives, all imprisoned as a punishment for their curiosity. The local populace is sure Bluebeard has murdered all of them. They rebel against his tyrannical rule and capture him, but Ariane sets him free. All the wives forgive him and remain with him in his castle.

Ariadne auf Naxos (a' ree AHD neh: owf NAH kso:s) Opera in a prologue and one act by Richard **Strauss**; libretto by Hugo von **Hofmannsthal**, suggested by Molière's *Le bourgeois gentilhomme*; Stuttgart Staatsoper, 1912; revised version, Vienna Hofoper (HO:F O: puh), 1916.

Singers perform an opera based on the myth of Ariadne (sop.) for a wealthy gentleman, who insists, over the objections of the composer (mezz.), that since time is of the essence, the commedia dell'arte company he has hired to present a play must perform simultaneously with the singers.

arietta (ah' ree EHT tah) *n.* [Italian: little air; breeze; small aria] A brief aria or melody, perhaps with two or three short verses. [French: *ariette* (ah *r*ee EHT)]

arioso (ah' ree O: soh) *n.*, *adj.* [Italian: airy; like an **aria**] —*n.* **1.** A lyrical, melodic passage, often one that grows directly out of a **recitative**. —*adj.* **2.** A tuneful or melodic setting, or way of composing a recitative passage in an opera; i.e., resembling an aria.

Arlen, Harold (1905–1986) Prolific American songwriter, film and stage composer. Among his Broadway shows are *Hooray for What!* (1937), ***Bloomer Girl*** (1944), and *Jamaica* (1957), all written with E. Y. **Harburg**. He wrote many film musical scores, as well as the songs "Over the Rainbow" for *The Wizard of Oz* (1939) and Groucho Marx's comic hit "Lydia, the Tattooed Lady."

See also MERCER, JOHNNY.

Arlesiana, L' (The Woman from Arles) (lahr leh:' zee AH nah) Opera in three acts by Francesco **Cilea**; libretto by poet Leopoldo Marenco (1831–1899) (le:' o: PO:L do: mah REHN ko:), based on French writer Alphonse Daudet's (1840–1897) (do: DEH:) *L'Arlésienne* (lah*r* lé ZYEHN); Milan, Teatro Lirico, 1897.

Federico (feh' deh REE ko:) (ten.), a young man from the countryside of Provence, is in love with a woman (mezz.) from Arles. His mother's (mezz.) godchild, Vivetta (vee VEHT tah) (sop.), is in love with him, and the two women show him compromising letters revealing that the woman from Arles had been the mistress of Metifio (meh TEE fee yo:) (bar.). Federico commits suicide on the eve of his wedding to Vivetta.

Armida (ahr MEE dah) At least ten operas based on Torquato Tasso's (1544–1595) (to:r KWAH to: TAHS so:) Italian Renaissance poem *Gerusalemme Liberata* (Jerusalem Liberated) (dgeh roo' sah LEHM me: lee be: RAH tah) were composed, including those by **Salieri** (1771), **Haydn** (1784), **Bianchi** (1802), **Rossini** (1817), and **Dvořák** (1904).

arme Jonathan, Der (Poor Jonathan) Viennese operetta by Karl **Millöcker**.

Armide (ahr MEED) Opera in five acts by Christoph Willibald Ritter von **Gluck**; libretto by Philippe **Quinault**, based on Tasso's poem; Paris Opéra, 1777.

The sorceress Armide (sop.) and Hidraot (ee' drah O:T) (bass-bar.), King of Damascus, plot the assassination of the victorious Crusader general Renaud (reh NO:) (ten.), but Armide falls in love with him. She works her charms and spells upon him, but Renaud's loyal Crusaders save him.

Arne, Thomas Augustine (1710–1778) English composer of songs and light operas; serious operas, including *Artaxerxes*; and the **pasticcio** *Love in a Village* (1762). His most famous composition is undoubtedly "Rule, Britannia!" His son, Michael Arne (1740–1786), was also a composer, with eighteen operas to his credit.

Arnold, Samuel (1740–1802) English music editor, composer, and producer of more than 100 musical stage pieces; remembered for his operas *The Maid of the Mill* (1765) and *Inkle and Yarico* (1787), with a libretto by George **Colman "the Younger,"** with whom he wrote several operas; and as the editor of the complete works of **Handel**, an edition which remained unfinished at Arnold's death.

See also POLLY.

arrangement *n.* A **version** of a score that includes melody and harmony and is orchestrated for different instruments and/or voices than the original composition, e.g., the **vocal score** of a musical comedy, with voice parts and **piano reduction** of the orchestral **score**; or the reduction for a small ensemble of a number from an operetta, suitable as dance music—common practice in the 19th c. Hence, *arranger*: the person who puts together the written musical arrangements. Cf. **orchestrator**.

Artaserse (ahr' tah SEHR seh:) A libretto by Pietro **Metastasio** that had more than 100 operatic settings, including those by **Gluck** (1741; his first opera); Niccolò **Piccinni** (1762); and **Cimarosa** (1781).

Artabano (ahr' tah BAH no:), who longs to become King of Persia, kills King Serse and attempts to poison the king's son, Artaserse, heir to the throne. Artabano's son, Arbace (ahr BAH che:), a faithful retainer of the royal house, frustrates his father's efforts. Arbace is in love with Serse's daughter, Mandane (mahn DAH neh:). Artaserse is in love with Artabano's daughter, Semira (seh MEE rah). Eventually the complicated threads of the plot are untangled, and Artabano is sent off to a well deserved exile.

Artaxerxes (ahr' tah ZUHRK seez) Opera in three acts by Thomas **Arne**, who translated Metastasio's libretto into English; London, Covent Garden, 1760.

articulation *n.* **1.** In diction, the formation and utterance of vowel and consonant sounds. Precise articulation is an important aspect of vocal technique. **2.** In music, an aspect of **phrasing**: how a singer joins notes together to form phrases.

Artists and Models Six Broadway musical **extravaganzas**, the first four being *Artists and Models of 1923* (Shubert Theatre; 312 perf.); *Artists and Models of*

1924 (Astor Theatre; 519 perf.), featuring music by Sigmund **Romberg**; *Artists and Models of 1925* (Winter Garden Theatre; 416 perf.), again with music by Romberg, among others; and *Artists and Models of 1927* (Winter Garden Theatre; 151 perf.). The revues sometimes had a slender story, built on the pretext of using artists and models as characters. The first one was produced by the Shuberts as competition for the **Earl Carroll Vanities**; the last Shubert production, on a smaller scale, was in 1930 (Majestic Theatre; 55 perf.). Other producers took over for a short-lived revue in 1943 (Broadway Theatre; 27 perf.), with Jane Froman (1907–1980), who had also performed in the 1934 **Ziegfeld Follies**, and comedian Jackie Gleason (1916–1987) in the cast. There were also two musical films: *Artists and Models* (1937) and *Artists and Models Abroad* (1938), both starring comedian Jack Benny (1894–1974), playing a different character in each one, with two different all-star casts and with singing and dancing integrated into the slender plots.

art rock An American musical form that incorporates the features of rock music, such as the use of electric instruments and amplification, but is harmonically more complex and textured, even occasionally adapting well known classical pieces; used in musical comedy where rock music is the required idiom. Also called *progressive rock.*

art song A composed vocal piece of brief duration, usually written in several verses and meant to be performed in a **concert** or **recital**, combining a sung line with a subtle instrumental **accompaniment**, usually for piano.

Ashman, Howard (1950–1991) Lyricist who collaborated with Alan **Menken** on Disney's animated film musicals *The Little Mermaid* (1989) and *Beauty and the Beast* (1991), both later mounted as Broadway shows. The team also wrote the Off-Broadway hit musical *Little Shop of Horrors* (1982).

aspirate *n.* (AS puh riht') A vowel or consonant characterized by an extra, exhaled puff of air, sometimes audible at the beginning of some vowels, and after or as part of some softly articulated consonants. In singing **coloratura** passages, a slight aspirate ("h") sound is sometimes heard; it can be, but is not always, a technical fault: "ah ha ha ha" instead of "ah ah ah ah."

As Thousands Cheer Broadway musical revue by Irving **Berlin**; book by Moss **Hart**; Music Box Theatre, 1933 (400 perf.); Off-Broadway revival: Greenwich House, 1998 (six-week limited run). This sparkling revue was directed by English-born former actor and Broadway powerhouse director Hassard Short (1877–1956). The book links a series of topical satirical sketches with music; each sketch is preceded by a newspaper headline. The score includes the instantly recognizable "Heat Wave," "Easter Parade," "Supper Time," and "Harlem on My Mind."

atonality *n.* The characteristic quality of the kind of music in which the traditional scales and **harmonic** structures are abandoned in favor of a loose arrangement of pitches, e.g., using Arnold Schoenberg's twelve tone scale; no key signature is used. Hence, the adj. *atonal,* applied to such music.

attack *n., v.* —*n.* **1.** The initial approach to the playing or singing of a piece. **2.** The style with which a piece is interpreted. **3.** The actual beginning of singing, and the way a singer begins to sing; i.e., the moment the tone of the voice is sounded and heard: the *onset* or *tonal onset* of the sung line (terms preferred by Richard Miller in *Solutions for Singers*). —*v. t.* **4.** To begin singing or playing with a particular energy: *The tenor attacked the aria "Di quella pira" from Verdi's* **Il trovatore** *with vigor.* (From that pyre) (dee' KWEHL lah PEE rah)

Auber, Daniel-François-Esprit (1782–1871) (dah NYEHL fraw*n* SWAH ehs P*R*EE o: BEH:*R*) French composer of ca. fifty operas and operettas. His works are little performed nowadays, but the overtures to a number of his operas remain popular, among them *Les diamants de la couronne* (The Crown Diamonds) (1841) (leh: dee ah MAH*N* duh lah koo *R*UHN), *Le cheval de bronze* (The Bronze Horse) (1835) (luh shuh val' duh B*R*O:*N*Z) , and *Le domino noir* (The Black Domino) (1837) (luh do:' mee no: NWAH*R*), all with libretti by Eugène **Scribe**. *La muette de Portici* (The Mute Girl of Portici) (1828) (lah mü EHT duh paw*r*' tee SEE), libretto by Scribe and dramatist Germain Delavigne (1790–1868) (zheh*r* ma*n*' duh lah VEE nyuh), is occasionally revived, but his most well-known work is *Fra Diavolo* (Brother Devil) (1830) (FRAH dee AH vo: lo:), libretto by Scribe; it was made into an amusing Laurel and Hardy film in 1933 [Comedy team, Stan Laurel (1890–1965) and Oliver Hardy (1892–1957)]. The story of this **opéra comique** in three acts concerns the bandit known as Fra Diavolo (ten.), who disguises himself as a marquis and arrives at an inn, where he hopes to steal the jewels of a wealthy English lord (ten.) and lady (mezz.), who are traveling in the Neapolitan countryside. But he is betrayed, and killed. The story is based loosely on the character of the real-life brigand and guerrilla leader Michele Pezza (1771–1806) (mee KEH: leh: PETS tsah), known as Fra Diavolo, who was captured by the Napoleonic French occupying forces and hanged.

See also ELISIR D'AMORE, L'.

Auden, W. H. (1907–1973) [b. Wystan Hugh Auden] English poet who wrote the libretti for several operas, including *Paul Bunyan* (1941) by Benjamin **Britten**; Igor Stravinsky's *The Rake's Progress* (1951), in collaboration with Chester Kallman (1921–1975); and *Elegy for Young Lovers* (1960) by Hans Werner **Henze**.

Audran, Edmond (1840–1901) (ehd MO:*N* o: D*R*AH*N*) French composer of some three dozen operettas, now known principally for his great success, the hilarious, tuneful, and adorable *La mascotte*.

Aufstieg und Fall der Stadt Mahagonny (Rise and Fall of the City of Mahagonny) (OWF shteek' *oo*nt FAHL deh: SHTAHT mah hah GO:N nee) Opera in three acts by Kurt **Weill**; libretto by Berthold **Brecht**; Leipzig, Neues (NOY ehs) Theater, 1930.

With elements of jazz and music hall, as well as memorable operatic songs, this **Newgate pastoral** takes place in the city of Mahagonny, founded by three escaped convicts, as a place where hedonism and pleasure may reign supreme. A group of prostitutes headed by Jenny (sop.), and the Alaskans Jimmy Mahoney (ten.) and his friends arrive, and anarchy prevails. The only crime is not having enough money to pay for one's pleasures. When Jimmy cannot pay for his drinks, he is condemned to death, but the citizens burn down the city before he can be executed.

Auftrittslied (OWF t*r*ihts LEET) *n.* [German: entrance-song] The introductory song a character sings about him- or herself, in 18th-c. **Singspiel**, e.g., Papageno's entrance aria in Mozart's ***Die Zauberflöte***; or in Viennese and German operetta, e.g., Siegfried's and Brunhilde's entrance songs in Straus's ***Die lustigen Nibelungen***.
See also ARIA (ARIA D'ENTRATA).

authenticity *n.* In music, accuracy of style in interpreting and performing a piece, and fidelity to the composer's intentions, as expressed by the **performance marks** in the score; hence, an *authentic* performance, i.e., one that is accurate and faithful to the composer's wishes. Trained musicians understand period styles in music, as well as the different styles required in different musical forms, e.g., jazz compositions, classical symphonies, 1950s musical comedy. The writing and interpretation of **ornamentation**, the way in which operatic recitatives are to be performed, and the variations in tempo are different in the different eras. See, for example, the authoritative book by Philip Gossett, *Divas and Scholars: Performing Italian Opera* (University of Chicago Press, 2006), which goes into great detail on the specific requirements for each composer, the way the works were performed, and the way they have been deformed and reinterpreted over time. Also invaluable is Clive Brown's *Classical and Romantic Performing Practice: 1750–1900* (Oxford University Press, 1999).
See also PERFORMANCE PRACTICE; STYLE; VERSION.

Avenue Q Broadway musical by Robert Lopez and Jeff Marx; book by Jeff Whitty; John Golden Theatre, 2003 (2556 perf.); in 2009, the show closed on Broadway and moved Off-Broadway to New World Stages, where it is still running as of this writing.
The setting is a tenement building in New York, and the musical unfolds using the ingenious device of a children's television show, along the lines of *Sesame Street*, with both human and puppet characters experiencing the problems of contemporary urban life.

B

Babes in Arms Broadway musical by **Rodgers and Hart**: music by Richard **Rodgers**, book and lyrics by Lorenz **Hart**; Shubert Theatre, 1937 (289 perf.); film, 1939.

Hit songs from the show include "My Funny Valentine," "I Wish I Were in Love Again," and "The Lady Is A Tramp."

During the Great Depression, a group of unemployed vaudevillians goes on the road, barnstorming. They leave their children at home, and the kids decide to mount a musical in order to make money and bring their parents back. But they lose money, and have to go to a work farm. A French aviator is forced to make an emergency landing in their midst. The resulting publicity turns things around and brings audiences flocking to the show put on by the "babes in arms."

Babes in Toyland Broadway operetta by Victor **Herbert**; book and lyrics by Glen **MacDonough**; Majestic Theatre, 1903 (192 perf.); Broadway revivals: Majestic Theatre, 1905 (21 perf.); Jolson's 59th Street Theatre, 1929 (32 perf.); Imperial Theatre, 1930 (33 perf.); extensive tours; filmed three times, most notably and delightfully in 1934 with Laurel and Hardy.

Little Jane and Allan are abandoned by their wicked Uncle Barnaby. He sets them adrift in a boat that comes to shore in Toyland, where they encounter characters from Mother Goose rhymes and fairy tales. Barnaby follows the children and falls in lust with the shepherdess Bo-Peep, who wants nothing to do with him because she is in love with Tom Tom, son of the old lady who lives in a shoe. Barnaby threatens to evict her as a way of blackmailing Bo-Peep. His plans are foiled by the inhabitants of Toyland, who bring him to justice at the Toy Factory.

Bach, Johann Christian (1735–1782) Youngest son of Johann Sebastian (1685–1750) and Anna Magdalena (1701–1760) Bach; composer of some dozen operas, very popular in their day in England, where he spent much of his career, and was music master to Queen Charlotte (1744–1818). Bach was known for the tasteful delicacy of his orchestrations, and for having made certain reforms in regard to formulaic composition, such as eliminating the **da capo aria** from his works.

Bacharach, Burt (b. 1928) American composer of popular songs, many with lyrics by Hal **David**; they co-wrote the Broadway show *Promises, Promises*.

backbeat *n.* A **rock** and **jazz** technique, consisting of emphasizing strongly the second and fourth (last) beats of a measure composed in 4/4 time, by attacking those beats loudly and sharply; esp. used by drummers.

backstage musical A motion picture and stage genre of stories, or an individual film or musical theater piece, dealing with the lives of performers in theater productions of musical comedies, e.g., Busby Berkeley's film *42nd Street* (1933), also done as a Broadway musical.

back-up *n.* **1.** Vocal **support** of a lead singer; also, the group of singers providing that support, called a *backup group*. **2.** Extra copies of music, extra props, extra copies of a recording used in a show, etc., in case they are needed because something goes wrong with the original.

balance *n.* **1.** The equalization of sound elements in recording music or the audio for a film. **2.** The adjusted sound levels between on-stage singers and the **pit orchestra** in a musical theater piece, so that the instrumentalists do not drown out the vocalists. **3.** In dancing, the optimal balanced posture necessary to ensure freedom of movement. **4.** In singing, the harmonious working together of all parts of the breathing and vocal apparatus.

balancé (ba' lah*n* SÉ) *n.* [French: balanced] In classical ballet, a rocking step, done in a series that consists of rocking back and forth, transferring the weight from one foot to the other, either from side to side or by crossing one foot in front of the other, in time to the music.

Balfe, Michael William (1808–1870) (BALF) Anglo-Irish opera singer and composer of thirty-five operas, among them *Falstaff* and *The Rose of Castile* (1857); his most notable success was the hugely popular *The Bohemian Girl*.

ballad *n.* **1.** A song in the form of a narrative poem; often, each stanza is followed by the same refrain, e.g., in the case of many folk songs. **2.** A song about love; a standard kind of number in musical comedy and operetta. **3.** *Hist.* [Fr. Old Provençal *baler (bah LEH:),* to dance] Originally, a song meant to be danced to; also, the melody or tune of such a song.

Ballad of Baby Doe, The Opera in two acts by Douglas S. **Moore**; libretto by John **Latouche**; Central City, CO, Opera House, 1956.

In the early 20th c., Horace Tabor (bar.), a rich Colorado mine owner married to Augusta (mezz.), falls in love with Baby Doe (sop.), who has left her husband. Horace divorces Augusta and marries Baby Doe. Having relied on the price of silver, which falls precipitously when the gold standard is adopted by the U.S., Horace finds himself ruined, but Baby Doe remains true to him, and he dies in her arms.

ballad opera *Hist.* An 18th-c. form from which today's **musical comedy** developed: a story told in dialogue interspersed with popular, well-known tunes drawn from folk ballads or operas, to which lyrics suitable to the story of the play were written, e.g., John Gay's *The Beggar's Opera*, first produced in 1728, and its sequel, *Polly*. The form had many practitioners, including the prolific Charles **Dibdin**. Although the genre was pretty much gone by the 19th c., W. S. **Gilbert** carried on the tradition with such comic pieces as *Dulcamara, or The Little Duck and the Great Quack* (1866), a burlesque of Donizetti's *L'elisir d'amore*; *Robert the Devil, or The Nun, the Dun, and the Son of a Gun* (1868), a satire of Meyerbeer's *Robert le Diable*; and many others, all of which had eclectic scores made up of well known opera airs, music hall songs, and other popular material, with amusing lyrics and silly dialogue by Gilbert. These works are more properly categorized as *ballad farce*: a ballad opera with an absurdly comical story.

ballerina *n.* A female ballet dancer.
See also PRIMA BALLERINA ASSOLUTA.

ballet *n.* **1.** A form of classical theatrical **dance** accompanied by music and using formalized steps, gestures, and movements that are precisely done and smoothly executed in a graceful, flowing, and expressive manner. The ballet originated in Renaissance Italy and was further developed in France in the 17th c. **2.** A theatrical entertainment consisting of either a full-length classical dance piece or drama, e.g., Tchaikovsky's *Swan Lake* (1877); or of a number of narrative or abstract shorter pieces. **3.** A dance **number** in 19th-c. operettas or operas.

ballet blanc (bah leh:' BLAH*N*) [French: white ballet] Any ballet in which the ballerinas are dressed in simple white tulle tutus and skirts, as in act 2 of *Giselle* (1841) or *La Sylphide* (1832), where the now classic fashion was first used.

ballet comedy [French: *comédie-ballet* (ko mé DEE ba LEH:)] *Hist.* A 17th-c. entertainment popular at the court of Louis XIV (1638–1715) that combined a spoken play with balletic interludes, e.g., Molière's *Le Bourgeois gentilhomme*, with music by Jean-Baptiste **Lully**.

ballet d'action (bah leh:' dak SYO:*N*) [French: ballet of action] A classical narrative dance piece that tells a dramatic story, and is meant to be performed with all the elements of character interpretation, on a full set, and in costume; e.g., Tchaikovsky's *Swan Lake*.

ballet de cour (bah leh:' duh KOO*R*) [French: court ballet] *Hist.* An elaborate dance and special effects **extravaganza**, with lavish scenery and costumes, such as those performed at Renaissance Italian courts, or at the 17th-c. court of Louis XIV.

ballet director The artistic head of a ballet company, often a retired dancer or a choreographer, who decides on casting, repertoire, and other artistic matters. Also called *artistic director*, as opposed to the company's *administrative director*, in charge of budget and other financial matters.

ballet girl *Hist.* In the 19th c., a female member of a chorus in an operetta or at the opera. The ballet girls were often courtesans, patronized by the scions of rich families who went to the opera to ogle them during performances and to meet them backstage afterwards.

ballet-héroique (bah leh: é *r*o: EEK) *n.* [French: heroic-ballet] A kind of **opéra-ballet** esp. popular at the court of Louis XV (1710–1774), in which the characters are heroes, noble figures, ancient gods and goddesses. **Rameau** wrote some superb ballets-héroiques, among them, *Les Indes galantes* and *Zaïs*.

ballet master; ballet mistress The person in charge of training the dancers in a ballet company.

24

ballet movements There are seven categories of movement, all with French names: *élancer* (é lah*n* SEH:): to dart, or move quickly; *étendre* (é TAH*N* dr*u*h): to stretch, to extend the limbs or body; *glisser* (glee SEH:): to slide, to glide; *plier* (plee EH:): to bend the body or limbs; *relever* (*r*uh luh VEH:): to lift up the body or the limbs, to raise; *sauter* (so: TEH:): to leap, to jump; *tourner* (too*r* NEH:): to turn, to turn around.

ballet-pantomime The narrative dance pieces of the romantic era, esp. in Paris, where pieces were created that combined ballet and the acting out of characters using gesture and other pantomimic techniques; the term **ballet d'action** is virtually interchangeable with ballet-pantomime, which usually refers to 19th c. ballets.

ballo (BAHL loh) *n.* [Italian: dance] **1.** *Hist.* The dances of the Italian Renaissance of the late 15th and 16th centuries. **2.** The Italian term for a grand soirée, a ball that includes dancing and refreshments, e.g., in Verdi's *Un ballo in maschera*.

ballroom dance Formal or informal dances, such as the **waltz** or the **tango**, done in the setting of an evening dance party or at a dance hall; ballroom dance scenes occur in many musical comedies and films, with a band sometimes playing at one end of a room on an elevated platform called a *bandstand*.

band *n.* **1.** A group or ensemble of musicians who play together: *rock band*; *jazz band*. **2.** The **pit orchestra** and/or onstage musicians who play for a musical theater piece.

band call *esp. Brit.* A rehearsal for the orchestra or band of a musical theater piece, without the singers, purely to go through the instrumental parts.

band car A rolling platform large enough to hold an orchestra, used in spectacles and extravaganzas. It is rolled behind the scenes onto an elevator platform, then lowered onto the stage, creating quite an effect; e.g., at New York's Radio City Music Hall.

bandmaster *n.* The conductor and **music director** of a band. Also called a *bandleader*.

band part The music, and the written score for an individual instrument in a band.

band room *esp. Brit.* The area under the stage near the **orchestra pit** where the musicians wait to take their places in the pit. Cf. **music room**.

Band Wagon, The Broadway musical revue; music by Arthur **Schwartz**; lyrics by Howard **Dietz**; skits by George S. **Kaufman**; New Amsterdam Theatre, 1931 (260 perf.); film, 1953, with a plot about show business difficulties added, and a screenplay by **Comden and Green**. The show was directed by Hassard Short. Still remembered is the song "Dancing in the Dark."

Barbe-bleue (Bluebeard) (bah*r*' buh BL*OO*) **Opéra bouffe** in three acts by Jacques **Offenbach**; libretto by Henri **Meilhac** and Ludovic **Halévy**; Paris, Théâtre des Variétés (teh: AH t*r*uh deh: vah *r*ee é TÉ), 1866.

Barbe-bleue (ten.), whose first five wives have all mysteriously died, marries the lusty peasant girl Boulotte (boo LO:T) (sop.), as her reward for having won the village Rose Queen contest. But he has his eye on Princess Hermia (eh*r*' mee YAH) (sop.), the long lost daughter of King Bobèche (bo BEHSH) (ten.). She has been discovered in the village on Barbe-bleue's estates by Count Oscar (os KAH*R*) (bar.), and escorted back to the royal palace, where Bobèche has ordered the sycophantic Oscar to put to death the six suspected lovers of Queen Clémentine (klé' mah*n* TEEN) (mezz.). Prince Saphir (sah FEE*R*) (ten.), Hermia's prospective bridegroom, arrives, and turns out to have been disguised as a shepherd whom she loved back in the village. Barbe-bleue enters to present Boulotte to the assembled court. She behaves scandalously, and he takes steps to have her poisoned so that he himself can marry Hermia; but his chemist, Popolani (po' po:' lah NEE) (bar.), saves her life, as he had those of all the other wives. Count Oscar had also saved the lives of the queen's suspected lovers, and all of them confront Bobèche and Barbe-bleue. There is a mass wedding, and everything is restored to its proper order.

Barber, Samuel (1910–1981) American composer, known for his lush orchestrations in a late romantic style; his operas include *Antony and Cleopatra* and *Vanessa*.

barbershop quartet A group of four male **a capella** singers who perform songs written in the "barbershop" style, i.e., in four-part harmony; originating in the early 20th c. with the Mills Brothers [John, Jr. (1910–1936) (bass; guitarist); Herbert (1912–1939) (ten.); Harry (1913–1982) (bar.); Donald (1915–1999) (lead ten.)], a famed African-American gospel music group from Ohio: they learned to sing in their father's barbershop. Such groups were sometimes featured in vaudeville. Typical well known barbershop songs include the **title song** from the Broadway show *Sweet Adeline*; and "Down by the Old Mill Stream."
See also GLEE.

Barbier, Jules (1822–1901) (zhül' bah*r* BYEH:) French librettist and collaborator with Michel **Carré** on such operas as Gounod's *Faust* and *Roméo et Juliette*; Meyerbeer's *Dinorah*; Thomas' *Hamlet*; and Offenbach's *Les contes d'Hoffmann*, based on the play he and Carré wrote.

barbiere di Siviglia, Il; ossia L'inutile precauzione (The Barber of Seville; or The Useless Precaution) (eel bahr BYEH: reh: dee see VEE [g]lyah; os SEE ah lee NOO tee leh preh:' kow zee O: neh) Opera in three acts by Gioachino **Rossini**; libretto by the poet Cesare Sterbini (1784–1831) (CHEH zah reh: stehr BEE nee), based on the play by iconoclastic playwright and merchant Pierre Caron de Beaumarchais (1732–1799) (PYEH:*R* kah *r*o:*n*' duh bo:' mah*r* SHEH:); Rome, Teatro Argentina, 1818.
Rossini's most famous opera was an immediate hit, supplanting a popular earlier version of the same story, composed in 1782 by Giovanni **Paisiello**, which had premiered at the Hermitage in St. Petersburg.
Count Almaviva (ahl' mah VEE vah) (ten.) falls in love with Rosina (ro: ZEE nah) (mezz. or sop.), the ward of Dr. Bartolo (BAHR to: lo:) (bass), who plans to

marry her and keeps her a virtual prisoner. With the connivance of the barber Figaro (FEE gah ro:) (bar.), Almaviva manages to enter the household disguised as a music teacher and supposed protégé of Bartolo's confidant, the scandalmonger Don Basilio (bah ZEE lee o:) (bass). Eventually, Almaviva and Rosina are united.

barcarole (BAHR kuh rohl') *n*. [Fr. Italian *barca* (BAHR kah): a skiff or boat; *barcarola* (bahr' kah RO: lah) or *barcaruola* (bahr' kah roo-O: lah): boatman's song] Originally, a simple boatman's song meant to accompany rhythmic rowing; esp., e.g., the song of the Venetian gondoliers; usually in a gentle, rocking 6/8 time; later imitated and adapted for artistic purposes, and used in operas; e.g., the "Barcarolle" (bah*r*' kah *R*O:L) [the French version of the word] in the Venetian act of Offenbach's *Les contes d'Hoffmann*, originally written as music for the Rhine in his opera *Les fées du Rhin* (1864).

baritone *n*. The medium-range mature male singing voice. A light or *lyric baritone* has a slightly higher range than a baritone; a *bass-baritone* has a slightly lower range.

barn dance An early 19th-c. rustic American dance in 4/4 time, popular at rural square dances and get-togethers, which were often held in barns; but the origin of the dance's name is the tune to which it was danced: "Dancing in the Barn."

Barnum Broadway musical by Cy **Coleman**; book by writer, director, and producer Mark Bramble (b. 1950); lyrics by Michael **Stewart**; St. James Theatre, 1980 (854 perf.).

The episodic story, presented in the style of a three-ring circus, is based very loosely on incidents in the life of 19th-c. mastermind showman, impresario, and circus magnate, P. T. Barnum (1810–1891), known for his outrageous fakery and hokum. The title role was memorably created by versatile star Jim Dale (b. 1935). Barnum, who is married to Charity, has an affair with the "Swedish Nightingale," famed opera singer Jenny Lind (1820–1887). The show ends with his forming a partnership with the Ringling Brothers, and running their circus.

barre (BAHR) *n*. [Fr. French: bar; railing] The horizontal length of metal piping installed as a hand railing against the wall of a ballet studio, often in front of a wall-size mirror; the dancers hold onto the barre while doing certain of their exercises, and when learning positions in ballet class.

barrelhouse *n., adj.* —*n*. **1.** An early type of free-form jazz **blues** with a 2/4 rhythm; first improvised on the piano; presumably first heard in bars, for which the slang word was "barrelhouse," fr. the fact that kegs of beer were stored there. Similar to **boogie-woogie**. **2.** A kind of piano playing in the style of that jazz. —*adj*. **3.** Pertaining to that kind of jazz: *barrelhouse jazz*.

Bart, Lionel (1930–1999) English composer and lyricist; wrote stage and television musicals, and film scores; best known for his West End and Broadway hit, *Oliver!*

Bartered Bride, The Comic opera by **Smetana**. See PRODANÁ NEVĚSTA.

Bartók, Béla Hungarian composer. See A KÉKSZÁKÁLLÚ HERCEG VÁRA (DUKE BLUEBEARD'S CASTLE).

basoche, La (The Law Clerks' Guild) (lah bah ZOSH) [French: the legal bar; fr. the name of the historical guild of lawyers' clerks, abolished during the French Revolution; in contemporary vocabulary, a pejorative term for the legal profession; the elected head of the guild assumed the title of King.] Operetta in three acts by André **Messager**; libretto by theater director Albert Carré (1852–1938) (ahl beh*r*' kah *RÉ*); Paris, Théâtre de l'Opéra-Comique, 1890.

   In 1514, in the Paris of King Louis XII (1452–1516), the law clerk and poet Clément Marot (1496–1544) (klé mah*n*' mah RO:) (ten.) is elected King of the Basoche, but under false pretenses: he is married, and one of the Basoche's rules is that the king must be a bachelor. He and his wife, Colette (sop.), pretend not to know each other, but his rival, Roland (bar.), is not fooled, and awaits the day when he can expose them. Princess Marie of England (mezz.) has been escorted to France by the duc de Longueville (dük' duh law*n*' guh VEEL) (bar.), who has married her by proxy on behalf of Louis XII (ten.), but she has given him the slip. Masquerading as a commoner, she takes rooms at an inn. Marot enters on horseback, and is acclaimed as king. Marie mistakes him for Louis XII. After many such misunderstandings, the situation is resolved. Roland becomes King of the Basoche; Marot and Colette leave for a second honeymoon.

bass *n.* The lowest-pitched mature male singing voice. A *basso cantante* (BAHS so kahn TAHN teh:) [Italian: singing bass] has a good top **register**, as well as an excellent low range; a *basso profundo* (pro FOON do) [Italian: deep bass] has a fine low register, and not a very high range.

basse dance (BAHS) A 15th and 16th-c. slow, stately court dance of Burgundian origin; there was a step to each beat of music, performed, presumably, by couples moving forward in a series of four slow steps to each four beats of music; the steps varied and, apparently, were often improvised.

Bat Boy Off-Broadway musical by Laurence O'Keefe; book by Keythe Farley (b. 1963) and Brian Flemming (b. 1966); first produced in Los Angeles; Union Square Theatre, 2001 (260 perf.); revivals in other cities.

   A half-feral creature, part boy, part bat, is discovered in the West Virginia hills. The sheriff takes him to the local veterinarian, Dr. Parker, where the creature is befriended by the doctor's wife, Meredith, and their teenage daughter, Shelley. They name him Edgar and see to his education, but Dr. Parker becomes insanely jealous. He kills Edgar and Meredith, then commits suicide, leaving his daughter to mourn them.

beat *n., v. —n.* **1.** In music, a rhythmic stress or metrical **accent**. **2.** The rhythm of a piece of music. **3.** In ballet, the hitting of one leg against the other. *—v. t.* **4.** To keep or conduct a musical piece in **tempo**: *to beat time.* See DOWNBEAT; UPBEAT.

5. In ballet, to hit one leg against the other when the dancer is in the air, or to hit one leg against the other when crossing both legs in the air.

Beauty and the Beast Broadway musical by Alan **Menken**; lyrics by Howard **Ashman**; book by Linda Woolverton (b. 1952); based on their 1991 Walt Disney cartoon, which owes more than a little to Jean Cocteau's (1889–1963) (zhah*n*' kok TO:) 1946 masterpiece film **version** of the famous Perrault (pe: *R*O:) fairy tale *La belle et la bête* (Beauty and the Beast) (lah BEHL eh: lah BEHT); lyrics to additional songs for the stage musical by Tim **Rice**; Palace Theatre, 1994 (5461 perf.).

Belle, the daughter of Maurice, begs the Beast to keep her as a prisoner in his grim, enchanted castle in exchange for her father, who had inadvertently stumbled into it when he was lost in the forest. The Beast agrees, and Belle resigns herself to a miserable fate, but enchanted objects in the castle come to life: Lumiere, the candlestick; Mrs. Potts, the teapot; and Cogsworth the clock persuade her that the Beast is really lovable. When Belle learns that Maurice is seriously ill, she begs the Beast to allow her to return to the village to care for him, which he does. Gaston, the narcissistic hunter who was in love with Belle, largely because she was the only village maiden to spurn his advances, leads an attack on the castle. It fails, but the Beast is mortally wounded. Belle tells him that she loves him, and the curse that turned him into the Beast dissipates. He is revealed as a handsome prince. The prince lives, they marry, and all ends happily ever after.

bebop; bop *n.* A form of 1940s' American **jazz** characterized by improvisational riffs and solos on various instruments, and esp. outstanding drumming; complicated melody with original harmonic changes; forceful, energetic rhythms and lively tempi. Among its most well known practitioners were "Dizzy" Gillespie (1917–1993) [John Birks Gillespie] and Charlie Parker (1920–1955) [Charles Parker, Jr.]. Cf. its opposite, **funky**.

Bee Gees [Barry (b. 1946), Maurice (1949–2003), and Robin (b. 1949) Gibb] Internationally famous Anglo-Australian singing trio: the three Gibb brothers composed and performed their own songs, beginning in the 1960s; wrote and recorded the original hit score for *Saturday Night Fever* (film, 1977; Broadway show, 1999). The name of the group was taken from Barry Gibb's initials.

Beeson, Jack (b. 1921) American opera composer and singer; one of his most famous works is ***Lizzie Borden***. He also wrote ***The Sweet Bye and Bye***; *Cyrano*, based on Edmond Rostand's play ***Cyrano de Bergerac***, and ***Captain Jinks of the Horse Marines***, based on the play by Clyde Fitch, both with libretti by Sheldon **Harnick**.

Beethoven, Ludwig van (1770–1827) German composer; born in Bonn; settled in Vienna. His adult-onset deafness did not stop him from continuing to compose masterpieces. Known for his tempestuous temperament and passionate music, this most famous of romantic composers was a great humanitarian who stood for liberty and justice and admired the advances in human rights made by the French

Revolution. He practically idolized Napoleon (1769–1821) as the embodiment of those ideals, until Napoleon betrayed them by declaring himself emperor. Beethoven's one opera, *Fidelio*, is centered on the themes of the abuse of political power and the tyrannical stifling of opposition. He composed incidental music to several plays and contemplated other opera projects, but none came to fruition.

Beggar's Opera, The First and best known of the popular genre of the **ballad opera**; music for its more than sixty-nine songs was adapted from various sources, including folk tunes and Handel operas, and arranged by the German-born English composer and pedagogue Dr. Johann Christoph Pepusch (1667–1752), who also composed some original music for it, including the overture; text and lyrics by John **Gay**; London, Lincoln's Inn Fields, 1728. There is a sequel called *Polly*. The idea for the story was suggested to Gay by his friend, the writer Jonathan Swift (1667–1745), author of *Gulliver's Travels*. Among several available recordings, the most fascinating and exquisite is that of the famous 1940 Glyndebourne Festival production, starring Michael Redgrave (1908–1985), directed by John Gielgud (1904–2000), on Pearl (GEMM CD 9917; 1991); the CD also contains a medley from *Lionel and Clarissa* by Charles **Dibdin**.

Meant to satirize Italian opera of the period, the eclectic score has its delights and refrains that became famous, among them, "How happy could I be with either / Were t'other dear charmer away!" The score has been arranged in various versions, and the story was adapted by **Brecht** and **Weill** for *Die Dreigroschenoper*. Among the most interesting arrangements are those by Benjamin **Britten** (1948) for eleven instruments. His arrangements reinforce the underlying darkness and current relevance of the piece.

This satiric **Newgate pastoral** is introduced by a spoken prologue delivered by the Beggar, who claims to have written the piece. Macheath (bar.), a gallant, swashbuckling highwayman, has married Polly Peachum (sop.). Her father, Peachum (bass), betrays Macheath to the police, and he is arrested and imprisoned at Newgate. Lucy Lockit (sop.), daughter of Lockit the jailer (bar.), falls in love with Macheath and helps the two-timing swaggerer to escape, but he is recaptured. The Beggar, maintaining that an opera must have a happy ending, ensures Macheath's reprieve, and he is released.

beguine (buh GEEN) *n.* A slow, sensuous, syncopated dance, much like a **rumba**; from the Caribbean islands of Martinique and Guadeloupe; first popularized in the 1930s, esp. with the Cole **Porter** song "Begin the Beguine" from his musical comedy *Jubilee* (1935), book by Moss **Hart**.

bel canto (behl' KAHN to) [Italian: beautiful singing] The style of singing esp. associated with mid-17th-c. baroque music through 19th-c. romantic opera; characterized by beautiful, even tones throughout the singer's range, as well by the technical skill and breath control required for negotiating the ubiquitous, florid **coloratura** passages, the smooth and seemingly effortless singing of high notes, and the ornamentation that is integral to dramatic expression. By extension, the style of composition that demanded such singing: *bel canto opera*.

30

bell kick In dance, or as a comic reaction of elation or triumph, a leap to the right or left side, with one foot kicking against the other as the leap is done; the person executing the bell kick first steps to the side, then jumps and almost simultaneously clicks one heel against the other; the outside leg may be fully extended.

belle Hélène, La (Beautiful Helen) (lah behl' é LEHN) **Opéra bouffe** by Jacques **Offenbach**; libretto by Henri **Meilhac** and Ludovic **Halévy**; Paris, Théâtre des Variétés, 1864.

Part of the great success of this piece was due to its star, Hortense Schneider (1833–1920) (o:*r* tah*ns*' shneh: DEH:*R*), a brilliant singing actress who gave Offenbach exactly the kind of performance he always wanted: great singing and a hilarious sense of tongue-in-cheek comedy. This is a sly romp through the myth of the origins of the Trojan War, and at the same time, a satire of the mores of the Paris of Napoleon III.

Orestes [Oreste (o: *R*EHST)] (mezz.) is a decadent young rake, given to frequenting prostitutes; Agamemnon (ah' gah' mehm NO:*N*) (bass-bar.) is an unbearable, hot-headed braggart; Calchas (kahl KAHS) (bar.), High Priest of Jupiter, is a fawning hypocrite; Achilles [Achille (ah SHEEL)] (ten.), is a vain narcissist; and the warrior brothers Ajax (ah ZHAHKS) (bass-bar.), are stupid louts. Helen, Queen of Sparta (sop.), immodestly refers to herself as the most beautiful woman in the world and attributes every dalliance of hers to Fate. Paris, Prince of Troy (pah *R*EES) (ten.), has been promised the most beautiful woman in the world by Venus, for awarding her the Golden Apple in a beauty contest with only three divine contestants. When the slyboots appears in Helen's bedchamber and tells her she is dreaming, she professes to believe it. Her husband, the feeble, weak-willed, easily manipulated King Menelaus (ten.) [Ménélas (mé' né LAHS)], unexpectedly returns home and discovers the pair—a major indiscretion, according to Helen, who says that he should have given her fair warning of his return, as any intelligent husband would in order to avoid scandal. Paris is forced to flee, but returns disguised as a High Priest of Venus, demanding that Helen accompany him on a voyage to Cytheraea. Menelaus consents, only to discover too late that his wife has gone off with none other than Paris. The Trojan War is now set to begin!

Belle of New York, The American musical comedy in two acts by German-born American composer and Broadway conductor and arranger, Gustave Adolph Kerker (1857–1923); book and lyrics by Hugh Morton (1865–1916); Casino Theatre, 1897 (56 perf.).

This was one of several collaborations between Kerker and Morton. Although not well received in New York, it was a phenomenon in Europe, with 697 West End perf. at the Shaftesbury Theatre, the first time an American musical theater piece had had such a long run; and successful productions in Paris and Berlin. It had two Broadway revivals (1900; 1921—in an expanded rewritten version called *The Whirl of New York*, with several collaborators contributing to the work of Kerker and Morton), and then promptly fell into obscurity until Hollywood producer Arthur Freed (1894–1973) rediscovered it and had it filmed in 1952, much changed, as a vehicle for Fred Astaire with new, pedestrian music by Harry **Warren** and lyrics by Johnny **Mercer**. The film's plot has only some points in common with the original, related here:

Surrounded by a cast of characters who could be right out of an 1890s' *Guys and Dolls*, Manhattan playboy Harry Bronson meets a Salvation Army lass, Violet Gray, who falls in love with him and wants to reform him, to the relief of his puritanical father, Ichabod, who had withdrawn his son's allowance. Ichabod will restore the allowance if Harry agrees to marry Violet and annul his marriage to Cora Angelique. But Violet realizes that Harry loves Cora, so she arranges to shock Ichabod by singing a risqué French number: "At Ze Naughty Folies Bergères (my feet zey fly up in ze air)." Her ruse works, and Ichabod is reconciled to Harry's marriage. This is a silly but rather cute number in a score that is often plodding, although there are some very listenable, lively, and even pretty tunes that surprise one like a sudden wave in a calm, dull sea. There is no sense of dramatic characterization in the score, which is mainly reminiscent of the music hall.

Bellini, Vincenzo (1801–1835) (veen CHEHN zo: behl LEE nee) Italian opera composer; one of the three greatest **bel canto** composers, along with **Rossini** and **Donizetti**. The epitome of romanticism, Bellini is known for his limpid, soaring, heartbreaking melodies. He wrote eleven operas, including *Il pirata* (The Pirate) (1827) (eel pee RAH tah); *La straniera* (The Foreign Woman) (1828) (lah strah NYEH: rah); *I Capuleti ed i Montecchi* (The Capulets and the Montagues) (1830) (ee kah' poo LEH tee ehd ee mon TEHK kee), based on Shakespeare's *Romeo and Juliet*; *Beatrice di Tenda* (bay' ah TREE che: dee TEHN dah) (1833); *La sonnambula*; and *Norma*—all with libretti by Felice **Romani**; and *I puritani*, libretto by Carlo Pepoli.

Bells Are Ringing Broadway musical by Jule **Styne**; book and lyrics by **Comden and Green**; Shubert Theatre, 1956 (924 perf.); Broadway revival: Plymouth Theatre, 2001 (104 perf.); film, 1960, with Judy Holliday (1924–1965) reprising the Broadway role that ensured the show's success.

Chatty, vivacious Ella Peterson, an answering service operator, likes to gossip with the customers. She falls in love with one of them, playwright Jeff Moss. Eventually, after a series of amusing mishaps, they end up together.

belly breathing A method of using the musculature for breath support during singing. This technique relies heavily on tensing the abdominal muscles to force the air in the lungs upwards. Maximum tension is created, which is one reason why this method is decried by such eminent theoreticians and teachers as Richard Miller in *Solutions for Singers*. Cf. its opposite, **appoggio**.

belly dancing A secularized version of medieval, pre-Islamic ceremonial solo dancing, called *raqs sharqi* (RAHKS SHAHR kee) [Arabic: eastern dance], originating in Egypt and spreading from there. Later, at the 18th-c. Ottoman court, it began to assume its present form as a kind of artistic dance. It is provocative and sexy, performed solo by women who sometimes wear face veils while displaying their bare, gyrating midriffs and employing provocative hip movements combined with graceful, undulating arm gestures. It has been used in modified form in ballets, and in such musicals as *Kismet* and *A Funny Thing Happened on the Way to the Forum*. Salome's "Dance of the Seven Veils" in Richard Strauss's opera *Salome* is sometimes done as a kind of belly dancing.

belt *v. t.* To sing out loudly and powerfully, using a lot of chest voice: *to belt a song*; *to belt out a song*; hence *belter*: a singer who belts. This style of singing is often called for in Broadway musicals.

Benatzky, Ralph (1884–1957) (beh NAHTS kee) [b. Rudolf Josef František Benatzki (FRAHN tih: shehk)] Czech-born Austrian composer of twenty-two Viennese operettas, among them *Im weissen Rössl (The White Horse Inn)*.

Benedict, Sir Julius (1804–1885) German-born English composer, conductor, pianist, and teacher; student and protégé of Carl Maria von **Weber**; conducted premiere of Wallace's *Maritana*; composed eight operas, of which the most successful was *The Lily of Killarney*, performed regularly until ca. 1930.

Berg, Alban Maria Johannes (1885–1935) (AHL bahn mah *R*EE ah yo HAHN ehs BEH[*R*]K) Austrian composer; he wrote two operas: *Wozzeck* (VO tsehk) (1925) and the unfinished *Lulu* (produced posthumously in 1937). Berg was much influenced by his musical studies with Arnold Schoenberg, innovative twelve-tone composer and fellow member of the Second Viennese School.

See EXPRESSIONISM.

bergamasque; bergomask *n.* [Fr. Italian *bergamasca* (behr' gah MAHS kah), from *Bergamo* (BEHR gah mo:'), the town where it originated] A popular 15th-c. Italian fast round dance, adopted in England and elsewhere in Europe.

Berlin, Irving (1888–1989) Russian-born American composer and lyricist of a host of the most famous popular songs and musicals ever written in the US. His first big hit, the song "Alexander's Ragtime Band" (1911), assured his reputation. He wrote for Broadway, Hollywood, **Tin Pan Alley**, and the *Ziegfeld Follies*. The *Music Box Revues* were devoted to presenting his songs. Among his most notable Broadway successes were *Watch Your Step* (his first Broadway show), *As Thousands Cheer*, *Of Thee I Sing*, *Louisiana Purchase*, *Annie Get Your Gun*, *Call Me Madam*, *This Is The Army*, *Yip Yip Yahank*, and *Face the Music*. He wrote the score for *The Cocoanuts* (1925), book by George S. **Kaufman** and Morrie Ryskind (1895–1985); this stage **vehicle** for the Marx Brothers became their first film, made in 1929. Berlin's family emigrated to New York's Lower East Side when he was five, and he grew up singing and composing songs, even though he had had no technical musical education beyond the fact that his father was a synagogue cantor. He composed some three dozen musical films and stage shows, as well as numerous songs that became standards, including the beloved "God Bless America."

Berlioz, Hector (1803–1869) (ehk to:*r*' beh*r*' LYO:Z) Innovative romantic French composer known for the dramatic style of his music; conductor; his operas include

Béatrice et Bénédict (1862) (bé ah TREES eh: bé' né DIHKT), to his own libretto, based on Shakespeare's *Much Ado About Nothing*; *Benvenuto Cellini* (1838) (behn' veh NOO to: chehl LEE nee), based loosely on the autobiography of the swashbuckling Italian Renaissance sculptor; the ambitious *Les Troyens*; and his "concert opera," *La damnation de Faust*, a "dramatic legend" meant to be sung with an orchestra in concert, rather than staged. His technical writings about music and his important *Memoirs* (1870; first translated into English in 1969; revised edition, Everyman's Library, 2002) make informative reading about the musical life of the period.

Bernstein, Elmer (1922–2004) Brilliant, award-winning American composer with wide-ranging interests in the arts; known primarily as the composer of more than 200 film and television scores. He composed two Broadway musicals, *How Now, Dow Jones* (1967) and *Merlin* (1983), the latter about the Arthurian wizard in his apprentice days. He was known as "Bernstein West," to distinguish him from Leonard Bernstein, who was nicknamed "Bernstein East."

Bernstein, Leonard (1918–1990) Preeminent, highly influential American composer; famous also as a teacher and symphony orchestra conductor; his works include ballet, musical comedies, operettas, and the opera *Trouble in Tahiti* (1952). Among his most celebrated works for the musical theater are *Candide*, *West Side Story*, and *On the Town* (1944). He also did a musicalized version of Barrie's *Peter Pan*. Bernstein made many recordings and was also well known for his series of concerts for young audiences.

Besoyan, Rick (1924–1970) American composer, writer, theater director, actor, and singer; best known for having written the music, book, and lyrics for the hit satirical musical *Little Mary Sunshine*.

Best Little Whorehouse in Texas, The Broadway musical comedy by Texas songwriter Carol Hall (b. 1939); book by Texas novelist, journalist, and playwright Larry L. King (b. 1929) and actor, director, and writer Peter Masterson (b. 1934); 46th Street Theatre, 1978 (1703 perf.); Broadway **return engagement**: Eugene O'Neill Theatre, 1982 (72 perf.); began as Off-Off-Broadway showcase; film, 1982.

This fun show was notable for Tommy Tune's (b. 1939) choreography.

Mona Stangley runs a successful brothel called the Chicken Ranch, established in 1840 and going strong ever since. It is frequented by Mona's friend Ed Earl Dodd, the local Sheriff, as well as by senators and other bigwigs. But the holier than thou, right-wing televangelist Melvin R. Thorpe mounts a hellfire crusade against the Chicken Ranch, and the establishment is forced to close.

Bettelstudent, Der (The Beggar Student) (deh: BEH tuhl shtoo DEHNT) Viennese operetta in 3 acts by Karl **Millöcker**; libretto by Friedrich **Zell** and Richard **Genée**, based on *Les Noces de Fernande* (Fernande's Wedding) (1870) (leh: no:s' duh fehr NAHND) by Victorien **Sardou**, and the five-act drama *The Lady of Lyons* (1838) by the English novelist and playwright, Edward Bulwer-Lytton (1803–1873); Vienna, Theater an der Wien (teh: AH tuh ahn deh VEEN), 1882.

A brilliant 1968 recording is available from EMI (7243 5 65387 2 6; 1994), complete with dialogue. The broad Saxon accents used by some of the actors add piquant flavor to the hilarious performance, and the enchanting music is beautifully sung.

In 1704, the occupying Saxon governor of Cracow, Colonel Ollendorf (O: lehn DAW[R]F) (bass), has been spurned by the young Polish aristocrat Laura Nowalska (LOW rah no: VAHL skah) (sop.) and insulted by her mother, Countess Nowalska (mezz.). He vows revenge and releases a young prisoner, Symon (ZEE mo:n) (ten.), disguising him as a wealthy aristocrat; Symon is to woo and wed Laura, and, as a reward, to receive his liberty and 10,000 crowns. The penniless student accepts the proposition, so long as his friend Jan (YAHN) (ten.) can accompany him, disguised as his secretary. Ollendorf agrees. Symon and Laura fall in love. He wants to confess everything but lacks the courage to do so, and they are married. Ollendorf then reveals the plot, and Laura realizes she has been the victim of his cruel revenge. But Symon and Jan, who is really an aristocrat in disguise, are involved in a plot to overthrow the Saxons. The Polish army besieges the city, and Ollendorf is obliged to surrender. The patriotic Symon is ennobled for his bravery and is reunited with Laura, who has forgiven him.

bharata natyam (BAH rah tah NAH tee ahm) A form of classical Indian dance, combined often with mime that tells a story based originally in Hinduism.

Bianchi, Giuseppe Francesco (1752–1810) (BYAH*N* kee) Distinguished Italian musician, singer, organist, conductor, and composer of more than seventy-five operas that were very popular and much admired in their day. He wrote six operas with Lorenzo **Da Ponte**, including *Armida* and *Antigona* (1794) (ahn TIH: go: nah) , the latter based on Sophocles' ancient Greek tragedy about the daughter of Oedipus and Jocasta. Bianchi also set libretti by Pietro **Metastasio**. He divided his time between Italy, Paris, and London. He committed suicide at his London home in Hammersmith.

Bickerstaffe, Isaac (1735–1812) [Also spelled Bickerstaff] Anglo-Irish librettist of some sixteen known works, including *The Maid of the Mill* (music by Samuel Arnold and others) and *Thomas and Sally* (music by Thomas Arne), and quite a few libretti for Charles **Dibdin**. After 1772, Bickerstaffe more or less disappears from history: He was hounded and persecuted in a homosexual scandal that involved several well known public figures, and he fled London, apparently dying in poverty. He is not to be confused with the pseudonymous Isaac Bickerstaff, a name adopted by Jonathan Swift as part of a hoax.

big band A large instrumental ensemble typically consisting of between twelve and twenty-five players; instruments included the trombone, saxophone, clarinet, trumpet (all of whom had solos), and a huge bass, drum, and percussion rhythm section; their heyday was in the 1930s and 1940s. Depending on the particular band, the music they played varied from jazz improvisation to dance music. Among the famous bandleaders: Paul Whiteman (1890–1967), known as the father of the big jazz band in the 1920s; jazz musician and composer Glenn Miller (1904–missing in action, 1944); the brothers, saxophonist and composer Jimmy (1904–1957) and trombonist Tommy Dorsey (1905–1956); William "Count" Basie (1904–1984); clarinetist Benny Goodman (1909–1986), known as the "King of Swing" and also for his playing of classical music; Harry James (1916–1983); trumpet and cornet player Louis Daniel Armstrong (1901–1971), affectionately known as "Satchmo" or "Pops"; composer Edward Kennedy "Duke" Ellington (1899–1974); Cabell "Cab" Calloway III (1907–1994); and jazz clarinetist and composer Artie Shaw (1910–2004) [b. Arthur Jacob Arshawsky]. The big bands played on stage, on the radio, and in Hollywood films.

Big Boy Broadway musical extravaganza; songs by prolific songwriter Buddy DeSylva (1895–1950), whose famous standards include "Button Up Your Overcoat" and "April Showers," and songwriter Joseph Meyer (1894–1987), whose songs include "California, Here I Come"; book by songwriter and librettist Harold Atteridge (1886–1938); Winter Garden Theatre, 1925 (56 perf.); film, 1930. This was a **vehicle** for Al Jolson (1886–1950), and it closed when he fell ill; he performed, as so often, in blackface

Gus, a stable boy for the Bedford family, is fired from his job due to the machinations of villains who want to fix the race at the Derby. But Gus manages to outwit them, and to ride Big Boy to victory.

On this thin plot, hit songs were hung, including "California, Here I Come!" (previously introduced by Jolson in the 1924 Broadway show *Bombo*) and "If You Knew Susie" (later, much more popular in the rendition by Eddie Cantor [1892–1964]). You can see excerpts from the film of *Big Boy*, as well as Eddie Cantor singing "If You Knew Susie," on YouTube.

Big River: The Adventures of Huckleberry Finn Broadway musical by Roger Miller (1936–1992); book by William Hauptman (b. 1942), based on the novel by Mark Twain (1835–1910); Eugene O'Neill Theatre, 1985 (1005 perf.); Broadway revival: American Airlines Theatre, 2003 (67 perf.), by Deaf West Theatre Company, as part of its national tour of the show, performed by both deaf and hearing actors, incorporating American Sign Language.

The runaway slave, Jim, joins his friend, Huck, when he escapes from his abusive alcoholic father. The two have many adventures along the Mississippi River, including an encounter with two con artists, the King and the Duke.

Billy Budd Opera in four acts by Benjamin **Britten**; libretto by English novelist E. M. Forster (1879–1970) and Eric Crozier (1914–1994), based on American writer Herman Melville's (1819–1891) story; London, Covent Garden, 1951.

During the Napoleonic era, the naïve, good-hearted innocent Billy Budd (bar.), afflicted with a stammer, has been pressed into service on the British man-o'-war H.M.S. *Indomitable*. His nemesis, the sadistic John Claggert (bass), master-at-arms, takes an immediate dislike to Budd, whom he hates because he is unconsciously attracted to him. He accuses Billy of treason. When Billy is summoned to answer the charge before Captain Vere (ten.), he stammers so dreadfully that he is unable to defend himself. In his frustration, he lashes out and kills Claggert, and he is sentenced to hang. Vere, who serves as narrator for the opera, has been haunted by what happened all his life: He had the power to commute the sentence, and he chose not to do so for reasons of expediency.

Billy Elliot: The Musical A highly successful musical comedy that opened in London in 2005 and on Broadway at the Imperial Theatre in 2008 (still running as of this writing); won the Tony® Award for Best Musical in 2009; music by Elton **John**; book and lyrics by Lee Hall (b. 1966), based on his screenplay for the 2000 film.

The lyrics are direct and forthright, and Elton John composed a beautiful score with wonderfully energetic dance music; touching, tuneful ballads; and stirring working-class anthems. The stage show is as emotionally uplifting and heart-warming as the film, with the story of Billy's own struggles set against the background of the sufferings and pride of the Yorkshire miners courageously standing up for their rights.

Billy Elliot is a boy from a Yorkshire coal-mining town who knows from an early age that he wants to be a ballet dancer. With the eventual support of his father and an understanding dance teacher, he overcomes the odds to realize his dream.

Bishop, Sir Henry Rowley (1786–1855) English composer and adapter of fifty-seven operas for the London stage, including Mozart's *Le nozze di Figaro* and Rossini's *Guillaume Tell*. His most well known original work is *Clari, or The Maid of Milan* (1823), containing the famous song "Home, Sweet Home."

Bitter Sweet An operetta in three acts by Noël **Coward**; libretto by the composer; London, Her Majesty's Theatre, 1929 (967 perf.); New York, Ziegfeld Theatre, 1929 (159 perf.); films: 1933, England; 1940, Hollywood, with the famous musical film team, soprano Jeannette MacDonald (1903–1965) and baritone Nelson Eddy (1901–1967). Coward is said to have wept when he saw the Hollywood movie, because he thought it so awful.

This operetta, popular with amateur societies, is also notable for an early documented use of the word "gay" to mean "homosexual," in the lyrics to a number sung by four dandies in act 3, "We All Wear a Green Carnation" (a well known symbol of homosexuality in the 1890s, worn in the lapel as a recognizable sign).

The elderly Marchioness of Shayne (sop.) reminisces about her earlier life, when she was studying singing in Vienna with the composer Carl Linden (bar.) and was madly in love with him. He was killed in a duel, and she returned to her native England, became a famous singer, and married the Marquis of Shayne. But she has never gotten over her first love.

Bizet, Georges (1838–1875) (zhawrzh' bee ZEH:) French composer of instrumental pieces and operas; studied with Charles **Gounod**. Bizet's most famous opera is *Carmen*; its initial failure probably contributed to his early death. Among his other operas are his first important work, *Les pêcheurs de perles* (The Pearl

Fishers) (1863) (leh: peh shuh*r*' de PEH*R*L); *La jolie fille de Perth* (The Fair Maid of Perth) (1867) (lah zho:' lee fee' yuh duh PEH*R*T), based on the novel of the same name by Sir Walter Scott (1771–1832); the unfinished *Ivan IV* (1862–1865), which contains some splendid music; the one-act masterpiece ***Djamileh*** (1872) (dgah MEE leh); *Le docteur Miracle* (Dr. Miracle) (1857) (luh dok tuh*r*' mee *R*AH kluh); and *Don Procopio* (1859) (don p*r*o ko' PYO:). Bizet married Geneviève **Halévy** (zheh nuh VYEHV ah' lé VEE) (1849–1926), daughter of the composer Halévy, and sister of the writer Ludovic Halévy, one of Offenbach's librettists. After his death she married the lawyer Emile Straus (ST*R*O:S; SHT*R*O:S) and became a noted society hostess; among her great friends was Marcel Proust (P*R*OOST) (1871–1922).

Black and Blue Broadway musical revue; Minskoff Theatre, 1989 (829 perf.). The revue featured well known and more obscure staged and choreographed **jazz** and **blues** numbers from the 1920s and 1930s. The African-American cast included such brilliant performers as Savion Glover (b. 1973), Tanya Gibson (b. 1960), and Carrie Smith (b. 1941). In 1993, Robert Altman (1925–2006) made a semi-documentary television film version, with both onstage and backstage scenes.

Black Crook, The American musical with an eclectic score consisting of songs by a number of contributors, arrangers, and adapters, headed by Thomas Baker, who wrote some original music for the show; much ballet music by G. Operti (?–1886); new songs were constantly being interpolated in the course of the run; book—"an Original Magical and Spectacular Drama in Four Acts"—by Charles M. Barras (1826–1873); New York, Niblo's Garden on Broadway and Prince Street, 1866 (475 perf.).

The *Black Crook* is often said to be the first American musical; it is certainly the first to have achieved widespread popularity, in an era when most shows ran for ca. thirty perf. The show was basically an excuse to exhibit as much of the female anatomy as was deemed respectable in that period, and the dancing chorus of "girls in pink tights" accounted for its appeal as one of the first **leg shows**. The myth is that the phenomenon of this dancing chorus came about by accident: In 1865, the Academy of Music had burned to the ground just at the point when a French ballet company had arrived to perform there, and the girls were stranded. The impresarios who had imported the company approached the manager of Niblo's Garden, William Wheatley (1816–1876), to see if they could rent the theater, and he decided to include the girls in the show, which was then in rehearsal. The reality is that renting Wheatley's theater was expensive, and the show's creators got a better deal at another theater, which burned down, so they went running back to Wheatley before he could have a chance to raise his prices. The show had already been put together, and the stranded ballet girls were part of it. Along with that attraction were the spectacular stage effects in a number of grandly elaborate transformation scenes, gorgeous scenery, and endless ballets. *The Black Crook* lasted more than five hours at its premiere; it was subsequently shortened, a bit. The show boasts the lamest lyrics and one of the worst written, most stilted, stupidest books ever penned for a musical—an opening night review in the *New York Times* called it "trashy," and that was an understatement. Barras, who took himself very seriously, was outraged when the producers who had signed a contract to present his play—and only then read the execrable script with mounting dismay, and realized what a potential flop they had on their hands—wanted to add music and turn it into a grand spectacle, but money purchased his acquiescence.

In the Harz mountains of Germany, the aging, crook-backed magician, Hertzog—the Black Crook of the title—has been promised another year of life for each soul he delivers to Zamiel, the Arch-Fiend. He ensnares the painter Rudolf (also spelled Rodolphe, depending on the issue of the program), who is in love with the peasant girl Amina, by promising to help him escape from the prison where he has been incarcerated after defying the evil Count Wolfenstein, who is also in love with Amina. Hertzog takes Rudolf to find a hidden treasure. On the way, Rudolf pauses to save the life of a dove, who turns out to be the Queen of the Golden Realm, Stalacta. She warns him that he is in danger, then sprits him away to Fairyland. Eventually, due to Stalacta's good offices, Rudolf is reunited with his beloved Amina, and Hertzog is "Foiled, tricked, crossed in the hour of my victory." After a "Grand procession of amphibea and gnomes, bearing in their arms and upon their heads salvers, shells, and quaint vases filled with gold and jewels," the conclusion calls for "an elaborate mechanical and scenical construction of the realms of STALACTA, occupying the entire stage. This scene must be of gradually-developing and culminating beauty ..."

The Black Crook had fifteen revivals, at least. The *New York Times* review of the 1873 revival called the original text "vacuous inanity," and said it had been "subjected to some compression" but "still preserves in its dialogue a fine capacity to bore." Still, the anonymous critic did love the special effects: "Some of the new effects, especially that produced by volumes of steam lighted up by calcium or other fires, are magnificent. The performing goat is wonderful ..." And the evening was a thunderously applauded success. In 1886, the revival included a "Mikado Ballet" (Gilbert and Sullivan's phenomenal hit had been produced the year before), and a performance by the Mignani family, who, as the *New York Times* reviewer said, "showed their ability at extracting music from paving stones, rammers, and broomsticks," on which they performed the "Triumphal March" from Verdi's *Aida*!

In 1954, *The Girl in Pink Tights*, an ahistorical, pedestrian Broadway musical by Sigmund **Romberg** about the creation of *The Black Crook*, with a book by Jerome Chodorov (1911–2004) and Joseph **Fields**, ran at the Mark Hellinger Theatre for 115 perf. The show is mainly notable for being Romberg's last effort, left uncompleted at his death; it was finished by Austrian-born American film actor and composer Charles Goldner (1900–1955), who also performed most amusingly as the ballet girls' manager: his is the only performance worth listening to on the original cast recording.

See also TRANSFORMATION SCENE.

39

Blackbirds of 1928 Broadway musical revue with songs by the prolific Jimmy McHugh (1894–1969) (music), who wrote 270 songs, including "I Can't Give You Anything But Love" and "On the Sunny Side of the Street"; and Dorothy **Fields** (lyrics); Liberty Theatre (518 perf.). The African-American cast included such famous stars as Bill "Bojangles" Robinson (1878–1949), one of the greatest tap dancers of all time; Adelaide Hall (1901–1993), who performed in Europe and the United States; Elizabeth Welch (1904–2003), who spent most of her career in England; and the Hall Johnson Choir. In 1930, 1933, and 1939, new *Blackbirds* revues were produced.

black bottom A vivacious 1920s dance, characterized by hip gyrations and sinuous moves in a rapid rhythm.

Blaemire, Nick (b. 1984) American singer, actor, composer and lyricist; he wrote the music and lyrics for Off-Broadway's *Glory Days* (2008), in which he also performed.

Blake, Eubie (1881–1983) [b. James Herbert Blake] American composer, songwriter, and musician. He often collaborated and performed with lyricist Noble **Sissle**, and the two wrote the musical *Shuffle Along* (1921), the first Broadway show written, produced, and performed by African-Americans, to be followed by four other hits, including *Elsie* (1923), *Chocolate Dandies* (1924), and two more *Shuffle Along* shows (1933; 1952). Blake also worked with other lyricists and performed internationally, having begun his career as a honky-tonk pianist.

Blane, Ralph (1914–1995) [b. Ralph Uriah Hunsecker] American composer, lyricist, and arranger; frequent collaborator with Hugh **Martin**. He contributed to the *New Faces* revue of 1936, and many other Broadway shows, including *Louisiana Purchase* and *Best Foot Forward* (1941), for which he and Martin did the music and lyrics.

bleat *n., v. —n.* **1.** The rapid alternation of a single note with variations in breath pressure; used in both singing and instrument playing; found in some **Monteverdi** operas, and used as late as the 19th c. in Richard Wagner's *Die Meistersinger*, in act 3, when the tailors tell their tale of the goatskin. Also called a *goat's trill*, from the sound imitative of the animal. *—v. i.* **2.** To alternate the same note rapidly, varying the breath pressure.
    See also TRILL.

Blitzstein, Marc (1905–1964) American writer, lyricist, and composer; wrote songs for the *Garrick Gaieties*; known for his translation/adaptation of Brecht and Weill's *Die Dreigroschenoper (The Threepenny Opera)*. Also composed the controversial leftist musical *The Cradle Will Rock*; and the opera *Regina* (1948), to his own libretto, based on the play *The Little Foxes* (1939) by Lillian Hellman (1905–1984), about the evil schemes of the covetous, power-hungry Southern matriarch Regina, who allows her husband Horace to die of a heart attack by refusing to give him his medication.

40

Blood Brothers West End, later Broadway musical by English composer/writer Willy Russell (b. 1947); London, Abbey Theatre, 1988 (still running at the Phoenix Theatre as of this writing); New York, Music Box Theatre, 1993 (840 perf.). Musically, the pop-rock score reflects the 1960s–'70s Beatles era, which is when the show takes place.

In Liverpool, fraternal twin boys are born to Mrs. Johnstone. Mickey remains with his mother, while the other is adopted by her employers, the wealthy Lyons family. Years later, Mickey Johnstone and Eddie Lyons meet each other but have no idea they are related, although they are surprised to learn they share a birthday, for which reason they make a pact to be "blood brothers." Eddie is pampered and Oxford-educated, while Mickey has become a despondent, petty criminal and serves a term in jail. Resenting his blood brother, Mickey invades the Lyons home and pulls out a gun. Mrs. Johnstone reveals the truth of their relationship in order to prevent tragedy, but the police rush in and shoot Mickey. As he falls, his gun goes off, killing Eddie.

Bloomer Girl Broadway musical by Harold **Arlen**; book by Fred **Saidy** and screenwriter Sid Herzig (1897–1985); lyrics by E. Y. **Harburg**; Shubert Theatre, 1944 (654 perf.).

Among the most memorable numbers from this delightful show are "Evelina" and the feminist protest **anthem** "It Was Good Enough for Grandma (But It Ain't Good Enough for Us)."

Set in 1861, during the Civil War, the musical was inspired by the life of Mrs. Amelia Bloomer (1818–1894), the writer, abolitionist, suffrage pioneer, and feminist reformer known, among other things, for her introduction of more comfortable, rational women's dress, esp. the bloomers (loose-fitting trousers gathered at the ankles) named for her. Her niece, Evelina Applegate, takes after her and is involved in the abolitionist and feminist movements, and in helping runaway slaves. Evelina's father, Horace, a wealthy hoop-skirt manufacturer, wants her to marry a slave-owning Southerner, Jeff Calhoun; but, although she is attracted to him, she will have nothing to do with him until he declares his adherence to the Union cause and the abolition of slavery, and frees his own slave Pompey. When he does, their love is assured.

Blossom, Henry (1866–1919) American stage writer, esp. of books for musical comedies, including many with Victor Herbert, among them *Mlle. Modiste* and *The Red Mill*. He was known as a solid writer and excellent lyricist, witty and sophisticated, and adept at drawing sharply delineated characters.

Blossom Time Broadway musical with a score by Sigmund **Romberg** adapted from music by Austrian romantic composer Franz Schubert (1797–1828); book and lyrics by Dorothy **Donnelly**, freely adapted from an internationally successful 1916 Viennese pastiche operetta, *Das Dreimädlerhaus* (The House of the Three Maidens) (dahs D*R*I MEH:DT luh[*r*] HOWS), with Schubert's music arranged by Hungarian Viennese composer Heinrich Berté (1857–1924) (beh[*r*] TÉ) and a libretto by Dr. Alfred Maria **Willner**, librettist and film director, Ernst Marischka

41

(1893–1963) (MAH rih:sh kah), and Heinz **Reichert**; also adapted in London as *Lilac Time*; Ambassador Theatre, 1921 (516 perf.); five Broadway revivals, including the only successful one, Jolson's 59th Street Theatre, 1924 (592 perf.); many national tours and amateur productions. A 1935 English film of the same name, with a completely altered plot and Schubert Lieder sung as originally written, in order to avoid paying for Romberg's version, starred idolized opera tenor Richard **Tauber** as Schubert.

The stage version of this **pastiche** (def. 2) operetta—which had so many schlock tours that it became a byword for the shabbily sentimental and the second-rate—presents a completely fictionalized, trivial account of Schubert's life. The composer of chamber music, symphonies, and more than 600 ethereally beautiful Lieder falls in love with a young lady named Mitzi Kranz. His rival is the wealthy Franz von Schober (in real life, one of Schubert's friends and patrons; they lived together for long periods of time), who wins Mitzi over by singing one of Schubert's songs to her. Schubert dies despairing, leaving his last symphony unfinished.

Bluebeard's Castle Opera by Béla Bartók. See A KÉKSZEKÁLLÚ HERCEG VÁRA.

bluegrass *n.* [Also used as an adj.: *bluegrass music*] A style of music first pioneered in the Kentucky bluegrass horse country; typically composed for a string **band** consisting of mandolin, guitar, fiddle (violin), bass, and piano; the music is lively, fast-paced, and often includes singing in harmony by a group; e.g., by the pioneers of bluegrass music, mandolin player, Bill Monroe (b. 1946) and his Blue Grass Boys, from Kentucky.

blues *n. pl.* [Used as a singular or pl. n.; fr. the slang use of the adj. *blue* to mean sad, unhappy, depressed: *I've got the blues*.] A style of song and music originally developed by African-American composers; e.g., the "Father of the Blues," the brilliant, much loved W. C. Handy (1873–1958) [William Christopher Handy], who established it as a popular art form. The blues dwells on the unhappiness of life, reflected in its lyrics, esp. bemoaning unrequited or lost love, and generally dealing with depressive, pessimistic states of mind. The music itself is characterized by its use of what came to be called the *blue note*; i.e., the third and seventh notes of a major scale, lowered by a semi-tone; and, in performance, by being crooned, rather than belted. There are various blues styles, including *country blues*, an early, simple form, beginning in the 19th c. and characterized by the use of the **ballad** and the acoustic guitar; and *urban blues*, originating in Chicago after World War II, with a vocalist accompanied by the electric guitar, harmonica, and percussion, esp. bass and drums.

bocca chiusa (BOK kah KYOO zah) [Italian: mouth closed] Humming, i.e., singing with the mouth closed; or, sometimes, with the lips open and the teeth closed. This is a technique that was used in teaching singing: The student would hum a line of music, and experiment with placement and breath control, so that when the mouth was opened, the student could sing the line with the feeling of placing the voice correctly in the **mask**. The technique of singing "bocca chiusa" is occasionally used in opera, as in the "Humming Chorus" in act 2 of Puccini's *Madama Butterfly*.

Boccaccio; oder Der Fürst von Palermo (Boccaccio, or The Prince of Palermo) (bo:k' KAH cho: O: deh:[r] deh:[r] FÜRST fon pah' LEHR mo:) Operetta in three acts by Franz von **Suppé**; libretto by Friedrich **Zell** and Richard **Genée**, based on a French play that is a fiction about the medieval Italian writer Giovanni Boccaccio (1313–1375), known for his book *The Decameron*; Vienna, Carl Theater, 1879. The music is brilliant, and this is usually considered von Suppé's masterpiece.

In Florence in 1331, Boccaccio is in love with Fiametta (fyah' MEHT tah) (sop.), adopted daughter of the grocer Lambertuccio (lahm' behr TOO cho:) (ten.), but the Duke of Tuscany (speaking role) has decided to acknowledge his paternity of Fiametta so that he can marry her to Pietro (PYEH: tro:), Prince of Palermo (ten.). She is taken to the palace, where Boccaccio has been commissioned to write a comedy to entertain the wedding guests. Its plot concerns a new suitor of Columbine, who must give her up so that she can marry a suitor with prior claims. Pietro, who has previously learned of the love of Fiametta and Boccaccio, understands the commedia's meaning immediately, as does the frowning Duke. He sternly condemns Boccaccio to life imprisonment ... as Fiametta's husband! And he appoints him Poet Laureate of his court, as a reward for his cleverness and ability.

Bock and Harnick Jerry Bock (b. 1928), composer; and Sheldon **Harnick**, lyricist and book writer; American musical comedy writing team, most famous for *Fiddler on the Roof*; they also wrote *Fiorello!* (1959), *Tenderloin* (1960), *She Loves Me* (1963), *The Apple Tree* (1966), and *The Rothschilds* (1970), their last collaboration before each decided to go his own way and work with other people.

bohème, La (lah bo: EHM) **1.** Opera in four acts by Giacomo **Puccini**; libretto by Giuseppe **Giacosa** and Luigi **Illica**, based loosely on the autobiographical novel *Scènes de la vie de bohème* (Scenes from Bohemian Life) (1847–1849) (SEHN duh lah vee' duh bo: EHM) by Henri Murger (1822–1861) (ahn ree' mür ZHEH:); Turin, Teatro Regio (REH dgo:), 1896.

Murger's novel was also adapted for a one-act **zarzuela**, *Bohemios* (Bohemians) (1904) (bo: EH:M ee o:s), by Amadeo **Vives**; and a Viennese operetta, *Das Veilchen von Montmartre* (The Little Violet of Montmartre) (1930) (dahs FIL khehn fon mo:n MAHR truh), by Emmerich **Kálmán**, with a libretto by Julius **Brammer** and Alfred **Grünwald**.

The story of this much loved and constantly performed **verismo** opera follows the lives and loves of a group of desperately impoverished artists in 19th-c. Paris. It is Christmas Eve. The poet Rodolfo (ro: DO:L fo:) (ten.) and his painter friend, Marcello (mahr CHEH:L lo:) (bar.), are freezing in the garret apartment they share, owned by Benoit (beh NWAH) (bass). Their friends, the musician Schaunard (sho: NAHR) (bar.), and the philosopher Colline (ko LEE neh) (bass), arrive with some food. Benoit comes to collect the rent, but they give him wine instead.

Rodolfo remains alone to finish his writing while the other three go out to a café. The seamstress Mimi (mee MEE) (sop.), their neighbor, comes in looking for a light for her candle, and the two fall instantly in love. At the Café Momus (mo: MÜS), Rodolfo introduces Mimi to his friends. The courtesan Musetta (moo ZEHT tah) (sop.) arrives with her wealthy, elderly patron, Alcindoro (ahl' chihn DO: ro:) (bass), but she leaves with her former lover, Marcello. Several weeks later, Mimi and Rodolfo have had a lover's quarrel; they decide that when the weather is warmer, in the spring, they will separate. Time passes, and the Bohemian friends have all met in the garret to have a festive time when Musetta enters and tells them that Mimi, dying of consumption, is nearly at the end of her life and wants to see Rodolfo once again. Mimi is brought in and put to bed. She dies, and Rodolfo is prostrate with grief.

2. Opera in four acts by Ruggiero **Leoncavallo**; libretto by the composer, based on the novel by Murger; Palermo, Teatro Massimo (MAHS see mo:), 1897.

See also RENT.

Bohemian Girl, The Opera in three acts by Michael William **Balfe**; libretto, based on a ballet scenario loosely adapted from Miguel de Cervantes' (1547–1616) novel *La gitanella* (The Gypsy Maid) (1613) (lah hee' tah NEH: yah), by theater manager Alfred Bunn (1796–1860), who produced several of Balfe's works in an attempt to establish opera in English; London, Drury Lane, 1844. The score contains some delightful melodies and exciting march and dance music.

Thaddeus (ten.), a Polish aristocrat in exile in Germany, falls in love with the gypsy maid Arline (sop.). Count Arneheim (bass) recognizes her as his long lost daughter, who had been kidnapped by gypsies. He rescues her, and she and Thaddeus are married.

Boieldieu, François-Adrien (1775–1834) (frahn SWAH ah dree EHN bo yehl DYOO) Much acclaimed, prolific French romantic opera composer. His best known work is *La dame blanche* (The White Lady) (1825) (lah dahm BLAHNSH); libretto by Eugène **Scribe**; the ten. aria, "Ah, quel plaisir d'être soldat!" (Ah, What a Pleasure to Be a Soldier!) (ah' kehl pleh ZEER deh truh sol DAH), was quoted humorously by Jacques **Offenbach** in *La Grande-Duchesse de Gérolstein*.

Boïto, Arrigo (1842–1918) (ah REE go: BO: ee to:) Italian librettist and **verismo** composer; wrote music and libretto for *Mefistofele*; wrote libretti for Amilcare Ponchielli's *La Gioconda* and Giuseppe Verdi's *Otello* and *Falstaff*. His unfinished opera *Nerone* (neh RO: neh:) (Nero), about the Roman emperor, was eventually completed by the celebrated conductor Arturo Toscanini (1867–1957) and others; Toscanini conducted its successful premiere in Rome in 1928.

bolero (bo: LEH: ro:) *n.* Spanish dance accompanied on castanets worked by the dancers, and by guitar and tambourine; in 3/4 time.

Bolton, Guy (1884–1979) Prolific Anglo-American writer who contributed to Hollywood musical films and wrote light-hearted, breezy, entertaining books for over fifty West End and Broadway musicals, including **Princess Theatre musicals**

with Jerome **Kern**, such as *Very Good Eddie*; and collaborations with P. G. **Wode-house**, among them *Anything Goes*, as well as *Oh, Boy!*, *Leave It to Jane*, and *Oh, Lady! Lady!* (1918). He also wrote the books for *Sally*, *Tip-Toes* and *Oh, Kay!*

Bombay Dreams West End and Broadway musical by A. R. Rahman. See MEEHAN, THOMAS.

Bones; Brudder [Brother] Bones *Hist.* In a **minstrel show**, the performer who sat on the end of the semicircle of minstrel singers and kept time by playing a pair of *bones*, a rhythm instrument consisting of two bones that were clacked together, or, more usually, two bone-shaped sticks of wood. He and the **Tambo** exchanged witty sallies and repartee with the **Interlocutor**. Also called the *pair of bones player*.

Bononcini, Giovanni (1670–1747) (bon' ihn CHEE nee) Italian composer of instrumental and sacred music; from a family of musicians; conductor and composer in Vienna at the Hapsburg court (1698–1712); wrote ca. thirty operas; internationally acclaimed for *Il trionfo di Camilla* (Camilla's Triumph) (1696) (ih:l tree ON fo: dee kah MEE lah). His most famous opera is *Griselda* (1722); excerpts starring Joan Sutherland (b. 1926) were recorded in 1966, available on Decca CD (448 977-2; 1996) along with highlights from *Montezuma* by **Graun**.

boogie-woogie *n.* A popular 1930s and early 1940s **jazz** and **blues** style, characterized by a strong, rhythmic **ostinato** bass accompaniment; originating as piano solos in the 1920s, with shifting chords for the left hand and ornamented variations on themes for the right hand. Boogie-woogie was sometimes played on three pianos, and was also played by big bands, esp. for dances.

book *n.*, *v.* —*n.* **1.** The text or libretto of a musical comedy or operetta. **2.** That part of the script of a musical comedy or operetta that includes the spoken dialogue and lyrics. **3.** The prompt copy of the script used by the stage manager. —*v. t.* **4.** To be hired for a particular job: *She booked the job*; hence, *booking*: an engagement for a job. **5.** To hire someone to do a job in entertainment and related fields, e.g., modeling; photography: *He booked the actor*. **6.** To buy tickets to an entertainment event: *to book seats*.

book number A song, dance number, or ensemble piece that helps to advance the story in a musical comedy or operetta.

book show A musical comedy, with its spoken dialogue and storyline, as opposed to a variety show or musical revue.

bop *n.*, *v.* —*n.* **1.** Short for and syn. with **bebop**. —*v. t.* **2.** To play or perform bebop music; by extension, to be "with it," *in the groove*, *in the know*. Cf. **rock**.

Boris Godunov (bah REES go' doo NOF) Opera in a prologue and four acts by Modest **Mussorgsky**; libretto by the composer, based on a dramatic narrative poem by Alexander Pushkin (1799–1837) and on *History of the Russian Empire* by Nikolai Mihailovich Karamzin (1766–1826) (nyih ko LI mih HAHEE lo vihch kah rahm ZEEN); composed in 1870; considerably revised by the composer in 1871; St. Petersburg, Mariinsky (mah' ree IH:N skee) Theater, 1874. The opera was revised twice after Mussorgsky's death by Nikolai **Rimsky-Korsakov**, in 1896 and 1906–1908; the now "standard version" was first produced at the Paris Opéra in 1908.

In 1591, nine year-old Dmitry (DMEE tree), heir to the throne of Ivan the Terrible, is murdered by Ivan's brother-in-law, the boyar Boris Godunov (bass). When Dmitry's brother Fyodor dies in 1598, Boris is offered the crown, which he pretends to decline, but finally accepts. Meanwhile, the ascetic monk Pimen (PYIH myehn) (bass), a former soldier who had witnessed the murder, is in his cell writing his history of Russia, which includes the slaying. He is aided by his assistant, the passionate Grigory (grih GO: ree) (ten.), who is the same age as Dmitry, and vows to avenge him. He poses as Dmitry and enters Russia through the Lithuanian border with the help of his two companions, the hedonistic monks Varlaam (VAHR lahm) (bass) and Missail (MEE sIl) (ten), who know nothing of his schemes. They are pursued by soldiers who are on the lookout, having heard rumors of the "false Dmitry." They manage to escape. Boris, having heard the rumors, thinks he may be going mad, but his confidant, Shuisky (shoo IH:S kee) (ten.), assures him that the boy had indeed been killed, and that this Dmitry is therefore obviously an imposter. When he leaves, Boris is prey to despair and hallucinations. Meanwhile, the restless people have begun to believe that Dmitry is still alive, and that he will soon arrive to claim his rightful place. Outside St. Basil's Cathedral, Boris is accosted by a Simpleton (ten.), who has been robbed of a kopek. He asks Boris to kill the thieves, as he had killed the boy, Dmitry. Boris is shocked, but retains his self-control and orders that the Simpleton remain free. Boris asks him to pray for him, but instead the Simpleton prays for the good of all Russia. Later, in the council chambers, the ministers are preparing a decree denouncing the imposter when Boris bursts in and collapses dead at their feet.

In Mussorgsky's revision, much weight is given to the love of Grigory, who has escaped to Poland, and the Polish noblewoman Marina (mah REE nah) (sop.), who wants to mount a revolution and rule Russia with Grigory, bringing about a Catholic renaissance and overthrowing Russian Orthodoxy.

Borodin, Alexander (1833–1887) (BO ro deen') Russian composer whose music was adapted for Broadway's *Kismet*. He never finished his projected operas, but *Knyaz Igor (Prince Igor)*, his masterpiece, was completed by Nikolai **Rimsky-Korsakov** and Alexander Glazunov (1865–1936) (GLAH zoo nof).

Boston *n.* A slow, sensuous **waltz**, popular in the early part of the 20th c. Also called hesitation waltz.

bossa nova (BAW sah NO: vah) [Portuguese: new trend] An innovative Brazilian dance with a combination of South American and American-style syncopated **jazz** music, played on the guitar, sometimes with drum accompaniment, and often with vocals; highly popular from about 1958 to 1963 in the United States.

Boublil, Alain (b. 1941) (ah la*n* boo BLIH:L) French librettist who usually writes with composer Claude-Michel **Schönberg**. The collaborated on two international hit musicals, *Les Misérables* and *Miss Saigon*. Less successful were *Martin Guerre* (1996) and *The Pirate Queen* (2006). Their collaboration began in 1973 with the spectacular **rock opera** *La révolution française* (The French Revolution) (lah *r*é vo: lü syo:*n*' frah*n* SEHZ).

bourgeois gentilhomme, Le (luh boo*r* zhwah' zhah*n* tee UHM) A **comédie-ballet** by Molière (1622–1673) (mo: LYEH:*R*) [Jean-Baptiste Poquelin (zhah*n* bah teest' po KLA*N*)] and Jean-Baptiste **Lully**; France, Chambord (shahm BO:*R*), 1670.

Known more today as one of Molière's most famous comedies than for Lully's droll music, the play centers around the efforts of the pretentious, ignorant Monsieur Jourdain (zhoo*r* DA*N*), played originally by Molière, to educate himself in the ways of the aristocracy in order to win the affections of a callous Marquise who connives with her aristocratic lover to bilk Jourdain of his money by flattering his ambitions. On the surface, the play seems to say that one should conform to the social class of which one is a member. But if the point of the satire were merely that, it would long ago have ceased to be performed; its more universal target, and its subversiveness, lie in mocking the cruelty of the system. Lully's music and the ballet sequences delighted the court of Louis XIV. The music is sprightly, lively, and original, much of it in the faux-Turkish mode of the day, popular since the Turkish ambassador's visit to the court of Versailles in 1669.

bourrée (boo *R*É)]French] **1.** A Renaissance French folk dance in 3/4 or 2/2 time; it features a skipping step alternating with jumps and slides. **2.** An aristocratic 17th- and 18th-c. dance with graceful skipping steps, performed at formal court functions by couples, often in alternation with a number of different dances in a series. **3.** In **ballet**, a series of small running steps, often performed **en pointe**.

box step A dance **combination** consisting of crossing the left foot over the right, stepping back on the right foot, then stepping to the left with the left foot, and ending by bringing the right foot parallel to the left foot. Often used as a basic step in musical comedy choreography. Also called a *jazz square*.

Boy Friend, The London, then Broadway musical by Sandy Wilson (b. 1924); book by the composer; Royale Theatre, 1954 (485 perf.); Broadway revival, Ambassador Theatre, 1970 (111 perf.); filmed in 1971, as a **burlesque** of a company putting on a production.

A spoof of the musicals of the 1920s and of the **Princess Theatre musicals**, the show parodies the delightful inanities and clichés of the high-living era. The role of Polly was played by Julie Andrews (b. 1935), making her Broadway debut.

In the sunny south of France at an exclusive boarding school for girls, Polly, from a family rich beyond the dreams of avarice, falls in love with the poor delivery boy Tony, who, in true P. G. **Wodehouse** fashion, is really a rich boy in disguise. Complications ensue, but all the intrigues are satisfactorily resolved as everyone bats their eyelashes and indulges in a Charleston.

Boy from Oz, The Broadway **jukebox musical**, with Peter Allen's 1970s pop songs; book by American screenwriter and playwright Martin Sherman (b. 1938) and Australian playwright Nick Enright (1950–2003); Imperial Theatre, 2003 (364 perf.).

The show is a biographical drama about the life and death of the award-winning gay Australian songwriter, singer, and celebrity entertainer Peter Allen (1944–1992), who died of AIDS. He was as famous for his relationships with Judy Garland (1922–1969) and her daughter Liza Minnelli (b. 1946), whom he married but later divorced—both are characters in the musical—as he was for his songs. But it was the performance in the title role of fellow Australian star Hugh Jackman (b. 1968), a superb actor and singer, that ensured the show's success.

Boys from Syracuse, The Broadway musical by **Rodgers and Hart**: Richard **Rodgers** (music) and Lorenz **Hart** (lyrics); book by George **Abbott** (who also produced and directed), adapted from *The Comedy of Errors* by William **Shakespeare**, who based his play on ancient Roman comedies; Alvin Theatre, 1938 (235 perf.); Off-Broadway revival, Theater Four, 1963 (502 perf.); Broadway revival: American Airlines Theatre, 2002 (107 perf.); filmed, in a highly truncated version, in 1940.

The score is a delightful romp, jazzy and funny, like the lyrics; its most well known song is "This Can't Be Love." Part of the fun comes from Abbott's anachronistic, 1930s dialogue; he used almost none of Shakespeare's writing in this, the first musical comedy from a Shakespearean source.

Antipholus and his slave, Dromio, travel from Ephesus to Syracuse. Unknown to each, they have twins who live there, with whom the Syracusans immediately confuse them. The Syracusan Antipholus and Dromio are married to Adriana and Luce, causing complications that are only resolved when the father of the twin Antipholus brothers, Aegon, sees them together and sets matters to right; the twins were separated in a shipwreck, and he is thrilled to see them again.

Braham, David (1834–1905) British-born American song and musical comedy composer; known as "The American **Offenbach**"; musical director and composer for the performing team Harrigan and Hart [actor, playwright, and composer Edward Harrigan (1844–1911) and performer Tony Hart (1855–1891); Harrigan married Braham's daughter]. The team appeared in Broadway musicals written by Braham, most of them with book and lyrics by Harrigan. Among the most successful of their shows were "The Mulligan Guards" series, inspired by Braham's 1873 hit song of that name, with Harrigan's lyrics set to a catchy, jaunty tune in 2/4 time: "We crave your condescension,/ We'll tell you what we know,/ Marching in the Mulligan Guards/ In the Seventh Ward below./ Our captain's name was Hussey,/ A Tipperary man./ He carried his sword like a Rooshian Duke/ When e'er he took command …" The song was a satire of the many pseudo-military "social clubs," complete with obligatory uniforms, that proliferated just after the American Civil War ended in 1865. The rapidly turned-out series of musicals began with *The Mulligan Guard Picnic* in 1878, and continued with ***The Mulligan***

Guards' Ball in 1879, followed that same year by *The Mulligan Guards' Chowder*. The year 1879 also saw the official D'Oyly Carte American production of Gilbert and Sullivan's *H. M. S. Pinafore*, previously seen in the U.S. in pirated versions; together with *The Brook* and Braham and Harrigan's shows, these were the big hits of that season. Two more in the series were produced the next year in quick succession: *The Mulligan Guards' Nominee* and *The Mulligan Guards' Surprise*. In 1881, the team produced *The Mulligan Guards' Silver Wedding*, and in 1883 they revived *The Mulligan Guards' Ball*, with new music added, and produced *Cordelia's Aspirations*, one of their most hilarious successes, with Cordelia Mulligan having delusions of grandeur and wanting to move uptown but deciding finally that the old downtown neighborhood is best. Braham and Harrigan wrote many other hit shows as well, among them *Old Lavender* (1885) and *Notoriety* (1894), and Braham wrote many songs and shows with other lyricists and librettists. For more on this colorful character and his delightful, now sadly all but forgotten music, see *David Braham: The American Offenbach* (Routledge, 2003) by John Franceschina.

Brammer, Julius (1877–1943) (BRAH muh) Austro-Hungarian librettist; often co-wrote libretti with Alfred **Grünwald** for operettas by Oscar **Straus**, Leo **Fall** (*Die Rose von Stambul*), and Emmerich **Kálmán**, including *Gräfin Mariza* and *Die Herzogin von Chicago*, among others. In 1943, during World War II, he was caught up in the Vichy dragnet in the south of France and murdered because he was Jewish.

branle (BRAHN luh) *n.* [French: shake] A French folk dance originating in medieval times; later popular in the 17th c. at the court of Louis XIV, and incorporated into the elaborate ballets presented there.

brass band A band composed of brass instruments: trumpet, horn, trombone, and so forth; sometimes with percussion added, but no woodwinds or strings.

Bray, Stephen (b. 1956) American songwriter, record producer (his label: Soultone records), and drummer; composed many songs in collaboration with singing star Madonna; co-composer and co-lyricist of the Broadway musical *The Color Purple*.

break *n., v.* —*n.* **1.** In singing, the place where one vocal **register** changes to the next one; e.g., where the chest goes into the head, or where the middle register becomes the high register: *where the voice breaks.* **2.** A **crack** in the voice or other momentary vocal imperfection due to undue tension or faulty singing technique. **3.** In playing brass or woodwinds, a momentary poor or imperfect tone, perhaps with a squeak, produced either by incorrect lipping technique for a brass instrument, or by an imperfection in the reed of a woodwind. **4.** A brief pause in the work of rehearsal or technical set-ups, esp. one meant to be a refreshing breather; hence, *to take a break.* **5.** A lucky opportunity or chance for an actor or singer to be noticed: *Being cast as Gilda in* **Rigoletto** *was her big break.* **6.** The interval between the large divisions of a stage piece; intermission; hence also, *act break*:

an intermission between acts, during a performance. —*v. i.* **7.** To change vocally from a childish **treble** to an adult voice: *The boy soprano's voice broke.* **8.** To end a workday in the theater, esp. during the rehearsal period: *to break for the day.*

breakdance; break dance; breakdancing *n.* A unique style of athletic urban street dance that originated in the 1970s in the African-American and Puerto Rican communities in New York City, esp. in Manhattan and the South Bronx; part of the **hip hop movement**. Its four basic moves are: 1) *toprock*: rhythmic, flexible, coordinated steps performed while standing; 2) *downrock*: steps involving footwork but performed on the ground or floor, using the hands as well, to move the body around; 3) *power moves*: athletic moves expressive of muscular power, involving momentum, using hands and feet, throwing the body around, and using the arms, e.g., in windmill-like gestures; 4) *freezes*: momentary stoppage of the dance, leaving the dancer in a pose from which he or she moves on to the next series of steps, many of them improvised. Having become well known nationally, breakdancing has been used in contemporary musical theater pieces. It is also taught in dance academies. Also called *breaking*; *b-boying*; hence, *breaker*, *breakdancer*, *b-boy*, *b-girl*: the person who breakdances.

breath control The management of the intake and outflow of air from the lungs, helped by diaphragmatic breathing: an important part of **vocal technique**.
See also DIAPHRAGM.

breathing mark A performance mark or symbol in a score indicating that a singer may or must breathe at that point. Also called *breath mark*.

breathing technique The method used to control the intake and outflow of air when singing, playing a musical instrument, or speaking on stage.

breath pause A very brief stop in singing, so that the singer can draw in air before continuing. Also called a *pause for breath*.

Brecht, Berthold (1898–1956) (BEH:[*R*] to:lt B*REKH*T) German playwright, librettist, and theoretician; known, among other things, for his collaborations with composer Kurt **Weill**, including *Die Dreigroschenoper (The Threepenny Opera)*, *Happy End*, and *Aufstieg und Fall der Stadt Mahagonny*. He also collaborated with other composers, among them Hanns **Eisler**. Brecht's iconoclastic ideas on theater were linked to his political ideas as a Communist: He thought theater that demanded the audience's rapt attention and elicited manipulated responses was a manifestation of bourgeois capitalism and called unconsciously for the basic acceptance of the system. He wanted to create what he called an "alienation," or "distancing effect," by which he meant a didactic, politicizing distantiation between audience and performance. To achieve this, Brecht used exposed lighting, ropes, sandbags, and other usually hidden production elements; and insisted that actors be directed to show, or indicate the character, rather than embodying it. The spectators were to be critical observers of the show, always aware that they were looking at a stage, and that a message was being conveyed.

Brel, Jacques Belgian songwriter and singer. See JACQUES BREL IS ALIVE AND WELL AND LIVING IN PARIS.

breeches part Syn. with **trousers role**, esp. in **opera**. Also called *pants part*; *pants role*.

Bricusse, Leslie (b. 1931) English composer and lyricist. Collaborated with Anthony **Newley** on *Stop the Word—I Want to Get Off* (1962), ***The Roar of the Greasepaint—The Smell of the Crowd***, and on a television version of ***Peter Pan***. Bricusse also wrote the lyrics for ***Victor/Victoria*** and the book and lyrics for Frank Wildhorn's *Jekyll and Hyde*.

bridge *n.* A brief transitional section between two important parts of a musical **number**, symphony movement, **opera scena**, etc.

Brigadoon Broadway musical by **Lerner and Loewe**: Alan Jay Lerner (book and lyrics) and Frederick Loewe (music); Ziegfeld Theatre, 1947 (581 perf.); Broadway revival: Majestic Theatre, 1980 (141 perf.); New York City Center Light Opera Company and New York City Opera productions, and innumerable summer stock presentations; film, 1954.

This was Lerner and Loewe's first big hit. Agnes de Mille's (1905–1993) masterful choreography helped ensure the show's success.

The enchanted village of Brigadoon, Scotland comes to life once every hundred years, its inhabitants having slept through each century-long protective night. Hunting in the Highlands, American tourists Jeff Douglas and Tommy Albright run across the village, which has just awakened. Tommy falls in love with a village lass, Fiona, and Jeff is pursued by the man chaser Meg. Harry, the spurned suitor of Fiona's sister, Jean, who is about to be married to Charlie, tries to leave the village, which would mean its demise: all the inhabitants are duty-bound to reside there, or the enchantment will be broken. But the vengeful Harry dies while trying to escape, so the village is safe. Jeff and Tommy return to New York, but Tommy longs for Fiona and goes back to Scotland. His love is so overwhelming that, by another miracle, the village comes to life for a moment, allowing Tommy to join Fiona in eternal bliss.

brigands, Les (The Brigands) (leh: b*r*ee GAH*N*) **Opéra bouffe** in three acts by Jacques **Offenbach**; libretto by Henri **Meilhac** and Ludovic **Halévy**; Paris, Théâtre des Variétés, 1869.

The almost **Brechtian** libretto represents the duo at their most wickedly satirical, and the vibrant, tuneful score is one of Offenbach's greatest. One of the best numbers is the song of the brigands, when they hear the perpetually late carabiniers in the distance: their tramping boots always give them away. W. S. **Gilbert** did a translation, *The Brigands*, published in 1871 but not produced until 1889, when it was mounted in New York at the Casino Theatre (113 perf.); it starred Lillian Russell (1861?–1922) as Fiorella.

In the forested mountains near Mantua, Italy, on the Spanish border (you can forget what you know of geography), the band of brigands led by Falsacappa (fahl' sah kah PAH) (bar.) is discontented and threatening revolt when Fragoletto (frah' go: leh' TO:) (sop.), in love with Falsacappa's daughter, Fiorella (fee o: reh' LAH) (sop.), captures a cabinet courier. The courier was on his way to the Prince of Mantua (ten.) to convey the news that his future bride and her entourage are journeying thither from Spain, expecting to collect three million as her dowry. Falsacappa waylays the expedition, imprisons them in an inn, and proceeds to the court with Fiorella masquerading as the Princess, only to discover that the Treasurer (bar.) has embezzled all the money to pay for his amours. The real Princess (sop.) and her entourage, having escaped from their confines, arrive at court, and things look very bad, until Fiorella reminds the Prince that they had met previously: the Prince had been lost in the forest and Fiorella had helped him to escape, saving his life. He is grateful, and pardons them all.

brindisi (BRIHN dee see) *n.* [Italian: from the southwestern Italian port of Brindisi] A drinking song or aria.

British Blondes *Hist.* A group of young ladies from England who toured the United States in the 1860s doing **leg shows** that were musical parodies of well known stories, such as "Ali Baba and the Forty Thieves"; their leader was the burlesque star Lydia Thompson (1836–1908); they performed in tights, showing off their legs, which were the main attractions.

Britten, Benjamin (Lord Britten of Aldeburgh; 1913–1976) Prolific English composer, conductor, and pianist; wrote many operas, among them *Paul Bunyan* (1941), his first, unsuccessful until its revival in 1976; *Peter Grimes*, his second, starring his life partner, ten. Sir Peter Pears (1910–1986); and his first big hit, *The Rape of Lucretia* (1946); ***Albert Herring***, ***Billy Budd***, ***The Turn of the Screw***, *A Midsummer Night's Dream*; the television opera *Owen Wingrave* (1971); and *Death in Venice*, his last. Britten did arrangements for a version of ***The Beggar's Opera***; and a two-piano version of Poulenc's ***Les mamelles de Tirésias***, in collaboration with the composer. A biographical documentary, *The Hidden Heart: A Life of Benjamin Britten and Peter Pears* (2001), with archival footage of Britten conducting and Pears in the original production of *Peter Grimes*, is available on DVD (EMI; 50999 2 16571 9 1; 2008).

See also VOLTA.

Broadway *n.* **1.** A north-to-south avenue in Manhattan; called "The Great White Way," because of the lights that illuminate it at night. **2.** New York City's main theater district, located in midtown.

Broadway swell *Hist.* A stock comic character in a **minstrel show**; he was very urban, brazen, conceited, bold-faced, and sporty, in flashy, dandified dress.

Brook, The; or, A Jolly Day at the Picnic Broadway musical comedy by the principal owner of William Cody's (1846–1917) "Buffalo Bill's Wild West" show, Nate Salsbury (1846–1902); written for his troupe, the Salsbury Troubadours, originating out of San Francisco; The San Francisco Minstrels' Hall, 1879.

Five friends decide to go on a picnic, where they perform songs, dances, and sketches for each other. They carry their props and costumes in their picnic baskets, along with lunch.

Brooks, Mel (b. 1926) Actor, writer, director, composer, lyricist; known for his hilarious comic shtick as a performer, and for his broad, satirical film comedies, two of which he turned into Broadway musicals: *The Producers* and *Young Frankenstein*. In 1962, he wrote the book for *All American*, a Broadway college football musical by Charles **Strouse**, with lyrics by Lee **Adams**.

Brown, Jason Robert (b. 1970) Broadway musical composer and lyricist; among his works are *Parade* (1998), book by Alfred Uhry (b. 1936), based on the historical events surrounding the anti-Semitic lynching of Leo Frank in Atlanta in 1913—the show was brilliantly directed by Harold Prince (b. 1928); the Off-Broadway, two-person show *The Last Five Years* (2001); and *13* (opened in Los Angeles, 2007; Broadway, 2008).

Bruch, Max (1838–1920) (MAHKS B*ROOKH*) German late-romantic composer of symphonies, violin concerti, chamber music and choral works; he wrote three operas: a **Literaturoper** in one act based on a text by Johann Wolfgang von Goethe (1749–1832), *Scherz, List und Rache* (Fun, Cunning, and Revenge) (1858) (SHEH[*R*]TS LIHST oont *R*AH kheh); *Die Loreley* (1863) (dee LO: *r*eh LI), which he called a "grosse romantische Oper" (G*R*O: seh *r*o: MAHN tih sheh O: peh[*r*]) (Grand Romantic Opera), about a love triangle that ends unhappily for all three protagonists, with the spirits of the Rhine claiming Lenore (leh: NO: *r*eh) (sop.), who had signed a pact with them; and *Hermione* (1872) (HEH[*R*] mee O: neh), in four acts, based on *The Winter's Tale* by William Shakespeare.

Brudder Bones One of the two **end men** in a **minstrel show**. See BONES.

Brudder Tambo One of the two **end men** in a **minstrel show**. See TAMBO.

Bruder Straubinger (Brother Straubinger) Viennese operetta by Edmund **Eysler**.

Bruneau, Alfred (1857–1934) [b. Louis Charles Bonaventure Alfred Bruneau (bo nah vahn tü*r*' ahl f*r*ehd' b*r*ü NO:)] French cellist, composer of art songs, sacred music; studied with **Massenet**, who influenced his musical style. Of his thirteen operas, most are based on legends and fairy tales; e.g., *Le jardin du paradis* (The Garden of Paradise) (1923) (luh zhah*r* d*a*n dü pah *r*ah DEE), based on the fairy tale by Hans Christian **Andersen**. His most famous work is the anti-war opera *L'attaque du moulin* (The Attack on the Mill) (1891) (lah tahk' dü moo LA*N*), based on a story by the naturalist writer Emile Zola (1840–1902), about an incident during the Franco-Prussian war of 1871. Zola, whom Bruneau supported politically, wrote several libretti for him.

Bubbling Brown Sugar Broadway musical revue, transferred from its Off-Broadway production; conceived by African-American producer and singer-actor Rosetta LeNoire (1911–2002), who appeared in many Broadway shows; ANTA

Playhouse, 1976 (766 perf.). This delightful "all-black" show revisits and celebrates the great days of the creative entertainers at Harlem's Cotton Club, and the Apollo Theatre on 125th Street; the revue features songs written mostly between 1920 and 1940.

buck dancing An early form of tap dancing, in which the dancers were relatively still from the waist up, while they stayed in one place and danced mostly on the balls of their feet, wearing shoes with wooden soles, rather than ones with metal taps.

buffo (BOOF fo:) *n., adj.* [Italian: comic; funny] —*n.* **1.** A singer of comic roles, e.g., *basso buffo*: a comic bass, such as the interpreters of Leporello in Mozart's ***Don Giovanni***, or Dr. Dulcamara in Donizetti's ***L'elisir d'amore***. Also called a *buffoon*. **2.** A comic actor; a comedian; a clown. —*adj.* **3.** Comic; droll; funny. **4.** Pertaining to comic roles: *buffo roles*.

bulerias (boo' lehr EE ahs) *n.* [Spanish] A Spanish **flamenco** dance: the concluding dance or dances at the end of a flamenco presentation, meant to show off the skills of the dancers in rapid movement. Also called *chuflas* (CHOO flahs) [boasting; showing off].

bump *n., v.* —*n.* **1.** A back and forward thrust of the pelvis, used in dance, esp. burlesque and other forms of provocative dance; also used in Broadway musical theater choreography. —*v. t.* **2.** To thrust the pelvis forward or back, as in the *bump and grind* movements of a striptease artist; the grind being a gyrating movement of the pelvis.

burden n. In music, another word for the **refrain** or **chorus** (def. 5) at the end of each verse of a song.

burlesque *n., v.* —*n.* **1.** A form of musical theater that combines comedy sketches, musical numbers, and ladies who strip for the audience; hence, *burlesque house*: a theater where such shows take place. **2.** A **parody** or **spoof** of a well known piece, or of an author's or composer's work. —*v. t.* **3.** To write, compose, or perform such a parody; to lampoon a work, author, or composer.

burletta (buhr LEH tuh) *n.* [Fr. Italian (boor LEH:T tah): little joke] *Hist.* A late 18th- and early 19th-c. English three-act farce with at least five songs, to get around the licensing laws that allowed spoken plays to be performed only at certain patent theaters.

Burnand, Sir Francis Cowley (1836–1917) [Wrote as F. C. Burnand] English humorist and librettist; editor of *Punch* magazine (1880–1906); wrote more than 100 texts for burlesques, operatic parodies, and comic operas; among them, the one-act *Cox and Box* (1867), with **Sullivan**; adapted Offenbach's ***La vie parisienne*** for the English stage.

Burrows, Abe (1910–1985) [b. Abram Solman Borowitz] American stage director and writer; wrote and/or doctored books for Broadway musicals, including ***Can-Can***, ***Guys and Dolls***, ***Silk Stockings***, and *How to Succeed in Business*

Without Really Trying (1961), about a window washer who uses a guide—hence, the title of the musical—to rise to a position of corporate prominence.

Busoni, Ferruccio (1866–1924) [Dante Michelangelo Benvenuto Ferruccio Busoni (DAHN teh: MIH: kehl AHN dgeh lo: behn' vehn OO to: fehr ROOCH cho: boo ZO: nee)] Innovative German-Italian pianist and composer; professor at the Akademie der Kunst (Academy of Art) (ah kah deh MEE deh[r] KOONST) in Berlin, where his pupils included Kurt **Weill**; wrote five operas, including *Doktor Faust* (composed from 1916 through 1924, and produced posthumously in 1925), for which he wrote his own libretto, based on 16th-c. puppet plays.

See also FAUST.

butoh (BOO to:) *n.* A contemporary, iconoclastic, expressionistic Japanese dance form that began at the end of the 1950s. Dancers perform in the nude, their faces painted white, their heads shaved. The deliberate, slow movements are bizarre and angular, expressive of repression and oppression, and, with some choreographers, meant to invoke the spiritual nature of man beyond the vision of the physical.

button *n. Slang.* **1.** The last, climactic note and moment of a musical **number** or musical comedy dance, delivered sometimes with a finalizing movement or gesture, so that the audience knows it is time to applaud. **2.** A joke's punch line, delivered in such a way as to cap the joke and make the audience laugh: *to put a button on it.*

By Jupiter Broadway musical by **Rodgers and Hart**: Richard **Rodgers** (music and book) and Lorenz **Hart** (book and lyrics), based on the play *The Warrior's Husband* (1932) by Julian F. Thompson (1888–1939); Shubert Theatre, 1942 (427 perf.). This was Rodgers and Hart's last collaboration, almost forgotten nowadays; Hart died a year after it was produced.

The story is based on the myth of Hercules, one of whose twelve imposed labors is to steal the magic girdle of the goddess Diana, now worn by Hippolyta, Queen of the Amazons, who rules Pontus together with her warrior Amazon women, while their husbands live the good life. When Hercules and Theseus lead the Greek army in an invasion, the Amazons fall in love with them. Hercules falls in love with Antiope, Hyppolyta's sister. The women cannot resist, and they surrender, leaving the kingdom to be ruled by men, with women as the power behind the throne—as the show maintains they always have been anyway.

Bye Bye Birdie Broadway musical by Charles **Strouse**; lyrics by Lee **Adams**; book by Michael **Stewart**; Martin Beck Theatre, 1960 (607 perf.); Broadway revival: Henry Miller's Theatre, 2009 (limited engagement); film, 1963. Among the delightful pop score's numbers, "Put on a Happy Face" remains a standard.

This silly but very funny show parodies sensational singing star Elvis Presley (1935–1977), who was still one of the great teenage heart-throbs when the show was written.

Conrad Birdie (an Elvis clone) is drafted by Uncle Sam, but before he leaves to begin his service, his manager, Albert, and Rose, Albert's fiancée, think it would be a great idea to garner publicity by having him sing a farewell song to one of his adoring teenage fans on national television. Kim, the selected fan, is ecstatic, but her boyfriend, Hugo, is less than thrilled. After a good many plot complications, they are reconciled. Conrad goes off to do his military duty, and Albert and Rose are married; she has convinced him to pursue his dreams, so he leaves show business to become a high school English teacher.

Byron, H. J. (1835–1884) [b. Henry James Byron] English writer of more than 100 musical pasticcios, burlesques full of puns, and operatic parodies with silly titles like *Lucia di Lammermoor, or the Luckless Laird, the Lovely Lady, and the Little Lover* (1865); translated Lecocq's ***La fille de Madame Angot*** (1873) and Offenbach's *La jolie parfumeuse* (1874) for the English stage.

C

cabaletta (kah' bah LEHT tah) *n.* [Italian: galloping section of music, in imitation of a horse's movement] The concluding, often fast-paced section of an **aria** or **opera scena** in a 19th c. opera.

cabaret (kab' uh RAY) *n.* [Fr. French] **1.** A French nightclub, with entertainment in the form of singing and dancing. **2.** A show at a nightclub or in a public room set aside for entertainment; covered in many cases by an Actors' Equity cabaret contract.

Cabaret Broadway musical by **Kander and Ebb**: John **Kander** (music) and Fred **Ebb** (lyrics); book by Joe **Masteroff**, based on English playwright John Van Druten's (1901–1957) *I Am a Camera* (1951), itself based on *The Berlin Stories* by Anglo-American writer Christopher Isherwood (1904–1986); Broadhurst Theatre, 1966 (1165 perf.); Broadway revivals: Imperial Theatre, 1987 (261 perf.), Kit-Kat Club [Studio 54], 1997 (2377 perf.); film, 1972. The original production, directed by Harold Prince, was a sensation; Prince also directed the 1987 revival.

In Berlin at the time of the Nazi takeover in 1933, the American writer Clifford Bradshaw is fascinated by the city's free-wheeling lifestyle, with its decadent cabaret life and easy sex. He lodges at a rooming house run by Fräulein Schneider (a role created by Lotte Lenya), who is being wooed by the Jewish grocer Herr Schultz. Clifford falls in love with the British nightclub singer Sally Bowles at the Kit-Kat Club. They have a casual fling, and Sally becomes pregnant. Clifford offers to marry her and take her back to the States, but, unprepared to accept motherhood, she has an abortion, deciding to remain in Berlin and pursue her career. Clifford leaves Berlin, and, in the worsening political climate, Fräulein Schneider breaks off her engagement to Herr Schultz. But life at the Kit-Kat goes on.

Cabin in the Sky Broadway musical by Vernon **Duke**; book by screenwriter Lynn Root (1905–1997), based on his story "Little Joe"; lyrics by John **Latouche**; Martin Beck Theatre, 1940 (156 perf.); film, 1943, with a screenplay co-written by Root and Joseph Schrank (1900–1984), and extra songs by Harold **Arlen** and E. Y. **Harburg**. Both the stage production and the film starred the brilliant actor and singer Ethel Waters (1896–1977) as Petunia.

This African-American fantasy folktale begins as the miscreant and gadabout Little Joe Jackson is dying. Petunia, his faithful wife, prays to God to give him another chance, and the Lawd gives him six months to prove his worth, with the help of the Lawd's General. The devil, Lucifer, Jr., tempts Joe with the seductress Georgia Brown, but he does not succumb to her wiles.

cabriole (KA bree ohl') *n.* [Fr. French: a goat-like leap] **1.** In ballet and dance, a kind of jump or leap that begins and ends in a **demi-plié** position. **2.** A 16th- and 17th-c. French dance, featuring a leaping step.

cachucha (kah CHOO chah) *n.* Vivacious Spanish dance in 3/4 or 3/8 time; used in ballets, and featured in a lively number in act 2 of Gilbert and Sullivan's *The Gondoliers*: "Dance a cachucha, fandango, bolero …"

cadence *n.* The ending **phrase** or phrases of a melody.

cadenza (kuh DEHN zuh) *n.* [Italian (kah DEHN zah): cadence] **1.** In opera or other vocal music, a brief, brilliant, elaborately composed section, near the end of an aria or other vocal piece, that shows off the singer's technical prowess. **2.** In a concerto, a section near the end of the first or last movement, performed by the soloist in a display of virtuosity.

cakewalk A 19th-c. African-American dance in syncopated rhythms, featuring improvised steps, including a strutting walk, and high kicks in a **can-can** style; used in the latter part of the c. as part of a **minstrel show**; and featured in *Clorindy; or The Origin of the Cakewalk* as well as in other Broadway musicals, such as *Watch Your Step* (1914). Originally, the dance, invented by slaves, was performed on plantations in the master's mansion, and a piece of cake was awarded to the most original and versatile of the dancers.

Caldara, Antonio (1670–1736) (kahl DAH rah) Prolific Italian composer; resident at the Hapsburg court in Vienna as vice-**Kapellmeister**, 1716–1736; wrote sacred and instrumental music, and ca. seventy-five operas, including a version of *La clemenza di Tito* (1734).

Call Me Madam Broadway musical by Irving **Berlin**; book by playwrights **Lindsay and Crouse**: Howard Lindsay and Russel Crouse; Imperial Theatre, 1950 (644 perf.); film, 1953.
George **Abbott** directed and Jerome Robbins (1918–1998) choreographed. Part of the show's success was due to Ethel Merman as Mrs. Sally Adams; she reprised her role for the film. The character is based on socialite and political party-giver Perle Mesta (1889–1975), called "The Hostess with the Mostes'," Truman's appointee as ambassador to Luxembourg.
Sally Adams, "The Hostess with the Mostes' on the Ball," is a millionaire Texas oil widow, known for her lavish parties and appointed by President Truman as Ambassador to the tiny European country of Lichtenburg. Sally falls in love with Prime Minister Cosmo Constantin, but offends him by throwing American money around. Her assistant, Kenneth Gibson, falls in love with Princess Maria. Sally helps him win her love, and Cosmo and Sally forgive each other and remain together.

Call Me Mister Broadway musical revue by Harold **Rome**; National Theatre, 1946 (734 perf.); film, much altered, 1951. This great hit revue, which starred former soldiers and USO entertainers, centered around the lives of the soldiers in World War II; the songs and sketches ranged from the satirical to the sober and serious.

calypso Music of the Caribbean, influenced by American jazz idioms; popular in the U.S. in the 1950s and '60s; featured in some musicals, e.g., *Once on This Island*.

Camelot Broadway musical by **Lerner and Loewe**: music by Frederick **Loewe**; book and lyrics by Alan Jay **Lerner**, based on the comic Arthurian fantasy novel *The Once and Future King* (1958) by English author T. H. White (1906–1964) [b. Terence Hanbury White]; Majestic Theatre, 1960 (873 perf.); Broadway revivals: New York State Theatre at Lincoln Center, 1980 (62 perf.), with Richard Burton; Winter Garden Theater, 1981 (72 perf.); George Gershwin Theatre, 1993 (60 perf.); film, 1967.

The show was directed by Moss **Hart**, and starred Julie Andrews as Guenevere; Welsh classical actor Richard Burton (1925–1984) as Arthur; and singer Robert Goulet (1933–2007) as Sir Lancelot.

King Arthur and his best friend, Sir Lancelot, both love Arthur's wife, Queen Guenevere. In order to prevent war, Arthur organizes the Knights of the Round Table in his city of Camelot. He is disillusioned about human goodness because of Lancelot and Guenevere's love affair. War beaks out anyway, due to the machinations of the villainous Mordred, Arthur's natural son. The king knights young Thomas, bequeathing him the legacy of Camelot and what it stands for: nobility, chivalry, and peace.

Cammarano, Salvadore (1801–1852) (sahl vah DO: reh: kah' mah RAH no:) [also spelled "Salvatore" in some sources] Italian poet, dramatist, and librettist; wrote texts for several operas by Gaetano **Donizetti**, including *Lucia di Lammermoor*; several for Giuseppe **Verdi**, including *La battaglia di Legnano*, *Luisa Miller*, and *Il trovatore*; as well as libretti for Giovanni **Pacini** and Saverio **Mercadante**, among them *La vestale*.

canary *n.* **1.** *Hist. Slang* A chorus singer in a musical comedy. **2.** *Slang* A female singer. **3.** A 16th-c. dance, largely done at aristocratic courts, in 3/4 or 6/8 time; lively, jaunty, and fast; so named because of its presumed origin in the Canary Islands. Also spelled "canarie."

can-can *n.* A dance in 2/4 time, popularized in 19th-c. French cabarets and music halls; lines of can-can girls would titillate and entertain the patrons, particularly with the celebrated *can-can kick* that exposed the underwear beneath the dancers' voluminous long ruffled skirts, which they held up as they kicked high, holding one leg up high from the waist and turning in a circle on the other leg. The dance usually begins with a run forward, holding the ruffled skirts and shaking them with both hands before beginning to do a series of high kicks, alternating legs, then proceeding to the can-can kick and ending in a **split**. It was featured at the famous cabaret the Moulin Rouge on the Place Pigalle in Paris, where Toulouse Lautrec made drawings of the dancers. But the most famous example is Offenbach's can-can in *Orphée aux enfers*.

Can-Can Broadway musical by Cole **Porter**; book by Abe **Burrows**; Shubert Theatre, 1953 (829 perf.); many stock productions; film, 1960.

Set in Paris in 1893, when the puritanical regime has outlawed the lascivious can-can, the story unfolds in the cabaret owned by La Mome Pistache (The Pistachio

Kid), who sings the quintessential paean to the City of Light, "I Love Paris." Rumors that she has defied the law and is still putting on the can-can are investigated by the strait-laced judge Aristide Forestier, who falls in love with her. He defends her so well that the can-can is allowed again, and they end up in each other's arms.

Candide Broadway comic operetta by Leonard **Bernstein**; book by celebrated American playwright Lillian Hellman (1905–1984), based on the novel of the same name by the iconoclastic French Enlightenment writer Voltaire (1694–1778); lyrics by the composer; noted Molière translator, poet, and scholar Richard Wilbur (b. 1921); John **Latouche**; and wit and writer Dorothy Parker (1893–1967); Martin Beck Theatre, 1956 (73 perf.); Broadway revivals: Broadway Theatre, 1974 (740 perf.), new book by Hugh **Wheeler**, with some new lyrics by Stephen **Sondheim**, directed by Harold Prince; George Gershwin Theatre, 1997 (123 perf.), directed by Harold Prince.

The score is full of verve and originality, so that this piece remained alive in public consciousness despite the obvious problems with the unwieldy book and the lack of success of the original production. Concert versions and recordings have proved popular.

The naïve, low-born Candide, in love with the aristocratic Cunegonde (a virtuosic soprano role), is thrown out of the castle where he has resided, and where he has been tutored by the hack philosopher Dr. Pangloss: "This is the best of all possible worlds." After journeying hither and yon in order to obtain enlightenment, Candide arrives back home and wins his beloved Cunegonde, having resolved to "cultivate his own garden," which is all that anyone can really do.

cantabile (kahn TAH bee leh:) *adj.* [Italian: singable] **1.** Pertaining to music that is mellifluous and melodious. **2.** A performance mark: to be performed in the style of smooth singing, e.g., *andante cantabile*: slow and lyrical.

cantata (kahn TAH tah) *n.* [Fr. Italian: sung] A full-length dramatic work for voices and orchestra; a sung drama, secular or religious, but one meant to be performed in concert, not staged as a drama.

cantilena *n.* (kahn' tee LEH: nah) [Italian: little song] A brief song, or a short melody or ballad; or a brief, melodious instrumental passage.

canto fiorito (KAHN to: fyo: REE to:) [Italian: lit., flowered song; ornamented song or singing] The style of ornamentation composed for arias in **bel canto** romantic operas; esp. used in the variations heard in repeats; hence, singing with added ornamentation.

canto spianato (KAHN to: spyah NAH to:) [Italian: smooth song; spun-out singing] A legato style of singing, without added ornamentation; the opposite of *canto fiorito*.

canzone (kahn DZO: neh:) *n.* [Italian: song] A song for several voices, as in a madrigal or part-song; hence, the diminutive, *canzonetta* (kahn tso: neh:' tah): a brief part-song.

Captain Jinks of the Horse Marines 1. Popular song composed and performed by William Horace Lingard (1839–1927), an English music hall singer and female impersonator; published 1868, and still popular ca. 1900; also used as an American square dance: "I'm Captain Jinks of the Horse Marines/ I feed my horse on corn and beans/ And sport young ladies in their teens/ Tho' a captain in the army."

2. Hit Broadway play by the prolific American dramatist Clyde Fitch (1865–1909), who wrote ca. sixty plays; 1902; also made into a silent film, 1916.

Having gone to Europe to pursue a career as an opera singer, Aurelia Johnson returns to America in triumph as Madame Trentoni (she hails from Trenton, NJ). When she lands in New York, her enchanting personality captivates everyone, including Captain Robert Carrolton Jinks, who wagers with his friends that he can win her love. He does, but on the night of her debut, she learns of the wager and is so upset that she feels she cannot go on. However, she overcomes her distress, and her American debut performance is a triumph. Jinks convinces her that, although everything started as a cynical wager, he now truly loves her.

3. Opera in three acts by Jack **Beeson**; libretto by Sheldon **Harnick**, based on Clyde Fitch's play; Kansas City, MO, Kansas City Lyric Theatre, 1975.

In the opera, the character is called Jonathan Jinks, and, when he and his friends Willie and Charlie go to the docks to see the arrival of Aurelia Trentoni, they goad him into the bet because they are jealous of his success with women. Jinks tries to help speed Aurelia's luggage through customs by bribing a customs officer, and is arrested for doing so. Out on bail, he succeeds in becoming her fiancé, and she makes a triumphant debut as the consumptive heroine in *La traviata*. But she learns of the bet, and is naturally upset. The police come looking for Jinks, who has failed to show up for his trial. He convinces her that he really loves her, and she plays Violetta in real life, persuading the police that Jinks had only jumped bail in order to minister to her in her mortal illness.

4. Broadway musical comedy, called *Captain Jinks*, with music by Lewis E. Gensler (1896–1978) and Stephen O. Jones; book by Frank Mandel (1884–1958) and Laurence Schwab (1893–1951), based on Fitch's play; lyrics by B. G. **De Sylva**; Martin Beck Theatre, 1925 (167 perf.).

Cardillac (kahr dee YAHK) Opera in three acts by Paul **Hindemith**; libretto by Swiss journalist and writer Ferdinand Lion (1883–1968) (LEE o:n), based on the story "Das Fräulein von Scuderi" (Mademoiselle de Scudéry) (dahs FROY lIn fuhn skoo DEH: ree) (skü' dé REE), by E. T. A. **Hoffmann**; Dresden, Staatsoper, 1926. Turned by the composer into a four-act opera, with a libretto adapted by Hindemith from Lion; Switzerland, Zurich Stadttheater, 1952.

The fascinating score is a combination of darkly expressionistic, driving, very powerful, densely orchestrated music full of odd Handelian echoes, with textures and tonalities reminiscent of the baroque period, but transformed with nightmarish bizarreness.

In 17th c. Paris, the populace is restless and anxious because of a series of unexplained murders. The jeweler Cardillac (bar.) is so in love with his own creations that he follows all his departing customers and stabs them to death, so that he can repossess the jewelry. An Officer (bass) ardently woos Cardillac's Daughter (sop.), and, without thinking twice, he tells her to marry the man, so indifferent is he to her fate. But she is torn between her love for her father and her desire for the Officer, who buys a gold chain from the jeweler. Cardillac follows him in disguise, and stabs him in order to recover the chain. As the Officer is dying, a Gold Dealer (bass) who has witnessed the murder tells the crowd what has happened. The Officer, out of a sense of pity for the Daughter, accuses the Gold Dealer of the murder. But the psychopath, who cannot bear to owe anything to anyone, not even his life, confesses his crimes, and the enraged mob tears him to pieces.

Carmen (kah*r* MEHN) Opera in four acts by Georges **Bizet**; original **opéra comique** libretto with dialogue by Henri **Meilhac** and Ludovic **Halévy**, based on the novella of the same name by the playwright, historian, short story writer, and archaeologist Prosper Mérimée (1803–1870) (p*r*os PEH:*R* mé *r*ee MÉ); Paris, Théâtre de l'Opéra-Comique, 1875; dialogue adapted as recitative and set to music in 1875 by Ernest **Guiraud** for the Vienna production. The opera, which is the most frequently performed of all the standard operas world-wide, is usually done now in Bizet, Meilhac and Halévy's **opéra comique** version, although for much of the 20th c. it was performed in Guiraud's **through-composed** edition.

On a hot, lazy day in the summer of 1820, the sweltering passers-by go about their business in a crowded plaza in Seville. A shy, naïve country lass, Micaëla (mee' kah eh LAH) (sop.), comes looking for her fiancé, Don José (do:n zho: ZÉ) (ten.), a soldier. He will shortly be there on guard duty, so she is told, but, instead of waiting, she goes off to find him. Soon, he arrives to take up his post. The girls who work in the cigarette factory just off the plaza come outside to take a break. Among them is the hot-headed, seductive gypsy girl Carmen (mezz.). José obviously finds her bewitching, and she throws a flower to him on her way back to work. After she is arrested in the factory for stabbing another girl in a fight, José is detailed to take her off to jail, but he allows her to escape, and he is arrested and imprisoned. On his release, he goes to join her at Lilas Pastia's inn, where she is dancing and where the gypsy smugglers meet to plan their escapades. The famous toreador Escamillo (ehs' kah mee' YO:) (bar.) enters, and is immediately drawn to Carmen. So is Captain Zuniga (zoo nyee' GAH) (bass), José's superior officer, who comes looking for her. José has heard the signal to return to barracks, but Carmen teases him and he refuses to go, even when the captain orders him to. Instead, he draws his sword and threatens the officer. Now his life is in danger, and he flees to the mountains with Carmen and the band of gypsy smugglers. There, Escamillo joins them, having fallen madly in love with Carmen, who by now is bored with José. Micaëla also makes her way to the gypsies' retreat, with the news that José's mother is on her deathbed, and he leaves with her. In Seville on the day of Escamillo's big bullfight, he and Carmen are warned that Don José is in the crowd, looking for vengeance. Escamillo enters the bullring, leaving Carmen outside. José finds her, and when his desperate protestations of love and his pleas that she return to him have no effect, he stabs her to death.

Carmen Jones Broadway musical using Bizet's score, modernized and arranged by Broadway orchestrator Robert Russell Bennett (1894–1981); book and lyrics by Oscar **Hammerstein**, who updated the story to World War II and set it in the African-American community in the South; Broadway Theatre, 1943 (503 perf.); film, 1954.

Carmina Burana Scenic cantata by Carl **Orff**.

Carmines, Reverend Al (1936–2005) [b. Alvin Allison Carmines, Jr.] Innovative American composer, music director, choral conductor; a prime influence in New York's Off-Off Broadway theater; founded the Judson Poets' Theater at the Judson Memorial Church, of which he was pastor. Among his ca. ten musicals are the ground-breaking *In Circles* (1968), book by the composer, based on Gertrude Stein's *A Circular Play* (1920); and the absurdist, avant-garde *Promenade* (1969), with a book by Maria Irene Fornes (b. 1930).

Carousel Broadway musical by **Rodgers and Hammerstein**: Richard **Rodgers** (music) and Oscar **Hammerstein** (book and lyrics), based on the play *Liliom* (1909) (LIH: lee om) by Hungarian-born American playwright Ferenc Molnár (1878–1952) (FEH rehnts MO:L nah:r); Majestic Theatre, 1945 (890 perf.); Broadway revivals: Majestic Theatre, 1949 (32 perf.); Vivian Beaumont Theatre at Lincoln Center, 1994 (322 perf.); New York City Center Light Opera Company revivals; West End revival, 2008; numerous tours and revivals; film, 1956.

Billy Bigelow, a carnival barker, and Julie Jordan, a local mill worker, fall in love with each other and marry. The jealous carnival owner, Mrs. Mullin, fires Billy. Meanwhile, Julie's friend Carrie Pepperidge and the fisherman Mr. Snow get married; they will have a large family. But Billy can't find a job, and he and Julie are obliged to live off the charity of her Aunt Nettie. When Julie becomes pregnant, Billy is simultaneously elated and ashamed, and determined to do something to help the family. He falls in with the evil-minded Jigger Craigin, who persuades Billy to join with him in robbing a payroll courier; but everything goes wrong, and Billy kills himself by falling on his own knife. He arrives in heaven, and the Starkeeper kindly lets him return to earth so that he can let Julie know how much he loves her and help their daughter, Louise, by giving her the confidence to do something with her life.

Carr, Frank Osmond (1858–1916) English composer of West End musical comedies, of which the most famous were *Morocco Bound* (1893) and *Go-Bang* (1894), written with Adrian **Ross**. He collaborated with W. S. **Gilbert** on *His Excellency* (1894). Carr's pedestrian score is largely imitative of Sullivan. As Gilbert remarked to D'Oyly Carte, "If I had had the benefit of your expensive friend Sullivan's music, it would have been a second *Mikado*."

Carré, Michel (1819–1872) (mee SHEHL kah RÉ) French poet and librettist for operas by Giacomo **Meyerbeer**, Charles **Gounod**, Georges **Bizet** and Ambroise **Thomas**; often worked with Jules **Barbier**, with whom he co-wrote the play on which the libretto to Offenbach's *Les contes d'Hoffmann* is based.

Caryll, Ivan (1861–1921) [*nom de théâtre* (theater name) (non duh té AH truh) of Félix Tilken (fé LIH:KS TEEL kehn)] Belgian-born English conductor and composer of more than two dozen West End and Broadway musical comedies; esp. known for his participation in the series of Edwardian **Gaiety musicals**. Caryll's music is generally lively, melodious, and rhythmically captivating, even if it tends sometimes to be rather formulaic and facile. Despite its faults, it is a shame that none of it is heard nowadays. The wonderful scores to *Little Christopher Columbus* (1893); the deliciously tuneful and vivacious *The Shop Girl* (1894); *The Circus Girl* (1897); the splendid *The Duchess of Dantzic* (1903), with its **Offenbachian** echoes; *Oh! Oh! Delphine* (1912), reminiscent in a happy way of **Lecocq**; and *Chin-Chin* (1914) are only some among many delectable bonbons, although their books do seem rather dated and verbose. Caryll's Broadway shows include the **ragtime** musical *Temple Bells* (1914) and *The Girl Behind the Gun (Kissing Time)* (1918), with book and lyrics by P. G. **Wodehouse** and Guy **Bolton**.

See also CELLIER, ALFRED; ÉTOILE, L'.

casino *n.* An establishment where legalized gambling takes place, e.g., in Atlantic City, NJ or Las Vegas, NV. Live variety shows are part of the entertainment, as well as productions of musical comedies.

castrato (kah STRAH to:) *n.* [Italian: castrated] A male contralto or soprano singer who was castrated as a boy. The practice of castrating choirboys with unusually beautiful soprano voices, in order to preserve the voice, was fairly common in the late 17th through the early 19th centuries, and was even continued in rare cases through the early 20th. In the early 18th c., castrati were much in demand in opera houses, where they sang the florid, heroic roles specially composed for them in baroque operas. Nowadays, their roles are often sung by mezzo-sopranos or contraltos; e.g., in **Handel** operas.

Catalani, Alfredo (1854–1893) (ahl FREH: do: kah' tah LAH nee) Italian **verismo** opera composer, best known for *La Wally* (1892).

Catered Affair, A Broadway musical; music and lyrics by John Bucchino; book by Harvey **Fierstein**, based on the 1956 film *The Catered Affair*, with a screenplay by prolific author Gore Vidal (b. 1925), adapted from a television drama by American stage and screen writer Paddy Chayevsky (1923–1981); Walter Kerr Theatre, 2008 (143 perf.).

The plot centers around the conflicts in a dysfunctional family in the Bronx, and the tensions between the blasé taxi driver Tom and his wife, the frustrated, world-weary Aggie (who have had their marital problems) over whether to give their daughter Jenny and her fiancé, Ralph, a big, fancy wedding that would virtually use up their savings, or a modest, inexpensive affair. Aggie wants a big celebration; Tom does not, and Jenny professes to be on his side. Meanwhile, Aggie's gay brother, Winston (played by Harvey Fierstein), who lives with them, enjoys gossiping with the neighbors; he wants a big wedding, but feels left out when he is not invited because he is not "immediate family." Haunting all of the characters is the death of Aggie and Tom's son in the Korean War (1950–1953).

cattle call In the musical theater, an audition for chorus and dance positions at which crowds of people try out. Cf. **group audition**; **open call**.

Cats West End and Broadway musical by Andrew Lloyd **Webber**; book by the composer, who set poet T. S. Eliot's (1888–1965) *Possum's Book of Practical Cats* to music; opened on Broadway in 1982 at the Winter Garden Theater. When it closed in 2000 after 7485 perf. (and 13 previews), it was one of the longest-running Broadway musicals.

Felines dance and sing their way through the tuneful show, which was done with spectacular special lighting effects. The only semblance of a story is when Grizabella dies at the midnight festivities, and Old Deuteronomy, sage philosopher, guides her to the life beyond this one.

Cavalleria rusticana (Rustic Chivalry) (kah' vah leh REE ah roos' tee KAH nah) Opera in one act by Pietro **Mascagni**; libretto by Guido Menasci (1867–1925) (GWEE do: meh NAH shee) and Giovanni Targioni-Tozzetti (1863–1934) (dgo: VAHN nee tahr DGO: nee to:t TSEHT tee), based on the play of the same name by Italian **verismo** writer Giovanni Verga (1840–1922) (VEHR gah), adapted from his short story; Rome, Teatro Costanzi (ko: STAHN dzee), 1890. The passionate score serves this melodramatic tale of jealousy and vengeance perfectly.

In front of the church during Easter Mass in a tiny Sicilian village, ca. 1880, the distraught and jealous Santuzza (sahn T*OO*T tsah) (sop.) is deeply upset that her lover, Turiddu (too RIH:D doo) (ten.), has deserted her for the younger and more attractive Lola (LO: lah) (mezz.). She reveals the affair to Lola's husband, Alfio (AHL fyo:) (bar.), who swears to avenge the insult to his honor and challenges Turiddu to a duel. After taking farewell of his mother, Lucia (loo CHEE ah), Turiddu, despite his terror, keeps their appointment, and Alfio kills him.

Cavalli, Pietro Francesco (1602–1676) (PYEH tro: frahn CHEHS ko: kah VAHL lee) Italian composer of more than forty operas, many on mythological subjects; e.g., *Didone* (1641) (dee DO: neh:), which is based on the same story as ***Didone abbandonata***, with a libretto by Giovanni Busenello (1598–1659) (boo' zeh NEHL lo:), available on a DVD from Dynamic (33537; 2007). Among his other outstanding works is the three-act *La Calisto* (1651) (lah kah LIH:S to:) [title character: a follower of the goddess Diana], with a libretto by impresario Giovanni Faustini (1615–1651) (fow STEE nee), based on stories from Ovid's *Metamorphoses*, available on a DVD from Harmonia Mundi (HMD 9909001.02; 2006).

cavatina (kah' vah TEE nah) *n.* [Italian] **1.** An **aria** sung by and often introducing a principal character in the first act of a 19th-c. Italian opera; the first part of an **opera scena**. **2.** A simple, short aria in an 18th-c. opera.

Cellier, Alfred (1844–1891) (seh LYEH:) English conductor and composer with several successful operettas to his credit, including *Dorothy* (1886), which rivaled

The Mikado in popularity. In 1891, Cellier began to compose the music to *The Mountebanks* by **Gilbert** after Sullivan had rejected the libretto; the score was completed after the composer's death by Ivan **Caryll**; it was produced in 1892, with fair success.

Cellier, François (1849–1914) English composer, orchestrator, and conductor; brother of Alfred Cellier; music director and principal conductor for the D'Oyly Carte original productions and earliest revivals of the **Gilbert and Sullivan** comic operas; his operettas *Bob* (1903) and *Ladyland* (1904) were West End successes.

Cenerentola, La, ossia La bontà in trionfo (Cinderella, or Goodness Triumphant) (lah chehn' eh REHN to: lah os SEE ah lah bo:n TAH ihn tree O:N fo:) Opera in two acts by Gioachino **Rossini**; libretto by Jacopo Ferretti (1754–1852) (YAH ko: po: fehr REHT tee), based on Perrault's fairy tale and libretti for two other operas; the recitatives and three of the numbers are by another composer, whose help Rossini requested, the church musician Luca Agolini (LOO kah ah' go: LEE nee); Rome, Teatro Valli (VAHL lee), 1817. One of Rossini's great triumphs, the enchanting score demands the utmost technical agility from its singers.

Angelina (ahn' dgeh LEE nah) (mezz.) is forced to be a serving maid by her wealthy father, the pompous Don Magnifico (do:n mahn YEEF ee ko:) (bass), and to cater to every whim of her two supercilious stepsisters, Clorinda (klo: RIH:N dah) (mezz.) and Tisbe (TIH:Z beh:) (sop.), who call her "Cinderella." Searching for a suitable wife, Prince Ramiro (rah MEE ro:) (ten.) arrives, disguised as his own valet, Dandini (dahn DEE nee) (bar.), who pretends to be the prince. Ramiro falls in love with Cinderella, and the Prince's tutor, Alidoro (ah' lee DO: ro:) (bass), wanting to help the match succeed, makes sure she is suitably attired and can attend the ball, which she was not supposed to go to. The glass slipper is replaced by a silver bracelet, and the story then follows more or less the same course as the fairy tale. Angelina prevails upon Ramiro to pardon all those who have mistreated her, forgives them herself, and expresses her joy over the change in her life in a splendid **coloratura** aria, "Naqui all'affano e al pianto" (I was born to care and weeping) (NAH kwee ahl ahf FAHN no: eh: ahl PYAHN to:), which Rossini is said to have composed in fifteen minutes while he was drinking with friends in a tavern in Rome—a story that is probably apocryphal.

cercar la nota (chehr KAHR lah NO: tah) [Italian: to seek, or look for the note] In singing, to anticipate the next ornamentation or note, esp. in florid **bel canto** passages; the anticipation is necessary in order to be able to breathe properly.

Chabrier, Emmanuel (1841–1894) (eh mah nü EHL shah bree EH:) French composer, much influenced by Wagner's music; wrote ten musical theatre pieces, of which the most well known are his masterpiece, *L'étoile*; the opera *Gwendoline* (1886) (gwehn do: LEEN); the **opéra comique** *Le roi malgré lui* (The King in Spite of Himself) (1887) (luh *R*WAH mal gré LÜI); and the operetta *Une education manqué* (A Missed Education) (1879) (ün é dü kah syo:*n* mah*n* KÉ), libretto by Leterrier and **Vanloo**.

chaconne (shah KUHN) *n.* [French, fr. Spanish *chacona* (chah KO: nah)] Dance in 3/4 or 3/8 time, probably of Spanish origin; sensuous in nature, with undulating movement; used in 17th-c. ballets. One of Offenbach's most popular pieces was the "Chaconne" from *M. et Mme. Denis* (1862) (muh s*yoo* eh: mah dahm duh NEE).

chaîné (sheh NÉ) *n.* [French: chained; linked] In dance, a series of continuous steps in which the body quickly rotates, as the feet, held as close together as possible, perform rapid alternate turns, moving along in a straight line.

chamber opera A small-scale, intimate piece with a small cast and with minimal orchestral accompaniment, often provided by a simple chamber music ensemble; e.g., *La serva padrona* by Giovanni **Pergolesi**; *The Turn of the Screw* by Benjamin **Britten**; *Les malheurs d'Orphée* by Darius **Milhaud**.

See also FUX, JOHANN JOSEPH.

chang (DGAHNG) *n.* [Mandarin Chinese: to sing] **1.** A song. **2.** The sung portions or a single sung passage of a **xiqu** (music-drama). **3.** Skill in singing.

character dance 1. Choreography in a ballet, musical comedy, or other musical theater piece that is characteristic or expressive of and danced by a particular personage or group. **2.** The general term for any form of dance that is not strictly classical or modern classical; e.g., folk dances or national dances.

character song A number in a musical comedy, opera, operetta, or comic opera that introduces a particular personage to the audience or portrays that personage in some way; usually sung by the performer playing the part; e.g., the introductory **patter** songs in **Gilbert and Sullivan**, such as Sir Joseph Porter's "When I Was a Lad," from act 1 of *H. M. S. Pinafore*; Annie's song, sung with her kid brothers and sisters, "Doin' What Comes Naturally," from Irving Berlin's *Annie Get Your Gun*.

Charleston A popular, jazzy, syncopated 1920s dance, named for the city of Charleston, SC, where it originated in the African-American community; characterized by the famous step of hands crossing over knees.

Charpentier, Gustave (1860–1956) (güs TAHV shah*r* pah*n* TYEH:) French composer; studied with Jules **Massenet**; known for his opera *Louise* (1900), filmed in 1939.

Charpentier, Marc-Antoine (1645/50?–1704) (mah*r* kah*n* twahn' shah*r* pah*n* TYEH:) French composer of ca. twenty-six works for the musical theater, including **pastoral** works, divertissements, and dramatic operas; worked with Molière on two comédie-ballets: *Le mariage forcé* (The Forced Marriage) (1672) (luh mah *r*ee ahzh fo:*r* SÉ); and *Le malade imaginaire* (The Imaginary Invalid) (1673) (luh mah lahd' ee mah zhee NEH:*R*).

Chausson, Ernest (1855–1899) (eh*r* nehst' sho: SO:*N*) Prolific French composer of songs and chamber pieces. The most well known of his full-scale works is the opera *Le Roi Arthus* (King Arthus) (composed during 1886–1895) (luh *r*wah ah*r*

TÜS), based on the love triangle story of King Arthur, Queen Guinevere, and Sir Lancelot.

Cherubini, Luigi (1760–1842) (loo EE dgee keh roo BEE nee) Influential Italian composer, teacher, and administrator; friend of major 19th-c. composers, including **Bellini**, **Donizetti**, Brahms, Chopin, Mendelssohn, and **Rossini**; spent most of his life in Paris. He wrote church music and ca. thirty operas, including his first great success, *Lodoïska* (1791) (lo do: EES kah), a resounding hit in French Revolutionary Paris, superbly recorded on Sony CD (82K 47290; 1991); and the opera many consider his masterpiece, *Médée* (Medea) (1797) (mé DÉ), about Jason and his unhappy marriage to Medea; libretto by prolific librettist and critic François-Benoît-Henri Hoffman (1760–1828) (*f*rahn swah beh nwah hahn *r*ee' o:f MAHN) [variously spelled Hoffmann, Hofman, and Hofmann], based on the 1635 tragedy by Pierre Corneille (1606–1684), in turn based on ancient Greek tragedies. From 1821 to 1841, Cherubini was head of the Paris Conservatoire (ko:*n*' seh*r* vah TWAH*R*), where he oversaw the studies of **Auber**, **Halévy**, the rebellious **Berlioz**, and **Offenbach** (one of the only foreign students ever admitted), among many others.

chest voice The lower register of a person's vocal range, the vibrations of which are felt in the upper chest when a performer speaks or sings.

Chicago Broadway musical by **Kander and Ebb**: John Kander (music); Fred Ebb (book and lyrics), with famed choreographer Bob Fosse (1927–1987) collaborating on the book, based on the 1926 satirical play *Chicago* by Maureen Dallas Watkins (1896–1969); 46th Street Theatre, 1975 (898 perf.); Richard Rodgers Theatre, phenomenal 1996 Broadway revival (more than 5000 perf. so far, and still running at the Ambassador Theatre as of this writing); film, 2002.

The story, done as a vaudeville show, unfolds in the Chicago of the 1920s Prohibition era, with its gangsters and speakeasies. The tawdry performer Roxie Hart (played originally by the brilliant, sassy Gwen Verdon [1926–2000]), shoots her lover because he has decided to leave her. She is defended by sleazy, big time lawyer Billy Flynn. Her fellow sleazebag killer Velma Kelly (a role created by the magnificent Chita Rivera [b. 1933]), wants her name in the headlines, just as Roxie does. The two of them wind up doing a vaudeville act together.

Chi pronuncia bene, canta bene. (kee:' pro: N*OO*N chah BEH: neh KAHN tah BEH: neh) [Italian: Who pronounces well, sings well.] An 18th-c. saying, meaning that if a singer has good, clear diction and excellent **articulation**, he or she can sing well; without excellent pronunciation and enunciation (in any language), not a chance.

See also DECLAMATION; SINGING.

choreographed facials Expressions done simultaneously as part of a number in a musical comedy, or by all the actors at once in a farce, e.g., jaws dropped open and eyebrows raised in surprise.

choreographer *n.* A person who devises, arranges, stages, and rehearses dances.

choreography *n.* **1.** The art of devising, arranging, and staging dances; hence, *to choreograph*: the act of doing so. **2.** The dances, taken as a whole, in a ballet, musical comedy, opera, operetta, etc.: *Marius Petitpa's (1818–1910) original choreography for Tchaikovsky's* Swan Lake. **3.** The order of steps in a particular dance: *the choreography of the minuet.* **4.** The movements and blocking of actors, esp. in crowd scenes; hence, *choreographed movement.*

chorister *n.* A member of a chorus, esp. one that performs classical music.

chorus *n.* **1.** A group of characters, usually of one type, such as citizens, soldiers, or officials, who comment on the action in ancient Greek tragedy. **2.** The ensemble performers who sing and/or dance as a group in a musical theater piece. In **Gilbert and Sullivan**, the male and female choruses play groups of characters, e.g., the crew of sailors (male) and Sir Joseph's sisters, cousins and aunts (female) in *H.M.S. Pinafore*; and they usually have all kinds of opinions about what is going on. **3.** A group of singers who sing together, either by themselves in concert, e.g., in liturgical music performed at church services by a choir; or as part of a larger ensemble, as in Handel's *Messiah*, written for instrumentalists, solo singers, and a chorus of men and women. Hence, the adj. *choral*: pertaining to the chorus; e.g., *a choral work*; *choral singing*. **4.** A piece of music sung by the chorus: *the "Hallelujah" Chorus.* **5.** The **refrain** of a song, or of a number in a musical theater piece.

chorus boy; chorus girl The male and female ensemble performers in a musical theater piece, esp. a musical comedy; occasionally used in a somewhat demeaning way.

Chorus Line, A Broadway musical by Marvin **Hamlisch**, lyrics by Edward Kleban (1939–1987); developed by cast members in workshops with choreographer Michael Bennett (1943–1987); opened at the New York Shakespeare Festival, played 101 perf. before being transferred to Broadway; Shubert Theatre, 1975 (6137 perf.); Broadway revival: Gerald Schoenfeld Theatre, 2006 (777 perf.); film, 1984.

Eighteen hopeful performers are interviewed by the director, Zach, as they audition for eight slots in the chorus of a new Broadway musical. The audience gets to know each of them as a person, with all their hopes, doubts and fears. Eight are finally chosen, and everyone participates in the show's rousing finale.

The documentary film *Every Little Step* (2009) details the story of how the show was put together.

chorus master The person who rehearses and conducts the chorus during perf. of classical choral works; or who rehearses the opera chorus.

Chris and the Wonderful Lamp Broadway operetta in three acts by John Philip **Sousa**; book and lyrics by Glen **MacDonough**, based on a popular 1895 children's novel, serialized in the *St. Nicholas* magazine, by Albert Stearns (1855–1919)—

the novel was also filmed, in 1917; opened in New Haven, 1899; Victoria Theatre, 1900 (84 perf.).

The score of this completely forgotten show, which garnered rave reviews, is inventive, rollicking, and tuneful. As with *The Black Crook* and, later, *Chu Chin Chow*, there was plenty of opportunity for marvelous, extravagant production numbers.

Young Chris Wagstaff (a **trousers role**), a "boy about town," is in love with Fanny Wiggins, but she is sent away to school, and he despairs of seeing her again. At a village auction, he buys an antique lamp, and when he rubs it, the Genie of the Lamp appears. The astonished Chris is granted the usual wishes. He and the Genie make their way to Prisms' Academy and kidnap Fanny, who is the "star pupil," coddled by Miss Prisms herself. They are magically transported, together with Scotty Jones, a "Boy-of-all-work" at the Academy, to Prince Aladdin's palace in the fairy kingdom of Etheria, where, as the *New York Times* review of the original New Haven production says, "there are high old goings on."

Christiné, Henri Marius (1867–1941) (k*r*ihs tee NÉ) Swiss-born French composer of musical comedies; revitalized musical theater in France after World War I. His greatest successes were *Phi-Phi* (1918) and *Dédé* (1921), the latter starring Maurice Chevalier (1888–1972), who also stars in the 1953 recording, which he introduces with an account of the original production (Musidisc 461 961-2; 2001). The delicious music tastes of the brightest cabaret tradition, with its bouncy rhythms and merry tunes. The hilarious book and lyrics for both musicals are by Albert **Willemetz**.

Chu Chin Chow: A Musical Tale of the East West End, later Broadway musical comedy by composer, singer, and variety monologist Frederick Norton (1869–1946); book by Australian-born actor-manager Oscar Asche (1871–1936)—who also produced, directed, and starred—based on *The Thousand and One Nights* tale "Ali Baba and the Forty Thieves"; London, His Majesty's Theatre, 1916 (2235 perf.); New York, Manhattan Opera House, 1917 (218 perf.); film, 1934.

Aside from telling its complicated story, *Chu Chin Chow* was an extravaganza, pantomime, and variety show with elaborate, periodically changed specialty acts introduced in the palace banquet scene and in the act 2 bazaar scene. The lively, tuneful score, although full of faux "Orientalism," has much to recommend it. An interesting CD includes some of the original cast recordings, as well as tracks from the film, along with modern studio recordings (EMI; 0777 7 89939 2 6; 1984).

Kasim Baba (brother of the impoverished Ali Baba) welcomes Chu Chin Chow of China, a wealthy merchant, by giving him an extravagant banquet, with a slave auction to be held as a special attraction. But Chu Chin Chow is in reality Abu Hassan (originally played by Asche), chief of the Forty Thieves, who has killed Chu Chin Chow in order to be able to enter Kasim's mansion and acquire his fortune. Abu Hassan has forced the beautiful Zahrat to become a spy for him in Kasim's house, by holding her lover hostage. After many complications, Zahrat foils his plans, kills the Forty Thieves by a ruse, and stabs Abu Hassan. She and her lover are reunited at last.

Ciboulette (see boo LEHT) Operetta in three acts by Reynaldo **Hahn**; libretto by Robert de Flers (1872–1827) (ro: beh*r*' duh FLEH*R*S) and Francis de Croisset (1877–1937) (f*r*ahn sees' duh k*r*wah SEH:); Paris, Théâtre des Variétés, 1923.

An original cast recording is available on a CD album entitled *L'Opérette Française 1921–1934 par ses Créateurs* (French Operettas 1921–1934 by Their Creators) (lo pé *r*eht f*r*ahn SEHZ pah*r* seh: k*r*é ah TUH*R*) (EPM Musique 982 482; 1992).

In the Paris of Napoleon III (1808–1873), Viscount Antonin de Mournelon (ah*n* to: NA*N* duh moo*r* nuh LO:*N*) (ten.) is engaged to Zénobie (zé no: BEE) (sop.), who is in love with a young lieutenant, Roger (*r*o ZHEH:) (ten.). His friend Duparquet (dü pah*r* KEH:) (bar.), one of the directors of the market center at Les Halles (leh: AHL), comforts him. At Les Halles, Antonin meets and falls in love with Ciboulette (sop.), who works there. She quits her job and pursues a singing career, becoming famous as a Spanish singer, Conchita Cibulero. In the audience one night is the still unmarried Antonin; he recognizes Ciboulette and sends her a note proposing marriage, which she accepts.

Cimarosa, Domenico (1749–1801) (do: MEHN ee ko: chih:' mah RO: zah) Prolific, much loved Italian composer of ca. eighty operas that were very popular in their day, among them the delightful *Il matrimonio segreto* and the tragic drama *Gli Orazi e I Curiazi* (The Horatii and the Curatii) (1796) ([g]lee o: RAH tse eh: ee k*oo* ree AH tsee), set in ancient Rome, a subject later also treated by Saverio **Mercadante**. Cimarosa was better known for his comic operas than for his serious works.

ciseaux (see ZO:) *n.* [French: scissors] A kind of dance movement involving crossing the feet in a scissors-like fashion, either when leaping into the air or when moving **en pointe**; the feet are in **second position**.

classical ballet The form of ballet that originated in the 17th c. See BALLET.

Clay, Frederic Emes (1838–1889) [usually called Frederic Clay] English composer of songs and musical theater pieces, including four he wrote with W. S. **Gilbert**, among them *Ages Ago* (1869), an early version of what became *Ruddigore*; and *Princess Toto* (1875), for which Clay and Gilbert had high hopes, but Gilbert is not at his best, and the score, though pleasant, is uninspired. Clay also worked on the English version of *The Black Crook*. He was a great friend of Arthur **Sullivan**, and introduced him to Gilbert.

clean up 1. To work on a musical theater number, e.g., a chorus number or ensemble dance piece, until the singing is absolutely in unison or the dance movements crisp, clear, and in time to the music, with all the kicks at the same height and with no extraneous or distracting movement; also, to work on solo pieces or dialogue scenes in order to eliminate everything extraneous and unnecessary. **2.** *Slang* To make a profit; to rake in the money: *The producers cleaned up on that show!*

clemenza di Tito, La (Titus's Clemency) (lah kleh MEHN dzah dee TEE to:) [Roman Emperor, Titus Flavius Vespasianus, known as Vespasian, 9–79 (TEE toos FLAH wee oos wehs' pah see AH noos) (vehs PAY zhuhn)]

1. Libretto by Pietro **Metastasio**, based on various classical sources, set by forty different composers, among them **Caldara** (1734), **Hasse** (1735) and **Galuppi** (1760), whose score contains some splendid pages: The recitatives are similar to Mozart's, but the arias are quite different and, while energetic, not nearly so beautiful or ethereal.

2. Brilliant last opera in two acts by Wolfgang Amadeus **Mozart**; libretto by Metastasio, adapted by poet and prolific librettist, Caterino Mazzolà (1745–1806) (kah the REE no: maht tso: LAH); Prague, National Theatre, 1791.

In ancient Rome, ca. 80 CE, Vitellia (vee TEHL lee ah) (sop.), daughter of an empress, has been rejected by the Emperor Tito (ten.), who plans to marry the foreign Queen Berenice. Vitellia involves Sesto (SEHS to:) (sop. or c-ten.) [Sextus], who loves her, in a plot to launch a conspiracy and kill the emperor. But Tito has changed his mind, for political reasons, and now plans to marry Sesto's sister, Servilia (sehr VIH:L ee ah) (sop.), who is loved by Sesto's friend, Annio (AH nee o:) (sop. or c-ten.) [Annius (AH nee oos)]. When Servilia tells Tito that she loves Annio, he allows them to be united. Meanwhile, Sesto, not knowing of this and further goaded by Vitellia, plans to carry out the assassination. When he is arrested and brought before Tito, Sesto dare not give an explanation without implicating Vitellia, who now nobly confesses that she is the instigator of the conspiracy. Tito pardons everyone, and all rejoice in his clemency.

Cloches de Corneville, Les (The Chimes of Corneville) Operetta by Robert **Planquette**.

clog dance A folk dance of English origin, also associated with Holland; performed in wooden-soled shoes that make a percussive sound; used occasionally in ballet or in musical theater. Cf. **tap**.

Clorindy; or The Origin of the Cakewalk Broadway musical **afterpiece** to the vaudeville show *Rice's Summer Nights*; music by Will Marion Cook (1869–1944), who later composed a number of African-American Broadway shows; book and lyrics by noted poet, short story writer, and novelist Paul Lawrence Dunbar (1872–1906); Casino Theatre, 1898 (55 perf.). Produced by Edward E. **Rice**, this show, billed as an "African singing and dancing novelty," was written and performed by African-Americans; it constituted the beginning of breaking down the color barrier on Broadway.

club *n.* A performance venue for cabaret, musical acts, singers, and variety entertainment; a nightclub.

coda *n.* End section of a piece of music.

Cohan, George M. (1878–1942) [George Michael Cohan] American star of stage musicals that he wrote for himself as vehicles; producer, director, songwriter.

Among his great hits were his first Broadway musical, *Little Johnny Jones* (1904), and *Forty-Five Minutes from Broadway*. He also starred in *I'd Rather Be Right*. His life was celebrated in the biopic *Yankee Doodle Dandy* (1942), for which he was technical adviser, so that James Cagney's (1899–1986) portrayal of Cohan, the staging of the shows, and the dancing are as authentic as possible. A biographical Broadway musical, *George M!*, by Michael **Stewart** and John (1933–1981) and Francine Pascal (b. 1938), using Cohan's songs and starring Joel Grey (b. 1932), opened in 1968 and ran for 427 performances.

Colman "the Younger," George (1762–1832) English dramatist and memoirist; devised the form of entertainment called the **jumble**. His father, the playwright and essayist George Colman "the Older" (1732–1794), also known as "George the First," had been manager of the Haymarket, and his son took over the position. Colman wrote the libretto for an anti-slavery opera, ***Inkle and Yarico*** (1787), with composer Samuel **Arnold**, with whom he also collaborated on several other pieces.

   See also POLLY.

Coleman, Cy (1929–2004) [b. Seymour Kaufman] American songwriter and theater composer, known for the ebullience of his music and his sense of lively rhythm; among the shows he wrote are ***Barnum***; *The Life* (1997); ***Little Me***; ***On the Twentieth Century***; *The Will Rogers Follies* (1991); *Wildcat* (1960), with a book by N. Richard Nash (1913–2000) and lyrics by Carolyn **Leigh**, about a character named Wildcat "Wildy" Jackson (played by Lucille Ball [1911–1989] in her only Broadway show), who hopes to strike it rich in the Texas oilfields in 1912; *Sweet Charity* (1966), with a book by Neil Simon (b. 1927), about an optimistic dance hall hostess named Charity Hope Valentine (played by Gwen Verdon, for whom the show was a great **vehicle**) and her unhappy love life; and *Seesaw* (1973), book by Michael Bennett, who also directed and choreographed, and lyrics by Dorothy **Fields**.

color *n., v.* —*n.* **1.** In singing or speaking, the tone of voice as influenced by a particular emotion or feeling. Also called *coloration*. **2.** In music, a particular effect achieved, e.g., by the use of chromatic notes, or by composing in a major or minor key. —*v. t.* **3.** To influence the way the voice sounds when speaking or singing by infusing a particular feeling or emotion into it, such that the emotion is clearly understood by the listening audience. **4.** To compose a musical passage with a particular effect in mind.

coloratura (ko:' lo: rah TOO rah) *n., adj.* [Italian: coloring; coloration] —*n.* **1.** Ornamentation of a line of music, e.g., elaborate grace notes, trills, roulades, runs, and scales, in order to show off the singer's technical prowess and beauty of tone; esp. used from the 17th c. through the early 19th, e.g., in the **bel canto** operas of the romantic era. **2.** A singer who performs this music. —*adj.* **3.** Pertaining to the kind of music just described: *a coloratura passage*. **4.** Pertaining to the singer who displays the vocal agility necessary in performing such music: *a coloratura soprano*.

Color Purple, The Broadway musical; songs by singer and songwriter, Brenda Russell (b. 1949), Allee Willis, and Stephen **Bray**; book by Marsha Norman (b.

1947), based on the novel of the same name by Alice Walker (b. 1944); Broadway Theatre, 2005 (910 perf.).

The music is strong on characterization, as well as being lively and interesting, although it is lacking in variety; the cast and perf. were superb, and made up for any lapses in the writing.

In the southern United States, Celie, an African-American teenager, grows up and becomes a strong black woman, fighting against the chauvinism of the tough black men she encounters and forming enduring relationships with wise, knowledgeable women who, like herself, have been through rough times.

combination *n.* In dance, a repeatable pattern of steps. Also called a *dance combination*.

Comden and Green: Betty Comden (1915–2006) and Adolph Green (1915–2002) Musical comedy writing team; native New Yorkers who wrote the book and/or lyrics for such Broadway shows as *On the Town* (1944); *Wonderful Town* (1953); *The Will Rogers Follies* (1991), *Bells Are Ringing*, *Applause*, and *On the Twentieth Century*, among many other collaborations. They also wrote the screenplay for the film *Singin' in the Rain* (1952), which was later adapted as a stage musical that played in London and on Broadway.

comédie à ariettes (ko mé dee ah ah ree EHT) [French: comedy with little songs] French 18th-c. form of operetta, ballad opera, comic opera, or musical comedy.

comédie-ballet 17th-c. French court entertainment. See BALLET COMEDY.

comédie-en-vaudeville (ko mé DEE ahn vo:d VEEL) [French: comedy in vaudeville style] French 18th-c. farces or comic plays with some interpolated songs and/or dances.

comic opera An **opera** or **operetta** with a light, romantic story that ends happily, featuring love ballads and duets, patter songs, big ensemble numbers, and other ingratiating, often beguiling music.

Company Broadway musical by Stephen **Sondheim** (music and lyrics); book by George Furth (1932–2008); Alvin Theatre, 1970 (690 perf.); Broadway revivals: Vivian Beaumont Theatre at Lincoln Center, special revival with original cast, 1993 (2 perf.); Criterion Center Stage Right, 1995 (103 perf.); Ethel Barrymore Theatre, 2006 (280 perf.).

This emotionally edgy show is about loneliness and the difficulty of commitment in relationships. The score is a perfect psychological reflection of the characters' states of mind, exemplified in the heart-wrenching number "Being Alive," full of pathos, yearning, and uncertainty. Harold Prince directed, and Michael Bennett choreographed.

The narcissistic loner Robert is about to turn thirty-five. His reminiscences and memories, and the people in his life, swirl about him in an expressionistic way in a series of episodes as the story of his journey through life evolves.

compose *v. t.* To write music.

composer *n.* A person who writes music.

composition *n.* **1.** A piece of music: *a musical composition*. **2.** The act of composing music: *According to legend, the composition of* **Il barbiere di Siviglia** *took* **Rossini** *just thirteen days*.

comprimario (ko:m' pree MAH ree oh) *n.* [Italian; also used as an adj. in English: *comprimario role*] A secondary, supporting role in an opera; and the singer who performs it.

concept musical A musical comedy that, rather than telling its story as a straightforward narrative, is built around a particular presentational idea, such as a narrative framework in which the story is told as if it were part of another setting; e.g., **Cabaret**, **Chicago**; or told with flashbacks, e.g. **Follies**. Also included in this broad category are shows that are expressionistic in nature and abstract in presentation; e.g., **Company**, **Lady in the Dark**; such a musical may deal in generalizations and abstracted stories, e.g., **Pacific Overtures**.

concept production A director's presentation of an opera that departs from its original setting, time period, or the style in which the piece was intended to be presented, presumably in order to illuminate the material in some way, but sometimes, so it seems, simply for the sake of doing something different.

concert *n.* A public performance of instrumental, orchestral, choral or vocal music; dance; or of a spoken arts event, by one or more individuals: *a jazz concert*; *a rock concert*; *a classical music concert*; *a poetry concert*. Classical music concerts usually take place in a specially built *concert hall*, such as Carnegie Hall, but also sometimes in such outdoor venues as the Hollywood Bowl or New York City's Central Park. Concert performances of operas are often done, without scenery, costumes, or physical acting.

conduct *v. t.* To lead the instrumental ensemble and/or singers in a performance, using a stick called a *baton* or the hands to communicate tempo, dynamics, and aesthetic, expressive aspects of the musical presentation; hence, the n., *conductor*: the person who does this: *music conductor*; *orchestra conductor*. Conducting involves setting the tempo, cuing the entrances for the different instruments and singers, and preparing the music in rehearsal with the performers, including setting dynamics and bringing out musical textures in the orchestration, thus ensuring a unified performance with everyone working together. Before the mid-19th c., the conductor was also often one of the chief musical performers; e.g., the first violinist, the pianist playing a concerto. **Berlioz**, the first interpretive conductor in the modern sense, and **Wagner** initiated conducting practices as we know them today. In 1847, Wagner began the practice of standing in front of the orchestra when conducting. Before that, conductors stood at the back of the orchestra directly in front of the stage, where the singers could see them from a short distance.

Contact Broadway dance musical conceived by Susan Stroman (b. 1954) and John **Weidman**; book by Weidman; choreographed and directed by Stroman, to recordings of classical and **popular music**; Vivian Beaumont Theatre, 2000 (1041 perf.).

There is no singing, and very little dialogue, in the show. Three stories are told: In 1754, an aristocrat, disguised as a servant, pursues a lady on a swing. In 1954, a gangster's abused wife, dining at an Italian restaurant in Queens, escapes into a fantasy world. In 1999, a suicidal man pursues a young lady all around New York City, and discovers that she lives in the apartment above his.

contes d'Hoffmann, Les (The Tales of Hoffmann) (leh: KO:*N*T do:f MAHN) Opera in five acts (prologue; three acts; epilogue) by Jacques **Offenbach**; libretto by Jules **Barbier**, based on a play he wrote with Michel **Carré**, using several stories by E. T. A. **Hoffmann**; Paris, Théâtre de l'Opéra-Comique, 1881.

Although he had originally envisioned the opera as **through-composed**, with recitatives, Offenbach rewrote it as an **opéra comique** with spoken dialogue, because the Opéra-Comique had decided to produce it; it was later performed in a through-composed **version** with recitatives mostly by Ernest **Guiraud**. There is no **definitive edition** or performing version of this opera, which premiered after the composer's death; but an altered version that included interpolated numbers became standard for a long time. The music had been completely conceived, but not fully orchestrated; the task of finishing it was confided to Guiraud. Although the opera calls for multiple roles sung by one sop., they are performed just as often by different individuals for each role.

At Luther's tavern, near the Nuremberg opera house, the venal politician Councilor Lindorf (lihn DO:*R*F) (bass or bar.) inveigles the key to the opera star Stella's dressing room from her servant, Andrès (ah*n* D*R*EHS) (ten.). The poet Hoffmann (ten.) arrives with a crowd of students to await his latest love, Stella, who is singing that evening. His Muse (mezz.), who assumes the identity of his friend, Nicklausse (nee KLO:S), is unhappy about the dissolute life of which the poet is so fond. Hoffmann sees Lindorf and recognizes in him an eternal rival. In telling the students the tale of the dwarf Kleinzach (KLIN ZAHK), Hoffmann begins to think of his past amours, each of whom represents a different characteristic of love: His first was the cold, unfeeling Olympia (o: la*n* pee AH) (sop.), who turned out to be a mechanical doll; his second, the passionate singer Antonia (ah*n*' to: nee AH) (sop.), more in love with her art than with him; his third, the faithless Venetian courtesan Giulietta (dgoo lee eht TAH) (sop.)—this is act 3, but it has often been performed as act 2, perhaps because the drama, both musical and theatrical, of the Antonia act is a stronger ending before the epilogue. Each woman has an evil genius who manipulates her and helps to prevent Hoffmann from finding satisfaction. In act 1, it is the cantankerous doll maker Spalanzani (spah lahn zah NEE) (bass or bar.); he has financial problems with his former partner Coppélius (ko: pé lee ÜS) (bass or bar.), who destroys Olympia in revenge for having been fobbed off with a worthless check from Spalanzani that was supposed to be his share of the profits from the mechanical doll. In act 2, Dr. Miracle (mee *R*AH kluh) (bass or bar.) forces the ill Antonia to sing until she collapses and dies. In act 3, Hoffmann is betrayed by Giulietta in conjunction with her lover, Schlemihl (shleh: MEEL) (bar.), whom he kills in a duel, and the magician Dapertutto (dah peh*r* TOO to:) (bar. or bass). Having tried to steal Hoffmann's reflection for Dapertutto in return for a diamond ring, Giulietta ends up in the arms of her bizarre servant, Pitichinaccio (pih: tih: shih: NAH cho:) (ten.), where Hoffmann finds her. In the end, he is even disillusioned by Stella, who has gone off with Lindorf. The Muse consoles him as best she may.

See also BARCAROLLE.

contraction and release One of the prime techniques of the doyenne of American dance, Martha Graham (1894–1991); consisting of the intake of breath (the release) and its total exhalation, causing or allowing the contraction of the body.

contralto *n.* Syn. with **alto**.

Converse, Frederick Shepherd (1871–1940) American composer and teacher; he wrote four operas, two of them never performed; in 1910, *The Pipe of Dreams* was done at the Metropolitan Opera, the first by an American composer. Converse was known for his lush orchestrations, much influenced by Richard **Strauss**.

cool *adj.* Pertains to a particular school of 1950s jazz that concentrated on low-volume, soft melodic improvisations, danceable rhythms, and old-fashioned development of riffs: *cool jazz*. Also used as a n.: *They played cool*; *Miles Davis's (1926–1991) Birth of the Cool recordings, made in 1949–1950*.

Copland, Aaron (1900–1990) American classical composer; studied composition with Rubin **Goldmark**; known for the wealth of his orchestral music, using themes from American folk tunes, e.g., in his most famous piece, the ballet *Appalachian Spring* (1944). He wrote two operas, *The Second Hurricane* (1937) and *The Tender Land*.

copy *v. t.* To **transcribe** or write out music, using an existing score and writing out the music from that score on a blank sheet of music paper.

copyist *n.* The person who copies out the parts for each instrument in an ensemble. Also called *music copyist*.

copyright performance *Brit.* The presentation of a theater piece, usually not fully mounted or rehearsed, to insure the author or authors' legal rights to the property, esp. in the 19th c., when plays and musical theater pieces were pirated and unauthorized productions were mounted, e.g., in the case of Gilbert and Sullivan's *H.M.S. Pinafore*, which was widely pirated in the U.S. As a result, G&S went to New York for the premiere of their next work, *The Pirates of Penzance*, in order to ensure the American copyright and thus prevent **piracy**, while premiering the production in England simultaneously to preserve their English copyright.

Cordelia's Aspirations Broadway musical by David **Braham**.

77

Corigliano, John (b. 1938) Award-winning American classical composer of film scores, chamber music, symphonies, known for his eclectic and varied styles. Among his dramatic works are the experimental one-act opera *Naked Carmen* (1970), an "electric rock opera" based on Bizet's *Carmen*. His two-act opera about the French Revolution, *The Ghosts of Versailles* (1991), with a libretto by William F. Hoffman (b. 1939), uses characters from the third play of Beaumarchais' "Figaro" trilogy, *La mère coupable* (The Guilty Mother) (1792) (lah mehr koo PAH bluh). In the opera, the ghost of Beaumarchais himself falls in love with Marie Antoinette. This was the first new American work presented at the Metropolitan Opera since Samuel Barber's *Antony and Cleopatra*.

Cornelius, Peter (1824–1874) (ko:[r] NEH: lee *oo*s) German composer; friend of Hector **Berlioz**; wrote three operas, of which the best known is the jaunty comic opera *Der Barbier von Bagdad* (1858) (deh bah[r] BEE[R] fuhn BAHK daht), to his own libretto in two acts, based a story from *The Thousand and One Nights*.

corps de ballet (ko:r' duh ba LEH:) [French: lit., body of ballet] **1.** Originally, an entire company of ballet dancers, including the principals; now, dancers who perform as a group, e.g., in a full-length theatrical ballet (the equivalent of a chorus of singers in a musical theater piece), as opposed to soloists. **2.** The group of dancers who are members of an opera company and who perform the ballets or other dances that are part of some operas, often as particular groups of characters; e.g., the Hungarian dancers in the "Csárdás" number in act 2 of *Die Fledermaus*.

coryphée (KO: rih FÉ) *n.* [French (ko:' *r*ee FÉ): Female chorus dancer] **1.** The female leader of the corps de ballet. **2.** A female ballerina who does small roles.

Così fan tutte (Thus Do All Women) [Full title: *Così fan tutte, ossia La scuola degli amanti* (Thus Do All Women, or The School for Lovers) (ko: ZEE fahn' TOOT teh: o: SEE ah lah SKooO: lah deh' [g]lee ah MAHN tee)] Opera in two acts by Wolfgang Amadeus **Mozart**; libretto by Lorenzo **Da Ponte**; Vienna, Burgtheater, 1790.

In Naples near the end of the 18th c., Don Alfonso (DON ahl FO:N zo:) (bass) tells his friends, Guglielmo (goo [G]LYEHL mo:) (bar.), engaged to Dorabella (do:' rah BEHL lah) (mezz.), and Ferrando (fehr RAHN do:) (ten.), engaged to Fiordiligi (fyo:r' dee LEE dgee) (sop.), that the two sisters they love and believe faithful are in reality as fickle as all other women. They scoff at him, but go along with a little scheme he has concocted to prove it: They will pretend to leave with the army, will return in disguise, and each will try to seduce the other's fiancée. They succeed, and a double marriage is arranged with the help of the maidservant Despina (dehs PEE nah) (sop.), who is roped into participating by Don Alfonso and is disguised as a notary. The joke is revealed, and everyone has a wry laugh.

cotillion; cotillon *n.* **1.** A formal ball, meant to enable young men and women of high social class to meet, and where young ladies make their debuts in society. **2.** A fast-paced, intricate 18th-c. French dance. **3.** The last dance or finale of an 18th-c. or 19th c. ball, usually a kind of round dance done by couples who change partners throughout, as a kind of farewell; e.g., in act 2 of Tchaikovsky's *Yevgenyi Onegin*.

count *n., v.* —*n.* **1.** In music and dance, the number of beats: *on a count of four*. **2.** In dance, another word for **beat**: *Move forward on the fourth count.* —*v. t.* **3.** In music, to go through the beats, starting at a particular point in the score, usually silently to oneself, in order to make an entrance at the right time: *to count the beats*. **4.** In dance, to go through choreographed steps in order, usually silently to oneself. When a choreographer is staging a dance number, he or she will often count the steps out loud while rehearsing with the dancers.

countertenor *n.* An adult male singer with a contralto range. Also called a *male alto*. Many countertenors are experts in baroque music and sing in opera houses, performing roles written in some cases for castrati.

Countess Mariza Viennese operetta by Emmerich Kálmán. See GRÄFIN MARIZA.

country music; country-western music; country & western music Songs, both solo and ensemble numbers, often performed with guitar or small band accompaniment, originating in the American middle west and south, e.g., in Nashville, TN—the virtual home of such music, with its major performance venue, the Grand Ole Opry House. The songs are often of a sentimental or nostalgic nature, all about love, fidelity, and hard or easy times. They are characterized by easily comprehensible lyrics; simple, memorable melodies, often sung with a throb and a vibrato, sometimes with a **scoop** or two; and by simple harmonic modulations. Some songs are crooned, others belted.

couplet *n.* A set of two rhymed lines, conventionally used in verse drama, e.g., in concluding a scene in Shakespeare; and in lyrics; often used in the plural to refer to certain lyrics in musical theater pieces, esp. in French (koo PLEH:), e.g., the "Couplets du caissier" (koo PLEH: dü keh SYEH:) (The Treasurer's Couplets) in Offenbach's *Les brigands*.

courante (k*oo* RAHNT) *n.* [Fr. French adj., female gender: running] A dance in 3/4 or 3/8 time, with running steps, esp. a 16th and 17th-c. French court dance, also popular in England.

covered tone In singing, the technique of modifying vowel sounds in the upper register, so that they are veiled, with a placement that is less bright, i.e., not pitched directly in the front of the **mask**, but using the area slightly in back as a **resonator**, causing the voice to resonate in the soft palate. The musical tone is thus more pleasing and beautiful to the listener, and the transitional tones more intense. Cf. **open tone**.

Coward, Noël (1899–1973) Prolific English playwright, composer of songs and musicals, director, stage and film performer, known for his wit, intelligence, and incisive, pithy dialogue. Among his many works for the musical theater are ***Bitter Sweet*** (1928); *Conversation Piece* (1934); *Sail Away* (1961); *The Girl Who Came* *to Supper* (1963); and *High Spirits* (1964), a musicalization of his play *Blithe Spirit* (1941), which he also directed.

crack *n., v.* —*n.* **1.** A sudden, unexpected break in the voice due to tension or faulty vocal technique, e.g., as when a tenor cracks on a high note. In act 2 of Gilbert and Sullivan's **Utopia Limited**, the tenor lead, Captain Fitzbattleaxe, sings "A Tenor All Singers Above," in which he explains that a tenor "must keep himself quiet, attend to his diet," or else "he can't do himself justice," and he cracks on his high notes. —*v. i.* **2.** To have a sudden break in the voice, caused by vocal tension: *Her voice cracked.*

Cradle Will Rock, The Broadway musical by Marc **Blitzstein**; book by the composer; Windsor Theatre, 1938 (108 perf.); Broadway revival: Mansfield Theatre, 1947 (34 perf.); film, *Cradle Will Rock* (1999), about the creation of the show, the controversy surrounding it, and the attempts to prevent its being put on because of its leftist political themes.

The show was produced by John Houseman (1902–1988), directed by Orson Welles (1915–1985), and mounted under the auspices of the Federal Theatre Project (FTP) (1935–1939), which had been started as part of Roosevelt's New Deal. The production was shut down under government pressure just as it was about to open on Broadway, ostensibly due to budget cuts, but probably because of the political controversy surrounding its perceived pro-Communism. Injunctions were slapped on the actors, and the theater itself was locked and guarded, but the courageous Welles rented another theater and had the audience march there with him to see the opening night performance, done with no costumes, scenery, or orchestra, and with Blitzstein accompanying on the piano. After the show's exciting reception, Welles did it as a series of Sunday evening readings at his famed Mercury Theater, and finally, the show began regular performances. The original cast recording, with Blitzstein narrating and playing the piano, is available on a CD from Pearl (GEMS 0009; 1998).

Reminiscent of works by **Brecht** and **Weill**, this parable about conditions at the height of the Great Depression is set in Steeletown, USA, owned and run by Mr. Mister, the epitome of the greedy, self-interested capitalist, who controls the media, the church, and the lives of the inhabitants through his cynically named Liberty Committee. The labor organizer Larry Foreman leads a revolt of the steel workers, and they win the day.

crescendo *n.* [Italian: growing] Becoming gradually louder.

croon *v. t.* To sing in a low, soft, evenly modulated, soothing voice, drawing out the sounds almost seductively, using more of the head voice than the chest voice; the opposite of **belt**; hence, *crooner*: a **vocalist** who sings this way; *crooning*: the style and act of singing in this manner.

csárdás; czardas (CHAHR dahsh') *n.* A two-part Hungarian national dance for couples; originated in the mid-19th c. The dance begins with a slow, stately, melancholy movement, its music often in a minor key; and then goes into a quick, fast-paced, energetic and lively movement; used in ballet and opera, e.g., in Tchaikovsky's ballet *Swan Lake*; Strauss's *Die Fledermaus* and *Der Zigeunerbaron*.

Csárdásfürstin (The Csárdás Princess) (CHAH*R* dahsh FÜ*R* stih:n) Viennese operetta by Emmerich **Kálmán**; libretto by Leo **Stein** and Béla Jenbach (1871–1943) (BEH: lah YEHN bahkh) [b. Béla Jakobovits (yah KO: bo: vihts)]; Vienna, Johann Strauss Theater, 1915.

This is one of the greatest Viennese operettas. There is a vibrant 1971 recording on EMI Classics CD (7243 5 66170 2 5; 1988).

At a café in Budapest, the singer Sylvia Varescu (VAH rehsh koo) (sop.), nicknamed the "Csárdás Princess," is finishing her last show before going off to New York for a booking. The waiters clear the space for a farewell supper party thrown for her by Count Boni Kancsianu (BO: nee KAHN chee ah noo) (bar.). He tells his friend, Count Feri von Kerekes (FEH ree fuhn KEHR eh kehsh) (bar.), how surprised he is that Edwin Lippert-Weylersheim (LIH peh[*r*]t VI leh[*r*]s HIM) (ten.) is not going to be there. Edwin's father, the Prince (bass), has been trying to get him to end his romantic pursuit of Sylvia, esp. since he is already engaged to Princess Stasi (SHTAH zee) (sop.), and perhaps it has worked. Edwin finally appears, and we learn that he plans to go to New York with Sylvia, but his cousin arrives with orders for him to report immediately for military duty. Edwin asks for half an hour's grace, sends for a notary, and has the guests witness his oath that he will return and marry Sylvia within two months. He then leaves for Vienna, and Boni tells Sylvia that Edwin cannot possibly marry her because the family will insist on his marrying Stasi. Upset and not knowing what else to do, she leaves for New York. Two months later, at a party in the Lippert-Weylersheim palace in Vienna, Boni and Sylvia arrive. At first sight, Boni falls madly in love with Stasi! Edwin presents Sylvia to his father as a countess, and she thinks he is ashamed of her, so she announces who she really is, shows everyone the marriage contract, and tears it up. Edwin's father is upset because there is no engagement to Stasi, who has been compromised, but Boni says that he loves her and wants to marry her. Out of family pride, the Prince will not allow Edwin to marry Sylvia, until Feri reveals that the Prince's second wife was once an actress. The Prince relents, and a double wedding takes place.

Cui, César (1835–1918) (sé ZAHR KOO ee) Russian composer, one of **The Five**; his works include several operas on Russian historical and literary themes, as well as *William Ratcliff* (1869) and *Angelo* (1876), the latter based on the same drama by Victor **Hugo** that was the basis for *La Gioconda*.

Cunning Little Vixen, The Opera by Leoš **Janáček**. See PŘÍHODY LIŠKY BYSTROUŠKY.

curtain call The appearance of actors at the end of the performance to acknowledge the audience's appreciative applause. Many curtain calls are staged or choreographed, particularly in the case of musical comedies.

curtain music Live or recorded instrumental music played just before the beginning of a play, signaling that the curtain is about to open.

curtain raiser 1. A short play, operetta, or sketch that is performed before the main performance event of the evening. **Gilbert and Sullivan** comic operas, for instance, were often preceded during their original runs by one-act operettas written by someone else. Their one-act comic opera *Trial by Jury* has itself been used as a curtain raiser for *H.M.S. Pinafore* or *The Pirates of Penzance.* **2.** The opening act in a vaudeville variety show.

Curtains "A Great Big New Musical Comedy" and "A Musical Whodunit" by **Kander and Ebb**: John Kander (music) and Fred Ebb (lyrics); original book and concept by Peter **Stone**; book by British-born writer, composer, and orchestrator Rupert Holmes (b. 1947); Al Hirschfeld Theatre, 2007 (537 perf.). Since Stone had died in 2003 and Ebb in 2004, the book and lyrics were polished and put together by Holmes and other collaborators, including the show's director, Scott Ellis (b. 1957).

The year is 1959. A Broadway-bound musical, *Robbin' Hood of the Old West*, has just taken its curtain call after a Boston tryout when the star, the temperamental and untalented Jessica Cranshaw, is poisoned onstage and rushed to the hospital, where she dies. Lieutenant Cioffi, the investigating officer, suspects everybody, since they all hated Jessica, including her rich husband, Sidney, and their ambitious daughter, Bambi. Cioffi interrogates everyone and falls in love with the understudy, Niki Harris. Then there are two more murders. The murderer turns out to be a theater critic!

cut-off *n.* A music conductor's hand signal: a gesture that serves as a cue, telling the musicians to stop playing and/or singing at the end of a piece, which they must do in **unison**. There is no set version of such a signal, but each conductor uses his or her own.

Cyrano de Bergerac There are a number of musical theater pieces based on the play *Cyrano de Bergerac* (1897) by Edmond Rostand (1868–1918). The plot: The poet and street brawler Cyrano is ashamed of his unusually large nose and thinks he will never find happiness. He is in love with his cousin, Roxane. His friend, young Christian, extremely handsome but tongue-tied, is also in love with her. Since she is attracted to romantic eloquence, Cyrano helps Christian to win her affections by telling him what to say, and by writing love letters for him. Christian is killed in battle and Roxane enters a convent, still cherishing her love for him. There, Cyrano visits her daily. One day, he arrives wounded, having been attacked by people working for his enemies. Only when he actually recites one of the love letters he has written, and that she has kept next to her heart, does she realize the true situation. But it is too late, and he dies in her arms. Victor **Herbert** wrote a bouncy, tuneful, gorgeous operetta titled *Cyrano de Bergerac* (1899). The distinguished English writer Anthony Burgess (1917–1993) wrote the book for the 1973 Broadway musical *Cyrano*, with energetic, melodious music by Michael J. Lewis (b. 1939). It starred Christopher Plummer (b. 1929) in a Tony® Award–winning performance in the title role, but the show only ran for 49 perf. *Cyrano: The Musical* (1993), translated from a Dutch musical by Koen van Dijk (b. 1959)

(KO:N fahn DIK), with English lyrics by performer and lyricist Peter Reeves and more music by Ad van Dijk to additional lyrics by Sheldon **Harnick**, was not much more successful on Broadway and closed after 175 perf. Harnick had also written the libretto to the opera *Cyrano* (1990) by Jack **Beeson**. Two further operas, both entitled *Cyrano de Bergerac*, were composed, one by Franco **Alfano** (1936) and the other by Walter **Damrosch** (1913).

D

da capo (dah' KAH po:) [Italian: from the beginning] Usually short for *da capo al fine* (ahl FEE neh:): from the beginning to the end. The performer starts over again at the beginning of a section that has just been performed, and repeats it through to the end.

da capo aria An opera aria constructed in three parts, the third of which is a repetition of the first; the form was introduced in the 17th c., with the operas of Claudio **Monteverdi**, and had become ubiquitous in the 18th c. The second section was in a different key from the first, and the third, repeat section was subject to variations and to coloratura ornamentation that showed off the singer's voice and technique.

Dalayrac, Nicolas (1753–1809) [b. Nicolas-Marie d'Alayrac] (nih: ko lah' mah *r*ee' dah leh: *R*AHK) Lawyer turned prolific French composer of chamber music and ca. fifty operas and opéras comiques, of which the only one that remains in public consciousness is *Nina, ou La folle par amour* (Nina, or The Love-Crazed Maiden) (1786) (nee NAH oo lah FOL pah*r* a MOO*R*), the basis for the opera by **Paisiello**.

dal segno (dahl SEH: nyo:) [Italian: from the sign] A **performance mark** indicating that part of a piece where a singer or instrumentalist should begin playing a recapitulated passage. Abbrev., D.S.

dal segno aria A version of the **da capo aria**, providing for a repetition starting not at the beginning of the first section, but at a **performance mark** placed over a bar partway through it.

Dames at Sea Off-Broadway musical by Jim Wise (1919–2000); book and lyrics by George Haimsohn (1926–2003) and Robin Miller; Bouwerie Lane Theatre, 1968 (578 perf.).

The show launched the career of Bernadette Peters (b. 1948).

In this spoof of 1930s Hollywood musicals, with every hilarious cliché in the book, Ruby (Bernadette Peters) arrives in New York City from Utah, determined to become a Broadway star. She falls in love with Dick, a sailor and songwriter, and gets a job in the chorus of a show starring Mona Kent. Also on hand are the wisecracking trouper Joan and her boyfriend, Lucky, another sailor who happens to be Dick's friend. When the theater has to be torn down, Dick and Lucky persuade their Captain to allow the show to be done on the ship. Mona gets seasick, and Ruby takes her place, becoming a star.

Damn Yankees Broadway musical with music and lyrics by Richard **Adler** and Jerry **Ross**; book by George **Abbott** and Douglass Wallop (1920–1985), based on his 1954 novel *The Year the Yankees Lost the Pennant*; 48th Street Theater, 1955 (1019 perf.); Broadway revival: Marquis Theatre, 1994 (718 perf.); film, 1958.

The success of this classic show was ensured by George Abbott's direction and the stunning choreography of the legendary Bob Fosse. A perennial favorite, this light-hearted musical is a version of the **Faust** legend:

Joe Boyd, an avid fan of the Washington Senators baseball team, is so upset by their losing streak that he would do anything to save the day. Mr. Applegate—hilariously played by Ray Walston (1914–2001) on both stage and screen—appears out of nowhere: He is Satan, disguised as a respectable businessman. Boyd sells his soul to the devil in order to secure the pennant, and is transformed into the champion slugger Joe Hardy. But he misses his wife, so he wants to give it all up and go home. Applegate, however, has a heavy investment in winning, so he summons a seductress who gets whatever she wants, Lola—played with all the wily art at her command by Gwen Verdon in both the original stage production and the film—to seduce Hardy and prevent him from returning home. But Lola's wiles fail to tempt the lovesick champion, who cleverly wriggles his way out of the satanic compact, wins the important game, and, changed back into his old self, goes happily home to his wife.

Damrosch, Walter (1862–1960) German-born American composer and conductor; son of distinguished violinist and conductor Leopold Damrosch (1832–1885); founded the Damrosch Opera Company in 1894; known for conducting American premieres of Richard Wagner's operas; composed several operas, among them *The Scarlet Letter* (1896), based on Nathaniel Hawthorne's novel, and ***Cyrano de Bergerac*** (1913).

dance *n., v.* —*n.* **1.** The art of moving in a choreographed or improvised rhythmic pattern, usually in time to music; hence *dancer*: one who practices the art of the dance. **2.** A particular pattern of steps done in a preset, consecutive series, e.g., **minuet**; **waltz**. **3.** The music to which such a pattern is executed by the dancers, or listened to as music by itself: *a waltz by Johann* **Strauss**; *a dance suite*. **4.** Choreographed movement in a musical theater piece or in a ballet, modern dance, or other program. —*v. t.* **5.** To move or step in a rhythmic, choreographic pattern, often to music.

See also BALLET; CHOREOGRAPHY.

dance band Group of instrumentalists who play at social events, weddings, and in dance halls or other venues.

dance captain The member of a musical comedy chorus appointed to be in charge of the dance numbers, and to make sure they are maintained as rehearsed; an honored position in every Broadway show.

dance director Syn. with **choreographer** in a musical comedy.

dance notation A system of written signs and symbols indicating the choreography of a ballet, musical comedy sequence, modern or other dance; there are several such systems.

See NOTATION.

Dancin' Broadway dance **revue** conceived, written, choreographed and directed by Bob Fosse, using music by George M. **Cohan**, Sigmund **Romberg**, John Philip **Sousa**, Harry **Warren**, and others; Broadhurst Theatre, 1978 (1787 perf.).

danse macabre (dahns' mah KAH bruh) [French: macabre, sinister dance] The dance of death, allegorically personified as a skeleton wielding a scythe in medieval painting and on stage in morality plays and contemporary ballets; performed in a black costume with a skeleton painted on it in white. Among composers who have written danse macabre pieces are Camille **Saint-Saëns**, Franz Liszt (1811–1886), Modest **Mussorgsky**, and Arnold Schoenberg. There is a notable danse macabre in Kurt Jooss's (1901–1979) (KOO[R]T YO:S) avant-garde 1932 ballet, *The Green Table*.

Da Ponte, Lorenzo (1749–1838) (lo: REHN zo: dah PO:N teh:) [b. Emmanuele Conegliano (eh mah' noo EH: leh: ko:' neh: [*G*]LYAH no:)] Italian poet and librettist of thirty-six operas; immortalized esp. as the author of the texts for three of Mozart's greatest operas: *Le nozze di Figaro*, *Don Giovanni*, and *Così fan tutte*. Born a Jew in the Republic of Venice, he converted to Catholicism and studied for the priesthood, but was expelled from the seminary for committing adultery. He left Italy for Vienna, where he became a leading light in the city's operatic world, providing libretti for all of the major composers of the period, including Antonio **Salieri**. Eventually, after a colorful life, which he relates in fascinating detail in the four volumes of his amusing autobiographical memoirs, Da Ponte left Europe for New York, where he became Columbia University's first professor of Italian literature.

See also GARCÍA, MANUEL.

David, Hal (b. 1921) American lyricist, known for the many pop songs he has written with Burt **Bacharach** and for the Bacharach-David musical *Promises Promises* (1968).

Death in Venice Opera in two acts by Benjamin **Britten**; libretto by art critic and writer Myfanwy Piper (1911–1997) (muh VAHN wee) [b. Mary Myfanwy Piper], based on the novella *Der Tod in Venedig* (1912) (deh: TO:T ihn vehn EH: dikh), by Thomas Mann (1875–1955), which was in turn based on real incidents in the writer's life; England, Snape, The Maltings, 1973.

Although written in two acts, the opera is really a series of disparate scenes with musical interludes in between them, often including dances that are a kind of variation on the **danse macabre**, which prominently underscore Aschenbach's increasing disorientation and near madness.

The closeted homosexual author Aschenbach (AH shehn BAKH) (ten.) goes to Venice for a vacation and a respite from the tensions of his life in Munich. There he is passionately attracted to a beautiful young Polish boy, Tadzio (Polish pron.: TAH dzhoo; German pron.: TAH dzee o:) (a dance role), who is on the beach at the Lido (LEE do:) with his family. A cholera epidemic breaks out, which almost nobody will admit is happening; Aschenbach tries to flee the city but is forced to remain because of a problem with his luggage. From a safe distance, he gazes with infinite longing at Tadzio playing with his friends. Aschenbach collapses onto a bench and dies.

Debussy, Claude (1862–1918) [b. Achille-Claude Debussy (ah sheel' klo:d' duh bü SEE) Innovative late-romantic French composer of impressionist music; worked on several operatic projects but composed only one opera, a masterpiece, *Pelléas et Mélisande*.

decrescendo (DEE kreh SHEHN do:) *n.* [Fr. Italian: growing softer] A gradual decrease in volume.

definitive edition The final, full, accurate, reliable **version** of a musical score, determined and set by musicologists or the composer(s) of the piece before it is published. But it is very difficult, if not impossible to determine what constitutes the definitive edition of many works, from earlier pieces through the 20th c. Conflicting or varying versions of many pieces exist: e.g., arias in Rossini's operas that he wrote or rewrote for particular singers, any of which might be used in a modern production. In performance, some musicals and operas are done with the published edition cut or otherwise altered, and some adhere to it faithfully. It is sometimes hard to determine a composer's final intentions, for various reasons; e.g., the destruction of the prompt books for the original (posthumous) production of Offenbach's *Les contes d'Hoffmann* when the Opéra-Comique burned down; the differences between autograph scores and early printed versions; extant multiple versions of a piece, e.g., Verdi's *Don Carlos*. For an interesting discourse on the subject of definitive versions of Italian operas, see Philip Gossett's *Divas and Scholars: Performing Italian Opera* (The University of Chicago Press, 2006).

de Koven, Reginald (1859–1920) [b. Henry Louis Reginald de Koven] American operetta composer, music critic, and conductor; most famous for his operetta *Robin Hood*; among his other works, highly popular in their day, are the operettas *Rob Roy* (1894), *The Mandarin* (1896), and *The Highwayman* (1898); and his opera *The Canterbury Pilgrims*, produced at the Metropolitan Opera in 1917.

Délibes, Léo (1836–1891) (lé o:' dé LEEB) French composer; student of Adolphe **Adam**; wrote two ballets that are still widely performed, *Coppélia* (1870) and *Sylvia* (1876); of the approximately two dozen operas and operettas he composed, only *Lakmé* still holds the stage.

Delius, Frederick (1862–1934) [b. Theodore Albert Frederick Delius] English composer; his six operas include *A Village Romeo and Juliet* and *Irmelin*. Many of Delius's operas, all written in the early part of his career, include orchestral interludes that are played as part of concert programs.

demi *n.* [Fr. French: half] In dance, any partially executed movement, or a position not fully realized; e.g., a demi-plié.

demi-plié (Anglicized: DEH mee PLEE ay) *n.* A **plié** in which the legs are bent only halfway.

descending *n.* [Also used as an adj.] **1.** Going down the steps of a scale. **2.** A falling tone in singing, going from high to low, either in a **legato** or **staccato** manner.

designer run A run-through rehearsal esp. for the benefit of the set, costume, wig, makeup, and lighting designers, e.g., of an opera that has elaborate effects, costume changes, and makeup that needs to be checked; a kind of technical rehearsal.

De Sylva, B. G. (1895–1950) [b. George Gard De Sylva; sometimes spelled DeSylva] Prolific American writer, producer, and stage and screen lyricist; wrote books for *Du Barry Was a Lady*, *Louisiana Purchase* (co-written with Morrie Ryskind); *Panama Hattie* (1940); wrote songs for *George White's Scandals*. Among his famous lyrics are "California, Here I Come" (see BIG BOY) and "Look for the Silver Lining," music by Jerome **Kern**, from the show *Sally*.

dialogue *n.* **1.** In dramatic material, the spoken words of a text; i.e., those uttered by the actors. **2.** In music, the alternation of sung lines between opposing characters or choruses; esp. refers to early music.

Dialogues des Carmélites (Dialogues of the Carmelites) Opera by Francis **Poulenc**.

Diavolessa, La (The She-Devil) (lah dee ah' vo: LEHS sah) Comic opera (**opera buffa**) in three acts by Baldassare **Galuppi**; libretto by Carlo **Goldoni**; Venice, Teatro di San Samuele (dee sahn sah moo EH: leh:), 1755.

A stylish CD recording that captures the opera's humor perfectly is available from CPO (999 947-2; 2004).

This is a whimsical and droll masterpiece about a penniless couple who elope to Naples: Dorina (do: REE nah) (sop.), who hopes eventually to come into an inheritance, and Giannino (dgahn NEE no:) (bar.). Giannino has a great idea! He knows of a well-heeled nobleman, Don Poppone (don pop PO: neh:) (bass), who is goodhearted but a bit obsessive about his hobby, treasure hunting. In order to earn some money, the couple will offer their services to him as "treasure hunters." Don Poppone is about to be annoyed by visiting aristocrats, Count Nastri (NAHS tree) (contr. or c-ten.) and his wife (sop.), who will prevent him from pursuing his treasure hunt—and this time, he is sure he has actually discovered one! His loving housekeeper, Ghiandina (gyahn DEE nah) (sop.), rolls her eyes and puts up with his eccentricities. Giannino and Dorina arrive, and Don Poppone mistakes them for the Count and Countess, who arrive shortly thereafter. He mistakes them for his "treasure hunters!" Everyone get embroiled in one misunderstanding after another, but everything is satisfactorily straightened out in the end.

Dibdin, Charles (1745–1814) Prolific English composer, actor, singer, writer, songwriter, and theater manager; one of the most important and influential figures in the 18th-c. English musical theater, with more than 100 works to his credit. He collaborated fruitfully with Isaac **Bickerstaffe** on a number of projects, including *The Ephesian Matron* (1769) and *The Recruiting Sergeant* (1770), as well as the **pasticcio** *Love in the City* (1767). On his own, Dibdin wrote the ballad operas *The Waterman, or The First of August* (1774) and *The Quaker* (1775), celebrated in their day. He also adapted French and Italian works for the English stage, among them operas by **Philidor** and **Grétry**, and *La serva padrona* by **Pergolesi**, produced in 1770 as *The Maid and the Mistress*. His most famous work was *Lionel and Clarissa* (1768), with a libretto by Bickerstaffe; a fascinating medley of a 1920 London production is available on Pearl (GEMM CD 9917; 1981); the CD includes *The Beggar's Opera*.

Didone abbandonata (Dido Abandoned) A libretto by Pietro **Metastasio**, based on book 4 of Virgil's (70–19 BCE) *Aeneid* (29–19 BCE) and book 3 of Ovid's (43 BCE—17/18 CE) unfinished *Fasti* (Days of the Roman Calendar) (FAH stee); 1724. This libretto was set by ca. fifty-five composers, including **Albinoni** (1725), **Galuppi** (1740; second version, 1764), **Hasse** (1742), **Jommelli** (1747; 1749; 1763, revised 1777–1783), **Sarti** (1762; new version, 1782), Niccolò **Piccinni** (1770), **Paisiello** (1794), **Paër** (1810), and **Mercadante** (1823). It was Metastasio's first original libretto.

The story, like that of *Dido and Aeneas* (1689) by Henry **Purcell**, *Didon* (1783) (dee DO*N*) by Piccinni, and the much earlier *Didone* (1641) by **Cavalli**, concerns the love of Dido (DI doh), Queen of Carthage, for the Trojan hero, Aeneas (ee NEE uhs), who has fled the burning city of Troy and will eventually arrive in Italy, where he will found Rome. In Metastasio's complicated story, Iarbas (ee YAHR bahs), King of the Moors, arrives at Dido's court disguised as his own minister, Arbaces (ahr BAY seez), and offers peace if Dido will marry Iarbas and have Aeneas killed. She refuses. Iarbas orders his confidant, Araspes (ah RAS peez), to kill Aeneas, but Araspes is in love with Dido's sister, Selene (seh LEE neh), and refuses. Fighting between Moors and Trojans erupts, and Aeneas bests Iarbas but spares his life. Selene reveals her love for Aeneas, but he and the fleet depart, while Araspes brings news that the Moors have set Carthage aflame. Iarbas renews his offer of marriage, but the despairing Dido refuses yet again, and hurls herself into the flames.

Dietz, Howard (1896–1983) Prolific American writer and lyricist; worked regularly with Arthur **Schwartz**, with whom he collaborated on *The Band Wagon*; supplied additional lyrics for *Oh, Kay!*; worked with Jerome **Kern** and Vernon **Duke**; contributed to numerous Hollywood musical films. For more than thirty years, he was the executive in charge of publicity for MGM. In 1974, he published his autobiography, *Dancing in the Dark: Words by Howard Dietz* (Quadrangle). "Dancing in the Dark" is the title of one of the most famous songs he and Schwartz wrote together.

diminuendo (dih mihn' yoo EHN doh) *adj.* [Italian: diminishing] Growing gradually softer. Cf. *decrescendo*.

89

director *n.* The person who oversees all aspects of a production in any entertainment venue, and stages the show.

Disney musicals A phenomenon since the 1990s, stage musicals based on Walt Disney features have proved immensely popular on Broadway and on tour. Three became megahits: *Beauty and the Beast*, *The Lion King*, and *Mary Poppins*. *The Little Mermaid* was less successful, as was *Tarzan* (2006), with music and lyrics by Phil Collins (b. 1951) and a book by David Henry **Hwang**, based on the 1999 animated feature: It got terrible reviews, but still managed to run at the Richard Rodgers Theatre for 35 previews and 486 perf.

dithyramb (DIH*TH* ih ram', or ramb') *n. Hist.* In ancient Greece, a choral ode or hymn, originally to celebrate the lubricious god Dionysus (DI o: NI suhs) at his annual Athenian festival, the Dionysia (DI o: NIHSH uh); and by extension, any formal choral ode or hymn.

Dittersdorf, Carl Ditters von (1739–1799) (DIH: tuhs fuhn DIH: tuhs dawf) Austrian composer of instrumental music and thirty-six operas, including *Die lustigen Weiber von Windsor* and *Die Hochzeit des Figaros* (The Marriage of Figaro) (1789) (dee HOKH TSIT dehs FEE gah RO:S), to his own libretto, based on the same play by Beaumarchais that **Da Ponte** used for the libretto to Mozart's *Le nozze di Figaro*. One of his most well known works is *Doktor und Apotheker* (The Doctor and the Apothecary) (1786) (DOK to:[*r*] *oo*nt ah' po: TEH: kuh[*r*]); libretto by German actor, playwright, and librettist Gottlieb Stephanie (1741–1800) (GOT leep SHTEH fah nee), a Romeo and Juliet story with a happy ending.

diva (DEE vah) *n.* [Italian] Originally a neutral term, meaning female opera star; now often derogatory, as when applied to male and female performers who are egotistical, spoiled, pampered, and demanding. Cf. **prima donna**.

divertissement (dih VUHR tihs muhnt') *n.* **1.** *Archaic.* An entertaining interlude in the middle of a longer entertainment; popular in 17th- and 18th-c. European theater. **2.** A short instrumental piece of free-form music.

divo (DEE vo:) *n.* [Italian] A male opera star.

Dixieland jazz A popular 1920s style of jazz, named for its area of origin, ca. 1915, in Dixie, the southern part of the United States. It is characterized by syncopation, dotted rhythms, and deliberately created dissonance, with instruments playing against each other rather than in close harmony, and by improvisation in performance. The Dixieland jazz band typically includes piano, drums, banjo, bass, trumpets, and clarinets.

Djamileh (dgah MEE LEH:) Opera in one act by Georges **Bizet**; libretto by Louis Gallet, based on the poem *Namouna* (1832) (nah moo NAH) by Alfred de Musset (1810–1857) (duh mü SEH:); Paris, Théâtre de l'Opéra-Comique, 1872.

This exquisite, all but forgotten masterpiece deserves to be heard more often. Its slender plot is invested with the most ethereal and beautiful music, much of it meant to evoke the world of 19th-c. Egypt. Gorgeously and sensitively orchestrated, the graceful, atmospheric score is full of lovely melody.

Living in his palace in Cairo, Haroun (ah *R*OON) (tcn.) insists on having a new mistress every month, and discards the old one. The mistresses are procured for him at the slave market in Cairo by his servant Splendiano (spleh*n*' dee ah NO:) (bar.). The slave merchant Hassan (ah SAH*N*) (speaking role) even sometimes comes to the palace to display the girls for his delectation. Djamileh (sop.), one of the mistresses, has fallen in love with Haroun. With the connivance of Splendiano, she returns in disguise and tries to get him to take her again. Haroun is so touched that he accepts her love. In fact, he had already fallen in love with her himself, but refused to give in to his own desires.

Dr. Atomic Opera in two acts by John **Adams**; libretto by Peter **Sellars**, drawn from various sources, including government documents; premiered 2005 at San Francisco Opera; produced at the Metropolitan Opera in 2008.

The story of this grim piece concerns the making of the atomic bomb during World War II and the conscience of Dr. J. Robert Oppenheimer (1904–1967), the Dr. Atomic of the title. The first act takes place a month before the bomb is tested; the second, on the day of the test.

Do I Hear a Waltz Broadway musical by Richard **Rodgers**; lyrics by Stephen **Sondheim**; book by Arthur **Laurents**, adapted from his play, *The Time of the Cuckoo* (1952), which was filmed as *Summertime* (1955); 46th Street Theatre, 1965 (220 perf.).

The American spinster Leona Samish falls in love with the married Venetian shopkeeper Renato di Rossi. Leona knows she will experience love if she hears a waltz, and she does, but the affair is doomed from its inception.

Doktor und Apotheker (The Doctor and the Apothecary) Singspiel by Carl Ditters von **Dittersdorf**.

Don Carlos (Don Carlo) Opera in five acts by Giuseppe **Verdi**; libretto by dramatist François-Joseph-Pierre-André Méry (1797–1865) (mé *R*EE), who died with the libretto unfinished, and theater director, administrator, librettist, and friend of Verdi, Camille du Locle (1832–1903) (kah MEE yuh dü LO kluh), based on the play *Don Karlos, Infant von Spanien* (Don Carlos, Infante of Spain) (1787) (do:n KAH*R* lo:s ihn FAHNT fuhn SHPAH nyehn) by Friedrich von Schiller (1759–1805) (*F*REED *rikh* fuhn SHIH luh), and several other sources; first produced in 1867 in French at the Paris Opéra as *Don Carlos*, then revised, under the composer's supervision, for the Italian version, produced that same year.

In 1568, Don Carlo (ten.), heir to the Spanish throne, is sent to France to meet his future bride, Elizabeth de Valois (sop.), daughter of the French king. They fall in love, but the king of France changes his mind and decides that, to cement the political alliance, the princess will marry King Philip II (bass). His son goes nearly mad with grief, and is comforted by his friend Rodrigo (bar.), Marquis of Posa, a political activist opposed to Spanish policy in occupied Flanders. Rodrigo tries to convince Carlo to forget his unhappy love and to join him in seeking relief for Flanders. The queen arranges to meet Carlo alone in the public garden, and makes it clear that she must remain a faithful wife. Princess Eboli (EH: bo: lee) (mezz.), in love with Carlo, sends him an unsigned note arranging a nighttime tryst, but he thinks he is meeting the queen. Wounded by this revelation of his feelings, and burning with the desire for revenge, Eboli betrays Carlo and the queen by stealing her jewel box, which she gives to the king. He forces Elizabeth to open it, and she finds the miniature of his son that he knows is there. The king is deeply depressed, for he now has proof of what he had suspected: the queen has never loved him. The ancient, blind Grand Inquisitor (bass) demands an audience with the king and warns him that something must be done about his son and Rodrigo. The king decides that his son must die. Rodrigo is now imprisoned, and is assassinated in Carlo's presence. He has managed to inform Carlo that the queen will wait for him at the monastery of San Yuste (SAHN YOO steh). They meet to say a final farewell. Carlo is on the point of being arrested when he is spirited away by a mysterious monk, whom everyone presumes to be the ghost of his grandfather, Charles V.

Don Giovanni [Full title, originally: *Il dissoluto punito, ossia il Don Giovanni* (The Dissolute One Punished, or Don Giovanni) (ihl dih:s' so: LOO to: poo NEE to: os: SEE ah ihl DO:N dgo: VAHN nee)] Opera in two acts by Wolfgang Amadeus **Mozart**; libretto by Lorenzo **Da Ponte**; Prague, National Theatre, 1787.

The action unfolds in Seville in the 17th c. While attempting to seduce Donna Anna (sop.), the masked Don Giovanni (bar.) is surprised by the entrance of her father, the Commendatore (ko:m MEHN dah TO: reh:) (bass), and kills him. He flees with his valet, Leporello (leh po: REHL lo:) (basso buffo), who has been keeping watch outside. Anna's fiancé, Don Ottavio (ot TAH vee o:) (ten.), vows to help her find the killer. Meanwhile, the abandoned Donna Elvira (ehl VEE rah) (sop.), still in love with Giovanni, is seeking him everywhere. Leporello explains that his master has seduced and abandoned hundreds of women—and in Spain alone, 1003—but this is of no account to Elvira, who still adores him. Running into a celebration of the nuptials of the peasants Zerlina (tsehr LEE nah) (sop.) and Masetto (mah ZEHT to:) (bar.), the incorrigible seducer decides that she is fair game, and manages to catch her alone. He falsely offers her marriage if she will go with him. Anna, Ottavio, and Elvira happen upon them just in time to prevent disaster, and vow to expose Giovanni's shocking behavior. As he is leaving with a mocking laugh on his lips, Anna recognizes him as the murderer. Giovanni gives a grand party, at which three masked guests—Anna, Ottavio, and Elvira— show up, intending to unmask him for his crimes. When Masetto, hearing Zerlina's cries, attempts to break down the bedroom door, pandemonium breaks loose, and Giovanni and Leporello flee. After several misadventures, Leporello and Giovanni meet in a cemetery before the statue of the Commendatore, whom Giovanni mockingly invites to dinner. The next evening, Giovanni is feasting when Elvira bursts in and tries to persuade him to return to her, only to be thrown out unmercifully. She nearly bumps into the statue of the Commendatore, who has arrived to accept the proffered invitation. Giovanni bravely offers his hand, which the statue seizes and holds fast, enjoining the malefactor to repent. When Giovanni adamantly refuses, the Commendatore drags him down to hcll. Anna, Ottavio, and Elvira arrive to denounce him, and Leporello tells them everything that has transpired. The opera ends with a tacked-on, moralistic chorus sung by all the principals: this is the proper end that awaits those who do evil.

Don Pasquale (DON pahs KWAH leh:) Comic opera in three acts by Gaetano **Donizetti**; libretto by the composer and Giovanni Ruffini (1807–1881) (roo FEE nee), based on the libretto by Angelo Anelli (ah NEHL lee) for *Ser Marc Antonio* (1810) by Stefano **Pavesi**; Paris, Théâtre Italien (ih: tah LYEH*N*), 1843.

This Molièresque satire takes place in 19th-c. Rome, where Don Pasquale (basso buffo), a rich, elderly bachelor, wants to marry in order to prevent his nephew Ernesto (ehr NEHS to:) (ten.) from inheriting his estate. Pasquale disapproves of his nephew's infatuation with the young widow Norina (no: REE nah) (sop.), whom Pasquale has never deigned to meet. A friend to all of them, Dr. Malatesta (mah' lah TEHS tah) (bar.), concocts a scheme to knock sense into Pasquale. He will present Norina to Pasquale as his sister, fresh out of the convent—a perfect prospect for marriage. Pasquale is enchanted, and a marriage ceremony is held. Norina proceeds to make Pasquale's life a living hell: she overspends on jewelry and clothing, and orders him around. Finally, he surprises his "wife" and his nephew together in the garden and orders her to leave his house, which she refuses to do. Malatesta suggests to his miserable friend that he can have his way only if Ernesto and Norina marry, and if she replaces his own wife as mistress of the house. Pasquale agrees, and is astounded when Norina shows up for the ceremony. Everything is now revealed. Pasquale, happy that he was not really married, laughs it all off, forgives everyone, and gives Ernesto and Norina his blessing.

Doña Francisquita (DO: nyah frahn' sees KEE tah) Zarzuela by Amadeo **Vives**; libretto by the prolific writing team Federico Sarachaga Romero (1886–1976) (feh deh REE ko: sah rah CHAH gah ro: MEH: ro:) and Guillermo Fernández Shaw (1893–1965) (gee YEHR mo: fehr NAHN dehs SHAW), based on the play *La discreta enamorada* (The Discreet Woman Enamored) (1653) (lah dees KREH: tah eh: nah mo: RAH dah) by Lope de Vega (1562–1635) (LO: peh theh: VEH gah); Madrid, Teatro Apolo, 1923. This wonderful, infectious **zarzuela** is bursting with energy, enthusiasm, and tunefulness.

In 19th-c. Madrid during carnival season, Francisquita (sop.) is enamored of the student Fernando (fehr NAHN do:) (ten.), but he has eyes only for the disdainful actress Aurora (ow RO: rah) (mezz.), whom his friend Cardona (kahr DO: nah) (ten.) advises him to avoid. Matías (mah TEE ahs) (bass), Fernando's widowed father, woos Francisquita. To make Fernando jealous, Francisquita pretends to accept his father's offer of marriage, while Fernando himself proceeds to flirt with her, in order to make Aurora jealous. He finds himself attracted to Francisquita the more she pretends to be indifferent, and he succeeds in making Aurora jealous by flirting passionately with Cardona, disguised as a woman at the carnival. Fernando and Francisquita dance a **mazurka**, and Matías dances with Aurora. The intrigues continue apace, the plot thickens, but the complications are finally resolved, and Fernando and Francisquita are united.

Donaldson, Walter (1893–1947) American stage and film composer; often collaborated with Gus **Kahn**, e.g., on *Whoopee!*. Among his famous songs are "Love Me or Leave Me," "My Blue Heaven," and "How Ya Gonna Keep 'Em Down on the Farm?"

Donizetti, Gaetano (1797–1848) (gah' eh TAH no: don ih: DZEHT tee) Prolific, versatile Italian composer of ca. sixty-five operas, i.e., there are some operas of which he did several revised versions. His most well known works are the dramas *Lucrezia Borgia* (1833) (loo KREH: tsyah BO:R dgah), ***Anna Bolena***, ***Maria Stuarda***, *Roberto Devereux* (1837) (deh vuh R*OO*), *La favorite* (1840) (lah fah vo: REET), *Linda di Chamounix* (1843) (shah moo NEE), and ***Lucia di Lammermoor***; and the comic operas *La fille du regiment* (The Daughter of the Regiment) (1840) (lah fee' yuh dü *r*é zhee MAH*N*), ***Don Pasquale***, and ***L'elisir d'amore***. Together with **Bellini** and **Rossini**, he is one of the triumvirate of major romantic-era **bel canto** opera composers, each of whom has a distinctive, individual style. Donizetti's captivating melodic gift, and his talent for variously setting dramatic or comic situations to compelling music, put him above most of his contemporaries, as interesting and talented as many of them were.

Donnelly, Dorothy (1880–1928) American actress, brilliant stage writer and lyricist; wrote book and lyrics for Romberg's ***Blossom Time*** and ***The Student Prince***, and other Broadway shows; close friend of the **Romberg** family.

doo wop A style of pop singing that developed esp. in the 1950s; characterized by rhythmic background vocal accompaniment, in close harmony, using syllables such as "doo wop" to set off and punch up a solo line.

Dostal, Nico (1895–1981) (DO: stahl) [b. Nickolaus Josef Michael Dostal] Austrian composer of sacred music, chamber music, numerous film scores and some two dozen operettas, of which the most famous are *Clivia* (1933) (KLEE vee ah) and *Die ungarische Hochzeit* (The Hungarian Wedding) (1939) (dee *oo*n GAH *r*ih: sheh HO:KH TSIT), both rather unoriginal and schmaltzy. He also did arrangements for Oscar **Straus**, Franz **Lehár**, and Robert **Stolz**.

double time 1. In music, the time signature 2/4, indicating two quarter notes to a measure. Also called *duple time*. **2.** In dance, music, or movement, something that is to be done twice as fast as it was done previously.

downbeat *n.* **1.** The first, strongest beat in a measure, marked off by a bar directly before it in the **score**. **2.** The first, strongest beat at the beginning of a musical composition; consequently, the conductor's cue to the musicians to start performing; hence, *on the downbeat*: starting to play or sing on such a beat or cue.

drag *n.* [Conjecturally, fr. 1870s theater slang, in the days when women's long skirts dragged on the ground] **1.** Women's dress worn by a male; men's dress worn by a woman. Playing roles in drag is as old as theater: in ancient Greece, actors played female parts using costume pieces, nor were women allowed on the European stage before the 17th c. The old-style British Christmas pantomime would not be complete without more than one *drag role*: the fairy godmother or a witch played by a man; the **principal boy**. In cabaret and nightclub shows, female impersonators may lip sync to women's recorded voices; some clubs are devoted entirely to this form of entertainment. The dénouement of the plot of Verdi's ***Rigoletto*** depends on a woman disguised as a man. And the story of Gilbert and Sullivan's *Princess Ida* hinges on men disguised as women. In opera, there are male roles composed for women— called breeches, pants, or **trousers roles**—such as the title role in Rossini's ***Tancredi*** and Octavian in Richard Strauss's ***Der Rosenkavalier***. In the ballet, the role of the Wicked Stepmother in Prokofiev's Cinderella is danced by a man. Albin in ***La Cage aux Folles*** makes his living doing a drag act in the nightclub that the play is named for, and also disguises himself as his partner's son's mother. **2.** In music, a phrase of three notes played on the snare drum: two short notes are played with one hand, the third, longer note with the other, all in one continuous phrase.

Draghi, Antonio (1634–1700) (DRAH gee) Italian librettist and composer of instrumental and sacred works, and 118 operas, many in one act; spent time at the Hapsburg court in Vienna; much of his life was spent in Venice, where he composed celebratory stage pieces for the carnivals. His stately **oratorio**, *La vita nella morte* (Life in Death) (1688) (lah VEE tah nehl lah MO:R teh), a gorgeous example of baroque music, and a huge success at the Hapsburg court, is beautifully performed on a CD from Auvidis (E 8616; 1998).

dramma eroicomico (DRAHM mah eh RO: ee KO: mee ko:) [Italian: heroic-comic drama] In the 18th c. esp., an **opera buffa** that had heroic elements as part of its story; e.g., *Orlando paladino* (Orlando the Knight) (1782) (o:r LAHN do: pah' lah DEE no:) by Franz Joseph **Haydn**.

dramma per musica (DRAHM mah pehr MOO zee kah) [Italian: drama for music] A written text meant to be set to music; an operatic libretto.

dramma tragicomico (DRAHM mah TRAH dgee KO: mee ko:) [Italian: tragi-comic drama; tragicomedy] In the 18th c. esp., an opera that mixed comic and serious elements; another term for **opera semiseria**.

Dreamgirls Broadway musical by Henry **Krieger**; book and lyrics by Tom Eyen (1941–1991); Imperial Theatre, 1981 (1531 perf.); Broadway revival: Ambassador Theatre, 1987 (184 perf.); film, 2006.

Directed and choreographed by Michael Bennett, the show told the story of the careers and personal lives of an African-American **Motown** singing trio (based loosely on the Supremes), under the management of Curtis Taylor, Jr., who thinks nothing of discarding one of the singers, his former girlfriend, and replacing her with someone he thinks will be better for business.

Dreigroschenoper, Die (The Threepenny Opera) (dee D*R*I G*R*O: shehn O:puh) Musical in three acts by Kurt **Weill**; libretto by Berthold **Brecht**, adapted from John Gay's **ballad opera**, *The Beggar's Opera*; Berlin, Theater am Schiffbauerdamm (SHIH:F BOW uh DAHM), 1928; filmed with the original cast in 1931. In the translation by Marc **Blitzstein** of this **Newgate pastoral**—less raw and gritty than the original—it opened Off-Broadway at the Lucille Lortel Theatre in 1956 (2707 perf.), starring Weill's wife, Lotte Lenya, who had performed in the original production and reprised her role as the streetwalker Pirate Jenny in the 1931 film.

A compelling Marxist portrayal of the cynical hypocrisy that prevails in capitalist society, as exemplified in the way people use each other for their own purposes, this adaptation is similar thematically to its 18th-c. source material. Weill's earthy, raunchy score is full of memorable numbers, including the well known "Ballad of Mack the Knife" and the haunting **tango** "In einer Zeit" (There Was a Time) (ihn I nuh TSIT), as well as the fantasy songs for Jenny.

Macheath, a mysterious underworld cad, two-timer, and killer nicknamed "Mack the Knife," wants to wed Polly Peachum, daughter of the crime boss, Jonathan Peachum. But Peachum and the prostitute Jenny Diver betray him to the police, and he is condemned to be hanged. Queen Victoria's reprieve arrives just in time.

Dreimädlerhaus, Das Viennese **pastiche** (def. 2) operetta, using the music of Franz Schubert. See BLOSSOM TIME.

drinking song A rousing number in a musical theater piece, accompanying the imbibing of a beverage, usually an alcoholic one; e.g., "Libiamo" (Let's drink) (lee BYAH mo:) from act 1 of *La traviata*.

Drowsy Chaperone, The A Canadian, then Tony® Award–winning one-act Broadway musical (2006, Best Original Score, Book, Scenery, Costumes, Featured Actress); music and lyrics by writer and comedian Bob Martin (b. ca. 1963), who also performed in the show as "Man in Chair," and actor-writer Don McKellar (b. 1963); book by actor, writer, and humorist Lisa Lambert (b. 1962) and writer and composer Greg Morrison (b. 1965); opened in Toronto, 1998; New York, Marquis Theatre, 2006 (706 perf.).

In this parodistic tribute to the 1920s Jazz Age, a Broadway musical enthusiast, the Man in Chair, tries to cure his agoraphobia by listening to recordings of a (fictitious) 1928 show called *The Drowsy Chaperone*, which comes to life in his apartment. We watch the **pastiche** (def. 2) and learn about the intriguing Man in Chair.

Dr. Seuss' How the Grinch Stole Christmas Broadway musical by Mel **Marvin**; book by novelist and playwright Thomas Mason, based on the book *How the Grinch Stole Christmas!* (1957) by celebrated children's author Dr. Seuss (1904–1991) [b. Theodor Seuss Geisel]; original production conceived and directed by Jack O'Brien; Hilton Theatre, 2006 (129 perf.); reopened, St. James Theatre, 2007 (109 perf.).

That curmudgeonly malcontent, the Grinch, a cat-like troglodyte, is envious of the noisy, joyous Christmas festivities he hears emanating from Whoville, the village in the valley far below his cave on Mt. Crumpit. He decides to destroy people's pleasure by stealing everyone's toys and decorations. But the Whos, upset as they are, celebrate Christmas just the same. The Grinch, realizing that Christmas is more than just presents and decorations, returns them. His heart, which was "two sizes too small," has now grown three sizes larger, and he is welcomed by the Whos as a Christmas guest.

drum roll A continuous playing of rapid, successive beats on a drum; used as an introduction for a master or mistress of ceremonies, a well known comedian, or other stage personality, or as part of a musical introduction in a musical theater piece.

Du Barry Was A Lady Broadway musical by Cole **Porter**; book by Herbert **Fields** and B. G. **De Sylva**; 46th Street Theatre, 1939 (408 perf.); film, 1943.

The show starred burlesque, stage, and film comedian Bert Lahr (1895–1967) [b. Irving Lahrheim], best known for his portrayal of the Cowardly Lion in the film *The Wizard of Oz* (1939), as Louis Blore, the washroom attendant at the swanky Manhattan Club Petite, who dreams he is King Louis XV of France; and Ethel Merman as the chorus girl May Daly, who becomes his mistress, Madame du Barry. May is attracted to Alex Barton, and Louis puts knockout drops in his cocktail but mistakenly drinks it himself. Even in his dream, May eludes him, and he awakens just in time to avoid being assassinated. The delightful, vintage Porter score includes the well known songs "Friendship" and "But in the Morning, No!"

duet *n.* A number for two singers, usually with instrumental accompaniment; sometimes performed against a choral background. Also sometimes called a *duo*.

Dukas, Paul French composer. See ARIANE ET BARBE-BLEUE.

Duke Bluebeard's Castle Opera by Bela Bartok. See A KÉKSZÁKÁLLÚ HERCEG VÁRA.

Duke, Vernon (1903–1969) [b. Vladimir Dukeksky] Russian-born, classically trained American stage and film composer; wrote songs for the *Ziegfeld Follies*; collaborated with lyricists Howard **Dietz**, Ira **Gershwin**, and John **Latouche**, with whom he wrote *Cabin in the Sky*. Among his famous songs are "April in Paris" and "Autumn in New York."

Dvořák, Antonín Leopold (1841–1904) (AHN to: neen LEH: o pold DVO:R zhahk) Czech composer known for his lyricism and for his part in the nationalist movement in Czech music; wrote ten operas, of which several exist in a number of revised versions, e.g., one of his masterpieces, *Jacobin* (The Jacobin) (1889, 1898) (YAH ko: been); in the U.S., his most famous opera is *Rusalka*; his last opera was a setting of the *Armida* story (1904).

dynamics *n. pl.* In music, the loudness or softness of the music in performance, and the transitions between levels of loudness or softness.

E

ear training Teaching music students to learn to hear, distinguish, and identify notes accurately; e.g., when learning *sight-singing*; part of the musical education of instrumentalists and vocalists. One of the objects of such education is to enable the musician to write down in musical notation the melody, harmony, and meter he or she hears: this aspect or ear training is called *dictation*.

See also SIGHT-READ.

Earl Carroll Vanities A series of nine Broadway revues, rivaling *Artists and Models*, the *Ziegfeld Follies*, and *George White's Scandals*; produced between 1923 and 1940 by Earl Carroll (1892–1948), who also wrote the music and lyrics for the first two revues, all of which ran at the Earl Carroll Theatre, except as indicated. The 1923 edition ran for 204 perf.; the 1924 revue opened at the Music Box Theatre before transferring to the Earl Carroll (133 perf.); 1925 (199 perf.); 1926 (200 perf.); 1928 (200 perf.), with W. C. Fields (1880–1946), who also wrote sketches; New Amsterdam Theatre, 1930 (215 perf.), with music by Harold **Arlen** and lyrics by E. Y. **Harburg**, and with Jack Benny, making his Broadway debut; 1931 (300 perf.), music by Burton **Lane**; 1932 (87 perf.), music by Arlen, and featuring comedian Milton Berle (1908–2002) and actress Helen Broderick (1891–1959), who had performed in the 1907 *Ziegfeld Follies* and would play Mrs. Smith in the movie of *No, No, Nanette*; St. James Theatre, 1940 (25 perf.). They were mild burlesque shows, with the reputation of being more risqué than they probably were. There were also two musical films: *Earl Carroll Vanities* (1945), with a slender love story plot; and *Earl Carroll Sketchbook* (1946), a **backstage musical**, with music by Arlen and songs by Jule **Styne** and Sammy Cahn (1913–1993).

Ebb, Fred (1928–2004) American writer and lyricist who collaborated with John Kander, writing the lyrics for such hit shows as *Cabaret*, *Chicago*, and *Kiss of the Spider Woman*.

See KANDER AND EBB.

ecossaise (é kos SEHZ) *n.* [French: Scottish] A **contredanse** in 2/4 time for two couples, in imitation of Scottish dances; popular in France and Germany in the early romantic era.

Edwards, Gus (1879–1945) [b. August Simon] Prolific German-born American songwriter, vaudeville performer and producer, conductor of his own orchestra, and music publisher; wrote songs for the *Ziegfeld Follies*; owned the Gus Edwards Music Hall in New York City, which featured vaudeville with the most famous stars of the day. His hit Broadway musical comedies include *Breaking into Society* (1905), *When We Were Forty-One* (1905), *Merry-Go-Round* (1908), and the revue *Hip! Hip! Hooray!* (1907). Among his well known songs is "By the Light of the Silvery Moon."

Einstein on the Beach Opera in four acts and five "knee plays" (intermezzos) by Philip **Glass** and the avant-garde director associated with productions of Glass's operas, Robert Wilson (b. 1941); libretto by Christopher Knowles, Lucinda Childs, and Samuel Johnson; France, Avignon Festival, 1974–1976.

This long opera—running time: ca. four hours and forty minutes—is done without regular intermissions, but the audience is told that they may wander in and out at will. The chorus enters the orchestra pit, where the sixteen-piece orchestra is also placed, and the proceedings begin. There is no plot to this "music-theater" piece, but there is a constant barrage of visual images and musical references, with texts arranged from the works of autistic poet Christopher Knowles (b. 1959), with whom Wilson had worked as a teacher; writings by choreographer Lucinda Childs (b. 1940); and texts by Samuel Johnson (1709–1784)—all revolving around the ideas of Albert Einstein (1879–1955).

Eisler, Hanns (1898–1962) (HAHNS I sluh) German composer known for his leftist politics; wrote music for thirty-eight plays, among them ten by Berthold **Brecht**, his lifelong friend; studied with Arnold Schoenberg. He emigrated to America during the Nazi era, but was expelled in 1947 after he was called before the House Un-American Activities Committee. Returning to East Berlin, Eisler pursued his musical life and worked on *Johann Faustus*, a three-act opera based on Goethe's **Faust**, left uncompleted at his death because of his discouragement after the controversy surrounding the iconoclastic libretto, published in 1952.

elisir d'amore, L' (The Elixir of Love) (leh lee ZEER dah MO: reh:) Comic opera in two acts by Gaetano **Donizetti**; libretto by Felice **Romani**, based on a libretto by Eugène **Scribe** for *Le philtre* (The Love Potion) (1831) (luh FIH:L *tr*uh) by **Auber**; Milan, Teatro Cannobiana (kahn no: bee AH nah), 1832.

In a Tuscan farming village in the early 19th c., Nemorino (neh mo: REE no:) (ten.) is smitten with the landowner Adina (ah DEE nah) (sop.). She reads the story of Tristan and Isolde and the magic love potion to the villagers, and Nemorino wishes he could find such an elixir! A traveling quack doctor, Dulcamara (d*OO*l kah MAH rah) (bass), arrives and expatiates on the wonders of his encyclopedic mind before selling his cure-all medications. Nemorino asks him if he has an elixir of love. The con artist sells him a bottle of Bordeaux, telling him it is a love potion that will only have its full effect twenty-four hours after it is taken—enough time for Dulcamara to decamp. Nemorino drinks, and is soon intoxicated. Adina is so annoyed at his belligerent behavior that she agrees to marry his rival, Captain Belcore (behl' KO: reh:) (bar.). When Nemorino begs her to wait twenty-four hours, she refuses. He can't afford another bottle of the elixir, and he is in despair until Belcore tells him that if he enlists in the army, he will immediately be paid "venti scudi" (twenty pieces of money) (VEHN tee SKOO dee). Nemorino enlists, takes the money, and procures another bottle. Meanwhile, he is the only one who hasn't heard that his rich uncle has died and he is now wealthy. But the village maidens have heard, and they surround him, much to his astonishment. He sees Adina, slightly off in the distance. When he is alone, he sings the heartbreakingly beautiful aria "Una furtiva lagrima" (A furtive tear) (OO nah foor TEE vah LAH gree mah), all about that little drop he noticed trembling on Adina's eyelash. He now knows that she loves him. But he will be departing soon as a soldier! Adina buys Nemorino's way out of the army and marries him, amidst general rejoicing.

embellishment *n.* In music, syn. with ornament, **ornamentation**, esp. grace notes.

enchainement *n.* In ballet and other forms of dance, a series of linked movements of different kinds, done one after the other in continuous execution.

encore *n., v.* [French: again] —*n.* **1.** The repeat of a **number**, usually at the request of the audience, who shout "Encore!" The French, however, do not use this word in the theater: instead, they shout "*Bis!*" (bih:s), which means the same thing. —*v. t.* **2.** To repeat a number.

Encores! An annual season of concert revivals at the New York City Center of Broadway musical comedies and operettas; established 1994. The series mission is to offer the public an opportunity to enjoy rarely heard musicals. Over the years, the presentations have become more elaborate, and simple readings have given way to semi-staged, choreographed performances.

end men In a **minstrel show**, the two performers who sat at either end of the semicircle: **Brudder [Brother] Bones** and **Brudder [Brother] Tambo**.

Enesco, Georges (1881–1955) (ZHO:RZH eh NEH sko:) [b. George Enescu] Prolific Romanian-born French conductor, teacher, violinist, pianist, composer of instrumental music; wrote one opera, *Œdipe* (Oedipus) (composed 1910–1931; premiere, 1936) (é DEEP), a masterpiece; libretto by French poet Edmond Fleg (1864–1973) (ehd mo:*n*' FLEHG), based on the Sophoclean trilogy. There is a magnificent 1990 CD recording on EMI (2 08633 2; 2008).

Engländer, Ludwig (1851–1914) [U.S. spellings: Englaender (*New York Times*); Englander] Austro-American composer of thirty-two works for the Viennese and Broadway stages, including a Broadway musical, *1776*; emigrated to New York in 1882, returning to Vienna in 1910. His biggest Broadway success was *Miss Innocence*; book by Harry B. **Smith**; 1908 (176 perf.); produced by Florenz **Ziegfeld** as a vehicle for his wife, Anna Held (1873–1918).

en pointe (ah*n* PWA*N*T) [French: lit., on point] In ballet and dance, standing on the tips of the foot, called the **points**, i.e., the row of toes.

ensemble *n., adj.* [Fr. French: together] —*n.* **1.** The company of performers in a production. **2.** The chorus in a musical theater piece. **3.** A **number** for more than one singer, e.g., **duet, trio**, etc. —*adj.* **4.** Together as a group: *ensemble acting*; *ensemble singing*; *an ensemble piece*.

entr'acte *n.* (AHN trakt) *n.* [French: (o:*n* TRAHKT); lit. between-act; interval] **1.** Intermission; interval between the acts of a play. **2.** A piece of music played during the interval.

entrechat (ahn' truh SHAH) *n.* A leap or jump during which the dancer, with legs held close to each other, quickly crosses the legs in front of and behind each other while still up in the air. If the number of crosses is even, the dancer lands on both feet; if it is odd, the dancer lands on one foot.

entrée *n.* [French: entry; entrance] **1.** The opening dance in a ballet. **2.** An individual dance during a ballet; an entrée can be for one or more principal dancers, and is separate from a number that includes the entire corps de ballet.

entry *n.* In music, the place in the score where a singer begins singing, or a particular instrument begins playing. Also called *entrance.*

equal voices Singers of the same vocal category used in a polyphonic ensemble; e.g., all sopranos only, singing in harmony; or, sometimes, all male or all female voices only.

equalization *n.* The attainment of a correct tonal balance of voices and instruments, or of voices singing alone, as in an **a capella** chorus; or of instruments playing alone in a band or orchestra; esp. as regards recording, but also for sound design in a theater.

Erkel, Ferenc (1810–1893) (EHR kehl FEH rehnts) Leading Hungarian composer; of his nine operas, the most famous are *Bánk bán* (Viceroy Bánk) (1861) (BAHNK BAHN) and *Hunyadi László* (1844) (HOON yah dee LAHS lo:)—extraordinary, exciting works. Erkel is known for his amazing melodic gift, his innovative use of Hungarian folk music and church modes, rich harmonies, and brilliant orchestrations. Superb recordings are available on Hungaroton CD: *Bánk bán* (HCD 11576-77; 1994); *Hunyadi László* (HCD 12581-83; 1995).

Erminie Comic opera by Edward **Jacobowski**.

Ernani (ehr NAH nee) Opera in four acts by Giuseppe **Verdi**; libretto by Francesco Maria **Piave**, based on the melodrama *Hernani* (1830) (ehr' nah NEE) by Victor **Hugo**; Venice, Teatro La Fenice (lah feh NEE cheh:), 1844.
    In 16th-c. Spain, Elvira (ehl VEE rah) (sop.), immured in the castle of her elderly fiancé, da Silva (dah SEEL vah) (bass), is in love with Ernani (ten.), outlawed for offenses against the crown. King Carlo (bar.) also loves Elvira, and removes her from the castle, ostensibly to keep her safe but really to attempt to make her his. Ernani, having entered the castle, is challenged to a duel by da Silva, but he obtains the favor of a postponement so that he can seek revenge against the king. As a token of fealty, he gives da Silva a horn: should da Silva sound it, Ernani's life will be forfeit. Carlo is elected Holy Roman Emperor, and Elvira begs him to begin his reign with an act of clemency, rescinding the sentence of outlawry against Ernani. Carlo does so, and Elvira and Ernani are married. But on their wedding night, da Silva's horn sounds. He offers Ernani a choice of poison or dagger. Ernani stabs himself and falls, mortally wounded.

escravo, O (The Slave) (oo ehsh KRAH voo) [Italian title: *Lo schiavo* (lo: SKYAH vo:)] Opera in four acts by Carlos **Gomes**; libretto by novelist and poet

Rodolfo Paravicini (1828–1900) (ro: DO:L fo: pah rah vih: CHEE nee), based on an idea of the important Brazilian writer, historian, and politician Alfredo d'Escragnolle Taunay, Visconde de Taunay (1843–1899) (ahl FREH: do: dehs krahn YO:L to: NEH: veesh KO:N duh duh: to: NEH:) [Portuguese: *Visconde*: viscount]; Rio de Janeiro, Teatro Lirico, 1889.

Set in Rio de Janeiro in 1567, the story concerns the love of the nobleman Américo (ah MÉ ree ko:) (ten.) for the Indian servant Ilara (ee LAH rah) (sop.), also loved by the Indian Iberé (ee BEHR é) (bar.), and centers around a planned Indian revolt.

étoile, L' (The Star) (lé TWAHL) Opéra bouffe in three acts by Emmanuel **Chabrier**; libretto by writing team Eugène Leterrier and Albert **Vanloo**; Paris, Théâtre des Bouffes-Parisiens (deh boof' pah *r*ee ZYEH*N*), 1877. *L'étoile* was produced in 1899 at the Savoy Theatre by D'Oyly Carte, as *The Lucky Star*, with a revised score by Ivan **Caryll**, and a book based on an 1890 American version, *The Merry Monarch*, by J. Cheever **Goodwin** and Woolson Morse; the English lyrics were by Adrian **Ross** and Aubrey Hopwood (1863–1917), who often collaborated with Lionel **Monckton**; the dialogue was by Charles H. E. Brookfield (1857–1913) [Charles Hallam Elton Brookfield], who also wrote the adapted book for the Savoy production of Offenbach's *La Grande-Duchesse de Gérolstein*; and the whole project was assembled and revised by H. L. [Helen Lenoir; i.e., Mrs. Helen D'Oyly Carte (1852–1913)].

Chabrier's merry, titillating score—his first for the stage—has tinges of sadness as well as wit, elegance, originality, and charm. It is unique in not being imitative of other operetta composers, yet it remains within the **opéra bouffe** tradition.

King Ouf (OOF) (ten.) wanders about incognito, trying to foment revolution among his people so as to procure a victim for execution in order to set an example, but everyone recognizes him and praises him and his government. He lights upon the hapless, impoverished street peddler Lazuli (lah' zü LEE) (ten.), who insults Ouf when the king's suit for the hand of Princess Laoula (lah oo LAH) (sop.) is rejected. But the execution has to be canceled because the court astrologer, Siroco (see *r*o: KO:) (bass), informs Ouf that the stars have predicted that he will die twenty-four hours after Lazuli, who is therefore immediately confined to the palace under guard and treated with the utmost care. But he and Laoula escape from the palace together, and disappear. The news of a shipwreck is announced, and Lazuli is said to have perished in it. Ouf waits to die, but twenty-four hours pass, and he is still alive! He is so overjoyed that he forgives Siroco for being an incompetent fraud. Lazuli and Laoula reappear, safe and sound, and he gives them his blessing.

Evangeline; or, The Belle of Arcadia Musical by Edward E. **Rice**; book and lyrics by J. Cheever **Goodwin**; 1874; numerous revivals and tours; ran at Niblo's Gardens, where *The Black Crook* had run.

A spoof of the well known narrative poem by Henry Wadsworth Longfellow (1807–1882), on which it is as loosely based as possible, this **burlesque** show capitalized on the spectacle of the girls in pink tights in the megahit *The Black Crook* by providing another of the **leg shows** that were to prove so popular. It toured constantly and was one of the best known, most loved musicals of the last quarter of the 19th c.

The story, if one can call it that, follows the vicissitudes and travels of the lovers Evangeline and Gabriel (a **trousers role**) until they are reunited happily ever after at the end. Evangeline visits the Wild West, where she dances with a heifer played by two actors inside either end of a cow costume, in the most popular number in the show. She is also followed at one point by a lustful whale, and the story takes her to Africa and more adventures. A featured, ubiquitous character was the Lone Fisherman, much loved by audiences, who found his taciturnity hilarious: he never said much, but he was periodically there, making a quick entrance, peering through his telescope, then exiting.

Evita West End and Broadway **through-composed** musical by Andrew Lloyd **Webber**; lyrics by Tim **Rice**; Broadway Theatre, 1979 (1567 perf.); national tours for several years; film, 1996.

The show, superbly directed by Harold Prince, is about the rise and fall of Argentine dictator Juan Perón (1895–1974) and his second wife, María Eva Duarte de Perón (1919–1952) (mah REE ah EH: vah DWAHR teh: deh: peh RO:N), popularly known as Evita. Evita's rise from poverty to acclaimed radio actress to wife of the President of Argentina, with his manipulative populist approach to politics, is commented on throughout by Che, a character modeled after the Argentine Marxist revolutionary Che Guevara (1928–1967) (CHEH: geh: VAH rah), who is most closely associated with Castro's Cuban revolution.

execution *n.* The way or manner in which a musical piece is performed.

excerpt *n.* A selection extracted from a longer piece; e.g., arias and ensemble pieces from an opera, often found on recordings or done in concert.

exit music 1. A theme played as a performer is leaving at the end of a routine, sometimes in the form of **traveling music**; often a **signature tune**. Also called a *chaser.* **2.** Instrumental composition meant to accompany a performer or performers as they leave a scene.

expression *n.* In music, the communication by a performer of the interpretation of a passage or piece of vocal or instrumental music; the way in which a piece is performed. Expression involves the communication of ideas and feelings; e.g., the interpretation of expression marks, **dynamics**, and so forth.

See also PERIOD; STYLE.

expressionism A German arts movement lasting from ca. 1900–1930, with influences on European and American arts; its precursors include works of the Swedish playwright August Strindberg (1849–1912) and such plays as German dramatist Georg Büchner's (1813–1837) *Woyzeck* (1836) (GEH: awk BÜ*KH* neh[*r*]; VOY tsehk), the basis of Berg's opera *Wozzeck*. In German music, it included the introduction of the twelve-tone system compositions of Arnold Schoenberg. Expressionistic music is iconoclastic and often ignores traditional harmonies. In terms of musical theater, its repercussions are felt in the pieces of **Brecht** and **Weill**, and in 20th-c. American and Hungarian opera.

See also JAZZ-VAUDEVILLE.

expression mark A **performance mark** consisting of a written direction in a musical score regarding interpretation, as opposed, for instance, to one that indicates tempo; e.g., *aufgeregt*: (OWF geh *R*EH:KT) [German] excitedly; *furioso*: (foo ree O: zo:) [Italian] furiously; *lagrimoso*: (lah gree MO: zo:) [Italian] tearfully.

extension *n.* **1.** In dance, the lifting of a leg as high as it can go, e.g., high enough to touch the ear. The higher a leg can be lifted, the better the extension: *He has a good extension.* **2.** In singing, notes that are beyond a singer's expected range; e.g., good high notes above the usual range of a mezzo-soprano: *She has a good extension.*

extravaganza *n.* **1.** An elaborate, spectacular show with a large cast, e.g., *The Black Crook*, the *Ziegfeld Follies*, the Radio City Music Hall presentations in New York. **2.** *Hist.* In 19th-c. England, esp. beginning in the early 1830s, a form of light **burlesque** (def. 2) with music, but with less emphasis on broad parody and more on musical and dance entertainment, with whimsical stories based on legends and fairy tales; a precursor of the **pantomime**. One of its major practitioners was **Planché**, the scripts of whose extravaganzas distinctly resemble the **jumble** of George **Colman "the Younger"**; e.g., in both their versions of the Bluebeard story.

Eysler, Edmund (1874–1949) (EHD m*oo*nt IS luh) [b. Edmund Eisler] Prolific Austrian composer of fifty-six Viennese operettas; known for his melodic gift. Although seldom done today, his most famous operetta, and his first great success, is *Bruder Straubinger* (Brother Straubinger) (1903) (B*R*OO duh SHT*R*OW bihng uh), libretto by Moritz West (1840–1904) [pseudonym of Moritz Nitzelberger (MO: *r*ih:ts NIH:TS uhl BEH[*R*] guh)] and Ignaz Schnitzer (1839–1921) (IHG nahts SHNIH tsuh), about a young man whose identity papers are stolen by an army deserter. He has to make do with his grandfather's papers, which would make him 114 years old, until all is set to right. Eysler's music was banned by the Nazis because he was Jewish; the composer was able to go into hiding during World War II, and so survived. Afterwards, he was the "grand old man" of the Vienna opera stage, and his works were revived with great success.

F

Face the Music Broadway musical by Irving **Berlin**; book by Moss **Hart**; New Amsterdam Theatre, 1932 (165 perf.).

The most famous song from this show is "Let's Have Another Cup of Coffee," but every number is a gem! Moss Hart's lyrics are brilliant, romantic, clever, and mirthful, and Berlin's music displays his customary vibrant melodic and rhythmic gifts. The show, directed by Hassard Short, is a satirical look at the Great Depression.

Hal wants money to produce a show, so he goes to the automat where all the millionaires now dine, and he manages to secure backing from Mrs. Martin Van Buren Meshbesher, whose husband, as it turns out, is a corrupt police official. Scandal and complications ensue, but when the show is a great success, everything is resolved happily.

Fach (FAKH) *n.* [German: division, specialization, branch] In opera esp., a singer's voice category, i.e., soprano, tenor, baritone, contralto; or, sometimes, the specialty of a singer, e.g., **coloratura** soprano, *basso cantante*, **Heldentenor**.

fade-out *n.* In music, a gradual diminution of the level of sound until the piece is over.

Fairy Queen, The Semi-opera in a prologue and five acts by Henry **Purcell**; libretto adapted anonymously from Shakespeare's *A Midsummer Night's Dream*; London, Queen's Theatre, Dorset Garden, 1692. The score, quite a beautiful one, was lost in 1701; a reward was advertised for whoever might find it, but it was not actually recovered until 1901, and then in an incomplete state. The work was not performed until 1946. This **semi-opera** follows Shakespeare's play fairly closely.

fait historique (feh:' ee staw *R*EEK) [French: historic deed; fact; happening] *Hist.* A term applied esp. to the opéras comiques produced during the French Revolutionary period (1789–ca. 1800). These works, mostly on revolutionary subjects or about true happenings during the period, were largely ephemeral; some were written by famous composers, e.g., Luigi **Cherubini**; others by now obscure composers, such as Pierre **Gaveaux**.

fake a curtain To do an encore of a musical number even though the applause has not indicated that the audience wants one; or to continue to bow at a curtain call even though the audience has virtually stopped applauding.

Fall family (FAHL) Austrian operetta composer, bandmaster, and conductor **Moritz Fall (1848–1922)**, many of whose shows were first mounted in Berlin, where he had settled, was the father of the famous **Leo Fall (1873–1925)**, a prolific composer of thirty-six operas and operettas that proved very popular in Berlin, Vienna (where he spent most of his life), and elsewhere internationally, esp. London and New York. Composer and conductor Harold Vicars (1876–1922), General Musical Director for prolific producer Charles Frohman (1856–1915), who produced Fall's operettas on Broadway, was interviewed in a *New York Times* article of September 17, 1911, "Glimpses of Leo Fall." Apparently, the composer of so many comic works did not have a wonderful sense of humor; nevertheless, "I had occasion to meet him many times … and found him one of the most lovable of men." His hobby was raising bulldogs, and he was a great admirer of the music of **Wagner**, Brahms, and Richard **Strauss**. Produced in Vienna in 1907, Leo Fall's most famous piece is *Die Dollarprinzessin* (The Dollar Princess) (dee DO: lah[*r*] p*r*ihn TSEHS ih:n), written before Lehar's more celebrated *The Merry Widow*, which it resembles. He had a brilliant gift for beguiling melody, captivating waltzes, and utterly charming orchestrations, as shown, for instance, in *Die Rose von Stambul* (The Rose of Stamboul) (1916) (dee *R*O: zeh fun STAM BOOL), with a libretto by Julius **Brammer** and Alfred **Grünwald**; and in *Madame Pompadour* (1922), book and lyrics by Ernst Welisch (1875–1941) (VEH lihsh), playwright and dramaturge at the Berlin's Berliner Theater (where the operetta was first produced), and the prolific Rudolf Schanzer (1875–1944) (SHAHN tsuh). Although it has little to do with the historical Madame de Pompadour (1721–1764) (po:*n* pah DOOR), mistress of Louis XV (1710–1774), the operetta is adorable. In an English translation by Frederick Lonsdale and Harry Graham, it opened at Daly's Theatre in London in 1923 and ran for 469 perf.; the original English cast recording is available on a CD from Pearl (GEMM CD 9068). In an American adaptation by Clare Kummer (1872–1958), *Madame Pompadour* ran at the Martin Beck Theatre in New York for 80 performances. Another very charming work is *Die Kaiserin (The Empress)* (1915), with music that is suitable to the environment of the merry 18th-c. Hapsburg court. Also delightful is the totally different *Der fidele Bauer* (The Faithful Peasant) (1905) (deh fee DEH: leh BOW uh), with a libretto by Victor **Leon** and a score that reflects perfectly the rural environment of the story. Leo's brother, **Siegfried Fall (1877–?)**, was a composer of serious music. The third brother, **Richard Fall (1882–1943)**, was a conductor and composer of film scores and revues, and wrote more than a dozen operettas; one of his big successes was *Arms and the Girl* (1912), on the London stage. In 1938, he left Nazi Germany for the US, but he went to France in 1943, and was arrested because he was Jewish, then was sent to Auschwitz, where he was murdered. Librettist Rudolf Schanzer, who was also Jewish, tried to escape the Nazis, but was caught and committed suicide on his arrest by the Gestapo in 1944.

Falla, Manuel de (1876–1946) (mah NWEHL deh: FAH yah) Prolific Spanish composer. He wrote zarzuelas and several dramatic pieces, among them *La vida breve* (The Short Life) (1913) (lah VEE thah BREH ve:), one of his most celebrated; and an unfinished dramatic **cantata**, *L'Atálantida* (lah TAH lahn TEE thah).

falsetto *n.* The high range of a voice, esp. the c-ten. male voice, above the natural register.

Falsettos Broadway musical by William **Finn**; libretto by the composer and James **Lapine**, who also directed; John Golden Theatre, 1992 (487 perf.); three Off-Broadway productions preceded the Broadway show.

Marvin leaves his son Jason and his wife Trina, and moves in with his male lover, Whizzer. Trina goes into therapy with Marvin's psychotherapist, Mendel, and they fall in love and marry. Whizzer leaves Marvin because Marvin is so insecure, neurotic and demanding. After Whizzer is diagnosed with AIDS, Jason is bar mitzvahed in Whizzer's hospital room, because he really wanted him to be at the ceremony along with his next-door neighbors, a lesbian couple. Marvin and Whizzer are reconciled, and realize how much they had meant to each other.

Falstaff 1. Seventeen operas, all based on Shakespeare's *The Merry Wives of Windsor*, were composed with this title, including works by Antonio **Salieri** (1799); Michael William **Balfe** (1838); and Adolphe **Adam** (1856). **2.** Opera in three acts by Giuseppe **Verdi**; libretto by Arrigo **Boito**; Milan, Teatro alla Scala, 1893.

This was Verdi's last opera, and one of his greatest masterpieces.

The amorous, portly, and bibulous Sir John Falstaff (bar.) attempts to seduce Mistress Alice Ford (sop.), wife of the irascible, jealous Ford (bar.), and Mistress Meg Page (mezz.), to whom he has sent identical love letters. The women show the letters to each other, and have no intention of giving in to Falstaff. He gets his comeuppance with the connivance of Mistress Quickly (mezz.), innkeeper at the Garter, where Falstaff spends all his time in the company of his low-life companions and henchmen, Bardolph (ten.) and Pistol (bar.). The young Ford daughter, Nanetta (sop.), ends up betrothed to her beloved, Fenton (ten.).

See also LUSTIGEN WEIBER VON WINDSOR, DIE.

fandango (fahn DAHN go:) *n.* Lively, sinuous Spanish dance in 3/4 or 6/8 time, usually with guitar and castanet accompaniment; periodically, the tempo speeds up, comes to a sudden stop, and then starts again slowly. There are wonderful fandangos in **zarzuela**; e.g., in act 3 of ***Doña Francisquita*** by Amadeo **Vives**.

fanfare *n.* An instrumental **flourish** or call, usually played on trumpets, to announce the arrival of someone important, or to announce the beginning of some important event.

Fanny Broadway musical by Harold **Rome**; book by famed director Joshua Logan (1908–1988), who also staged the show, and playwright S. N. Behrman (1893–1973), based on the trilogy of plays, later made into films, by French writer Marcel Pagnol (1895–1974) (pah NYO:L); Majestic Theatre, 1954 (888 perf.); film, 1961.

The original French films are captivating, romantic classics that bring a tear to the eye and gladden the heart; the musical is less convincing, particularly considering the rather pedestrian score, although it does contain two or three attractive numbers, and the adaptation of the story is well done. The production—Broadway producer David Merrick's (1911–2000) first—was notable for the performances of renowned opera singer Ezio Pinza (1892–1957) as César and the charming

Hollywood character actor Walter Slezak (1902–1983), son of the internationally famous Austrian opera tenor Leo Slezak, (1873–1946), as Panisse.

Marius, who works at a waterfront café in Marseilles owned by his father, César, and frequented by colorful local characters, yearns for the life of a sailor. He is in love with Fanny, who is pregnant by him but has not told him. One day, Marius sneaks off, and sails away. Panisse, an elderly sail maker who adores Fanny, marries her and agrees to raise the child as his own. He provides a good home for them. Many years later, Marius returns to Marseilles. He and Fanny still love each other, and he is shocked to learn that he has a son, Césario. Panisse, who is dying, enjoins Marius to marry Fanny and blesses their union.

Fantasticks, The Legendary Off-Broadway musical, with a beautiful score that is by turns wistful, romantic, sprightly, and full of verve, by Harvey **Schmidt**; book and charming, memorable lyrics by Tom **Jones**, based on the play *Les Romanesques* (The Fantasticks) (1894) (lé *ro:'* mah NEHSK) by Edmond Rostand; 1960 (17,162 perf.), at the 144-seat Sullivan Street Theatre; Broadway revival: Snapple Theatre Center, 2004 (return engagement still running as of this writing), with Jones playing the Old Actor; numerous productions; television version: 1964; film: directed by Michael Ritchie and completed in 1995 but re-cut by Francis Ford Coppola and released in 2000, screenplay by Jones.

Matt and Luisa grow up next door to each other. Their fathers, Bellomy and Hucklebee, pretend to be feuding; they have put up a wall between their two properties, so as to fuel their children's supposedly forbidden love for each other. The fathers hire the bandit El Gallo to kidnap Luisa, so that Matt can save her. He does, but they fall out of love. Matt goes off to explore the world, where he fares badly; Luisa, enamored of El Gallo, is abandoned by him. Matt and Luisa, older and wiser, rediscover their love for each other.

farandole (fah *rahn* DO:L) *n.* A vivacious Provençal skipping dance in 6/8 time, performed by couples, originally as part of medieval street festivals; used in some ballets, such as Tchaikovsky's *Sleeping Beauty*; and in some operas, e.g., **Offenbach** and Sardou's *Le Roi Carotte*.

Farnie, H. B. [Henry Brougham] (1836–1889) Scottish expert writer on golf; prolific librettist with some sixty works to his credit, including his own original libretti and translations of French comic operas and operettas for the London and Broadway stages, among them many **Offenbach** pieces and several by Charles **Lecocq**, such as *La fille de Madame Angot*; Edmond **Audran**, among them *La mascotte*; and Robert **Planquette**, including *Les cloches de Corneville*.

Fauré, Gabriel Urbain (1845–1924) (gah bree EHL ür ban' fo: RÉ) French composer, considered the greatest of his generation; wrote in all genres; best known for his chamber music, his numerous art songs, and his magnificent *Requiem*; student of Camille **Saint-Saëns**; wrote two operas, both masterpieces: *Prométhée* (Prometheus) (1900) (pro mé TÉ), and *Pénélope* (Penelope) (1913) (pé né LOP), both based on ancient Greek myths.

Faust (FOWST) **1.** The aged scholar and alchemist of a moralistic Renaissance legend, Faust sells his soul to the devil in exchange for youth and beauty, in order to win the woman with whom he has fallen in love, and pays the bitterest price for having done so. The legend has been retold in at least twenty operas adapted from its most famous modern version, the epic verse drama by the German literary genius Johann Wolfgang von Goethe (1749–1832); Part One was published in 1806, and revised in 1828/29; Part Two was published posthumously in 1832. The work was actually an armchair drama, not meant to be performed, but to be read. Hector **Berlioz** adapted it into a dramatic symphonic poem, *La damnation de Faust* (lah dahn nah syon' duh FO:ST) (1846). Fourteen other operas based on the legend, but not on Goethe, were also composed, including those by Ludwig **Spohr** (1816), considered a landmark of romantic operatic composition; and Ferruccio **Busoni**: *Doktor Faust* (1925)—incomplete at the composer's death and performed posthumously. In Prokofiev's *Ognenniy angel (The Fiery Angel)*, Faust and Mephistopheles are characters, seen in fantasy.
2. Opera in five acts by Charles **Gounod**; libretto by Jules **Barbier** and Michel **Carré**, based on Goethe's poem; Paris, Théâtre Lyrique, 1859. The score, with its sustained, compelling drama, is Gounod's greatest triumph, and the four principal roles all have superb musical showpieces: Faust (ten.); Marguerite (sop.); Mephistopheles (bass); and Valentin (vah lahn TAN) (bar.), Marguerite's protective soldier brother.

See also EISLER, HANNS; HERVÉ; MEFISTOFELE.

Favart, Charles-Simon (1710–1792) (fah VAHR) Influential, highly regarded French theater producer, librettist, dramatist, and composer of ca. eighty musical theater pieces in various genres. His wife, Marie-Justine-Benoîte Favart (1727–1772) (mah ree zhüs teen' behn WAHT), was a singer and playwright who often collaborated with her husband. They are both characters in Offenbach's witty operetta, *Madame Favart*, based on real incidents in their colorful lives.

favola in musica (FAH vo: lah ihn MOO zee kah) [Italian: fable/story in music] *Hist.* A 17th c. term, meaning a mythological subject or other kind of story set to music; an early operatic form, exemplified in Monteverdi's *La favola d'Orfeo* (lah FAH vo: lah do:r FEH: o:) (1607), based on the legend of Orpheus and Eurydice.

Fedora (feh DO: rah) Opera in three acts by **verismo** composer Umberto **Giordano**; libretto by Arturo Colautti, based on the play by Victorien **Sardou**; Milan, Teatro Lirico, 1898.

In St. Petersburg in 1881, a Russian nihilist activist, Count Loris Ipanov (LO: rees ee PAH nof) (ten.), kills Count Vladimir Andrejevich (ahn DRAY uh vihch), who was having an affair with his wife. Princess Fedora Romanov (ro MAH nof) (sop.), who was to have married Andrejevich the next day, seeks vengeance on the murderer and follows him to Paris, where he confesses the crime to her but explains the reason for it, and also tells her that Andrejevich had fired at him first. Loris has fallen in love with Fedora, and she with him. But his explanation of the murder, as well as their falling in love, have come too late, because she had already written to the Czarist police denouncing him. The information she has supplied causes the death of Loris's brother and mother. When he swears to avenge them, Fedora, knowing he will soon discover the truth, commits suicide and dies in his arms at their villa in Switzerland.

Fela! Innovative, unique "Afrobeat" dance-drama musical conceived and put together by the team of book writers Jim Lewis, who also supplied additional lyrics; Bill T. Jones, the show's choreographer-director; and producer-writer, Stephen Hendel; music and lyrics by revered Nigerian poet, composer, political activist, and performer, Fela Anikulapo-Kuti (1938–1997), based on his life; additional music by Aaron Johnson and Gordon McLean; music arranged and performed by the Antibalas Afrobeat Orchestra, based in Brooklyn; opened Off-Broadway, 37 Arts Theatre B (September 2008), ran for one month, and won 2009 Lucille Lortel Award for Outstanding Musical; moved to Broadway, Eugene O'Neill Theatre, 2009 (still running as of this writing). The show revolves around the efforts mounted by 1000 soldiers to put an end to Kuti's shows at the legendary Shrine nightclub in Lagos, Nigeria.

Festspielhaus (FEHST shpeel HOWS) *n.* [German: festival playhouse] A theater specially built for festival perf., e.g., the Bayreuth Festspielhaus, constructed for the perf. of Wagner's operas.

Fiddler on the Roof Highly successful, much acclaimed Broadway musical by Jerry **Bock**; lyrics by Sheldon **Harnick**; book by Joseph **Stein**, based somewhat loosely on Yiddish writer Sholom Aleichem's (1859–1916) *Tevye the Dairyman* stories; Imperial Theatre, 1964 (3249 perf.); Broadway revivals: Winter Garden Theatre, 1976 (168 perf.); Lincoln Center New York State Theatre, limited engagement, 1981 (56 perf.); George Gershwin Theatre, 1990 (259 perf.); Minskoff Theatre, 2004 (817 perf.); film, 1971.

Based on the spoken stage play, a Yiddish film, *Tevye* (1939), starring the brilliant Maurice Schwarz (1890–1960), shows us a rather different character than the Tevye of the musical: tired from overwork, more serious and world weary, more perceptive and less naïve, and with a wry, ironic, intolerant, yet appealing and sometimes cynical sense of humor, as opposed to the more overtly comic, shoulder-shrugging, charming, and good-hearted humor of the musical comedy dairyman. Zero Mostel's (1915–1977) performance as Tevye in the musical was famous, and the role was later excellently played on stage by such wonderful actors as Herschel Bernardi (1923–1986); [Chaim] Topol (b. 1935), who did the film version as well; and Harvey **Fierstein**. The show was also notable for Jerome Robbins's (1918–1998) choreography and direction.

In the late 19th c., Tevye, an impoverished dairyman, and his wife, Golde, cling to Jewish traditions in the village of Anatevka in Czarist Russia. However, their daughters are not so set in their ways, and decide to break with tradition by finding husbands without using the services of Yente the matchmaker or asking for their parents' permission. The youngest daughter falls in love with a young man of the Russian Orthodox faith, and marries him, whereupon Tevye disowns her. The czar expels all the Jews from Anatevka, and they leave with sadness, but also with hope for the new lives they will make in America.

Fidelio; oder Die eheliche Liebe (Fidelio; or Conjugal Love) (fee DEH: lee o: O: duh dee EH: eh lih' *kh*eh LEE beh) Opera in two acts by Ludwig van **Beethoven**; libretto by Josef Sonnleithner (1766–1835) (YO: zehf ZON LIT nuh), based on a libretto by the writer and French Revolutionary politician Jean-Nicolas Bouilly (1763–1842), (ZHAH*N* nee' ko LAH boo YEE), drawn from actual events that transpired during the French Revolution, and set to music by Pierre **Gaveaux** in 1798. Beethoven's only opera was first produced in 1805 at Vienna's Theater an der Wien. The **Singspiel** libretto for this **rescue opera** was rewritten twice: in a two-act version by poet Stefan von Breuning (1774–1827) (SHTEH fahn fuhn B*R*OY ning), produced in 1806 at the Theater an der Wien. The final version, by the poet and translator Friedrich Treitschke (1776–1842) (F*R*EED *r*ikh T*R*ITSH keh) was produced in 1814 at the Kärntnertortheater (KEH[*R*]NT nuh TO:[*R*] teh: AH tuh).

Beethoven's opera is also famous for its four overtures: the usual one for the opera, called the *Fidelio* overture; and the three *Leonora* overtures: the first was composed for a performance in Prague; the second was actually the one used at the premiere; and the third was played at an 1806 revival.

The Spanish nobleman Florestan (FLO: reh STAHN) (ten.), a political activist and opponent of the regime, has been secretly imprisoned near Seville. His wife, Leonora (leh:' o: NO: rah) (sop.), gains admittance to the prison disguised as a boy called Fidelio, under the pretext of seeking employment. The aged jailer, Rocco (ROK: ko:) (bass), hires her, and his daughter, Marzelline (mahr' tseh LEE nah) (sop.), falls in love with Fidelio, to the annoyance of the gatekeeper Jacquino (zhah KEE no:) (ten.), who hopes to marry Marzelline. Rocco allows the prisoners out of their cells to enjoy the warm weather. He trusts Fidelio enough to have him help with a prisoner in solitary confinement, none other than Florestan. When Don Pizarro (pee TSAHR ro:) (bar.), the minister who has illegally had Florestan incarcerated, arrives and is about to kill him, Fidelio/Leonora draws a pistol and saves her husband's life. The government minister arrives and has Pizarro arrested. Florestan and Leonora are reunited, and Marzelline and Jacquino are reconciled.

Ferdinando **Paër** wrote an opera on the same subject in 1804. Johann Simon **Mayr** also set the story, to an Italian version of the French libretto by Gaetano **Rossi**: *L'amor coniugale* (Conjugal Love) (1805) (lah MO:R kon yoo GAH leh:), which he called a "farsa sentimentale" (a sentimental farce) (FAHR sah sehn tee mehn TAH leh:); Padua, Teatro Nuovo (NWO: vo:), 1805. For this version, the story was reset in Poland. The music is engaging and exciting, and moves along briskly, but is hardly on the passionate level of Beethoven. Still, it is worth redis-covering. A live performance was recorded in 2004 and is available on a Naxos CD (8.660198-99; 2008).

See also ARIA DI VENDETTA.

Fields family Dorothy, Herbert, and Joseph were the daughter and sons of famed comedian and producer **Lew Fields (1867–1941)** of the Weber and Fields vaudeville team [Joe Weber (1867–1942)]. All three had long and distinguished careers as stage and film writers. **Dorothy Fields (1904–1974)**, a brilliant lyricist, collaborated with well known composers, among them Jerome **Kern** and Irving **Berlin**, on additional songs for films of many of their stage musicals, and wrote the lyrics for many Broadway shows, including the hits, *A Tree Grows in Brooklyn*, *Redhead* by Albert **Hague**, and Sigmund Romberg's *Up in Central Park* (1945), the latter two with books by her and her brother **Herbert Fields (1897–1958)**. Her career began when songs that she wrote with Jimmy McHugh were introduced at Harlem's famed Cotton Club in 1927; the following year, the two collaborated on *Blackbirds of 1928*, which was a huge hit, and in 1929, Herbert wrote the book for Cole Porter's first big success, *Fifty Million Frenchmen*. He also wrote books for **Rodgers and Hart**, including *Dearest Enemy* (1925) and *A Connecticut Yankee* (1927), and the books for *Panama Hattie* (1940) and *Du Barry Was A Lady*, as well as working with his sister on many hits, including Irving Berlin's *Annie Get Your Gun*. **Joseph Fields (1895–1966)** wrote Broadway hit plays, sketches for the *Ziegfeld Follies*, and co-wrote *Gentlemen Prefer Blondes*, *Wonderful Town*, and Rodgers and Hammerstein's *Flower Drum Song*. All three Fields siblings collaborated on the book for Cole Porter's *Mexican Hayride*.

Fierstein, Harvey (b. 1954) Noted film and Tony® Award–winning stage actor, writer, and librettist/lyricist for several Broadway musical comedies, among them *La Cage aux Folles* (1983) and *A Catered Affair* (2008).

fifth position In dance, the placement of the feet so that they are completely in front of each other, with the heel of one foot touching the toes of the other; or, alternatively, so that the heels touch just inside the joint of the big toe, where it joins the rest of the foot.

Fifty Million Frenchmen Broadway musical by Cole **Porter**; book by Herbert **Fields**; Lyric Theatre, 1929 (254 perf.). The score is really fantastic, and the lyrics are snappy, witty and brilliant. Songs include "You Do Something to Me" and "The Tale of the Oyster."
   This clever show, Porter's first big hit, tells the slender story of an American millionaire, Peter Forbes, who makes a bet that within one month he can win the favors of Looloo Carroll, an American tourist in Paris, without using or even alluding to any of his money. He poses as a guide, but he falls in love with her, and withdraws from the bet.

figure *n.* **1.** A musical phrase, or note grouping, that forms part of a melody, and is recognizable on its own. **2.** In dance, a particular, repeatable series of steps.

filar il tuono (fee LAHR eel TWO: no:) [Italian: to prolong or draw out the tone or note] To dwell on, draw out, or prolong a sung note, beginning softly at a low volume, swelling in volume, then gradually going back down to a lower volume, all on one breath: a technique used to great effect in opera. Also called *filar la voce* [Italian: draw out or prolong the voice (lah VO: che:)].

Fille de madame Angot, La (Madame Angot's Daughter) (lah FEE yuh duh mah dahm ah*n* GO:) Operetta in three acts by Charles **Lecocq**; libretto by Louis François Nicolaie Clairville (1811–1879) (nee ko: LEH: uh kle:*r* VEEL), Paul Siraudin (1813–1883) (see *ro*: DA*N*), and Victor Koning (1842–1894) (ko NIH:NG), based on a 1796 **opéra comique** by le Citoyen Antoine-François Eve *dit* Maillot (1747–1814) (luh sih: twah YEH*N* [the Citizen] ah*n* twahn' *fr*ah*n* SWAH EHV dee [called] mah YO:) [Also called Démaillot (dé mah YO:)]; Brussels, Théâtre des Fantaisies-Parisiennes (deh: fah*n* teh: zee' pah *r*ee ZYEH*N*), 1873.

In Paris, during the Directory (1795–1799), the florist Clairette (kleh: *R*EHT) (sop.), daughter of Madame Angot, works in the marketplace where her fellow workers arrange for her to marry Pomponnet (pawn po NEH:) (bar.), barber-hairdresser to Mademoiselle Lange (LAH*N*ZH) (mezz.), a famous actress. But Clairette is in love with Ange Pitou (ah*n*zh' pee TOO) (ten.), a royalist poet who writes satirical anti-government songs, particularly critical of the wealthy Larivaudière (lah *r*ee vo: DYEH:*R*) (bar.), secret lover of Mademoiselle Lange. She is the mistress of Barras (bah *R*AHS), one of the five Directors. Larivaudière is deathly afraid that, thanks to Pitou, Barras will discover the affair. So he bribes Pitou not to sing his latest lampoon. But Clairette has learned it from him, and, wanting to delay her marriage to Pomponnet, sings it, and is promptly arrested. Wanting to know why she is being satirized, Lange has Clairette brought to her, and they recognize each other as old school friends. She explains to Lange about Pitou, who presently arrives, and Lange falls in love with him. As it turns out, she, Larivaudière, Pitou, and Barras are all royalist conspirators. A meeting of the conspirators is scheduled for that same evening, and they are all about to be arrested when Lange saves the day by pretending they are all there for a ball, to which she invites the Hussars who were supposed to arrest them. At the ball, Clairette and Lange realize they are both in love with Pitou. Clairette discovers them together, renounces Pitou, and marries Pomponnet.

finale *n.* The concluding section of an act in an opera, operetta, or musical; or of a movement in a symphony, concerto, or other musical composition.

fine (FEE neh:) *n.* [Italian: end; closing] **1.** The end of a musical composition, or of a section of it, as in the instruction to play or sing *da capo al fine*; i.e., from the beginning to the end. **2.** The concluding section of a **quadrille** or other **square dance**.

Finian's Rainbow Broadway musical by Burton **Lane**; book by E. Y. **Harburg** and Fred **Saidy**; lyrics by Harburg; 46th Street Theatre, 1947 (725 perf.); two New York City Center Light Opera Company revivals, and many stock productions; Broadway revival, St. James Theatre, 2009 (92 perf.); film, 1968, starring Petula Clark (b. 1932) as Sharon and Fred Astaire as Finian, his last major film role.

Finian McLonergan steals a pot of gold from the leprechaun Og. He and his daughter Sharon escape to America, where McLonergan wants to plant the crock near Fort Knox so it can grow. Og follows them, and every day he becomes more human, as long as he cannot recover his pot. Sharon falls in love with the radical political organizer Woody Mahoney, who is mobilizing black and white share-croppers against the racist Senator Billboard Rawkins. When Rawkins is turned into an African American, he learns the stupidity of his ways and the harm he has done, and reforms. Og, in love with a mortal, decides to remain human. Woody and Sharon are united.

Finn, William (b. 1952) Tony® Award–winning American composer, lyricist, and playwright whose works often deal with the conditions of being gay and Jewish in America; among his musicals are ***Falsettos*** and ***The 25th Annual Putnam County Spelling Bee***.

fioritura (fyaw' rih TOO rah) *n.* [Italian: floweriness; "flowery" musical orna-mentation] Florid ornamentation or embellishment; e.g., grace notes, trills, appoggiaturas, or other adornments in **bel canto** operas.

first position In dance, the placement of the feet so that they form a line, with the heels touching.

Five, The A group of romantic nationalist Russian composers, also called "The Mighty Handful" [Russian: *moguchaya kuchka* (mo: GOO chah' yah KOOCH kah): mighty heap, group], who wanted to revive music and opera in Russia using native music, including folk motifs. The founding members of the group were Mili Balakirev (1837–1910) (MEE lee BAH lah KEE rehf) and César **Cui**, who met together in 1856. Modest **Mussorgsky** joined them in 1857, followed by Nicolai **Rimsky-Korsakov** in 1861, and finally, by Alexander **Borodin**, who joined in 1862. They did not call themselves "The Five," but were so referred to by others; Rimsky-Korsakov refers to them in his memoirs, *The Chronicle of My Musical Life* (1909), as "Balakirev's circle" or sometimes as the "Mighty Handful," an expression made fun of by the group's enemies.

Flaherty, Stephen (b. 1960) and Lynn Ahrens (b. 1948) Songwriting team well known in the 1980s and 1990s; they wrote ***Ragtime***; *Seussical* (2000), based on characters from the stories of children's author, Dr. Seuss; and ***Once on This Island***, among many other musicals.

flam *n.* Snare drum stroke of one long and one short note in succession; much used in **jazz**.

flamenco *n.* Spanish dance form that evolved from Andalusian gypsy dancing, influenced by North African dance; it includes the use of the voice in undertones, with nasal humming and undulating melodies, rhythmic stamping of the feet, and sometimes abrupt, sometimes smooth, always supple gesticulation with the arms and hands. Intensity of expression and intense concentration, singing, and hand clapping are integral to flamenco, as are the use of castanets to click out rhythms and guitars to reinforce the dancers' moods as they invent and improvise new movements and vary the rhythm of each dance. There are many different kinds of flamenco dances, including the four main, basic ones: the ***alegrias***, the *soleare* (so:' leh: AH reh:), the *buleria* (boo' leh: REE ah), and the *ferruca* (feh: ROO kah).

fling *n.* A Scottish dance in various rapid rhythms; e.g., the Highland fling, usually danced to the music of bagpipes; the dancers wear the traditional kilt as they do the steps in place using arm and foot movements. There steps include back-stepping, stepping toe to heel, rocking, crossing one foot over the other and back, and shaking and turning. Variations on the Highland fling were used in the big dance numbers in the musical ***Brigadoon***.

Fledermaus, Die (The Bat) (dee FLEH: duh MOWS) Operetta in three acts by **Johann Strauss II**; libretto by lyricist and poet Carl Haffner (1804–1876) (HAHF nuh) and Richard **Genée**, based on the play *Le réveillon* (luh *r*eh veh: YO:*N*) (1872) (The New Year's Eve [or Christmas Eve] Celebration) by Henri **Meilhac** and Ludovic **Halévy**, who based their typical French boulevard farce on actor and playwright Julian Roderick Benedix's (1811–1873) comedy *Das Gefängnis* (The Prison) (1851) (dahs guh FEHNGK nih:s); Vienna, Theater an der Wien, 1874.

The sparkling, effervescent score is as frothy and bubbling as the champagne it extols, and full of heady delights and famous waltzes—a joyous romp from beginning to end, as shown, for instance, in the marvelous production directed by Dona D. Vaughn at the Manhattan School of Music in 2009, where the fresh, youthful, and thoroughly professional double casts put on a version full of vivacity and ebullient high spirits thoroughly worthy of this classic piece—too often disgraced by stodgy pedestrian revivals.

Dr. Falke (FAHL keh) (bar.) has decided to revenge himself on his friend, Gabriel von Eisenstein (GAH b*r*ee ehl fuhn I' zuhn SHTIN) (ten. or bar.), for a practical joke Eisenstein had played on him three years before, after a costume party where the drunken Falke had been dressed as a bat. Eisenstein had left him all night on a bench in front of the hospital, prey to the mockery of his colleagues. Falke per-suades the unsuspecting, philandering hedonist—who is supposed to report to prison to begin serving a sentence on minor charges—to accompany him to a ball given by Prince Orlofsky (o:r LO:F skee) (mezz.), where Eisenstein will meet women of easy virtue while he masquerades as a French aristocrat; he can report to prison after midnight, with nobody any the wiser. As soon as he takes leave of his wife, Rosalinde (RO: zah LIH:N deh) (sop.), her admirer, the opera singer Alfred (ten.), enters and is comfortably ensconced when the prison director, Frank (F*R*AHNK) (bass-bar.), arrives to escort Eisenstein personally to jail. To protect Rosalinde's reputation, Alfred has no choice but to pretend to be Eisenstein, so off he goes. Falke has arranged for Frank, also disguised as a French aristocrat, to be at Orlofsky's, along with Eisenstein's servant, Adele (ah DEH: leh) (sop.), and Ros-alinde, disguised as a masked Hungarian countess. Eisenstein does not recognize her, and tries to seduce her. She manages to filch the watch he uses as an entice-ment. The next morning, when Eisenstein arrives at the prison, all is revealed, Rosalinde shows him the watch, and everything ends in laughter and merriment.

floor show Entertainment at a nightclub, esp. in the space surrounded by tables, or at one end of the room, where there may also be a raised platform or bandstand; usually consisting of singing and/or stand-up comedy routines, and sometimes of lines of dancing girls.

Flora, the Red Menace Notable as the first Broadway musical by **Kander and Ebb**: music by John Kander; lyrics by Fred **Ebb**; book by George **Abbott**, who also directed, and Robert Russell (1912–1992), later revised by David Thompson, based on Lester Atwell's (1909–2001) novel *Love Is Just Around the Corner*; Alvin Theatre, 1965 (87 perf.).

Liza Minnelli (b. 1946) made her Broadway debut as Flora Meszaros, an art school graduate who has trouble finding a job as a fashion illustrator during the Great Depression. Her boyfriend, Harry Toukarian, a member of the Communist Party, convinces her to join with him in trying to reform the world. Although she finds no work as an artist and breaks up with Harry, Flora remains optimistic about the future, due in part to the good offices of her friend, Mr. Weiss, who persuades her that she can only find true peace and fortitude within herself.

Florodora An immense West End and Broadway musical comedy success; music and lyrics by Leslie **Stuart**, with extra songs and/or lyrics by Edward Boyd-Jones, Frank Clement, and Paul **Rubens**; book by Owen Hall (1853–1907) [Pseudonym of theater critic James Davis, when he wrote for the stage]; London, Lyric Theatre, 1899 (455 perf.); New York, Casino Theatre, 1900 (553 perf.); Broadway revivals: Broadway Theatre, 1905 (32 perf.), Century Theatre, 1920 (150 perf.); many touring productions.

On the Philippine island of Florodora, Cyrus Gilfain, an elderly perfumer, is in love with Dolores, the daughter of a man he hornswoggled. Dolores loves Frank Abercoed, the perfume company manager. Cyrus wants Frank to marry Angela, Cyrus's daughter, but Angela loves Captain Arthur Donegal. Cyrus buys a supposedly haunted castle in Wales, and thither they all repair. The superstitious Cyrus is inveigled into allowing the couples who want to be together to get married.

Original cast recordings were made in 1900—the first in history—and they are available on Opal CD 9835, produced for Pearl Records in 1989. The show was famous for an intriguing, attractive sextet of gorgeous dancing girls, called the "Florodora girls": each one became well known, and married a millionaire!

Flotow, Friedrich von (1812–1883) (FREED *rikh* fuhn FLO: tow) German composer of some dozen operas, among them the lyrical romantic drama *Alessandro Stradella*, about the adventurous life of the Italian composer. Von Flotow's greatest success, still constantly performed, is the tuneful, captivating *Martha*. He spent much of his life in Paris, where the light style of appealing, romantic music and the great melodic gifts of this sophisticated, genial German aristocrat were immensely appreciated.

Flower Drum Song Broadway musical comedy by **Rodgers and Hammerstein**: music by Richard **Rodgers**; book by Oscar **Hammerstein** and Joseph **Fields**, who did the original adaptation of the novel *The Flower Drum Song* by Chinese-American writer, C. Y. Lee (b. 1917) and proposed the project to Rodgers and Hammerstein; lyrics by Oscar **Hammerstein**; St. James Theatre, 1958 (600 perf.); Broadway revival, Virginia Theatre, 2002 (169 perf.), book rewritten and updated by playwright David Henry **Hwang**; film, 1961.

Considered advanced in its day for putting a story with an Asian-American cast on stage, the show was ultimately considered unintentionally racist because it dealt in stereotyped characters and stereotypical situations, which the new text by Hwang attempted to eliminate.

In San Francisco's Chinatown, nightclub entrepreneur Sammy Fong is in love with sexy singer Linda Low, who clearly enjoys "being a girl." But he is engaged in a traditional, arranged match to Mei Li, who arrives from China accompanied by her father, Dr. Li. Sammy gets Mei Li and the Chinese American Wang Ta together in the hope that she will fall in love with the young man and want out of the arrangement. Although Wang Ta is engaged to Linda Low, he does fall in love with Mei Li, and they end up together. Sammy and Linda are also married.

In Hwang's rewritten version, the lyrics were not changed, but they were put in a different context. And the pleasant score was retained.

Mei Li and her father escape from Communist China, and she goes to work as an actress in a traditional Chinese theater in San Francisco, managed by Wang Chi-Yang. She falls in love with Ta, his son, who is enamored of Linda Low, a nightclub chanteuse and a modern girl. The theater is losing business, so Wang, with the help of the agent Madam Liang (Wang Ta's stern aunt in Hammerstein and Fields' original book), turns it into a nightclub that puts on satirical cabarets in which Linda performs. The disappointed Mei Li plans to leave for Hong Kong, but Ta, realizing he loves her, convinces her to stay.

Floyd, Carlisle (b. 1926) American opera composer, whose first great success was *Susannah* (1955). He also composed *Wuthering Heights* (1958), based on the novel by Emily Brontë (1818–1848), with its agonizing story of Catherine and Heathcliff and their doomed love; and *Of Mice and Men* (1970), based on the 1937 play by John Steinbeck (1902–1968).

Floyd Collins Off-Broadway musical by Adam **Guettel**; book by Tina Landau (b. 1962), who also directed; Playwrights Horizons limited run, 1996 (25 perf.); many regional productions.

The story is based on a sensational news event of 1925. Floyd Collins, a Kentucky farmer, is trapped in a cave he has been exploring, and all attempts to rescue him are in vain. The story makes national headlines, and hordes of journalists and curiosity seekers arrive on the scene. Before the rescue party can reach him, Collins dies of exposure.

folk music Songs, ballads, round songs, and the like that are part of a people's tradition, whether they are anonymous or by a known composer, e.g., Stephen Collins Foster (1826–1864).

folk rock An eclectic musical genre that is a combination of the simple kind of melodies and refrains used in folk songs with elements of rock music band arrangements, e.g., for twelve-string guitar and percussion, modifying the folk element accordingly by melding its tunes with a rock sound; began in the 1960s in Great Britain; some of the music by the Beatles may be said to be in this genre.

follies *n. pl.* [Used as a singular or pl. n.] *Hist.* A lavishly staged revue or series of revues featuring dance numbers, songs, comedy routines, and, esp., gorgeous young women in spectacular costumes slowly and seductively walking down staircases; popular in the early 20th c. in the U.S., e.g. the ***Ziegfeld Follies***.

Follies Broadway musical by Stephen **Sondheim**; book by James Goldman (1927–1998); Winter Garden Theatre, 1971 (552 perf.); Broadway revival: Roundabout Theatre limited run, 2001 (116 perf.).

The lavish original production, with gorgeous costumes, was notable for Harold Prince's and Michael Bennett's co-direction, and Bennett's choreography.

Two married couples who have known each other since the women were chorus girls and the men were their suitors meet again at a nostalgic reunion hosted by the producer of the eponymous *Weismann Follies* at his old theater, soon to be torn down. The story shifts between the present and the ghosts of a past life: the characters' young selves are seen as they were then. The marriage of Ben Stone and his wife Phyllis seems to be on the rocks, and Sally, who is married to traveling salesman Buddy Plummer, is still in love with Ben. The show turns into a dreamlike recreation of the *Follies*, which mirrors their relationships. After coming back to reality, they decide to give things another try.

follow spot A lighting instrument worked by a trained technician, called the *follow spot operator*; used to track a performer's movements during a stage show; much used in musical comedies, burlesque, and vaudeville.

Forbidden Broadway A series of satirical revues that parody Broadway musical comedies; started in 1981; done in various venues and with different casts over more than twenty-five years.

Forever Plaid Off-Broadway musical entertainment written and compiled by Stuart Ross, who also directed; featuring songs of the 1950s and 1960s, with vocal and instrumental arrangements by James Raitt (1953–1994); Triad Theatre, 1990 (1811 perf.); film, 2008. The show offered a satirically affectionate look at the all-male, four-part harmony groups, such as the Four Aces, the Four Freshmen, and the Four Lads, that proliferated in the early 1950s and lasted through the 1960s.

Forty-Five Minutes from Broadway Hit Broadway musical by George M. **Cohan**, who wrote the music, book, and lyrics, and directed the show; New Amsterdam Theatre, 1906 (90 perf.). The rambunctious score is full of varied delights, and the show rollicks along full tilt. It is perhaps worth a Broadway revival!

In New Rochelle, NY, forty-five minutes north of Times Square, Tom Bennett, having inherited his uncle's estate, is planning to use it to win the affections of the famous actress Flora Dora Dean. Meanwhile, Dan Cronin has been wooing Mary Jane Jenkins, former maid and nurse of the deceased uncle, because he is sure that the estate has been left to her. Kid Burns, Tom's secretary, arrives in New Rochelle to go through the papers, and falls in love with Mary. In the course of his work, he finds an authentic will that does indeed leave everything to her, and that was made after the other will. But he is afraid she will think he is just after her for her money. She loves him, too, and, in order to test him, she destroys the will. He proposes, and she knows that he adores her. Tom inherits the money.

42nd Street Broadway musical comedy adapted from the Warner Brothers **backstage musical** film of 1933, directed by Lloyd Bacon (1889–1955); music for the film by film and stage composer Harry **Warren**, lyrics by his collaborator on many Hollywood musical films, the Swiss-born American lyricist Al Dubin (1891–1945); music for the stage show by Harry Warren, interpolating songs from other films of his; book by Michael **Stewart** and Mark Bramble (b. 1950), adapted from the screenplay by Rian James (1899–1953) and James Seymour (1895–1976), based on a novel by Broadway dancer and novelist Bradford Ropes (1905–1966); Winter Garden Theatre, 1980 (3486 perf.); Broadway revival: Ford Center for the Performing Arts, 2001 (1524 perf.).

The title song was an immediate hit, and the film was also notable for the innovative choreography of Busby Berkeley (1895–1976) [b. William Berkeley Enos]. For the Broadway show, the superb choreography was by veteran Gower Champion (1920–1980).

During the Great Depression, naïve Peggy Sawyer arrives in New York from Sioux City, Iowa, all starry-eyed over Broadway. She is hired by producer Julian Marsh to be in the chorus of his new musical, *Pretty Lady*. She makes friends with a couple of the other dancers, who teach her the ropes. When the show's star breaks her ankle, Peggy goes on in her place, and her performance is a triumph.

forza del destino, La (The Force of Destiny) (lah FO:R tsah dehl dehs TEE no:) Opera in four acts by Giuseppe **Verdi**; libretto by Francesco Maria **Piave**, based on the Spanish melodrama *Don Alvaro, o la fuerza del sino* (Don Alvaro, or The Force of Destiny) (1835) (do:n ahl VAH ro: o: lah FWEHR sah thehl SEE no:) by Angel de Saavedra Ramirez de Banquedano, Duke of Rivas (1791–1865) (AHN hehl theh: sah VEH: drah rah MEE rehs theh: bahn keh: DAH no:) (REE vahs), and on a scene from the play *Wallensteins Lager* (Wallenstein's Camp) (1799) (VAH luhn SHTINS LAH guh) by Friedrich von Schiller; Milan, Teatro alla Scala, 1862.

In the 18th c., in a castle in Spain, the Marquis de Calatrava (kah' lah TRAH vah) (bass) enters his daughter's bedroom and surprises her and her lover, Don Alvaro (ten.), as they are about to elope. But Leonora (sop.) and Alvaro have been chaste, and the young man affirms Leonora's innocence, throwing his pistol to the floor. It discharges and kills Calatrava. The lovers manage to escape, but they are separated. To protect herself, Leonora disguises herself as a man. In an inn, she discovers her brother, Don Carlo (bar.), disguised as a university student. He

119

relates to the assembled customers the story of what happened, and makes clear his determination to kill the murderer. Leonora decides to become a hermit and to live in a cave near the desert monastery of Hornachuelos (O:R nah CHWEH: lo:s). Padre Guardiano (gwahr' dee AH no:) (bass), the monastery's Father Superior, agrees to supply the penitent with food and drink. Meanwhile, Alvaro, believing Leonora dead, has become a captain in the Spanish army, which Carlo has joined as well. In the campaign, the wounded Alvaro is rescued by Carlo, who has become his best friend, neither knowing the true identity of the other. In a moving duet, "Solenne in quest'ora" (Solemnly in this hour) (so: LEHN neh: ihn kwehst O: rah), Alvaro, believing he is about to die, confides the key to his trunk to Carlo, telling him to take out a sealed packet and burn it, should he indeed pass away. Carlo opens the packet and finds a portrait of Leonora. When Alvaro recovers, Carlo challenges him to a duel; but they are prevented from fighting by soldiers on patrol, who take Carlo off as Alvaro flees. Alvaro takes the name Don Raphael, and enters the monastery at Hornachuelos. Carlo, who has been looking for Alvaro for five years, finds him and again challenges him to a duel. But the monk refuses, until Carlo goads him with racist taunts about Alvaro's Indian blood. In the ensuing swordfight, Alvaro wounds Carlo and asks for help from the nearby hermit. They are astounded to recognize each other. When Leonora goes to help her dying brother, he stabs her to death.

Fosca (FO:S kah) Opera in four acts by Carlos **Gomes**; libretto by Antonio **Ghislanzoni**, based on the novel *La festa delle Marie* (The Feast of the Marians) (1869) (lah FEHS tah DEHL leh: MAH ree eh:) by Luigi Capranica (1821–1891) (kah PRAH nee kah); Milan, Teatro alla Scala, 1873.

In this exciting and emotional opera, set in 10th-c. Venice, pirates have abducted the Venetian nobleman Paolo (PAHO: lo:) (ten.), with whom Fosca (sop.), sister of the pirate chief Gajolo (gah YO: lo:) (ten.), is in love—a recipe for the unhappiness that ensues.

Foss, Lukas (b. 1922) German-born American opera composer; his operas include *The Jumping Frog of Calaveras County* (1950), based on the story of the same name by Mark Twain (1835–1910); and *Griffelkin* (1956), originally done for television, about a little devil who visits the earthly plane on his tenth birthday and learns about life.

Four Saints in Three Acts "An opera to be sung" in a prologue and four acts by Virgil **Thomson**; libretto by Gertrude Stein (1874–1946), American writer domiciled in Paris, based on a scenario by painter Maurice Grosser (1903–1986), Thomson's companion; 1934. The opera premiered at the Wadsworth Athenaeum in Hartford, CT with an all-black cast, and was directed by John Houseman (1902–1988) and choreographed by Frederick Ashton (1904–1988), distinguished English dancer and director of the Royal Ballet; Broadway: 1934, 44th Street Theatre (60 perf).

This symbolic, allegorical story, if there can be said to be a story, unfolds in Spain, and actually involves only three principal saints in four acts!: Two St. Theresas—St. Theresa I (sop.) and St. Theresa II (mezz.)—who are surrounded by men who perhaps wish to learn from them, and St. Ignatius (bar.), who is surrounded by women who perhaps wish to learn from him, help each other to become saints. There are other saints as well: the photographer St. Settlement, who takes their pictures; and St. Chavez, who acts as a kind of social director, organizing a party. Periodically, the Commère (mezz.) [French (ko:m MEHR): gossip] and the Compère (bass) [French (ko:n PEHR): comrade, accomplice] appear and smile benignly, or argue with each other. In front of the curtain, before act 4, they quarrel over whether or not there should be a fourth act. There is. We see all the saints in heaven, and they are singing happily.

fourth position In dance, the placement of the feet so that one is in front of the other, a foot's length apart, and more or less open, i.e., crossed or in a more parallel line; similar to **third position**.

foxtrot; fox trot A popular American ballroom dance originating around the beginning of the 20th c.; internationally popular as well through the 1920s; usually a slow dance with a **ragtime** accompaniment in duple or quadruple time, but can be faster.

Fra Diavolo (Brother Devil) The most well known **opéra comique** by Daniel-François-Esprit **Auber**.

Francesca da Rimini The most well known opera by Riccardo **Zandonai**.

Franchetti, Alberto (1860–1942) (ahl BEHR to: frahn KEHT tee) Italian **verismo** opera composer; among his operas are his first, *Asrael* (1888) (AHZ rah EHL), much influenced by Wagner; his two most well known, *Germania* (1902) (dgehr MAH nee ah) and *La figlia di Jorio* (Jorio's Daughter) (1906) (lah FIH: [g]lyah dee YO: ryo:), with a libretto by Gabriele d'Annunzio (1863–1938) (gah' bree EH: leh dah NOON dzee o:), Italian poet, politician, and librettist of seven operas.

Frau Luna (Madam Moon) Berlin operetta by Paul **Lincke**.

Frauen haben das gern (Women Like That) Berlin operetta by Walter **Kollo**.

free jazz Improvisational music by an entire ensemble, often dissonant and with riffs and spontaneous solos, without attention paid to the regular harmonics of any particular key; popular in the 1960s and 1970s.

Freischütz, Der (The Freeshooter) (deh[r] FRI SHÜTS) Opera in three acts by Carl Maria von **Weber**; libretto (written at Weber's suggestion) by the composer's friend, the lawyer, poet, short story writer, and librettist Johann Friedrich Kind (1768–1843) (YO: hahn FREED rikh KIHNT), based on "Der Jägerbraut" (The Hunter's Bride) (deh YEH: guh BROWT), a story in *Gespensterbuch* (A Book of Ghosts; i.e., Ghost Stories) (five-vol. anthology, published 1811–1817) (geh SHPEHN stuh BOOKH) by author, lawyer, and librarian Johann August Apel (1771–1816) (OW goost AH pehl) and prolific popular novelist Friedrich Laun (1770–1849) (LOWN) [Pen name of Friedrich August Schultze (SHOOL tseh)]; Berlin, Schauspielhaus (SHOW shpeel HOWS), 1821.

121

The opera is set in the wilds of devastated Bohemia, just after the Thirty Years War (1618–1648). Max (ten.), a hunter, is in love with Agathe (ah GAH teh) (sop.), daughter of the head forest ranger, Cuno (KOO no:) (bass). Cuno warns Max that if he loses the next day's contest, the winner of which will inherit the post of head ranger, he cannot marry Agathe. Meanwhile, Max's friend Caspar (bass) has sold his soul to the Devil, Samiel (ZAH mee ehl) (speaking role). To save himself, he must bring Samiel another victim. Seeing the emotional state Max is in, Caspar realizes he will be easy prey. He gets Max drunk, and then astonishes him when he has Max shoot down a passing bird. Caspar explains that this exploit was brought about by the use of a *Freikugel* (free, i.e., magic bullet) (FRI KOO guhl). This was his last one of seven, each of which ensures a winning shot; and he persuades Max that he can have seven if only he goes with him to the dreaded Wolf's Glen at midnight. There, Caspar forges the magic bullets—a scene parodied by **Gilbert and Sullivan** in *The Sorcerer*. The last bullet will hit whatever target Samiel wishes, but Max is not informed of this. At the decisive shooting contest, Max wins every round. He is down to his last bullet when Prince Ottokar (O to: KAHR) (bar.), amazed at his marksmanship, orders him to shoot a passing dove. Agathe, arriving in her white wedding gown, begs him not to do so, for she senses that she is the dove; but he fires anyway, and she falls as if struck. However, it is Caspar who has been hit, betrayed by Samiel, who directed the bullet at him. Max, full of remorse, confesses his pact with the Devil, and Ottokar banishes him; but a holy Hermit (bass) intervenes on his behalf, and Ottokar relents, giving Max a year in which to prove himself worthy.

Friml, Rudolph (1879–1972) [b. Charles Rudolph Friml] Czech-born American composer of very successful Broadway musicals and operettas, Friml settled in the US in 1906. His important works include his first great success, *The Firefly* (1912), as well as *High Jinks* (1913), ***Rose-Marie*** (1924), ***The Vagabond King*** (1927), and *The Three Musketeers* (1928).

Full Monty, The [Expression derived either from the name of Field Marshal Bernard Montgomery (1887–1976), nicknamed "Monty" by his troops in World War II, known for his meticulousness and fully planned military strategies; or from the name of haberdasher Montague Maurice Burton (1885–1952), founder of Burton's Menswear, known for the full three-piece suit] Broadway musical by composer and lyricist David Yazbek (b. 1960); book by Terrence **McNally**, based on the 1997 British film of the same name; Eugene O'Neill Theatre, 2000 (770 perf.).

With its setting changed from the industrial north of England (in the film) to Buffalo, NY, the story of the musical involves a group of unemployed workers who decide to put on a strip show with full frontal nudity in order to raise money. Their wives are not too happy about this, but when they finally put the show on, it is a huge hit, and everyone rejoices.

funk *n.* A kind of **jazz** that was popular starting in the 1950s; characterized by old-fashioned melody, rhythmic variety, and blues-like compositions. By extension, a particular mood, usually a bad one: *in a blue funk*. Hence also the adj. *funky*: applied to such music, and, by extension, to a bad or unpredictable mood or frame of mind: *funky jazz. They played funky music. He's in a funky mood*. Cf. its opposite, **bebop**.

Funny Girl Broadway musical by Jule **Styne**; lyrics by Bob **Merrill**; book by playwright and screenwriter Isobel Lennart (1915–1971); Winter Garden Theatre, 1964 (1348 perf.); film, 1968. Based very loosely on the life of famed comedienne Fanny Brice (1891–1951), who appeared regularly in the ***Ziegfeld Follies*** and on radio, the show was a star **vehicle** for Barbra Streisand (b. 1942), who also did the film, making her reputation on both stage and screen. She starred as well in the less successful film sequel, *Funny Lady* (1973). The backstage story revolves around Brice's unhappy marriage to gambler and con artist Nicky Arnstein (1879–1965), but the show is really an excuse for the marvelous musical numbers that showed Streisand off to supreme advantage.

Funny Thing Happened on the Way to the Forum, A Broadway musical by Stephen **Sondheim** (music and lyrics); book by Larry **Gelbart** and writer and television and stage director Burt Shevelove (1915–1982), based on ancient Roman comedies by Plautus (254–184 BCE); Alvin Theatre, 1962 (964 perf.); Broadway revivals: Lunt-Fontanne Theatre, 1972 (159 perf.); St. James Theatre, 1996 (715 perf.); film, 1966.

This delightful romp through ancient Rome starred Zero Mostel as the slave Pseudolus—a name that sounds made up, but is actually the title of one of Plautus's plays. In 1972, Pseudolus was played by veteran burlesque, stage, and television comedian Phil Silvers (1911–1985), who had played the whoremaster, Marcus Lycus—whose brothel is just next door to the house of Senator Senex Senior [*Senex*: Latin for "old man"]—in the film version of the musical. Nathan Lane (b. 1956) played Pseudolus in the 1996 revival. Hysterium was originally played by Jack Gilford (1907–1990). The performances of Mostel and Gilford are preserved in the film.

Pseudolus contrives to win his freedom from slavery to Senex Senior and his domineering wife, Domina [Latin: mistress] by assuring their son, Hero, that he will procure the virgin, Philia [Greek: love; Latin, *filia*: daughter], whom Hero has seen next door, as his wife. Philia is also the object of Senex's lust, and has been purchased from Marcus Lycus by the vainglorious general Miles Gloriosus (MEE leh:s glo: ree OH soos). The general is arriving to claim her, and, while Domina is away, Senex hopes to have his way with Philia. Pseudolus ropes his fellow slave, Hysterium, into pretending to be the corpse of Philia. While Hysterium is playing dead at the mock funeral arranged by Pseudolus, Hero and Philia will have the opportunity to elope. Despite the ensuing complications and misadventures, Hero is united with Philia, and Pseudolus obtains his freedom.

fusion music A combination form of **jazz** and **rock**, originating in the late1960s; characterized by the use of amplified instruments played at a high volume, and jazz-like improvisations. Also called *jazz-rock*.

Fux, Johann Joseph (1660–1741) (F*OO*KS) Prolific Austrian composer of sacred, operatic, and instrumental music, with nineteen operas to his credit, including a version of the Orpheus and Eurydice legend, *Orfeo ed Euridice* (1715) (o:r FEH: o: ehd eh: OO ree DEE cheh:); **Kappelmeister** to the Hapsburg court; wrote important, influential treatise on counterpoint, *Gradus ad Parnassum* (The Ascent to Parnassus) (1725) (GRAH d*oo*s ahd pahr NAH s*oo*m). His **chamber opera** *Dafne in Lauro* (Daphne [Transformed] into Laurel) (1714) (DAHF neh: ihn LOW ro:) is a splendid example of baroque composition; it is available on CD (Nuova Era, 6930/31, 1995).

G

Gaiety musicals A series of late Victorian and Edwardian musical comedies produced at the Gaiety Theatre in London by theater owner George Edwardes (1855–1915) [b. George Joseph Edwards], who for three decades, from 1875 on, ran a West End theater empire that included Daly's Theatre, the Prince of Wales, the Lyric, and the Adelphi. He also produced *Dorothy* by Alfred **Cellier**, at the Lyric. Many of the Gaiety musicals by his stable of composers and librettists had the word "girl" in the title, because Edwardes liked that and thought it was a box office draw: *A Gaiety Girl* (1893) by Sidney **Jones**; *The Shop Girl* (1894), *The Circus Girl* (1896), and *A Runaway Girl* (1898), all by Ivan **Caryll**; *The Sunshine Girl* (1912) by Paul A. **Rubens**. *Our Miss Gibbs* (1909) by Ivan Caryll and Lionel **Monckton** was another huge hit. Similar musicals were produced at Edwardes's other theaters, e.g., the hugely successful shows *The Geisha* (1896) by Jones, and *San Toy* (1899), *A Country Girl* (1902), and *The Cingalee* (1904) by Rubens, produced at Daly's; and *The School Girl* (1903) by Rubens, produced at the Prince of Wales. At the Apollo, Edwardes mounted *The Girl from Kay's* (1902) by Caryll and Rubens, et al., and *The Quaker Girl* (1910) by Monckton. Despite the misnomer, these shows are also thought of as Gaiety musicals. They tended after a time to be formulaic. Some of them are quite shallow, superficial, and pedestrian, and they sound very much alike, with trite love ballads and unfunny, hack comic songs imitative of **Gilbert and Sullivan**.

galliard *n.* An energetic 16th-c. dance in 3/4 or 3/8 time; very popular in aristocratic circles, and esp. at the court of the English queen, Elizabeth I (1533–1603). It usually followed a **pavane**. In the version done during presentation of a **masque** at court, partners were chosen from the audience to perform with the masquers. Its variant is the *volta*.

galop *n.* A lively 19th-c. round dance in 2/4 time, originating in Germany; popular from the 1820s on at balls and dances; music often arranged from well known operas and operettas; used as well in dances in operas and in ballets. At the end of each musical phrase, the dancer does a brief hopping or skipping step; hence, the name of the dance. It was included in the **quadrille** later on in the century.

Galuppi, Baldassare (1706–1785) (bahl' dahs SAH reh: gah LOOP pee) [Called *il Buranello* (ihl boo rah NEHL lo:), from his native town, Burano (boo RAH no:), near Venice.] Prolific Italian composer of all kinds of instrumental music, sacred music, and more than 100 serious and comic operas. He spent much of his life in Venice, but was internationally famous and traveled to London and St. Petersburg, where he spent two years at the court of Catherine the Great (1729–1796). Many of his operas were on the same subjects as those of the other composers of his era, sometimes using libretti by Pietro **Metastasio**; e.g., *Artaserse* (1749; second version, 1751); *Didone abbandonata*; *La clemenza di Tito*—both **Mozart** and Galuppi used Metastasio's libretto (much altered in Mozart's case);

Semiramide riconosciuta (1749). The story of *Idomeneo* (1756) was also set by Mozart. And in 1768, Galuppi composed *Iphigenia in Taurus*, a version of which was also set by **Gluck**. He wrote seventeen comic operas to libretti by Carlo **Goldoni**, among them the sprightly and engaging *La Diavolessa* **(The She-Devil)**.

Ganne, Louis (1862–1923) (loo ee GAHN) French composer of military marches, ballets, and ca. twenty operettas, of which the best known is the vivacious *Les saltimbanques* (The Acrobats) (1899) (leh: sahl ta*n* BAH*N*K), about an abandoned child, Suzanne, who is taken into a circus and treated brutally by the circus manager. She runs away with several other members of the troupe. Eventually, she is recognized as the long lost daughter of an aristocrat, and they are reunited.

García, Manuel (1775–1832) (mah NWEHL gahr SEE ah) Spanish tenor, teacher of **bel canto**, composer of songs and operas, and founder of a notable musical family of singers, composers, and teachers; created roles for **Rossini**, including Count Almaviva in *Il barbiere di Siviglia* (written for him). In 1825, he premiered Italian operas in New York: Rossini's *Il barbiere di Siviglia*, *La Cenerentola*, and *Otello* (his most famous role); and Mozart's *Don Giovanni*, in which he sang the transposed title role. With him in the company were his second wife, Joaquina (1780–1854) (hwah KEE nah) (sop.); son Manuel (1805–1906) (bar.); and daughter Maria Felicia Malibran (1808–1836) (mezz.). All four performed in *Don Giovanni*, with **Da Ponte** himself in the audience. Maria Malibran was one of the most famous and acclaimed opera singers of her day. She had an amazing range, and aside from singing Desdemona and Cenerentola, her roles included the title roles in Bellini's *Norma* and Rossini's *Semiramide*.

Garrick Gaieties, The Intimate Broadway musical revues that played at the Garrick Theatre on West 35th Street. *The Garrick Gaieties of 1925* had seven songs by Richard **Rodgers** and Lorenz **Hart** (launching their careers), as well as songs by other writers, satirical sketches of topical interest by a team of humorists, and a linking book by young actors of the Theatre Guild company, which produced the show. The first of the series, it was originally intended for only two fund-raising perf. for the Theatre Guild, but it proved so popular that its run was continued and it lasted for 211 perf. Done by the same creative team, *The Garrick Gaieties of 1926* was mounted for 174 perf., and a show combining music and sketches from both productions began touring in late 1926. There was also a *Garrick Gaieties of 1930*, with songs by the **Gershwin** brothers, Marc **Blitzstein**, Johnny **Mercer**, E. Y. **Harburg**, and Vernon **Duke** (but none by Rodgers and Hart).

Gassmann, Florian Leopold (1729–1774) (GAHS MAHN) Bohemian opera director and composer of sacred music, ballets, and ca. twenty serious and comic operas, many to libretti by **Goldoni** and **Metastasio**; his career was spent at the Hapsburg court in Vienna, where he taught music; Antonio **Salieri** was one of his students. There is a delightful recording of his lively comic opera *Die junge Gräfin* (The Young Countess) (1770) (dee Y*OO*N geh G*R*EH fih:n) [Italian title: *La Contessina* (lah ko:n tehs SEE nah)], with a libretto by Goldoni, revised by librettist

Marco Coltellini (1719–1777) (ko:l tehl LEE nee) and translated into German by composer and writer on music Johann Adam Hiller (1728–1804); Bayer Records (BR 100 252/3; 1995).

gaucho drama (GOW cho:) [Fr. South American Spanish: cowboy] Argentinean and Uruguayan folk melodrama, with stories about noble-minded outlaws of aristocratic origin, based on the model of Robin Hood. The form originated in the early 19th c.; these musical plays include dances and songs accompanied on guitars.

Gaveaux, Pierre (1761–1825) (pee EH:*R* gah VO:) French opera tenor; outstanding **opéra comique** composer and music publisher; among his operas is *Léonore; ou L'amour conjugal* (Leonora, or Conjugal Love) (lé' o NO:*R* oo lah moo*r*' ko:*n* zhü GAHL) (1798), the original inspiration for Beethoven's ***Fidelio***; Gaveaux himself created the role of Florestan in his opera. Aside from his many opéras comiques, he also composed in the genre of the **fait historique**.

gavotte (gah VOT) *n*. [Fr. *gavot* (gah VO:): the name for an inhabitant of the Pays de Gap (peh:ee' duh GAHP), where the dance supposedly had its origins in 14th-c. peasant dances] A formal, stately, 18th-c. French dance in 4/4 time, very popular at court balls, along with the **minuet**. It is used in ballet, opera, and operetta, e.g., in act 2 of Gilbert and Sullivan's *The Gondoliers*, "I am a courtier grave and serious": "Now a gavotte perform sedately / Offer your hand with conscious pride."

Gay Divorce Broadway musical by Cole **Porter** (music and lyrics); book by Dwight Taylor (1902–1987) [son of famed actress Laurette Taylor (1884–1946)]; Ethel Barrymore Theatre, 1932 (248 perf.). The show was renamed for the 1934 film version, *The Gay Divorcee*, which was much different from the stage show, even though it had a screenplay by Taylor. Only the hit standard "Night and Day" was retained from Porter's score. The movie starred Fred Astaire, reprising what turned out to be his last Broadway role. He and Ginger Rogers (1911–1995) played leading roles together for the first time.

Mimi Bratt wants a divorce, so she and her lawyers arrange for her to be caught at a seaside resort hotel in flagrante with a professional, paid co-respondent, Tonetti. In love with Mimi, Guy Holden (played by Astaire) follows her to the hotel, where he is mistaken for Tonetti. The resulting complications are all resolved; Mimi gets her divorce, and Guy gets Mimi.

Gay, John (1685–1732) English writer and theater manager, best known for ***The Beggar's Opera*** and its lesser known sequel, ***Polly*** (1728). He also wrote the libretto for Handel's ***Acis and Galatea***.

Gelbart, Larry (1928-2009) American playwright; known for his television writing, Broadway comedies and screenplays; wrote books for several musicals, notably ***A Funny Thing Happened on the Way to the Forum***.

Genée, Richard (1823–1895) (REE *kh*ah*r*t zheh NÉ) [b. Franz Friedrich Richard Genée] German librettist, noted conductor, and composer of more than thirty now forgotten operettas, for which he often wrote his own libretti or collaborated with

Friedrich **Zell**, e.g., on Johann Strauss's *Eine Nacht in Venedig*; translated works by **Offenbach**, **Lecocq**, and **Sullivan**; co-wrote libretto for *Die Fledermaus*, and helped **Strauss** compose the music; co-wrote libretto with Zell for Millöcker's *Der Bettelstudent* and for several operettas by von **Suppé**, including *Boccaccio*. He usually wrote the lyrics, while his collaborators wrote the dialogue, after they had worked together on the construction of the libretto.

Generalprobe (gehn' eh: R*AHL* P*R*O: buh) *n.* [German: general rehearsal; called in French a *générale* (zhé né R*AHL*), and, in France, also applied to an invited dress rehearsal of a play] The final, usually invited dress rehearsal of a production in a German opera house. Guests of the singers and management, some critics, and perhaps school groups may be invited to what would be the first preview performance in an American theater.

Gentlemen Prefer Blondes Broadway musical by Jule **Styne**; lyrics by screen and stage lyricist Leo Robin (1900–1984); book by Joseph **Fields** and Anita Loos (1888–1981), based on her hilarious 1925 novel of the same name; Ziegfeld Theater, 1949 (740 perf.); Broadway revival: Lyceum Theatre, 1995 (40 perf.); film, 1953, with the story and time period altered.

It's the Roaring '20s. The gold-digging, blonde flapper Lorelei Lee—"Just a little girl from Little Rock"—and her friend, brunette Dorothy Shaw, embark on an ocean liner bound for Europe with all expenses paid by Lee's sugar daddy, the button manufacturer Gus Esmond. While at sea, Lorelei falls in love with a diamond tiara owned by a wealthy English lady, Mrs. Henry Spofford; so she proceeds, very indiscreetly, to try to seduce the rather stuffy Mr. Spofford. They finally arrive in Paris, where the intrigues continue and lawyers get involved. The two young beauties secure jobs performing in a cabaret; and Gus, still in love with Lorelei in spite of everything, forgives her indiscretions, so it's not going to be "Bye, Bye, Baby." It seems, nevertheless, that "Diamonds Are a Girl's Best Friend."

George M! Broadway musical about the life of George M. **Cohan**.

George White's Scandals A series of Broadway revues that rivaled the *Ziegfeld Follies*; produced by George White (1890–1968) [b. George Weitz], who also performed in the shows, wrote lyrics and sketches, and hired composers, among them George **Gershwin**. There were three Hollywood **backstage musical** films with the same title (1934, 1935, both produced and directed by White; 1945, produced by White), using material from the shows. The thirteen stage revues were produced in the years 1919–1928, 1931, 1932, 1936 and 1939 at the Liberty, Globe, and other theaters. Aside from the first revue, the most notable in the series were those of 1922, which included music by George Gershwin and lyrics by B. G. **De Sylva**, including the hit number "I'll Build a Stairway to Paradise"; 1926 (424 perf.), in which Gershwin's *Rhapsody in Blue* and the song "St. Louis Blues" by W. C. Handy were interpolated; 1931 (202 perf.), with Ethel Merman, production numbers in the Ziegfeld manner, and songs by Lew Brown (1883–1958) and Ray Henderson (1896–1970), including "Life Is Just a Bowl of Cherries."

German, Sir Edward (1862–1936) English operetta composer; considered the successor to Sir Arthur **Sullivan**, although he never quite lived up to the promise; completed Sullivan's *The Emerald Isle* (1901), with a libretto by Basil **Hood**, after the composer's death; composed *Tom Jones*, **Merrie England**, and several other pieces for the musical stage, among them *A Princess of Kensington* (1903), with a libretto by Hood and *Fallen Fairies* (1909), with a libretto by Sir W. S. **Gilbert**.

Gershwin, George (1898–1937) American composer. He wrote orchestral pieces, among them *Rhapsody in Blue* (1924) and *American in Paris* (1928), and dozens of stage and screen musicals; known for his innovative use of jazz and blues; composed "Swanee," made famous by Al Jolson in 1919; wrote songs for *George White's Scandals*. With his brother Ira, he wrote the Broadway musicals *Lady, Be Good!*, *Tip-Toes*, *Oh, Kay!*, *Funny Face* (1927; film, 1957), *Strike Up the Band*, *Girl Crazy*, and *Of Thee I Sing*, among others; they also wrote the opera *Porgy and Bess* together, in collaboration with DuBose Heyward.

Gershwin, Ira (1896–1983) Noted American stage and film lyricist. Aside from his numerous collaborations with his brother George, Ira wrote songs with Vernon **Duke** for the *Ziegfeld Follies*; his first Broadway show, *Two Little Girls in Blue* (1921), with a score by Vincent **Youmans**; and *Lady in the Dark*, with Kurt **Weill**; as well as collaborating on several projects with Harold **Arlen** and Jerome **Kern**.

Ghislanzoni, Antonio (1824–1893) (gih:s' lahn DZO: nee) Italian opera librettist and baritone, best known for his libretto to Verdi's *Aida*. When he lost his singing voice, he turned to writing as a career, and wrote libretti for **Catalani**, **Gomes**, and **Ponchielli**, among many others.

Ghosts of Versailles, The Opera by John **Corigliano**.

Giacosa, Giuseppe (1847–1906) (dgoo ZEH peh dgah KO: zah) Italian professor of drama, librettist, and **verismo** playwright; co-author with Luigi **Illica** of libretti for Puccini's *Tosca*, *Madama Butterfly*, and *La bohème*.

Gigi Broadway musical by **Lerner and Loewe**: composer Frederick Loewe and lyricist-librettist Alan Jay Lerner; based on their 1958 film of the same name, adapted from *Gigi* (1944) (zhee ZHEE), a novella by French writer Colette (1873–1954); Uris Theatre, 1973 (103 perf.); many regional and school productions.

In Paris, during the Belle Époque, Gaston is bored with the high living and devil-may-care attitude of his bon vivant uncle Honoré. He prefers the company of Gigi, a tomboy and the granddaughter of the wealthy Madame Alvarez, a retired demi-mondaine and Honoré's former mistress. The wayward Gigi is being brought up by her aunt Alicia to be a courtesan, and Gaston toys with the idea of making her his mistress, but, since he really loves her, he decides to marry her instead.

gigue (ZHEEG) *n.* A popular early 18th-c. French dance, with folk origins, in 6/8 or 1/8 time; later used also in ballets with pastoral settings; similar to an Irish **jig**.

Gilbert, Sir William Schwenck (1836–1911) English lawyer, dramatist, humorist, librettist, and stage director; known for his caustic wit and acerbic barbs; most famous for the Gilbert and Sullivan comic operas; published several collections of *Bab Ballads* (1868; 1872; 1876; 1882; 1890; 1898)—"Bab" was his nickname as a baby—satiric light verse, which he illustrated himself; originally published in *Fun* magazine, beginning in 1861; some of the poems form the basis for certain of the G & S operas; the later editions included lyrics from them.

See also BALLAD OPERA; BRIGANDS, LES; CARR, FRANK OSMOND; CELLIER, ALFRED; CLAY, FREDERICK; GERMAN, EDWARD; GROSSMITH, GEORGE; REED, THOMAS GERMAN.

Gilbert and Sullivan 1. Sir William S. Gilbert and Sir Arthur S. **Sullivan**, the team that composed famous comic operas. **2.** [Short for *Gilbert and Sullivan comic opera*] The comic operas of Sir W. S. Gilbert, who wrote the libretti and directed the productions, and composer, Sir Arthur S. Sullivan; produced by Richard D'Oyly Carte (1844–1901): a musical theater phenomenon that took the Anglophone world by storm in the latter part of the Victorian era. Although there are still professional productions from time to time, Gilbert & Sullivan is now largely the preserve of American and British amateur companies. Also called *G & S*.

The fourteen Gilbert and Sullivan comic operas:

1871 *Thespis, or the Gods Grown Old*
1875 ***Trial by Jury***
1877 (revised, 1884) *The Sorcerer*
1878 ***H.M.S. Pinafore, or The Lass That Loved A Sailor***
1879 ***The Pirates of Penzance, or The Slave of Duty***
1881 ***Patience, or Bunthorne's Bride***
1882 ***Iolanthe, or The Peer and the Peri***
1884 *Princess Ida, or Castle Adamant*
1885 ***The Mikado, or The Town of Titipu***
1887 ***Ruddigore, or The Witch's Curse***
1888 ***The Yeomen of the Guard, or The Merryman and His Maid***
1889 *The Gondoliers, or The King of Barataria*
1893 ***Utopia Limited, or The Flowers of Progress***
1896 *The Grand Duke, or The Statutory Duel*

See also COPYRIGHT PERFORMANCE; PATTER; SAVOYARD; SAVOY OPERAS.

Gilbertian (gihl BUHRT ee uhn) *adj.* Pertaining to the topsy-turvy, paradoxical, whimsical wit exemplified in the G & S comic operas and other works of Sir W. S. Gilbert.

Gille, Philippe (1831–1901) (fee leep' ZHIH:L) French playwright and librettist; wrote six libretti for Jacques Offenbach, including *Le docteur Ox* (Doctor Ox) (1877) (luh dok tuh*r'* O:KS), based loosely on a novel by Jules Verne (1828–1905); five libretti for Léo **Délibes**, including *Lakmé*; and the text for Jules Massenet's *Manon* (with Henri **Meilhac**).

Giménez, Jerónimo (1854–1923) (heh RO: nee mo: hee MEH nehs) Spanish conductor and composer; studied in Paris and Rome; composed more than 100 zarzuelas, many in one act; also collaborated with Amadeo **Vives** on ca. twelve zarzuelas. His most famous work is *La tempranica* (The Woman Who Gets Up Early) (1900) (lah tehm PRAH nee kah).

Ginastera, Alberto (1916–1983) (ahl BEHR to: hee' nah STEH rah) Argentine composer of instrumental work, two ballets, and four operas: *Don Rodrigo* (1964); *Bomarzo* (1967) (bo: MAHR so:); *Beatrix Cenci* (1971) (beh: ah TREEKS CHEHN chee), commissioned for the opening of the Kennedy Center in Washington, DC; and the unfinished *Barabbas* (1977). As a defender of civil liberties, he was twice exiled from Argentina by the Perón government, but he returned to assume various preeminent academic posts.

Gioconda, La (The Joyful Woman) (lah dgo: KO:N dah) Opera in four acts by Amilcare **Ponchielli**; libretto by Arrigo **Boito** under the penname "Tobia Gorrio," based on the drama *Angélo, tyran de Padoue* (Angelo, Tyrant of Padua) (1835) (ah*n* zheh: LO: tee *r*ah*n*' duh pah DOO) by Victor **Hugo**; Milan, Teatro alla Scala, 1876.

In late Renaissance Venice, Enzo Grimaldo (EHN dzo: gree MAHL do:) (ten.), a Genoese nobleman, is in love with the Venetian lady Laura (LOW rah) (mezz.), wife of Alvise Badoero (ahl VEE zeh: bah' do: EH: ro:) (bass). Enzo plans to elope with her. The street singer La Gioconda (sop.) is in love with him, but overcomes her jealousy because of Laura's goodness to Gioconda's blind mother (contr.), and helps Enzo and Laura escape. Instead of giving herself to the Inquisition spy Barnaba (BAHR nah bah) (bar.), in return for his help, as she had promised, Gioconda commits suicide.

Giordani, Tommaso (1730–1806) (to:m MAH zo: dgo:r DAH nee) Italian composer of some twenty-five operas. He emigrated from Naples to Ireland, and also worked in London, where he composed operas, as he did in Dublin, to libretti in English. The entire Giordani family, except the composer, were singers, and formed their own opera company, which performed in Dublin in 1764. The following year, Giordani composed a version of *The Maid of the Mill*.

Giordano, Umberto (1867–1948) (oom BEHR to: dgo:r DAH no:) Italian **verismo** opera composer, whose works include the often revived *Fedora* and *Andrea Chénier*.

Girl Crazy Broadway musical by George **Gershwin**; lyrics by Ira Gershwin; book by Guy **Bolton** and John McGowan (1894–1977); Alvin Theatre, 1930 (72 perf.); Broadway revival: Shubert Theatre, 1992, with many alterations, renamed *Crazy for You* (1622 perf.); filmed three times: 1932; 1943; 1966 (completely altered and retitled *When the Boys Meet the Girls*). The show made stars of Ginger Rogers and Ethel Merman, making her Broadway debut.

To keep his playboy son, Danny Churchill, out of mischief, his father sends him from New York City to Custerville, a remote Arizona desert town where there are no gambling dens or nightclubs, and, most importantly, no loose women—in fact, hardly any women at all. Danny arrives in a NYC cab, having been driven the entire distance by Gieber Goldfarb. It doesn't take Danny long to turn the whole town into a dude ranch and to fall in love with the postmistress, Molly Gray (played by Ginger Rogers). Gieber has the time of his life, talks to the Indians in Yiddish, and runs for sheriff. Everybody just has a grand old time! And so does the audience, listening to all those hilarious jokes and marvelous hit songs, including "I Got Rhythm" and "Embraceable You."

The Girl in Pink Tights Broadway musical by Sigmund **Romberg**. See BLACK CROOK, THE.

Giroflé, Girofla (zhee *r*o: FLÉ zhee *r*o: FLAH) Operetta in three acts by Charles **Lecocq**; libretto by writing team Albert **Vanloo** and Eugène Leterrier; Brussels, Théâtre des Fantaisies-Parisiennes, 1874.

An excellent CD recording of this brilliantly silly operetta, complete with the hilarious dialogue, is available from Gaité Lyrique (201842 MU744; 1991).

Don Boléro d'Alcarazas (do*n* bo: lé *R*O: dahl kah *r*ah ZAHS) (light bar.), governor of a North African Spanish coastal province, and his wife, Aurore (o *R*O:*R*) (mezz.), have identical twin daughters (both sop.; usually played by one singer) who are both engaged to be married on the same day: Giroflé to Marasquin (mah *r*ah SKA*N*) (ten.), the son of a wealthy banker to whom Don Boléro is heavily in debt; and Girofla to the irascible Mourzouk (moo*r* ZOOK) (bar.), chief of a Moorish tribe that has been a threat to the province's security. Marasquin duly shows up, but Mourzouk sends word that he will not arrive until the next day, because he has an awful toothache; so Giroflé, her parents, and Marasquin set off for the church, leaving Girofla at home in case Mourzouk should appear after all. Soon after their departure, the dreaded pirates who are the scourge of the region invade the house and kidnap Girofla and the butler, Pedro (ten.). Don Boléro begs Admiral Matamoros (mah tah mo: *R*O:S) (silent, mostly offstage role) to rescue Girofla before Mourzouk arrives. But it is too late! Mourzouk shows up early, with trumpet fanfares and his entourage! Aurore persuades Giroflé to masquerade as Girofla, and another wedding takes place. She is now married to both Marasquin and Mourzouk! The endless problems that result are finally resolved when the door bursts open and a beaming Matamoros enters with Girofla! He has beaten the pirates, rescued the girl, and saved the day!

Giulio Cesare in Egitto (Julius Caesar in Egypt) Opera by George Frideric **Handel**.

Glass, Philip (b. 1937) American composer with several operas to his credit, including *Akhnaten* (1983), *Einstein on the Beach* (1976), and *Satyagraha* (1980); known for his neo-baroque themes, simple and repetitive, which can be lulling and hypnotic, with repeated, rippling arpeggios; but the repetition is actually quite complex and the cumulative effect is riveting.

glee *n.* A part-song for three or more voices, secular in nature; e.g., those used for **barbershop quartet** singing.

Glinka, Mikhail (1804–1857) (mee KHAYL GLIHN kah) Russian composer; his operas include *Zhizn za tsarya (A Life for the Tsar)* and *Ruslan i Lyudmila* (Ruslan and Lyudmila) (1842) (ROOS lahn ee lyood MEE lah), based on Pushkin's poem. He was a pioneer in Russian nationalist music, using such Russian instruments as the balalaika, and incorporating themes from folk music into his compositions.

glissade (glee SAHD) *n.* [Fr. French n., feminine gender: slide; slip] In dance, a kind of traveling step in the form of a smooth slide or glide in any direction.

glissando (glee SAHN do:) *n.* [Italian: sliding] A series of ascending or descending notes that are to be played or sung smoothly in succession, as a kind of slide. In vocal music, a kind of **coloratura** passage, consisting of a legato vocal slide that includes all the notes through which the voice passes when going from one note to a higher or lower one.

Gluck, Christoph Willibald, Ritter von (1714–1787) (KHRIH:S to:f VIHL ih bahlt' RIH tuh fuhn GLOOK) German composer, whose superb sense of melody and deeply felt musical characterizations influenced the operatic composition not only of his contemporaries, but also of the romantic **bel canto** composers. Among his more than forty operas are *Alceste*, *Armide*, *Iphigénie en Aulide (Iphigenia in Aulis)*, *Iphigénie en Tauride (Iphigenia in Tauris)*, and *Orfeo ed Euridice (Orpheus and Eurydice)*.

Godard, Benjamin (1849–1895) (go: DAHR) French composer, violist, professor at the Paris Conservatoire; wrote eight operas; now remembered for the "Berceuse" (Lullaby) (behr SOOZ) from his opera *Jocelyn* (1888) (zho suh LAN).

god light The shaded lamp on a conductor's music stand that shines on the score and allows the conductor to be seen by the orchestra.

Godspell Off-Broadway musical by Stephen **Schwartz**; book by American dramatist and director John-Michael Tebelak (1948–1985), who also directed; Cherry Lane Theatre, 1971 (2118 perf.); Broadway transfer: Broadhurst Theatre, 1976 (527 perf.); frequent summer stock and school productions; film, 1973. The title is an archaic spelling of the word "gospel," and the show, which tells the story of Jesus's life, is based on the *Gospel According to St. Matthew*. It is free-spirited and lends itself to innovative staging, and the score is bright and engaging.

Goetze, Walter Wilhelm (1883–1961) (GÖT seh) German composer of musical revues and ten very popular Berlin operettas, of which the most famous is the tuneful, lively *Adrienne* (1926), about the French actress Adrienne Lecouvreur, also the subject of the **verismo** opera by **Cilea**; wonderful 1956 recording on CD by Membran Music (23708; 2007), with highlights from Goetze's *Liebe im Dreiklang* (Love in Three Notes) (1950) (LEE beh ihm DRI KLAHNG).

Golden Age of Operetta, The [In German, *die Goldene Operettenzeit* (dee GO:L deh neh o: peh REHT tehn TSIT)] The name frequently given to the heyday of

Viennese operetta, from roughly the 1860s, beginning with the work of von **Suppé**, through about 1899, the year Johann **Strauss** died. The following years saw the birth of the **transatlantic operetta**, and the work of **Abraham**, **Fall**, Oscar **Straus**, **Stolz**, **Lehár** and **Kálmán**—often called the "Silver Age."

Goldmark family Karl Goldmark (1830–1915) (KAH[*R*]L GO:LT mah[*r*]k) Hungarian composer. The son of a Jewish cantor, Goldmark's interest in music began in childhood. He was raised in Austria and spent most of his life in Vienna, where he became a friend of Johannes Brahms (1833–1897) and was a staunch supporter of the music of Richard **Wagner**. Of his six operas, the only one still performed is *Die Königin von Saba (The Queen of Sheba)*. His brother, **Leo Goldmark**, was a librettist who emigrated to the U.S., where, among other works, he wrote the book to the musical *1776*. Leo's son, **Rubin Goldmark (1872–1936)**, born in New York, was a noted American musician, pianist, composer, and teacher of composition at the Juilliard School. He studied composition with Antonín Dvořák. Among Goldmark's students were George **Gershwin** and Aaron **Copland**.

Goldoni, Carlo (1707–1793) (KAHR lo: go:l DO: nee) Prolific Venetian playwright and librettist; known for his cleverly plotted plays in *commedia dell'arte* style. [Italian: comedy of art (kom MEH: dee ah dehl AHR teh:)] It was he who coined the term, to distinguish his scripted comedies from the *commedia dell'improviso* [Italian: comedy of improvisation (kom MEH: dee ah dehl ihm pro: VEE zo:)], the improvisational pieces performed by commedia troupes. Goldoni wrote many comic operas with Baldassare **Galuppi**, from whom his name is inseparable, and with Florian Leopold **Gassmann**.

See also DIAVOLESSA, LA (THE SHE-DEVIL).

Gomes, Carlos (1836–1896) (KAHR los GOO mehs) Wonderful Brazilian composer; son of a band leader who began his son's musical training, which included learning to play various instruments. Gomes spent most of his life in Italy. While sometimes using Brazilian musical themes, particularly in early works, his operas are composed after Italian models, esp. those of **Verdi**, whom he admired. Of his three operettas and nine operas, one of his two greatest successes was *Salvator Rosa*; the music displays great melodic and orchestral originality. His other great triumph is *Il Guarany*, and *Fosca* is equally rewarding. Even more splendid in its heartfelt passion is *O escravo*.

Goodwin, J. Cheever (1850–1912) [Joseph] American actor and writer, born in Boston; considered the first American to make a successful career as a librettist; author of more than a dozen shows, including *Evangeline, or The Belle of Arcadia* and *Wang*; translator of the libretto for *1776*, retitled *The Daughter of the Revolution*.

gopak (GO: pahk) *n.* A strenuous, energetic Ukrainian dance in 2/4 time; used in some Russian ballets.

gorgheggio (go:r GEH dgoh:) n. [Italian: throaty warbling] A coloratura embellishment consisting of a rapid, warbling oscillation between higher and lower notes, sung in a sort of yodeling fashion; very popular in opera from the late 17th through the mid-19th centuries.

gospel music African-American religious music, comprising spirituals, hymns and the like, sung by both individual soloists and choirs, or both together, either during church services or in concerts. Paul Robeson (1898–1976), one of the greatest bass singers of the 20th century, included superb spirituals and gospel hymns among his many, diverse recordings.

Gossec, François-Joseph (1734–1829) (go SEHK) Influential Netherlands-born Walloon French composer; friend of **Gluck**; wrote ca. twenty operas; director of the singing school at the Opéra in Paris; ardent supporter of the French Revolution, for which he composed the highly popular musical **divertissment** *Le triomphe de la République* (The Triumph of the Republic) (1793) (luh t*r*ee O*N*F duh lah *r*é pü BLEEK), combining ballet, folk dances such as the **polonaise**, sung recitative, and song, with full orchestral accompaniment. There is a complete recording of this stirring, fascinating, and very beautiful piece on Chandos CD (CHAN 0727; 2006).

Götterdämmerung The fourth and last opera of Richard Wagner's **Ring Cycle**.

Gounod, Charles (1818–1893) (SHAH*R*L goo NO:) [Charles-François Gounod] French composer of two symphonies, chamber music, opera and sacred music, including his famous *Ave Maria* (1859); conductor, choral director; student of Fromental **Halévy**; wrote a dozen operas, including *Mireille* (five acts, 1864; revised to two acts, 1889) (mee *R*EH:YUH), with a libretto by Michel **Carré**, based on the epic poem, *Mireiou* (1859) (mee *R*EH: yoo) by the Provençal poet Frédéric Mistral (1830–1914) (f*r*é dé *r*ih:k' mih: ST*R*AHL). The opera takes place in 19th-c. Arles, and concerns the love of Vincent (va*n* SAH*N*) (ten.) and Mireille (sop.), which her father Ramon (*r*ah MO:*N*) (bass) opposes, preferring Vincent's rival, Ourrias (oo *r*ee AHS) (bar.); in the 1864 version, Mireille dies, but in the revised version, Vincent and Mireille are happily united at the end. Two of Gounod's operas are repertory standards: *Faust* and *Roméo et Juliette* (1867) (*r*o: mé O: eh: zhü LYEHT), both with libretti by Jules **Barbier** and Michel **Carré**, the latter work based on the play by **Shakespeare**. Toward the end of his life, Gounod wrote his fascinating *Mémoires d'un artiste* (Memories/Memoirs of an Artist) (Calmann Lévy, 1896; posthumously published) (mé MWAH*R* duh nah*r* TEEST).

Goyescas (goy EHS kahs) Opera in three scenes (one act) by Enrique **Granados**, using music scored from his 1911 piano suite inspired by the paintings of Francisco José de Goya y Lucientes (1746–1828) (frahn SEES ko: ho: SÉ theh: GO: yah ee loo SYEHN teh:s); libretto by Fernando Pèriquet Zuaznábar (1873–1940)) (fehr NAHN do: pehr ee KEHT soo ahs' NAH bahr); composed, 1915; premiere, New York, Metropolitan Opera, 1916.

In Madrid, ca. 1800, the renowned bullfighter Paquiro (pah KEE ro:) (bar.) welcomes the arrival of his fiancée, Pepa (PEH: pah) (sop.). Paquiro invites Rosario (ro SAH ree o:) (sop.) to a dance at the local tavern that evening. Rosario's fiancé, Fernando (ten.) also arrives, and says he will accompany her himself. Meanwhile, Pepa is jealous of the attentions being paid to Rosario by Paquiro. At the dance, Paquiro and Fernando quarrel, and agree to fight a duel. In Rosario's garden, Fernando swears his eternal love for her. He goes to fight the duel, in which he is fatally stabbed, and dies in her arms.

Graf von Luxemburg, Der (The Count of Luxembourg) (deh[r] GRAHF fuhn LOOK sehm BOO[R]K) Operetta in three acts by Franz **Lehár**; libretto by A. M. **Willner**, Leo **Stein**, and Robert Bodanzky (1879–1923) (bo: DAHN tskee); Vienna, Theater an der Wien, 1909; adapted for the London stage in 1911, and performed at Daly's Theatre (240 perf.), with lyrics and libretto by Adrian **Ross** and Basil **Hood**; opened on Broadway at the New Amsterdam Theater in 1912 (120 perf.), with lyrics by Ross and Hood and a new libretto by Glen **MacDonough**.

Having run through a fortune while living a Bohemian life in Paris, René, Count of Luxembourg (ten.), readily agrees to a scheme proposed by the Russian Prince Basil Basilovitch (BA zihl ba ZIH:L o vih:ch) (ten.): He will pay René a lot of money to marry a street singer with whom the Prince is in love. She will become Countess of Luxembourg, and René must vow to divorce her within a few months, so that the Prince can marry her, which he cannot do while she remains a commoner. The marriage with Angèle Didier (ahn ZHEHL dih: DYEH:) (sop.) is duly conducted in the atelier of René's friend, the artist Brissard (bree SAHR) (bar.), without the identity of either being revealed to the other, but from the touch of their hands when they exchange rings through a hole in a canvas on Brissard's easel, they fall in love. Several months later, Angèle gives a grand party, and René and Brissard are among the guests. René and Angèle are immediately attracted to each other. Much discomfited by this, and to prevent things from going further, Prince Basil announces his forthcoming marriage to Angèle. Brissard reveals that she is already married, since René has yet to fulfill his vow to divorce her. Although she is secretly delighted, Angèle has her pride, and she expresses her contempt for marriages undertaken only for money. Because of her attitude, René refuses to have anything more to do with her. Prince Basil is commanded by the Czar to marry Princess Stasa Kokozoff (STAH zah KO: ko: zo:f) (mezz.), so he releases René from his vow to divorce Angèle. Meanwhile, René has come into some property, and he pays Prince Basil back all the money he had received. Unable to bear being parted from Angèle any longer, René tells her that he truly loves her, and she is overjoyed, because she has loved him all along.

Gräfin Mariza (Countess Mariza) (GREH fih:n MAH rih: tsah') Operetta in three acts by Emmerich **Kálmán**; libretto by Julius **Brammer** and Alfred **Grünwald**; Vienna, Theater an der Wien, 1924; Broadway: Shubert Theatre, 1926 (321 perf.), book and lyrics adapted by Harry B. **Smith**.

There is a superb 1972 recording on CD (EMI Classics: 7243 5 65974 2; 1996).

Countess Mariza (sop.) arrives at her Hungarian country estate to give a banquet celebrating her engagement to Baron Koloman Zsupán (KO lo: mahn TSHOO pahn), whom she has invented, borrowing the last name of the boorish pig farmer from Strauss's *Zigeunerbaron*. She simply wants to discourage any suitors. She and the bailiff, Bela Török (BEH: lah TÖ rök) (ten.), are attracted to each other. He is really Count Tassilo Endrödy-Wittemburg (TAH shee lo: EHN drö dee VIH: telım BEH[R]K), forced to take a job under an assumed name because his family has lost its fortune. His main object is to save enough money for a dowry for his sister, Lisa (LEE zah) (sop.). A real Baron Koloman Zsupán (bar.) shows up with his friend, Prince Popolescu (PO: po: lehs' koo) (ten.), who knows Mariza and how eccentric she can be. The Baron was as surprised by the announcement of the engagement as Mariza is to learn that such a person really exists. Also surprised is Lisa, one of the guests, to see her brother acting as bailiff and butler. She had had no idea what he was up to, but she agrees not to reveal his identity. Tassilo behaves insolently, and Mariza fires him. But since she has fallen in love with him, she rehires him. Eventually, with the true state of affairs revealed, Tassilo and Mariza are united, and Lisa marries Zsupán.

Granados, Enrique (1867–1916) (ehn REE keh: grah NAH do:s) Spanish composer known for his piano and orchestral works; wrote ca. ten pieces for the musical theater, including recently rediscovered Catalan operas; his greatest theatrical triumph was *Goyescas*.

Grand Hotel Broadway musical, music and lyrics by Robert Wright and George Forrest, with extra songs by Maury **Yeston** and Wally Harper; book by Luther Davis (1916–2008), based on the novel, *Menschen im Hotel* (People in the Hotel) (1929) (MEHN shuhn ihm ho: TEHL) by Austrian-born American writer Vicki Baum (1888–1960); 1989 (1077 perf.). The show was directed and choreographed by award-winning actor-singer-dancer-choreographer-director Tommy Tune (b. 1939). Set in Berlin in 1928, the musical follows the stories of a number of people of different social classes.

grand jeté (grahn zheh TÉ) [French: great leap; lit., thrown] In dance and ballet, a spectacular leap up, with both legs thrown at a ninety-degree angle to the hips; preceded by a preparatory step, e.g., a **glissade**. Used in ballet and musical comedy dancing.

grand opera The great 19th-c. French spectacle operas, such as those by **Meyerbeer**, produced at the Paris Opéra: the lavish, grandiose productions, usually in five acts, included obligatory lengthy ballets and huge choruses.

Grande-Duchesse de Gérolstein, La (The Grand Duchess of Gerolstein) (lah grahnd dü shehs' duh zhé ro:l SHTIN) **Opéra bouffe** in three acts by Jacques **Offenbach**; libretto by Henri **Meilhac** and Ludovic **Halévy**; Paris, Théâtre des Variétés, 1867.

The immense success of this satirical, anti-militarist piece, mounted during the Paris Exposition, was due in part to the star for whom it was written, Hortense Schneider. Every crowned head in Europe came to see it, and, so it is rumored, to have his turn with her in her dressing room, which was maliciously nicknamed *le passage des Princes* (Prince's Alley) (luh pah SAHZH deh: PRANS).

The capricious Grand Duchess (sop.) of Gérolstein is attracted to Private Fritz (ten.), who, unknown to Her Highness, is engaged to Wanda (sop.), on whom General Boum (BOOM) (bar.) has his roving eye. The Grand Duchess promotes Fritz to the rank of General, much to the fury of Boum and the Court Chamberlain, Puck (bar.), who has been trying to promote her marriage to Prince Paul (ten.). The Grand Duchess gives Fritz hint after obvious hint that she would love to love him, but they go right over his head. Then she discovers that he loves Wanda! On his wedding night, they will murder him... but, no! The Grand Duchess changes her mind when she is attracted to Baron Grog (bar.), the foreign envoy sent to plead the case for Prince Paul. As long as Grog stays at court, she will marry Paul! And she will allow the others to play a practical joke on Fritz, which they do. The Grand Duchess restores Boum to his generalship, while Fritz and Wanda are reunited. Even the Grand Duchess is reconciled to her lot, although she has learned that Grog is married and will be returning home. "If you can't have what you want, you had better want what you have!" says she.

See also SAVOY OPERAS.

grapevine *n.* A dance **combination** often used in choreographing musical comedies and operettas, e.g., seen frequently in **Gilbert and Sullivan**. The grapevine is basically a traveling step, consisting of stepping to the right on the right foot, crossing the left foot in front of the right, stepping to the right on the right foot, crossing the left foot in back of the right foot, stepping to the right on the right foot again, and repeating the combination as many times as necessary, traveling across the stage while doing so. The combination may be repeated to the opposite side, starting off on the left foot, and done to either side, going back and forth, or simply traveling in one direction.

Graun, Carl Heinrich (1702/3–1771) (GROWN) Prolific German opera composer, whose brothers were also noted musicians; wrote three dozen operas, six of them to libretti by Pietro **Metastasio**, also set by other composers, among them *Artaserse*. Most of his operas were written to libretti by Leopoldo de **Villati**. Graun spent much of his life in Berlin, where he was **Kapellmeister** of the Berlin Opera under King Frederick II (1712–1786), known as Frederick the Great, of Prussia. Frederick wrote several libretti for him, including that for *Montezuma* (1755), based on Voltaire's play *Alzire, ou Les Américains* (Alzira, or The Americans) (1736) (ahl ZEER oo leh: zah mé ree KAN), also the basis for Verdi's *Alzira*. Highlights from *Montezuma* are available on a Decca CD (448 977-2; 1996) with Joan Sutherland; included are excerpts from *Griselda* by **Bononcini**.

Grease Broadway musical by Jim Jacobs (b. 1942) and Warren Casey (1935–1988), with additional songs, used in the subsequent film version and several major stage revivals, by Barry Gibb of the **Bee Gees**, John Farrar (see **Xanadu**), and conductor, arranger, and composer Louis St. Louis; started in Chicago as an amateur production; opened Off-Broadway (128 perf.) and transferred to Broadway, Eden (1972) then Broadhurst Theater (3400 perf.); Broadway revivals: Eugene O'Neill

Theatre, 1994 (1503 perf.); Brooks Atkinson Theatre, 2007 (585 perf.); national tours and hundreds of school productions; film, 1978.

In Chicago in the 1950s, at Rydell High School, the "greasers" hold sway. Cool, hip Danny Zuko is enamored of Sandy Dumbrowski, a virtuous square, instead of falling for Betty Rizzo or one of the other street-savvy Pink Ladies. Lots of peer pressure is applied, and when Sandy learns to be more streetwise and cool, she is accepted by the gang, and by Danny.

Great Waltz, The Spectacular Broadway biographical **extravaganza** about the life of Johann **Strauss II**; music by Johann Strauss and Johann Strauss II; lyrics by English lyricist and screenwriter Desmond Carter (1895–1939); book by Moss **Hart**, based on the libretto for the biographical **pastiche** (def. 2) operetta *Walzer aus Wien* (Waltzes from Vienna) (1930) (VAHL tsuh ows VEEN) by Dr. Alfred Maria **Willner**, Ernst Marischka, and Heinz **Reichert** (the trio that wrote the libretto to the pastiche operetta on which *Blossom Time* was based), as translated for the London stage production, *Waltzes from Vienna* (1931), by Desmond Carter and Caswell Garth; 1934 (298 perf.); not to be confused with the 1938 MGM film of the same name, which is also a biopic about the Strauss family, but has nothing to do with the Broadway musical script: Oscar **Hammerstein** wrote lyrics for the film. The show, directed by Hassard Short, concerns the jealousy of the father for the son, who triumphs at Vienna's Dommayer's Gardens, with the father finally applauding his son's success.

Green, Johnny (1908–1989) American film and stage composer, conductor, and orchestrator; did arrangements for the stage show *By Jupiter* and the film versions of *West Side Story* and *Oliver!*

Grétry, André-Ernest-Modeste (1741–1813) (ahn dré' ehr nehst mo dehst' gré TREE) Belgian Walloon French composer whose career was spent in Paris; composed ca. seventy operas. His first great success was the **comédie-ballet** "mêlée de chants et de danses" (mixed with songs and dances) (meh lé duh SHAHN eh: duh DAHNS) in four acts, *Zémire et Azor* (1771) (zé MEER eh: ah ZO:R), a version of the *Beauty and the Beast* story in which Prince Azor (ten.) has been transformed into the Beast and Zémire (sop.) redeems him from enchantment; the libretto is by the French writer and librettist Jean-François Marmontel (1723–1799) (zhahn frahn swah' mahr mo:n TEHL), who wrote several other libretti for Grétry, and also did texts for **Rameau**. While the piece has a certain ingratiating charm, it lacks real drama, and the word that comes to mind in describing it is "decorous." On the other hand, *Pierre le Grand* (Peter the Great) (1790) (pee eh:r luh GRAHN) is very delightful and musically engaging. The subject is Tsar Peter's incognito work in the shipyards in Holland, as in Lortzing's *Zar und Zimmermann*; the libretto, in four acts, is by Jean-Nicolas Bouilly, based on Voltaire's history of Russia. The piece was banned briefly during the French Revolution because of its sympathetic portrait of the tsar. It is available on a DVD from ArtHaus Musik (101 097; 2002). An excellent 1978 recording of the lively, tuneful three-act **opéra comique** *Richard Coeur de Lion* (Richard the

Lion-Heart) (1784) (*ree* SAH*R* kuh*r* duh lee O*N*) is available from EMI (5 75266 2; 2002); also included on the CD is *Le devin du village* by **Rousseau**.

See also GUILLAUME TELL.

Grey Gardens Broadway musical by Scott Frankel; lyrics by Michael Korie; book by Doug Wright, based on the 1975 documentary film of the same name; Walter Kerr Theatre, 2008 (341 perf.).

This unlikely story for a musical was movingly played in a tour de force by the virtuosic Christine Ebersole (b. 1953) as Mrs. Beale in act 1—with Erin Davie in her Broadway debut as Edie—and Edie in act 2, with the brilliant Mary Louise Wilson (b. 1932) as Mrs. Beale in act 2. The score is engaging, with exciting pastiches of 1940s songs in act 1 and appropriately contemporary, eerie, dissonant touches in act 2.

In 1941, at Grey Gardens, a Long Island mansion inhabited by Jacqueline Kennedy Onassis's (1929–1994) aunt, Edith Ewing Bouvier Beale (1895–1977), and her family, Mrs. Beale is all set to announce the engagement of her daughter Edie (1917–2002) to Joe Kennedy, Jr. (1915–1944). Mrs. Beale is planning to sing some of her favorite songs at the engagement party, but when her husband telephones to announce that he is going to Mexico to get a divorce, the party breaks up and the engagement is off. Act 2 takes place thirty years later, and Mrs. Beale is still living in the mansion with her now middle-aged daughter. They argue about the past, and Edie is still trying to get away from Grey Gardens, but we know she never will.

Grossmith, George (1847–1912) English comedian, actor, singer, writer, composer; wrote eighteen comic operas, including *Haste to the Wedding* (1891), libretto by W. S. **Gilbert**; almost 100 musical sketches, and more than 600 comic songs and piano pieces, as well as three books, including the very amusing comic novel, *Diary of a Nobody* (1892), in collaboration with his brother, the actor and author Weedon Grossmith (1854–1919). George Grossmith is best known for having created the patter-song roles in most of the original **Gilbert and Sullivan** productions, from John Wellington Wells in *The Sorcerer* through Jack Point in *The Yeomen of the Guard*. His performing career spanned four decades, and included innumerable solo appearances in which he performed his own material. He wrote two fascinating memoirs: *A Society Clown: Reminiscences* (1888), and *Piano and I: Further Reminiscences* (1910), important for anyone interested in the history of the Victorian musical theater. His son, George Grossmith, Jr. (1874–1935), was an actor, songwriter, and producer of Edwardian musicals.

grotesque dance; grotesque dancing *Hist.* Originating in Italy in the 18th c., and soon becoming popular on the English stage, this was a form of entertainment that combined **ballet** steps with athletic prowess; hence, *grotesque dancer*: one who performed this sort of dance. Dances of this genre were done as discreet entertainments, like evenings at the ballet, and influenced the use of dance as part of a musical theater piece, e.g., in the physical acting out in dance of emotion, passion, and character.

group *n.* **1.** A series of notes that form a coherent phrase. **2.** A number of musicians who sing and/or play instruments together, e.g., a **band**, a **barbershop quartet**, or a singing group.

group audition Casting session in which several performers try out at the same time. Dance and chorus auditions are often group auditions; the choreographer will teach the dancers a **combination**, which they then do for the casting personnel.

growl *n.* In **jazz**, a distorted low, rough, rumbling sound, played on a bass; even more distorted when amplified.

Grünwald, Alfred (1884–1951) (GRÜN vahlt) Austrian-born American writer, journalist, dramatist, and librettist of some forty operettas; with Julius **Brammer**, he co-wrote the books for Fall's *Die Kaiserin*, Kálmán's *Gräfin Mariza* and *Die Herzogin von Chicago*, among others, as well as libretti for Oscar **Straus**, Paul **Abraham**, Robert **Stolz**, and Franz **Lehár**. Because he was Jewish, he emigrated with his family to the United States in 1940, during World War II, and worked for the U.S. army. From 1988 to 1990, he was U.S. ambassador to Austria. His papers are in the Billy Rose Theatre Division of the New York Public Library.
See also BOHÈME, LA.

gruppetto (groo PEHT toh) *n.* [Italian: little group] An ornamentation or embellishment in a vocal line consisting of a group of three notes, two of which are subordinate to the main note; very popular from the late 17th through the 19th centuries.

Guarany, Il (The Guarani) (eel GWAH rah nee') [A Brazilian Indian nation] Opera in four acts by Carlos **Gomes**; libretto by Antonio Scalvini (1820–1890) (skahl VEE nee) and Italian librettist and impresario Carlo d'Ormeville (1840–1924) (do:r muh VEEL); Milan, Teatro alla Scala, 1870.
This magnificent opera takes place in Brazil in 1560, and involves a complicated love story set against the background of the conflicts between the Portuguese and the Indians.

Guettel, Adam (b. 1964) Broadway musical composer; among his works are *The Light in the Piazza* and *Floyd Collins*; grandson of Richard Rodgers.

Guillaume Tell (William Tell) (gee YO:M TEHL) **1.** Opera—*drame mis en musique* (drama set [lit. put into] to music) (DRAHM mee zahn mü ZEEK)—by André-Ernest-Modeste **Grétry**; libretto, based on the life of the legendary Swiss resistance hero, by Michel-Jean Sedaine (1719–1797) (mee shehl zhahn' suh DEHN), playwright and author of some two dozen libretti for major French composers; Paris, Comédie-Italienne (Salle Favart) (ko mé dee' ih: tah LYEHN sahl fah VAHR), 1791.
2. Opera in four acts by Gioachino **Rossini**; libretto by Victor-Joseph Étienne de **Jouy**; revised by anti-monarchist dramatist Hyppolite-Louis-Florent Bis (1759–1855) (ee po LEET loo ee' flo: rahn BEES) and his fellow republican, journalist, one-time mayor of Paris, and legislator Armand Marrast (1801–1852)

141

(ah*r* mah*n*' mah *R*AH), based on Friedrich Schiller's romantic drama, *Wilhelm Tell* (1804), based on the legend; translated into an Italian version as *Guglielmo Tell* (*goo* [*G*]LYEHL mo: TEHL); Paris Opéra, 1829.

In 1307, Switzerland is occupied by the Austrians and governed by the ruthless Gessler (GEHS luh) (bar.). The Swiss resistance movement is led by William Tell (bar.) and supported by Melcthal (MEHLK tahl) (bass), whose son Arnold (ten.) loves the Austrian princess Mathilde (mah TIH:LD). Melcthal dies, and Arnold joins the resistance to honor his father's memory. In the square of the village of Altdorf, Gessler demands that the populace bow down before his hat, placed on a spear for all to see. Tell defies him. Gessler commands Tell to shoot an apple off his son's head. Jemmy (zheh MEE) (sop.) stands bravely while his father takes aim and succeeds in shooting an arrow clean through the apple without harming his son. He declares that he had reserved an arrow for Gessler in case of failure, whereupon he is arrested and taken to the fortress of Küssnacht (KÜS NAKHT) in the middle of Lake Lucerne. Arnold organizes an uprising, and Mathilde make sure Jemmy is safe, together with his mother Hedwig (mezz.). Tell is freed, and when his boat reaches shore, he assassinates Gessler. The overthrow of the Austrian occupiers is assured.

Guys and Dolls One of the great classic Broadway musicals; music by Frank **Loesser**; book by Abe **Burrows**, based on characters and several stories by New York writer Damon Runyon (1880–1946); 46th Street Theatre, 1950 (1200 perf.); numerous revivals, including the Broadway revivals at the Martin Beck Theatre, 1992 (1143 perf.) and the Nederlander Theatre, 2009 (121 perf.); film, 1955. The original production was directed by George S. **Kaufman** and choreographed by Michael Kidd (1915–2007).

The perpetually broke Nathan Detroit runs a popular crap game, but he is always having problems finding a location for it because the police keep closing the game down. His girlfriend, Adelaide, a nightclub singer, wants him to reform and to marry her already! Their relationship is contrasted with that of "Sky" Masterson, a handsome gambler, and Sarah Brown, a Salvation Army girl. Sarah and her father run the Save-a-Soul Mission. Seeing his opportunity to raise money to rent a place for the crap game, Nathan bets Sky that he can't seduce Sarah into going with him to Havana. He takes the bet and wins it, but he doesn't want to collect the money because he has fallen in love with Sarah. In the end, after several complications are resolved, Nathan finally marries Adelaide, and Sky marries Sarah.

See also BELLE OF NEW YORK, THE.

gypsy *n. Slang* Broadway musical comedy performer, esp. a member of the **chorus**. It is a time-honored custom to give the performer with the most Broadway credits temporary custody of the *gypsy robe* in order to ensure the success of a Broadway musical that is about to open. The robe, decorated with emblems from each show whose cast has contributed to it, is given away by its previous possessor during a backstage ceremony in the new production's theater.

Gypsy Broadway musical by Jule **Styne**; lyrics by Stephen **Sondheim**; book by Arthur **Laurents**, based very loosely on the autobiography of Gypsy Rose Lee (1914–1970); Broadway Theatre, 1959 (704 perf.); Broadway revivals: Winter Garden Theatre, 1974 (124 perf.); St. James Theatre, 1989 (499 perf.); Shubert Theatre, 2003 (488 perf.); St. James Theatre, 2008 (369 perf.); film, 1962. The original production, with dance music arranged by John **Kander**, was directed and choreographed by Jerome Robbins.

Rose, a real stage mother, pushes her daughters, June and Louise, to become **vaudeville** child stars, and goes on the road with them and a variety act. Vaudeville is dying, but Rose's boyfriend, Herbie, their manager, somehow gets them bookings. June elopes with one of the boys, Tulsa, and Rose pushes the untalented, reluctant Louise into burlesque; this disgusts Herbie, who leaves Rose. Louise eventually becomes the great striptease star Gypsy Rose Lee. Rose bitterly lashes out at Louise, whom she considers ungrateful, but the two women are reconciled in the end.

Gypsy Baron, The Operetta by Johann **Strauss**. See ZIGEUNERBARON, DER.

H

habanera (ah' bah NEH: rah) *n.* [Fr. Spanish: a woman native to or residing in Havana, Cuba] A Cuban dance and song form originating in Havana in the 19th c.; in slow 2/4 tempo, with the typical musical **figure** of a dotted eighth note followed by a sixteenth note and two more eighth notes to complete the measure; influenced the development of the Argentine **tango**; popular in Central America, Spain, and the rest of Europe. Georges **Bizet** wrote a famous habanera for the title character in act 1 of *Carmen*.

Hagen, Daron (b. 1961) American composer of orchestral works, chamber music, song cycles, choral works; among his eight operas is the absorbing *Shining Brow* (2006), in a prologue and two acts, libretto by Paul Muldoon (b. 1951), about architect Frank Lloyd Wright (1867–1959); recording on Naxos CD (8.669020-21; 2009). Hagen's style is eclectic, but basically tonal, using a blend of musical idioms.

Hague, Albert (1920–2001) [b. Albert Marcuse] German-born American television and stage composer. Obliged to escape the Nazis, since he was Jewish, he went first to Rome and then emigrated to the U.S., where he composed some half dozen Broadway musicals; of these, the most well known are *Plain and Fancy* and *Redhead* (1959), the latter with a book by Dorothy and Herbert **Fields**, Sidney Sheldon (1917–2007), and David Shaw (1916–2007), and lyrics by Dorothy Fields. This murder mystery musical was a vehicle for Gwen Verdon, who had been a sensation in *Damn Yankees*.

Hahn, Reynaldo (1874–1947) (*r*eh: NAHL do: AHN; HAHN) Venezuelan-born French conductor, singing teacher, writer, music critic; noted composer of many songs, including the much recorded "Si mes vers avaient des ailes" (If My Verses Had Wings) (see meh: VEH*R* ah veh: deh: ZEHL), which he wrote when he was only fourteen; several operas, and some dozen operettas, among them *Ciboulette*. Hahn was the first lover and then lifelong friend of writer Marcel Proust (1871–1921). He was raised as a Catholic, but since his father was Jewish, the Nazis banned his music and he was forced to flee south during the Second World War, where he remained in seclusion. After the war, he became director of the Paris Opéra. He published several books, including memoirs of his friend actress Sarah Bernhardt (1844–1923), *La grande Sarah* (lah g*r*ahnd' sah *R*AH) (Hachette, 1930); and his collected lectures on singing, *Du chant* (dü SHAH*N*) (On Singing; Gallimard, 1920), translated as *On Singers and Singing* (Amadeus Press, 2003).

See also SHAKESPEARE, WILLIAM.

Hair Psychedelic musical by Galt **MacDermot**; book and lyrics by Jerome Ragni (1935–1991) and James Rado (b. 1932), both of whom also performed in the show; premiered Off-Broadway in 1967 for a six-week limited engagement; opened on Broadway, Biltmore Theatre, 1968 (1750 perf.); Broadway revivals:

Biltmore Theatre, 1977 (43 perf.); Al Hirschfeld Theatre, 2009 (still running as of this writing); film, 1979.

The iconoclastic show, with a brilliant score, was known for its far out advocacy of flower power, the psychedelic drug culture, and anti-war activism, as well as for its onstage nudity and its advocacy of sexual freedom. It was superbly directed by Tom O'Horgan (1926–2009). Among its many memorable numbers is "Aquarius," about the dawning of a new age when peace and love will finally prevail.

The story concerns the anti-war hippie Claude (played by Rado), who is about to be drafted into the army to go fight in Vietnam. His pal Berger (played by Ragni) and the other members of his "tribe" urge him to burn his draft card. He is drafted nevertheless, and killed in action in Vietnam.

Hairspray Broadway musical by composer, arranger, lyricist, and performer Marc Shaiman (b. 1959) (music and lyrics) and director and lyricist Scott Wittman (b. 1955) (lyrics); book by Mark **O'Donnell** and Thomas **Meehan**, based on John Waters's 1990 film of the same name; Neil Simon Theatre, 2002 (2500 perf.); film, 2007, with a screenplay by O'Donnell and Meehan. The show is fantastic: lively and entertaining, with a wonderful sociocultural theme about emerging civil rights, set to energetic, engrossing music.

In Baltimore, in 1962, the plump teenager Tracy Turnblad has only one desire: to appear on local television on the Corney Collins dance show, a segregated program. The show sponsors a Miss Teenage Hairspray contest, which Tracy's overweight mother Edna, fearing that her daughter will be deeply hurt, reluctantly helps her to enter. Tracy has to learn how to dance better; noticing that some of the black students are a lot freer and more inventive at dancing than the white students, she asks for their help, which they give, although they are wary. Tracy then protests the exclusion of "Negroes" from the contest, which Amber Von Tussle, daughter of the snob Velma, is contriving to win. Eventually, Tracy and her black friends are allowed to dance on the show along with the white kids for the first time. Tracy wins the contest as well as the admiration of her new boyfriend, Link Larkin, the heartthrob teen who has all the girls at the high school (including Amber) at his feet.

See also RETURN ENGAGEMENT.

Halévy, Fromental (1799–1862) [Jacques-François-Fromental-Élie Halévy (zhahk' frahn swah' fro: mahn TAHL é lee' ah lé VEE)] French opera composer of ca. forty works, many of them grand operas for the Paris Opéra; studied with **Cherubini**. His only well known opera is *La Juive*, which for a century was one of the mainstays of the French repertoire worldwide.

Halka Opera by Stanisław **Moniuszko**.

Halle, Adam de la (1237?–1288) (ah dahn' duh lah HAHL) Medieval French composer; wrote the piece often considered the very first opera: the fascinating and lively *Le Jeu de Robin et Marion* (The Play of Robin and Marion) (1275) (luh zhuh duh ro BAN eh: mah ree O:N), a **light opera** about Robin Hood and Maid Marian; recorded on a Harmonia Mundi CD (ZZT 040602; 2003).

Hamlisch, Marvin (b. 1944) Prolific American film and stage composer, arranger, and pianist; composed the score for *A Chorus Line*; did vocal and/or dance arrangements for *Funny Girl* and many other shows; published an informative, entertaining autobiography, *The Way I Was* (Scribner, 1992).

Hammerstein II, Oscar (1895–1960) [Usually called Oscar Hammerstein] American book writer and lyricist; collaborated with Jerome **Kern**, Sigmund **Romberg**, Rudolf **Friml**, and Vincent **Youmans**; and with Richard **Rodgers** on **Rodgers and Hammerstein** musicals; son of influential German-born American opera impresario Oscar Hammerstein I (1847–1919).

Handel, George Frideric (1685–1759) [b. Georg Friedrich Händel] Influential, prolific, very great German-born English baroque composer whose vast output of instrumental music, operas and oratorios, some of which were meant to be staged, is still widely performed. His beloved *Messiah* (1742) is one of the most popular orato- rios ever written, done annually during the Christmas season. His forty-five operas include *Alcina*; *Ariodante* (1724); *Giulio Cesare in Egitto* (Julius Caesar in Egypt) (1724) (DGOO lyo: CHEH: zah reh: ihn eh: DGIH:T to:), about Caesar and Cleopa- tra [Usually called simply *Giulio Cesare*]; *Il pastor fido* (The Faithful Shepherd) (1712) (ih:l PAH sto:r FEE do:); *Radamisto* (1720); *Rinaldo* (1751); and *Rodelinda, regina dei Langobardi* (Rodelinda, Queen of the Langobards) (1725) (ro:' deh LIH:N dah reh DGEE nah deh:'ee LAHN go: BAHR dee). Handel also composed three masque operas: *Acis and Galatea*, *Semele* (1744), and *Hercules* (1749). And he wrote several pieces in the genre of the **pasticcio**, among them *Elpidia* (1725).

Handelian (han DEHL ee uhn) *adj.* Characteristic of the distinctive baroque musi- cal style of George Frideric Handel, with its graceful ornamentations, marvelous orchestral textures, and pure, fluid melodic line.

Hanson, Howard (1896–1981) Prolific, much honored American composer, acclaimed for his symphonic writing; wrote one opera, an engrossing if grim masterpiece that was produced to great acclaim at the Metropolitan Opera in 1934: *Merry Mount*; libretto by music critic Richard L. Stokes (1882–1957), based loosely on the story *The Maypole of Merry Mount* (1837) by Nathaniel Hawthorne (1804–1864), about the hypocrisy of the 17th-c. New England Puritans; superb CD recording on Naxos (8.669012-13; 1996).

Harbach, Otto (1873–1963) [b. Otto Abels Hauerbach] American playwright and lyricist; wrote ca. forty musicals with such composers as Jerome **Kern**, Rudolf **Friml**, Vincent **Youmans**, George **Gershwin**, and Sigmund **Romberg**; worked with Oscar **Hammerstein**, to whom he taught lyric writing, on Friml's *Rose-Marie* and Romberg's *The Desert Song* (1926); wrote the books for Karl Hoschna's *Madame Sherry* and Jerome Kern's *Roberta*, and co-wrote the book for Youmans's *No, No, Nanette*.

Harburg, E. Y. "Yip" (1896–1981) [b. Edward Yipsel Harburg] American lyricist; worked with many composers, including Burton **Lane** (*Finian's Rainbow*).

146

harmonic *adj.* **1.** Pertains to the theory and practice of the kind of music that works within a tonal system of key relationships: *harmonic music*. **2.** Pertains to an individual musical scale and/or chords used in that kind of music: *a harmonic scale*.

harmony *n.* **1.** The relationship of musical pitches to each other, whether individual notes heard in succession or notes sounded together as a consonant or dissonant chord. **2.** The texture of a musical composition: *two-part harmony*; *three-part harmony*. **3.** Unison; ensemble; e.g., singing *in harmony*, i.e., with all the vocal lines in consonance with and complementing each other, all in the same key.

Harnick, Sheldon (b. 1924) American writer and lyricist; wrote lyrics for *Fiddler on the Roof* and other shows with Jerry **Bock**, including *She Loves Me, Fiorello!* (1959), *Tenderloin* (1960), *The Apple Tree* (1966), and *The Rothschilds* (1970); and libretti for *Captain Jinks of the Horse Marines* (1975) and *Cyrano* (1990), with scores by Jack **Beeson**.
    See also BOCK AND HARNICK; CYRANO DE BERGERAC.

Harrigan, Edward American actor, composer, and lyricist. See BRAHAM, DAVID.

Hart, Lorenz (1895–1943) Prolific American lyricist and book writer; known for his fruitful collaboration with composer **Richard Rodgers**.
    See RODGERS AND HART.

Hasse, Johann Adolf (1699–1783) (HAHS seh) Prolific, influential German composer of more than sixty operas; friend of librettist Pietro **Metastasio**, many of whose libretti he set, including *Didone abbandonata*.

hat boi (HAHT BOY) [Vietnamese: sung drama] The traditional Vietnamese classical form of opera or sung drama, often with comic or satiric content; based originally on Chinese models; there are eight kinds, and there are six major categories of songs; e.g., *hat khach* (HAHT KHACH): [song of strangers], performed in scenes of joyous meetings; *hat nam* (HAHT NAHM) [southern song], a sort of sad ballad; *hat nieu* (HAHT NY*OO*), miscellaneous songs, including love songs, songs of sacrifice, and students' songs. Also called *hat bo* (HAHT BO:); *hat tuong* (HAHT TWO:NG) (sung play).

hat cheo (HAHT CHAY o:) [Vietnamese: sung satirical drama] A northern Vietnamese genre of musical play that includes dance and slapstick farce; a form of *hat boi*.

hayashi (hah YAH shee) *n.* [Japanese: wind and percussion ensemble] **1.** The wind and percussion instruments that serve to provide incidental music and accompaniment for plays and dances, including **noh** and **kabuki** theater. **2.** The traditional ensemble of three drums and a flute that accompanies noh and some kabuki perf. **3.** The instrumentalists who perform in these situations. Also called *hayashi kata* (KAH tah) [hayashi person].

Haydn, Franz Josef (1732–1809) Much loved, prolific Austrian classical composer of symphonies, chamber music, masses and other sacred music; oratorios, including *Die Schöpfung* (The Creation) (composed between 1796 and 1798) (dee SHÖP foong). Haydn wrote ca. twenty-five musical theater pieces in the genres of the **Singspiel** and **through-composed** opera, including *L'anima del filosofo/ Orfeo ed Euridice* and *L'infedeltà delusa (Deluded Unfaithfulness)*. A great friend and admirer of Mozart, "Papa" Haydn was also known for his genial, sunny disposition.

heavy metal An unsubtle, simplistic, incredibly loud kind of **rock** music, relying on heavy amplification of electric and electronic guitars and other instruments; frequently characterized by lyrics full of bigotry, including misogyny; sometimes used in contemporary musical comedies, e.g., elements of the musical aspects (not the contents of the lyrics) of *Rent*.

Hedwig and the Angry Inch Off-Broadway cult **rock musical** by Stephen Trask; book and lyrics by John Cameron Mitchell (b. 1963), who also starred in the title role; Jane Street Theatre, 1998 (857 perf.); film, 2001, directed, written by, and starring Mitchell.

Hedwig, born Hansel in East Berlin, marries an American soldier and has a sex change operation to make the marriage official, but the doctors make a mess of it, leaving Hedwig with an inch of undetermined fleshy material for his/her genitals. The soldier leaves her, and she sings rock music to make a living.

Heldentenor (HEHL dehn teh NO:[R]) *n.* [German: hero-tenor] Heroic tenor; i.e., one who sings such leading dramatic roles as Tristan in Richard Wagner's *Tristan und Isolde*, which require extraordinary lung power and the ability to sustain a difficult vocal assignment.

Hello Again Off-Broadway musical by Michael John **LaChiusa**; book by the composer, suggested by the play *La Ronde* (1900) [German title: *Reigen* (Round Dance) (RI gehn)] by Austrian writer and dramatist Arthur Schnitzler (1862–1931) (SHNIHTS luh); limited Lincoln Center engagement, 1993 (65 perf.).

The varied, delicate, yet pointed score of this quiet, effective musical sets off the story of a series of ten sexual encounters in which one of the partners in the previous episode appears as a partner in the next one. Beginning in 1900, each episode takes place in a succeeding decade.

Hello, Dolly! Broadway musical by Jerry **Herman**; book by Michael **Stewart**, based on the comedy, *The Matchmaker* (1955) by distinguished playwright Thornton Wilder (1879–1975); 1964 (2844 perf.); Broadway revivals: 1975 (45 perf.), starring Pearl Bailey; 1978 (152 perf.), starring Carol Channing; 1995 (127 perf.), starring Carol Channing; film, 1969, starring Barbra Streisand. In the long-running original production, Channing (b. 1921) was replaced by a series of stars including Ginger Rogers and Ethel Merman. In 1967, the show's producer, David Merrick, remounted the show, which had been starting to lose business, with an all African-American cast led by Pearl Bailey (1918–1990).

It's the 1890s Belle Époque. Wealthy Yonkers merchant Horace Vandergelder hires a matchmaker, the widow Mrs. Dolly Levi, to find him a wife, unaware that she herself wants to marry him. Horace had been thinking of marrying the rich milliner Irene Molloy, so Dolly matches her up with Vandergelder's store clerk, Cornelius Hackl. Along with Horace's niece, Ermengarde, who is in love with the artist, Ambrose Kemper, they all meet in New York City at the Harmonia Gardens, which features dancing and singing. There are many plot complications, but Horace eventually proposes marriage to Dolly, and she accepts. All the right couples end up together at the end of this vibrant, vivacious musical, one of Jerry Herman's best.

Henze, Hans Werner (b. 1926) (HAHNTS VEH nuh HEHN tsuh) Innovative German composer of symphonies, concertos, chamber music, incidental music for the theater, ca. fourteen ballets, including *Undine* (1958), and ca. thirteen operas. Among his best known operas are *Boulevard Solitude* (1952); *Der Prinz von Homburg* (The Prince of Homburg) (1960) (deh PRIHNTS fuhn HOM boo[r]k); *Elegy for Young Lovers* (1961), with a libretto by W. H. **Auden** and Chester Kallman; and *Der junge Lord* (The Young Lord) (1963) (deh Y*OO*NG eh LO:[*R*]T). Attracted to all the art and music that the Nazis considered degenerate, Henze suffered psychologically under the regime, even more so because he was gay. He was drafted in 1944, serving in Poland. After the war, he completed his musical education and wrote pieces that reflect his horror of militarism and fascism. His music is gorgeous, and eclectic in style, relying heavily on twelve-tone techniques.

Herbert, Victor (1859–1924) [b. Victor August Herbert] Irish-born, German-raised and educated, exceptionally gifted, prolific American composer of instrumental, choral, and musical theater works; distinguished symphony orchestra conductor (Director of the 22nd Regimental Band of the New York National Guard, 1893–1900; conductor of the Pittsburgh Symphony, 1898–1904; founded the Victor Herbert Orchestra, 1904); teacher at the National Conservatory of Music in New York City; noted cellist. When his German wife, the opera singer, Therese Förster (1861–1927) (teh *R*EH: zeh FÖ[*r*'] stuh), was hired to sing at the Metropolitan Opera, he decided to emigrate to the U.S., and played cello in the Met orchestra. He had previously been a member of several European orchestras, including the **Strauss** Orchestra in Vienna. Herbert wrote two operas, forty-three operettas, and numerous songs, and is one of the fathers of the American musical theater. He was also an activist interested in musicians' and composers' rights, and in 1914 was one of the founders of the American Society of Composers, Authors and Publishers (ASCAP). Herbert's first operetta was *Prince Ananias* (1894). His operettas include *Babes in Toyland*, *The Fortune Teller* (1898), *Cyrano de Bergerac*, *Mlle Modiste*, *Naughty Marietta*, *The Red Mill*, and *Sweethearts*. He also wrote numbers for the *Ziegfeld Follies*, and composed *Sally* in collaboration with Jerome **Kern**.

Herman, Jerry (b. 1931) Very popular, highly successful musical comedy composer and lyricist. His first show was an Off-Broadway musical revue, *I Feel Wonderful* (1954), and a decade later he had his first megahit, *Hello, Dolly!* In collaboration with critic and writer Marilyn Stasio, he wrote an autobiography, *Showtime: A Memoir* (Dutton, 1996).

Complete list of Jerry Herman's Broadway shows:
1960 *From A to Z* (musical revue; contributed one song)
1961 *Milk and Honey*
1964 *Hello, Dolly!*
1964 *Ben Franklin in Paris* (contributed two songs)
1966 **Mame**
1969 *Dear World*
1974 *Mack and Mabel*
1979 *The Grand Tour*
1980 *A Day in Hollywood/A Night in the Ukraine* (contributed two songs)
1983 **La Cage aux Folles**
1985 *Jerry's Girls* (retrospective revue)
2001 *Jerry Herman on Broadway* (retrospective revue)

Hérold, Ferdinand (1791–1833) (feh*r* dee nah*n*' eh *R*OLD) [b. Louis Joseph Ferdinand Hérold] French composer; studied composition with **Méhul** and **Salieri**; of his ca. two dozen opéras comiques, the most well known works are *Zampa*, esp. its overture; and *Le pré aux clercs* (The Monks' Meadow) (1832) (luh pré o: KLEH*R*), based on a story by Prosper Mérimée. His ballet, *La fille mal gardée* (The Poorly Watched Daughter) (1828) (lah FEE yuh mahl gahr DÉ), still holds the stage in various versions.

Hervé (1825–1892) (her VÉ)[b. Louis Auguste Joseph Florimond Ronger (loo ee' o: güst' zho: zehf flo: *r*ee MO*N* ro:*n* ZHEH:)] French musician, actor-singer, and composer of more than 100 operettas and opéras comiques, many of them in one act; one of the fathers of operetta. His brilliant melodic and rhythmic gifts are much in evidence in one of his masterpieces, **Mam'zelle Nitouche**. Among Hervé's other great works are the three-act opéra-bouffe *Chilpéric* [title role] (1868; revised, 1895) (sheel pé *R*IH:K), a burlesque of medieval France; and an **opéra bouffe** in four acts, *Le petit Faust* (The Little Faust) (1869) (luh puh tee FO:ST), a hilarious **parody** of the *Faust* legend and esp. of the opera by Gounod, produced ten years earlier; the libretto was co-written by Hector-Jonathan Crémieux, and the music sparkles and bounces. You can see excerpts from a recent production on YouTube. Hervé himself starred in the title roles in both pieces. His sense of humor and satire were outrageous, and his performances, as well as the works themselves, elicited roars of appreciative laughter in Paris and in London, where he also wrote for the English musical theater.

Herzogin von Chicago, Die (The Duchess of Chicago) (dee HEH[*R*] tso: gihn fuhn shih: KAH go:) Viennese **transatlantic operetta** by Emmerich **Kálmán**; libretto by Alfred **Grünwald** and Julius **Brammer**; Vienna, Theater an der Wien, 1928. The score uses the famous **Charleston** dance tune and is full of vivacious **jazz** textures.

Miss Mary Lloyd (sop.) of Chicago makes a bet with the members of the Eccentric Young Ladies Club that she can bring back from Europe the most expensive thing that any of them has ever beheld. Meanwhile, Crown Prince

Sándor Boris (ten.) of Sylvania agrees to marry Princess Rosemarie (sop.) of Morenia, but they do not love each other. Mary arrives in Budapest and meets Bondy (ten.), the Prince's aide-de-camp. She arranges with him to buy the royal palace, and she wants the prince that goes with it. They meet and fall in love. Bondy and Princess Rosemarie are also in love, and they elope. But when the prince reads a letter Mary has written to her father, it looks as if she is only buying him instead of loving him. So he dumps her, and decides he wants to marry Rosemarie after all. In Budapest on her way home, Mary meets an American producer who wants to make a movie about the romantic story of Mary and the prince, but not without a happy ending. So the prince and Mary get married, and do a **foxtrot** to seal the deal.

Heuberger, Richard (1850–1914) (HOY beh[r] guh) Austrian composer, music critic, choral conductor, music teacher; wrote five Viennese operettas, of which the most famous and successful was his first, *Der Opernball* (The Opera Ball) (1898) (deh O:P uh[r]n BAHL). He was the first composer to whom the libretto for *Die lustige Witwe (The Merry Widow)* was offered but, apparently, he had too many commitments to accept the job.

high kick In dance, a movement of one of the legs upward, from a standing position; the toe is usually pointed and the leg is stretched and, usually, lifted rapidly as high as possible; often, the legs are kicked up in alternation in a series. The high kick is used both by soloists and by lines of dancers in a chorus, a revue, or a musical comedy, e.g., in the **can-can**; in extravaganzas, such as the shows featuring the famous Rockettes, the corps of young lady dancers who kick in unison at the Radio City Music Hall in New York City; as well as in ballet sequences.

Highland fling A Scottish dance. See FLING.

hillbilly music The folk music of American mountain areas, e.g., the Appalachians, the Ozarks; consisting of simple instrumental compositions, whether for a combination of instruments (guitar and fiddle) or for an individual instrument; and simple songs, often with guitar accompaniment.

Hindemith, Paul (1895–1963) (POWL HIHN deh MIHT) German composer, violinist, music teacher; fell into disfavor with the Nazis for his so-called "degenerate art," and emigrated to the U.S. in 1940, returning to settle in Switzerland after the war; composed several operas, including *Cardillac* and *Mathis der Maler* (Mathis the Painter) (1933–1935) (MAH tees deh: MAH luh), to his own libretto in seven scenes, about the painter Matthias Grünewald (1470–1528) (mah TEE ahs GRÜ neh VAHLT) and the conflict between leading the life of an artist and political involvement; the opera is set at the time of the Peasants' War (1524–1525), an economic and religious uprising. In 1934, Hindemith had composed his *Mathis der Mahler Symphony*, which formed the basis of the opera's music.

hip hop A movement in music and dancing, originating in the 1960s in the African-American and Hispanic communities of New York City, partly as an outgrowth of

rap music. Hip hop numbers are characterized by a combination of song and recitation; complicated lyrics and rich, textured musical accompaniments, featuring the development of riffs. Beginning in the 1970s, hip hop was popular internationally as well as in the U.S. Hip hop is used wonderfully in the musical *In the Heights*.

See also BREAKDANCE; RIFF.

hira-gasy (HEE rah GAH see) *n.* [Malagasy: Malagasy song] Malagasy performers in Madagascar who do a popular form of short musical play, consisting of dialogue, dances, and songs which are either traditional moral narratives or songs adapted from French cabaret and music hall.

His Excellency Comic opera by W. S. **Gilbert** and Frank Osmond **Carr**.

Hit the Deck Broadway musical by Vincent **Youmans**; book by Herbert **Fields**, based on the play *Shore Leave* (1922) by Canadian writer Hubert Osborne (1881–1958); lyrics by Leo Robin (1900–1984), Clifford Gray (1887–1941), and Irving Caesar (1895–1996); Belasco Theatre, 1927 (352 perf.); three films: 1930, an adaptation of the stage show, with additional songs by Youmans; 1936, retitled *Follow the Fleet*, starring Ginger Rogers and Fred Astaire, with seven additional songs by Irving **Berlin**; 1955, with a different plot that includes an actress who wants a role in the stage production of *Hit the Deck*. Among the hit songs from this delightful and silly romp are "Hallelujah," "Sometimes I'm Happy," and "Join the Navy."

Loulou Martin runs a dockside coffeehouse in Newport, RI, and appears not to have a care in the world. She adores the sailor Bilge Smith and follows him all the way to China, where she presents him with his own ship, for which she has evidently saved her money for years. But he doesn't get it: Just how rich is she? Is she going to take care of him, or he of her? It looks as if they will break up, until she agrees to give all her money to their first child. Bilge is mollified, and they happily head to the chapel.

H.M.S. Pinafore, or The Lass That Loved A Sailor "An Entirely Original Comic Opera" in two acts by **Gilbert and Sullivan**; London, Opera Comique, 1879.

This was a megahit, with pirated productions proliferating so rapidly in America, in the days before copyright laws, that D'Oyly Carte decided to send an "official" production to New York, along with Gilbert and Sullivan themselves.

Captain Corcoran (bar.) of the H.M.S. Pinafore, at anchor in Portsmouth Road, has betrothed his only daughter, Josephine (sop.), to the First Lord of the Admiralty, Sir Joseph Porter (bar.), but she is in love with the sailor Ralph Rackstraw (ten.). Sir Joseph arrives, accompanied by his sisters, cousins, and aunts, led by his cousin Hebe (mezz.). He shows far more interest in the sailors, who all ought to dance hornpipes, according to him, than to his prospective bride. He finds Ralph particularly handsome, and the ugly sailor Dick Deadeye (bass) thoroughly repulsive. Ralph and Josephine decide to elope, but their plans are foiled by Deadeye, and Ralph is sent to what Sir Joseph, who is not up on his nautical terminology, calls the "dungeon." But now Little Buttercup (contr.), the bumboat woman who sells sundries to the sailors and is in love with the captain, reveals her guilty secret: the captain and Ralph were exchanged shortly after birth, since she accidentally switched them when she was nursemaid to both, so that the captain is really the lowborn one, and Ralph ought by now to be captain. There is therefore no obstacle to Josephine and Ralph being wed, since Sir Joseph certainly would not marry a lowly tar's daughter. Little Buttercup will no doubt wed the former captain, and Hebe promises to comfort Sir Joseph in his declining years—a prospect that does not appear to make him happy.

Hoffmann, E. T. A. (1776–1822) [Ernst Theodor Amadeus Hoffmann] (EH*R*NST TEH: o do:*r*' ah' mah DEH: *oo*s HO:F MAHN) German romantic fantasist writer, conductor, and composer whose short stories have provided material and inspiration for more than a dozen operas and ballets, including Offenbach's *Les contes d'Hoffmann* and *Le Roi Carotte*; Paul Hindemith's *Cardillac*; and Léo **Délibes'** 1870 ballet *Coppélia* (ko: pé' lee AH), which uses the stories "Der Sandmann" (The Sandman) (deh: ZAHNT mahn) and "Die Puppe" (The Doll) (dee *P*OO peh), also adapted for act 1 of *Les contes d'Hoffmann*. Aside from chamber music and other instrumental works, Hoffmann's fourteen operas include *Scherz, List, und Rache* (1801–1802; since lost), after Goethe, which was also set by Max **Bruch**; and an 1816 opera based on the legend of the sprite *Undine*. He also appears as a character in several pieces, most famously in Offenbach's opera.

Hofmannsthal, Hugo von (1874–1929) (HOO go: fuhn HOF mahns TAHL), Austrian poet, playwright, and librettist, best known for his collaboration over twenty-three years with Richard **Strauss**. The Strauss operas for which he wrote libretti are their first, *Elektra* (1909), *Der Rosenkavalier*, *Ariadne auf Naxos*, *Die Frau ohne Schatten*, *Arabella*, and *Die ägyptische Helena*. They had a good working relationship despite numerous artistic disagreements. Much of it was conducted in a voluminous correspondence which shows that Strauss helped shape the libretti to a great degree.

Hoiby, Lee (b. 1926) American pianist and composer of instrumental and vocal music, and ten operas, among them several one-act pieces, including the amusing musical monologue for mezz., *Bon Appétit!* (1989), libretto by Julia Child (1912–2004), based on her PBS-TV cooking show; recording on Albany Records CD (TROY 1028; 2008), which includes the one-act *This is the Rill Speaking* (2008). He also composed the full-length operas *The Tempest* (1986) and *Romeo and Juliet* (2004), based on the plays by **Shakespeare**. His best-known opera is *Summer and Smoke* (1971), with a libretto by distinguished playwright Lanford Wilson (b. 1937), based on the 1948 play by Tennessee Williams (1911–1983).

Hood, Basil (1864–1917) English librettist and (occasional) stage director; wrote texts for Sir Arthur Sullivan's *The Rose of Persia* (1899) and *The Emerald Isle* (1901), score completed by Edward **German**, for whom Hood wrote the libretti to *Merrie England* and *A Princess of Kensington* (1903). He adapted *Die lustige*

Witwe (The Merry Widow) and *Der Graf von Luxemburg (The Count of Luxembourg)* by Franz **Lehár**, *Ein Waltzertraum (A Waltz Dream)* by Oscar **Straus**, and *Die Dollarprinzessin (The Dollar Princess)* by Leo **Fall** for the English stage.

hoofer *n. Slang* A professional dancer, esp. a nightclub or Broadway musical dancer.

Hook, James (1746–1827) English piano teacher, organist, music director; composer of ca. fifty pieces for the musical theater, including many for the miniature stage of the Vauxhall pleasure garden; wrote many songs. Hook was a child prodigy who composed his first opera when he was eight. His greatest success was *The Fair Peruvian* (1786).

Horne, Lance (b. 1977) American singer, pianist, lyricist, and Emmy Award–winning composer of instrumental pieces, songs, classical rock, dance compositions, chamber works, and musical theater pieces, among them the vocal arrangements for the Broadway show *Little Women* (2005); the musical *Back in the Day* (2007), with lyricist and playwright Kate Rigg, with whom he also collaborated on *Pictures of Dorian Gray* (1999); *Rachel Said Sorry* (2009; book by Gina Gianfriddo), first presented for the 24 Hour Musicals; and *The Strip* (2010).

hot *adj.* Pertains to a particular kind of **jazz**, as opposed to **cool**; characterized by loud volume, compelling rhythms, and brilliant, virtuosic improvisation: *hot jazz*.

Hot Mikado, The Broadway musical adaptation of Gilbert and Sullivan's *The Mikado*; Broadhurst Theatre, 1939 (85 perf.); with an African-American cast including the tap-dance king, Bill "Bojangles" Robinson (1878–1949), in the title role; **swing** orchestrations of Sullivan's music by noted Broadway orchestrator Charles L. Cooke (1891–1958); directed by Hassard Short. Readapted as *Hot Mikado* in 1986 by director, choreographer, lyricist, and writer David H. Bell (book) and Rob Bowman (orchestrations), it ran briefly on Broadway and in the West End. There was also a version called *The Swing Mikado*, done in Chicago in 1938, which was so successful at the Chicago World's Fair of 1939 that it inspired the creation of *The Hot Mikado* under the auspices of Broadway producer Mike Todd (1909–1958).

How to Succeed in Business Without Really Trying Broadway musical by Frank **Loesser** and Abe **Burrows**.

Hugo, Victor (1802–1885) Towering, iconic romantic French novelist, poet, playwright, and political activist whose writings inspired more than sixty-five works for the musical theater, including Donizetti's *Lucrezia Borgia* (loo KREH: tsyah BO:R dgah)—both Hugo's play, *Lucrèce Borgia* (lü krehs bo:r ZHYAH), and the opera were written in 1833; Verdi's *Ernani* and *Rigoletto*; Ponchielli's *La Gioconda*; operas by **Balfe** (*The Armourer of Nantes*; 1836) and **Gomes** (*Maria Tudor*; 1879), based on Hugo's play, *Marie Tudor* (Mary Tudor) (1833) (mah ree tü DO:R); Broadway's *Les Misérables*; and the hit French-Canadian musical *Notre-Dame de Paris* (no truh DAHM duh pah REE) by French-Italian composer

Riccardo Cocciante (b. 1946) (ree KAHR do: ko: CHAHN teh:), with lyrics by French-Canadian Luc Plamondon (b. 1942) (lük' plah mo:*n* DO:*N*). First mounted in Paris in1998, it is based on IIugo's 1831 novel of the same name, the title of which is usually translated as *The Hunchback of Notre Dame*.

Humperdinck, Engelbert (1854–1921) (EHNG ehl beh[*r*]t HOOM peh[*r*] DIHNK) German composer, music critic, music editor, teacher; met **Wagner** in 1880, and helped at Bayreuth with preparations for *Parsifal*. Of his nine operas, the two best known are *Königskinder* (King's Children) (1910) (KÖ ni*kh*s KIHN duh); and his first, the beloved *Hänsel und Gretel* (Hansel and Gretel) (1893) (HEHN zuhl oont G*R*EH: tuhl).

Huszka, Jenö (1875–1960) (YEH nö HOOS kah) [Also called Eugen Huszka (OY gehn)] Hungarian violinist; lawyer and government official; composer of fourteen popular Budapest operettas, displaying his great romantic melodic gift; his tunes are reminiscent of lush Viennese waltzes, as well as of Hungarian folk music. All but one were written to libretti by playwright Ferenc Martos (1875–1938) (FEH rehnts MAHR tosh). A recording of delightful excerpts from several operettas, including two of his greatest hits, *Bob herceg* (Prince [lit. Duke] Bob) (1902) (BOB HEHR tsehg) and *Lili bárónö* (Baroness Lili) (1919) (LIH: lee BAH ro: nö), is available from Hungaroton (HCD 16807; 1996).

Hwang, David Henry (b. 1957) American playwright, known for his plays on Asian and Asian-American themes, e.g., his great success, *M. Butterfly* (1988), film, 1993; co-author of the book for Elton John's Broadway musical *Aida*; author of rewritten version of Rodgers and Hammerstein's *Flower Drum Song*.

hymn *n.* A sacred or religious song of praise to a deity; often one in several verses meant to be sung by a congregation during a service. Hymns are also used in musical theater pieces; e.g., the opening hymn to Venus in Offenbach's *La belle Hélène*, or some of the Druidic ceremonial music in Bellini's *Norma*.

I

Ibert, Jacques (1890–1962) (zhahk' ee BEH*R*) French composer; wrote seven operas, including two with the Swiss composer Arthur Honegger (1892–1955) (o: neh GEH*R*): *L'aiglon* (The Eaglet) (1937) (leh GLO:*N*), based on the play by Edmond Rostand, about Napoleon's son; and *Les petites cardinal* (The Little Cardinals) (1939) (leh: puh teet kah*r* dee NAHL). His most appreciated work is the farce *Angélique* (1927) (ah*n* zhé LEEK), in the genre of 19th-c. operetta.

I Can Get It for You Wholesale Broadway musical by Harold **Rome**; book by Jerome **Weidman**, based on his unsentimental, satirical novel and 1951 screenplay of the same name, about the garment industry in New York; Shubert Theatre, 1962 (300 perf.). Barbra Streisand made her memorable Broadway debut as the secretary, Miss Marmelstein.

Garment manufacturer Harry Bogen will do anything to get to the top, and when all his machinations lead only to his collapse, he has nobody left but his mother and his compassionate girlfriend, Ruthie, to stand by him.

I Do, I Do Broadway musical by Harvey **Schmidt**; book by Tom **Jones**, based on the play *The Fourposter* (1951) by Dutch-born American playwright Jan de Hartog (1914–2002); 46th Street Theatre, 1966 (560 perf.). The show, produced by David Merrick and directed by Gower Champion, starred Mary Martin (1913–1990) and Robert Preston (1918–1987).

This two-hander follows the story of a married couple, Agnes and Michael, from their wedding through their entire married lives and the raising of their children, until they finally sell their house and their old fourposter bed.

I'd Rather Be Right Broadway musical by **Rodgers and Hart**: Richard **Rodgers** (music) and Lorenz **Hart** (lyrics); book by George S. **Kaufman**, who also directed; Alvin Theatre, 1937 (290 perf.).

This satirical comedy starred George M. **Cohan**, returning to Broadway after an absence of a decade and performing for the first time in a show he had not written himself. Cohan played President Franklin D. Roosevelt (1882–1945), whom he loathed. He was not terribly fond of Rodgers or Hart either, and rehearsals were apparently not very enjoyable.

Roosevelt appears in a dream to a young couple, Phil Jones and Peggy Barker, who cannot get married until he balances the budget. In the dream, various well known figures of the time appear, and Roosevelt tries everything he can think of to solve the country's financial problems, but he just can't seem to manage the unruly Depression economy. He advises the couple to get married anyway: better times are sure to come.

I Love You, You're Perfect, Now Change Off-Broadway musical revue by pianist and musician Jimmy Roberts; lyrics and sketches by playwright Joseph "Joe" DiPietro (b. 1960); Westside Theatre (Upstairs), 1996 (5003 perf.; closed 2008);

many productions in summer, community, and dinner theaters; many international productions. In a series of vignettes, the show deals satirically with the nature of heterosexual relationships and marriage, with four actors portraying all the characters.

Illica, Luigi (1857–1919) (loo EE dgee IH:L lee kah) Prolific Italian poet and opera librettist; wrote ca. eighty libretti, including *La Wally* by **Catalani**, *Andrea Chénier* by **Giordano**; collaborated with Giuseppe **Giacosa** on Puccini's *Manon Lescaut* (also co-written by Giulio Ricordi [1840–1912] [DGOO lyo: ree KO:R dee] and others), *La bohème*, *Madama Butterfly*, and *Tosca*. He introduced the French practice of including extensive stage directions in Italian opera libretti.

I Married an Angel Broadway musical by **Rodgers and Hart**: Richard **Rodgers** (music) and Lorenz **Hart** (book and lyrics), with contributions by the show's director, Joshua Logan (see FANNY), based on the fantasy comedy *Angyalt vettem feleségül* (I Married an Angel) (1932) (AHN dyahlt VEHT tehm FEH lehsh é:' gül) by Hungarian playwright and screenwriter Vaszary János (1899–1963) (VAH sah ree YAH nosh) [János Vaszary]; Shubert Theatre, 1938 (338 perf.); film, 1942, starring Nelson Eddy and Jeannette MacDonald in their last movie together. The show was full of risqué jokes, which the film avoided, although the screenplay was by the usually irrepressible Anita Loos. Still remembered are the title song and "Spring Is Here."

The philandering Count Willie Palaffi, a Budapest banker, breaks off his engagement to the aggravating Anna. He is so annoyed that he swears he will only marry an angel, and, lo and behold, an angel named Angel descends from heaven. Willie falls in love and marries her; she loses her wings when they make love, but she remains as angelic and naïve as ever. Meanwhile, Willie's sister, Countess Peggy Palaffi, has taken Angel in hand, teaching her the ways of the world, since her honesty and lack of ability to dissemble have caused endless problems for Willie. Peggy also saves her brother's bank from financial disaster by making a deal with rival banker Harry Szigetti.

imbroglio (ihm BRO: [g]lyo:) *n.* [Italian: entanglement; involved, complicated situation. Fr. the name Broglio (BRO: [g]lyo:): the arcade running the length of the Doge's Palace in Venice, the scene of intrigues and plots; hence, lit., in the Broglio] **1.** A scene or musical number in an opera where the plot complications and entanglements are reflected in the music; e.g., the act 2 scene in Mozart's *Don Giovanni* where Leporello is mistaken for his master, and the various characters accost him and meet each other by chance. **2.** A complicated plot, or an involved situation that forms part of a plot, full of entanglements that must be sorted out.

impresario *n.* **1.** *Hist.* Originally, the manager or artistic director of an Italian opera company. **2.** A producer, esp. of great individual musical artist's tours, ballet, opera, or visiting foreign companies.

impressionism in music Deriving from the mid-19th c. French movement in the visual arts (an outgrowth of romanticism), this early 20th-c. movement in music was characterized by the experimental use of textures, harmonies, a free sense of modulation, and occasional dissonances, all however within the context of standard **harmonic** music, esp. as developed by such composers as **Berlioz** and **Wagner**. The composers wanted to provide an "impression" of events or phenomena, evoking a mood and creating an atmosphere, rather than a programmatic tone picture. In both the concert hall and the musical theater, Claude **Debussy** is the impressionist composer par excellence, e.g., in his opera *Pelléas et Mélisande*.

Im weissen Rössl (The White Horse Inn) (ihm VI suh *RÖ* sl) [Old spelling, still sometimes seen: *Im weissen Röβl*] Berlin operetta in three acts by Ralph **Benatzky**; lyrics by Robert Gilbert (1899–1978); libretto by writer Hans Mueller-Einigen (1882–1950) (MÜ luh I nih gehn) and Berlin theater director Erik Charell (1895–1974) (shah *R*EHL), based on the 1897 farce of the same name by German stage director Oscar Blumenthal (1852–1917) (BLOO mehn TAHL) and actor Gustav Kadelburg (1851–1925) (*G*OO stahf KAH dehl BOO[*R*]K); additional numbers by Robert **Stolz**, Bruno Granichstaedten (1879–1944) (GRAH ni*kh* SHTEH:D tuhn), and Viennese composer Hans von Frankowski (1888–1945) [b. Johann de Cruce Edler von Frankowski (YO: hahn deh K*R*OO tseh EH: dluh fuhn f*r*ahn KOF skee)]; Berlin, Grosses Schauspielhaus (G*R*O: sehs SHOW shpeel HOWS), 1930; filmed seven times, the latest in 1994, a film of a live Berlin production. Hugely acclaimed in Vienna, where it remains perennially popular, this joyous, sunny operetta was also successful on Broadway, opening at the Center Theatre in 1936 and running for 223 perf., starring Kitty Carlisle Hart (1910–2007) as Josefa [Josepha]; and in London's West End, where it opened in 1931 and ran at the London Coliseum for 651 perf.

In the Austrian Salzkammergut (ZAHLTS KAHM muh GOOT) region, life is good at the White Horse Inn in St. Wolfgang, located on the shore of the Wolfgangsee (VO:LF gahng ZEH:), with a dock for boats bringing guests to the inn. The headwaiter, Leopold Brandmayer (B*R*AHNT MI uh) (ten.), is in love with the inn's owner, Josefa Vogelhuber (yo: ZEH fah FO: guhl HOO buh) (sop.), but, while she thinks he is wonderful at his job, she also thinks he is just another typical gold-digger, so she rejects his advances. She is waiting for one of her regular guests, the lawyer Dr. Erwin Siedler (ZEET luh) (ten.), hoping that this year he will finally propose marriage to her. Siedler arrives, and the other guests include his client Sülzheimer's silly, self-important son, Sigismund Sülzheimer (ZEE gihs mo*o*nt ZÜLTS HI muh) (bass); Sülzheimer's business rival, Wilhelm Giesecke (GEE zeh keh) (speaking role); and Giesecke's daughter, Ottilie (o TEE lyuh) (sop.), with whom Siedler falls in love. Giesecke soon gets the idea of marrying Ottilie to Sigismund, which would end his financial problems and merge their businesses. But Ottilie requites Siedler's love and refuses to marry Sigismund, who, in any case, has fallen for Klärchen (KLEH[*R*] *kh*en) (sop.), accompanying her father, Professor Dr. Hinzelmann (HIHN tsehl MAHN) (speaking role), on a tour of the Salzkammergut region. Leopold is disgusted by all the carrying on and decides to quit, but Josefa has been taking a good hard look at him and has decided to accept his marriage proposal. They receive news that Emperor Franz

Josef (1830–1916) (speaking role) will arrive for a short visit and will be staying at the inn. Josefa, nearly prostrate with nervousness, begs Leopold to stay on at least for that, and he agrees. In a wonderful scene, the Emperor arrives and is greeted with rejoicing. He acts as a kind of deus ex machina and a father figure, and talks sense into everyone. All the right couples end up together.

At the Volksoper (FO:LKS O: puh), the operetta theater in Vienna where I saw this marvelous show ca. thirty years ago, the audience went wild when Franz Josef entered, nostalgic as they were for the pre-World War I days. He spoke with a very heavy Viennese accent, and in quiet, fatherly tones that delighted them even more. The music of this piece is jubilant, and the show plays beautifully. One of the funniest numbers is the song sung by Sigismund in the third person, "Was kann der Sigismund dafür, dass er so schön ist?" (vahs kahn deh[r] ZEE gihs moont dah FÜR dahs eh[r] zo: SHÖN IHST) (How can Sigismund help it, if he's so handsome?).

In the Heights Broadway musical by actor and Tony® Award–winning composer Lin-Manuel Miranda (b. 1980) (music and lyrics); book by award-winning playwright Quiara Alegria Hudes; Off-Broadway, 2007 (year-long run), transferred to Broadway, 2008 (still running at the Richard Rodgers Theatre as of this writing).

The compelling Latin rhythms and harmonic variations of the brilliant score for this show—the first by Hispanic-Americans to come to Broadway—about the Dominican-American community in Washington Heights perfectly and joyously tell the story of the struggles to rise above poverty and to deal with the emotions of love in this close-knit New York City neighborhood. **Hip hop**, **rap music**, **salsa**, **merengue** and **soul music** are the idioms used to create the atmosphere of the neighborhood and to characterize its inhabitants.

Usnavi (played by Lin-Manuel Miranda) owns a bodega in Washington Heights—he was named by his parents for the first ship they saw when they arrived in the U.S. from the Dominican Republic: what they saw was "US Navy." He has practically been raised by the neighborhood matriarch, Abuela Claudia, a second mother to him, and he is in love with Vanessa, but he lacks the courage to ask her out. He dreams of returning to the land where he was born, and of owning a beachfront bar. Vanessa, a beautician, also dreams of leaving the barrio and of moving downtown. Benny, the only African-American in the community, dreams of having his own car-wash business. He and Vanessa's friend, Nina are in love. Nina's over-protective father owns a car service company, and her mother, Camila, dreams of having her own restaurant. Abuela wins $96,000 in the lottery. By the end of the second act, we have seen the end of an era, and we know the neighborhood will continue to change, as it always has: the sign for Rosario's Car Service is gone, and we see the signs for the old Irish car service and the even older Jewish bakery that used to be there. Abuela dies, and Usnavi decides to remain in the neighborhood. He is home.

incidental music Background accompaniment, usually instrumental, for a stage drama.

Incoronazione di Poppea, L' (The Coronation of Poppea) (lih ko: ro: nah' tsee O: neh: dee po: PEH: ah) Opera in a prologue and three acts by Claudio **Monteverdi**, assisted by other, unknown composers; libretto by Gian Francesco Busenello, based on ancient Roman senator and historian Tacitus's (56–117) *Annals*; Venice, Teatro SS Giovanni e Paolo, 1643. This is one of the great masterpieces by the father of opera.

During the prologue, Fortune and Virtue argue which of them is the greatest, but Love maintains that the story they are about to see shows that he is greater than either. The Roman Emperor, Nero (sop.) [Nerone (neh RO: neh:)], has taken Poppea (sop.) as his mistress. Otho (mezz.) [Ottone (o TO: neh:)], a "most noble lord," is deeply distressed, for he loves her himself, and the Empress Octavia (sop.) [Ottavia (ot TAH vee ah)] is grief-stricken. Nero announces that he wishes to banish the Empress and marry Poppea. Seneca (bass), his former tutor, says that the Emperor has gone mad. Nero sentences him to death, and Seneca commits suicide. Otho, with the connivance of Octavia, plans to assassinate Nero and Poppea. He borrows clothing from Drusilla (sop.), who is in love with him, and enters Poppea's chamber, but the murder is prevented by the god Love. Drusilla and Otho are arrested, and banished, together with Octavia. Watched over by Love and his mother, Venus (sop.), Poppea is now crowned Empress of Rome.

Indes galantes, Les A **ballet-héroique** by Jean-Philippe **Rameau**.

Indian Queen, The Semi-opera by Henry **Purcell**.

Indy, Vincent d' (1851–1931) (van SAHN dan DEE) French composer; wrote one operetta and twelve operas, heavily influenced by **Wagner**, including *La légende de St. Christophe* (The Legend of St. Christopher) (1920) (lah lé zhahnd duh san kree STOF), in three acts, to his own libretto.

L'infedeltà delusa (Faithlessness Outwitted) (lih:n feh: dehl TAH deh: LOO zah) Opera in two acts by Franz Joseph **Haydn**; libretto by Marco Coltellini; Hungary, Eszterhàza (EHS tehr hah' zah), 1773. This "burletta per musica" (boor LEHT tah pehr MOO zee kah), with an entrancing score, has a complicated farcical plot:

Outside Filippo's house, the old peasant Filippo (fee LEEP po:) (ten.), the wealthy farmer Nencio (NEHN cho:) (ten.), the young peasant Nanni (NAHN nee) (bass), and Nanni's sister, Vespina (veh SPEE nah) (sop.), in love with Nencio, are basking in the late evening sunshine. Nanni is in love with Filippo's daughter, Sandrina (sahn DREE nah) (sop.), and he wonders where she is, while his sister is sure that Filippo and Nencio are up to something. Indeed, at her father's forcing, Sandrina agrees to marry Nencio and give up Nanni. Nanni and his sister swear vengeance. They go through a series of machinations, with Vespina disguised as different characters, but all the trickery is finally revealed. Filippo and Nencio accept the situation, and Sandrina is now free to marry Nanni, while Nencio agrees to marry the clever Vespina.

ingénu; ingénue *n.* [French] The young male and female leads, respectively, esp. in comic opera or musical comedy. The female role was often that of a sentimental, sensitive heroine; the male either that of an ardent young lover or a young, simple-minded fool.

Inkle and Yarico Opera in three acts by Samuel **Arnold**; libretto by George **Colman "the Younger,"** based on a 1711 essay on the relative merits of the sexes by Richard Steele (1672–1729), published in his journal *The Spectator*, the essay in turn having been based on traveler Richard Ligon's (1585?–1682) book *True and Exact History of the Island of Barbadoes* (1673), in which an incident is related about the enslavement of an American Indian girl named Yarico; London, Little Theatre in the Haymarket, 1787.

The opera proved very popular, and was performed for at least fifty years after its premiere. The extensive spoken dialogue, with songs and ensembles scattered throughout, makes this piece more of a play with music than a true opera; and the dialogue itself is verbose in the tedious style of the period, in need of a Sheridan or a Goldsmith to liven it up. It was the first anti-slavery piece, when slavery was a current subject of debate.

Inkle (ten.) is a British adventurer engaged to a young English lady, Narcissa (sop.), and torn between his love for her and for the "noble savage" Yarico (sop.), who has rescued him from danger in "an American forest." Nevertheless, he tries to sell Yarico to slavers, but the sale is prevented by the governor of Jamaica, and the crestfallen Inkle acknowledges that he loves her: "Love's convert here behold, / Banish'd now my thirst of gold, / Bless'd in these arms to fold / My gentle Yarico."

instrumentation *n.* **1.** The particular arrangement of parts for musical instruments used in any particular musical piece; another word for **orchestration**. **2.** The theory and practice of orchestration.

Interlocutor *n.* In a **minstrel show**, the performer who sat in the center of the semicircle and served as both presenter (master of ceremonies) and straight man in comedic exchanges. He exchanged remarks and bantered with the **Bones** and the **Tambo**. Also called the *middleman*.

interlude *n.* **1.** A brief entertainment, usually a musical one, presented between the acts of a play. **2.** A brief instrumental piece of music played between the acts of a play or the verses of a song. **3.** *Hist.* An entertainment presented between the courses of a medieval or Renaissance banquet; a comic sketch performed between the acts of a medieval mystery or morality play; hence, a farcical sketch or short play.

intermezzo (ihn' tuhr MEH tsoh) *n.* [Fr. Italian] **1.** A brief instrumental interlude in a larger work, e.g., the piece played between the two scenes of Pietro Mascagni's *Cavalleria Rusticana*. **2.** *Archaic.* Music played as the audience was returning to their seats after the intermission. **3.** *Hist.* In Renaissance Italy through the 18th c., a spoken or sung comic entertainment performed as an interlude between the acts of a tragedy or **opera seria**, in order to lighten the mood. See also PERGOLESI, GIOVANNI BATTISTA.

interpolation *n.* Inserted material not written for the particular project, e.g., an interpolated **aria** that may have been written for another opera, as in the Metropolitan Opera production of Offenbach's *La Périchole*, in which the Grand Duchess's "Saber Aria" from the finale of act 1 of *La Grande-Duchesse de Gérolstein* was inserted.

interval *n.* **1.** The distance in pitch between two notes. **2.** *Brit.* The intermission between the acts of a piece, the two halves of a concert or recital, etc.

intonation *n.* **1.** The melodic or pitch pattern of a language, or of an individual utterance: *intonation pattern*. **2.** In playing an instrument or singing, the way in which the correct pitches (tones) are produced.

Into the Woods Broadway musical by Stephen **Sondheim** (music and lyrics); book by James **Lapine**, who also directed; Martin Beck Theatre, 1987 (765 perf.); Broadway revival, Broadhurst Theatre, 2002 (279 perf.). This bitter-sweet, intriguing story is set to some of Sondheim's most compelling and evocative music.

Life is not happy-go-lucky for the fairy-tale characters living in the forest. Actions have consequences. Someone who kills a giant must be punished. And if you marry a prince you are hardly acquainted with, what will the marriage be like? We all want a happily ever after ending, but is there one? If the first act ends on the childish idea that everyone has found his or her happy ending, the second shows that one needs maturity and understanding to achieve it.

introduction *n.* **1.** A short **overture** played before the curtain rises, or a brief piece of music played just after it rises. **2.** A brief piece of music played before the main section of a number, song, etc., that is part of the number and leads directly into it. Called an *intro*, for short.

in unison 1. Singing or playing instruments in complete accord and **harmony**; also, group singing of the same note simultaneously, harmonizing precisely in different octaves (e.g., the note C, sung on a low pitch by basses and altos and on a high pitch by tenors and sopranos), no matter what the voice category. **2.** Dancing all together; e.g., when everyone in a **corps de ballet** does the same steps at the same time.

See UNISON.

Iolanthe, or The Peer and the Peri Operetta in two acts by **Gilbert and Sullivan**; London, Savoy Theatre, 1882.

This libretto is the closest Gilbert came to real political satire, and he wrote a delightfully topsy-turvy story. And Sullivan's rhythmically varied, brilliantly orchestrated score is one of his best.

In an Arcadian meadow, Iolanthe (mezz.), a Fairy, is being reinstated by the Fairy Queen (contr.) into the Fairy band. She had been banished for marrying a mortal, something forbidden by Fairy law. Her son, the Arcadian shepherd Strephon (bar.), and Phyllis (sop.), an Arcadian shepherdess, are engaged to be married. But Phyllis is a ward in chancery. The Lord Chancellor (bar.) will decide her fate, and he is not happy about Strephon. That august official now appears on the scene with the entire House of Lords, preceded by a military band. They have come to see for themselves what is going on. Earl Tololler (ten.) and the Earl of Mountararat (bass-bar.) are interested in Phyllis, who knows nothing of Strephon's Fairy origins. He has never told her that he is half a Fairy—he was waiting for the right time—so she is shocked when they tell her they have seen Strephon kissing a young lady in St. James's Park. He explains that she is his mother, but nobody believes him. Phyllis tells Strephon they must part, and asks Tololler and Mountararat to decide which of them will be her husband. Strephon summons the Fairy Queen and her band, so that she can explain matters, but the Lord Chancellor and the Peers defy her. To punish them, she makes Strephon a member of Parliament. In the Palace Yard, Westminster, with the Houses of Parliament looming in the background, the sentry, Private Willis (ten.), philosophizes. The sleepless Lord Chancellor has almost decided to marry Phyllis himself, when Iolanthe, defying Fairy law yet again, appears to plead for her son, who is also his son, for it was he whom she had married! Having thought her dead, the Lord Chancellor is not only shocked, but deeply moved to have found her again. But she must once more be punished, and this time the death sentence may not be commuted. However, all the Fairies have fallen in love with all the Peers, and the Fairy Queen with Private Willis. The Lord Chancellor has an inspiration: Change the law! Instead of its reading that every Fairy shall die who marries a mortal, let it read, "Every Fairy shall die who *doesn't* marry a mortal." This is done. They all get married, and Phyllis is united with Strephon. They all go flying off to Fairyland, for "Every Peer is now a Peri."

Iphigénie en Aulide (Iphigenia in Aulis) (ih:f ee zhé NEE ahn o: LEED) The story of Agamemnon's sacrifice of his daughter Iphigenia (ih fih dgeh NI uh), over the horrified objections of Clytemnestra (klI tehm NEHS trah), in order to secure propitious winds for the voyage to Troy and a favorable outcome to the war, is the subject of eight operas, the most famous being the one in three acts by Christoph Willibald Ritter von **Gluck**; libretto by Bailli Leblanc du Roullet (1716–1786) (ba yee' luh blah*n*' dü *r*oo LEH:), based on Jean Racine's (1639–1699) version of Euripides' play; Paris Opéra, 1774.

Iphigénie en Tauride (Iphigenia in Tauris) (ih:f ee zhé NEE ah*n* to: *R*EED) Based on Euripides' play, the story of Iphigenia rescued by the gods and taken to the island of Tauris is the subject of five operas, the most well known being the 1779 work in four acts by **Gluck**, with a text by librettist Nicolas-François Guillard (1752–1814) (nih: ko: lah f*r*ah*n* swah gee YAH*R*)—this was, in fact, his first libretto; it premiered at the Paris Opéra.

Irene Broadway musical by composer Harry Tierney (1890–1965), with lyrics by his usual songwriting partner, Joseph McCarthy (1885–1943); book by James Montgomery (1888–1966), based on the Cinderella story; Vanderbilt Theatre, 1919 (675 perf.); Broadway revivals: Jolson's 59th Street Theatre, 1923 (16 perf.); revised version, Minskoff Theatre, 1973 (607 perf.); film, 1940.

All three members of the creative team also wrote material for the ***Ziegfeld Follies***. The most famous songs in this fabulous show, full of jazzy rhythms and textures, with great brass solos and wonderful Broadway tunes, are the title number and "Alice Blue Gown."

The beautiful Irish lass Irene O'Dare, an upholsterer's assistant in New York, is sent out to the Marshall estate on Long Island to repair cushions. She falls in love with the Marshall son and heir, Donald. Madame Lucy, a male fashion designer, agrees to help her by supplying her with a gown that she will wear to a swank society party at the mansion, where she is the cynosure of all eyes. Naturally, she marries Donald.

Irish step An early form of tap dancing, used by Ruby Keeler (1909–93) in some of the first Hollywood movie musicals. There were no metal taps on the shoes, which had wooden soles, and the steps were fairly light.

Irish stepdance; step dancing A form of Irish folk dancing, performed solo and in groups, in hard or soft shoes. There are organizations in Ireland that hold step dancing contests, and concerts of such dances have been popular entertainments; e.g., the *Riverdance* shows, which include intricate patterns and unison dancing of reels, jigs, hornpipes and the like, accompanied by traditional Irish music; they played on Broadway in 1996 and 2000.

Irma la Douce (ee*r* mah lah DOOS) [French: Irma the Sweet] Paris, then West End and Broadway musical by Marguerite Monnot (1903–1961) (mah*r* guh *R*EET mon NO:); book and lyrics by Alexandre Breffort (1901–1971) (ah lehk SAH*N* d*r*uh b*r*ehf FO:*R*); translation by British writers Julian More (b. 1928), David Heneker (1906–2001), and Monty Norman (b. 1928); Plymouth Theatre, 1960 (524 perf.); film, 1963. This show is hilarious, very sexy and delightful, and the music is lively and tuneful.

Nestor, a Parisian law student, is in love with the prostitute Irma-la-Douce, and he is jealous, so he disguises himself as wealthy, elderly Oscar, and convinces her to give up her clients and marry him. She falls in love with Oscar, which makes Nestor jealous. So he kills off his alter ego, and is convicted of the murder. Sent to Devil's Island, Nestor escapes and makes his way back to France, where he is able to prove that he didn't do it, or, rather, that he did, but he didn't actually kill himself. He and Irma, who is charmed, are united at last.

Irmelin Opera in three acts by Frederick **Delius**; libretto by the composer, based on fairy tales; posthumously produced, Oxford, New Theatre, 1953.

Nils (ten.) is a prince disguised as a swineherd. He is searching for his true love, whom he is told he will find where a silver stream ends. He goes there and finds Irmelin (sop.), a princess who is also waiting for her true love.

Ivanhoe 1. Novel written in 1819 by Sir Walter Scott; set in 12th-c. England. Its story is the subject of at least six operas. They include an **opéra comique**, *Ivanhoé* (ee vah' no: É) [the French version of the name], by Gioachino **Rossini** (1826), which is a **pasticcio** of his own gorgeous music. The plot of Scott's novel was highly distorted by its librettists: leading romantic poet Emile Deschamps (1791–1871) (deh: SHAH*N*) and writer and politician Gabriel-Gustave de Wailly (1804–1878) (duh vI YEE). Also based on the novel are *Der Templar und die Jüdin* by Heinrich **Marschner** and *Ivanhoe* (1832) by Giovanni **Pacini** (1832), libretto by Gaetano **Rossi**.

2. Opera in five acts by Sir Arthur Seymour **Sullivan**; libretto by the American-born English noted amateur athlete, novelist, poet, and librettist Julian Russell Sturgis (1848–1904); London, Royal English Opera House, 1891.

Wilfred of Ivanhoe (ten.), a Saxon knight, returns in disguise from the Holy Land, where he has been fighting for the Norman King Richard the Lionheart (bar.), who has a sterling reputation for fair-mindedness and evenhanded treatment of both Norman and Saxon. Ivanhoe claims his rightful inheritance and the hand of Lady Rowena (sop.), betrothed at the behest of his father Cedric (bar.) to the last of the disinherited Saxon royal line. The Jewish heroine Rebecca (sop.) loves Ivanhoe, whom she has helped in his time of need, and the evil Norman knights De Bracy (ten.) and De Bois Guilbert (bar.) are in love with her. They imprison Rebecca and her father, Isaac of York (bar.), in Torquilstone Castle, which is then besieged by Ivanhoe and Robin Hood (bar.) and his Merry Men. Rebecca is accused of witchcraft, but Ivanhoe, in a trial by combat, kills Gilbert, saving her life. King Richard the Lionheart returns and overthrows his evil brother, Prince John (bass). He allows Ivanhoe to marry Rowena.

Ivan Susanin Opera by Mikhail **Glinka**. See ZHIZN ZA TSARYA (A LIFE FOR THE TSAR).

J

Jacques Brel Is Alive and Well and Living in Paris Off-Broadway musical revue constructed from the songs of Belgian composer-singer Jacques Brel (1929–1978); 1968 (1847 perf.); Broadway revival, 1972 (limited engagement, 54 perf.); filmed as a kind of elaborate music video, on location in Paris, in 1975, with Brel himself doing a number; a 2006 Off-Broadway revival, in a revised version, ran for more than a year at the Zipper Theatre. The show, which was presented at the Village Gate, a New York City cabaret, mostly used the English translations and adaptations of Brel's lyrics by Eric Blau and Mort Shuman (he also performed in the show), but some of the songs were done in French, or in French followed by English. All the numbers were presented dramatically, each singer playing a character for the particular song.

Jacobowski, Edward (1858–1929) English composer of sixteen musical comedies; studied music in Vienna. His great hit, an international success, was *Erminie* (1885), a comic opera in three acts, based on popular French plays about the roguish thief and libertine Robert Macaire, presumed to have been a real person in the late middle ages.

jam (to); jam session To improvise instrumental music, esp. popular with jazz bands or small groups or bands doing country or popular music; either in rehearsal or just for fun.

Janáček, Leoš (1854–1928) (LEH: osh YAH nah: chehk) Innovative, strikingly original Czech composer; his ten operas include the three-act *Jenůfa* (1904), a melodramatic love story; *Káta Kabanová*; *Příhody Lišky Bystroušky (The Cunning Little Vixen)*; a story about mortality versus immortality, *Věc Makropulos* (The Makropulos Affair) (1926) (VEHNTS mah KRO: poo lo:s'), in three acts, based on the 1922 play of the same name by Czech playwright, Karel Čapek (1890–1938) (KAH rehl CHAH pehk); and *Z mrtvého domu* (From the House of the Dead) (1930) (zuh MUHRT vé kho: DO: moo), in three acts, based on the 1862 novel of the same name by Russian writer, Feodor Dostoevsky (1821–1881); libretti for all five by the composer.

janger; djanger (DGAHN gehr) *n.* [Indonesian: humming] A form of Balinese dance-drama with traditional, rhythmic vocal accompaniment; performed by women; also, the traditional songs that accompany the dance-drama.

jazz *n.* A major form of American instrumental music, later expanded to include vocal music; created by African-Americans. Jazz, which has links to a variety of African tribal musics, European-American **march** music, **blues** and **ragtime**, began in New Orleans around the turn of the 20th c. Its characteristics include complex harmonic and rhythmic structures; daring and complicated polyphony; virtuosic, improvised, spontaneous solos; and free-wheeling melody. There are many schools, styles, and kinds of jazz, which has had an enormous influence on composition for the musical theater, e.g., **bebop**, **cool**, **free jazz**, **funk**, **hot**, **Latin jazz**, **New Orleans jazz**; **swing**.

jazz band A group of instrumentalists who play jazz music; it usually consists of percussion, brass and wind instruments, as well as a double bass, but no other strings.

jazz opera An opera that uses jazz as its principal musical idiom; e.g., Gershwin's *Porgy and Bess*. Jazz also plays a major role in Křenek's *Jonny spielt auf* and is important in certain numbers in *Die Dreigroschenoper (The Threepenny Opera)*; it influenced Igor **Stravinsky** and Paul **Hindemith** as well as the operatic work of Virgil **Thomson** and Leonard **Bernstein**, whose *Trouble in Tahiti* (1952) features a **scat** trio for a chorus. Marc **Blitzstein** utilized jazz in his opera *Regina* and in other works, e.g., *The Cradle Will Rock*.

jazz square A kind of dance combination. Syn. with **box step**.

jazz-vaudeville drama *Hist.* A 1920s American form of left-wing political protest musical play, employing **jazz** as its musical idiom; much influenced by **expressionism**; e.g., dramatist John Howard Lawson's (1894–1977) *Processional: A Jazz Symphony of American Life* (1925). Although Lawson felt he had discarded expressionism, there are expressionistic elements in the play, which he characterized as "essentially vaudevillesque in character" and informed by "a formalized arrangement of jazz music."

Jenůfa Opera by Leoš **Janáček**.

Jersey Boys Internationally successful Broadway **jukebox musical** with a book by Academy Award–winning screenwriter Marshall Brickman (b. 1941) and Rick Elice (b. 1956), featuring the songs of Frankie Valli (b. 1934), from Belleville, NJ, and the Four Seasons; August Wilson Theatre, 2005 (still running as of this writing). The show originated at the La Jolla Playhouse in California, and was directed by Des McAnuff (b. 1952). The Four Seasons were a popular 1950s and '60s singing quartet from New Jersey, who left a life of petty street crime to become huge stars, introducing a new sexy, sound to pop music. The other three members of the group were Tommy DeVito (b. 1936), from Belleville; Nick Massi (1935–2000), from Newark; and Bob Gaudio (b. 1942), born in the Bronx, NY, and raised in Bergenfield, NJ.

Jessel, Leon (1871–1942) (LÉ on YEHS suhl) German conductor, musical director, and composer of eighteen Berlin operettas, of which the best known is *Schwarzwaldmädel* (The Black Forest Girl) (1917) (SHVAH[*R*]TS vahlt' MEH: duhl); libretto by August **Neidhart**; it ran for 900 perf. Jessel is also known for his march, "Parade of the Tin Soldiers" (1905). He wrote songs for the 1924 *Ziegfeld Follies*. As a Jew, he was imprisoned by the Gestapo in 1941 for having written in 1939, in a letter to his librettist, Wilhelm Sterk (1880–?) (SHTEH[*R*]K), that he couldn't work in an era when Jews were being annihilated, and as long as he did not know what terrible destiny awaited them and him. At the age of seventy, he was tortured so brutally by the Gestapo that he died in the Berlin Jewish Hospital shortly after his release.

Jesus Christ Superstar Broadway musical by Andrew Lloyd **Webber**; lyrics by Tim **Rice**; Mark Hellinger Theatre, 1971 (720 perf.); Broadway revivals: Longacre Theatre, concert version, 1977 (96 perf.); Ford Center for the Performing Arts, 2000 (48 perf.); film, 1973. The highly theatrical production was directed by Tom O'Horgan, and the album was a best seller. This is a Biblical **rock musical** about the life of Jesus Christ during the last seven days of his life, when he decides to allow himself to be betrayed and crucified, so that he can save his disciples.

jeté (zheh TAY) *n.* [Fr. French, past participle of *jeter* (zhuh TÉ; to throw): thrown] In dance and ballet, a leap: a springing movement that requires the dancer to jump up using one foot, and to land on the other.
   See also GRAND JETÉ; TOUR JETÉ.

ji (DGEE) *n.* [Japanese: chorus] **1.** In **noh** theater, a chorus of eight or ten men who sing parts of the play in unison while seated, often in a semicircle at the back of the stage. Also called *ji utai kata* (OO TI KAH tah) [chorus song person]. **2.** The sections of a noh play sung by the *ji.* Also called *ji utai* [chorus song]

jig *n.* **1.** A lively dance in 3/4 or 3/8 time, expressive of excitement and joy, e.g., the traditional Irish jig; also, a lively song performed while doing such a dance. See also GIGUE; IRISH STEPDANCING. **2.** *Hist.* A short musical **afterpiece** in the Elizabethan theater, consisting often of obscene or ribald songs and dances.

Jin Xiang (b. 1935) (DGIHN SHAHNG) Chinese composer and teacher. After being sent to work as a farm laborer for twenty years, he was able to practice music and to teach composition at the Chinese Music Conservatory. His operas include *A Warm Breeze Outside* (1980), *Savage Land* (1987), and *Sunrise* (1990).

jitterbug *n., v.* [From *jitters,* slang for "nerves"; because of the frenetic movement the dance could have] —*n.* **1.** A kind of **swing** dance, originating in the 1930s; the partners hold one or both hands briefly, often letting go while swinging away from and toward each other, in time to a lively jazz beat. Cab Calloway popularized the term with his recording of the song "Call of the Jitter Bug" (1935). —*v. i.* **2.** To do the dance just described.

jive *n., v.* —*n.* **1.** A 1940s African-American ballroom dance in 4/4 time, and the music that accompanied it; a variation of the jitterbug. —*v. i.* **2.** To play or swing along with a band or jazz combo.

jo (DGO:) *n.* [Japanese: introduction] **1.** The stately, slow musical **overture** or **introduction** to a Japanese theater presentation. In traditional *bugaku* (boo GAH koo) [dance-drama], the dancers enter as the *jo* is played. **2.** The first part of a **noh** play, presenting an important secondary character. **3.** The first in a series of five noh plays; it is always about one of the gods.

John, Sir Elton (b. 1947) Prolific, much loved British rock star, musician, performer, and film and stage composer of such Broadway and West End hits as *Billy Elliott*, *Aida*, and *The Lion King*; also performed in the film *Tommy* (1989).

Jonny spielt auf (Jonny Strikes Up) (DGO:N nee SHPEELT OWF) A **Zeitoper** by Ernst **Křenek**; libretto by the composer; Leipzig, Neues Theater, 1927.

The haunting score is eclectic and diverting, and ranges over the history of music, with lots of experimentation, jazz, touches of expressionistic dissonance, Austrian folk **ländler**, and 19th-c. romantic operatic composition. It was considered scandalous when first produced in Leipzig, but in 1928, it was produced at the Metropolitan Opera, and it was a great success there and worldwide. It was banned by the Nazis as "degenerate."

In Paris, Jonny (bar.), "a black jazz-band violinist," is having an affair with Yvonne (sop.), a hotel maid, who is two-timing him with the classical violinist, Daniello (bar.), who is carrying on with the opera singer Anita (sop.), who has been having an affair with the composer Max (ten.), whom she met near a glacier and who has composed an opera for her. When Daniello's violin is stolen, Jonny is accused of the theft, but he protests his innocence. Yvonne is accused of the theft, and fired. She goes to Austria as Anita's maid, and, out of revenge for being accused, betrays Daniello and Anita by revealing their affair to Max, who breaks up with her. But when he hears her singing on the radio, he resumes their affair. Jonny did steal the violin, and they cross the ocean to America, all except Daniello, who is crushed by the locomotive taking them to the ship.

Jommelli, Niccolò (1714–1774) (nee' ko: LO: yo:m MEHL lee) Prolific and influential Italian opera composer; known for his musical and dramatic innovations in the presentation of opera, of which he wrote around eighty, in addition to his instrumental and liturgical music. He was one of the most admired composers of his day, considered by many to be one of the greatest of the century.

See also DIDONE ABBANDONATA.

Jones, Sidney (1861–1946) [b. James Sidney Jones] English clarinetist, conductor, and composer of ca. twenty musical comedies; most well known for his contributions to the series of **Gaiety musicals**, including *The Geisha* (1896), perhaps his most successful musical comedy, and *A Gaiety Girl* (1893), which inaugurated the series. The son of a military bandmaster, he grew up learning to play a variety of instruments, and later studied music formally at Trinity College in Dublin. He toured the English provinces conducting operettas, and also conducted musicals in the West End.

Jones, Tom (b. 1928) American writer, lyricist, actor; most famous for *The Fantasticks*, written with Harvey **Schmidt**; wrpte lyrics and/or books for a dozen other musicals, including *110 in the Shade* (1963), *I Do, I Do* (1966), *Celebration* (1969), all with Schmidt; and *Harold and Maude* (2004).

Joplin, Scott (1868–1917) Innovative American composer, noted esp. for his **ragtime** compositions, many of which are for the piano. Joplin was known as "King of the Ragtime Composers." He also wrote the opera *Treemonisha*, which he struggled without success to have performed in his lifetime; in 1972 it was finally produced.

Joseph and the Amazing Technicolor Dreamcoat West End, then Broadway musical by Andrew Lloyd **Webber**; lyrics by Tim **Rice**; based on their 1968 **cantata**; transferred from Off-Broadway to Broadway; Royale Theatre, 1982 (747 perf.); Broadway revival, Minskoff Theatre, 1993 (231 perf.).

The subject of this colorful **rock musical** is the familiar Biblical story of Joseph, betrayed by his brothers and sold into slavery in Egypt, where he rises eventually to become Pharaoh's confidant.

Jouy, Victor-Joseph Étienne de (1764–1846) (vih:k to:r' zho ZHEHF é tyehn' duh zhooWEE) French dramatist and librettist; wrote texts for Gioachino **Rossini**, for whom he co-authored the libretto to *Guillaume Tell (William Tell)*, and for Gaspare **Spontini** (*La vestale*), as well as libretti for **Cherubini** and **Méhul**.

Juive, La (The Jewess) (lah ZHÜEEV) Opera in five acts by Fromental **Halévy**; libretto by Eugène **Scribe**; Paris Opéra, 1835.

This compelling, majestic grand opera was part of the standard repertoire for a hundred years but has rarely been revived since, despite the amazing impact of its melodramatic, hair-raising music and the wrenching tragedy of its story. Its most well known aria is the heartbreaking "Rachel, quand du seigneur" (Rachel, when from the Lord) (*r*ah SHEHL kah*n* dü she NYUH*R*), sung in the last act by the Jewish goldsmith Eléazar (ehl é ah ZAH*R*) (ten.); the aria was made even more famous when celebrated tenor Enrico Caruso (1873–1921), in his last new role, recorded it in 1920, near the end of his life. In *Swann's Way* (1913), the first volume of Marcel Proust's *A la recherche du temps perdu* (In Search of Lost Time) (ah lah *r*uh SHEH*R*SH dü tah*n* peh*r* DÜ), the Narrator's grandfather, in a mild display of anti-Semitism, hums it under his breath whenever the Narrator's Jewish friend Bloch arrives at the house.

The story is set in Konstanz, Switzerland in the year 1414, on the day when the Council of Constance is to begin deliberating on theological issues besetting Christianity, and when the Protestant Hussites have been defeated by the army led by Prince Léopold (lé o POLD) (ten.). The Jewish goldsmith Eléazar's daughter, Rachel (sop.), has fallen in love with Samuel, a Jew who works in the shop. He is actually the disguised Léopold, and he is smitten with her. Rachel invites Samuel to their Passover Seder. Léopold's wife, Princess Eudoxie (*oo* duhk SEE) (sop.), orders a special gold chain as a present, to honor and celebrate his victory. Léopold, who is now filled with remorse, reveals that he is a Christian, and Rachel says she does not care. Eléazar, who is horrified at first, gives them his blessing. But Samuel disappears mysteriously. When the chain is delivered by Eléazar and Rachel, she recognizes Léopold. Mad with rage and jealousy, knowing that what she is about to say is a lie and that it will condemn her to death, she announces that the two of them have been lovers. Cardinal Brogni (b*r*o: NYEE) (bass), president of the Council of Constance, orders that they be tried, and

Eléazar with them as a co-conspirator. They are found guilty and condemned to death, but Léopold's sentence is commuted to exile because Rachel, in remorse, and persuaded by Eudoxie, tells the truth at last. The Cardinal had suffered years before, in Rome, before he had taken holy orders, when his wife had died in a fire and his daughter had been spirited away by an unknown Jew. He now offers, in memory of his lost daughter, to save Rachel's life if she will renounce her faith, but she will not, nor will Eléazar renounce his. He tells the Cardinal, who had persecuted him when they both lived in Rome, that he knows all about his daughter, but the secret will go with him to his grave. The Cardinal begs him to reveal it, but he is adamant. On the day of the execution, Brogni asks Eléazar if his daughter is still alive. "Yes," says Eléazar. "Where is she?" asks Brogni. "She is there!" shouts Eléazar, pointing to the flames that are engulfing Rachel. He throws himself onto the pyre, leaving the Cardinal horror-stricken.

jukebox musical A stage or screen musical comedy whose score consists of the popular songs of a particular composer, performer, or singing group, e.g., *Mamma Mia* (1999; film, 2008); *Jersey Boys* (2005).

jumble *n. Hist.* An odd form of musical theater devised in the 18th c. by the manager of the Haymarket Theatre in London, dramatist and memoirist George **Colman "the Younger."** The jumble combined opera, farce, and tragedy, and was a hodge-podge of entertaining and ludicrous juxtapositions. A title from 1811: *The Quadrupeds of Quedlinburgh*, billed as a "tragico-comico-anglo-germanico-hippo-ono-dramatico romance," in two acts. Cf. **extravaganza**; **pasticcio**.

jump split In dance, an athletic move used in musical comedy and sometimes in ballet, consisting of leaping off the stage floor, extending the legs, one all the way to the front, the other all the way to the back, and landing in that position; a spectacular way of ending a dance, esp. when done by the entire chorus of dancers; e.g., in the can-can numbers of **Offenbach** or in Cole Porter's *Can-Can*.

K

kabuki (kah' BOO kee') *n.* A form of traditional Japanese musical theater, founded in the 17th c., and still very popular with commercial troupes in many Japanese cities. Its characteristics include standardized characters wearing stylized makeup; presentational choreography and acting, using traditional movements and gestures; gorgeous, flowing costumes; and stylized scenery. All parts are played by male actors; "women-style" roles and the actors playing them are both called *onnagata* (ON nah GAH tah), some of whom perform specified roles in a flamboyant style called *aragoto* (AH ruh GO: to:), which includes a stylized freeze pose called a *mie* (MEE eh:), used at significant moments; or in the chanting-singing style called *gidayu* (guh DAH yoo); the chanter himself is also a *gidayu*. Gentle, romantic male characters perform in a restrained style called *wagoto* (WAH go' to). The stage is curtained off with the traditional striped *hikimaku* (HIH kuh MAH koo). Musicians play classical Japanese music **accompaniment** in a stage-right, partially enclosed box called a *geza* (GEH: zah). Spectacular special entrances and dramatic exits are made down a runway called a *hanamichi* (HAH nuh MEE chee) that runs the length of the auditorium. The audience expresses its approval with *kakegoe* (KAH keh GO: eh): traditional shouts.

    See also HAYASHI.

Kahn, Gus (1886–1941) German-born American **Tin Pan Alley** lyricist and pop songwriter; collaborator on many musicals with various composers, including George and Ira **Gershwin**, on *Show Girl* (1929); and Walter **Donaldson** on *Whoopee!* Among his most famous songs: "Toot Toot Tootsie," "It Had To Be You," "Love Me or Leave Me," and "Yes, Sir, That's My Baby."

Kaiserin, Die (The Empress) (dee KI zeh *r*ihn') Operetta in two acts by Leo **Fall**; libretto by Julius **Brammer** and Alfred **Grünwald**; Berlin, Metropoltheater (meh' t*r*o: PO:L teh: AH tuh), 1915.

    This wonderful operetta boasts a vivacious and exhilarating score, and a witty, insouciant libretto. A 1953 recording is available on CD from Membran Music (231707; 2007); it includes highlights from *Der fidele Bauer* (The Faithful Peasant), recorded in 1954.

    Some time in the early 18th c., at the Hapsburg palace of Schönbrunn (shön B*R*OO*N*), near Vienna, the young and willful future Austrian Empress Maria Theresia (sop.) has finally married her darling Franzl (F*R*AHNTSL), Prince August Franz von Lothringen (LO: t*r*ihng ehn) (ten.). They adore each other, but he has become her Prince Consort, and she has to deal as a public figure with foreign diplomats, and as a private person with her husband. A bit lost, she gets the advice of the worldly Princess Adelgunde (AH dehl GOO*N* deh) (sop.), and everything works out for the best.

Kálmán, Emmerich (1882–1953) (EHM uh rihk KAHL mahn) [Imre (IHM reh:) Kálmán] Great Hungarian composer of two dozen Viennese operettas, known for his tuneful and vibrant scores. Among his enthralling successes are the exciting, vibrant *Die Zirkusprinzessin* (The Circus Princess) (1926) (dee TSEER koos prih:n TSES sih:n), available on CD in a spirited 1955 recording from Membran Music (231709; 2007); *Csárdásfürstin*, *Gräfin Mariza*, and *Die Herzogin von Chicago*.

Kalmar, Albert "Bert" (1884–1947), and Harry Ruby (1895–1974) [b. Rubinstein] American songwriting team; composers/writers of several Hollywood musical films and of Broadway musicals, including *Animal Crackers* (1928), starring the Marx Brothers, and later filmed. Among their most popular song hits are "Who's Sorry Now?" and "I Wanna Be Loved By You."

Kammersänger; Kammersängerin (KAH muh ZEHNG uh;—*r*ihn) *n.* [German: chamber-singer of the male and female genders, respectively] An honorary title given by the German and Austrian governments to distinguished singers; succeeded the title bestowed at the royal or princely courts in the 18th and 19th centuries: *Hofkammersänger* (HOHF–; court-chamber-singer).

Kander and Ebb John Kander (b. 1972), and Fred Ebb (1928–2004). American team who wrote more than fifteen Broadway musicals and musical films; Kander wrote the exciting, memorable music, Ebb the clever, pointed lyrics.

Major works of Kander and Ebb:
1965   *Flora, the Red Menace*
1966   *Cabaret*
1968   *Zorba*
1971   *70, Girls, 70*
1975   *Chicago*
1978   *The Act*
1981   *Woman of the Year*
1984   *The Rink*
1991   *And the World Goes Round*
1992   *Kiss of the Spider Woman*
1997   *Steel Pier*
1999   *Fosse*
1999   *Over and Over (All about Us)*
2001   *The Visit*
2007   *Curtains*

Kapellmeister (kah' PEHL MI stuh) *n.* [German: chapel-master] The choir director of a chapel at a royal German or Austrian court; also, *Hofkapellmeister* (HOHF—; court-chapel-master); at one time, the general word for a conductor or music director, e.g., of an opera house.

Káta Kabanová (KAH tah KAH bah no vah') Opera in three acts by Leoš **Janáček**; libretto by the composer, based on *The Storm* (1859) by the Russian playwright Alexander Ostrovsky (1823–1886); Brno, National Theatre, 1921.

Káta (sop.), her husband Tichon (TEE khon) (ten.), and her mother-in-law Kabanicha (KAH bah nee chah) (mezz.), who detests Káta, live together. Káta is prey to feelings of guilt because she is in love with Boris (ten.), with whom she has a secret tryst while Tichon is traveling on business. As a storm rages outside, she confesses all, then runs away to see Boris one more time before drowning herself.

Katerina Izmaylova Opera by Dmitri **Shostakovich**. See LEDY MAKBET MTSENSKOVO UYEZDA.

kathak (KAH tahk) *n.* [Fr. Hindi *katha* (KAH tah): story] A classical northern Indian narrative dance told with gesture and accompanied by music; performed by virtuosic dancers and noted for the fast turns they make, and for its stamping steps. Kathak deals with stories of the Hindu gods and goddesses.

kathakali (KAH tuh KAH lee) *n.* A classic Indian form of mime-dance-drama originating in the 17th c. in Kerala in the north of India; performed by actors in exquisite costumes and elaborate makeup, with vocal and instrumental music played by four musicians.

Kaufman, George S. (1889–1961) [George Simon Kaufman] Brilliant American wit, raconteur, humorist, satirist, and writer of hit Broadway comedies, many with writing partner Moss **Hart**. He co-wrote and stage directed *I'd Rather Be Right* and *Of Thee I Sing*, and was also a collaborator on two Marx Brothers hits: *The Cocoanuts* (1925) and *Animal Crackers* (1928), as well as on *Strike Up the Band* (1930).

Kelly, Michael (1762–1826) Irish theater manager, composer, and tenor; studied music first with his musical family in Dublin—he was the eldest of fourteen children—and later in Milan. He was invited to sing in a new Italian company in Vienna at the Hapsburg court, where he stayed from 1783–1787. There, he met and befriended **Mozart**, for whom he originated the roles of Don Curzio (KOOR tsee o:), the magistrate, and Don Basilio in *Le nozze di Figaro*. He was also a friend of Paisiello, and created the role of the Count in *Il barbiere di Siviglia*. He returned to England, and made his debut at Drury Lane in *Lionel and Clarissa* by Charles **Dibdin**. His greatest success as a composer was the opera *The Bard of Erin* (1811), in which he gave his last performance. His *Reminiscences of Michael Kelly, of the King's Theatre, and the Theatre Royal Drury Lane* (1826) make great reading. They are full of droll anecdotes about everyone he knew in the world of music, including Dr. **Arne**, Charles Dibdin, Samuel **Arnold**, Paisiello, and, of course, Mozart, whom he describes at rehearsals of *Le nozze di Figaro* as enthusiastic, encouraging, and altogether charming.

Kern, Jerome (1885–1945) [b. Jerome David Kern] Innovative, highly gifted American composer of more than forty acclaimed Broadway and film musicals and numerous songs; collaborated with such writers as P. G. **Wodehouse** and Guy **Bolton** on the **Princess Theatre musicals**, including *Very Good Eddie* and *Leave It to Jane*; Otto **Harbach** on *Roberta*; and Oscar **Hammerstein** on *Music in the Air*, *Show Boat* (his masterpiece), and *Sweet Adeline*. He also co-composed *Sally* with Victor **Herbert**. His first Broadway show was *The Girl from Utah* (1914), a

British import by Paul A. **Rubens** and Sidney **Jones**, for which Kern added songs, including a very influential ballad in 4/4 time, "They Didn't Believe Me," the first time such a change from the usual waltz songs was made.

Khovanshchina (kho VAHN shchee nah) Opera in five acts by Modest **Mussorgsky**; libretto by the composer in collaboration with architect, jurist, acerbic critic, playwright, and novelist Vladimir Stasov (1824–1906) (vlah DEE meer STAH so:f); unfinished at the composer's death and completed by Nicolai **Rimsky-Korsakov**; St. Petersburg, Amateur-Musical-Dramatic Club, 1886.

As Peter the Great becomes czar of Russia in 1682, the various political factions have continued to pursue their own ends. Opposed to Peter's attempted reforms are the Old Believers, led by Dosifei (DO see fay') (bass), in collaboration with Prince Ivan Khovansky (ee VAHN kho VAHN skee) (bass); among the Old Believers are the lovers Andrei Khovansky (ahn DRAY) (ten.), Ivan's son, and the prophetess Marfa (MAHR fah) (mezz.). Ivan is assassinated by a traitor, and when Peter's political victory is assured, Marfa, Andrei, and other Old Believers commit suicide.

Kienzl, Wilhelm (1857–1941) (KEEN tsl) Austrian composer of numerous choral works, piano pieces, chamber music, songs, and ten operas; much influenced by **Wagner**, but developed a more individual musical idiom with his best known opera, the magnificent *Der Evangelimann* (The Evangelist Preacher) (1895) (deh EH vahn GEH: lee MAHN), with a libretto by the composer, about an evangelist who forgives his dying brother's betrayal; superb 1981 CD recording (EMI; 5 66370 2; 1997).

King and I, The Musical comedy by **Rodgers and Hammerstein**: music by Richard **Rodgers**; book and lyrics by Oscar **Hammerstein**, based on Margaret Landon's (1903–1993) novel *Anna and the King of Siam* (1944); St. James Theatre, 1951 (1246 perf.); Broadway revivals: Uris Theatre, 1977 (719 perf.); Broadway Theatre, 1984 (207 perf.); Neil Simon Theatre, 1996 (807 perf.); film, 1956. The role of the Welsh widow Anna Leonowens (1831–1915) was created by Gertrude Lawrence (1898–1952), who, having purchased the stage rights to the biographical novel for herself, suggested the project to Rodgers and Hammerstein. Yul Brynner (1920–1985) created the role of the King of Siam and played it in the 1977 and 1985 Broadway revivals, as well as in the film version.

Anna and her son Louis arrive in Siam, where she will be tutor to the many children of the polygamous King. She and the King quarrel immediately, and she thinks of leaving, but she falls in love with her charges. The tutor and the King make their accommodations; although stubborn and at times intractable, he learns about tolerance from her. After the performance of *Uncle Tom's Cabin*, denouncing tyranny, which his slave Tuptim has written for a reception of foreign diplomats, the slave flees the palace with her lover, but she is captured and brought back to face punishment. Anna pleads her case with the King, who cannot bring himself to whip the girl. Gravely ill, he takes to his deathbed, admonishing his son to be a strong and just ruler. Anna remains in Siam to help guide the new monarch.

King Priam (PRI uhm) Opera in three acts by Michael **Tippett**; libretto by the composer based on Homer's Iliad; London, Covent Garden, 1962.

Prince Paris of Troy (ten.), having abducted Helen (mezz.), wife of King Menelaus (bass) of Sparta, sets off the Trojan War. The libretto follows incidents in the ten-year siege of Troy. After the Greek hero Achilles (ten.) kills the Trojan prince Hector (bar.), and the war is lost, King Priam (bass) chooses death over dishonor.

King Roger Opera by Karol **Szymanowski**. See KRÓL ROGER, PASTERZ.

King's Henchman, The Opera in three acts by Deems **Taylor**; libretto by lyric poet Edna St. Vincent Millay (1892–1950); New York, Metropolitan Opera, 1927.

The opera was a huge national success in the United States, and was revived for three seasons in a row at the Metropolitan Opera, which also performed it on tour; its enthusiastic reception was due largely to the performance of Eadgar by famed baritone Lawrence Tibbett (1896–1960), a superb singing actor with an outstanding voice. But the late-romantic score, vaguely reminiscent of Wagner's *Tristan und Isolde*, is not terribly interesting. The same can be said of the libretto: Millay is a wonderful poet whose instincts have here betrayed her into writing pompously.

In the 10th c., King Eadgar (EHD guhr) (bar.) of Britain sends his retainer Aethelwold (EHTH uhl wold') (ten.) to arrange a marriage with Princess Aelfrida (ehl FREE duh) (sop.) of Devon, renowned for her beauty. The vassal and the princess fall in love, and are married. Aethelwold sends word to the king that, in reality, Aelfrida is ugly and the rumors of her beauty false. When, after time has passed, the suspicious king journeys to visit his friend and discovers the truth, he is deeply upset by the betrayal, and Aethelwold commits suicide in shame and remorse.

Kismet Broadway operetta with music adapted from Alexander **Borodin** by musicians and lyricists Robert Wright (1914–2005) and George Forrest (1915–1999); book by screenwriters Charles Lederer (1910–1976), who also produced the show, and Luther Davis (1916–2008), from novelist, screenwriter, and playwright Edward Knoblock's (1874–1945) stage play *Kismet* (1911); Ziegfeld Theatre, 1953 (583 perf.); numerous summer stock and other revivals; film, 1955.

The complicated plot involves the foiling of the evil Wazir's machinations to wed the Caliph of Baghdad to one of the three princesses of Ababu, in order to enrich himself. But the Caliph has fallen in love with Marsinah, daughter of a wily and clever beggar-poet who has been mistaken for the poet Hajj by brigands, whose chief, Jawan, Hajj had cursed. The false Hajj promises to remove the curse in return for money, which will allow Jawan to find his son, kidnapped many years before. Jawan is arrested and discovers that his long lost son is none other than the Wazir, who now has his own father executed. Lalume, the Wazir's wife, has fallen in love with Hajj, who had also been arrested and condemned to a horrible punishment; she helps him to escape. Eventually, after many more complications, Hajj kills the Wazir in self defense and is pardoned by the Caliph, who marries Marsinah.

Kiss Me Again American version of *Mlle. Modiste.*

Kiss Me, Kate Broadway musical by Cole **Porter** (music and lyrics); book by Bella and Sam **Spewack**, based on William Shakespeare's *The Taming of the Shrew*; New Century Theatre, 1948 (1070 perf.); Broadway revival, Martin Beck Theatre, 1999 (909 perf.); countless summer stock productions; film, 1953.

Not only are the book and lyrics brilliant, but the score is possibly Cole Porter's greatest. The music and lyrics for the *Taming* scenes are often delightfully anachronistic, while the backstage scenes have contemporary music, such as the duet "Why Can't You Behave," for Lois and Bill; and the **pastiche** (def. 1) Viennese operetta songs "Wunderbar" and "So in Love," for Fred and Lilli.

The two stars of a musical version of *Taming of the Shrew* playing in Baltimore, Fred Graham and Lilli Vanessi, performing Petruchio and Kate, used to be husband and wife. They bicker onstage, while in character, and off, while in the dressing room. Lois Lane and Bill Calhoun, who play Bianca and Lucentio, are in love with each other, but Bill has a gambling problem that lands him in hot water. Two rather literary gangsters show up backstage to collect money for their boss from Fred, on an IOU that Bill has signed with his name. But they love Shakespeare, and they help keep Lilli in the show when she wants to walk out. They also give the good advice to "Brush Up Your Shakespeare" if you want to be successful with women. Finally, everything is straightened out, and Fred and Lilli, who really adore each other, are reconciled.

Kiss of the Spider Woman Broadway musical by **Kander and Ebb**; music by John **Kander**; lyrics by Fred **Ebb**; book by Terrence **McNally**, based on the novel *El beso de la mujer araña* (The Kiss of the Spider Woman) (1976) (ehl BEH: so: theh: lah moo HEHR ah RAHN yah) by Manuel Puig (1932–1990) (mah NWEHL PWEEG), and the 1985 film of the same name; Broadhurst Theatre, 1993 (906 perf.).

In a South American prison, cellmates Valentin Arregui Paz, a revolutionary who dreams of rejoining his comrades, and Luis Alberto Molina, a gay hairdresser who fantasizes as a way of escaping his situation, become friends, despite the fact that they are such different people. When Valentin is tortured, Molina takes care of him afterwards. The prison warden promises to release Molina if he can get Valentin to reveal the name of his girlfriend, but Molina will not betray him. As he confesses his love to Valentin, Molina is shot by the prison warden.

klezmer music (KLEHZ muhr) [From Yiddish: *kley* (kleh:) (instrument) and *zemer* (ZEH mehr) (song); derived from Hebrew] Secular Jewish instrumental folk music of Ashkenazi (Eastern European) origin; usually for a small band of *klezmorim* (klehz MAW rihm), klezmer musicians, who played originally at weddings and other celebratory occasions; characterized by lively melodies suitable for dancing, and by imitation of the human voice, esp. that of the cantor singing ornamented liturgical music. Some of the music in *Fiddler on the Roof* is inspired by klezmer music.

Knickerbocker Holiday Broadway musical by Kurt **Weill**; book by playwright Maxwell **Anderson**; Ethel Barrymore Theatre, 1938 (168 perf.); film, 1944, with the mordant satire removed and only the romantic plot retained.

The show is set in New Amsterdam during the governorship of Pieter Stuyvesant (1612–1672), implicitly compared to President Franklin D. Roosevelt, who was extremely popular at the time. It was not a success, despite the beautiful Weill score, still remembered for "September Song."

Stuyvesant falls in love with one of the colonists, Tina Tienhoeven, daughter of a city councilor and in love with the radical, Brom Broeck. He sentences Broeck to be hanged for his political activities, but, with an eye towards history's view of him, pardons Brom and even blesses his marriage to Tina.

Knyaz Igor (Prince Igor) (KNYAHZ EE go:r) Opera in a prologue and four acts by Alexander **Borodin**; libretto by the composer; St. Petersburg, Mariinsky Theatre, 1890.

The Polovitsians (po:' lo: VIH tsee anz) are a nomadic, northwest Asian Russian tribe who have founded their own state on the Black Sea and conquered southern Russia. The year is 1185. Prince Igor (bar.) and his son Vladimir (vlah DEE meer) (ten.) are captured by the Polovitsians. Their leader, Khan Konchak (KAHN KO:N chak) (bass), entertains his royal guests with the magnificent "Polovitsian dances." He offers to free them if they agree not to fight the Polovitsians, but Igor refuses. He escapes, leaving Vladimir behind. While Igor goes back to his wife, Yaroslavna (yah ro: SLAHV nah) (sop.), Vladimir marries the Khan's daughter, Konchakovna (KO:N chah ko:v' nah) (mezz.), with whom he has fallen in love.

Kodály, Zoltán (1882–1967) (ZO:L tahn KO: dI) Hungarian composer, ethnomusicologist, linguist, teacher; composed orchestral, chamber, and choral music, as well as *Háry János* (1926) (HAH ree YAH no:sh), an impressionistic, complex, richly orchestrated "Hungarian folk opera," a **Singspiel** with spoken dialogue.

Kollo, Walter (1878–1940) [b. Walter Ellmar Kollo (VAHL tuh EHL mah[r] KO:L lo:)] German conductor and prolific composer of revues, film scores, and some forty Berlin operettas, including *Wie einst in Mai* (1913), on whose libretto Romberg's *Maytime* is based. His most well known operetta is *Frauen haben das gern* (Women Like That) (1931) (FROW uhn HAH buhn DAHS GEH[R]N), libretto by writing team Franz Arnold (1878–1960) and Ernst Bach (1876–1929), lyrics by Dr. Fritz **Oliven** (Rideamus). The story concerns a wealthy manufacturer who wants his daughter to marry his best friend. Naturally, she has other ideas.

Königin von Saba, Die (The Queen of Sheba) (dee KÖ nih gihn fon ZAH bah) Opera in four acts by Karl **Goldmark**; libretto by prolific writer Salomon Hermann, Ritter von Mosenthal (1821–1877) (ZAH lo: mo:n HEH[R] mahn RIH tuh fuhn MO: zehn TAHL); Vienna, Hofoper, 1875.

King Solomon's (bar.) favorite, Assad (ten.), falls in love with the Queen of Sheba (mezz.) when he sees her on the occasion of her state visit. Solomon forces

Assad to marry Sulamith (sop.). Assad serves a prison sentence for having committed sacrilege during the marriage ceremony. Released from prison, he goes into the desert to seek his unhappy wife, from whom he begs forgiveness before dying in her arms.

Korngold, Erich Wolfgang (1897–1957) Gifted Austro-Hungarian-born American opera and film composer, considered one of the great composers of his day; forced as a Jew to flee the Nazi onslaught; most famous for his many Hollywood film scores. Among his operas, all rarely performed, is the celebrated *Die tote Stadt*.

krakowiak (krah KO: vyak) *n.* A Polish dance, named for the city of Cracow [Kraków (KRAH koof)]; more often known by its French name, *cracovienne* (krah ko: VYEHN); there is a wonderful example in Glinka's *Zhizn za tsarya (A Life for the Tsar)*.

Kreisler, Fritz (1885–1962) Austrian-born American virtuoso concert violinist, conductor, and composer; studied in Paris with Léo **Délibes**; known for his numerous violin compositions, many of which he recorded himself; wrote two operettas, both considered masterpieces: *Apple Blossoms* (1919) and *Sissy* (1932). Because of his Jewish ancestry, he went from city to city, one step ahead of the Nazis, and finally left Europe on the eve of World War II, becoming a U.S. citizen in 1943.

Křenek, Ernst (1900–1991) (EH:NST KSHEH nehk) [Usually spelled "Krenek" (KREH nehk)] Austrian-born American composer of works for the musical theater, including comic operas; an expressionist opera, *Orpheus und Eurydike* (Orpheus and Euridice) (1926) (AW*R* foys *oo*nt oy' *r*ih DEE keh); and a number of *Zeitopern*, most famously the **Zeitoper** *Jonny spielt auf*.

Kreutzer, Conradin (1780–1849) (kon *R*AH deen K*R*OY tsuh) Prolific German conductor and composer of instrumental and vocal music; wrote ca. forty operas, of which the only one that remains well known is the stirring, romantic *Das Nachtlager in Granada* (The Night Encampment at Granada) (1834) (dahs NAKHT LAH guh ihn g*r*ah NAH dah), which owes much to **Weber**; excellent recording on Capriccio CD (60 029-2;.1993).

Krieger, Henry (b. 1945) Grammy® and Tony® Award–winning American stage and screen composer; wrote scores for *The Tap Dance Kid*, *Dreamgirls*, and *Side Show* (1997). He also wrote *Romantic Poetry* (2008), with a book and lyrics by playwright and screenwriter John Patrick Shanley (b. 1950); limited run at the Manhattan Theatre Club; the story concerns two different couples and the complications in their love affairs.

Król Roger, Pasterz (King Roger, Shepherd) (krool RO zhehr PAHSH tezh) [In English, usually called *King Roger*] Opera in three acts by Karol **Szymanowski**; libretto by the composer and Polish poet Jarosław Iwaszkiewicz (yah RO swahf ee vash KYEH vihch; 1894–1980); Warsaw Opera, 1926.

In 12th-c. Sicily, at the court of King Roger (bar.), his wife, Queen Roxane (sop.), falls in love with the itinerant Indian prophet (ten.) of an obscure Dionysian cult, who converts both the king and queen. They renounce Christianity over the protests of the Archbishop of Palermo (bass). The opera ends with a bacchanalian feast.

kuchipudi (KOO chee POO dee) *n.* An Indian form of dance-drama, incorporating music and mime.

kujawiak (koo YAH vyak) *n.* A fast-paced Polish dance, similar to a **mazurka**.

Künneke, Eduard (1885–1953) (EHD wahrt KÜ neh keh) German composer of instrumental works, operas, and some dozen operettas; student of Max **Bruch**; worked in New York in 1924–1925 for the Shuberts on a **pastiche** (def. 2) biographical operetta, *Offenbach*, and other projects, and learned about American musical theater; known for his rousing, jazzy, energetic style, exemplified in such works as the exciting, delightful *Lady Hamilton* (1926), about the love of Lord Nelson and Lady Emma Hamilton. The operetta may be set in the Napoleonic era, but it has all the musical hallmarks of the United States in the 1920s. A rousing 1953 recording—authentic in style, since it is conducted by Franz Marszalek (1900–1975) (mah[r]' SHAH lehk), who officiated at the operetta's premiere—is available from IMC Music (GL 100.774; 2007); included in the album are highlights from Künneke's *Traumland* (Dreamland) (1941) (TROWM LAHNT). His greatest success is the hilarious ***Der Vetter aus Dingsda***.

kuse (KOO seh:') *n.* [Japanese: story] The narrative at the heart of a **noh** play that is either danced and sung, or else only sung by the **ji** (the **chorus**); it recounts the background of the story.

L

La Cage aux Folles (lah KAHZH oh FOL) [The French word *folle* means "mad-woman," and is also homosexual slang for "queen" or "**drag** queen"] Broadway musical by Jerry **Herman**; book by Harvey **Fierstein**, based on the hilarious 1978 French film and stage play of the same name; Palace Theatre, 1983 (1761 perf.); Broadway revival, Marquis Theatre, 2004 (229 perf.).

Above La Cage aux Folles (The [Drag] Queens' Cage), a nightclub on the French Riviera, is the apartment of its gay owners, partners Albin (ahl BA*N*) and Georges (ZHAW*R*ZH). Albin is the talented female impersonator who stars in the club's drag show. Georges's son, Jean-Michel (zhahn' mih SHEHL), is engaged to be married to Anne, daughter of a right-wing politician. Jean-Michel insists that his parents conceal the true nature of their relationship, redecorate to get rid of any gay ornamentation; and enlists the help of his biological mother, who is late for the dinner to which the prospective in-laws have been invited. By the time she shows up, Albin, in drag as Jean-Michel's mother, has nearly blown the cover-up. All attempts at concealment backfire in any case, since the press has managed to follow the politician to the club. He avoids publicity by escaping in drag.

LaChiusa, Michael John (b. 1962) (lah KYOO zah) Highly gifted American composer and writer, known for his brilliant sense of style and challenging, original music. Among his many musicals are *Hello Again* (1993); *The Petrified Prince* (1994), performed at New York's Public Theater; *Marie Christine* (1999); and *The Wild Party*.

Lady, Be Good Broadway musical by George **Gershwin**; book by Guy **Bolton** and Fred Thompson; lyrics by Ira Gershwin; Liberty Theatre, 1924 (330 perf.); film, 1941.

This was the first Broadway collaboration of the Gershwin brothers, and it starred Fred Astaire (1899–1987) and his sister Adele (1896–1981). The silly plot did not prevent the show from being a hit, and the score is particularly felicitous, with such songs as "Fascinating Rhythm" and "Oh, Lady Be Good."

The wealthy real estate owner Josephine Vanderwater has been spurned by Dick Trevor, who is in love with Shirley Vernon. In revenge, Josephine has Dick and his sister Susie evicted from their apartment. They are forced to live on the sidewalk temporarily, but their lawyer, "Watty" Watkins, comes up with a scheme to make money. Although the scheme results in complications, Dick and Susie win out.

Lady Hamilton Operetta by Eduard **Künneke**.

Lady in the Dark Broadway musical by Kurt **Weill**; book by Moss **Hart**; lyrics by Ira **Gershwin**; Alvin Theatre, 1941 (162 perf., and in a **return engagement** the same year, 305 perf.); film, 1944.

The show, co-directed by Hart and Hassard Short, starred Gertrude Lawrence, and featured Danny Kaye (1913–1987) in a patter song, "Tschaikovsky."

The troubled magazine editor Liza Elliott no longer seems to be able to make business or editorial decisions, so she decides to go into therapy with Dr. Brooks. During the course of her analysis, she relates her dreams, and much of the musical is devoted to surreal dream sequences. By the end of her therapy, Liza has regained her functionality and her love for her work, as well as her ability to feel love for her advertising manager, Charley Johnson.

Lady Macbeth of the Mtsensk District, The Opera by Dmitri **Shostakovich**. See LEDY MAKBET MTSENSKOVO UYEZDA.

Lakmé (lahk MÉ) Opera in three acts by Léo **Délibes**; libretto by Philippe **Gille** and prolific playwright and librettist Edmond Gondinet (1828–1888) (ehd mo:*n*' go:*n* dee NEH:), based on the novel *Le mariage de Loti* (Loti's Marriage) (1880) (luh mah *r*ee ahzh' duh lo: TEE) [Original title, *Rarahu* (*r*ah' *r*ah Ü), the title character, a Tahitian girl with whom Loti is in love] by writer and traveler Pierre Loti (1850–1923) (pee ehr' lo: TEE) [pseudonym of Julien Viaud (zhü lyeh*n*' vee O:)]; Paris, Théâtre de l'Opéra-Comique, 1883.

In mid-19th c. British-occupied India, the English officer Gérald (zhé *R*AHLD) (ten.) falls in love with Lakmé (sop.), daughter of Nilakantha (nee lah' kah*n* TAH) (bar.), the Brahmin high priest. He is ready to abandon his duty to his regiment for her. Torn between her religion and her desires, she loves him in return, but her father is furious at the violation of his temple, and swears revenge. He forces his daughter to sing at the local bazaar, knowing that her song will cause her unidentified lover to reveal himself. When Gérald appears, Lakmé involuntarily gives him away by fainting. Nilakantha stabs him, but fails to kill him, and he is spirited away to a secret hideout, where Lakmé nurses him back to health. He is found by his friend and colleague, the officer Frédéric (fré dé *R*IH:K) (bass), who persuades him to return to his duties. When Lakmé realizes what is happening, she takes poison.

Lalo, Édouard (1823–1892) (é dwah*r*' lah LO:) French composer of great melodic gifts, and a brilliant master of orchestration; he wrote four operas, of which the most well known is the gorgeously orchestrated *Le roi d'Ys* (The King of Ys) (1888) (luh *r*wah DEES), based on the Breton legend of the submerged city of Ys (EES).

lament *n.* [Fr. Italian *lamento* (lah MEHN to:): lament] An aria in which a character mourns some person or happening; esp. associated with baroque opera. The lament is always in a slow tempo; it sometimes resembles recitative, and always involves a pause in the action of the opera. There are famous examples in *Dido and Aeneas* by Henry **Purcell**, and in *Orlando* (1753) by **Handel**.

Land des Lächelns, Das (The Land of Smiles) (dahs LAHNT dehs LEH*KH* uhlnts) Operetta in three acts by Franz **Lehár**; libretto by dramatist and gynecologist Ludwig Herzer (1872–1939) (HEH*R* tsuh[*r*]) [pen name of Ludwig Herl (HEH*R*L)] and Fritz **Löhner**; considerably revised version of *Die gelbe Jacke* (The Yellow Jacket) (1923) (dee GEHL buh YAH kuh); Berlin, Metropol-Theater,

1929. The role of Sou-Chong was written for Richard **Tauber**, who sang and recorded one of Lehár's most well loved songs, "Dein ist mein ganzes Herz" (My Whole Heart Is Yours) (DIN ihst mIn GAHN tsehs HEH*R*TS).

In Vienna in 1912, at a ball given by Count Lichtenfels (L*I*KH tehn FEHLS) (speaking role), his daughter Lisa (LEE zah) (sop.) finds herself increasingly bored. But among the guests is the Chinese Prince Sou-Chong (ZOO CHO:NG) (ten.), whose tales of China intrigue her. He must soon return home, but it is clear that they love each other, and she goes with him to Peking, where there is an elaborate ceremony in which he dons a yellow jacket as a symbol of his new office as prime minister. Sou-Chong is obliged to marry four wives, but he cannot bear the idea, because his heart is given solely to Lisa: "Dein ist mein ganzes Herz." Meanwhile, Lisa's friend Gustl (G*OO* stl) (sop.) has arrived, and Lisa, who chafes under the restrictions imposed on women in China, feels nostalgic for Vienna. She decides to go home, but Sou Chong orders her to stay. Gustl and Lisa concoct an escape plan. They are discovered, and she begs Sou Chong to let her go. With deep sorrow, which he hides, he does so, and she and Gustl return to Austria.

ländler (LEHNDT luh) *n.* [Fr. German *Land* (LAHNT): country; countryside; land] An 18th- and 19th-c. Austrian or German country dance in 3/4 or 3/8 time; similar to the **waltz**, of which it was the predecessor; sometimes used in operas and ballets.

Landstreicher, Die (The Tramps) Viennese operetta by Carl Michael **Ziehrer**.

Lane, Burton (1912–1997) American film and stage songwriter and composer; wrote music for the 1931 edition of ***Earl Carroll Vanities***; among his many shows are ***Finian's Rainbow*** and ***On a Clear Day You Can See Forever***.

Lapine, James (b. 1949) American director and writer; collaborator on several projects with William **Finn**, whose ***Falsettos*** and ***The 25th Annual Putnam County Spelling Bee*** he directed; and with Stephen **Sondheim**: He directed *Sunday in the Park with George*, and directed and co-wrote ***Into the Woods*** and *Passion*.

La Plume de Ma Tante Broadway revue. See PLUME DE MA TANTE, LA.

largo (LAHR go:) *adv.* [Italian: broad; wide] A performance mark: at a slow, broadly open tempo, with sustained stateliness and a broad, emotional touch; expansively.

Later the Same Evening Opera by John **Musto**.

Latin jazz South and Central American music derived from the **jazz** forms cultivated in the United States, esp. associated with the 1940s and with popular South American dances such as the **mambo**; characterized by strong percussion and syncopated rhythms.

Latouche, John (1917–1956) American lyricist and librettist; wrote the text for ***The Ballad of Baby Doe*** and many Broadway musicals, among them the revue ***Pins and Needles***, as well as some lyrics for Bernstein's ***Candide***.

Laurents, Arthur (b. 1918) American stage and screen writer and director; wrote books for *Gypsy*, of which he directed several revivals; *West Side Story*; Stephen Sondheim's *Anyone Can Whistle* (1964); and *Do I Hear a Waltz?* by Richard **Rodgers**; directed Jerry Herman's *La Cage Aux Folles*.

Lawrence, Jerome (1915–2004) American playwright; together with Robert Edmund **Lee**, he did the books for two projects by Jerry **Herman**: *Mame* and *Dear World* (1969). They also wrote the hit Broadway play *Inherit the Wind* (1955).

lead sheet A list in order of the musical cues in a show, used by the music director in place of a full score.

leader *n.* The musical conductor, esp. of a band or small jazz or pop music orchestra, e.g., a dance orchestra. Also called a *bandleader. Brit.* Concertmaster (the first violinist).

Leave It to Jane A **Princess Theatre musical** in style, if not in actuality, by Jerome **Kern**; book and lyrics by Guy **Bolton** and P. G. **Wodehouse**, based on the play *The College Widow* (1915) by American novelist, humorist, and dramatist George Ade (1866–1944); Longacre Theatre, 1917 (167 perf.); Off-Broadway revival, Sheridan Square Playhouse, 1958 (928 perf.).

The daughter of the president of Atwater College, Jane Witherspoon, cynosure of all undergraduate eyes, connives at gaining victory by the Atwater football team over Bingham College: She convinces halfback Billy Bolton to enroll at Atwater and not at Bingham, as he had originally planned. He wins the game, and he gets the girl.

Leave It to Me! Broadway musical by Cole **Porter**; book by Sam and Bella **Spewack**, based on their 1932 comedy, *Clear All Wives*; Imperial Theatre, 1938 (291 perf.).

This was Mary Martin's Broadway debut. One of the best known numbers from the sparkling score is "My Heart Belongs to Daddy," a strip-tease that Martin did as the secretary Dolly Winslow. Written and produced in the grim era preceding World War II, the show contained humor that was at first appreciated; but as things began to look worse and worse, and the Hitler-Stalin pact was signed, it lost its appeal, and the show closed.

The reluctant ambassador to Soviet Russia, Alonzo P. Goodhue, only got the appointment because his society hostess wife gave a great deal of money to President Franklin D. Roosevelt's re-election campaign. The fledgling ambassador is so desperate to return home that he misbehaves, hoping to be recalled. He even shoots a brash politician right in Red Square. But everything he does backfires, and he is considered a hero. Then he lights on a sure plan: He will try to reconcile everyone and secure world peace. This is considered so stupid that he is immediately summoned back to the United States and relieved of his ambassadorship.

Lecocq, Charles (1832–1918) (shah*r*l' luh KOK) One of the greatest French operetta composers. He was a near rival of **Offenbach** (whom he sometimes imitated shamelessly), but Lecocq was noted more for sentimental, elegant, and stylish comic operas than for satire. His style of operetta became very popular after the end of Napoleon the Third's empire and the defeat of France in the Franco-Prussian war of 1870–1871. Among Lecocq's masterpieces are *Le petit duc*, *La Fille de Madame Angot*, and *Giroflé, Girofla*.

See also UNDINE.

Ledy Makbet Mtsentskovo uyezda (Lady Macbeth of the Mtsensk District) (LEH' dee mahk BEHT MTSEHNSK ko vo: oo YEHZ dah) (MTSEHNSK) Opera in four acts by Dmitri **Shostakovich**; libretto by the composer and poet, playwright, and librettist Alexander Preis (1905–1942) (PRIS), based on one of the most well known novels by Nikolai Semyonovich Leskov (1831–1895) (NIH' ko ll syem YON o vihch lyihs KO:F); Leningrad, Maly (MAH lee) Theatre, 1934; revised and retitled *Katerina Izmaylova* (kah' teh REE nah ihz' MI lo: vah) in 1963.

In the provincial city of Mtsensk in 1865, Katerina Izmaylova (sop.) is disenchanted with her rich merchant husband, Zinovy (zih NO: vee) (bar.). She also endures mistreatment by her boorish father-in-law, Boris (bo REES) (bass). While Zinovy is away on business, Katerina has an affair with their new servant, Sergei (sehr GAY) (ten.). Boris discovers what has been going on, and has Sergei beaten. Katerina poisons her father-in-law. When her husband returns, she and Sergei murder him as well, and hide the body in the cellar. They arrange to get married, but during the wedding feast, the body is discovered. They are arrested and sent to Siberia, where Sergei, already unhappy with Katerina, succeeds in seducing another prisoner, Sonyetka (SO nyeht kah) (con.). Katerina throws herself into the river, and pulls Sonyetka with her to a watery grave.

Lee, Robert Edwin (1918–1994) American lyricist and playwright; wrote plays and musical books with his usual writing partner, Jerome **Lawrence**, including the book and lyrics for *Shangri-La* (1956), a musical based on *Lost Horizon* (1933; film, 1937) by British novelist James Hilton (1900–1954), who worked with them on it; the music was by Harry **Warren**; it lasted for two weeks. The most famous Lawrence and Lee musical is *Mame*, with a score by Jerry **Herman**.

leg shows *Hist.* From the 1860s throughout the 19th c., American musical extravaganzas whose main feature was women in tights showing off their legs in dance numbers; the forerunner of 20th-c. **burlesque**.

Legally Blonde: The Musical Broadway musical with songs by Lawrence O'Keefe and Nell Benjamin; book by Heather Hach, based on the 2001 film of the same name; opened at the Palace Theatre, 2007 (625 perf.) after playing in San Francisco; taped for television before a live audience in 2008, while it was still running; several international productions and a successful national tour.

Warner Huntington III dumps his girlfriend, sorority president Elle Woods, because he thinks she is just another dumb blonde. To prove him wrong, she applies for and is accepted at Harvard Law School, where he has enrolled. Elle falls in love with Emmett Forest, a teaching assistant. Meanwhile, Warner has found another girlfriend, Vivienne, who is as nasty as can be to Elle. Elle becomes class valedictorian, and Vivienne applies to join the Peace Corps. Warner quits law to pursue a modeling career, and Emmett and Elle get engaged.

legato (leh GAH toh) *adj.* [Italian: linked] Pertains to smooth, even singing and playing, with the notes linked together and not separated.

legitimate singing The vocal technique and aesthetic style used by a singer trained to place the **voice** in the **mask**, and to control the changing muscular tensions involved in the shifts between the **chest voice** and the **head voice**; heard in classical music, opera, operetta, some Broadway musicals, and some popular music: *She belts, but she also sings legit.* Opera and many operettas require more expertise and agility than any other form of musical theater. Broadway musical comedy usually does not demand the same kind of control and flexibility that opera does, because—despite the variety of styles, e.g., rock, blues, popular ballads—the music does not have the great range or ornamented passages found in opera. Called *legit singing* or *legit,* for short. Cf. **belt.**

Lehár, Franz (1870–1948) (*FRAHNTS* LEH: hah[*r*]) [b. Lehár Ferenc (FEH rehnts)] Hungarian-born Austrian operetta composer, one of the greatest and most loved; conductor, who recorded a number of his own works. He wrote thirty Viennese operettas, among them *Die lustige Witwe (The Merry Widow)*; *Der Graf von Luxemburg (The Count of Luxembourg)*; *Das Land des Lächelns (The land of Smiles)*; *Zigeunerliebe* (Gypsy Love) (1910) (tsih GOY nuh LEE beh); *Eva* (1911); *Frasquita* (1922; revised 1933); *Paganini* (1925); *Der Zarewitsch* (The Czarevich) (1927) (deh tsah *REH*: vihch); *Friederike* (1928), a truly splendid score; and *Giuditta* (1934).

Lehrstück (LEH:[*R*] SHTÜK) *n.* [German: teaching-piece, play] *Hist.* During the 1920s and 1930s, a play with songs meant to inculcate a political lesson, usually Marxist in nature. Berthold **Brecht**, for instance, wrote such pieces, of which he may have been the inventor; among them, *Der Jasager* (The Yes-Man) (1930) (deh: YAH ZAH guh), music by Kurt **Weill**; and *Die Massnahme* (The Measures Taken) (1930) (dee MAHS NAH muh), music by Hans **Eisler.** Cf. **Zeitoper.**

Leigh, Carolyn (1926–1983) American lyricist; often wrote songs with Cy **Coleman**; did lyrics for several Broadway shows, including *Little Me* and *Peter Pan* (1954).

Leigh, Mitch (b. 1928) American composer, songwriter, director, and producer; esp. known for his hit show, *Man of La Mancha.*

Leitmotiv (LIT mo: TEEF) *n.* [German: lead, leading-theme, guiding motive; usual English spelling: leitmotif] In opera, the principal recurring musical theme associated with a character, or, sometimes, with a place or idea. The audience is reminded of the character every time the leitmotif is heard, whether the character is present or not; it sometimes heralds the character's arrival; famously used as a compositional device by **Wagner.**

186

Léon, Victor (1858–1940) (VIHK to:r LÉ o:n) [b. Viktor Hirschfeld] Austrian librettist, esp. known for his libretto to *Die lustige Witwe (The Merry Widow)* (in collaboration with Lco **Stein**) by Franz **Lehár**.

Leoncavallo, Ruggero (1857–1919) (roodg DGEH: ro: leh:' o:n kah VAHL lo:) Italian **verismo** composer of some twenty operas, best known for *Pagliacci*. Among his other works are a version of *La bohème* that fails to rival that of Puccini; his first opera, *Chatterton* (1876), about the romantic English poet; and the occasionally performed *Zazà* (1900).

Lerner and Loewe American librettist and lyricist Alan Jay Lerner (1918–1986) and composer Frederick **Loewe**: the writing team that produced such Broadway megahits as *Brigadoon*, *My Fair Lady*, *Paint Your Wagon*, *Camelot*, and, less successful in its Broadway production, *Gigi*, based on their film. Lerner also wrote books and lyrics for other composers, among them Kurt **Weill**.

Les Misérables [Popularly known as *Les Mis* or *Les Miz*] International and Broadway pop-opera by Claude-Michel **Schönberg**; adapted and expanded in a "rough translation" (his words) by South African-born English writer Herbert Kretzmer (b. 1925), from the French libretto of Alain **Boublil**, based on the novel of the same name by Victor **Hugo**; Paris, Palais des Sports (pah leh:' deh: SPO:*R*), 1980; London, Barbican Arts Center, then Palace Theatre, 1985 (still playing at Queen's Theatre as of this writing); New York: Broadway Theatre, later moved to Imperial, 1987 (6680 perf.); Broadway revival, Broadhurst Theatre, 2006 (479 perf.); many long-running tours.

In the Restoration France (1820s–'30s) of the Bourbons, Jean Valjean, sentenced to prison for stealing a loaf of bread, is released after serving a nineteen-year sentence; but he is pursued by police inspector Javert for the rest of his life, since Javert believes all former convicts are potential recidivists. Valjean has made every effort to change his life and disguise his identity, becoming the good M. Madeleine, mayor of a provincial town. He gives aid to Fantine, an unwed mother who is desperately ill. Then, after being unmasked as a released convict, he is forced to flee again, this time to the anonymity of life in Paris. He has also been raising Cosette, daughter of the deceased Fantine. Cosette falls in love with the young revolutionary Parisian student Marius, whose life Valjean saves during an uprising. Once again, Valjean's identity is revealed, and he decides to surrender to Javert. The inspector is thereby unmanned. Unable to bear the thought that he has been wrong all his life, and that the man he has considered a criminal is really a good, ethical person, he kills himself.

Leterrier, Eugène French librettist; writing partner of Albert **Vanloo**.

libretto (lih BREH toh) *n.* [Italian: little book.] The text, or **book** of an opera, comic opera, or operetta; hence, *librettist*: the writer of a libretto.

Lied (LEET) *n.*, *n. pl. Lieder* (LEE duh) [German: song] A song for a soloist, usually accompanied by the piano, sometimes by other instruments or the full orchestra; a German art song.

Liederspiel (LEE duh[*r*], or deh[*r*] SHPEEL) *n.* [German: songs-play] *Hist.* An early 19th-c. popular German light comedy or drama with interpolated songs.

Life Begins at 8:40 Broadway musical revue with twenty songs by Harold **Arlen**, lyrics by Ira **Gershwin** and E. Y. **Harburg**; Winter Garden Theatre, 1934 (237 perf.). The revue featured comic sketches and amusing songs, all centered around Depression-era themes. Among its beloved stars were Ray Bolger (1904–1987), Dixie Dunbar (1919–1991), Luella Gear (1907–1980), and Bert Lahr.

Life for the Tsar, A Opera by Mikhail **Glinka**. See ZHIZN ZA TSARYA.

Light in the Piazza, The Operatic Broadway musical by Adam **Guettel**; book by playwright, screenwriter, director and actor Craig Lucas (b. 1951), based on the novella of the same name by Elizabeth Spencer (b. 1921), also adapted for the screen in 1962; Vivian Beaumont Theatre, 2005 (504 perf.); final performance broadcast, 2006, on PBS-TV. The score is evocative, and there are many beautiful songs and some lovely moments in this nostalgic, moving show.

While vacationing in Florence, Margaret Johnson, a tourist from North Carolina, and her slightly brain-damaged, immature daughter Clara, meet the Nacarelli family. The son, Fabrizio, falls in love with Clara, and the suspicious Margaret tries to prevent their seeing each other. But, realizing they are deeply in love, she finally agrees to the marriage.

light opera Charming pieces that deal with light, amusing, romantic situations; **comic opera**; a catch-all term that applies to Viennese operetta, some musical comedy, and the comic operas of such composers as **Donizetti** or **Offenbach**.

Li'l Abner Broadway musical by pianist and songwriter Gene de Paul (1919–1988); lyrics by Johnny **Mercer**; book by the show's co-producers, screenwriters Norman Panama (1914–2003) and Melvin Frank (1913–1988), based on characters in the popular cartoon series of the same name by Al Capp (1909–1979); St. James Theatre, 1956 (693 perf.); film, 1959. The show is utterly silly and highly entertaining, and the boisterous, tuneful score is rambunctious and farcical.

Set in hillbilly Dogpatch, the story concerns the carryings-on of the local catch, Li'l Abner Yokum, spunky Mammy Yokum, henpecked Pappy Yokum, and Abner's sweet, old-fashioned girlfriend, Daisy Mae. The preacher Marryin' Sam, the loud-mouth General Bullmoose, and the siren Appassionata Von Climax are among the other characters. Appassionata wants what she can't have: Abner. But everything turns out all right, and the town is saved from being the site of an atomic bomb test, in the place the government considers the biggest waste in the entire country.

Lily of Killarney, The Opera in three acts by Sir Julius **Benedict**; libretto by play-wright, theater critic, and translator John Oxenford (1812–1877) and prolific Anglo-Irish playwright Dion Boucicault (1820?–1890) (DI o:n boo' sih KOH), based on his play *The Colleen Bawn* [Irish Gaelic, *bawn*: white, fair, blonde]; London, Covent Garden, 1867. The few recorded excerpts of this once internationally popular piece are very beautiful, with truly lovely melodies reminiscent of Irish folk song.

Hardress Cregan (ten.) is secretly married to a peasant lass, Eily O'Connor (I lee) (sop.). Mr. Corrigan (bass), who holds the mortgage on the Cregan estate, visits Hardress's widowed mother, Mrs. Cregan (contr.), and threatens to marry her unless the debt is paid. The only way out of this dilemma seems to be for Hardress to marry the wealthy heiress Ann Shute (sop.), so he goes to Eily and tries to get their marriage certificate from her. But, persuaded by the priest Father Tom (bass) and Myles na Coppaleen (ten.), who is in love with her, she will not give it up. Nevertheless, Cregan woos Ann, albeit reluctantly. His friend Danny Mann (bar.) offers to help him by murdering Eily, but Cregan is horrified. Danny goes in search of Eily, and drowns her (or so he thinks). On the way home, he is accidentally shot by Myles, out hunting, and he confesses to the murder before he dies. But Myles had heard her Eily's cries, and had rescued her. Soon, the day dawns when Cregan is supposed to marry Ann, but Corrigan and some soldiers arrive, and he is arrested for plotting the murder. He is about to be taken away, when Eily and Myles show up. Cregan realizes that he adores his wife, and announces to all present that he is married to Eily. Moved to tears, Ann bestows on the Cregans all the financial help they need.

Lincke, Paul (1866–1946) (POWL LIHN keh) [b. Carl Emil Paul Lincke] German operetta composer; wrote some dozen works; remembered for the Berlin anthem "Berliner Luft" (Berlin Air) (beh[r] LEE nuh LOOFT), from his most well known operetta, *Frau Luna* (Madam Moon) (1899) (FROW LOO nah); film, 1941; a party of Berliners take a trip to the moon and meet Frau Luna and her court. Other well known operettas of his are *Im Reiche des Indra* (In the Kingdom of Indra) (1899) (ihm RI kheh dehs IHN drah) and *Lysistrata* (1902), which contains the song "Glühwürmchen" (Little Glowworm) (GLÜ VÜ[R]M khen), arranged by Johnny **Mercer** as "Glow Little Glow Worm."

Lindau, Carl (1853–1934) (LIHN dow) [b. Karl Gemperle (GEHM peh[r] leh)] Austrian comic actor who switched careers to become a prolific Austrian librettist, with ca.100 original libretti and translations to his credit, many written in collaboration; e.g., ***The Yeomen of the Guard*** by **Gilbert and Sullivan**, which Lindau and Leo **Stein** translated in 1889 as *Capitän Wilson* (kah' pih: TEH:N). He also collaborated on translations of many Gaiety musicals, and on such original libretti as *Die Landstreicher* by **Ziehrer**.

Linley, Thomas (1733–1795) English composer; wrote a dozen operas; best known for the score to *The Duenna* (1775), to a libretto by his son-in-law, the Irish playwright and member of parliament Richard Brinsley Sheridan (1751–1816), married to Elizabeth Linley (1754–1792), a singer. She performed in the piece, and Linley's son, Thomas (1756–1778), a violinist and composer, collaborated with his father on the score.

Lion King, The Broadway musical by Elton **John** (music), Tim **Rice** (lyrics), and Irene Mecchi (book), based on their 1994 Walt Disney animated feature of the same name; new music, lyrics, and scenes added for the stage adaptation, variously contributed by Elton John and Tim Rice; the show's director, Julie Taymor (b. 1952); the show's choral director and vocal arranger, South African musician Lebo M. (b. 1964) [Lebohang Morake]; and others; additional music by Hans Zimmer (b. 1957), who wrote the background score for the film; New Amsterdam Theatre, 1997; later moved to the Minskoff, where it is still running as of this writing; international megahit.

The Lion King, Mufasa, and Queen Sarabi present their son, Simba, heir to the throne, to their assembled subjects at Pride Rock on the African savannah. Mufasa's evil brother, Scar, wants the throne for himself. When Simba visits him, he piques his nephew's curiosity by talking about the elephant graveyard, where Simba is forbidden to go. Accompanied by friends, they go anyway. Scar starts a stampede and tells Mufasa that his son is trapped in its path. When Mufasa hurries to rescue Simba, the king is trampled to death, and Scar insinuates to Simba that he is the cause. Simba runs away and grows up far from the court, while Scar mounts the throne and proves to be a terrible monarch. Rafiki, a wise old baboon who has befriended Simba, persuades him to return home to avenge his father's murder. There is a battle, and Scar is killed. Simba becomes king and marries his childhood sweetheart. Once again, all the animals come to pay tribute, and the king and queen present their new cub, heir to the throne.

Lindsay and Crouse Playwriting team Howard Lindsay (1869–1968) and Russel Crouse (1893–1966), best known for their Broadway hit play *Life with Father*, which opened in 1939 and ran through 1945; film, 1947, starring the urbane, polished William Powell (1892–1984), who played Florenz **Ziegfeld** in several films. Lindsay and Crouse wrote the books for Cole Porter's ***Anything Goes***; ***The Sound of Music*** by **Rodgers and Hammerstein**; and *Mr. President* (1962) by Irving **Berlin**.

lindyhop *n.* A jazzy 1920s American dance that was a variation of the **Charleston**. Called *lindy*, for short.

Literaturoper (lih:' teh: rah TOOuh[r] O: peh:[r]) *n.* [German: literature-opera] An opera set to an extant literary work, in which the script of a play or of a narrative poem is set to music virtually intact or with minimal alteration; e.g., Nicolai Rimsky-Korsakov's *Mozart and Salieri* (1898), a setting of the dramatic poem by Alexander Pushkin; Claude Debussy's ***Pelléas et Mélisande***; Ralph Vaughan Williams' *Riders to the Sea* (1937), set to the text of John Millington Synge's play.

Little Mary Sunshine Off-Broadway musical comedy by Rick **Besoyan**; book and lyrics by the composer; Orpheum Theatre, 1959 (1143 perf.).

This show is a hilarious parody of sentimental 1920s operettas, esp. those that were filmed with Nelson Eddy and Jeannette McDonald.

Mary Potts, nicknamed Little Mary Sunshine by the Kadota [Dakota] Indians, led by the sage Chief Brown Bear, her foster father, is an eternal Pollyannaish optimist. She owns and runs the Colorado Inn in the Rocky Mountains, where she is forever entertaining the customers with cheerful songs. The land on which the inn is located is the subject of a lawsuit between the Kadotas and the U.S. government. But Chief Brown Bear gives the inn to Mary, and the rest of the land is to be a national park. Meanwhile, Captain Jim Warington and the Forest Rangers, including Corporal Billy Jester, have played their valiant part in preventing trouble. Jim and Little Mary Sunshine end up in each other's arms.

Little Me Broadway musical by Cy **Coleman**; lyrics by Carolyn **Leigh**; book by prolific comedy writer Neil Simon, based on the novel of the same name by Patrick Dennis; Lunt-Fontanne Theatre, 1962 (257 perf.); Broadway revivals in revised versions, Eugene O'Neill Theatre, 1982 (101 perf.); Roundabout Theatre Company at Criterion Center Stage Right, 1998 (99 perf.).

The show was a star vehicle for comedian Sid Caesar (b. 1922), who played multiple roles; Simon was one of the writers on Caesar's hit television variety series, *Your Show of Shows* (1950–1954).

The notorious Hollywood star and social climber Belle Poitrine, widow of Fred Poitrine, a soldier killed in action in World War I, decides to collaborate with Patrick Dennis on writing her memoirs about how she got ahead by capitalizing on her various conquests. When she was a girl from the wrong side of the tracks in Venezuela, IL, she had fallen in love with Noble Eggleston, a boy from the right side of the tracks. In order to win his love, she had set out to attain fame and riches. In the end, Belle and Noble are reunited, and all ends happily ever after, after all.

Little Mermaid, The Broadway musical by Alan **Menken**; book by Doug Wright (b. 1962), based on the 1998 Walt Disney cartoon adapted from the fairy tale of the same name by Hans Christian **Andersen**; lyrics by Howard **Ashman**; Menken and Ashman also wrote the music and lyrics for the cartoon; Lunt-Fontanne Theatre, 2007 (685 perf.).

The silver-voiced mermaid Princess Ariel, daughter of King Triton, is unhappy in the undersea world and longs to live among the humans she has seen on land. She falls in love with Prince Eric and makes a pact with Ursula, the witch, to give up her beautiful voice in exchange for being changed into a human. But she must make Eric kiss her, or all will be lost, and she will be turned back into a mermaid and enslaved to Ursula. In order to ensure that Ariel will fail, the witch disguises herself as a beautiful woman and sings with Ariel's voice, but she is exposed in time and is slain by the prince. Ariel has, in fact, become a mermaid again, but her compassionate father turns her back into a human so that she can be reunited with Eric.

Little Night Music, A Broadway musical by Stephen **Sondheim**; book by Hugh **Wheeler**, based on Ingmar Bergman's (1918–2007) film comedy, *Smiles of a Summer Night* (1955); Shubert Theatre, 1973 (601 perf.); film, 1978. The title is a translation of the name of Mozart's famous, popular 1787 *Serenade Number 13 for Strings*, known as *Eine kleine Nachtmusik* (I' nuh klI' nuh nahkht' moo zeek').

Under Harold Prince's superb direction, this bittersweet, witty comedy of manners about the nature of love and its complicated desires, its disappointments and its joys, was an engrossing, lovely production, esp. with Sondheim's evocative, nostalgic score.

The wealthy Swedish lawyer Frederik Egerman has unwisely married the beautiful Anne, a shy young woman half his age. She is so sexually repressed that she has remained a virgin, and the frustrated and worldly Frederik is drawn to the charms of his former mistress, the famous actress Desiree Armfeldt, currently the mistress of Count Carl-Magnus Malcolm. The jealous Countess Charlotte tells Anne that Frederik is having an affair with Desiree. Meanwhile, Anne is attracted to Henrik, her stepson, who is her age. Desiree gets her mother, the aged former courtesan Madame Armfeldt, to invite Frederik, Anne, and Henrik to her country estate; Carl-Magnus and Charlotte also arrive, unexpectedly. On one enchanted moonlit night, Anne runs away with Henrik, Carl-Magnus and Charlotte rediscover their love for each other, and Frederik finds happiness in the arms of Desiree. Dear Madame Armfeldt slips quietly and peacefully out of this life.

Little Shop of Horrors Off-Broadway musical by Alan **Menken**; book by Howard **Ashman**, who also directed, based on the screenplay of the 1960 film *The Little Shop of Horrors*; Orpheum Theatre, 1982 (2209 perf.); Broadway revival, Virginia Theatre, 2003 (372 perf.), directed by Jerry Zaks (b. 1946); film, 1986. This grisly little offbeat spoof of horror pictures is a classic, and it is quite hilarious, accompanied by very funny and engaging music.

The repressed and nerdy botanist Seymour Krelbourn works in Mr. Mushnik's flower shop. Seymour is in love with the salesgirl, Audrey, but does not dare to let her know it. By chance, he happens upon a curious plant that survives on human blood. It brings him fame and fortune, but the plant is insatiable, and Seymour is obliged to feed it with Mr. Mushnik and parts of Dr. Orin Scrivello, a sadistic dentist who was Audrey's boyfriend. The plant eventually devours everyone, including Seymour and Audrey.

Little Women 1. Novel published first in two parts, 1868 and 1869, and then in 1880 as one book, by Louisa May Alcott (1832–1888), who based incidents in the story on her own family life. In Concord, MA, the sisters, Meg, Jo, Beth, and Amy March, and their mother, Margaret, known as "Marmee," are all left alone during the Civil War while their father, an army chaplain, is fighting at the front. They make do as best they can, and he writes letters home to them. Jo is a companion to her Aunt March, until she falls ill and Amy takes her place. Jo falls in love with and marries Professor Friedrich "Fritz" Bhaer, an impoverished German teacher, while Meg, the oldest, and Amy, the youngest, also marry. Beth dies of scarlet fever.
2. Opera in two acts by Mark **Adamo**; libretto by the composer, based on the novel; Houston Grand Opera, 1998; New York City Opera premiere, 2003. This critically acclaimed opera has had more than thirty-five productions world-wide, and was broadcast in 2001 as part of the series *Great Performances* on PBS.
3. Broadway musical by conductor, musical director, and composer Jason Howland, with vocal arrangements by Lance **Horne**; book by Alan Knee, based on the novel; lyrics by Mindi Dickstein; Virginia Theatre, 2004 (192 perf.).

Lizzie Borden Opera in three acts by Jack **Beeson**; libretto by Kenward Elmslie, based on a scenario by German-American writer Richard Plant (1910–1988); New York City Opera, 1965.

The opera is based on the facts of the sensational murder trial of Lizzie Borden (1860–1927) in Fall River, MA in 1892. She was accused of hacking her father, a rich banker, and her stepmother to death with an axe. She was acquitted, without being cleared in the public's mind.

Andrew Borden (bass-bar.) is a mean-spirited curmudgeon who refuses to give his daughters Lizzie (mezz.) and Margret (sop.) enough money to meet their expenses, and is under the thumb of his second wife, Abigail (sop.). He even refuses to give a church donation to his pastor, Rev. Harrington (ten.). Margret is courted by Captain Jason MacFarlane (bar.), and they elope. Andrew, who thinks Lizzie complicit in the elopement, is so upset that he tries to turn her out of the house, and her mind appears to be increasingly unhinged. Andrew and Abigail are both murdered, but offstage, in the manner of Greek tragedy, and children chant the famous nursery rhyme, "Lizzie Borden took an axe."

Lloyd Webber, Sir Andrew (b. 1948) Prolific English composer of musical theater shows; from a distinguished family of classical musicians. His pieces include the phenomenal international hits *Cats* and *The Phantom of the Opera*. His first show was *Joseph and the Amazing Technicolor Dreamcoat*. Among his other hits are *Evita*; *Sunset Boulevard* (1996), based on the 1950 film; and *Starlight Express* (London, 1984; New York, 1987).

Loesser, Frank (1910–1969) Prolific American lyricist and composer; wrote music and lyrics for such shows as *Where's Charley?* (1948), his first Broadway hit as a composer; *Guys and Dolls*; *How to Succeed in Business Without Really Trying*; and the semi-operatic *The Most Happy Fella* (1956).

Loewe, Frederick (1901–1988) American composer, born in Berlin to Viennese parents; child prodigy pianist; composer of much loved hit Broadway musicals, together with his writing partner, Alan Jay **Lerner**.

See LERNER AND LOEWE.

Löhner, Fritz (1883–1942) (FRIH:TS LÖ neh:[r]) Austrian lawyer, military officer, and classical scholar; satirical writer, under the pen names Beda (BEH: dah) and Löhner-Beda; wrote operetta libretti for Paul **Abraham** and co-wrote libretto for Franz Lehár's *Das Land des Lächelns (The Land of Smiles)*. After the Germans annexed Austria in 1938, Löhner, who was Jewish, was sent to Buchenwald concentration camp, then to Auschwitz, where he was gassed.

Lopez, Francis (1916–1995) (frahn sees lo: PEHZ) French composer of ca. forty musical comedies, including *La Belle de Cadix* (The Beautiful Woman of Cadiz) (1945) (lah behl' duh ka DEEKS), which ran for two years in Paris and starred Luis Mariano (1914–1970) (lü EES mah ree ah NO:), the highly popular Spanish-French tenor. Mariano also starred in Lopez's great stage and film hit, *Le chanteur de Mexico* (The Singer from Mexico) (1951) (luh shahn tuhr' duh mehk see KO:), which ran for 954 perf. You can see excerpts from the delightful 1956 film on YouTube. There is also an excellent 1977 recording on Universal Music Classics France (4769995; 2006); and fine recordings on the same label of excerpts from two more of his big hits, *Andalousie* (Andalusia) (1947) (ah*n*' dah loo ZEE) and *Méditerranée* (Mediterranean) (1955) (mé' dee teh' *r*ah NÉ) (4769989; 2006).

Loreley, Die Opera by Max **Bruch**.

Lortzing, Albert (1801–1851) German composer of twenty operas and operettas; librettist, conductor, singer, and actor. Lortzing had a great melodic gift and a feeling for effective, beautifully textured, imaginative orchestration. Among his most notable works are *Der Waffenschmied* (The Armourer) (1846) (deh WAHF ehn SHMEET), *Der Wildschütz* (The Poacher) (1842) (deh VIHLT SHÜTS), *Zar und Zimmermann*, and *Undine*.

Lost in the Stars Broadway musical by Kurt **Weill**; book by Maxwell **Anderson**, based on the novel *Cry, the Beloved Country* (1948) by South African novelist and political activist Alan Paton (1903–1988); Music Box Theatre, 1949 (273 perf.); Broadway revival, Imperial Theatre, 1972 (47 perf.); film, 1974.

This last musical by Weill is set in South Africa during the days of apartheid. Kumalo, a black minister, goes from his village to Johannesburg in search of his son, Absalom, from whom he has had no word in some time. Meanwhile, the impoverished young man, needing money to help his pregnant girlfriend, Irina, has participated in a robbery, during the course of which Arthur Jarvis, a white liberal, is killed. He is the son of James Jarvis, a rich white man who lives in the same village as Kumalo and Absalom. Absalom is executed, and Kumalo and James are united in grief.

Louisiana Purchase Broadway musical by Irving **Berlin**; book by Morrie Ryskind and B. G. **De Sylva**; Imperial Theatre, 1940 (444 perf.); film, 1942. The best known numbers from the sparkling score are "Fools Fall in Love" and "Wild about You."

This political satire, inspired by the carryings on of corrupt Louisiana governor Huey Long (1852–1937), takes the naïve Senator Oliver P. Loganberry to New Orleans to investigate the shady practices of the Louisiana Purchasing Company. In order to deflect the investigation and divert the senator, the company's president hires the sexy Viennese refugee Marina von Linden to vamp him, and the restaurateur Yvonne Bordelaise to satisfy his every gustatory need. Loganberry resists Marina and falls in love with Yvonne, whom he marries. A picket line prevents the senator from testifying against the company.

Louise Opera in four acts by Gustave **Charpentier**; libretto by the composer; Paris, Théâtre de l'Opéra-Comique, 1900; film, 1939; recorded in Paris in 1935, conducted by the composer: Nimbus Prima Voce CD (NI 7829; 1991).

Louise (sop.) and Julien (zhü LYEH*N*] (ten.) are in love, but her parents object to the relationship. Nevertheless, they move in together in Montmartre. But Louise's mother (mezz.) comes to tell her that her father (bass) is very ill, so she returns home to help nurse him. When he is well again, he and her mother refuse to allow Louise to return to Julien. After a bitter argument, her father throws her out of the house, and she is able to go back to the man she loves.

Love Life Broadway musical by Kurt **Weill**; book and lyrics by Alan Jay **Lerner**; 46th Street Theatre, 1948 (252 perf.). The eclectic score is virtually a history of the development of American musical styles.

The story of this **concept musical** concerns Sam and Susan Cooper, a married couple who never age as their lives progress from 1791 to 1948; each scene is introduced by a vaudeville sketch.

Love of the Three Oranges, The Opera by Serge **Prokofiev**. See LYUBOV' K TRYOM APEL'SINAM.

Lucia di Lammermoor (loo CHEE ah dee LAH mehr MOOR) Opera in three acts by Gaetano **Donizetti**; libretto by Salvadore **Cammarano**, based on the novel *The Bride of Lammermoor* (1815), by Sir Walter Scott; Naples, Teatro San Carlo, 1835.

One of the most heartbreakingly beautiful moments in this deeply felt score is the Sextet in the wedding scene, in which the characters express their conflicting emotions: "Che mi frena in tal momento" (What stops me at such a moment) (keh: mee FREH: nah ihn TAHL mo: MEHN to:), as Edgardo wonders aloud why he does not immediately avenge himself on Enrico.

Scotland in the late 16th-c. is in a state of political turmoil, in which private family feuds are mixed with public quarrels. The impressionable and sensitive Lucy (sop.) [Lucia (loo CHEE ah] is deeply in love with Edgar (ten.) [Edgardo (ehd GAHR do:)] of Ravenswood, a family that is the political enemy of her own. He must leave Scotland, and they meet to bid each other an emotional farewell. Lucy's brother, Lord Henry Ashton (bar.) [Enrico (ehn REE ko:)] forces her to marry the English lord Arthur Bucklaw (ten.) [Arturo (ahr TOO ro:)], but the ceremony is interrupted by the arrival of Edgar, who denounces Lucy for her faithlessness and makes good his escape. In their wedding chamber, Lucy stabs Arthur to death, and then goes completely mad. Edgar sees a funeral cortege bearing a coffin to its grave, and, upon inquiring, learns that it is Lucy, who has just died, whereupon he stabs himself to death.

Luders, Gustav (1865–1913) German-born American musician, conductor, arranger, and very popular composer of fifteen Broadway operettas, including *The Burgomaster* (1900), *King Dodo* (1902), and *The Prince of Pilsen* (1903), all with books by journalist, librettist, and screenwriter, Frank S. Pixley (1867– 1919); and *The Sho-Gun* (1904), with a book by George Ade. The failure of Luders's last piece, *Somewhere Else* (1913), presumably brought on his fatal heart attack, four days after the opening; the show lasted for only eight performances.

ludi Graeci thymelici (LOO dee GRI kee tee meh: LEE kee) [Latin: Greek musicians' games/entertainments; fr. Greek, *thymele* (*TH*EE meh: leh:): originally, a sacrificial altar, and, by extension, the orchestra, where it was located; by further extension, the musicians who performed in the orchestra, i.e., the orchestra in its modern sense of a group of instrumentalists] *Hist.* In ancient Rome, where there were many annual and periodic *ludi* (games; entertainments) of different kinds and in many venues, these were performances that included dancing, singing, and instrumental music, presumably inspired by Greek entertainment practices and from Greek musical sources, and perhaps done by Greek performing artists. These particular *ludi* were a form of musical theater, some of them undoubtedly done in open-air amphitheaters, some in an *odeum* (oh DEH: uhm) [Latin: a small, roofed theater building where musical perf. took place]. A performer was called a *ludio* (LOO dee o:); pl. *ludiones* (loo dee O: neh:s).

Lully, Jean-Baptiste (1632–1687) (zhah*n*' bah teest' lü LEE) [b. Giovanni Battista Lulli (dgo: VAHN nee baht TEES tah L*OO*L lee)] Italian-born French composer who collaborated with Philippe **Quinault** on ballets, and with Molière on several comédie-ballets; one of the greatest of baroque composers.

lustigen Nibelungen, Die (The Merry Nibelungs) (dee L*OO*S tih gehn NEE beh L*OO*NG ehn) "Burlesque operetta" in three acts by Oscar **Straus**; libretto by Rideamus (Dr. Fritz **Oliven**); Vienna, Carltheater (KAH[*R*]L teh: AH tuh), 1904.

This hilarious **Offenbachian** farce—Straus's first operetta—is the occasion for mordant anti-militarist, anti-nationalist satire. It sends up Norse mythology, and it is full of wonderfully disrespectful allusions to both the music and the endless plot complications of Wagner's **Ring cycle**. Straus's ebullient, joyously tuneful score is bound to keep all but the most jaded listener smiling and chuckling throughout, the more so because Rideamus's lyrics are hysterically funny. In 2008 and 2009, the operetta had successful revivals in Berlin, Vienna, and Zurich.

King Gunther (G*OO*N tuh) (bar.) of Burgund (BO*OR* G*OO*NT) is down in the mouth. In a moment of madness, he proposed marriage to Brunhilde (B*R*UN HIHL deh) (mezz.), Queen of Isenland (EE zehn LAHNT), who will only marry the person who can best her in hand to hand combat. Everybody else was proposing to her, not believing she would win, so he got on line, too. She knocked everybody flat. Now he has received a telegram from her: "Meet me at the train station at 4:25 precisely, and I'll knock you flat." Bound by the code of honor, he has no choice but to meet her. Uncle Hagen (HAH gehn) (bar.) has an idea: Invite the hero Siegfried (ZEEK f*r*eet') (ten.) to help fight her. He is the only man who has defeated her in the past, and he is invincible, because he bathes in dragon's blood and wears the magic Tarnhelm. He has also managed to steal the Rhine gold, which is now "mein Gold" (my gold) (MIN GO:LT), says he; and he has wisely invested it in the Rhine Bank at six per cent, so he is immensely wealthy, even if he did flunk out of the Gymnasium (high school)—"all that damn studying!" He would be a perfect match for Hagen's daughter, Kriemhild (K*R*EEM hihlt') (sop.), who is already in love with him. Siegfried arrives, and the match is arranged. Emboldened by Siegfried's mere presence, Gunther manages to knock Brunhilde out! So the two couples get married, but nothing is ever simple, and there are complications, lots of them. For one thing, Siegfried receives news that the Rhine

Bank has gone belly up. Just as he is congratulating himself on having married the wealthy Kriemhild, Hagen, who has decided he wants to inherit the Rhine gold, comes after him. He manages to foil Hagen's attempt on his life because a little bird told him he was going to be murdered. Meanwhile, Brunhilde is still feeling betrayed, and is not to be mollified by an offer of a share of the Rhine gold, because she has also heard that the bank crashed. All misunderstandings are eventually cleared up, and the whole clan is merry once again.

lustigen Weiber von Windsor, Die (The Merry Wives of Windsor) (dee LOOS tih geh:n VI buh[r] fuhn VIHND zo:[r]) **1.** Opera in three acts by Otto **Nicolai**; libretto by Salomon Hermann, Ritter von Mosenthal, based on Shakespeare's *The Merry Wives of Windsor*; Berlin, Königliches Opernhaus (Royal Opera House) (KÖN ih*kh* lih*kh*' ehs O: peh[r]n HOWS), 1849. The plot follows Shakespeare very closely, except that Bardolph, Pistol, and several other characters are eliminated. The husbands and wives are given German names: Fluth (FLOOT) (sop.) [Ford], and Reich (RI*KH*) (mezz.) [Page].
2. Singspiel in two acts by Carl Ditters von **Dittersdorf**; libretto by G. C. Römer (RÖ muh[r]), based on Shakespeare's play; Germany, Oels (ÖLS), 1796.

See FALSTAFF.

lustige Witwe, Die (The Merry Widow) (dee LOOS tih guh VIH:T veh) Operetta in three acts by Franz **Lehár**; libretto by Viktor **Léon** and Leo **Stein**, based on the comedy *L'attaché d'ambassade* (The Embassy Attaché) (1861) (la tah shé' dah*n* ba SAHD) by Henri **Meilhac**; Vienna, Theater an der Wien, 1905.

This is Lehár's most famous and loved operetta, produced innumerable times, filmed, and recorded; the sheet music sales alone made him a fortune.

The beautiful and rich Merry Widow, Hanna Glawari (HAH nah GLAH vah ree) (sop.), arrives in Paris from her impoverished Balkan country, Pontevedro (PO:N teh VEH dro:), intending to have a marvelous time. At the legation ball, Baron Mirko Zeta (MEER ko: ZEH: tah) (bar.), the Pontevedrian envoy to France, is not happy when French aristocrats pay her court, for he does not wish her to marry and so lose millions for his country. The baron sees a way to save the day: He will have the legation secretary, Count Danilo Danilowitsch (dah NEE lo: dah NEE lo: vihch) (ten.), woo her and wed her. But the baron does not know that Danilo and Hanna were once lovers, and when he proposes his scheme, Danilo refuses; he professes to prefer the pleasures of Maxim's, with its women of easy virtue and its flowing champagne. Danilo loves Hanna, but it is now beneath him ever to tell her so, since that would place him among the gold diggers who only want her for her money. At the party she gives at her home the next day, Hanna entertains the guests with traditional Pontevedrian folk dances done by dancers in native costume, and sings a lush Pontevedrian folk song about the Vilja (VEEL yah), the legendary Maiden of the Forest. Upset that Danilo appears to be avoiding her, she announces that she will marry the aristocrat Camille de Rosillon (kah mee' yuh duh *r*o: zee YO:*N*) (ten.), who is actually in love with Valencienne (va lah*n*' see YEHN) (sop.), the baron's wife. Danilo is thoroughly disgusted, particularly when he thinks that she has had a rendezvous with Camille in the summerhouse. But Valencienne is the one who had the rendezvous. She is a faithful wife to the baron, and had gone there to tell Camille that. Hanna and Danilo now understand each other and look forward to being united in wedded bliss.

lyric *n., adj.* —*n.* **1.** The words of a song, or part of a song; esp. used in the pl., and esp. pertaining to popular song, musical comedy, operetta, and comic opera: *the lyric to the second verse*; *the lyrics for the first verse*; *song lyrics*. **2.** In the pl., the texts of all the songs in a musical theater piece, taken together: *the lyrics for My Fair Lady*. —*adj.* **3.** Musical; melodious; meant to be sung, esp. as pertains to the drama, hence *lyric drama*: the class of plays, such as **opera**, that are sung instead of spoken; *lyric theater*: musical theater. **4.** Light in timbre and register: *a lyric soprano*, or *light soprano*; *a lyric baritone*, or *light baritone*; *a lyric tenor*.

lyricist *n.* A writer of the texts of songs for musical comedy, operetta, or comic opera; or of the words for individual popular songs.

Lysistrata 1. Classic Greek comedy by Aristophanes, in which the Athenian women, led by Lysistrata, refuse to have sexual relations with the men until they stop making war with Sparta. It has been used as the subject of several musical theater pieces, including a 1902 operetta by Paul **Lincke**; and *The Happiest Girl in the World* (1961), an **Offenbach** pastiche (def. 2) with lyrics by E. Y. **Harburg** and a book by Fred **Saidy**.
2. *Lysistrata or The Nude Goddess* is an opera in two acts by Mark **Adamo**; libretto by the composer; Houston Grand Opera, 2005. You can hear excerpts from the Houston Grand Opera's original production of this exciting, beautiful, dramatic work on Mark Adamo's website, www.markadamo.com.

Lyubov' k tryom apel'sinam (The Love of the Three Oranges) (lyoo BOF k TRYO:M ah pehl SEE nahm) Opera in four acts by Serge **Prokofiev**; libretto by the composer, based on a 1913 adaptation by famed theater director, teacher, and theoretician Vsevelod Meyerhold (1874–1940) of the comedy-fable, *L'amore delle tre melarance* (1761) (lah MO: reh: DEHL leh: TREH: meh:l' ah RAHN cheh:) by the Venetian aristocrat Carlo Gozzi (1720–1806) (GO:T tsee), playwright of theatrical fairy tales, who based it on a fairy tale by the Renaissance courtier and writer Giambattista Basile (1566? 1575?–1632) (dgahm' baht TEES tah bah ZEE leh:); Chicago Lyric Opera, in French, as *L'amour des trois oranges* (lah moor' deh: t*r*wah zo: *R*AH*N*ZH), 1921.

In a mythical country, the King of Clubs (ten.) arranges with his prime minister, Leandro (leh: AHN dro:) (bar.), to put on an entertainment that will cure the Prince's (ten.) hypochondriacal depression by making him laugh, and the king's jester, Truffaldino (troof' fahl' DEE no:) (ten.), is put in charge. But Leandro is conspiring with Clarissa (klah RIH:S sah) (sop.), the king's niece, to murder the prince, so that she may inherit the throne. The entertainments proffered by Truffaldino fail to elicit the prince's laughter, except when the witch Fata Morgana (FAH tah mo:r GAH nah) (sop.), Leandro's protector, enters to make sure the prince does not laugh, and, colliding with the jester, collapses, exposing her behind. The prince bursts into unseemly guffaws, and Fata Morgana punishes him by sending him on a mission to fetch three oranges from Creonta (kreh: O:N tah) (offstage role), another witch. The prince and Truffaldino are lost in the desert, but Celio (CHEH: lyo:) (bass), the king's protector, comes to their aid. He tells them that the three oranges, in which three princesses are imprisoned, are in Creonta's kitchen, and they find them and make off with them. In the desert, the oranges have grown huge. From two of them, princesses emerge, and they die of thirst, for there is no water. From the third, princess Ninetta (nee NEHT tah) (sop.) comes forth, but Fata Morgana turns her into a rat. When, eventually, Celio helps to foil all the plots against them and releases Ninetta from enchantment, she and the prince are united.

M

MacDermot, Galt (b. 1928) Canadian-born New York composer; songwriter. From a diplomatic family, he spent much time in South Africa, and its music influenced his own style of composition; among his many scores are *Hair* and *Two Gentlemen of Verona*.

MacDonough, Glen (1870–1924) American playwright, librettist and lyricist; wrote libretto for Victor Herbert's hit *Babes in Toyland*; author of some two dozen musicals, including five others with **Herbert**, and *Chris and the Wonderful Lamp* (1899/1900) with John Philip **Sousa**, as well as adaptations of operettas by Johann **Strauss** and Franz **Lehár**, among them, *Der Graf von Luxemburg (The Count of Luxembourg)*.

mad scene In certain operas, an extended aria and cabaletta with coloratura variations—sometimes in imitation of a flute that plays phrases the singer repeats (an *aria di imitazione*)—expressive of the heroine's delusional state of mind after she has gone insane (sometimes temporarily, sometimes not); e.g., in Donizetti's *Lucia di Lammermoor*, Bellini's *I puritani*.
   See also ARIA; OPERA SCENA.

Madama Butterfly (Madam Butterfly) (mah DAH mah BUH tehr FLI) Opera in two acts by Giacomo **Puccini**; libretto by Giuseppe **Giacosa** and Luigi **Illica**, based on the hit American play *Madame Butterfly* (1900) by New York writer-director-producer David Belasco (1853–1931), adapted from the short story of the same name by John Luther Long (1861–1927); Milan, Teatro alla Scala, 1904. This wrenching drama is based on the real facts Long used for his story.
   In Nagasaki, Japan, at the turn of the 20th c., the American naval lieutenant Pinkerton (ten.) marries Cio-Cio-San (CHO: CHO: SAHN) (sop.), a geisha known as "Madam Butterfly," but the American consul, Sharpless (bar.) sees that he does not take the marriage seriously. Pinkerton leaves with his ship, and Butterfly gives birth to their son, whom she names "Trouble." She hopefully and eagerly awaits Pinkerton's return, but when he does show up again, it is with his American wife, Kate (mezz.). Butterfly promises that she will give the child to Pinkerton and Kate so that he may be raised in America. When Pinkerton comes to take the child, he finds Butterfly dead. She has committed suicide.

Madame Chrysanthème (Madam Chrysanthemum) (mah dahm kree' sahn TEHM) Opera in a prologue, four acts, and an epilogue by André **Messager**; libretto by Georges Hartmann and André Alexandre, based on the novel of the same name by Pierre Loti; Paris, Théâtre de la Renaissance, 1893.
   In a story similar to that of Puccini's *Madama Butterfly*, a French naval officer, Pierre (ten.), marries a Japanese geisha called "Madame Chrysanthème" (sop.) in late 19th-c. Nagasaki, and leaves on his ship, not intending to return. She writes to him, and he is moved by the sincerity of her letter, but he does not go back to Japan.

Madame Pompadour Internationally successful Berlin operetta by Leo **Fall**.

Madame Sherry Broadway musical by Austro-Hungarian-born American composer Karl Hoschna (1877–1911); book and lyrics by Otto **Harbach**; New Amsterdam Theatre, 1910 (231 perf.). This was the last of six musicals that Hoschna and Harbach wrote together. The show's hit song is "Every Little Movement (Has a Meaning All Its Own)."

Edward Sherry runs the Sherry School of Aesthetic Dancing, where he teaches modern, impressionistic dance. It has been underwritten by his wealthy archeologist uncle Theophilus, who spends much of his time on digs in Greece, and to whom Edward has lied that he is married and has two children. Theophilus arrives with his niece Yvonne for an unexpected visit, and Edward ropes his housekeeper and two of his students into posing as his family. But Theophilus is not fooled for long. He cheerfully invites everyone for an outing on his yacht, and once they are out at sea, he demands to know the truth, or he will not return to shore. When he finds out what has been going on, he threatens to cut off the school's funding; but Yvonne is in love with the reprobate, and when Edward truthfully announces his engagement to her, the day is saved.

madcap musical A musical comedy whose principal element is its fast-paced, farcical plot, providing the composer with opportunities for patter songs, chase music, and the like; e.g., the **Princess Theatre musicals**.

madrigal *n.* A brief lyric poem set to music; sometimes performed **a capella**; meant for contrapuntal part-singing by a chorus or other ensemble, e.g., in the act 1 finale of Gilbert and Sullivan's ***Ruddigore***, and other G & S comic operas.

madrigal comedy *Hist.* A 16th-c. Italian form of musical entertainment, in which a series of related madrigals were sung, usually **a capella**, and often telling a story, preceded sometimes by a spoken prologue; performed on a stage, with painted scenic backdrops. The madrigal comedy is one of the forms from which opera developed.

maestro (MI stroh) *n.* [Fr. Italian: master] Conductor; also, a respectful term of address to a conductor, and, sometimes, to a master singing teacher or performer.

Maeterlinck, Maurice (1862–1949) (mo: *R*EES meh' teh*r* LA*N*K) Belgian Symbolist poet, essayist, playwright and librettist; he won the Nobel Prize for literature in 1911; wrote libretti for Debussy's ***Pelléas et Mélisande***, adapted from his own drama; and Dukas' ***Ariane et Barbe-bleue***.

Magic Flute, The Opera (**Singspiel**) by Wolfgang Amadeus **Mozart**. See ZAUBERFLÖTE, DIE.

Magic Show, The Broadway musical with music and lyrics by Stephen **Schwartz**; book by Australian musician and writer Bob Randall; Cort Theatre, 1974 (1920 perf.). This highly entertaining show was really an excuse to show off the prowess of Canadian star magician Doug Henning (1947–2000), with a framework provided by the financial troubles of the Passaic Top Hat, a nightclub in northern New Jersey. The managers hire the magician to help them attract customers.

Maid of the Mill, The Opera **pasticcio** in three acts by Samuel **Arnold**; libretto by Isaac **Bickerstaffe**, based on the novel *Pamela; Or, Virtue Rewarded* (1740), by Samuel Richardson(1689–1761), in which an earl marries his gamekeeper's daughter, and the Jacobean comedy *The Maid in the Mill* (1623), by John Fletcher (1579–1625) and Samuel Rowley (1585–1626); London, Covent Garden, 1765.

In English actor and printer William Oxberry's (1784–1824) introduction to the 1822 publication of the libretto—vol. 20 of the series *Oxberry's New English Drama*, which he edited and introduced—he extols the moral virtues of the story, in which love triumphs over class prejudice and Lord Aimsworth (ten.) marries the miller's daughter, Patty (sop.), after the convolutions of the complicated plot have been resolved: "From the practical virtues of *Lord Aimsworth*, which are worth a volume of precepts, irrational pride may derive a cure, and licentious love obtain an antidote... and *Patty* is so bright an incentive to the energies of female honor, that she cannot be seen too often, or too closely followed." The dialogue is verbose, in the usual manner of the period, but the verses are well written. An undated mid-18th-c. book of *English Songs and Duets*, vol. 2, contains one song from the opera by Arnold, one setting of a song using music by "Signr. **Galluppi**," and of another by the Elector of Saxony. Arnold's contribution, "Hist, hist, I hear my Mother call," a duet for Theodosia (sop.)—daughter of the aristocrat, Sir Harry Sycamore (bar.)—and her swain, Mr. Mervin (ten.), is quite a pretty melody.

Sir Harry has destined Theodosia for Lord Aimsworth, but she is in love with Mr. Mervin (whom Sir Harry does not consider a suitable match). Sir Harry has his daughter write a dismissive letter to Mervin, but all is set right in the end. Says Oxberry, "... in Sir Harry Sycamore, talkative ignorance may read a salutary lesson."

The opera, successfully staged at the Crow Street theater in Dublin, was also mounted in a rival production at the Smock Alley theater, with music to Bickerstaffe's libretto by Tommaso **Giordani**; all of his music to this opera has been lost.

Maid of the Mountains, The Comic opera in three acts by Harold Fraser-Simson (1878–1944); book by drawing-room comedy writer Frederick Lonsdale (1881–1954); lyrics by the prolific Harry Graham (1874–1936), with more than two dozen shows to his credit, including translations of Viennese operettas for the West End stage; additional lyrics by "Valentine" (1876–1961) [pen name of Archibald Thomas Pechey] and F. Clifford Harris (1875–1949); additional music by songwriter and conductor James Tate (1875–1922) [brother of opera singer Dame Maggie Teyte (1888–1976)], and the show's music director, Merlin Morgan; London, Daly's Theatre, 1917 (1352 perf.).

The show was directed by Oscar Asche, the director, author, and star of the other big English hit of World War I, *Chu Chin Chow*. But unlike *Chu Chin Chow*, this piece is musically not of very great interest, although it is often effective. There are some exciting moments, but the comic songs seem terribly dated, esp.

the pre-feminist lyrics. The more sentimental songs appealed to the sadness of the war-torn nation, and those are the most effective musical moments. There is an excellent CD recording on Helios (CDH55246; 2006).

Set in the mountains of Italy, the story concerns the heroic Teresa (sop.), "maid of the mountains," who is passionately in love with the brigand chief Baldassare (ten.). She is captured and imprisoned, but Baldassare and his band, disguising themselves as soldiers, rescue her. The brigand chief himself pretends to be the provincial governor, but when he displays his newfound love for the governor's daughter, Angela, the jealous Teresa exposes his masquerade, and he is imprisoned in an island fortress. Full of remorse, she leads a successful attack against the fortress, only to have Baldassare leave her for Angela.

The show's leading lady, West End and Broadway star Jose Collins (1887–1958) [stepdaughter of James Tate], hated this original "unhappy" ending, so she insisted that it be changed to a "happy" one, where Teresa leaves for the mountains with Baldassare after he realizes that his feelings for Angela were mere infatuation.

Maillart, Louis-Aimé (1817–1871) (loo ee' eh mé mI YAH*R*)French composer; studied with Fromental **Halévy**; wrote some half dozen operas, of which the best known is *Les dragons de Villars* (The Dragoons of Villars) (1856) (leh: d*r*ah GO:*N* duh vee LAH*R*), with a light, graceful, colorful score.

Makropoulos Affair, The Opera in three acts by Leoš **Janáček**.

malheurs d'Orphée, Les Opera by Darius **Milhaud**.

mambo A lively **ballroom dance** of Cuban origin; began in the 1930s, and became popular on the North American continent as well as the Caribbean islands.

Mame Broadway musical by Jerry **Herman**; book by Jerome **Lawrence** and Robert Edmund **Lee**, based on the semi-autobiographical comic novel *Auntie Mame* (1955) by Patrick Dennis (1921–1976); Winter Garden Theatre, then Broadway Theatre, 1966 (1513 perf.); Broadway revival, Gershwin Theatre, 1983 (48 perf.); film, 1974, starring Lucile Ball (1911–1989).

The show starred five-time Tony® Award–winning actor-singer Angela Lansbury (b. 1925); in the 1969 West End production, Ginger Rogers played the title role.

The eccentric and wealthy Auntie Mame takes as her motto, "Life is a banquet, and most poor sons-of-bitches are starving to death." When her brother dies, she raises her nephew, Patrick, who arrives at her Manhattan apartment at the age of ten, in a spirit of freedom and independence. Helping her are her "bosom buddy," actress Vera Charles; and Patrick's nanny, Agnes Gooch. Mame loses her money in the Depression and tries her hand at several jobs, all with disastrous consequences, but she refuses to give up. She falls in love with Beauregard Jackson Pickett Burnside, whom she marries after turning the bigoted world of his relatives on their Georgia plantation of Peckerwood upside down. During their honeymoon, Beauregard falls off one of the Alps, and the widowed Mame, wealthy once more, returns to New York; there she refuses to kowtow to the bigoted values of the upper middle-class Upsons, to whose snobby, priggish daughter, Gloria, Patrick has become engaged. Patrick thinks he is in love with Gloria, but his aunt quickly disabuses him of that notion. All ends happily as Patrick finds a more appropriate woman to wed, and Auntie Mame takes their son under her wing.

mamelles de Tirésias, Les (The Breasts of Tiresias) (leh: mah MEHL duh tee *r*é: zee AHS) Opera in a prologue and two acts by Francis **Poulenc**; libretto by poet Guillaume Apollinaire (1880–1918) (gee YO:M a po lih: NEH:*R*); Paris, Théâtre de l'Opéra-Comique, 1947; accompaniment arranged for two pianos by the composer and Benjamin **Britten** for the Aldeburgh Festival, 1958.

In his 1917 preface to the poem that would later be set to music, Apollinaire described it as "surrealistic," a word which he had coined. And, indeed, the opera is surrealistic, bizarre, deliberately confusing, and altogether delightful and hilarious, both dramatically and musically, with rhythmic echoes of **Offenbach** and melodious touches that come and go, like the characters in the story.

Based on the myth of the blind prophet Tiresias (tI REE see uhs), who had been both a man and a woman, the opera is set in Zanzibar, here surrealistically located somewhere around Monte Carlo on the French Riviera. The Director (bar.) tells us in a prologue that morals need reforming, and that people should have lots of children. He also tells us he can do whatever he wants, since time and space mean nothing. Thérèse (té *R*EHZ) (sop.), the wife of a Husband (ten.) [le Mari (luh mah *R*EE)] who demands his bacon, tells us that she is a feminist. Tired of being a subservient wife, she releases her breasts, which are two balloons, becomes a man, Tiresias, and leaves. He realizes that he must become a woman, and does so, but he assumes the joys of paternity, because he is really still a man. In other words, he is both a man and a woman—a hermaphrodite. He fathers 40,000 babies. Many of the babies cry incessantly, and he commands them in vain to be quiet. Two friends show up, quarrel, and shoot each other in a duel, but reappear later on riding scooters. A Gendarme (bar.) tries to help, and grows enamored of the Husband, but he reveals his manhood, and the Gendarme is vaguely disappointed. A Fortuneteller nearly strangles the Gendarme when he tells her that her profession is illegal. She then reveals that she is Thérèse, and she and her Husband are reunited. She is a woman again and he is a man—more or less.

Mamma Mia! Broadway **jukebox musical** with songs by **ABBA**; book by British playwright Catherine Johnson (b. 1957); Winter Garden Theatre, 2001 (still running as of this writing); film, 2008, with a screenplay by Johnson.

Sophie Sheridan is to be married on the Greek island where she lives, and she wants her father to be at the wedding. But who is her father? Her mother, the rock singer Donna, isn't sure. It could be any one of three men from her past, so Sophie invites all three to the island. Donna's former singing partners, Rosie and Tanya, are also invited, and this is the occasion for all three to sing their old songs and reminisce about the good old days. This slender thread of a non-plot is an excuse for the ever popular, joyous songs of ABBA.

Mam'zelle Nitouche (Miss Touch-Me-Not) (mahm zehl' nee TOOSH) Operetta (*vaudeville-opérette*) in three acts by **Hervé**; libretto by Henri **Meilhac** and Albert Millaud (1844–1892) (ahl beh*r* mee YO:); Paris, Théâtre des Variétés, 1883; films, 1931, 1954. A delicious 1968 CD recording is available from Universal Music (4769999; 2006), starring the supremely funny French film comedian Fernandel (1903–1971) (feh*r*' nah*n* DEHL).

Célestin (sé leh STA*N*) (bar.) plays the organ and gives singing lessons to the girls at a convent school. He leads a double life, writing farcical operettas under the name Florimond (flo: *r*ih MO:*N*). Denise (sop.), nicknamed Mam'zelle Nitouche for her prudishness, discovers his secret, and things get complicated, but everything ends in triumph for him, and for her: She marries a viscount (ten.).

Mancini, Henry (1924–1994) Prolific American film and television composer; also worked on the Broadway musical *Victor/Victoria*.

manipuri (mah' nee POO ree) *n.* A form of Indian classical dance that also involves song and simple musical accompaniment; originated in Manipur (MAH nee POOR), in northeast India; often on religious themes. Manipur also usually involves audience participation. The dancers' gestures and expressions are subtle, and they never strike the floor hard, so that the effect of the sounds they make is always soft and gentle.

Man of La Mancha Broadway musical by Mitch **Leigh**; book by Dale Wasserman (1914–2008), based on the *Don Quixote* books (1604, 1615) of Miguel de Cervantes (1547–1616) (mee GEHL deh sehr VAHN teh:s); ANTA Theatre, 1965 (2349 perf.); Broadway revivals: 1972 Lincoln Center limited engagement (140 perf.); Palace Theatre, 1977 (124 perf.); Marquis Theatre, 1992 (136 perf.); Martin Beck Theatre, 2002 (320 perf.); film, 1972, with a dubbed Peter O'Toole (b. 1932) in the title role.

The role of Don Quixote was created by Richard Kiley (1922–1999), who also played it in the first two revivals, and became identified with it. His rendition of the inspirational song "The Impossible Dream" helped make it a standard.

Cervantes and his servant are imprisoned by the Inquisition, and they act out the story of Don Quixote, the deluded Spanish aristocrat who believes himself to be a chivalrous knight errant in love with Dulcinea—in reality, the prostitute Aldonza. He tries to live the life of the medieval knights of old, fighting evil and doing good, as in the old romances. When he leaves his village in La Mancha, he is accompanied by the peasant who becomes his faithful squire, Sancho Panza. Eventually, Quixote's relatives take him in hand and try to cure him, and he returns to the sad reality of contemporary life. When they have finished their story, Cervantes and his servant are taken away to face the Inquisition.

Manon Lescaut 1. Controversial short novel published in 1731 by the Abbé Prévost (1697–1763) [Abbé Antoine François Prévost d'Exiles (ah bé' ah*n* twah*n*' frah*n* swah' pré vo:' deh GZEEL)] [Full title: *L'Histoire du chevalier des Grieux et de Manon Lescaut* (lee STWAH*R* dü shuh vah lyeh:' deh: g*r*ee *OO* eh: duh mah no*n'* lehs KO:)] The chevalier des Grieux recounts the story of his unhappy love for Manon Lescaut, for whom he has sacrificed his noble inheritance and the goodwill of his father. She was on her way to enter a convent when she met des Grieux at an inn. They had run away to Paris, where they lived together as man and wife, but without being married, and she had an affair. He became a priest, but Manon begged him to return to her, which he did. She left him two more times for richer men when his money ran out. Eventually, she was arrested for theft and prostitution, and sentenced to deportation to New Orleans. He followed her there, and soon asked the governor to marry them; but the governor's nephew fell in love with Manon, and his attentions to her prompted a duel in which des Grieux thought he had killed him, although he had only knocked him out. The couple fled into the desert wilderness, hoping to reach an English settlement, but Manon died of hunger and exhaustion.

Three operas have been based on the novel, altering the plot, and of necessity condensing it for the stage. In all three, Manon is a sop.; des Grieux, a ten. role.

2. *Manon Lescaut*, **opéra-comique** in three acts by Daniel-François-Esprit **Auber**; libretto by Eugène **Scribe**; Paris, Théâtre de l'Opéra-Comique, 1856.

The opera does not follow the novel closely at all. Manon leaves des Grieux for the Marquis d'Hérigny (dé *r*ee NYEE) (bar.). Because he cannot pay his debts, des Grieux is obliged to enlist in d'Hérigny's regiment. Manon goes to live with d'Hérigny. Des Grieux deserts and goes to find her. He wounds the marquis in a duel, and is sentenced to death, but he manages to get on a ship bound for New Orleans, following the one in which Manon is being deported for prostitution. When they arrive, they escape and flee New Orleans. In the desert, Manon dies in des Grieux's arms.

3. *Manon*, opera in five acts by Jules **Massenet**; libretto by Henri **Meilhac** and Philippe **Gille**; Paris, Théâtre de l'Opéra-Comique, 1884.

In this version, as in the novel, des Grieux becomes a priest after Manon has deserted him, but she goes to find him, and they run off together. Now leading a dissolute life, des Grieux is accused of cheating and is arrested at a gambling house, but eventually freed, while Manon is also arrested and sentenced to deportation as a prostitute. On the road to Le Havre, des Grieux bribes an officer to be allowed to speak with her. He tries to persuade her to escape with him, but she dies in his arms.

4. *Manon Lescaut*, opera in four acts by Giacomo **Puccini**; libretto by Domenico Oliva (1860–1917) (do: MEHN ee ko: o: LEE vah), Marco Praga (1862–1929) (MAHR ko: PRAH gah), Giulio Ricordi, Giuseppe **Giacosa**, and Luigi **Illica**; Milan, Teatro alla Scala, 1893.

The plot of this opera also differs from the novel. Having first deserted des Grieux for the wealthy Géronte (zhé RO*N*T) (bass), Manon takes up with him again when he enriches himself at gambling, but she steals Géronte's jewels. She is arrested for theft and prostitution and sentenced to deportation to New Orleans. Des Grieux sails with her, and they escape from New Orleans. But Manon, overcome with exhaustion, collapses and dies in his arms.

march *n.* A stirring musical composition, usually in 2/4, 4/4, or 6/8 time, meant to accompany people walking in rhythm and in **unison**, i.e., using the same steps and gestures at the same time; esp. associated with the military. Marches are usually composed with melodies in four, six, or eight measures, which are reprised, followed by a second march tune (called a *trio section*), and then reprised again.

Maria Stuarda (Mary Stuart) (mah REE ah stoo AHR dah) Opera in three acts by Gaetano **Donizetti**; libretto (the only one he ever wrote) by magistrate and future Prefect of Police Giuseppe Bardari (1817–1861) (bahr DAH ree), based on the 1830 Italian translation by poet, librettist, translator, art collector, and politician Andrea Maffei (1798–1885) (ahn DREH: ah mah FEH: ee) of the tragedy *Maria Stuart* (1800) by Friedrich von Schiller; Naples, Teatro San Carlo, 1834. Another of Donizetti's historical operas, like *Anna Bolena*, this one is based on the tragic story of Mary, Queen of Scots and her conflict with Queen Elizabeth I.

Maritana Grand opera in three acts by Vincent **Wallace**; libretto by Edward Fitzball (1792–1873), with extra lyrics contributed by Alfred Bunn ("In Happy Moments," Don José's beautiful act 2 aria; "Scenes that Are Brightest," Maritana's famous, very lovely act 3 ballad), based on the drama *Don César de Bazan* (1844) (do:*n* sé zahr' duh bah ZAH*N*) by French dramatist, novelist and librettist Adolphe Philippe d'Ennery (1811–1899) (dehn nuh *R*EE) and Philippe François Pinel Dumanoir (1806–1865) (pee nehl' dü mah NWAH*R*); 1845.

The conductor for the triumphant premiere at London's Theatre Royal, Drury Lane, was Julius **Benedict**. The libretto may be rather inept, and the verse is often doggerel, but the music is really glorious and deeply moving, the quintessence of the romantic sensibility, as the excellent recording on the Marco Polo CD demonstrates (8.223406-7; 1996). The plot device of the marriage of Maritana and Don Caesar inspired **Gilbert** when he was writing *The Yeomen of the Guard*.

In the late 17th c., the Spanish King Charles (bass), out among the people incognito, flirts with the street singer Maritana (sop.) as she performs in a plaza in Madrid. He is recognized by the courtier Don José de Santarem (bar.), who is in love with the queen, and thinks he can turn the flirtation to his advantage. The penniless nobleman Don Caesar de Bazan (ten.) is arrested for attacking the Captain of the Guard, so that Lazarillo (mezz.), a young friend of his, can escape their pursuit. Don Caesar is sentenced to death. Don José approaches Don Caesar in prison, and offers to make sure he is shot instead of hanged if he will only marry an unknown veiled lady (Maritana), to whom he promises compensation and instant widowhood. They both agree, and they are married. The execution takes place, but Lazarillo has managed to remove the bullets from the firing squad's rifles. Don Caesar decides to find out who his wife is. Meanwhile, Maritana has been taken to the palace of the king's friend, the Marquis de Montefiori (bass). Charles, whom Don José has informed of the wedding, awaits her there, and pretends that it is he who has married her; but she will have none of him, and says that she loves Don Caesar, whom she has seen in the plaza. Now, Don Caesar arrives, and Don José tries to make him sign away all claim on his wife, when he hears Maritana singing and recognizes her as his unknown bride. He knows he has been duped, and Don José, knowing he knows, has him imprisoned again. But he escapes, and goes to his own villa, where Maritana has been taken and where Don Caesar finds the king, who accosts him and pretends to be him. Raising an eyebrow, Don Caesar pretends to be the king, and learns that the king has pardoned him. Don José is now going to reveal the king's infidelity to the queen, but Don Caesar kills him. The king, deeply moved by Don Caesar's loyalty in spite of everything he has been through, gives him and Maritana his blessing, and makes him Governor of Valencia.

Mârouf, savetier du Caire (Mârouf, the Shoemaker of Cairo) (mah *R*OOF sah vuh tyeh:' dü KEH:*R*) Opera in four acts by Henri **Rabaud**; libretto by Lucien Népoty (1878–1945) (lü syeh*n* né po: TEE), based on a story in *The Thousand and One Nights*; Paris, Théâtre de l'Opéra-Comique, 1914.

Mârouf is a poor cobbler, who, persuaded to pose as a rich merchant awaiting the arrival of a caravan, marries one of the Sultan's daughters. When he admits the joke, he and the princess, who now loves him, flee, pursued by the Sultan and his guards, only to find that by the aid of a guardian spirit, he is a rich merchant after all.

Marschner, Heinrich (1795–1861) (HIN *rikh* MAH[*R*]SH nuh) German composer of romantic operas, among them *Hans Heiling* (1833) (HAHNTS HI lihng), based on a medieval legend; *Der Templar und die Jüdin* (The Templar and the Jewess) (1829) (deh TEHM plah*r oo*nt dee YÜ dih:n), based on Sir Walter Scott's *Ivanhoe*; and *Der Vampyr*.

Marseille operetta A genre of French musical comedy with stories that are set in the southern port city of Marseille; e.g., seven operettas by Marseillais composer Vincent **Scotto**, including his first big hit, *Au pays du soleil* (In the Country of the Sun) (1931) (o: pehEE dü so LEH:ee). Many of the characters speak in the colorful Marseille accent, and the lively music is replete with folk idioms and American-influenced jazz motifs; the charming orchestrations often include the accordion. The first Marseille operettas, produced in that city and often later done with huge success in Paris, were composed in the 1890s; but the genre flourished esp. from the late 1920s through the early '60s.

Martha, oder Der Markt von Richmond (Martha, or Richmond Market) (MAH[*R*] tah O: duh deh: MAH[*R*]KT vuhn *R*IHCH mont) Opera in four acts by Friedrich von **Flotow**; German libretto by Friedrich Wilhelm Riese, adapted from a ballet for which von Flotow had composed the first act; often sung in Italian translation; Vienna, Kärntnertortheater, 1849.

The famous tenor aria, "M'appari" (She appeared to me) (MAHP pah REE)— in German, "Ach, so fromm" (Ah, so pious) (AKH zo: F*R*O:M)—taken from von Flotow's *L'âme en peine* (The Soul in Pain) (1846) (lahm ah*n* PEHN), was first interpolated in 1865 for a Paris production. The beautiful score makes the implausible plot almost believable; among its lovely, romantic melodies is "Letzte Rose"

(LEHTS teh *RO*: zeh) (Last Rose), a traditional Irish air, "The Last Rose of Summer," with lyrics by the Irish poet Thomas Moore (1779–1852), published in *Irish Melodies* (1813).

Lady Harriet (sop.) and her maid Nancy (mezz.), bored with life at the court of Queen Anne (1665–1714), disguise themselves as the peasants Martha and Julia, respectively, and go to the country fair at Richmond. Lyonel (ten.) and Plunkett (bass), two young farmers, hire them as servants and fall in love with them. But the ladies are obliged to sneak off and return to court, where they realize that they have fallen in love with their humble swains; they nevertheless refuse to recognize Lyonel and Plunkett when they come across them during a royal hunt, causing Lyonel to be perceived as a madman when he tells the courtiers what had happened. But, after some further complications, Lady Harriet arranges for a replica of Richmond Fair to be constructed near Lyonel's farmhouse. There Lyonel finds his "Martha," and both couples are happily reunited, esp. since Queen Anne has discovered that Lyonel is the son and heir of the Earl of Derby, unjustly banished.

Martin, Hugh (b. 1914) American songwriter, music arranger, film and stage composer; did vocal arrangements for *Cabin in the Sky*, *Du Barry Was a Lady* and *The Boys from Syracuse*; frequent collaborator with Ralph **Blane**, e.g., on *Louisiana Purchase*, *Meet Me in St, Louis*.

Martin, Jorge (b. 1959) Prolific, Cuban-born American composer of orchestral, chamber, choral, solo vocal, and operatic works; among his operas are *The Composer's Nightmare, or Puss in Boots* (1998–1999), a comic opera, revised from the earlier *Puss in Boots*; *Beast and Superbeast* (1996), an evening of four brilliant, tuneful comic chamber operas based on short stories by the English writer Saki (1870–1916) [Hector Hugh Munro]; and *Before Night Falls* (composed 2003-2005), world premiere at the Fort Worth Opera Festival, 2010.

Martinů, Bohuslav (1892–1959) (BO: hoo slahf MAHR tee noo) Czech composer; wrote fifteen operas, including three radio operas, sometimes using **jazz** idioms; some of his works are very difficult to perform and to listen to, but his more accessible works include his first great stage success, *Julietta* (1938) (YOO lyeht' tah), to his own libretto; *Hry o Marii* (Miracle Plays of Mary) (1935) (KHREE o: MAH ree ee); and the radio opera, *Hlas lesa* (The Voice of the Forest) (1935) (KHLAHS LEH sah).

Martin y Soler, Vicente (1754–1806) (vee SEHN teh mahr TEEN ee so LEHR) Spanish composer; wrote in the genre of **zarzuela**; composed some thirty operas, including three with libretti by Lorenzo **Da Ponte**, among them his most well known opera, *Una cosa rara, o sia Bellezza ed onestà* (A Rare Thing, or Beauty and Honesty) (1786) (OO nah KO: zah RAH rah o: SEE ah behl LEHT tsah ehd o:' nehs TAH).

Marvin, Mel (b. 1941) American musical arranger, conductor, performer, and composer known for his tuneful scores, including incidental music for many classic and modern plays; his musical theater contributions include his collaboration on the revue *Tintypes* (1980); ***Dr. Seuss's How the Grinch Stole Christmas***; and the dance music and incidental arrangements for ***Applause***.

Mary Poppins West End, then Broadway musical; music and lyrics by Richard M. (b. 1928) and Robert B. (b. 1925) Sherman, with new songs by Anthony Drewe and George Stiles; book by Julian Fellowes, based on the 1964 Walt Disney feature film starring Julie Andrews, adapted from children's stories by Australian writer P. L. Travers (1899–1996); New Amsterdam Theatre, 2006 (still running as of this writing).

In London in 1910, the wind brings Mary Poppins to the home of the dysfunctional Bank family on Cherry Tree Lane, where she fills the position of governess to the Banks children, Jane and Michael. Mary and the children have many magical adventures in company with her friend, Bert, a chimney sweep and sidewalk chalk artist. Having helped to heal the family, Mary Poppins leaves when the wind changes.

Mascagni, Pietro (1863–1945) (PYEH tro: mahs KAH nyee) Italian **verismo** opera composer and conductor, best known for his often performed one-act tragedy *Cavalleria rusticana*. Among his sixteen operas, several others continue to hold the stage in occasional productions, including the three-act **pastoral** comedy *L'amico Fritz* (Friend Fritz) (1891) (lah MEE ko: FRIH:TS), the four-act tragedy *Guglielmo Ratcliff* (William Ratcliff) (1895) (goo [G]LYEHL mo: RAHT klihf), and the three-act melodrama *Iris* (1911) (EE rees). He can be heard in a 1940 recording giving a spoken introduction to and conducting *Cavalleria rusticana*, starring Italian ten. Beniamino Gigli (1890–1957) (behn' yah MEE no: GEE [g]lee), often considered Caruso's successor; available on a CD from EMI (CHS 7 69987 2; 1989), which includes Gigli singing arias from *Iris* and *L'amico Fritz*.

mascotte, La (The Mascot) (lah mahs KOT) Opéra comique in three acts by Edmond **Audran**; libretto by Alfred Duru (1829–1890) (dü *RÜ*) and Henri Charles Chivot (1830–1897) (shee VO:), who collaborated on ca. forty operetta libretti, including Offenbach's *Madame Favart* and *La fille du tambour-major*; Paris, Théâtre des Bouffes-Parisiens, 1880.

This has got to be one of the funniest operettas ever written, and the music is rollicking and merry throughout. There is an excellent 1956 recording, complete with the hilarious dialogue, on Musidisc CD (465 877-2; 2000).

In 17th c. Piombino (pyo:m BEE no:), a principality near Pisa, the farmer Rocco's (*r*o: KO:) (ten.) terrible luck changes when his brother Antonio sends him his turkey-keeper, Bettina (beh tee NAH) (mezz.), to be his good luck mascot, with a caveat: She must remain a virgin, or her ability to bring good luck will cease! The eternally unlucky Prince Laurent XVII of Piombino (lo: *RAHN*) (bar.) stops at the farm for refreshments during an afternoon hunt and appropriates Bettina for himself, taking Rocco to court as chamberlain and leaving the farm in the care of Bettina's boyfriend, the shepherd Pippo (pee PO:) (bar.). Pippo goes to the castle disguised as a strolling entertainer, and finds that the Prince is about to marry her. That way she will remain a virgin, because, as he sings in a hilarious number, he is impotent: "Je suis incapable!" (zhuh süee zan kah PAH bluh). Laurent's daughter, Princess Fiametta (fyah meht' TAH) (sop.), wants to marry Pippo, and breaks off her engagement to Prince Fritellini (frih: teh' lee NEE) (ten.) of Pisa. Pippo and Bettina jump through the castle window into the river. In act 3, Pisa has declared war on Piombino, and Pippo and Bettina (disguised as a man) have joined the Pisan army. With the mascot accompanying them, victory is assured. Laurent has now been deposed, but he, Fiametta, and Rocco have escaped down the back stairs and disguised themselves as strolling singers; they are so inept that they are starving. They find Pippo, who is soon to be married to Bettina. He doesn't care that she is a mascot; he still wants to marry her. Fiametta, seeing Fritellini, decides that she loves him, and, since he loves her, there will soon be a double wedding. Pippo consoles Laurent by telling him that although Bettina will no longer be a virgin, her powers will be passed on to their children, because a mascot's powers are hereditary. Laurent and Fritellini hope the happy couple will have twin daughters—one for each of them to bring up!

mask *n.* The area of the face around the cheeks and nasal cavities, used as a vocal **resonator**, where actors and singers place the **voice** for maximum effect.
  See also COVERED TONE; OPEN TONE.

masque *n. Hist.* An Elizabethan or Jacobean court drama using elaborate costumes and sets, with music and dance as its principal elements.

Massé, Victor (1822–1884) (vih:k TO:*R* mahs SÉ) French composer; student of **Halévy** at the Paris Conservatoire; wrote twenty-three operas and operettas, of which the most well known is *Les noces de Jeannette* (Jeannette's Wedding) (1853) (leh: NOS duh zhah NEHT), with a libretto by Jules **Barbier** and Michel **Carré**.

Massenet, Jules (1842–1912) (ZHÜL mahs [suh] NEH:) Prolific French opera composer, known for his lush orchestrations and rich characterizations. Of his thirty-six operas, the most well known are *Manon*, based on the novel ***Manon Lescaut***; *Thaïs*; and *Werther*. Also outstanding are: *Hérodiade* (Herodias) (1877) (é ro: dee AHD); *Le roi de Lahore* (The King of Lahore) (1877) (luh *R*WAH duh lah O:*R*); *Le Cid* (The Cid) (1885) (luh SIH:D); *Cendrillon* (Cinderella) (1898) (sahn dree YO:N); *Le jongleur de Notre-Dame* (The Juggler of Notre-Dame) (1901) (luh zho:n GLUH*R* duh NO truh DAHM); *Chérubin* (Cherubino) (1904) (shé rü BA*N*); and *Don Quichotte* (Don Quixote) (1909) (do:n kee SHOT).

master class In the world of music education, a session during which students perform prepared pieces for a noted professional artist in the students' field, in order to get input and advice, and to hear a critique of their work, e.g., one given by a famous opera singer, who hears and critiques arias or songs. Often, there is an invited audience of students, teachers, other professionals, and, sometimes, members of the general public. Some master classes have also been shown on television, or recorded on CD, e.g., those given by Maria Callas at the Juilliard School in 1971–1972.

Masteroff, Joe (b. 1919) Tony® Award–winning American playwright and librettist; wrote books for Broadway's *Cabaret* and *She Loves Me*, and the unsuccessful *70, Girls, 70* (1971); wrote libretti for an opera based on *Desire Under the Elms* by American playwright Eugene O'Neill (1988–1953); and for *Paramour*, based on the play *Waltz of the Toreadors*, by French dramatist Jean Anouilh (1910–1987).

Mathis der Maler (Mathis the Painter) Opera by Paul **Hindemith**.

matrimonio segreto, Il (The Secret Marriage) (eel mah tree MO: nee o: seh GREH: to:) Opera in two acts by Domenico **Cimarosa**; libretto by Giovanni Bertati (1735–1815) (behr TAH tee), based on the comedy *The Clandestine Marriage* (1766) by famed actor, David Garrick (1717–1779) and George **Colman** "the Elder"; Vienna, Burgtheater, 1792.

Geronimo (bass), a wealthy citizen of Bologna, is eager to marry his daughter, Elisetta (eh: lee ZEHT tah) (sop.), to the English Count Robinson (bass). But he loves the other daughter, Carolina (sop.). Carolina has secretly married a young business associate of her father's, Paolino (pah' o: LEE no:) (ten.). And Geronimo's spinster sister, the Argus of the home, Fidalma (fee DAHL mah) (mezz.), is in love with Paolino! Needless to say, after many intrigues and complications, everything is straightened out. The happy Count is glad to marry Elisetta, Fidalma still rules the roost, and that is that!

Mayr, Johann Simon (1763–1845) (YO: hahn ZEE mo:n MI*R*) [Often known as Giovanni Simone Mayr, the Italian form of his name] German singing teacher, author of books on music, and composer of Italian operas. Most of his career was spent in Italy, where he was highly successful. Mayr wrote dozens of operas; his composing style was modeled on those of Gluck and Rossini, and he had a great melodic gift. Among his operas, still sometimes performed, are what many consider his masterpiece, *Medea in Corinto* (Medea in Corinth) (1813) (meh: DEH: ah ihn ko: RIHN to:), libretto by Felice **Romani**. His first opera, well received, was *Saffo* (Sapho) (1794) (SAH fo:); and his first great success was *Ginevra di Scozia* (Ginevra of Scotland) (1801) (dgih NEH: vrah dee SKO: tsee ah).

See also FIDELIO.

May Night Opera by Nicolai **Rimsky-Korsakov**.

Maytime Broadway operetta by Sigmund **Romberg**; lyrics and book by writer and performer Rida Johnson Young (1869–1926) [b. Ida Louise Johnson], adapted from a Berlin operetta, *Wie einst im Mai* (As Once in May) (1913) (vee INST ihm MI), by Walter **Kollo**; Shubert Theatre, 1917 (492 perf.); many touring companies and stock productions; film, starring Jeannette MacDonald and Nelson Eddy, 1937, with only one song from the stage show ("Will You Remember"), and songs from other operettas.

The New York millionaire Colonel Van Zandt breaks up his daughter Ottilie's romance with the working-class Richard Wayne. Persuaded by her father, she marries Claude, her cousin. Fifteen years later, Richard has become a wealthy businessman, and is married. He and Ottilie run into each other at Madame Delphine's nightclub. They regret what might have been. Twenty-five years later, Ottilie is a debt-ridden widow, and has even had to sell her home. At auction, Richard buys it and makes her a present of it. Five years after that, they have both died. Their grandchildren, Dick and Ottilie, have fallen in love, and are engaged. They meet in the garden of the house to plan their future.

mazurka Lively Polish national dance of 16th-c. origin, in 3/4 or 6/8 time, often with an extra accent on the third beat; popular at formal dances and society parties throughout Europe in the 19th c. There is also a slow, sentimental version. The mazurka has been used often in ballet, e.g., Tchaikovsky's *Swan Lake*, Délibes' *Coppélia*; and in musical theater, e.g., Glinka's *Zhizn za tsarya (A Life for the Tsar)*, and in the great carnival scene in the **zarzuela *Doña Francisquita***. The dance is meant for couples, and includes foot stamping and heel clicking.

McNally, Terrence (b. 1939) Prolific American playwright and librettist; known for his brilliant dramas, among them *The Lisbon Traviata* (1989), involving a coveted recording of a live performance by Maria Callas in 1958; and *Master Class* (1995), with Callas giving master classes at Juilliard; his books for musicals include *The Rink* (1984) and ***Kiss of the Spider Woman***, by **Kander and Ebb**; ***Ragtime***; and ***The Full Monty***.

medley *n.* A potpourri; an arbitrary mixture of tunes linked together and played or sung one after the other, often by the same composer, and from a particular show. See also QUODLIBET.

Médée (Medea) Opera by Luigi **Cherubini**.

medieval musical drama An ancestor of contemporary musical theater, medieval liturgical dramas centered on religious subjects. They were performed with simple accompanying instrumental music (drum, flute) and simple vocal melodies, evolved out of an expanded liturgy, in ca. the 10th c. Alongside them, a secular drama, often using religious stories, developed. It included incidental music and some vocal interpolations, with, later, the addition of minstrel and troubadour songs, and specialty juggling and acrobatic acts.

Medium, The Opera in two acts by Gian Carlo **Menotti**; libretto by the composer; New York, Columbia University, 1946.
Madame Flora (contr.), a medium, is assisted by her daughter Monica (sop.) and her mute servant, Toby. They help her to defraud her customers. During one séance, she is chilled to feel a hand on her throat; unhinged, she confesses that she is a cheat and a fraud. Her clients will not believe her, but she is unnerved and takes to drink. Toby is in love with Monica, and she throws him out of the house. But he returns, and hides behind the curtain from which the "spirits" used to

appear. Madame Flora sees it move. She grabs a gun and shoots, thinking she is killing a ghost. Toby falls dead at her feet.

Meehan, Thomas (b. 1929) Tony® Award–winning American stage and film writer; did books for Broadway musicals *Cry-Baby* (1980), ***Hairspray*** (both with Mark **O'Donnell**), ***Annie***, *I Remember Mama* (1979), *The Producers*, and ***Young Frankenstein*** (the last two with Mel Brooks), as well as revising the book for *Bombay Dreams* (2002), the London hit by Indian film composer A. R. Rahman, lyrics by Don Black (b. 1938), when it came to Broadway in 2004, where it ran for 284 perf.; the story concerns a young man from the slums of Bombay who dreams of becoming a Bollywood star.

Mefistofele (Mephistopheles) (MEH fee STO: feh: leh:) Opera in a prologue, four acts, and an epilogue by Arrigo **Boito**; libretto by the composer, based on the legend of **Faust**, as told in both parts of Goethe's dramatic epic poem; Milan, Teatro alla Scala, 1868.

In the prologue, Mefistofele (bass) wagers with God that he can win Faust's (ten.) soul. He persuades the elderly scholar to sell his soul by promising him one moment of perfect happiness. Under the name Enrico, Faust, now young and invigorated, woos Margherita (mahr geh REE tah) (sop.), an innocent young girl who gives birth to Faust's son, then goes mad, poisons her mother and kills the baby. Imprisoned, Margherita, in a brief moment of sanity, refuses Mefistofele's offer to free her, and dies. Faust travels to Greece, where Helen of Troy (silent role) offers him her love, which turns out to be a chimera. As he dies, Faust prays to be delivered from the evil one, and his prayers are answered.

Méhul, Étienne-Nicolas (1763–1817) (é tyehn' nee ko: lah' mé ÜL) French composer of four symphonies, instrumental music, and ca. forty operas; composed patriotic songs during the French Revolution, including the military march "Le chant du depart" (The Song of Departure) (luh shahn' dü dé PAHR), which became the Napoleonic anthem, used by **Offenbach** in *La fille du tambour-major*; friend of Napoleon, who championed his work; also in high favor during the Bourbon Restoration after Napoleon's defeat. His works were very popular and highly regarded by professional musicians. Among his most well known operas is *Joseph* (1807), based on the story of Joseph in the Book of Genesis.

Meilhac, Henri (1831–1897) (ahn ree' me: YAHK) Prolific French playwright and librettist; often collaborated with Ludovic **Halévy**, their most famous and atypical work being the libretto for Bizet's ***Carmen***; they also wrote libretti for **Offenbach**, among them ***Barbe-bleue***, ***La belle Hélène***, ***La vie parisienne***, ***La Grande-Duchesse de Gérolstein***, ***Les brigands***, and ***La Périchole***. Meilhac had the outrageous sense of humor and satire reflected in the lyrics, while Halévy was a craftsman in constructing and arranging the libretti. They did a number of libretti for Lecocq, including ***Le petit duc***. Meilhac also worked with other writers, and collaborated on the libretti for Herve's ***Mam'zelle Nitouche*** and Massenet's ***Manon***.

Meistersinger von Nürnberg, Die (The Mastersingers of Nuremberg) (dee MI stuh ZIHNG uh vuhn NÜ[*R*]N be:k) Opera in three acts by Richard **Wagner**; libretto by the composer; Munich, Königliches Hof- und Nationaltheater (Royal Court and National Theater) (KÖN ih*kh* lih*kh* ehs HO:F oont NA[T]S yo: NAHL teh: AH tuh), 1868.

Considered one of Wagner's more accessible works, this opera, which takes place in 16th-c. Nuremberg, is a paean to German nationalism and nationalistic art, and, by extension, to the transformative power of art, and esp. music.

Walther von Stolzing (VAHL the fuhn SHTO:L tsihng) (ten.) loves Eva (sop.), daughter of the goldsmith Veit Pogner (FIT PO:G neh[*r*]) (bass), who insists that she become engaged to whoever wins the great singing contest, to be held the next day by the Mastersingers. Walther is not a member, and he must audition by singing for the town clerk, the acerbic, dictatorial, not terribly talented Beckmesser (BEHK MEH suh) (bass-bar.), who also loves Eva and therefore gives Walther bad marks, eliminating him from the contest. But the philosophical and fatherly cobbler Hans Sachs (HAHNS ZAHKS) (bass-bar.), half in love with Eva himself, recognizes Walther's talent and originality, and decides to help them. When Walther relates a dream to Sachs, he writes it down and turns it into two verses of a song, and when Eva visits Walther in the cobbler shop, Walther himself is inspired to add a third verse. Beckmesser comes to the shop and sees the song lying about. He asks to use it, sensing that it could be the prize song, and he is given permission. At the contest, Beckmesser makes a hash of the song with his terrible singing, and Walther is invited to show how it should be sung. He sings sublimely and wins the prize. His beloved Eva will now be his bride, and he is invited to be a Mastersinger.

Mèlesville (1787–1865) (meh luhs VEEL) [Pen name of Anne-Honoré-Joseph Duveyrier (ahn o no: *ré*' zho: zehf' dü veh: *R*YEH:)] Prolific, very popular French librettist and dramatist; author of more than 300 plays, vaudevilles, melodramas, and **opéra comique** libretti, including that for *Zampa* by **Hérold**; libretti for **Adam** and **Auber**, some of them in collaboration with **Scribe**; and several one-act pieces for **Offenbach**.

melisma (meh LIHZ muh) *n.* A group of musical notes, or an extended passage consisting of groups of musical notes, all sung on one syllable; e.g., on the second syllable of the word "exalted" in the sentence "Ev'ry mountain shall be exalted" in *Messiah* by **Handel**; common in medieval liturgical music, such as Gregorian chant, and in opera arias, e.g., in bel canto **ornamentation**. Hence, the adj. *melismatic*: pertaining to music composed using melismas.

melodrama *n.* Originally, a play with music; later, a particularly lurid form of drama, noted for one-dimensional, stereotypical characters and overdone, perfervid emotion. Hence, the adj., *melodramatic*: pertaining to the overdone and simplistic in story lines, characterizations, and the musical portrayal of emotion and situations. The word is not purely pejorative, however, and may be used in a positive way, to mean dramatic, moving, and heartfelt, although the aspect of one-dimensionality is still the major underlying connotation.

melody *n.* Tune; air; a rhythmic progression or sequence of musical tones or pitches; hence, the adj. *melodic*: pertaining to melody, e.g., to a tuneful score: *a composer's melodic gift*; *melodious*: tuneful and pleasing to the ear.

Menken, Alan (b. 1950) Award-winning American stage and film composer and songwriter, known for his musical comedy *The Little Shop of Horrors*, and for the scores to the Walt Disney screen and stage musicals *Beauty and the Beast* and *The Little Mermaid*, all three in collaboration with librettist and lyricist Howard **Ashman**; also wrote the scores for other Disney animated features.

Menotti, Gian Carlo (1911–2007) Italian-born American composer; his operas include *Amahl and the Night Visitors*, *The Telephone* (1947), *The Consul* (1950), *The Saint of Bleecker Street* (1954), *The Unicorn, the Gorgon, and the Manticore* (1956), and *The Medium*.

Mercadante, Saverio (1795–1870) (sah VEH: ree o: mehr' kah DAHN teh:) Prolific, melodically gifted Italian composer of ca. sixty operas, among them his masterpiece, *La vestale*. He wrote with the best librettists of his day, including Felice **Romani**, Francesco Maria **Piave**, and Salvadore **Cammarano**. His operas include *Orazi e Curiazi* (Horatii and Curatii) (1846) (o: RAH tse eh: koo ree AH tsee), with a libretto by Cammarano, recorded superbly on CD for Opera Rara (ORC 12; 1995). The story is also the subject of an opera by **Cimarosa**. Set in ancient Rome, it concerns two families who are political enemies and are related by marriage: the Horatii of Rome and the Curatii of Alba. When war between the two cities breaks out again, after a period of truce, the murderous political rivalry predominates over the family ties.
See also DIDONE ABBANDONATA; SHAKESPEARE, WILLIAM.

Mercer, Johnny (1909–1976) [b. John Herndon Mercer] American lyricist and songwriter. He composed songs for the *Garrick Gaieties* and *Blackbirds of 1939*; composed Broadway musicals *St. Louis Woman* (1946) and *Saratoga* (1959), in collaboration with Harold **Arlen**; co-wrote songs for *Li'l Abner* with Gene de Paul; wrote scores for many Hollywood musical films.
See also BELLE OF NEW YORK, THE; LINCKE, PAUL.

merengue (meh REHN geh:) *n.* [From the Spanish dessert, meringue (meh RIHN geh:): beaten egg whites and sugar] A kind of fast music and gyrating dance with small steps done close together in a circular motion, in 2/4 time, originating in the Dominican Republic and popular all over North and South America. There are many types of merengue, and there are merengue bands and dance orchestras. Merengue is one of the idioms used in the Broadway musical *In the Heights*.

Merrie England Operetta in two acts by Edward **German**; libretto by Basil **Hood**; London, Savoy Theatre, 1902. This is often said to be German's masterpiece, and, indeed, the music is sparkling and lively, and shows his considerable melodic gift.
Sir Walter Raleigh (ten.) and the Earl of Essex (bar.) are rivals for the favors of Queen Elizabeth (mezz.). When the jealous queen discovers that Raleigh loves

216

her Lady-in-Waiting, Bessie Throckmorton (sop.), she conspires to destroy her. But her machinations are foiled by Essex, who arranges a masque in Windsor Forest. Herne the Hunter appears at the legendary Herne's oak (which plays so prominent a part in *The Merry Wives of Windsor*), and Essex pretends he does not see him. The superstitious Elizabeth takes this for a sign and pardons Jill-All-Alone (mezz.), a May Day reveler she had accused of witchcraft, and Bessie. Essex escorts the queen away, and the others continue to dance round the oak.

Merrill, Bob (1921–1998) [b. Henry Robert Merrill Lavan] Prolific American stage and film composer and lyricist; collaborated with Jule **Styne**, writing lyrics for *Funny Girl*; wrote scores for *New Girl in Town* (1957), based on Eugene O'Neill's (1888–1953) play *Anna Christie* (1921); *Carnival* (1961), based on the Hollywood film *Lili* (1953); and *Take Me Along* (1959), based on O'Neill's *Ah, Wilderness!* (1933); known also for his hit song, "How Much Is That Doggie in the Window?"

Merry Widow, The Operetta by Franz **Lehár**. See LUSTIGE WITWE, DIE.

Merry Wives of Windsor, The Operas by Otto **Nicolai** and Carl Ditters von **Dittersdorf**. See LUSTIGEN WEIBER VON WINDSOR, DIE.

messa di voce (MEHS sah dee VOH che:) [Italian: mass of the voice] A gradual **crescendo** followed by a gradual **diminuendo** on the same sustained sung note; a technique much used in opera, particularly in **bel canto** singing.
     See also FILAR IL TUONO.

Messager, André (1853–1929) [b. André Charles Prosper Messager (ahn dré' shah*r*l' p*r*o:s peh*r*' mehs' sah ZHEH:)] French composer of thirty operettas and ca. ten ballets. *La basoche* and *Madame Chrysanthème* are masterpieces, as is his most famous operetta, *Véronique*. Other notable works include the **Savoy opera** *Mirette* (1894), *Les p'tites Michu* (The Michu Girls) (1897) (leh: pteet mee SHÜ), *Fortunio* (1907) (fo:*r*' tü NYO:), and *Monsieur Beaucaire* (1919) (muh syoo bo: KEH:*R*).

metaphor aria; simile aria In **opera seria**, an aria in which the singer compares him- or herself or the situation to something else, often a phenomenon of nature; e.g., a raging tempest or a lion. In Handel's *Giulio Cesare*, Caesar sings the aria "Va tacito e nascosto" (Go quietly and hidden) (vah TAH chee to: eh: nahs KO:S to:), about a hunter, implicitly compared to a conspirator.

Metastasio, Pietro (1698–1782) (PYEH: tro: meh' tah STAH zee o:) Much admired Italian poet and librettist, almost all of whose ca. sixty texts were set many times each by different composers; e.g., *Artaserse*, *La clemenza di Tito*; *Didone abbandonata*; *Semiramide riconosciuta*.

meter *n.* 1. The **tempo** or **rhythm** of a line of poetry, i.e., iambic pentameter; hence, *metrical*: pertaining to meter: *metrical verse*. 2. The objective tempo of a measure of music, indicated by its time signature, as opposed to the tempo— faster or slower—at which it may be performed.

Mexican Hayride Broadway musical by Cole **Porter**; book by Joseph, Herbert, and Dorothy **Fields**; Winter Garden Theatre, 1944 (481 perf.). Two of the show's big hits were "I Love You" and "Count Your Blessings."

The show was a vehicle for comedian Bobby Clark (1888–1960), who played the hapless Joe Bascom, down in Mexico on the run from the FBI. He cooks up a numbers scheme with Mexican gangster Lombo Campos. When everything goes wrong, Bascom has to assume any number of disguises to avoid being caught.

Meyerbeer, Giacomo (1791–1864) (French pron.: dgah' ko: MO: meh:' yuh*r* BEH:*R*; English pron.: DGAH kuh moh MI uhr BEER) Gifted German composer whose grand operas, written to French libretti, many by **Scribe**, were enormously popular in Paris and set the standard for such works. Despite some gorgeous if sometimes facile melodies, and beautiful, lush orchestrations, his vast panoramas are generally out of fashion today. His sixteen grand operas include *Semiramide*; *L'Africaine*; *Robert le Diable* (Robert the Devil) (1831) (*r*o beh*r* luh DYAH bluh); *Les Huguenots* (The Huguenots) (1836) (leh: zü guh NO:); and *Le prophète* (The Prophet) (1849) (luh p*r*o FEHT).

mezzo-soprano *n.* The medium range of the female voice; the singer with that range, without the soprano's high notes or the contralto's low notes; many leading roles have been written for mezzos, and then transposed for soprano; e.g., Rosina in Rossini's *Il barbiere di Siviglia*. Called a *mezzo*, for short.

Midsummer Marriage, The Opera in three acts by Michael **Tippett**; libretto by the composer; London, Covent Garden, 1955.

The symbolist allegory unfolds on midsummer's day. Jennifer (sop.), who is engaged to Mark (ten.), feels she cannot go through with the wedding until she knows herself better. Separately, Mark and Jennifer wander into a cave, which turns out to be a place of mystery. They are involved in rituals and ceremonies that include her father, the gangster King Fisher (bar.), and his secretary, Bella (sop.), as well as Bella's boyfriend, Jack (ten.). The clairvoyant Madame Sorostris (contr.) arrives and sees visions of the couples. When King Fisher tries to prevent the union of Jennifer and Mark, he dies. And when they come out of the cave, Jennifer and Mark are now reborn and ready to be wed.

Midsummer Night's Dream, A 1. Comedy in five acts by William **Shakespeare**. The story features three interconnected plots: Two pairs of lovers find themselves, for various reasons, in the Athenian woods on the eve of a festival during which a group of rustics are to present a play, which they are rehearsing in a clearing in the woods. The Fairy King and Queen, Oberon and Titania, are quarreling, and they use their powers of enchantment to manipulate the pairs of lovers and the rustic amateur players for their own ends, aided by the sprite, Puck. In the end, everything is set to right; the couples, temporarily separated or at odds, are reunited, and the enchantments lifted.
2. Opera in three acts by Benjamin **Britten**; libretto by the composer and Peter Pears, based on the play; England, Aldeburgh, 1960.

3. Incidental score for Shakespeare's play with ballet interludes, composed in 1843 by Felix Mendelssohn-Bartholdy (1809–1847); the *Overture to Shakespeare's A Midsummer Night's Dream* had been written in 1826.

Mignon (mee NYO:*N*) Opera in three acts by Ambroise **Thomas**; libretto by Jules **Barbier** and Michel **Carré**, based on Goethe's *Wilhelm Meisters Lehrjahre* (Wilhelm Meister's Formative Years) (1795–1796) (VIHL hehlm MI stuhs LEH[*R*] YAH *r*eh); Paris, Théâtre de l'Opéra-Comique, 1866.

In search of his long lost, abducted daughter, the deranged wandering minstrel Lothario (bass) strays far and wide in Germany, and then goes south to Italy. He comes across a band of gypsies, who force the young Mignon (mezz.) to entertain them by dancing. When she resists, they start to beat her, but she is rescued by Wilhelm Meister (ten.); he buys her from the gypsies, who had kidnapped her when she was a small child, and makes her his page. Wilhelm is in love with the actress Philine (sop.), and Mignon, who has fallen in love with him, grows jealous. Her new friend, Lothario, hears her say that she wishes a fire would consume the castle where Philine is acting. He sets fire to the castle, which Mignon has entered. Wilhelm rescues her, and with the help of Lothario, nurses her back to health. Lothario, having suddenly regained his full mental powers, remembers that he is actually a count, and he recognizes Mignon as his daughter, Sperata. Wilhelm has now realized that he loves Mignon, and they are united forever.

Mikado, The, or The Town of Titipu Comic opera in two acts by **Gilbert and Sullivan**; London, Savoy Theatre, 1885; films, 1939, 1967, under the auspices of the D'Oyly Carte Opera Company; there have been any number of television and DVD presentations: consult the IMDb for listings.

This is Gilbert and Sullivan's most enduring and popular comic opera. The libretto is a satire of the British class system and of Victorian sexual mores. There is no intention to satirize Japan or Japanese culture, customs, and ways of behaving, which, however, form the marvelous, colorful setting and background to the story, and which Gilbert took great pains to make authentic in the original production. See *Topsy-Turvy* (1999), Mike Leigh's (b. 1943) film about the creation and staging of *The Mikado*; period details and rehearsal conditions are shown with great accuracy.

Ko-Ko (bar.), condemned to death for the capital crime of flirting, has been promoted to the post of Lord High Executioner. He was next in line to have his head chopped off, so there will be no more executions, because Ko-Ko can't very well cut his own head off. But the Mikado (bass-bar.) is planning a state visit to Titipu, and he expects an execution. A victim must be found immediately! The newly arrived wandering minstrel Nanki-Poo (ten.) agrees to be the victim, provided he may leave Titipu with Yum-Yum (sop.), whom Ko-Ko was planning to marry, and whom Nanki-Poo loves. A fake death certificate will be shown to the Mikado as proof of his execution. But when he sees that Nanki-Poo was the victim, the Mikado condemns to death Ko-Ko, Pitti-Sing (mezz.), and Pooh-Bah (bar.), who described the execution to him, for Nanki-Poo is his son, who fled the court to avoid marrying the elderly, unattractive Katisha (contr.). The only solution is for Ko-Ko to woo and win Katisha, which he does, with the utmost reluctance and a nice metaphor, comparing himself to a bird that committed suicide for love. Nanki-Poo then conveniently reappears with his Yum-Yum.

See also HOT MIKADO, THE.

military band A group of instrumentalists attached to a branch of the armed services; often a marching band led by a drum major; instruments include a portable bass drum to keep time, brasses, sometimes a glockenspiel, and some woodwinds, e.g., flute, piccolo, clarinet, saxophone; usually the oboe, bassoon, French horn, and strings are not included.

Milhaud, Darius (1892–1974) (dah RYÜS mee YO:) French avant-garde composer; studied with Paul Dukas and Vincent **D'Indy** at the Paris Conservatoire; wrote incidental music to many plays, and ca. fifteen operas, including several chamber operas on mythological subjects; among these is probably his best known, *Les malheurs d'Orphée* (The Misfortunes of Orpheus) (1926) (leh: mahl uh*r'* do:*r* FÉ), a **chamber opera** in three acts, with a libretto by Armand Lunel (1892–1977) (ah*r* mah*n'* lü NEHL), Milhaud's childhood friend, collaborator with him on other operas, and the last known native speaker of the now extinct Jewish language Judeo-Provençal (Shuadit). The opera is a reworking of the story of Orpheus and Eurydice. It is available on a CD, conducted in 1956 by Milhaud himself (ADES 13.284-2; 1996). As a Jew, Milhaud fled the Nazis for America in 1940, when they occupied France, returning to Europe in 1947.

Millöcker, Karl (1842–1899) (KAH[*R*]L MIH: LÖ kuh) Austrian composer, conductor, and flautist; known for his brilliant melodic gift. He wrote ca. twenty operettas, including the vivacious *Der arme Jonathan* (Poor Jonathan) (1890) (deh[*r*] AH[*R*] meh YO: nah tahn'), a huge hit in London and New York, as well as in Vienna. The intriguing libretto, which is full of sardonic humor, is by the prolific team of playwrights and librettists Hugo Wittmann (1839–1923) (HOO go: VIH:T mahn) and Julius Bauer (1853–1941) (YOO ly*oo*s BOW uh). A complete recording of a live 1980 perf. is available from IMC Music (GL 100.781; 2006). The operetta takes place in the United States—a setting considered exotic when the piece was first mounted—and involves the millionaire Vandergold (bar.), who changes places with his cook, Jonathan (ten.). The ingratiating *Gräfin Dubarry* (Countess du Barry) (G*R*EH fih:n dü BAH *r*ee) was one of the great successes of 1879. It was revised for Berlin in 1931, and renamed *Die Dubarry* (The Dubarry); elegant, complete recording from Membran Music (231713; 2007); translated into English, it was a big hit in London in 1932. An Austrian film version was made in 1951, and a West German one in 1975. Another great success was the exciting, melodramatic *Gasparone* (1884) (gah spah RO: neh:), which takes place in Sicily in 1820; excellent 1956 complete recording from Membran Music (231712; 2007). But Millöcker's most well known work remains ***Der Bettelstudent (The Beggar Student)***. The latter three were all written to libretti by Richard **Genée** and Friedrich **Zell**.

Minnesinger (MIH neh ZIHNG uh) *n*. A medieval German traveling minstrel.

minstrel *n*. A performer: the general medieval term, which originally was more specifically applied to those who sang, often composing their own material and accompanying themselves on a stringed instrument; but those who recited stories, played instrumental music, danced, and did acrobatics were also called minstrels. They usually traveled from venue to venue; hence, the term *wandering minstrel*.

minstrel show *Hist.* An American form of variety entertainment with skits and *minstrel songs* purporting to be African-American; it began in the 1840s and was almost gone by the end of the century. The shows were stereotypical and inauthentic, although some of the music was quite wonderful. A minstrel show was usually divided into three parts, with the performers, who sang and played instruments such as the banjo, ukulele, and guitar, sitting in a semicircle. First, the **Interlocutor**, in the middle, bantered with the two **end men**, the **Bones** and the **Tambo**. Then came the variety portion of the entertainment, including specialty acts and songs, with the performers rising and moving to the center of the semicircle. Finally, there was a comic sketch, often featuring the **Broadway swell**, among other characters; and, frequently, there was a parody of a current hit musical show; a rousing number ended the proceedings. Popular on both sides of the Atlantic, the shows were performed mainly by white actors in blackface makeup or, after the Civil War, sometimes by African-Americans in blackface. In Gilbert and Sullivan's *Utopia Limited*, one of the best numbers is the act 2 cabinet meeting scene, done as a lively minstrel show song, very ingeniously orchestrated by Sullivan.

minuet *n*. A formal, stately18th-c. dance in 3/4 time, done with graceful movements; much used in opera, operetta, and historical films.

Mireille Opera by Charles **Gounod**.

Miss Hook of Holland Edwardian musical in two acts by Paul A. **Rubens** (music and lyrics); book by the composer, director and librettist Austen Hurgon (1868–1942), with whom Rubens did several shows; London, Prince of Wales Theatre, 1907 (462 perf.); New York, Criterion Theatre, 1907 (119 perf.); national US and Australian tours.

The musical was commissioned by its producer, Frank Curzon (1868–1927), as a vehicle for his wife, star Isabel Jay (1879–1927), who had performed many **Gilbert and Sullivan** roles with the D'Oyly Carte Opera Company. The pleasant score displays a charming, facile gift for melody, but a rather plodding sense of rhythm, with occasional flashes of rhythmic interest (e.g., in the opening chorus of act 2, "Any time you're passing"; # 19, act 2, a "concerted number" called "Mr. Hook had arranged his house").

This "Dutch Musical Incident" has a rather convoluted plot about little Miss Sally Hook of Zuyder Zee, who invents a liqueur called "Cream of the Sky" that makes a fortune for her and her widowed father, Mr. Hook, a distiller. When the recipe is lost, Mr. Hook offers a reward. Eventually it is returned, and all of the plot's romantic complications are resolved as well.

Miss Saigon West End, then Broadway musical by Claude-Michel **Schönberg**; book and lyrics by Alain **Boublil**, translated and adapted by Richard Maltby, Jr.; Broadway Theatre, 1991 (4097 perf.); extensive tours and international perf. in fifteen languages. The show is a reworking of the *Madama Butterfly* story, set in the era of the Vietnam War (1959–1975). The musical, with its powerful score, is **through-composed**, like the collaborators' *Les Misérables*.

The story begins at the end of the war, in April, 1975, when the Marines are preparing to leave Vietnam. Chris, an American soldier, falls in love with the young Vietnamese prostitute Kim, but as the Americans leave, the two are separated. Kim has his child, and many years later, she and her son try to get to America with the help of the Engineer, a sleazy French-Vietnamese club owner, who had employed her. But they only make it as far as Bangkok, where Kim and Chris meet again. He is now married to Ellen, an American woman. Kim leaves the boy with Chris, and, in order to make sure that he will take his son with him, she kills herself.

Mlle. Modiste Broadway operetta by Victor **Herbert**; libretto by Henry **Blossom**; Knickerbocker Theatre, 1905 (202 perf.); filmed as *Kiss Me Again* in 1931, named for the show's most famous song. The plot, so typical of operettas world-wide, remains nevertheless most enjoyable, and the music is Herbert at his extraordinary best.

Fifi (sop.) is a stage-struck sales clerk in a millinery shop on Paris's fashionable Right Bank. Her employer, Mme. Cécile (mezz.), disapproves of the attentions paid to her by one of the customers, Captain Etienne de Bouvray (ten.). His uncle, the Comte de St. Mar (bar.), also disapproves. But a wealthy American tourist, Hiram Bent (bass), is so impressed with Fifi's talent that he pays for singing lessons. A year later she has become the toast of Paris under her stage name, Mme. Bellini. The Comte de St. Mar throws a gala party, and hires Mme. Bellini to entertain the guests. He recognizes her as Fifi, and is so charmed by her beauty and her singing that he withdraws his objections to his nephew marrying her.

modern dance Contemporary choreography, often free in form and abstract, that explores the possibilities for movement without the set patterns of classical dance or **ballet**. Individual modern dance companies have established their own movement styles, often under the aegis of a famous choreographer.

modulation *n.* Transition from one key to another.

Monckton, Lionel (1861–1924) English composer, associated with the series of Edwardian musical comedies called the **Gaiety musicals**; his highly successful seventeen musicals include *The Arcadians*, *A Country Girl* (1902), *The Orchid* (1903), *Our Miss Gibbs* (1909), and *The Quaker Girl* (1910). He also contributed music to other projects produced by George Edwardes. Monckton's musical style is facile but appealing, full of catchy, popular melodies and engaging rhythms. It is also a good deal more superficial than that of earlier Victorian composers, such as Sir Arthur **Sullivan**, and than some of his contemporaries on the continent.

Moniuszko, Stanisław (1819–1872) (stah NEE swahf mo NYOOSH ko:) Polish composer of more than twenty operas, of which the best known is the internationally successful *Halka* (1846–1847), with a libretto by Włodzimierz Wolski (1824–1882) (vwo: DZHEE myehzh VO:L skee). The opera tells a contemporary triangular love story in which the heroine, Halka (HAHL kah) (sop.), ends by committing suicide. Its music is stirring, and its soaring melodies are very moving. Nearly all of Moniuszko's operas are set in Poland during various historical eras, and they are notable for the incorporation of such Polish dances as the **mazurka** and the **krakowiak**.

Monsigny, Pierre-Alexandre (1729–1817) (mo:*n* see NYEE) French composer; wrote ca. fifteen operas, forgotten today, but highly regarded in his own time. He was known for his emotional nature, and for his courteous manners, modesty, and elegance. He composed with some difficulty, which may have been for any of several reasons, including poor eyesight. He gave up composing in 1777, after the great success of his three-act **opéra comique**, *Félix, ou L'enfant trouvé* (Felix, or The Foundling) (fé LEEKS oo lah*n* fah*n* t*r*oo VÉ), with a libretto by Michel-Jean Sedaine, but he remained involved in the world of music as a teacher and school inspector. After having suffered impoverishment during the French Revolution, Monsigny was later much honored as one of the founders of the Opéra-Comique. Under Napoleon, his operas had a nice revival. He had a delightful melodic gift and wrote lively, engaging music, less formulaic than some of his contemporaries. There is a marvelous CD recording on TOWO Records (MO 195; 1993) of several "Ouvertures" to his operas.

Montemezzi, Italo (1875–1952) (IH: tah lo: MO:N teh METS tsee) Italian composer and conductor; taught harmony at the Milan Conservatory. Of his seven operas, the best known is *L'amore dei tre re (The Love of Three Kings)*, considered one of the great masterpieces of early 20th-c. opera.

Monteverdi, Claudio (1567–1643) (KLOW dee o: MO:N' teh VEHR dee) Italian composer of some of the earliest operas, including *L'incoronazione di Poppea*.
　　See also FAVOLA IN MUSICA.

Montezuma Opera by Carl Heinrich **Graun**.

Moore, Douglas (1893–1969) American opera composer; studied in Paris with Vincent **D'Indy** and French composer, conductor, and teacher Nadia Boulanger (1887–1979). Of his thirteen operas, the most well known is *The Ballad of Baby Doe*. Other works of note include *The Devil and Daniel Webster* (1939) and *The Wings of the Dove* (1961). Moore wrote several children's operas, including *The Emperor's New Clothes* (1949) and *Puss in Boots* (1950).

Morris dance [Fr. a corruption of the adj. *Moorish*: pertaining to the Moors of North Africa] In the 16th c., the general English term for dance that was part of a theatrical presentation. The term was generalized from late medieval English dances done for festivals: the dances were supposed to resemble those of North Africa, and the performers blackened their faces.

Moses und Aron (Moses and Aaron) (MO: zehs oont A *ro*:n) Unfinished opera in two acts, with a third act left incomplete, by Arnold **Schoenberg**; libretto by the composer, based on the Book of Exodus; Zurich Opera House; 1957.

Most Happy Fella, The Broadway musical by Frank **Loesser**; book and lyrics by the composer, based on the play *They Knew What They Wanted* (1924) by dramatist and screenwriter Sidney Howard (1891–1939); Imperial Theatre, 1956 (676 perf.); Broadway revivals: Majestic Theatre, 1979 (76 perf.); Booth Theatre, 1992 (252 perf.); sometimes produced by opera companies.

Tony, an elderly Italian vintner in California's Napa Valley, writes a letter proposing marriage to a young San Francisco waitress, Rosabella. He has enclosed a picture of his handsome young foreman, Joe, and she accepts. When she arrives at the vineyard, she is naturally shocked by the deception. However, Tony is so sweet, that she learns to love him, despite the temptations in her path.

Mother of Us All, The Opera in three acts by Virgil **Thomson**; libretto by Gertrude Stein, with no indication of staging; scenario, written after the libretto to allow the opera to be staged, by Maurice Grosser; New York, Columbia University, Brander Matthews Hall, 1947.

This engrossing, surrealistic piece, with an eclectic score reminiscent of American folk music and richly orchestrated, concerns the life of the feminist and suffragette Susan B. Anthony (1820–1906) (mezz. or dramatic sop.). Characters who lived when she did, such as John Adams (1735–1826)—Stein says "presumably John Quincy Adams" (1767–1848) (ten.); Daniel Webster (1782–1852) (bass); and Ulysses S, Grant (1822–1885) (bass-bar.), appear and have their own social issues to deal with. Gertrude S. (sop.) and Virgil T. (bar.) also put in an appearance. The opera begins with Susan B. Anthony and her companion, Anne (contr.), sitting peacefully at home. Susan is putting together a scrapbook of newspaper clippings, while Anne sits opposite her and knits. After that, there are political protests, rallies, and meetings, and Susan is congratulated. The opera ends with Virgil T. unveiling her statue in Washington, DC, surrounded by ghosts of the past.

motif; motive *n.* A recognizable musical theme in the form of a particular melody or rhythmic figure; it may reappear in altered but still identifiable form.

See also LEITMOTIV.

Motown *n.* [Nickname for the city of Detroit, MI; a shortening of Motortown; Detroit is the center of the auto industry] The style of popular music created by African-American singers and instrumentalists in the 1960s and '70s in Detroit, and associated with the famous record label of the same name, founded there by Barry Gordy, Jr. (b. 1929), with an $800 loan. Celebrated Motown singers include Stevie Wonder (b. 1950) [b. Steveland Hardaway Judkins], as well as such groups as the Temptations, and Diana Ross (b. 1944) and the Supremes. The music, which is derived from a combination of gospel and rhythm and blues, is characterized by close harmony and part-singing, as well as fluid, attractive melody. During live performances, the singing is often accompanied by a slight swaying movement, done **in unison**. The "Motown sound" is heard in some Broadway musicals and films, e.g., *Dreamgirls*.

motto aria In baroque opera composition, an aria that begins with a motif based on the aria's principal melody; the motif is repeated, and the melody is then fully unfolded, before the singer begins the vocal part of the aria.

movement notation Syn. with dance **notation**.

Mozart, Wolfgang Amadeus (1756–1791) (VOLF gahng ah mah DEH: *oo*s MO: tsahrt) [b. Johann Chrysostom Wolfgang Amadeus Mozart] Austrian musical genius, child prodigy, and one of the most beloved composers of all time.
Wolfgang Amadeus Mozart's operas:
1767 *Apollo et Hyacinthus* (Apollo and Hyacinth) (ah po lo:' eh: ee ah san TÜS)
1768 *Bastien et Bastienne* (Bastien and Bastienne) (bah STYEH*N* eh: bah STYEHN)
1769 *La finta semplice* (The Feigned Simpleton) (lah FEEN tah SEHM plee che:)
1770 *Mitridate, re di Ponto* (Mithridates, King of Pontus) (mee' tree DAH teh: REH: dee PO:N to:)
1771 *Ascanio in Alba* (ahs KAH nyo: ihn AHL bah)
1772 *Il sogno de Scipione* (Scipio's Dream) (ihl SO: nyo: dee shee PYO: neh:)
1772 *Lucio Silla* (Lucius Silla) (LOO cho SEE lah)
1775 *La finta giardiniera* (The Feigned Gardener) (lah FEEN tah dgahr' dee NYEH: rah)
1775 *Il re pastore* (The Shepherd King) (eel REH: pah STO: reh:)
1779–1780 (Unfinished; completed 1866) *Zaide* (zah EE deh)
1781 *Idomeneo, re di Creta* (Idomeneo, King of Crete) (ee do:' meh NEH: o: REH: dee KREH: tah)
1782 *Die Entführung aus dem Serail* (The Abduction from the Seraglio) (dee ehnt FÜ *roo*ng ows deh:m zeh *R*I)
1783 (Unperformed) *L'oca del Cairo* (The Goose of Cairo) (LO: kah dehl KI ro:)
1783 (Unperformed) *Lo sposo deluso* (The Deluded Husband) (lo: SPO: zo: deh: LOO zo:)
1786 *Der Schauspieldirektor* (The Impresario) (deh:[*r*] SHOW SHPEEL dee *R*EHK to:[*r*])
1786 *Le nozze di Figaro*
1787 *Don Giovanni*
1790 *Così fan tutte, ossia La scuola degli amanti*
1791 *Die Zauberflöte*
1791 *La clemenza di Tito*

Mozartean (mo: TSAHR tee uhn) *adj.* **1.** Pertaining to and characteristic of Mozart's music, with its liveliness, innate grace, verve, rhythmic facility, and brilliant melody; or to music which resembles or is reminiscent of his in having similar characteristics. **2.** Pertaining to singers and instrumentalists who specialize in the Mozartean **repertoire**, or to fans, scholars and students of his life and work.

mudra (MOO drah) *n.* Hindu dance gesture in which the sinuous, continual, rhythmic movements of the arms and hands accent the rhythm of the body movement.

Muette de Portici, La Opera in two acts by **Auber**.

Müller, Adolf (1801–1886) (MÜ luh) Austrian opera singer, conductor, arranger, and extraordinarily prolific composer, with ca. 600 scores for incidental music to plays and musical theater projects in all genres, esp. the **Posse** and the **Singspiel**. In 1825, his very first Singspiel brought him fame: *Wer andern eine Grube gräbt, fällt selbst hinein* (He Who Digs a Grave for Others Falls into It Himself) (veh[r] AHN duhn I neh G*R*OO beh G*R*EH:PT FEHLT ZEHLPST hih: NIN).

Mulligan Guards' Ball, The Broadway musical comedy by David **Braham**; book and lyrics by Edward Harrigan, expanded from their **vaudeville** sketch; Theatre Comique, 1879 (138 perf.—a lot for those days). Braham and Harrigan's 1873 hit song, "The Mulligan Guards," is one of the show's great numbers.

Dan Mulligan (played by Harrigan), head of the Irish-American social club known as the Mulligan Guards, plans to hold a ball on the ground floor of a rental facility. In the same building, the Skidmore Club, an African-American social group, is hosting its own festivities, which they are obliged to hold on the second floor. Mulligan is an all-round ludicrous bigot, but a loveable curmudgeon nonetheless (much in the manner of Archie Bunker in the 1970s television series *All in the Family*): He can't stand the fact that his son Tommy (played by Harrigan's vaudeville partner, Tony Hart) is carrying on a romance with a German-American girl, Katy Lochmuller. In addition, Dan's wife, Cordelia, hates Katy's mother. During the ball, the Skidmore Club dances so vigorously that the floor collapses, and in the ensuing confusion and melee, Tommy and Katy manage to extricate themselves and run away to be married.

musette *n.* **1.** A kind of bagpipe. **2.** A stately dance in 2/4 or 3/4 time, popular at court functions and society balls in France in the 18th c.; similar to the **gavotte**.

music and opera festivals Gala, celebratory events taking place periodically and seasonally, often during the summer, at a particular place, during which concerts, recitals, operas, and other musical perf. are given. Among the well known summer festivals are the Spoleto Festival in Italy; the Avignon Festival in France; the Caramoor Festival of classical music, not far from New York City; the Chautauqua, Glimmerglass, and Lake George Opera Festivals in upstate New York; the Mostly Mozart Festival at Lincoln Center in New York City; the Glyndebourne Opera Festival in England; the Salzburg Festival in Austria, devoted mostly to Mozart; and the Bayreuth Festival in Germany, which presents the works of Richard Wagner.

Music Box Revues Small-scale, intimate revues presented at the Music Box Theatre on West 45th Street in New York City, built by Irving **Berlin** and producer Sam H.

Harris (1872–1941) for the purpose of presenting them. There were four: 1921 (440 perf.), with a huge cast that included Berlin himself; 1922–1923 (330 perf.), with Bobby Clark; 1923 (273 perf.), with opera singer Grace Moore (1898–1947); 1924 (184 perf.), with Fanny Brice, Bobby Clark, and Grace Moore. Directed by Hassard Short, the revues featured Berlin's songs. In the 1923 revue, humorist and actor Robert Benchley (1889–1945) performed his famous and hilarious monologue "The Treasurer's Report," which he filmed in 1928.

music conductor The person who leads the orchestra by rehearsing and performing with them. Also called an *orchestra conductor*; *conductor*, for short.
See CONDUCT.

music contractor The person whose job is to hire musicians for an orchestra or band, e.g., a Broadway **pit orchestra**.

music cue 1. A signal for some action or movement to begin, as music begins to play; i.e., the entrance of a character or of the chorus in a musical theater piece; marked by a particular rhythmic pattern or melody. See also VAMP. **2.** A signal in the theater, e.g., in a musical theater piece, for the orchestra or band to begin playing, or for singers to begin singing; given by the conductor on a signal from the stage manager or other person in charge of telling the orchestra when to start. **3.** The marking in a stage manager's prompt script indicating where music is to start, and where it is to stop; e.g., in the case of **incidental music** in a play.

music director The person in charge of all aspects of the music in a film or theater project; he or she may function as a conductor, as well. Also called a *musical director*.

music drama An opera **through-composed**, without many clearly separate arias differentiated from recitatives, and with the drama therefore continuous, e.g., the operas of Richard **Wagner**.

music hall *esp. Brit.* **1.** A theater where variety entertainment was presented, up through about the 1960s; similar to American vaudeville theaters. Supper or dinner was served at 19th-c. music halls, and the entertainment took place while a meal or drinks were being served. Also called a *hall*. **2.** The entertainment presented in such a theater.

Music in the Air Broadway musical by Jerome **Kern**; book and lyrics by Oscar **Hammerstein**; Alvin Theatre, 1932 (342 perf.); Broadway revival, Ziegfeld Theatre, 1951 (56 perf.); film, 1934.
The composer Karl Reder, a student of Dr. Walther Lessing, is in love with Lessing's daughter, Sieglinde. They leave their small Bavarian town together, bound for Munich, where they hope to have a song of theirs published, and to attend the premier of an opera that Karl has written. In Munich, Frieda Hatzfeld, the prima donna who is to star in the opera, sets her predatory sights on Karl, and the composer Bruno Mahler pursues Sieglinde. When Frieda is indisposed on opening night, Sieglinde takes her place, but her performance is a failure. The

three return to their small town, determined to have nothing more to do with the big city, and to make music as they have always done.

Music Man, The Broadway musical by Meredith **Willson** (music and lyrics); book by the composer and Franklin Lacey (1917–1988); Majestic Theatre, 1957 (1375 perf.); Broadway revival, Neil Simon, 2000 (721 perf.); numerous summer stock productions and revivals; film, 1962, with Robert Preston, who had created the part of Harold Hill on Broadway in this perennially popular and delightful masterpiece.

The glib, fast-talking "Professor" Harold Hill arrives in River City, Iowa, and the town is transformed when he forms a boys' marching band, supposedly to keep them away from sin and the temptations of the local pool emporium. Hill's game is to collect money for instruments and uniforms, and then skedaddle. Mayor Shinn and the town officials are suspicious of Hill, but they can't prove a thing, and he gives them the run-around. The local piano teacher, Marian Paroo, sees right through him, but, as she is about to expose him, a trainload of instruments arrives. Everyone is thrilled, including Marian's kid brother, Winthrop. She doesn't dare say a thing, and, besides, she has fallen in love with the music man. But the fraud is revealed anyway, and the furious townspeople are practically ready to tar and feather Hill, when Marian reminds them of all the pleasure he has given them. They are not impressed, but at that point, the boys, dressed in their band uniforms, heave into view and begin squeaking away on the instruments Hill was supposed to teach them to play. All is forgiven, if not forgotten, as they march gleefully down the street.

music plot A list of the music cues in the stage manager's prompt copy of a script.

music rights Legal entitlement to present or perform a piece of music, obtained from the copyright owner or owners, who give the performer or producer clearance, e.g., for those wishing to use a copyrighted song in a movie or television show; royalties or a fee must be paid. Performance rights organizations that handle requests for such entitlement include the American Society of Composers, Authors and Publishers (ASCAP); and Broadcast Music Incorporated (BMI). Also called *musical rights*; *performance rights*.

music room 1. The enclosed space backstage in a theater where instruments can be stored; also, the location where musicians can gather prior to going into the pit. **2.** *Hist.* **a.** The place in an Elizabethan or Restoration theater where the musicians were assembled; the word "room" often meant "place" in a general way in the 17th c. **b.** Conjecturally, the overhanging balcony (called the *inner above*) at the back of the stage, where the musicians played. **3.** *Hist.* In 18th-c. English taverns or other establishments, a back room where musical events and entertainments were performed. See also SONG AND SUPPER ROOMS. **4.** A large or small salon generally reserved for musical activities in a private home; a salon or hall in a mansion, palace, or other aristocratic venue, where concerts and recitals of vocal music can be performed.

music schools and programs There are many noted schools in the United States where students may obtain college and advanced degrees in various fields of music, from instrumental to vocal. They include the Academy of Vocal Arts (AVA) in Philadelphia, PA; The Curtis Institute of Music in Philadelphia; the Eastman School of Music in Rochester, NY; the Carnegie Mellon School of Music in Pittsburgh, PA; the Pittsburgh Music Academy (PMA); and, in New York City, the Manhattan School of Music (MSM); Mannes College the New School for Music; and the Juilliard School. There are also many excellent university programs throughout the country, such as those at Northwestern University in Evanston, IL; the University of Indiana at Bloomington; the Loyola University College of Music in New Orleans; the Conservatory of Music at Oberlin College in Ohio; and the University of Maryland School of Music in Baltimore.

See also YOUNG ARTISTS PROGRAMS.

music stand An adjustable pole resting on three steady feet, and holding at its top an adjustable, flat, metal, rectangular shelf with a lip at its bottom to hold a score.

music tent/circus A summer theater that presents arena stagings of musical comedies under a circus tent, e.g., St. John Terrell's Music Circus, now defunct, in Lambertville, NJ. Also called *musical tent theater*.

music theater Syn. with **musical theater**.

musical adaptation A version of a play, novel, or other material, rewritten for the stage or screen, with songs and ensemble numbers added; e.g., *My Fair Lady*, *The Mystery of Edwin Drood*, *The Phantom of the Opera*, *West Side Story*. Also called *musical version*; *musicalization*.

musical comedy; **musical** A **comic opera**, **light opera** or **operetta** in the form of a stage play or film in which vocal and instrumental music and dances are an essential part of the show, with spoken dialogue in between the numbers. Although there are many English and European examples of musical comedy, the term is often used to refer to the American, esp. Broadway, variant of the operetta, distinguished by its use of American musical idioms, including popular song, ragtime, jazz, folk music, gospel, and rock. Many Broadway shows have been adapted for the screen, and many musical comedies were written directly for the movies, esp. in the 1930s and 40s, the "golden age" of the Hollywood movie musical. Also sometimes called a *musical play*. There are many original and revival cast recordings available on CD. A series of four albums produced by Pearl Records, *Broadway Through the Gramophone*, with recordings dating from 1900 to 1929, is of great historical interest (GEMS 0082–GEMS 0085; 2000).

See also BELT; LEGITIMTE SINGING.

musical play A drama with music, both incidental and in the form of songs. Also called *musical drama*; *a play with music*.

musical theater 1. Any form of drama in which vocal and instrumental music are an essential part of the entertainment, including **musical comedy**, **opera**, and operetta; the **lyric** drama. **2.** Broadway and Broadway-style musical comedy; e.g., West End shows; the term is often limited in scope to mean only this genre of the lyric drama.

musicalize *v. t.* To turn a spoken play or other material into a musical theater piece; to write a **musical adaptation**; hence, the n. *musicalization*: the result of the activity just described: *the musicalization of Hugo's* **Les Misérables**.

musician *n.* A person who makes a living as a creator, teacher, or performer of instrumental and/or vocal music.

Mussorgsky, Modest (1839–1881) (mah DYEHST moo SAWRK skee) Russian composer; one of **The Five** who hoped to regenerate Russian music and infuse it with national feeling; composed eight operas, including **Boris Godunov**, of which Nicolai **Rimsky-Korsakov** did two revised versions, and **Khovanshchina**.

Musto, John (b. 1954) American recording artist, pianist, composer of instrumental and orchestral works, and of operas, including *Later the Same Evening* (2007), based on paintings by American artist Edward Hopper (1882–1967), with characters and their stories imagined from those in the paintings; it was superbly produced in 2008 at the Manhattan School of Music. He also composed *Volpone* (2004), based on the play by Ben Jonson (1572–1637); and *Bastaniello* (2008), based on an Italian folktale. Mark Campbell wrote the libretti to all three.

mute *n., v., adj.* —*n.* **1.** A silent actor or role; a mime; a pantomimist: a person who simulates various situations in silent performance, using movement and gesture. **2.** A cone or cylinder made of pasteboard and covered with cloth or leather, inserted into a trumpet or horn to change or deaden the sound. **3.** A piece of metal fitted onto the bridge of a violin or other string instrument to soften the sound; hence, for both brass and strings, the Italian performance directions *con sordini* (kon so:r DEE nee): with the mute [in place]; *senza sordini* (SEHN dzah so:r DEE nee): without the mute, i.e., with the mute removed. —*v. t.* **4.** To deaden or alter the sound of an instrument using such a device. —*adj.* **5.** Silent; pertaining to a non-speaking role, or to a person unable to speak, for whatever reason.

My Fair Lady Broadway musical by **Lerner and Loewe**: music by Frederick Loewe; book and lyrics by Alan Jay Lerner, adapted from George Bernard Shaw's play *Pygmalion* (1914); Mark Hellinger Theatre (later Broadhurst, then Broadway Theatres), 1956 (2717 perf.); Broadway revivals: St. James Theatre, 1976 (384 perf.); Uris Theatre, 1981 (124 perf.); Virginia Theatre, 1993 (165 perf. followed by national tour); many tours, summer stock productions, international megahit; film, 1964.

The sparkling, varied score is brilliant in its musical characterizations, with lively patter for Higgins and a lovely ballad for Freddy, "On The Street Where You Live"; the waltz tunes are reminiscent of Viennese operetta.

Professor Henry Higgins, a phonetics expert and a confirmed bachelor, makes a bet with his friend, Colonel Pickering, that he can pass off the ignorant Cockney flower girl Eliza Doolittle as a duchess within six months, simply by teaching her how to speak like one. Liza shows up at his home and takes speech lessons with Higgins, the martinet. As an experiment, he takes her to the Ascot races. There she meets Freddy Eynsford-Hill, who falls madly in love with her. As a culmination, Higgins and Pickering take her to an embassy ball, and the whole thing works like a charm, But Liza now wants to be treated like the lady she has been taught to be, and Higgins scolds and berates her until she is so exasperated that she walks out on him. Only then does he realize that he loves her. In a comic subplot, her father, Alfred Doolittle, a Cockney dustman, is forced to get married and become a respectable gentleman, with an inheritance to boot.

Mystery of Edwin Drood, The: The Solve-It-Yourself Broadway Musical
Broadway musical by Rupert Holmes; book and lyrics by the composer, adapted from Charles Dickens's (1812–1870) last, uncompleted novel; Imperial Theatre, 1985 (632 perf.); many summer stock and regional productions.

This ingenious musical, presented as if it were a British **music hall** show done by the "Music Hall Royale" under the leadership of Chairman Cartwright, called for audience participation: With the question of who murdered Edwin Drood not having been answered by Dickens, the audience gets to vote on the solution to the crime, and on the identity of the mysterious stranger Dick Datchery. The show then comes to an end based on the culprit chosen by them. Throughout, the Victorian actors break character to comment on the proceedings and address the audience directly, or to interpolate a music hall song.

In the town of Cloisterham, young Edwin Drood (**trousers role**) makes himself cordially disliked, with his arrogance and quarrelsome nature. When he disappears after a Christmas Eve snowstorm, presumably murdered, the suspects include his uncle, the secretive choirmaster John Jasper, an opium addict, in love with Rosa Bud, who has been engaged to Drood since birth. Neville Landless, newly arrived from Ceylon with his sister, Helena, is also attracted to Rosa. Other characters include Princess Puffer, who runs the opium den frequented by Jasper, and the prim Reverend Crisparkle.

N

native air opera A Nigerian form of musical religious theater. Syn. with **Yoruba opera**.

Naughty Marietta Broadway operetta by Victor **Herbert**; book by Rida Johnson Young; New York Theatre, 1910 (136 perf.); film, 1935, starring Jeannette MacDonald and Nelson Eddy. The songs from this favorite score include "Tramp! Tramp! Tramp!" and "Ah, Sweet Mystery of Life."

In 1780, the Countess d'Alena has escaped from France and made her way to New Orleans, disguised as the peasant girl Marietta (sop.). She falls in love with Etienne (ten.), the son of the Lieutenant Governor. Pirates, led by the mysterious Bras Pique, are wreaking havoc, and the king has hired Captain Dick Warrington (bar.) to destroy them. Dick falls in love with Marietta, and discovers who she really is. He has also been ordered to escort her back to France, but she is captured by Bras Pique, who turns out to be Etienne in disguise. Dick sets out to rescue her, and Etienne and his cutthroats escape. Marietta now realizes that she loves Dick, and they board the ship for France.

Nedbal, Oskar (1874–1930) (OS kah[r] NEHD bahl) Czech composer and symphony orchestra conductor; wrote one comic opera and seven Viennese operettas, of which the best known is *Polenblut* (Polish Blood) (1913) (PO: lehn BLOOT), an international success; libretto by Leo **Stein**. The story concerns a Polish count who flouts his fiancée by flirting with another woman right in front of her, after which she cleverly punishes him. He finds that he loves her after all, and proposes marriage all over again, which she is happy to accept.

Neidhart, August (1867–1934) (OW go*o*st NIT hah[r]t) Prolific Austrian dramatist and librettist, with forty-five operetta libretti to his credit, including *Schwarzwaldmädel* by Leon **Jessel**, for whom he did several other texts as well. He also wrote libretti, sometimes in collaboration with others, for Edmund **Eysler**, Walter **Kollo**, Eduard **Künneke**, and Leo **Fall**. A year after the Nazis came to power, Neidhart committed suicide.

Nessler, Viktor Ernst (1841–1890) (NEHS luh) Alsatian composer, choral director; studied music in Germany; composed eleven operas, of which the most famous is the militaristic *Der Trompeter von Säckingen* (The Trumpeter of Säckingen) (1884) (deh t*r*om PEH tuh fuhn ZEHK ihng ehn), with almost every number in a minor key; CD recording on Capriccio (60 055 2; 1997).

New Faces musicals A series of seven Broadway musical revues produced in 1934 (149 perf.), 1936 (193 perf.), 1943 (94 perf.), 1952 (365 perf.), 1956 (220 perf.), 1962 (30 perf.), and 1968 (68 perf.). They introduced fresh, then unknown performers and writers; e.g., Imogene Coca (1908–2001) and Henry Fonda (1905–1982) in 1934; songwriter Ralph **Blane** and Van Johnson (1916–2008) in 1936; "Professor" Irwin Corey (b. 1912) in 1943; Alice Ghostley (1926–2007), Paul

Lynde (1926–1982), Eartha Kitt (1927–2008), and Carol Lawrence (b. 1934), songs by Sheldon **Harnick**, and sketches by Mel **Brooks**, in 1952; Jane Connell (b. 1925), and sketches by Neil Simon in 1956; Marian Mercer (b. 1935) in 1962; Madeline Kahn (1942–1999) and Robert Klein (b. 1942) in 1968. There are two films based on the revues: *New Faces of 1937* (1936 [*sic*]), and *New Faces* (1954; based on *New Faces of 1952*).

Newgate pastoral [From London's Newgate prison] A **parody** of the pastoral genre, replaced from the countryside to an urban setting, where the sweetness and innocent naiveté of shepherds and shepherdesses is satirized in the cynicism and self-serving greed of crooks and whores masquerading as innocents; e.g., *The Beggar's Opera*, *Die Dreigroschenoper (The Threepenny Opera)*, *Aufstieg und Fall der Stadt Mahagonny*, *The Rake's Progress*.

Newley, Anthony (1931–1999) Prolific English performer, comedian, songwriter, composer; a star in the U.S. and the UK. With Leslie **Bricusse**, he collaborated on *Stop the World—I Want to Get Off* (1962), *The Roar of the Greasepaint—The Smell of the Crowd*, and other projects. Among his well known songs are "What Kind of Fool Am I?" and "Who Can I Turn To?"

New Orleans jazz The earliest, original form of **jazz**, starting ca. the beginning of the 20th c. and evolving from earlier improvisational **blues** and **ragtime** forms in the city of New Orleans, LA. It features improvisation by a group, sometimes with dissonant harmonies, as instruments improvise against each other, one or another suddenly standing out, then submerging back into the dense texture of the music. The usual instruments in a jazz band are piano, drums, bass, guitar, banjo, clarinet, saxophone, trumpet, and trombone.

New Wave music A 1970s American version of punk rock, exemplified in the work of such bands as the Talking Heads, with songs featuring symbolic poetry and simple melodies.

Next to Normal Broadway musical by Tom Kitt; book and lyrics by Brian Yorkey; Booth Theatre, 2009 (still running as of this writing); first opened Off-Broadway in 2008, in a different version that was less relentless and more comedic. The eclectic score includes elements of rock, country-western, and old fashioned lyricism.

Diana Goodman is a suburban housewife with bipolar disorder, which of course affects her husband, Dan, her daughter, Natalie, and her teenage son, Gabe, who is alternately good and unkind in his relationship with her. The family members tear each other apart in bitter arguments. The story contains successive revelations about the origin and onset of Diana's disorder, and scenes of various treatments and fantasies; there is no plot in the old-fashioned sense of the word, but rather an ongoing sense of living.

Nicolai, Otto (1810–1849) [b. Carl Otto Ehrenfried Nicolai (EH *r*ehn FREET NIH: ko: LI)] German conductor and composer, best known for his opera *Die Lustigen Weiber von Windsor*.

233

Nina, o sia La pazza per amore (Nina, or The Love-Crazed Maiden) (NEE nah o SEE ah lah PAHT tsah pehr ah MO: reh:) Opera in one act (1789; premiere, Caserta [kah ZEHR tah]), revised to two acts (1790; premiere, Naples. Teatro dei Fiorentini [deh:' ee fyo:r' ehn TEE nee]) by Giovanni **Paisiello**; libretto by Giambattista Lorenzi (1719–1805) (DGAHM baht TEES tah lo: REHN zee), based on an Italian translation of the libretto to a very popular French **opéra comique** by Nicolas **Dalayrac**, *Nina, ou La folle par amour* (Nina, or The Love-Crazed Maiden) (1786) (nee NAH oo lah FOL pah rah MOOR), text by Benoît-Joseph Marsolliers des Vivetières (1750–1817) (beh nwah' zho: ZEHF mahr so LYEH: deh: vee vuh TYEHR).

Nina (sop.) is a sensitive young lady in love with Lindoro (lih:n DO: ro:) (ten.). He is the Count (bar.), her father's prospective choice of a bridegroom, but her father changes his mind and chooses a richer fiancé for her. The two rivals fight a duel, and when Nina thinks Lindoro has been killed, she goes mad and loses her memory. Finally, Lindoro reappears and she regains her sanity.

9 to 5 Broadway musical by famed country singer and actress Dolly Parton (b. 1946); book by Patricia Resnick (b. 1953), based on the film *Nine to Five* (1980), starring Dolly Parton, Jane Fonda (b. 1937), and Lily Tomlin (b. 1939); Marquis Theatre, 2009 (still running as of this writing).

Violet, a department supervisor, and Judy, a newly hired secretary, work in a company run by Franklin Hart—an impossible, hypocritical, male chauvinist bigot who is gross and disgusting to them and to Doralee (played by Dolly Parton in the film), his private secretary. The women conspire to give him his comeuppance by imprisoning him in his own home and running the company better than he ever did. They also discover that he has been embezzling from the corporation. When his wife returns early from a cruise, she frees Hart, and he threatens to send the women to jail. But the big boss of the corporation shows up and admires the new, better productivity of the department, so he sends Hart on a special project to Brazil. Hart is in no position to reveal the truth, since the ladies did everything in his name. They can't take credit for the improvements, but he can, so he reveals nothing, and they don't expose his embezzlement. Hart departs; Violet takes his place; Judy quits her job and marries the Xerox repairman; and Doralee becomes a country singer.

noble position In singing, the alignment of head, neck, and torso in an upright posture, which permits correct breathing technique; much used, esp. in classical singing and opera; the singer should not remain in a rigid, inflexible position, e.g., when acting on stage, but must be aware of and maintain the optimal posture necessary for producing the most agreeable and resonant sound.

noh theater [Also spelled "nō"] A traditional form of Japanese dance-drama, originating in the 14th c., using classical Japanese music and performed on a bare wooden stage by masked actors.

See also HAYASHI; JI; JO; KUSE.

No, No, Nanette Broadway musical by Vincent **Youmans**; book by Otto **Harbach**, Irving Caesar (1895–1996), and Frank Mandel, based on the play *My Lady Friends* (1919) by Mandel and Emil Nyitray (?–1922), adapted from the short story *Oh, James!* by playwright May Eddington (1883–1957) [b. May Edginton] and Rudolf Besier (1878–1942) [known for his play, *The Barretts of Wimpole Street* (1931)]; Globe Theatre, 1925 (321 perf.); Broadway revival, 46th Street Theatre, 1971 (874 perf.); films, 1930, 1940.

This vivacious tea party of a show—one of its famous songs is "Tea for Two"—is completely silly and endearing.

The Bible publisher Jimmy Smith lives an irreproachable life at home with his spendthrift wife Sue, his orphaned niece, Nanette, and his impertinent maid, Pauline. While traveling for business, Jimmy has met Winnie, Betty, and Flora in three different cities, and he is supporting all three financially, because he can't bear for them to be unhappy. But they are becoming demanding, so Jimmy decides to put an end to the situation with the help of his friend and lawyer, Billy. He arranges to meet all three women in Atlantic City. Nanette has a boyfriend, Tom, Billy's assistant; they have a fight, so she too goes traipsing off to Atlantic City. Everyone turns up there, including Lucille, Billy's wife, who is led to believe that Billy is having an affair with the three women. In order to protect Jimmy, he does not deny it. Sue wonders what is going on, and pandemonium breaks loose. Eventually, matters are explained to Lucille and to Sue. But Jimmy hasn't actually done anything wrong, so Sue pardons him and puts herself in charge of all his money—no more spending it to support unhappy ladies! Tom and Nanette make up.

Norma Opera by Vincenzo **Bellini**; libretto by Felice **Romani**, based on the verse tragedy *Norma* (1831) by poet and champion of romanticism Alexandre Soumet (1788–1845) (soo MEH:); Milan, Teatro alla Scala, 1833.

In the time of the Roman occupation of Gaul, Norma (sop.), daughter of the Druid chief Oroveso (o: ro: VEH: zo:) (bass), is a vestal priestess of Irminsul (eer' meen S*OO*L), and vowed to chastity. But she has fallen so passionately in love with the Roman proconsul, Pollione (po: lee O: neh:) (ten.), that she has broken her vow and has actually had two sons by him. Now, he has fallen in love with another vestal, Adalgisa (ah dah DGEE zah) (mezz.), and abandoned Norma and their children. In the majestic aria "Casta diva" (Chaste goddess) (KAH stah DEE vah), Norma prays to the goddess of the moon for peace with the Romans, but there is no peace in her heart. Adalgisa, deeply troubled, comes to confess to Norma that she has broken her vows, not yet finalized, and to ask for her help. Norma is sympathetic, and wants to know who her lover is; but when she learns that it is Pollione, she is enraged. She decides to kill her two innocent little sons, but she cannot bear to do it, and instead summons Adalgisa, telling her she may go to Rome with Pollione and marry him, provided she take the boys with her. But Adalgisa will not accept this, and instead tries to persuade Pollione to return to Norma. He refuses, and when Norma learns that he plans to invade the temple and kidnap Adalgisa, the furious priestess rushes there and strikes the great gong, summoning the Gauls, whipping them into a war frenzy, and inciting them to revolt against the Romans. The proconsul, taken in the vicinity of the temple, is condemned to death by fire. But Norma can still save him, and she offers to do so if he will renounce all thought of Adalgisa. This he will not do. Norma now confesses her crimes against the goddess, and, confiding her sons to the care of Oroveso, ascends the pyre. With his love for her reborn, Pollione joins her in death.

No Strings Broadway musical by Richard **Rodgers**.

notation *n.* **1.** A standardized system of writing down music so that it can be read and/or performed. **2.** A system of writing down dance steps (**dance notation**) so that they can be reproduced.

Novello, Ivor (1893–1951) [b. David Ivor Davies] Popular Welsh composer, songwriter, playwright, recording artist, singer, actor, and matinee idol; wrote fourteen musical theater pieces. He also contributed songs to revues. With book writer Christopher Hassall (1912–1963), he collaborated on six musicals, their first being *Glamorous Night* (1935), which Novello also produced and starred in. Among Novello's famous songs is the World War I inspirational tune, "Keep the Home Fires Burning" (1915), which immediately made him famous. Novello was known for his lush, romantic, sentimental style.

nozze di Figaro, Le (The Marriage of Figaro) (leh: NOT tseh: dee FIH: gah ro:) Opera in four acts by Wolfgang Amadeus **Mozart**; libretto by Lorenzo **Da Ponte**, based on the play *La folle journée, ou Le marriage de Figaro* (The Mad Day, or The Marriage of Figaro) (written, 1778; produced, 1784) (la fol zhoo*r* NÉ oo luh mah *r*ee AHZH duh fee gah *R*O:) by Pierre Caron de Beaumarchais; Vienna, Burgtheater, 1786.

In this sequel to the story of *Il barbiere di Siviglia*, Count Almaviva (bar.) is unhappily married to Rosina (sop.), now Countess Almaviva, to whom he appears to have grown indifferent, although he remains jealous and possessive. He flirts outrageously with her lady's maid, Susannah (sop.), who is engaged to Figaro (bass), now the Count's servant and living in the ancestral castle near Seville. The Countess's adolescent page boy, Cherubino (keh' roo BEE no:) (sop. or mezz.), only recently post-pubescent, doesn't know what to do with his feelings, and he has a crush on her. The Countess devises a plan, helped by Cherubino, Figaro and Susannah, to trap the Count and make him mend his ways: Susannah will arrange a rendezvous with him in the garden at night, but the disguised Cherubino will take her place. There are numerous mistaken identities, due to the darkness and to people wearing each other's clothing, but by the end, everything is straightened out. The Count, not realizing that he was flirting with his own wife until she revealed herself, begs her forgiveness and vows to lead a blameless life in future.

See also DITTERSDORF, CARL DITTERS VON.

number *n.* An individual song, aria, ensemble, etc. in an opera, operetta, or musical comedy.

number opera An opera in which each aria or ensemble can be separated out from the whole and performed as a discreet selection, e.g., in a concert; the individual numbers are linked by sung **recitative** or, in the case of the **ballad opera**, **Singspiel**, or **opéra comique**, by spoken dialogue. The number opera was the usual kind of opera until the arrival of Richard **Wagner** and his **through-composed** music dramas, which influenced later Verdi operas, e.g., *Otello* and *Falstaff*, and the Italian **verismo** school later in the 19th and early 20th centuries.

O

obbligato (ob' blee GAH to:) *n.* [Italian: obliged; German spelling: *obligato*; also used as an adj.: *obbligato accompaniment*] Absolutely required; necessary; music that must be performed and may not be omitted, e.g., an instrumental accompaniment written for particular instruments to accompany a solo singer, as in some of Mozart's operas; or the clarinet obbligato in Schubert's **lied** for soprano, piano, and clarinet, *Der Hirt auf dem Felsen* (The Shepherd on the Rock) (deh: HEE: uh[r]t owf de:m FEHL zuhn).

Obersteiger, Der Operetta by Carl **Zeller**.

O'Donnell, Mark (b. 1954) Tony® Award–winning American humorist and writer; with Thomas **Meehan**, he co-wrote the books for the Broadway musicals *Cry-Baby* (2008) and *Hairspray*, and the screenplay for the film version of the latter.

Oedipus Rex Opera-oratorio in two acts by Igor **Stravinsky**; libretto by Jean Cocteau, based on the tragedies *Oedipus the King*, *Antigone*, and *Oedipus at Colonus*, written ca. 435–425 BCE by Sophocles (496–406 BCE); first performed in Paris, Théâtre Sarah Bernhardt, 1927, as an **oratorio**; first staged in Vienna, Staatsoper, 1928, as an opera. The music and libretto are static, and the work really is more an oratorio than an opera.

The story follows closely that in Sophocles' first play about the myth of Oedipus, who grows up to slay his father, King Laius, not knowing who he is, and becomes king of Thebes in his place. He marries Laius's widow Jocasta, ignorant of the fact that she is his own mother. When Oedipus and Jocasta discover the truth, she kills herself, and Oedipus puts out his own eyes. He wanders forth in agonizing guilt, accompanied by their daughter, Antigone, who remains with him, faithful to the end.

Offenbach, Jacques (1819–1881) (ZHAHK o:' fehn BAHK; anglicized: AWF ehn bahk') [b. Jacob Offenbach; his father, the synagogue cantor and musician, Isaac Juda Eberst (1779–1850), known as "der Offenbacher" (the man from the town of Offenbach) (deh O: fehn BAH khuh[r]), had taken Offenbach as his last name] Prolific German-born French composer of full-length and one-act comic operas, operettas, and three operas, with more than 100 stage works to his credit, as well as art songs and instrumental pieces, including those for cello, of which Offenbach was a virtuoso player; the musical voice of the Second Empire of Napoleon III; known for his beguiling melodic gift, his vivacious rhythms, his twinkling humor, and his brilliant orchestrations. Even his works that are considered less important contain wonderful, ear-tickling, bewitching music, among them the utterly sweet, charming one-act operetta *La chanson de Fortunio* (Fortunio's Song) (1861) (lah shahn SO:*N* duh fawr tü NYO:) and the splendid, full length operettas *La diva* (1869) (lah dee VAH) and *Belle Lurette* (Beautiful Lurette)

(1880) (behl' lü REHT), the latter completed by Léo **Délibes** after the composer's death. There is an interesting CD, *La Grande Époque: Rare Recordings of Delmas, Héglon, Lafitte, Simon-Girard*, that includes 1903 recordings by Juliette Simon-Girard (1859–1954) (see mo:n' zhee RAHR), who worked with the composer and created the title roles in *La fille du tambour-major* and *Madame Favart*, from which she recorded one of the great numbers, the "Ronde des vignes" (Grapevine Rondo) (ro:nd' deh: VEE nyuh); available from Pearl (GEMM 9113; 1994). The recordings show what Offenbach, who directed most of his own productions, wanted from his singers: superb singing, and a true sense of droll, tongue-in-cheek comedy.

Important full-length works by Offenbach:

1858 (revised, 1874) ***Orphée aux enfers***

1859 (revised 1868, 1875) *Geneviève de Brabant* (Genevieve of Brabant) (zhehn uh VYEHV duh brah BAHN)

1861 (revised, 1868) *Le pont des soupirs* (The Bridge of Sighs) (luh po:n deh: soo PEER)

1864 ***La belle Hélène***

1864 *Les fées du Rhin* (The Rhine Fairies) (lé fé' dü RAN)

1866 ***Barbe-bleue***

1866 ***La vie parisienne***

1867 ***La Grande-Duchesse de Gérolstein***

1867 *Robinson Crusoé* (ro' ban SO:N krü' zo: É)

1868 ***La Périchole***

1869 ***Les brigands***

1869 *La princesse de Trébizonde* (The Princess of Trebizond) (lah pran sehs' duh tré' bee ZO:ND)

1868 *Le château à Toto* (Toto's Chateau) (luh shah to:' ah to: TO:)

1869 *Vert-Vert* (Greenie, the Parrot) (vehr' VEHR); German title: *Kakadu* (KAH kah DOO)

1872 *Fantasio* (fahn tah ZYO:)

1872 ***Le Roi Carotte***

1873 *La jolie parfumeuse* (The Pretty Perfume Girl) (lah zho: lee' pahr fü MOOZ)

1874 *Madame l'archiduc* (Madam Archduke) (mah dahm' lahr shee DÜK)

1875 *Le voyage dans la lune* (The Trip to the Moon) (luh vwah yahzh' dahn la LÜN)

1878 *Madame Favart* (mah dahm' fah VAHR)

1879 *La fille du tambour-major* (The Drum-Major's Daughter) (lah fee' yuh dü tahn boor' mah ZHAWR)

1881 ***Les contes d'Hoffmann***

Offenbachian (o:f' ehn BAHK ee uhn) *adj.* Pertaining to the kind of lilting, sparkling, rhythmically effervescent and melodically fertile music, as heady and intoxicating as champagne, and the iconoclastic, satiric wit and gaiety exemplified in the captivating comic operas of Jacques Offenbach.

Of Thee I Sing Broadway musical by George **Gershwin**; lyrics by Ira Gershwin; book by George S. **Kaufman**, who also directed, and Morrie Ryskind; Music Box Theatre, 1932 (473 perf.); Broadway revival, also directed by Kaufman, Ziegfeld Theatre, 1952 (72 perf.); sequel, by the same creative team: *Let 'Em Eat Cake* (1933; 90 perf.).

This landmark, **Gilbertian** satirical show, produced the year before Franklin D. Roosevelt was elected, roundly mocks the inefficiency and hypocrisy of the Depression-era government. "Love Is Sweeping the Country" was one of the great hits of the jaunty, rollicking, good-humored score.

During the presidential campaign, candidate John P. Wintergreen and his cronies come up with a winning idea: The campaign will sponsor a national beauty contest, and whoever wins will marry Wintergreen and become First Lady. However, Wintergreen has married his secretary, Mary Turner, whom he loves for her corn muffins—he has never tasted better. So when Wintergreen wins the election and the quintessential Southern belle, Diana Devereaux, wins the contest, she is outraged and sues him for breach of promise. Since she is of French descent, the French ambassador gets involved, and it looks as if an embarrassing international incident is in the offing. In order to avoid this, the Senate decides to hold an impeachment trial. But Mary is expecting, and it won't look good to try an expectant father, so the case is dismissed. Meanwhile, Diana marries the Vice President, a blank nonentity named Alexander Throttlebottom—and nobody doubts that she will make him live up to his name.

Oh Boy! A **Princess Theatre musical** by Jerome **Kern**; book and lyrics by P. G. **Wodehouse** and Guy **Bolton**; Princess Theatre, 1917 (463 perf.).

This silly, bubbly show tells the intricately plotted tale—which could be right out of a Wodehouse novel—of the rather muddled George Budd, who has secretly married his inamorata, Lou Ellen, daughter of the stern Judge Carter, and doesn't know how to break the news to his rich battleaxe Aunt Penelope, his guardian—one of an army of such formidable aunts created by Wodehouse in his novels. While the happy couple is gone, George's friend, the dapper, polo-playing country club type Jim Marvin, and his glamorous girlfriend, Jackie, together with all their friends, decide to use the Budds' place out in Long Island for a party celebrating their victory in the latest polo match. They are surprised that George is not there. The Budds arrive in due course, and they have no idea that they have guests, nor do the guests know the Budds have returned. Aunt Penelope, who has sent a telegram warning George not to marry Lou Ellen and telling him of her imminent arrival, shows up, and so does the irascible Judge Carter. The resulting confusion and mistaken identities are, of course, happily resolved by the end of this bouncy show, which boasts "Till the Clouds Roll By" among its hit numbers.

Oh, Kay! Broadway musical by George **Gershwin**; lyrics by Ira **Gershwin**; additional lyrics by Howard **Dietz**; book by Guy **Bolton** and P. G. **Wodehouse**; Imperial Theatre, 1926 (256 perf.); Broadway revival produced by David Merrick, rewritten for an African-American cast and set in Harlem, Richard Rodgers Theatre, 1990 (112 perf.).

The part of Lady Kay was written as a **vehicle** for Gertrude Lawrence. Gershwin composed a jazzy, lively, cheerful score and his brother wrote snazzy, optimistic lyrics about how the 1920s were here to stay—very optimistic, just a few years before the dark time of the Great Depression. "Chin up!" as they sing, and "Keep muddlin' through!" Famous songs from this show include "Someone to Watch Over Me" and "Do, Do, Do (what you done, done, done before)."

The impoverished Duke of Durham and his sister, Lady Kay, over in the U.S. from England, happens to know that Jimmy Winter, a millionaire, is seldom to be found at home on his waterside Long Island estate. Kay volunteers this information to her bootlegger acquaintances, Shorty McGee, and his sidekick, Larry Porter, who decide to use the place for their crooked activities, while Kay figures to enjoy the fantastic digs for a while and to make up for the loss she has incurred paying taxes back home. But then Jimmy unexpectedly shows up with the socialite, Constance Appleton, whom he has theoretically married. Since there is some sort of legal problem, they will not be spending the night together. Thinking quickly on her dancing feet, Kay masquerades as the new maid, and Shorty becomes the butler. Naturally, Kay falls in love with Jimmy, and he finds her very attractive indeed. The feds raid the premises and find the illegal liquor. They are about to deport Kay when Jimmy reveals that he has secretly married her! Everyone but Kay is astonished.

Oklahoma! Broadway musical by **Rodgers and Hammerstein**: music by Richard **Rodgers**; book and lyrics by Oscar **Hammerstein**, based on a play produced by the Theatre Guild: *Green Grow the Lilacs* (1931), by Lynn Riggs (1899–1954); St. James Theatre, 1943 (2212 perf.); Broadway revivals: Broadway Theatre, 1951 (100 perf.); 1953, limited City Center engagement (40 perf.); 1969, limited Lincoln Center engagement (88 perf.), produced by Rodgers; Palace Theatre, 1979 (302 perf. and national tour), directed by William Hammerstein (1918-2001), the librettist's son; George Gershwin Theatre, 2002 (413 perf.); international productions, national tours, and numerous revivals, including, notably, those in 1958, 1963, and 1965 by the New York Light Opera Company; film, 1955.

Superbly directed by Georgian-born Armenian-American stage and film director Rouben Mamoulian (1897–1987), the show was notable also for the choreography of Agnes de Mille (1905–1993), which was recreated for the movie. This masterpiece is possibly Rodgers and Hammerstein's greatest show, and it had a formative influence on the **book musical** in the American theater for the remainder of the 20th c.

Oklahoma would become a state in 1907, but when our story begins, it is still the Oklahoma Territory, still rough frontier country, although well settled and farmed, and there is conflict between the cowmen and the farmers. The show opens on a bright, sunny morning, to find a handsome cowboy, Curly McLain, wandering nonchalantly through the cornfields and onto the farm where the girl of his dreams, Laurey Williams, lives with her Aunt Eller. The strange, brooding, disturbed farmhand who works for them, Jud Fry, is also in love with Laurey. Curly takes Laurey's affection for him a bit too much for granted, and to punish him gently, she agrees to go to the big event, a box social, with Jud. But she regrets her decision almost as soon as she makes it, and has a nightmare involving Jud. At the party, where people bid for prepared picnic hampers, Curly outbids Jud for Laurey's hamper, staking everything he owns to win it. When Jud menaces them, Laurey fires him. There is now no obstacle to Curly and Laurey getting married, but at the wedding party, Jud appears, drunk, and threatens Curly with a knife. They fight, and Jud falls on the knife, killing himself. At Aunt Eller's urging, there is a quick murder trial, obligatory, although Curly is actually guilty of nothing, and he is acquitted. Statehood is declared for Oklahoma, and there is a double celebration as the exuberant townspeople, cowmen, and farmers exult in this happy event, while Laurey and Curly can now celebrate the beginning of their life together. A delightful subplot involves the gal "who cain't say no," Ado Annie, and her flirtations with the peddler Ali Hakim, much to the annoyance of her boyfriend, Will Parker.

Old Chelsea Operetta by Richard **Tauber**.

Oliven, Dr. Fritz (1874–1956) (o: LEE vehn) German lawyer, humorist, lyricist, cabaret writer, and librettist of Berlin operettas, among them Oscar Straus's *Die lustigen Nibelungen* and *Der Vetter von Dingsda* by Eduard **Künneke**. His sense of humor was hilarious and infectious, and he was known under his pen name as a humorist, Rideamus (REE deh: AH moos), Latin for "Let us laugh." When the Nazis came to power, Oliven, who was Jewish, left Germany, and spent the rest of his life in Brazil.

Oliver! London, then Broadway musical by Lionel **Bart**; book by the composer, based on Charles Dickens's much adapted second novel, *Oliver Twist* (1838); Imperial Theatre, 1963 (782 perf.); Broadway revivals: Martin Beck Theatre, 1965 (64 perf.), following the national tour; Mark Hellinger Theatre, 1984 (30 perf.); film, 1968.

The music appropriately reflects the Victorian **music hall**. In the novel the portrait of Fagin is decidedly anti-Semitic, but in the show, Fagin's Jewishness is downplayed, and he becomes a twinkly rascal.

In early Victorian London, where the divisions between the wealthy, educated middle class and the hungry poor, dwelling in the slums, are stark, the orphaned Oliver Twist is taken under the wing of the petty thief and fence Fagin, who trains boys to be thieves and pickpockets. Among Fagin's cronies are the violent criminal Bill Sykes and his long-suffering girlfriend, Nancy, whom he will end by murdering. Oliver is eventually found by his relatives and rescued from a life of misery and crime.

ombra scene [Italian (O:M brah): shadow; shade; ghost] An opera scene that usually takes place in the underworld and involves the appearance of a shade; esp. in early operas, e.g., those about the legend of *Orfeo ed Euridice*, when Eurydice appears to Orpheus.

On a Clear Day You Can See Forever Broadway musical by Burton **Lane**; book by Alan Jay **Lerner**, loosely based on the play *Berkeley Square* (1929) by John S. Balderston (1889 1954); lyrics by Lerner; Mark Hellinger Theatre, 1965 (272 perf.); national tours; 2000 **Encores** presentation; film, 1970, starring Barbra Streisand.

The bizarre story of this strange musical, with a wonderful score, revolves around the problematic ideas of reincarnation and ESP. To please her fiancé, Warren, the loquacious Daisy Gamble, who has ESP, goes to psychiatrist Dr. Mark Bruckner to be hypnotized into giving up smoking. He discovers that in a past life she was Melinda Wells, an 18th-c. Englishwoman, and he is convinced that Daisy is the reincarnation of Melinda, who was on her way to Boston with her husband, the portrait artist Edward Moncrief, when the ship was wrecked and they drowned. Daisy and Mark fall in love with each other. Although he is ridiculed by his fellow psychiatrists, Mark goes public with the case. When Daisy discovers that it is about her, she and Mark quarrel, but she forgives him, dumps her fiancé, and returns to him.

on the downbeat A music cue. See DOWNBEAT.

On the Twentieth Century Broadway musical by Cy **Coleman**; book and lyrics by **Comden and Green**, based on the screwball comedy film *Twentieth Century* (1934), directed by Howard Hawks (1896–1977), with a screenplay adapted by Ben Hecht (1894–1964) and Charles MacArthur (1895–1956) from their stage play *Twentieth Century* (1932); St. James Theatre, 1978 (453 perf.).

Everyone travels from Chicago to New York on the *Twentieth Century* train. The down-at-heels Broadway producer Oscar Jaffe, former lover of the now famous star Lily Garland, whom he discovered, wants her to appear in his next play so that he will get the backing it needs to succeed. Mrs. Primrose, a religious fanatic, agrees to back the play, which is about Mary Magdalene; however, she turns out to be not only nutty as a fruitcake, but also without a dime to her name. Oscar, who feels he might as well drop dead, decides to fake a deathbed scene, and Lily is so upset that she agrees to appear in the play.

On Your Toes Broadway musical by **Rodgers and Hart**: music by Richard **Rodgers**; book by the composer, with George **Abbott**, who also directed, and Lorenz **Hart**; lyrics by Hart; Imperial Theatre, 1936 (315 perf.); Broadway revivals: 46th Street Theatre, 1954 (64 perf.), Virginia Theatre, 1983 (512 Broadway perf., national tour, exported to London), both directed by Abbott; film, 1939.

The choreography was by Russian-born American ballet and show choreographer George Balanchine (1904–1983).

Phil Dolan, Jr., a former dancer, is teaching at Knickerbocker University, while his girlfriend, Frankie Frayne, writes songs, and one of his students, Sidney Cohn, composes ballets. Phil encourages Peggy Porterfield, a rich patron of the arts, to persuade Sergei Alexandrovich to produce Cohn's new ballet for his company. During rehearsals, the prima ballerina, Vera Barnova, flirts with Phil, who is also dancing in the ballet. This upsets both Frankie and Vera's own boyfriend and dancing partner, Konstantine Morrosine, who hires two gangsters to dispose of Phil. "Slaughter on Tenth Avenue" is proceeding when Phil receives a note warning him that he will be shot as soon as it ends. He keeps on dancing until the police arrive and the plot can be foiled.

Once on This Island Broadway musical by Stephen **Flaherty**; book and lyrics by Lynn **Ahrens**, based on the novel *My Love, My Love: The Peasant Girl* (1985) by Trinidad-born American writer Rosa Guy (b. 1925); Booth Theatre, 1990 (478 perf.); Winter Garden Theatre, special benefit, 2002 (2 perf.).

The music of this show appropriately reflects its Caribbean setting, with elements of **calypso** and island folk dance; it is performed by an all African-American cast.

On an island in the Antilles, storytellers act out the tale of the beautiful, poor girl Ti Moune, who offered her soul to the gods in exchange for the life of the wealthy Daniel after he has been in an auto accident. He recovers and they fall in love, but he is forced by his family to marry a rich girl whom they think more suitable. Ti Moune dies and is turned into a tree that overlooks their dwelling.

Once Upon a Mattress Off-Broadway, then Broadway musical by Mary **Rodgers**; book by Jay Thompson, Dean Fuller, and Marshall Barer (1923–1998), based on the fairy tale "The Princess and the Pea," by Hans Christian **Andersen**; lyrics by Barer; Phoenix Theatre, 1959 (460 perf.); Broadway revival, Broadhurst Theatre, 1996 (223 perf.).

The original show starred Carol Burnett (b. 1933) as Winifred, a role she reprised in two television versions of the show, in 1964 and 1972; she played the Queen in a 2005 TV version. Burnett brought the house down when she brassily sang about how she has always been shy.

The year is 1482, and Prince Dauntless must marry. Until he does, nobody else in the land will be allowed to. But as far as his mother the Queen is concerned, nobody is good enough for her little boy. Clever, feisty Princess Winifred, known as "Fred," manages to outwit the Queen; and the King, who hasn't spoken in so long that everyone thinks he is mute, finally tells his wife to shut up.

One Touch of Venus Broadway musical by Kurt **Weill**; book by humorist S. J. Perelman (1904–1979) [b. Sidney Joseph Perelman] and poet [Frederick] Ogden Nash (1902–1971), suggested by the novel *The Tinted Venus: A Farcical Romance* (1885), by F. Anstey (1856–1934) [pen name of English novelist and humorist Thomas Anstey Guthrie]; lyrics by Nash; Alvin Theatre, 1943 (567 perf.); film, 1948.

This show was notable for the performance of Mary Martin, appearing for the first time in a starring role as Venus. The most well known song from this beautiful score is "Foolish Heart."

Engaged to the domineering Gloria, the meek barber Rodney Hatch—a "Yes, dear" man if ever there was one—buys her an engagement ring. When he tries it on the finger of a statue of Venus, the statue comes to life and immediately falls in love with him. He is in bliss, but Venus is less convinced the more she learns what life in the modern world is like, and the position women are in. In fact, she is so annoyed that she prefers life as a statue, and turns back to stone. Rodney, meanwhile, has learned a thing or two, and he breaks up with Gloria.

open tone In singing, the bright, ringing sound produced by placing the voice in the front of the **mask**, used as a resonator. Cf. **covered tone**.

opera *n.* [Latin: works; pl. of *opus*: a single artistic work] A play set to music, and meant to be sung and acted on stage with orchestral accompaniment. Most operas are **through-composed**, i.e., almost every word is set to music. There is solo and, in most cases, ensemble singing, with the dialogue being sung in **recitative**. But in many operas, the dialogue is spoken, e.g., in **opéra comique** and **Singspiel**. The singers must be trained in classical vocal technique requiring great control, agility, and beauty of tone, as well as the flexibility necessary to express vocally the range of emotions demanded by the musical settings.

See also LEGITIMATE SINGING.

opera ballet A dance sequence that takes place in an opera. At the Paris Opéra in the nineteenth century, it was de rigeur to have a ballet in the third act, and many patrons arrived late in order to see it and their favorite ballet dancer, with whom they might be hoping to have an affair. Often, ballets were stuck into the opera for no particularly good reason. When operas such as Verdi's *Il Trovatore* were produced in Paris, a ballet had to be interpolated and new music composed.

opéra-ballet *n. Hist.* A performance piece that combines dance and singing in almost equal measure; esp. popular in the 17th c. at the court of Louis XIV and in the 18th at the court of Louis XV; several were composed by **Lully**. Later, **Rameau** also wrote in this genre, esp. in its sub-genre the **ballet-héroique**; e.g., *Zaïs* and *Les Indes galantes*.

opéra bouffe (o: pé *r*ah BOOF) [French] The French 19th-c. term for comic opera; also, an individual example of the genre. The 18th-c. term *opéra bouffon* (boo FO:*N*) means the same thing. Lively, melodious music, comedy, satire, and a happy ending are always part of such pieces.

opera buffa (O: peh rah BOO fah) [Italian] The Italian term for comic opera; also, an individual example of the genre.

opéra comique (o pé *r*ah ko MEEK) [French] The French term for operas with spoken dialogue, which includes some very serious pieces, as well as operetta; not to be confused with "comic opera," which is *opéra bouffe*. The term applies to the genre in general, and to individual examples of it.

opera di obbligo (dee O:B blee go:) [Italian: lit., opera of obligation; obligatory opera] *Hist.* In 9th c. Italy, an opera that the management felt obliged to schedule as one of its principal operas of the season; a **warhorse** that was expected to generate income.

opera di ripiego (dee ree PYEH go:) [Italian: lit., opera of reserve; opera held in reserve] *Hist.* In 19th c. Italy, a fully prepared and mounted production of an opera that the management could put on any time; it was held in reserve in an emergency, such as the illness or incapacity of a star or the state of unpreparedness of a scheduled opera.

opera di sentimento (dee sehn' tee MEHN to:) [Italian: opera of feeling; sentimental passion; sensitivity] In the 18th c. esp., an opera with a romantic love story and a happy ending.

opéra-féerie (o' pé *r*ah fé' uh *R*EE) *n.* [French: opera-fairy-spectacle, or fairy-tale-like extravaganza] An opera or operetta with elements of fantasy and spectacle; i.e., elaborate scenery, costumes, special effects, and a large cast including a **corps de ballet** and singing **chorus**; e.g., Offenbach's *Le voyage dans la lune*, *Le Roi Carotte.*

opera house A theater where operas and ballets are presented.

opera scena (O: peh: rah SHEH: nah) [Italian: opera scene] A solo portion of an opera, esp. in **bel canto** romantic pieces, consisting usually of an **aria** that begins with a **cavatina** section, often **cantabile**; continues with a **bridge** that may be in the form of a **recitative**; and concludes with a **cabaletta**.

opera semiseria (SEH mee SEH ree ah) In the mid-18th c. esp., an opera buffa that had serious elements, as in certain libretti by Carlo **Goldoni**; e.g., Galuppi's *La Diavolessa (The She-Devil)* (1755). Also called **dramma tragicomico**.

opera seria (SEH: ree yah) [Italian: serious opera] The term is usually applied only to 18th-c. spectacle operas on classical, heroic or tragic themes.

operetta *n.* [Italian: little opera] A musical theater piece that includes spoken dialogue; stories that are comic or seriocomic, and often romantic in nature, with lush ballads and vivacious dance tunes, e.g., those of the Viennese school by Johann **Strauss**, Franz **Lehár**, and Emerich **Kálmán**; the French operettas of Charles **Lecocq** and Jacques **Offenbach**; and the pieces of **Gilbert and Sullivan**. The American variant that developed from it, incorporating American musical elements, such as jazz and popular song, is usually referred to as a **musical comedy** or musical. Operetta includes not only the European varieties, but also American pieces by such composers as Victor **Herbert**, Jerome **Kern**, and Sigmund **Romberg**. It requires **legitimate singing**, i.e., operatic vocal technique, as opposed to the techniques demanded in many Broadway shows, which often need singers who can **belt** and who have the versatility to sing in various **popular music** styles, e.g., rock, blues, ballads, crooning.

oratorio *n.* A religious drama set to music; performed by soloists, chorus and orchestra, but usually without being acted out, and with no scenery or costumes; e.g., Handel's *Messiah* (first performed in 1742). In 1997, opera stage director Jonathan Miller (b. 1934) directed a fully staged production of Johann Sebastian Bach's *St. Matthew Passion* (1727) at the Brooklyn Academy of Music; it was revived in the same venue in 2009.

Orazi e Curiazi (Horatii and Curatii) Opera by Saverio **Mercadante**.

orchestra *n.* [Fr. ancient Greek: the open place in front of a stage where the chorus danced, often to musical accompaniment. Fr. *orkesthai* (o:r KEHS *th*I'): to dance. Cf. the word "orchesography": the art of dancing described] **1.** In the musical theater, a large group of instrumentalists, including strings, brass, woodwinds, and percussion, who play for performances of stage pieces in theaters, opera houses, and other venues. **2.** The downstairs seating area in an American theater.

orchestra dress [Short for *orchestra dress rehearsal*] A dress or tech-dress rehearsal of a musical theater piece on a completely set and lit stage, with the full orchestra playing in the pit.

orchestra pit The sunken well in front of a theater stage where the musicians perform for a musical theater event; called the *pit*, for short. *Brit.* orchestra well.

orchestra rail/railing The bar or barrier that separates the orchestra pit from the rest of the auditorium.

orchestra stands The music stands in the orchestra pit, with lights attached to the top rim, shining down onto the music.

orchestration *n.* The arrangement of parts for the instruments in a musical piece, giving it **texture**; the determination of what instruments are to play what musical lines, solo or in combination, and when; another word for instrumentation.

orchestrator *n.* The person who scores and arranges the instrumental parts for music that has already been composed; hence *orchestrations*: the musical arrangements. Composers may be their own orchestrators, taking their skeleton or outline scores, adding ornamentation, and filling in which instruments are to play what parts. In the contemporary musical theater, a score is often orchestrated from a composer's piano version by someone hired especially for that purpose. Cf. **arranger**.

Orfeo ed Euridice (Orpheus and Eurydice) (o:r FEH: o: ehd ayoo' rih DEE che) [*Orphée et Eurydice* (o:r FÉ eh: uh *r*ee DEES)] **1.** Opera in three acts by Christoph Willibald Ritter von **Gluck**; libretto by Ranieri de' Calzabigi, based on the ancient Greek myth; Vienna, Burgtheater, 1762.

The most well known aria from this beautiful opera is Orpheus's moving "Che farò senza Euridice" (What will I do without Euridice?) (keh: fah RO: sehn dzah eh: OO rih: DEE cheh:); French title: "J'ai perdu mon Eurydice" (I have lost my Eurydice) (zheh: peh*r* dü' mo: NUH *r*ee DEE suh).

The widowed Orpheus (contr.; ten. in revised, French 1774 version) grieves so deeply for his dead wife, Eurydice (sop.) that Zeus, king of the gods, gives him permission to descend to Hades to bring her back to life, if, with the power of his musical art, he can convince Pluto to allow him to do so. But Orpheus may not so much as look at Eurydice until they have crossed the river Styx and are back in the land of the living. Orpheus enters the Elysian Fields, and finds Eurydice. But she cannot understand why he will not look at her, and he is not permitted to give her an explanation. She says he no longer loves her. In a momentary surge of emotion, he turns to her, and she falls dead at his feet. But the god of love, Amor (sop.), is so moved that he brings her to life again.

2. Opera in four or five acts by Franz Joseph **Haydn**; libretto by Carlo Francesco Badini (?–1793) (KAHR lo: frahn CHEHS ko: bah DEE nee); 1791–1792; not performed until 1951, in Florence. [Original title: *L'anima del filosofo* (The Philosopher's Spirit) (LAH nee mah dehl fih: LO: so: fo:)]

This was Haydn's last opera, and it presumably remained unfinished at his death. Plans to produce it at the King's Theatre in the Haymarket in London fell through. The philosopher of the original title is not named in the work, and the title's meaning and relevance remain unfathomable. The music is beautiful, but the slow-moving, poorly crafted libretto lacks dramatic impact and is so unwieldy that the opera appears unstageworthy. The superb recording on L'Oiseau-Lyre (452 668-2; 1997) shows that it would certainly be worth doing in concert form.

Creon (KREE on) (bar.) [Creonte (kreh: O:N teh:)] has agreed to allow his daughter Eurydice (sop.) to marry Orpheus (ten.), instead of her originally intended groom, Arideus (A rih DEE uhs). When she tries to escape from Arideus's pursuing men, she is bitten to death by a snake and descends to Hades. Orpheus follows her there, led by the Sybil (mezz.) [Genio (DGEH: nee o:)]. He enters Hades with the permission of Pluto (bass), and finds Eurydice, but is warned not to look at her or disaster will ensue. He accidentally does so, and she dies. Still grieving, he is given a cup of poison by the Bacchantes, which he takes.

See also FAVOLA IN MUSICA.

Orff, Carl (1895–1982) (AW[R]F) German composer; wrote nineteen operas or semi-operatic works, e.g., the "scenic cantata" in three parts, *Carmina Burana* (Songs of Beuren) (1937) (kahr MEE nah boo RAH nah), his most well known work, to 13th-c. Latin texts by the monks of Benediktbeuern (BEH neh DIH:KT BOY uh[r]hn). In 1943, he set texts of the ancient Roman writer Catullus (84–54 BCE) (kah T*OO* loos; anglicized: kuh TUH l*oo*s) to music, *Catulli Carmina* (Songs of Catullus) (kah T*OO* lee). His most well known operas include *Der Mond* (The Moon) (1929) (deh MO:NT) and *Der Kluge* (The Industrious One) (1943) (deh KLOO geh). Orff is known for his simple melodies, compelling rhythms, and densely textured harmonies; and also for a certain static, undramatic quality in his stage works.

ornamentation *n.* In music, the embellishment of a musical line or melody with an extra note or extra notes; e.g., such ornaments as the **appoggiatura**; the *backfall*, also called a *forefall*, used in baroque opera: gracing a note by preceding it with the note above it in the scale (it may or may not be followed by a trill or shake on the main note, lasting half the value of that note); the *grace note*: an unaccented note parenthetically added onto another note just before it; the **trill**; and the *roulade*: a run of notes from high to low, or from low to high, up or down the scale. Ornamentation of a vocal line is the hallmark of **coloratura** work, and in virtuosic vocal displays employing variations on a main theme during the cabaletta portion of an **aria**. The style, kind, and amount of ornamentation vary with the particular historical period and its known **performance practice**.

Orphée aux enfers (Orpheus in the Underworld) (o:*r* fé' o: zah*n* FEH:*R*) **Opéra bouffon** (comic opera) in two acts by Jacques **Offenbach**; libretto by Ludovic **Halévy**, later revised by Hector-Jonathan Crémieux (1828–1892) (ehk to:*r*' zho: nah tah*n*' k*r*é MY*OO*); Paris, Théâtre des Bouffes-Parisiens, 1858; revised and expanded to four acts, as an **opéra-féerie**, in1874, premiere at Théâtre de la Gaité.

The vitriolic bile that critics poured on Offenbach's head for daring to mock sacred antiquity brought the public flocking to the theater, and ensured the success of this enduring masterpiece. It runs amok through the conventions of classical drama and the ancient Greek myth of Orpheus, Father of Music, and his abiding love for his wife, Eurydice. But the real target of the satire is Napoleon III, the philandering emperor who was apparently more interested in palace chambermaids than in governing his realm—portrayed as blustering Jupiter.

Orpheus (ten.) and Eurydice (sop.) can't stand each other. He plays the violin. She hates the violin! When Pluto (ten.) carries her off to Hades, Orpheus is overjoyed. But the Goddess of Public Opinion (mezz.) insists that he plead with Jupiter (bar.) on Mt. Olympus for the safe return of his wife. Jupiter and the entire pantheon of gods and goddesses descend to Hades to investigate. In Hades, Eurydice languishes under the unwelcome ministrations of her jailer, John Styx (ten.), former King of the Boeotians (bee OH shuhns). Jupiter disguises himself as a fly, enters her chamber through the keyhole, and tries to seduce her, but they are interrupted. Orpheus arrives at a bacchanalian revelry to claim her, and Jupiter decrees that he may have her back, provided he does not look at her until they have reached the exit from Hades. Orpheus drags her away without looking, and Jupiter sends a bolt of lighting in his direction. He turns around, and Jupiter, in triumph, insists that Eurydice remain in the underworld. The festivities end with the *galop infernal* (ga luh' pa*n* feh*r* NAHL), the famous **can-can**.

ostinato (o:' stee NAH to:) *adj.* [Italian: obstinate, insistent] The continual repetition of a melody, theme, or accompanying figure, with little variation; e.g., *basso ostinato*: the repetition of a figure in the bass, i.e., underneath the main melodic line, accompanying it.

Otello (Othello) (o: TEHL lo:) **1.** *Otello, ossia Il moro di Venezia* (o: SEE ah ihl MO: ro: dee veh NEH: tsee ah) Opera in three acts by Gioachino **Rossini**; libretto by the prolific Neapolitan dilettante Francesco Maria Berio, marchese [marquis] di Salza (1765–1820) (frahn CHEHS ko: mah REE ah BEH ree o: mahr KEH: zeh: dee SAHL tsah), based loosely on the tragedy *Othello, The Moor of Venice* by William **Shakespeare**; Naples, Teatro del Fondo (FO:N do:), 1816.

In Venice, Otello (ten.) is acclaimed for his victory over the Turks, and the Doge (ten.) rewards him with citizenship. Otello has married Desdemona (dehz DEH: mo: nah) (sop.) secretly, since her father, Elmiro (ehl MEE ro:) (bass) [Brabantio in Shakespeare], objects to the marriage. Meanwhile, Iago (ee AH go:) (ten.) is jealous because he has been passed over for promotion, and he vows revenge, using the Doge's son Rodrigo (ro: DREE go:) (ten.), who is in love with Desdemona, to get at Otello, and employing a stolen letter of hers that is open to misinterpretation. Otello is jealous of Rodrigo, and thinks that he and Desdemona may be having an affair. She protests her innocence, but, goaded to a fury by his jealous passion, he does not believe her, and murders her.

2. Opera in four acts by Giuseppe **Verdi**; libretto by Arrigo **Boïto**, based closely on Shakespeare's tragedy; Milan, Teatro alla Scala, 1889.

This is one of Verdi's most ambitious and modern works, both dramatically and musically, and it is a departure for him, verging as it does on the through-composed music drama and **verismo** style that would later come into vogue.

The opera opens in Cyprus (rather than in Venice, as in Shakespeare), where the populace is anxiously awaiting the arrival of Otello (ten.), whose ship is seen in stormy seas. He lands safely and triumphantly. Iago (bar.), Otello's ensign, passed over for promotion to lieutenant in favor of Cassio (KAH syo:) (ten.), plots his revenge. Implying that Cassio's behavior in a drunken tavern brawl was less than honorable, he makes sure that Otello dismisses him. Later, he insinuates to Otello that Otello's wife, Desdemona (sop.) has been unfaithful with Cassio. When Desdemona pleads with Otello on Cassio's behalf, Otello starts to believe Iago's lies. As further "proof," Iago gives Otello Desdemona's embroidered hand-kerchief—a gift from Otello—which he gets from her lady's maid, his wife Emilia (mezz.). Iago tells him that he found it in Cassio's chamber. Believing him, and in a blind fury, Otello smothers Desdemona.

overture *n.* **1.** In musical theater, the instrumental introduction to an opera, operetta, or musical comedy, usually played before the curtain rises. It may be a fully developed composition using themes from the piece; or it may be a *medley overture*, i.e., a series of tunes from the piece. **2.** The instrumental introduction to an **oratorio**. **3.** A short instrumental piece composed for an orchestra.

P

pace *n.* The **tempo** or rate of speed at which a spoken or musical piece is played and performed. An integral part of pace is rhythmic intensity, created by the energy put into the performance.

Pacific Overtures Broadway musical by Stephen **Sondheim**; book by John **Weidman**; Winter Garden Theatre, 1976 (193 perf.); Off-Broadway revival, Promenade Theatre, 1984 (109 perf.); Broadway revival: Studio 54, Roundabout Theatre limited engagement, 2004 (93 perf.).

   This innovative work, with the original version produced and directed by Harold Prince, evokes Japan in 1853–1859 and its opening up to the Western world, moving on to the present day. The Japanese viewpoint is made clear by a narrator, the Reciter. Two characters represent the two divergent points of view prevailing at the time: the westernized Samurai Kayama and the anti-Western rebel Manjiro, Kayama's friend and later arch-opponent. The plot is the unfolding of historical events leading to the modernization of Japan.

Pacini, Giovanni (1796–1867) (dgo: VAHN nee pah CHEE nee) Highly successful Italian opera composer of some forty works, very popular in their day but seldom performed nowadays; recordings show him to have had a fertile, delightful, and even inspired melodic gift, and a felicitous, deliberately **Rossinian** style of composition: he was Rossini's contemporary, and, in his early phase, took Rossini as his model. Among his notable earlier successes are the tuneful *Alessandro nelle Indie* (Alexander in the Indies) (1824) (ah' lehs SAHN dro: NEHL leh: EEN dee e:) and the impressive *L'Ultimo giorno di Pompeii* (The Last Day of Pompeii) (1825) (*LOO*L tee mo: DGO:R no: dee pom PEH:ee), the latter often considered his masterpiece. *Maria, regina d'Inghilterra* (Mary, Queen of England) (1843) (mah REE ah re DGEE nah dihng' ihl TEH:R rah), a later triumph, has an early **Verdian** ring to it. Indeed, Pacini has been seen as a link between Rossini and Verdi.

package *n., v. —n.* **1.** An entertainment project, usually a musical, prepared esp. for touring, usually to summer theaters; hence, used as an adj., *package show*; *package house*: a summer theater that books packages or star packages. It may include a star and a few cast members in key roles; an entire company; or a star alone; hence, *star package*. The package show will add cast members and production elements when it arrives at the various theaters on the road; it is accompanied by an advance stage manager, who goes to the next theater on the tour to help prepare for the arrival of the package. —*v. t.* **2.** To put together such a show.

Paër, Ferdinando (1771–1839) (fehr' dee NAHN do: pah EHR) Italian opera composer of approximately forty works, many in the old-fashioned **opera semiseria** style; spent most of his life in Paris and taught composition; Franz Liszt was among his students; his use of the **crescendo** influenced the composing style of

Gioachino **Rossini**. Among his most successful works are his first hit, *Griselda* (1798) (gree ZEHL dah); *Leonora* (1804) (leh:' o: NO: rah), set to an Italian version of the opera by Pierre Gaveaux, which influenced Beethoven's ***Fidelio***; and *Sofonisba* (1805) (so' fo NEEZ bah), about which the German fantasist E. T. A. **Hoffmann** wrote a scathing critique, while others thought it brilliant. In fact, it is workmanlike, conventional, and unexciting; listen to the recording on Opera Rara (ORR237; 2006). *Le maître de chapelle* (The Choirmaster) (1821) (luh meh' truh duh shah PEHL) is considered Paër's masterpiece.

See also DIDONE ABBANDONATA.

Pagliacci (Clowns) (pah [*G*]LYAH: chee) Opera in two acts by Ruggiero **Leon-cavallo**; libretto by the composer; London, Covent Garden, 1892.

A supreme example of **verismo** opera, this short piece is usually presented with Mascagni's ***Cavalleria Rusticana***. The opera provided Enrico Caruso with one of his signature roles, which includes the wrenching aria that ends act 1, "Vesti la giubba" (Put On the Costume) (VEH stee lah DGOOB bah).

Tonio (TO: n[ee]yo:) (bar.), a travelling actor, tells the audience in a Prologue that they are about to see the unfolding of a true story. Nedda (NEHD dah) (sop.), the wife of Canio (KAH n[ee]yo:) (ten.), head of a traveling commedia troupe, has been having an affair with Silvio (SIH:L v[ee]yo:), a peasant who lives in the village where the company has arrived to perform, and she plans to run away with him. Tonio, whose advances Nedda had repulsed, sees her with Silvio. He runs to tell Canio, who has gone to drink with the locals at the inn. Canio demands to know who Nedda's lover is, but she denies everything. He is desperately upset, but the show must go on. He cannot contain his fury, and during the improvisational comedy, which resembles the real-life situation, Canio demands that Nedda, playing Columbine, tell him the name of her lover. Enraged when she pretends to be doing the play, he stabs her. Silvio runs up onto the stage to save her, and Canio knifes him as well.

Paint Your Wagon Broadway musical by **Lerner and Loewe**: Alan Jay Lerner (book) and Frederick Loewe (music); Shubert Theatre, 1951 (289 perf.); film, 1969.

During the California Gold Rush in 1853, Ben Rumson discovers gold on his land, and the rush is on. A mining town is established, and Ben's daughter, Jennifer, the object of everyone's attentions, falls in love with the Mexican prospector Julio Valveras, whom she marries after the lode runs out and the town is deserted.

Paisiello, Giovanni (1740–1816) (dgo: VAHN nee pIz YEHL lo:) Prolific Italian composer of ca. ninety operas; esp. known for his comic operas, among them *Il barbiere di Siviglia* (1782), with a libretto by Giuseppe Petrosellini (1727–ca. 1797) (dgoo ZEHP peh: PEH tro: sehl LEE nee), who also wrote texts for **Cimarosa**, **Galuppi** and **Salieri**. Paisiello's *Barbiere*, although very popular, was eclipsed by Rossini's version. One of his last serious operas, *Proserpine* (1803) is very beautiful, with a superbly orchestrated score; available on CD (Dynamic; 442/1-2; 2003). It was composed to a French libretto by Nicolas-François Guillard, based on an earlier one by Philippe **Quinault**, about the myth of the goddess Ceres, whose daughter Proserpine is abducted by Pluto. The opera was commissioned for and presented at the court of Napoleon I. Paisiello's most well known work is undoubtedly *Nina, o sia La pazza per amore (Nina, or The Love-Crazed Maiden)*.

See also DIDONE ABBANDONATA.

Pajama Game, The Broadway musical by Richard **Adler** and Jerry **Ross**; book by George **Abbott**, who also directed, and Richard Bissel (1909–1994), based on his novel *7 1/2 Cents*; St. James Theatre, 1954 (1063 perf.); Broadway revivals: Lunt-Fontanne Theatre, 1973 (70 perf.); American Airlines Theatre, 2006, limited engagement (170 perf.); film, 1957.

A satirical look at labor relations in the garment industry, the show is set at the Sleep-Tite Pajama factory in Cedar Rapids, Iowa. The factory's new manager, Sid, falls in love with Babe, the head of the union's grievance committee. This complicates the situation in the shop, since the workers want a raise, which they finally get. Other characters include Sid's secretary, Gladys, and her boyfriend, Hines, a time-study efficiency expert who is very proud of his expertise. Among the hit songs in the show are "Hey There" and "Hernando's Hideaway."

Pal Joey Broadway musical by **Rodgers and Hart**: Richard Rodgers (music) and Lorenz Hart (book and lyrics), based on stories by John O'Hara (1905–1970), written for *The New Yorker* magazine; Ethel Barrymore Theatre, 1940 (374 perf.); Broadway revivals: Broadhurst Theatre, 1952 (540 perf.); Circle in the Square Theatre, 1976 (106 perf.); Studio 54, Roundabout Theatre limited engagement, 2008 (122 perf.); film, 1957, starring Frank Sinatra (1915–1998).

George **Abbott** directed the original production of this great classic, which starred the marvelous Gene Kelly (1912–1996). Among the show's brilliant numbers is the standard "Bewitched."

"Pal" Joey is a cynical, two-timing, unapologetically amoral nightclub **hoofer** who thinks nothing of sleeping with every chorus girl in sight, and "borrowing" money from them. Linda, a secretary, seems a likely cash cow, so he goes after her and wins her affections, but dumps her for the wealthy, bored socialite Mrs. Vera Simpson. She and Joey understand each other; they are just in it for the sex. She gets bored with him, and when blackmailers try to horn in, she simply dumps him, and tells Linda she can have him back. But Linda has wised up. Joey goes his merry way.

pantomime *n.* **1.** Silent acting, using gesture and movement. Called *mime*, for short. **2.** A theater piece that is performed silently, sometimes with musical **accompaniment**. **3.** A popular British entertainment incorporating music, dialogue, and such diverse elements as comic turns, fairy-tale characters, melodrama, acrobatics, and special magical effects; usually seasonal, e.g., the Christmas pantomime. Called a *panto*, for short. See also EXTRAVAGANZA.

Parade Broadway musical by Jason Robert **Brown**.

parlando (pahr LAHN do:) *adj.* [Italian: speaking] In opera, imitating a declamatory tone of a voice when singing; i.e., giving the impression of speaking while singing, as in **recitative**.

parody *n., v.* —*n.* **1.** A mocking, satirical work that imitates the style and characteristics of an existing person, piece or genre; e.g., Offenbach's masterful, yet satirical imitation of Meyerbeer's *L'Africaine* in the musical **introduction** to act 2 of *Robinson Crusoé*; Sullivan's parodies of Verdi in *The Pirates of Penzance*. Hence, *parodist*: one who writes or performs a parody. —*v. t.* **2.** To write or perform such a **spoof** or **burlesque**.

See also NEWGATE PASTORAL.

pas de deux (pah duh D*OO*) [French: lit., step of two] In ballet and dance, a section of a scene or a separate number for two dancers together.

pas seul (pah S*OO*L) [French: lit., step alone] In ballet and dance, a solo dance.

passagio (pahs SAH dgo:) *n.* [Italian: passage] The pivotal place where the vocal **register** changes, e.g., from head to chest voice, meaning that the muscles are tensed and relaxed to make the transition.

passegio (pahs SEH dgo:) *n.* [Italian: passing by] The opening section of some 16th-c. Italian dances: the approach of the dancers to each other; their preliminary bows and curtsies, and their beginning steps.

passepied (pahs PYEH:) *n.* [French] *Hist.* A late 17th-c. court dance in 3/4 or 6/8 time, similar to the **minuet**, but faster; used in ballets by **Lully**.

pasticcio (pahs TEE cho:) *n.* [Italian: lit., pie; fig., mess, hotchpotch, jumble, gallimaufry] An opera put together using music by different composers, or using selections from different works by one composer. The practice of arranging such operas, which began in Italy in the 17th c. and was well established in the early 18th, became very popular in England. In some cases, singers would select their favorite arias, and linking recitative and ensemble numbers based on a popular, well known libretto or scenario would then be put together by a house composer or other staff member working for an opera company. In 1725 in London, George Frideric **Handel** selected works from currently popular operas—some of them from the repertoires of the singers who were to appear—and arranged them into an opera called *Elpidia*, using the outline of an extant libretto and adding music of his own for recitatives and perhaps some ensembles—all meant to cater to the taste of the moment. Some of the ballad operas or ballad farces of the 18th and 19th centuries, e.g., *The Beggar's Opera*, are pasticcio operas. A well known **pastoral** pasticcio from 1762 is *Love in a Village*, a "New Dramatic Opera," compiled by Thomas **Arne** from music by himself, Handel, Baldassare **Galuppi**, and a number of now obscure composers. Cf. **jumble**.

pastiche (pas TEESH) *n.* [Fr. French for Italian *pasticcio*] **1.** A piece in imitation of some work or style; sometimes a **burlesque** of an existing work. **2.** The usual English word for *pasticcio*; e.g., *Christopher Columbus* (1976), with an original libretto and lyrics by Don White, using music cobbled together by Patric Schmid from some of the more obscure **Offenbach** pieces: *a pastiche operetta* (e.g., ***Blossom Time***).

pastoral n. An artistic, literary, and theatrical genre of play or musical theater piece that is set in the countryside and features rural characters such as peasant lads and lasses, shepherds and shepherdesses; e.g., Offenbach's *Les bergers* (leh: beh*r* ZHEH:) (1865; The Shepherds), which included 18th-c. **pastiche** (def. 1) elements. The genre begins with the Greek myths of nymphs and shepherds, with which **Offenbach** had such fun. He wrote a number of parodies of the pastoral, e.g., in act 1 of ***Orphée aux enfers*** and act 1 of ***Barbe-bleue***. And Gilbert and Sullivan parodied the genre in act 1 of ***Iolanthe***. In the theater, the pastoral originated in the late 16th c., with such pieces as Handel's ***Acis and Galatea***. The 19th c. saw romantic pastoral operas, such as Bellini's ***La sonnambula***, Donizetti's ***L'elisir d'amore***, Smetana's ***Prodaná Nevěsta (The Bartered Bride)***, and Mascagni's *L'amico Fritz*.

See also NEWGATE PASTORAL.

Patience, or Bunthorne's Bride Comic opera in two acts by **Gilbert and Sullivan**; London, Opéra Comique, 1881; transferred to the newly built Savoy Theatre, the first production to be mounted there.

Gilbert parodied the Aesthetic movement and its adherents, including Oscar Wilde (1854–1900), whom D'Oyly Carte sent to the US on a lecture tour, to publicize *Patience*. Sullivan's score is one of his most memorable and amusing, with jaunty military airs for the Heavy Dragoons, and mournful tunes for the aesthetic maidens. The churchy quality of some of the music reflects the operetta's origins: Gilbert started out to satirize aestheticism, then changed his ideas and decided to lampoon the church, basing the new libretto on one of his Bab Ballads, "The Rival Curates": the two enemies would be competing clergymen. The project was well advanced when he got cold feet and reverted to his original idea.

The Heavy Dragoons, led by their Colonel (bass-bar.), are in love with twenty lovesick maidens, but the ladies are all in love with the aesthetic poet Reginald Bunthorne (bar.). He, however, is in love with the milkmaid Patience (sop.), who is in love with Bunthorne's rival, her childhood sweetheart, the poet Archibald Grosvenor (bar.), who captures the affections of the maidens. The clumsy efforts of the Dragoons to be aesthetic have little effect. The portly Lady Jane (contr.), who loves Bunthorne although he scorns her, encourages him to confront Grosvenor. When Bunthorne threatens to curse him, Grosvenor quails in terror, gives up his aestheticism, and returns to being a commonplace young man. He can now marry Patience. The maidens follow Grosvenor's example and become commonplace young ladies. They will marry the dragoons, and Lady Jane will wed the Colonel. Bunthorne will "have to be contented with a tulip or lily."

patter *n.* Words meant to be spoken or sung quickly, as in the patter songs in **Gilbert and Sullivan** or the many fast-paced solo and ensemble numbers in **Offenbach**; hence, *patter-song roles*, i.e., those played by the leading comedian in G & S, although patter songs are sung by other characters as well. Part of the effect of the complicated lyrics depends on their rapid-fire delivery; more important, however, is keeping the rhythm steady, and acting the songs as well as singing them.

pavane (pah VAHN) *n.* [French; probably fr. Italian *paduana* (pah doo AH nah): pertaining to the city of Padua, where the dance may have originated] A slow, stately, dignified, formal 16th- and 17th-c. processional court dance in 2/2 or triple time; in one of its moves, women glided around, holding their trains and sweeping them along gracefully. In a stylized walk, the dancers took two single steps forward, then one double step backward, then two forward steps, etc. Also sometimes called a *paduana*.

See also GALLIARD.

Pavesi, Stefano (1779–1850) (STEH fah no: pah VEH: zee) Italian conductor and prolific composer of ca. seventy operas, including the very successful *Ser Marc Antonio* (1810) (sehr MAHRK ahn TO: nyo:), on which ***Don Pasquale*** by **Donizetti** is based. Pavesi was an Italian patriot, exiled to France, but was able to return to Venice, where he resumed his career in music

peel off In dancing, a movement away from a formation or line of dancers, each dancer in succession moving off in tempo when his or her turn arrives.

Peking opera The most well known school of Chinese opera.

See also PROLETARIAN OPERA; XIQU.

Pelléas et Mélisande (Pelléas and Mélisande) (peh lé AHS eh: mé lee ZAH*N*D) Opera in five acts (twelve tableaux) by Claude **Debussy**; libretto by Maurice **Maeterlinck**, slightly altered from his play (1892); Paris, Théâtre de l'Opéra-Comique, 1902.

Golaud (go: LO:) (bar.), the grandson of King Arkel (ah*r* KEHL) (bass), marries a mysterious, aloof young maiden, Mélisande (sop.), whom he has found in the forest. Although Golaud's half-brother, Pelléas (ten.), falls in love with her, they dare not even speak of it, but their passion proves too strong. When they meet near the fountain where she had lost her wedding ring, Golaud, who has been spying on them, kills Pelléas, and Mélisande falls ill. She gives birth to a child, and when Golaud questions her about what had happened between her and Pelléas, she dies without answering him.

performance marks Indications in a musical score regarding how a piece or passage is to be played or sung, including indications of tempo and dynamics.

See also EXPRESSION MARKS.

performance practice 1. The skills, and knowledge of agreed, generally accepted conventions necessary in interpreting and presenting a work of dramatic, choreographic, or musical art. **2.** The way in which a work of entertainment is presented or performed. **3.** The way and style in which a work of entertainment was presented to the public in its historical period. Also called *performing practice*. **4.** The ways in which historical works are generally performed. For more on this subject as applied, for instance, to Italian operatic music, see Philip Gossett's magisterial *Divas and Scholars: Performing Italian Opera* (The University of Chicago Press, 2006). See also VERSION.

Pergolesi, Giovanni Battista (1710–1736) (pehr go: LEH: zee) Italian composer of instrumental and vocal music, famous for his lightness of touch and melodic gifts; of his ten operas, the best known is the comic **intermezzo**, *La serva padrona*.

Périchole, La (lah pé *r*ee KO:L) **Opéra bouffe** in two acts by Jacques **Offenbach**; libretto by Henri **Meilhac** and Ludovic **Halévy**, based on the comedy *Le carrosse du Saint-Sacrement* (The Carriage of the Holy Sacrament) (1829) (luh kah *R*OS dü sa*n* sak *r*uh MAH*N*) by Prosper Mérimée; 1868; second version in three acts, 1874; both premiered in Paris, Théâtre des Variétés.

Two famished street singers, La Périchole (sop.) and Piquillo (pee kee YO:) (ten.), entertain the crowd in the main plaza in Lima, Peru, but the people are not amused, in spite of two delightful songs. When a traveling troupe of acrobats shows up, the crowd joyously follows them, and Piquillo leaves in search of other places to sing. The smitten Viceroy, Don Andrès (don ah*n* D*R*EHS) (bar.), invites Périchole to accompany him to the palace. Although she and Piquillo are madly in love with each other, she is so hungry that she agrees, and writes him a farewell letter in a touching and beautiful waltz song: the "Letter Aria," "O mon cher amant, je te jure" (o: mo:*n* sheh*r* ah MAH*N* zhuh tuh ZHÜ *r*uh) (Oh, my dear lover, I swear to you). But there is a problem: Any woman residing in the palace as the Viceroy's favorite must be married, for the sake of keeping the court respectable. Périchole is taken away to be wined and dined, while the Viceroy's two henchmen, the Court Chamberlain, Comte Miguel de Panatellas (ko:*n*t mee GEHL deh: pah nah tehl LAHS) (bar.) [a *panatela* is a kind of cigar] and the Governor of Lima, Don Pedro (ten.), go in search of a husband. Piquillo returns and, not finding Périchole, is on the point of committing suicide when the two officials persuade him that life has more to offer. They get him drunk, and hire two inebriated notaries. Périchole, quite sated and drunk herself, is now not too happy about the approaching marriage, until she recognizes Piquillo. She is heavily veiled, and as soon as the marriage ceremony is over, the pair is torn apart and taken to separate rooms in the palace. The next day, Piquillo, now officially ennobled, must present his wife to the Viceroy in a court ceremony. When Piquillo sees Périchole, he becomes furious, and he is promptly hustled off to the prison for recalcitrant husbands, where she joins him. The Viceroy, transparently disguised as a jailer with a beard, arrives to offer her release if she will give in to him. She pretends to do so, so that she can steal his keys. Locking him in the cell, Piquillo and Périchole escape together with the Marquis de Santarem (sah*n* tah *R*EHM) (ten.), who has spent twelve years digging through his dungeon walls with a little penknife and wound up in their cell. Soldiers hunt for them without success, but they appear voluntarily before the Viceroy, in order to prevent harm befalling the three young ladies who had given them shelter in their popular cabaret. Moved by their love, the Viceroy pardons everyone.

Peter Grimes Opera in a prologue and three acts by Benjamin **Britten**; libretto by English poet, novelist and left-wing playwright Montagu Slater (1902–1956), based on "Letter XXII: Peter Grimes" from the 1810 poem *The Borough* by the naturalist and poet George Crabbe (1754–1832); London, Sadler's Wells Theatre, 1945.

This was Britten's first great success. The role of Grimes was played by his life partner, the eminent tenor Peter Pears.

In a tiny Suffolk fishing village, The Borough, Peter Grimes (ten.) is cleared of murder at an inquest after the death of his apprentice. He accepts as apprentice another young man, brought to him by the schoolmistress Ellen Orford (sop.). Several weeks pass, and Ellen learns that Peter has been treating the boy badly. She and Peter quarrel, and are overheard by the villagers emerging from church services. He goes back to his hut on the cliffs, and the villagers send a deputation to investigate the situation. Distraught and angry, Peter forces the boy through the back door onto the cliff, and he accidentally falls to his death. More time passes, and nobody has seen either the boy or Grimes, when he returns to the village in his fishing boat, having been out to sea. Meanwhile, a sweater has washed up onto the beach, and Ellen recognizes it as the one she had knitted for the boy. Peter is now out of his mind. Captain Balstrode (bar.) tells him to take his boat to sea and to sink it, and Grimes sets off.

Peter Pan There have been several musicalizations of the 1905 play by Sir James M. Barrie (1880–1937) about the little boy who didn't want to grow up, and, while searching for his shadow, arrives at the Darling house in London and flies away with Wendy and her brothers to Never-Never-Land, where he hopes Wendy will be a mother to him and the Lost Boys. She is kidnapped by Pan's nemesis, the pirate Captain Hook, and Pan fights a duel to save her. In 1950, Leonard **Bernstein** wrote a wonderful score and lyrics, simply adding songs to Barrie's original play, for a new production; it ran for 321 perf., opening at the Imperial Theatre, and starred Jean Arthur (1900–1991) as Peter Pan and Basil Rathbone (1892–1967) as Captain Hook. But in 1954, Bernstein's version was superseded by a production that featured a score by composer Mark Charlap (1928–1974) and lyricist Carolyn **Leigh,** with added songs by Jule **Styne** (music) and **Comden and Green** (lyrics). The show starred Mary Martin as Peter Pan and Cyril Ritchard (1898–1977) as Captain Hook; this version, which ran for only 152 perf. at the Winter Garden Theatre, gained in popularity as it received several television broadcasts. It enjoyed four Broadway revivals, including one in 1979 that ran at the Lunt-Fontanne Theatre for 551 perf., starring Sandy Duncan (b. 1946) in the title role, with George Rose (1920–1988) as Captain Hook. A new television version of Barrie's play was done in 1976, with music and lyrics by Leslie **Bricusse** and Anthony **Newley**.

petit duc, Le (The Little Duke) (luh puh' tee DÜK) Operetta in three acts by Charles **Lecocq**; libretto by Henri **Meilhac** and Ludovic **Halévy**; Paris, Théâtre de la Renaissance, 1878.

At Versailles, at the beginning of the 18th c., the fifteen year-old duc de Parthenay (pah*r*' tuh NÉ) (sop.) is being wed to his fifteen year-old bride (sop.) in a marriage of convenience, for she is a wealthy heiress. At the end of the evening, she is taken away to a lady's academy, the couple's parents having decided that they are too young to experience wedded bliss. The dispirited little duke is buoyed by the news that he has been appointed commander of the family regiment, and decides to start on maneuvers immediately. He leads his regiment to the academy and disguises himself as a peasant girl seeking asylum, escaping from the licentious soldiers. He demands that the Headmistress (mezz.) return his bride to him, but she makes him withdraw with his regiment. Two years later, in a military encampment, the unwary soldiers, drunk and disorderly, allow themselves to be attacked; but the day is saved by the arrival of the duke and his regiment. The duchess, having escaped from the academy, shows up at the camp, despite the prohibition against women being allowed on the grounds. When she is discovered, the duke is forced to surrender his sword for disobeying orders. But because of his heroism in battle, all is forgiven and the young couple is reunited at last.

petit Faust, Le An **opéra bouffe** by **Hervé**, parodying Gounod's *Faust*.

Phantom of the Opera, The Phenomenally long-running West End and Broadway musical by Andrew **Lloyd Webber**; book and lyrics by Richard Stilgoe and Charles Hart, loosely based on the novel *Le Fantôme de l'Opéra* (luh fah*n* to:m' duh lo pé *R*AH) by Gaston Leroux (1868–1927) (gah STO:*N* luh *R*OO); opened on Broadway in 1988 at the Majestic Theatre; more than 9,000 perf. and still running at the Majestic as of this writing in 2009; film, 2004. Incidentally, none of the versions of this much adapted novel is particularly faithful to the book, which is very much worth reading.

The show was brilliantly directed by Harold Prince, using staging that at appropriate times has similarities to the **grand opera** productions of 19th-c. Paris.

The disfigured and deranged Phantom, having built a hidden lair for himself in the deepest cellars of the opera house in Paris, kidnaps the singer he adores, Christine Daaé. She is rescued by her fiancé, Raoul; he has tried to protect her from the Phantom, who haunts and terrorizes staff and public alike, and has even gone so far as to cut a chandelier loose during a performance by one of her rivals. As the Phantom is about to be captured in his lair by an angry mob, he vanishes into thin air.

Philidor, François-André Danican (1726–1795) (f*r*ahn swah' ah*n* d*r*é' dah nee kah*n*' fih: lee DO:*R*) Brilliant French composer from a family of musicians; music teacher and copyist; noted chess player and author of treatises on the game. Composer of more than two dozen opéras comiques, many of them domestic comedies. He also composed an opera adapted from incidents in Miguel de Cervantes's *Don Quixote*, called *Sancho Pança dans son isle* (Sancho Panza on His Island) (1762) (sah*n*' sho: pah*n* SAH dah*n* so:n EEL); and *Tom Jones* (1765), based on Henry Fielding's novel of the same name.

phrase *n., v.* —*n.* **1.** In music, a group of musical notes that form an inseparable melodic and rhythmic pattern, usually extending over several measures; also, a discreet section of a melody. **2.** A choreographed pattern of steps in a dance that form a discreet, separable section of a larger dance, such that it may be worked on separately. —*v. t.* **3.** To interpret a piece of music by grouping melodic patterns together in an expressive way. **4.** To devise, choreograph, or arrange a pattern in a dance.

phrasing *n.* **1.** In music, the act and way of grouping the phrases in a musical piece for expressive and stylistic purposes: *a singer's phrasing of an* **aria**. *To phrase on the beat*: to group the notes of a melody beginning on the strongest accented note, and to maintain the phrasing by accenting the strongest notes. **2.** The act and way of arranging choreographed patterns of dance steps.

piano dress [Short for *piano dress rehearsal*] A dress, tech, or tech-dress rehearsal of a musical theater piece, with piano accompaniment only.

piano rag A **ragtime** composition for the piano.
　　See also JOPLIN, SCOTT.

piano reduction An **arrangement** for piano of a piece originally composed for an instrumental ensemble or orchestra; also, the printed **score** of that arrangement. The term is sometimes used as a syn. for the **vocal score** of an opera, operetta, or musical comedy, with the vocal line accompanied only by the piano arrangement: *the piano reduction of **La traviata**.*

piano rehearsal A run-through or work-through of a musical theater piece in a rehearsal studio or on stage, with piano accompaniment only.

piano score The arrangement for keyboard and voice of a musical theater piece or song.

piano-vocal score Syn. with piano score, but esp. used for that of a full musical theater piece

Piave, Francesco Maria (1810–1876) (frahn CHEHS ko: mah REE ah PYAH veh:) Italian poet and librettist; most noted for having written ten opera libretti in close collaboration with his friend Giuseppe **Verdi**, beginning with **Ernani** in 1844. He also wrote texts for Giovanni **Pacini** and the **Ricci brothers**, notably *Crispino e la comare.*

Piccinni family (pih:t CHIH:N nee) **Niccolò Piccinni (1728–1800)** Italian composer from a family of musicians; wrote ca. 120 operas, including *Alessandro nelle Indie* (1758; second version, 1774), *Artaserse* (1762), *Didone abbandonata* (1770), all with libretti by Pietro **Metastasio**. He spent much of his career in Paris, and composed operas to French as well as Italian libretti. His musical style is exciting and his melodic gift outstanding, as evidenced, for instance, by the CD recording of his comic musical "**intermezzo**" for four voices, *Le donne vendicate* (The Revenge of the Women) (1763) (leh: DO: neh vehn dee KAH teh:), libretto after Carlo **Goldoni**, on Chaconne (CHAN 0705(2); 2004). His third son, **Luigi Piccinni (1764–1827)** was a conductor and opera composer, with thirteen not terribly successful works to his credit. **Louis Alexandre Piccinni (1779–1850)**, the natural son of Niccolò's eldest son, **Giuseppe Piccinni (1758–?)**, was a French accompanist and rehearsal pianist, and the composer of twenty-six operas, as well as ballets and incidental music.

pick up 1. To speed things up: *Pick up the pace!* **2.** To hire extra musicians, dancers or actors for particular performances of a prepared musical, play, concert or ballet recital; hence, the n. *pick-up*: a musician or performer hired to fill out the orchestra or cast of an entertainment project, e.g., a Broadway musical that is on tour.

piece *n.* A written or musical composition, whether of long or short duration, meant or used for performance; e.g., a song, an opera, a play, a poem.

Pikovaya Dama (Pique Dame; The Queen of Spades) (PEE ko: vah yah DAH mah) Opera in three acts by Pyotr Ilyich **Tchaikovsky**; libretto by the composer's brother Modest Ilyich Tchaikovsky (1850–1916), based on Alexander Pushkin's (1799–1837) story; St. Petersburg, Mariinsky Theatre, 1890.

In Saint Petersburg in the 1790s, Gherman (GEHR mahn) (ten.) [Hermann], a military officer, is in love with Lisa (LEE zah) (sop.), but he is too poor and of too low a social class to marry her. In any case, she is betrothed to Prince Eletsky (yehl YEHT skee) (bar.). Lisa is the granddaughter of an aged Countess (mezz.), known as the Queen of Spades, who dwells on her past, when she was courted by all the young aristocrats. She gambled her nights away, and she is rumored to know the secret winning combination of three cards. When Gherman invades her bedroom late one night, in order to try to inveigle the secret from her so that he can win enough money to marry Lisa, she dies. Lisa flees in despair, and drowns herself in the Neva. The Countess's ghost reveals the secret: "Three, seven, ace." Gherman, even more insane by this time, goes to Eletsky's to gamble, and, after winning on the first two cards, loses on the third, which is the Queen of Spades. He kills himself, after seeing the ghost one more time.

Pins and Needles Broadway revue; sketches by Marc **Blitzstein** et al.; songs by Harold **Rome**; additional sketches by Arnold B. Horwitt; Labor Stage, 1937 (1108 perf.). Sponsored by the International Ladies Garment Workers' Union, this revue was revised two times: *Pins and Needles 1939*, *Pins and Needles 1940*. The revues dealt with labor relations and the garment industry in particular, as well as world politics, in a jocular and light-hearted way in the middle of the Great Depression. The huge cast consisted for the most part of talented amateurs.

Pippin Broadway musical by Stephen **Schwartz**; book by Roger O. Hirson (b. 1926); Imperial Theatre, 1972 (1944 perf.); innumerable summer stock and school productions.

The show was a spectacular hit, due in part to the direction and outstanding choreography of Bob Fosse (1927–1987).

Pippin, son of the emperor Charlemagne, has no understanding of life. He decides to learn by doing, and experiments with war and politics, until, having seen through the terrible counsels of the manipulative Leading Player, the show's narrator and commentator, he discovers that the only true happiness is to be found in our relationships with those who are dearest to us.

piracy *n.* **1.** The crime of the unauthorized use of copyrighted or patented material; copyright or trademark infringement; stealing artistic or intellectual property in order to make a profit. In the days before the strict enforcement of copyright laws, piracy was very common. See COPYRIGHT PERFORMANCE; POLLY. **2.** The act of stealing or plagiarizing such material. **3.** The crime of robbery on the high seas. Piracy from the 16th through the 18th centuries has provided the material for many films and musical theater pieces, mostly entirely fictitious, but some based on actual history.

Pirates of Penzance, The, or The Slave of Duty Comic opera in two acts by **Gilbert and Sullivan**. Simultaneous premieres, to avoid copyright problems and piracy in America: England, Paignton, Bijou Theatre, and New York, Fifth Avenue Theatre, 1879; opened in London, Opéra Comique, 1880; New York Shakespeare Festival revival at Delacorte Theatre in Central Park, with new, jazzed up orchestrations, moved to Uris, then Minskoff Theatre, 1981 (772 perf.); innumerable tours, revivals, summer and amateur performances, of the original version.

Along with *H.M.S. Pinafore* and *The Mikado*, this is one of the G & S megahits. The entrance of the Major-General's daughters in act 1, "Climbing Over Rocky Mountain," is taken directly from the score of Gilbert and Sullivan's first collaboration, *Thespis, or The Gods Grown Old*, where it was sung by the thespians as they climb Mt. Olympus. Most of the score to *Thespis* (some of which is said, conjecturally, to have been borrowed from Offenbach's *Orphée aux enfers*), has been lost; this sprightly chorus makes one rather regret that fact. Sullivan had unfortunately left his score for the first act in London, but apparently had copies of the Thespis score, which may even have been packed instead by mistake; hence, the use of the *Thespis* chorus in the new piece.

The story hinges on a paradox: Frederick (ten.), our hero, is bound by contract as an apprentice pirate until his twenty-first birthday, but he was born in leap year. He has just turned twenty-one years old, but "if we go by birthdays," he is "a little boy of five"—although this interesting fact is only revealed later on, when his nursemaid, Ruth (contr.), who mistakenly apprenticed him to the pirates in the first place, remembers it. Frederick, the very slave of duty, had happily left the pirate band, but now feels bound to serve the Pirate King (bass-bar.) once again. He must leave his beloved Mabel (sop.), the Major-General's (bar.) daughter, in order to do so, nor can he accompany the Sergeant of Police (bar.) and his force to help arrest the pirates, who, in any case, turn out to be noblemen "who have gone wrong." They are all pardoned, "because, with all their faults, they love their Queen," and they marry the Major-General's other daughters, as Mabel and Frederic are reunited.

pirouette (pih:' roo EHT) *n.* In ballet, a 360-degree turn executed on one leg, while the other leg is bent, often while the foot touches the knee of the working leg; such turns are often executed in a series, and **en pointe** (ah*n* PWA*N*T) [French: on point], i.e., while raising the body on the tip of the ballet shoe [*sur la pointe* (sür lah PWA*N*T); French: on the tip], with the foot bent straight to form a straight line with the leg.

pit *n.* **1.** Short for **orchestra pit. 2.** *Brit.* The rear part of the orchestra section of a theater auditorium; the seats located there are called *pit stalls.*

pitch *n., v.* —*n.* **1.** A particular musical note; such a note, with its basic tonality and timbre, within a range of notes; hence, *relative pitch*: the ability to hear mentally and reproduce a note in relation to another note at the correct interval; *perfect pitch*: the ability to hear mentally and reproduce any note. **2.** Each level in the range of musical notes. **3.** The timbre, or **register**, of the speaking voice, including its **range. 4.** The level at which the tonality of a musical instrument is set or tuned. Historically, standard pitch, pitches, and pitch levels have varied over the centuries, and have been higher or lower than they are today.

pit orchestra The group of instrumentalists playing in the orchestra pit.

pizzicato (piht' tsee KAH to:) *n.* [Italian: pinched; plucked] The technique of playing a violin or other stringed instrument by plucking the strings with a finger. Abbrev. in scores: pizz.

placement *n.* **1.** In voice work, directing the air carrying sound to a **resonator**, e.g., the **mask**, for maximum vocal resonance and effectiveness of voice projection: *forward placement.* **2.** In dance, the alignment of the body.

Plain and Fancy Broadway musical by Albert **Hague**; lyrics by Arnold B. Horwitt; book by Joseph **Stein** and Will Glickman; Mark Hellinger Theatre, 1955 (461 perf.). The score is delightful and lively, with some wonderful dance music and pretty ballads.

Dan King has inherited a barn in the Pennsylvania Amish country. He and his lady friend Ruth Winters go down there from New York to sell it. They get involved with the locals, among them Hilda Miller, who always wants to have a great time; and Papa Yoder, a farmer, who wants his daughter Katie to marry Ezra Reber. But Katie is in love with his brother, Peter Reber, an outcast who proves his innocence during a lively barn raising. In the end, the two New Yorkers get engaged.

Planché, James Robinson (1796–1880) English translator, adapter, and writer of pieces in the genre of the **extravaganza**; translated many operas for the London theater, including works by **Auber, Bellini, Marschner, Mozart, Offenbach**, and **Weber**.

Planquette, Robert (1848–1903) (*r*o beh*r*' plah*n* KEHT) French composer of ca. twenty operettas. His most famous piece, *Les cloches de Corneville* (The Chimes of Corneville) (1877) (leh: KLOSH duh ko:*r* nuh VEEL) [also called *The Bells of Corneville*; *The Chimes of Normandy*], translated into English by H. B. **Farnie**, has a very complicated plot involving the mysterious identities of some of the characters, love intrigues, and the rights to the castle of Corneville. Popular on the English stage were *Rip van Winkle* (1882) and *Nell Gwynne* (1884), both with libretti written in English by Farnie.

plié (PLEE ay) *n.* [Fr. French past participle of *plier* (plee É): to fold; to bend] In dance, esp. in ballet, bending the legs at the knees, which are turned outward at right angles to the body; a movement usually executed slowly and gracefully, as it is in ballet class, where it is a fundamental exercise for a muscular warm-up at the **barre**.
See also DEMI-PLIÉ.

Plume De Ma Tante, La (lah PLÜM duh mah TAH*N*T) Broadway musical revue that began as a Paris hit before moving to London and New York; music by Gérard Calvi (b. 1922) (kahl VEE); book by Robert Dhéry (1921–2004) (dé *R*EE), who also directed and performed in the show; French lyrics by Francis Blanche (1919–1974); English lyrics by Ross Parker, who also performed in the show; Royale Theatre, 1958 (835 perf.). The revue was a satire of things Gallic, and made fun of everything from French cuisine to French attitudes to love and sex.

points *n. pl.* The tips of a dancer's foot, i.e., the row of toes: *to be on point* (**en pointe**).

Polenblut (Polish Blood) Viennese operetta by Oskar **Nedbal**.

polka *n.* A popular round dance at 19th-c. balls and parties; originating in Bohemia; used in ballet and opera. The dance is in 2/4 time: three steps, then a hop. A variation is the polka **mazurka**.

Polly Ballad opera in three acts by Dr. Johann Christoph Pepusch and John **Gay**; 1728. *Polly* is a sequel to *The Beggar's Opera*, but it was banned by the Lord Chamberlain's censorship office. Nevertheless, the book and songs were published in 1729; it proved so popular that it was pirated, and Gay and his publisher, a Mr. Rich, managed to get seventeen injunctions against other publishers. The anti-slavery piece was not produced until 1777, at London's Little Theatre in the Haymarket, when it was not particularly successful. For that production, Samuel **Arnold** added some songs to the fifty-four already in the piece, and wrote an overture using well known tunes from *The Beggar's Opera*. George **Colman** "the Older" doctored the libretto.

Polly Peachum and Macheath are transported to the West Indies. They are separated, then reunited after various adventures involving the coffee planters, Mr. Ducat and his housekeeper, Mrs. Trapes (virtual mirror images of Mr. and Mrs. Peachum); and pirates with such names as Vanderbluff, Culverin, and Capstan.

polonaise *n.* Stately, slow, processional Polish national dance in moderate 3/4 time; originating in the 17th c.; used in ballet and opera; e.g., Glinka's *Zhizn za tsarya (A Life for the Tsar)*. It was often the first dance at a formal ball.

Ponchielli, Amilcare (1834–1886) (ah mih:l KAH reh: po:*n* KYEHL lee) Noted Italian conductor, accomplished organist, composer of sacred music and of some ten operas, of which the only one that still holds the stage is *La Gioconda*. He taught at the Milan Conservatory, where his students included **Mascagni** and **Puccini**.

popular music Songs, ballads, and other light musical entertainment with easily accessible tunes and song lyrics, meant to be enjoyed by a broad cross-section of the population.

Porgy and Bess Broadway folk opera in three acts by George **Gershwin**; lyrics by Ira Gershwin and Dubose Heyward (1885–1940); libretto by DuBose Heyward, based on his novel *Porgy* (1925) and the play adapted from it, also titled *Porgy* (1927), written with his wife, Dorothy Heyward (1890–1961); Alvin, Theatre, 1935 (124 perf.); Broadway revivals: Majestic Theatre, 1942 (286 perf.), followed by a national tour and two return engagements in New York, at the 44th Street Theatre, 1943 (24 perf.), and the City Center, 1944 (64 perf.); new production, Ziegfeld Theatre, 1953 (305 perf.), following an international tour; Houston Grand Opera productions, limited New York engagements, Uris Theatre, 1977 (129 perf.), Radio City Music Hall, 1983 (67 perf.); other notable opera company productions: New York City Light Opera, 1961, 1964; Metropolitan Opera, 1985; New York City Opera, 2000; film, 1959.

This powerful opera, George Gershwin's supreme achievement, was his last Broadway show. Among its well known classic numbers are "Summertime," "Bess, You Is My Woman Now," and "It Ain't Necessarily So." The piece is set in the African-American community on Catfish Row in Charleston, SC, naturalistically recreated in the original production.

The crippled Porgy (bass-bar.), who rolls around in a goat cart, is in love with Bess (sop.), who is restless, fickle, untrustworthy, and the girlfriend of tough guy Crown (bar.). In a heated dispute over a crap game, Crown kills Robbins (ten.), a neighbor, and runs away, leaving Porgy and Bess temporarily together. But Crown comes back, and Porgy kills him in a fight. The neighbors refuse to give him away, but he is asked to go and identify the body. He refuses and is jailed for contempt of court. Meanwhile, Bess has gone to New York with her new boyfriend, Sportin' Life (ten.), a cocaine dealer. When Porgy gets out of jail, he goes after her, rolling away in his goat cart.

portamento (po:r' tah MEH:N to:) *n.* [Italian: carrying] In singing, smooth gliding from one note to the next, including the intermediate pitches in the glide.
See also SCOOP.

port de voix (po:*r*' duh VWAH) [French: carrying of the voice] In singing, an ornament, usually performed using portamento, and applied sometimes to the singing of the **appoggiatura**, esp. in 19th-c. **bel canto**. The compound ornament consists of a note that is usually below the main, already ornamented note, and carries the voice smoothly up to ornament the ornament, as it were.

Porter, Cole (1891–1964) One of America's most celebrated composers of musicals for the stage and screen; brilliant, witty lyricist. His first big Broadway hit was the adorable *Fifty Million Frenchmen*. Among Porter's more than two dozen outstanding, memorable works for the stage are *Anything Goes*, *Du Barry Was a Lady*, *Gay Divorce*, *Mexican Hayride*, *Kiss Me, Kate*, *Can-Can*, and *Silk Stockings*, all later filmed. He wrote *Broadway Melody of 1940*, *You'll Never Get Rich* (1941), *The Pirate* (1948), and other Hollywood musicals directly for the screen.

position *n.* In dance and esp. in ballet, the placement of the arms and feet; there are five positions of the feet, numbered first through fifth. The arms are placed in various graceful positions, as a means of balancing the body.

    See FIRST POSITION; SECOND POSITION; THIRD POSITION; FOURTH POSITION; FIFTH POSITION.

Posse (PO:S seh) *n.* [German: farce, joke, foolery] In Vienna esp., a farcical operetta: *Posse mit Gesang* (farce with singing) (miht geh ZAHNG).

postillon de Lonjumeau, Le (The Coachman of Lonjumeau) (luh pos tee yo:*n*' duh lo:*n*' zhü MO:) Operetta in three acts by Adolphe **Adam**; libretto by writer and director "Adolphe de Leuven" (1800–1884) (luh VEH*N*) [Pen name of Count Adolphe von Ribbing] and "Brunswick" (1805–1859) [Pen name of Léon Lévy]; Paris, Théâtre de l'Opéra-Comique, 1836.

    The score of this delightful if implausible operetta is a tuneful masterpiece, best known for its difficult tenor aria, "Mes amis, écoutez l'histoire" (My friends, listen to the story) (meh: zah MEE é koo teh: lee STWAH*R*), with its high D at the end, beautifully negotiated by the American lyric tenor John Aler (b. 1949) on a 1985 recording of the complete work for EMI (557106-2).

    Chapelou (shah puh LOO) (ten.), a postilion (coachman), has a gorgeous voice that is noticed immediately by the head of the Paris Opéra, the Marquis de Corcy (duh ko:*r* SEE) (bar.), when he stops at the inn owned by Chapelou's new wife, Madeleine (sop.). De Corcy persuades Chapelou to go away with him to perform. Chapelou leaves his wife, changes his name to Saint-Phar (sa*n* FAH*R*) and becomes a famous singer. Ten years pass. Madeleine has come into an inheritance, and now calls herself Madame de Latour. She goes to Paris and meets Saint-Phar, who does not recognize her but falls instantly in love with her. His suit is so successful that they are married! Smitten and jealous, the Marquis de Corcy has not recognized Madeleine either, but he summons the police to denounce Saint-Phar as a bigamist. Madeleine puts on the old clothes she wore as an innkeeper. Astonished, and now remorseful, Chapelou at last recognizes the wife he had abandoned, and they fall into each other's arms.

Poulenc, Francis (1899–1963) (fra*h*n sees' poo LA*N*K) [b. Francis Jean Marcel Poulenc] French composer of songs and instrumental pieces; also wrote three operas, each one a masterpiece: *Les mamelles de Tirésias*; *Dialogues des Carmélites* (Dialogues of the Carmelites) (1953–1956) (dee ah LOG deh: kahr mé LEET), to his own libretto in three acts, based on a drama by French writer Georges

Bernanos (1888–1948) (beh*r* nah NO:S), about a group of nuns who go to the guillotine during the French Revolution; and *La voix humaine* (The Human Voice) (1959) (la vwah ü MEHN), for solo soprano, libretto in one act by Jean Cocteau, about a woman having a telephone conversation with the lover who has jilted her.

prelude *n.* **1.** A brief musical **introduction** or **overture** to a musical theater piece, or to a fugue, or to the movement of a longer piece. **2.** A brief, free-form musical composition.

prepared audition In the musical theater, arias or songs that an actor has rehearsed and that are ready for use when required, e.g., for a **musical comedy** casting session; for an opera audition for a season as a supporting principal, or for a chorus position; for one of the many **Young Artists Programs** that opera companies maintain; or for a music school's vocal program.

Příhody Lišky Bystroušky (The Cunning Little Vixen) (PSHEE kho: dee LEESH kee BEE strow shkee) [lit. The Tales of Vixen Sharpears] Opera by Leoš **Janáček**; libretto by the composer, based on the 1920s serialized novella *Liška Bystrouška* (LEESH kah BEE strow shkah) (Vixen Sharpears) with verses by Rudolf Těsnohlídek (1882–1928) (ROO dolf TEH*N*S no: hlee dehk), illustrated by Stanislav Lolek (1873–1936) (STAH nee slahf LO: lehk), for the Brno (BUHR no:) newspaper *Lidové Noviny* (LEE do vé NO: vee nee); Brno, Opera House, 1924.

The opera contrasts and compares the world of animals and that of human beings. In the woods near a Moravian village, the vixen Sharpears (sop.) is caught by the Forester (bar.), who keeps her as a pet. But she escapes in the confusion of the revolt of the hens against the Rooster (sop.) that she has fomented. She manages to throw the Badger (bass) out of his lair, and makes it her new home. The Forester is sad, because he had grown to love the vixen, and he is doubly melancholy because the mysterious woman he loves, Terynka (TEHR ihn kah) (silent role), to whom the local schoolmaster (ten.) is also attracted, will marry the poultry dealer Harašta (HAH rahsh tah) (bass). Meanwhile, Sharpears takes the fox Golden-back (sop.) as a mate, and they have a cub. The Forester, awaking from a nap one day, sees the cub, and the sight, reminding him of Sharpears, brings him some measure of comfort.

prima ballerina assoluta (PREE mah bah' leh: REE nah ahs' so: LOO tah) [Italian; lit., first ballerina absolute] In a ballet company, the principal female dancer: a term reserved, however, for only the greatest dancers.

prima donna (PREE mah DO:N nah) [Italian: first lady] Originally, a neutral term meaning the opera singer who had the principal female role; now also a derogatory term for an egotistical, demanding star, whether male or female. Cf. **diva**.

Prince Igor Opera by Alexander **Borodin**. See KNYAZ IGOR.

Princess Theatre musicals A series of Broadway musical comedies presented at the Shuberts' Princess Theatre, a 299-seat house on 39th Street near Sixth Avenue, from 1915–1919; the theater was too small for large Broadway spectacles or follies shows, but perfect for intimate musicals. The series was started by the theater's co-owner, producer F. Ray Comstock (1880–1949), and literary agent Elizabeth Marbury (1856–1933)—among her clients were Oscar Wilde and George Bernard Shaw. They asked composer Jerome **Kern** and author Guy **Bolton** to inaugurate it, and their first show was *Nobody Home* (1915; 135 perf.), with lyrics by Schuyler Green. The second was the hit *Very Good Eddie*. P. G. **Wodehouse** joined the team, and they produced *Oh, Boy!, Leave It to Jane*, and their last one, *Oh, Lady! Lady!* (1918; 219 perf.). Several other successful musicals were written, some by other writing teams. The final show, which was not a great success, was a revue by composer Richard A. **Whiting** and lyricist Ray Egan (1890–1952), called *Toot Sweet* (45 perf.), a pun on the French phrase *tout de suite* (too' duh SÜEET), meaning "right away." The style of the music and lyrics of the Princess Theatre musicals, as well as the stories, influenced the development of the Broadway musical comedy.

principal boy The young lady who plays the **trousers role** of Prince Charming in a British **pantomime**.

principal girl 1. The young heroine in a British **pantomime**. **2.** In **vaudeville** and **burlesque**, the comedienne who plays roles in skits, e.g., the nurse in a doctor act.

Prodaná Nevěsta (The Bartered Bride) (PRO: dah nah NEH vehn stah) Comic opera in three acts by Bedřich **Smetana**; libretto by Czech writer Karel Sabina (1811–1877) (KAH rehl SAH bee nah); Prague, Opera House, 1866; revised version, **through-composed** without dialogue, 1870. The appealing score has echoes of Czech folk music and sprightly dances, which are sometimes played as separate orchestral selections.

Mařenka (MAHR zhehn kah) (sop.), a peasant girl, loves Jeník (YEH neek) (ten.), who appears to have come out of nowhere. Her parents, working with the marriage broker Kecal (KEH tsahl) (bass), insist that she marry Vašek (VAH shehk) (ten.), son of the wealthy Tobias Mícha (TO: bee ahs MEE khah) (bass). Mařenka looks for the simple-minded Vašek. Pretending to be someone else, she persuades him that Mařenka would be the worst possible wife for him. Meanwhile, Kecal has persuaded Jeník to give up Mařenka in return for a handsome financial settlement, provided that she marry the eldest son of Tobias Mícha. This turns out to be himself. Everyone except the tricked Kecal rejoices, not least Vašek, who realizes his dream of joining a traveling circus.

production number A lavishly staged ensemble song and dance routine for principals and chorus in a musical theater piece or film.

projection *n.* In terms of acting and singing in the theater, throwing the voice, and making the intentions of the lines or of the emotions in a musical number clear to the audience; hence, the *v. t. project*: to throw the voice.

Prokofiev, Serge (1891–1953) (ser GAY prah KO fyehf) Prolific Russian composer of symphonies; ballets, among them *Cinderella*; and fifteen operas, including

Lyubov' k tryom apel'sinam (The Love of the Three Oranges); *Igrok* (The Gambler) (1917) (EE grok), based on the 1867 story of the same name by Feodor Dostoevsky (1821–1881); *Voyna y Mir* (War and Peace) (1943) (VI nah ee MEER), based on the 1865–1869 novel of the same name by Count Leo Tolstoy (1828–1910); and the bizarre *Ognenniy angel* (The Fiery Angel) (ahg NYEHN yee AHN gyehl) (1955), which involves witchcraft and the Inquisition.

See also UNDINE.

proletarian opera and ballet An opera or ballet that deals with working class life and the proletarian revolution; esp. popular in the U.S.S.R. and Communist China in the 20th c., e.g., such **Peking opera** pieces as *The Red Lantern* (1970), *Song of Dragon River* (1972), and *The Red Detachment of Women* (1964), a political ballet about women who are liberated when they join the People's Liberation Army (the piece was also filmed, 1970). Among the most famous Russian examples is the Soviet opera classic *Tikhy Don* (The Quiet Don [River]) (1935) (TEE khee DO:N) by Ivan Dzerzhinsky (1909–1978) (ee VAHN dzehr ZHIHN skee).

prologue *n.* **1.** The opening scene or scenes of an opera or a play, separate from the main action; the material often deals with what led up to the main story, and sets the scene for the audience. **2.** A speech or aria that introduces a play or opera, and that sometimes asks the audience's indulgence; e.g., the Prologue to Leoncavallo's *Pagliacci*.

Promises Promises Broadway musical by Burt **Bacharach**; lyrics by Hal **David**; book by playwright Neil Simon; based on Billy Wilder's 1960 film *The Apartment*; Shubert Theatre, 1968 (1288 perf.). This was the only venture of the famous songwriting team into the Broadway venue.

The ambitious bachelor Charles Chuck Baxter lends his apartment to the married higher-ups in his firm for lovers' trysts. He falls in love with a waitress who works in the company cafeteria, Fran Kubelik, with whom his boss, J. D. Sheldrake, has had an affair. Chuck and Fran start to go out together, when Sheldrake decides to resume the affair. After Fran's attempted suicide, Chuck decides to stop lending his apartment to the bosses, and invites Fran for a private New Year's Eve celebration.

prompt *v. t.* **1.** To give an actor lines, either during a rehearsal or during a performance, when the actor has had a lapse of memory. **2.** During an opera performance, to follow and conduct the score from the *prompt box*—the sunken, recessed compartment at the front of the stage where the prompter sits during a performance—along with the conductor, so as to give the singers their cues.

prompt book 1. The stage manager's marked copy of a script, prepared with lighting, scenery, and sound cues, furniture and set prop placement plans, and performers' moves; used to call a show. Also called *prompt copy*; *prompt script*. **2.** The prompter's prepared copy of a stage play or opera, with cues and moves written into it.

prompter *n.* **1.** The person who gives actors their lines when they have forgotten them during a rehearsal or performance. **2.** The person who gives opera singers their cues, and who follows and conducts the score along with the conductor for the singers' benefit.

Puccini, Giacomo (1858–1924) (DGAH ko: mo: poo CHEE nee) One of the most loved of all Italian opera composers; often considered the successor to Giuseppe **Verdi**, he was an enthusiastic exponent of the late-romantic **verismo** school.

Giacomo Puccini's operas:

1884 *Le Villi* (The Villi) (in one act; three more versions, in two acts: 1884, 1885, 1889) (leh: VEE lee)

1889 *Edgar* (in four acts; second version, in four acts: 1891; two three-act versions: 1892, 1905)

1893 *Manon Lescaut* (second, revised version: 1893)

1896 *La bohème*

1900 *Tosca*

1904 *Madama Butterfly* (four revised versions: 1904, 1905, 1906, 1920)

1910 *La fanciulla del West* (The Girl of the Golden West) (revised version, 1912) (lah fahn CHOO lah dehl WEHST)

1917 *La rondine* (The Swallow) (revised versions: 1920, 1924; 1994, with third act orchestration completed) (lah RO:N dee neh:)

1918 *Il trittico* (The Triptych) (ih:l TRIH:T tee ko:), consisting of three one-act operas:
Il tabarro (The Cloak) (ih:l tah BAHR ro:)
Suor Angelica (Sister Angelica) (swo:r' ahn DGEH: lee kah)
Gianni Schicchi (DGAHN nee SKEE kee)

1926 *Turandot*

Purcell, Henry (1659–1695) English composer; wrote incidental music to forty-four plays; composed the opera *Dido and Aeneas* (1689), with a libretto based on Virgil's *Aeneid*, in a prologue and three acts, by Irish poet Nahum Tate (1652–1715), poet laureate of England, in 1692; the opera became Purcell's most famous piece. Another of his masterpieces is *The Fairy Queen*, and one of his last great works, probably unfinished, is the semi-opera *The Indian Queen* (1695), with **masque** scenes, a trumpet symphony, and much spoken dialogue, the libretto adapted from a drama by poet laureate John Dryden (1631–1700) and his brother-in-law, Sir Robert Howard (1626–1698); it is a completely invented triangular love story about the Aztec king, Montezuma.

See DIDONE ABBANDONATA.

puritani di Scozia, I (The Puritans of Scotland) (ee poo' ree TAH nee dee SKO: tsyah) [Usually called simply *I puritani*] Opera in three acts by Vincenzo **Bellini**; libretto by Italian poet, patriot, and librettist Carlo Pepoli (1796–1881) (PEH po: lee), adapted from the 1833 French play *Têtes rondes et Cavaliers* (Roundheads and Cavaliers) (teht ro:nd' eh: kah' vah LYEH:) by Jacques Ancelot (1794–1854) (zhahk' ahn SLO:) and Xavier Boniface Saintine (1798–1865) (ksah VYEH: bo nee FAHS san TEEN); Paris, Théâtre Italien, 1835.

The French play was adapted from the 1816 novel *Old Mortality* by Sir Walter Scott, which takes place ca.1689, forty years after the period of the Civil War between the Cavaliers and the Roundheads—as the Puritans were called, on account of their short haircuts.

The bizarre title is reminiscent of the opening lines of Canadian humorist Stephen Leacock's (1869–1944) satire "Gertrude the Governess," in *Nonsense Novels* (1911):

> It was a wild and stormy night on the West Coast of Scotland. This, however, is immaterial to the present story, as the scene is not laid in the West of Scotland. For the matter of that the weather was just as bad on the East Coast of Ireland.
>
> But the scene of this narrative is laid in the South of England…

Indeed, the implausible narrative is laid in Plymouth in the 17th c., during the Civil War in which Cromwell and his Puritans defeated the Stuarts and their Royalist followers. Queen Henrietta Maria (mezz.) [Enrichetta (ehn' ree KEHT tah)], widow of the executed Charles I, is imprisoned in a fortress held by the Puritans and governed by Walter, Lord Walton (bass) [Gualtiero (gwahl' TYEH:R o:)]. His daughter, Elvira (ehl VEE rah) (sop.). is betrothed to the Cavalier, Lord Arthur Talbot (ten.) [Arturo (ahr TOO ro:)], who has an enemy in the bitterly jealous Puritan, Sir Richard Forth (bar.) [Riccardo (reek KAHR do:)], unrequitedly in love with Elvira, to whom he was engaged until Arturo came along. Arturo, using the special safe-conduct pass that allowed him, a Royalist, to enter the Puritan stronghold, helps the queen escape, disguising her in Elvira's bridal outfit and escorting her out of the fortress. He then rides "madly off in all directions" (like the nobleman in "Gertrude the Governess"). Elvira goes stark raving mad. Informed of her condition, Arturo cannot bear to abandon her, and returns to the castle to confront his fate. His execution is imminent when news providentially arrives of the defeat of the Royalists and the victory of Cromwell and his Puritans, together with an amnesty for all prisoners. Arturo's immediate release restores Elvira's sanity, and they rush passionately into each other's arms as the curtain falls on a celebratory note.

Q

quadrille *n.* **1.** A formal, early 19th-c. French ballroom dance for four couples, popular esp. in the period of Napoleon I; popular also in Great Britain at formal dances. See also GALOP. **2.** A kind of American square dance, popular in the late 18th- and early 19th centuries at balls and country dances; in 3/8, 6/8 or 2/4 time. In both Europe and America, the dance consisted of five figures and a **finale**.

quartet; quartette *n.* **1.** A group of four instrumentalists or singers. **2.** A composition for four instruments, e.g., a string quartet for two violins, a viola, and a cello; or for four voices, e.g., the quartet in act 1 of Beethoven's *Fidelio*, the quartet in act 4 of Verdi's *Rigoletto*.

Queen of Spades, The Opera by Pyotr Ilyich **Tchaikovsky**. See PIKOVAYA DAMA.

quickstep *n.* A march in 6/8 time.

Quinault, Philippe (1635–1688) (fee leep' kee NO:) Prolific French librettist who collaborated with a number of famous composers, most notably Jean-Baptiste **Lully**. Quinault wrote the scenarios for many of Lully's ballets, and the libretti for both Lully's *Alceste* and Gluck's *Armide*. For more information on this fascinating personage, see Buford Norman's magisterial *Touched by the Graces: The Libretti of Philippe Quinault in the Context of French Classicism* (Summa Publications, 2001).

quintet *n.* **1.** A group of five instrumentalists or singers. **2.** A musical composition for five instruments or five voices, e.g., the quintet in the last act of Wagner's *Die Meistersinger*.

quodlibet (KWOD lih BEHT) *n.* [Fr. Latin, quod: that; libet: pleases] **1.** *Hist.* From the 15th through the early 18th centuries, a musical game in which disparate pieces were played or sung in an improvised **medley**. **2.** An improvised or composed potpourri of popular themes by a particular composer, or of a singer's popular numbers, done as a medley, esp. popular in 19th-c. Vienna as part of an eclectic concert program.

quotation *n.* In musical terms, a brief musical passage that is included in the midst of a larger musical piece, taken from another piece expected to be well known to the audience; e.g., Mozart's quotations in the last act of *Don Giovanni* of his own popular success *Le nozze di Figaro* and *Fra i due litiganti* by **Sarti**; Gilbert and Sullivan's reference in the act 1 finale of *Utopia, Limited* to their huge triumph *H.M.S. Pinafore*.
See also ALLUSION.

R

Rabaud, Henri (1873–1949) (ah*n* *r*ee' *r*ah BO:) French composer and conductor; studied with Jules **Massenet**; Director of the Paris Conservatoire, 1920–1940; composed six operas; best known for his engaging "oriental" opera, *Mârouf, savetier du Caire*, with its clever orchestrations and insouciant melodies

ragtime *n.* An African-American style of syncopated, melodic music, jaunty and lively, often with march-like rhythms easily adapted to dancing; first associated with the piano, and esp. with the compositions of its brilliant, innovative composer Scott **Joplin**, known as the "King of the Ragtime Composers."

Ragtime Broadway musical by Stephen **Flaherty**; lyrics by Lynn **Ahrens**; book by Terrence **McNally**, based on the novel of the same name by E. L. Doctorow; Ford Center Theatre, 1998 (861 perf.).

The musical styles in this lively, brilliant score are eclectic, and include ragtime, cakewalks, patter songs, blues, and patriotic marches, as well as suitable musical idioms for each of the three groups represented—a kind of American melting pot, as has been said before elsewhere, suitable to the period and the material.

Americans from three different backgrounds at the beginning of the 20th c. are portrayed: Mother and Father, in an established white, Anglo-Saxon, Protestant (WASP) family in New Rochelle, NY, are very traditional in their views. Tateh [Yiddish: father], widowed father of a Jewish immigrant family, struggles to make ends meet and to help his daughter to a new and better life; he decides to begin making movies as a way out of his difficulties. The African-American ragtime pianist Coalhouse Walker is deeply wounded by the terrible racism he experiences, and goes over the edge when his fiancée Sarah is killed. Walker takes over the famous J. P. Morgan Library on New York City's 36th Street, threatening to blow it up, and the building is surrounded by police. Eventually, the educator and writer Booker T. Washington (1856–1915) persuades him to surrender. Walker is shot to death as he emerges from the building. Mother, deeply affected by all these events, decides to divorce Father, and marries Tateh, raising their children and the orphaned son of Sarah and Walker.

Historical characters in supporting roles lend verisimilitude, among them the scandalous Evelyn Nesbitt (1884–1967), who was involved in the murder of her former lover, the famed Beaux Arts architect Stanford White (1853–1906). He was killed by her first husband, Harry K. Thaw (1871–1947), found not guilty by reason of insanity—the tale is retold in a most amusing number sung by Nesbitt, "The Crime of the Century."

Rake's Progress, The Opera in three acts and an epilogue by Igor **Stravinsky**; libretto by W. H. **Auden** and Chester Kallman, based on the 1735 series of engravings by English artist William Hogarth (1697–1764); Venice, Teatro La Fenice, 1951.

This strange story is set to stranger music, which is dissonant and at times downright unpleasant, deliberately unsettling and disturbing.

In England in the 18th c., the lazy Tom Rakewell (ten.), in love with Anne Trulove (sop.), refuses a job in the city offered to him by her father, Trulove (bass). He succumbs to the blandishments of the seemingly omnipresent Nick Shadow (bar.), whom he hires as a servant. They go to London, where Rakewell indulges in a life of vice. He marries Baba the Turk (mezz.), a bearded lady, and makes unwise investments, bankrupting himself. Everything he owns is sold at auction by the auctioneer Sellem (ten.). Tom winds up in Bedlam, the insane asylum near London, and Shadow now reveals himself as Satan, claiming Tom's soul. They agree to gamble for it, and Tom wins. Shadow disappears, but before he does, he condemns Tom to madness. Anne comes to visit Tom in Bedlam, sings him to sleep, and then leaves; when he realizes she is gone, he dies.

Rameau, Jean-Philippe (1683–1764) (zhah*n* fih: lihp' *r*ah MO:) Distinguished, original French music theorist and composer who wrote in all genres, composing ca. thirty pieces for the musical theater. Among his great works is *Les Indes galantes* (The Gallant Indies) (1735) (leh: za*n*d gah LAH*N*T), a **ballet-héroique** in a prologue and four "entrées"—actually, an opera, which tells four love stories that take place in Turkey, Peru, Persia, and America, after the god Amor has been abandoned by the youth of France, Italy, Spain and Poland.

See also ZAÏS.

range *n.* **1.** The span of notes that a voice or instrument can encompass. **2.** The extent of notes usually encompassed in a particular voice category: *the soprano range*. **3.** The span of notes an individual singer is capable of: *He has a limited range*.

rap music; rap [Fr. rap: to talk] **A capella**, improvised, rhythmic rhyming talk-music, sometimes accompanied on the drums; began around the 1980s, in urban African-American settings, and is most often associated with black artists.

raqs sharqi A Middle Eastern dance form. See BELLY DANCING.

Ravel, Maurice (1875–1937) (*r*ah VEHL) French composer; wrote only two operas, both masterpieces: *L'heure espagnole* (The Spanish Hour) (1911) (luh *r*ehs pah NYOL) and *L'enfant et les sortilèges* (The Child and the Spells) (1925) (lahn fah*n*' eh: leh: so:*r* tih: LEHZH), which he spent five years composing (1920–1925).

Raymond, Fred (1900–1954) (*R*I mont) [b. Raimund Friedrich Vesely (*R*I mo*o*nt F*R*EED rih*kh* FEH zeh lee)] Austrian composer of eleven operettas; his greatest success was the intriguing, lively *Maske in blau* (The Blue Mask) (1937) (MAHS keh ihn BLOW), involving a woman disguised in a blue mask; recorded on CD by Membran Music (231714; 2007), with highlights from *Viktoria und ihr Hussar* by Paul Abraham.

recital *n.* **1.** An intimate, small-scale **concert** of vocal music with simple accompaniment, usually on the piano; or of instrumental music performed by individual artists: *a violin recital*. Recitals may take place in large concert halls, as well as in smaller theaters or rooms. **2.** A dance performance. **3.** A student presentation of vocal or instrumental music, to demonstrate the student's accomplishment in a particular field. **4.** A spoken arts entertainment featuring prose or poetry readings: *a dramatic recital.*

recitative (REH sih tah TEEV) *n.* [Italian: *recitativo* (reh' chih: tah TEE vo:); French: *récitative* (ré sih: tah TEEV)] Sung dialogue or soliloquy in an opera; the musical setting is supposed to mirror a conversational tone; some recitatives are underscored with dramatic music. Called *recit* (REH siht), for short.

Red Mill, The Broadway operetta by Victor **Herbert**; libretto by Henry **Blossom**; Knickerbocker Theatre, 1906 (275 perf.); Broadway revival: Ziegfeld Theatre, 1945 (531 perf.).

The score is as genial as the story, and delightfully melodic in Herbert's best vein. Two numbers that cannot help but make one smile remain well known: "Every Day Is Ladies' Day with Me" and "The Streets of New York (In Old New York)." The story, written for a famous team of comedians—Fred Stone (1873–1959) and Dave Montgomery (1870–1917), known for their slapstick vaudeville routines and rapid-fire repartee—is rather silly, and quite amusing:

Two Americans, Con Kidder and Kid Conner, recklessly spend all their money on a trip through Europe and end up penniless in a small Dutch village, Katwyk-aan-Zee, where they meet a sea captain, Van Damm, and the burgomaster's daughter, Gretchen, who is in love with him. Her father objects to the match and wants her to marry the provincial governor, so he imprisons her in the village's red mill. The Americans, after a series of misadventures in which they disguise themselves as various characters, manage to help her escape, and all is set to rights, especially since the governor loves Gretchen's aunt. The Americans are happy to have helped romance along, and, best of all, they manage to secure passage on a boat returning home.

Redhead Broadway musical by Albert **Hague**.

reduction *n.* An **arrangement** of an orchestral score for fewer instruments; e.g., the reduction of a musical theater piece full score for piano and voice.

Reed, Thomas German (1817–1888) English theater manager, producer; composer of several comic pieces to early libretti by W. S. **Gilbert** and F. C. **Burnand**. In 1855, Reed and his wife, the multi-talented contralto Priscilla Horton Reed (1818–1895), founded and ran German Reed's Gallery of Illustration, producing clean, decorous comic operettas by Frederick **Clay**, Alfred **Cellier**, **Sullivan**, Edward **Solomon**, and others, in which Mrs. Reed performed. The name was chosen to avoid the not quite respectable word "theater," associated with cheap burlesques and sexual innuendo, and therefore offensive to Victorian sensibilities; the attitude would be different thirty years later.

refrain *n.* **1.** The final, regularly recurring section of each strophe in a poem, or verse in a song, e.g., the **chorus** of a number in a musical theater piece. **2.** The melody or music of the regularly repeated section, which may be a memorable tune that becomes as popular as a catchphrase.

Regina Opera by Marc **Blitzstein**.

register *n.* **1.** The particular pitch or **range** of a singer's **voice**: *the soprano register*; *the bass register*. **2.** One of the **pitch** levels of any voice: *the high, middle and low registers*.

Reichert, Heinz (1877–1940) (HINTS *R*I *kh*uh*r*t) [b. Heinrich Blumenreich (HIN *r*ih*kh* BLOO mehn R*IKH*)] Austrian librettist who collaborated on many Viennese operettas with A. M. **Willner**, including *Das Dreimädlerhaus*, adapted for the American stage as ***Blossom Time***, and *Walzer aus Wien*, adapted as ***The Great Waltz***. They also wrote the libretto that was later adapted for Puccini's *La rondine* by Giuseppe **Adami**. Reichert was Jewish, and he left Nazi Austria for Hollywood, where he continued to write for the last years of his life.

Reinhardt, Heinrich (1865–1922) (HIN rih*kh R*IN HAH[*R*]T) Austrian pianist, organist, and composer of songs and piano pieces; studied with innovative Austrian composer Anton Bruckner (1824–1896); wrote one comic opera and eighteen Viennese operettas, the first being the highly successful *Das süsse Mädel* (The Sweet Girl) (1901) (dahs ZÜ she MEH: duhl).

relevé (REHL uh VÉ) *n.* [French (*r*uh luh VÉ): lifted up] In dance, rising from a flat foot to stand on half or full point, often with a slight springing step.

Rent Broadway musical by composer-librettist Jonathan Larson (1960–1996), based loosely on Puccini's *La bohème*; Nederlander Theatre, 1996 (5124 perf.); film, 2005. Tragically, Larson died just before the premiere. The rock score includes elements of folk music and blues.

In the 1990s, Roger Davis, a rock musician and composer, shares a tenement apartment in New York City's East Village with the video artist Mark Cohen. They and their friends deal with such issues as AIDS and poverty, and struggle through their unhappy straight and gay love affairs. Roger is in love with the dancer Mimi Marquez, while Mark's ex-girlfriend, Maureen Johnson, a performance artist, has an affair with legal aid worker Joanne Jefferson. Unlike Mimi in the original story, the Mimi in *Rent* survives, and they are all inspired to do something with their lives by the drag queen Angel Schunard, whose death from AIDS has left the college professor Tom Collins bereft.

repertoire *n.* **1.** An actor or singer's prepared roles or pieces: *Her repertoire included many bel canto roles*. **2.** The operas or ballets that a company has done, or is prepared to do. **3.** The collection of operas or other kinds of pieces available for performance: *the standard operatic repertoire*; *the Shakespearean repertoire*.

repetitor *n. Hist.* In 18th-c. English theater, the musician who trained and rehearsed the chorus, of which he was often a member.

reprise (ruh PREEZ) *n., v.* [French: taken again; sometimes incorrectly pronounced "ruh PRIZ"] —*n.* **1.** In musical comedy, the repetition of a musical number, in part or as a whole, that has been heard earlier in the show.   *v. t.* **2.** To repeat, in part or as a whole, a musical number that has been heard earlier in the show. **3.** To perform again a role that an actor has previously done, esp. in musical comedy: *Ethel Merman reprised her stage role as the ambassadress in the 1953 film of* **Call Me Madam**.

rescue opera An opera built around the theme of the saving or salvation of one person by another, often a woman in dire straits by the hero who loves her; e.g., Sullivan's **Ivanhoe**, Beethoven's **Fidelio**, in which that situation is reversed and a faithful wife rescues her wrongfully imprisoned husband.

return engagement 1. The performance or run of a play, musical comedy, or other project after a lapse of time, in the same theater or other venue where it had previously been done. **2.** The run of perf. of a leading role in a theater piece by an actor who has previously performed it, but who has been out of the cast for some time; e.g., Harvey Fierstein in the Broadway musical *Hairspray* (closed January 2009), who returned to **reprise** his Tony® Award–winning performance as Edna Turnblad for the end of the run.

révérence (*ré* vé *RAHNS*) n. [French: bow; show of reverence] **1.** *Hist.* The term, beginning in the 16th c., for the elaborate bow at the beginning of a dance, e.g., the **galliard**; made by a male dancer to his partner and to the assembled guests at a ball or formal dance. It was performed—as dance manuals of the period, such as *Orchésographie* (o:*r* ké so:' g*r*ah FEE) (Orchesography; 1589) by Thoinot Arbeau (1520–1595) (twah NO: ah*r* BO:) tell us—as follows: "You hold the left foot firmly on the ground, bending the shank of the right leg, carry the point of the right foot behind the said left foot: taking off your bonnet or hat and saluting the demoiselle and the company." **2.** *Hist.* The Elizabethan bow at the curtain call. **3.** The elaborate closing bow done by male and then female dancers at the end of a ballet class.

revival *n.* A production of a play or musical after its original production has been closed for some time, usually with a new cast, but sometimes with original cast members reprising their roles.

revue *n.* **1.** A prepared variety entertainment of sketches, songs, and dances that runs at a theater or cabaret; sometimes thematic, e.g., the series of *Forbidden Broadway* revues. **2.** A musical show that runs in a theater and consists of variety entertainment, e.g., Irving Berlin's **This Is the Army**, the **Ziegfeld Follies**, **New Faces of 1952**, **Pins and Needles**; or of an overview of a composer's work, e.g., *Cole*, a 1991 revue that featured the songs of Cole **Porter**.

Rezniček, Emil Nikolaus von (1860–1945) (EH: meel NIH: ko: lows' fuhn REHTS nih CHEHK) Austrian conductor and composer of fourteen operas and three operettas. His operas include *Ritter Blaubart* (Lord Bluebeard) (1920) (*R*IH tuh BLOW BAH[*R*]T), based on the same Bluebeard story used by **Offenbach**, Bartók, and Dukas; and his most famous work, the comic opera, *Donna Dianna* (1894), to his own libretto.

Rheingold, Das (The Rhine Gold) The first opera in Wagner's **Ring cycle**.

rhythm *n.* **1.** The arrangement or pattern of alternating slow and fast beats in music, depending on the length of each note. **2.** The **tempo** and **pace** of an acted scene; i.e., the slow or fast pacing of the dialogue and movement.

Ricci brothers: Federico (1809–1877); Luigi (1805–1859) (feh deh: REE ko:; loo EE dgee; REE chee) Italian opera composers from a family of professional musicians; the brothers wrote four operas together. Federico (who grew the most extraordinary, huge sideburns) wrote numerous art songs and fifteen operas on his own, many of them comic; as well as one of his great triumphs in drama: his first success, *La prigione di Edimburgo* (The Prison of Edinburgh) (1838) (lah prih DGO: neh: dee ehd' ihm BOOR go:); libretto by Gaetano **Rossi**, loosely based on *The Heart of Midlothian* (1818) by Sir Walter **Scott**. The beautiful, tuneful score is full of drama. Luigi wrote twenty-three masses and other liturgical music, as well as twenty-six operas on his own (with varying success over the years), and was much acclaimed several years before his younger brother became a composer. Federico launched his own career with their first collaboration, *Il colonello* (The Colonel) (1835) (ihl ko:' lo: NEHL lo:), a two-act **opera buffa**. In 1850, the brothers wrote their most enduring joint opera (most of it is supposed to have been composed by Luigi), *Crispino e la comare* (Crispino and the Good Fairy) (krihs PEE no: eh: lah ko: MAH reh:); libretto by Francesco Maria **Piave**, once as popular as Donizetti's ***L'elisir d'amore*** or Rossini's ***Il barbiere di Siviglia***; it has some very charming music, but not the sustained felicity of either *Elisir* or *Barbiere*.

Rice, Edward E. (1848/9–1924) [b. Edward Everett Rice] Prolific, Boston-born producer of popular musicals, and composer of eighteen full-length musical burlesques and musical comedies; his two greatest hits were the phenomenal ***Evangeline; or The Belle of Arcadia*** and ***Adonis***. He was also one of the first to break Broadway's color barrier, when he produced ***Clorindy; or The Origin of the Cakewalk*** in 1898.

Rice, Tim (b. 1944) [Timothy Miles Bindon Rice] Prolific lyricist who has collaborated with such composers as Andrew **Lloyd Webber** and Elton **John**.

riff *n.* A repeated, short melodic theme: a **motif**; often done with wide-ranging improvisational variations when repeated, esp. a **jazz** or rock riff.

Rigoletto (ree' go LEHT to:) Opera in four acts by Giuseppe **Verdi**; libretto by Francesco Maria **Piave**, based on the romantic melodrama *Le roi s'amuse* (The King Amuses Himself) (1832) (luh *r*wah' sah MÜZ) by Victor **Hugo**; Venice, Teatro La Fenice, 1851.

So popular had Verdi become that while this opera was in rehearsal, the Duke of Mantua's aria "La donna è mobile" (Woman Is Fickle) (lah DON nah eh: MO:

bee leh:) had to be kept secret, lest the tune leak out before it was supposed to be heard.

The hunchbacked court jester Rigoletto (bar.), loathed for his viper-tongued jibes, mocks old Count Monterone (mo:n' teh RO: neh:) (bar.), whose daughter has been seduced by the licentious Duke of Mantua (ten.). Monterone curses them both. The disquieted Rigoletto is returning home through the dark and deserted streets when he is accosted by an assassin for hire, Sparafucile (spah' rah foo CHEE leh:) (bass), who, having overheard Rigoletto's mutterings, offers his services just in case. Meanwhile, the courtiers have hatched a scheme to abduct Rigoletto's daughter, Gilda (DGIH:L dah) (sop.), thinking she is his mistress. Hoodwinking Rigoletto, they have him participate in the abduction, and they carry Gilda off as booty for the duke. Rigoletto returns to the ducal palace and tries without success to get them to tell him where his daughter is. Some time before these events, the Duke, disguised as a poor student, had gone out in search of sexual conquests, and had seen Gilda at her church. He had courted her, and she had fallen in love with him, but she had concealed this from Rigoletto. At the palace, she is naturally as surprised to see the Duke as he is to see her. Delighted to have the nubile Gilda in his clutches, the Duke seduces her, and she rushes away, ashamed and upset, into her father's waiting arms. Rigoletto arranges with Sparafucile to have the Duke killed. The bait to lure him to the assassin's deserted inn is Sparafucile's sister, Maddalena (mah' dah LEH: nah) (contr.), whom the duke tries to seduce. She falls hard for his facile, seedy charms, so she persuades her brother to give up the plan to kill him, and to murder instead the first stranger who arrives at the inn. Disguised as a man, for safety, Gilda, led there by her father so that she can see for herself what the Duke is really like, overhears their plan. As a storm rages, she enters the inn, where Sparafucile stabs her to death and puts her body in a sack. Rigoletto comes to collect the body, and is dragging the sack away to dump it in the river when he hears the duke singing in the distance. Shocked, he opens the sack and discovers his daughter, who dies in his arms. Monterone's curse has been fulfilled!

Rimsky-Korsakov, Nicolai (1844–1908) Russian pianist and composer of vocal and instrumental music, known for his symphonic suite *Scheherazade* (1885) (sheh HEH reh ZAHD), based on the *Thousand and One Nights*, which displays his special gift for rich orchestral textures and coloration. He was one of **The Five**, and most of his eighteen operas are on Russian themes. Among them are his first, *Pskovityanka* (The Maid of Pskov) (PSKO viht yahn' kah), which was revised several times and finalized in 1898; *Mlada* (1872) (MLAH dah); *Mayskaya noch'* (May Night) (1878) (MI skI ah NOCH); *Snegurochka* (The Snow Maiden) (1881) (SNYEH GOO roch kah); *Tsarskaya nevesta (The Tsar's Bride)*; *Sadko* (1895) (SAHT ko:); *Motsart i Sal'yeri* (Mozart and Salieri) (1897) (MO: tsahrt ee sah LYEH ree), in one act, with Pushkin's 1830 "little tragedy" of the same name as its libretto; and *Zolotoy petushok* (The Golden Cockerel) (1906) (ZO lo TOY pyeh TOO shok). He revised works by other composers, e.g., Mussorgsky's ***Boris Godunov***; and helped finish Borodin's ***Knyaz Igor (Prince Igor)***.

Ring cycle: *Der Ring des Nibelungen* **(The Ring of the Nibelungs)** Tetralogy by Richard **Wagner**, with libretti by the composer, based on Norse mythology and the ancient saga *Nibelungenlied* (Song of the Nibelungs) (nee' beh LOONG ehn LEET); first presented as a cycle over four days at the Bayreuth **Festspielhaus**, 1876:

1869 *Das Rheingold* (The Rhine Gold) (dahs *R*IN GO:LT): prologue in one act (four scenes) to the trilogy of succeeding operas; premiere: Munich, Königliches Hof- und Nationaltheater

1870 *Die Walküre* (The Valkyrie) (dee vahl KÜ *r*eh): three acts; premiere: Munich, Königliches Hof- und Nationaltheater

1871 (composition finished) *Siegfried* (ZIH:K F*R*EET); three acts; premiere: Bayreuth Festspielhaus, 1876

1874 (composition finished) *Götterdämmerung* (Twilight of the Gods) (GÖ tuh DEHM uh ROONG): prologue and three acts; premiere: Bayreuth Festspielhaus, 1876

Das Rheingold opens in the river Rhine—*in it*, as the hilarious Anna Russell (1911–2006) says in her comic retelling of the Ring cycle story. The Nibelung dwarf Alberich (AHL beh *r*ih*kh*) (bass-bar.), having renounced love, steals the gold guarded in the Rhine by the three Rhine Maidens (sop., sop., mezz.) and takes it below to the workshop of Nibelheim (NEE behl HIM) to forge a Ring that will make him master of the world. Meanwhile, Wotan (VO: tahn) (bass-bar.), chief of the gods, is having the palace of Valhalla (val HA lah) constructed by the giants, brothers Fasolt (FAH zo:lt) (bass) and Fafner (FAHF nuh) (bass), who are unhappy because he cannot pay them the promised amount. Wotan goes to Nibelheim, where he obtains both the Ring, which he wishes to keep, and the rest of the Rheingold, with which he will pay the giants. Furious, Alberich curses the Ring. Wotan ends up giving it to the giants, adding it to the already enormous pile of gold. Fasolt and Fafner immediately fight over it, and Fafner kills Fasolt, leaving with the Ring, the magic helmet called the Tarnhelm (TAHRN HEHLM), and the pile of gold. The gods now enter Valhalla.

Die Walküre The back story: Wotan has had to devise a means of keeping Valhalla safe, so he begets nine daughters: the Valkyries, who guard Valhalla and take dead heroes there, revivifying them so that they, too, can defend it. In order to secure Valhalla completely, Wotan needs to ensure that the curse of the Ring is lifted by giving it and the Rheingold back to the Rhine maidens. To that end, he fathers Siegmund (ZIH:G m*oo*nt) (ten.) and Sieglinde (ZIH:G lihn deh) (sop.). Siegmund's mission will be to kill Fafner, obtain the gold, and return it. The twins are separated, and, while Siegmund wanders the earth, Sieglinde is forced by the repulsive Hunding (HOON dihng) (bass) to marry him. As the curtain rises, we see Hunding's hut, with a giant tree in the middle, in which Wotan has embedded the sword Nothung (NO: t*oo*ng), which can only be withdrawn by a hero. Seeking shelter from the winter storm, Siegmund enters the hut. He and Sieglinde do not recognize each other, but are strangely attracted. Hunding comes home to find Siegmund, and challenges him to fight the next day. Siegmund withdraws

Nothung, and he and Sieglinde flee. Hunding finds them, and in the ensuing fight, Wotan's daughter, the Valkyrie Brünhilde (BRÜN HIHL deh) (sop.), sides with her half-brother Siegmund, although ordered not to. Wotan shatters Nothung, and Siegmund is killed. Brünhilde collects the pieces and gives them to Sieglinde, who will bear Siegmund's child, Siegfried. As punishment for her disobedience, Wotan takes away Brünhilde's immortality and puts her to sleep, surrounded by a ring of magic fire that only a hero can penetrate.

Siegfried The back story: Sieglinde has died in childbirth, and Siegfried (ten.) is raised by the Nibelung dwarf Mime (MEE meh) (ten.), Alberich's brother, in his house and blacksmith shop, not far from the cave where Fafner, who has transformed himself into a dragon by using the magic Tarnhelm, guards the Rheingold. Mime wants to forge Nothung again from the fragments and have Siegfried kill Fafner with it, so that Mime can get the Ring and the Rheingold for himself. And now, as the story continues, we are in the blacksmith shop. Siegfried forges Nothung, and he and Mime seek Fafner, whom Siegfried kills, burning a finger with the dragon's blood. Sucking it, he realizes that he can now understand the language of the birds, as a forest bird (sop.) warns him that Mime plans to kill him and tells him about Brünhilde and the ring of magic fire. Siegfried kills Mime. Wotan the Wanderer tries to bar his path, but he breaks the Wanderer's staff with Nothung. Taking the Ring and the Tarnhelm, Siegfried follows the bird to Brünhilde, whom he awakens and claims as his wife. ("She's his aunt, by the way," Anna Russell informs us.)

Götterdämmerung The three Norns (NAW[R]N) (Fates) (sop., mezz., contr.) predict the end of the gods. Longing for adventure, Siegfried leaves Brünhilde, confiding the Ring to her care. He arrives at the Hall of the Gibichungs (GIH bih choong), ruled by Alberich's son, Hagen (HAH gehn) (bass), who lives there with his half-brother and half-sister, Gunther (GOON tuh:) (bar.) and Gutrune (goo TROO neh) (sop.). Hagen is aware of all that has transpired, and he hatches a plan to avenge himself on Siegfried by giving him a drink that will make him forget Brünhilde and induce him to marry Gutrune. He will then send the oblivious Siegfried to fetch Brünhilde as a bride for Gunther, and so obtain the Ring. Siegfried accomplishes his mission, seizes the Ring, and takes Brünhilde with him to Hagen. Brünhilde denounces him for his betrayal, and conspires with Hagen and Gunther to kill Siegfried during a hunt. Hagen spears him in the back. Brünhilde orders a funeral pyre to be lit for Siegfried on the banks of the Rhine, seizes the Ring from his finger, and gallops into the flames herself. The Gibichung Hall is now on fire. When Hagen tries desperately to snatch the Ring from Brünhilde, the Rhine overflows its banks, inundating everything, and he is dragged by the Rhine Maidens to his watery doom. Valhalla collapses. The reign of the old gods is now over.

See also LUSTIGEN NIBELUNGEN, DIE.

Road Show Off-Broadway musical (formerly titled *Bounce*); music and lyrics by Stephen **Sondheim**; book by John **Weidman**; New York Shakespeare Festival's Public Theatre, limited two-month engagement, 2008.

The story spans several decades, from the Alaskan Gold Rush to the Florida land boom of the 1930s, and tells the story of two brothers in their quest to fulfill the American dream. The themes of ethics and sound judgment inform the story, as the brothers' lives change in surprising ways.

Roar of the Greasepaint, The—The Smell of the Crowd Broadway musical by Leslie **Bricusse** and Anthony **Newley**; Shubert Theatre, 1965 (231 perf.).

Still well remembered from the vibrant, engaging score are "Who Can I Turn To?" and "A Wonderful Day Like Today."

In this world, there are the "haves" and the "have nots." Cocky (played by Newley) is a "have not," and Sir is a "have." Cocky loses at everything, whereas Sir wins at everything. But Cocky realizes that without people like him, Sir would be nowhere, and this gives him a measure of self-respect and confidence.

Roberta Broadway operetta by Jerome **Kern**; book and lyrics by Otto **Harbach**; New Amsterdam Theatre, 1933 (295 perf.); film, 1935, with much of the score eliminated, and two new songs by Kern, with lyrics by Dorothy **Fields**: "Lovely to Look At" and "I Won't Dance."

The original stage score is memorable for one number in particular, "Smoke Gets In Your Eyes." But the rest of it deserves to be heard as well. Hassard Short directed, and there were extravagant production numbers with choreography by the famed Mexican-born American dancer and choreographer José Limon (1908–1972).

Having inherited a Paris dress shop named "Roberta" from Aunt Minnie, John Kent, a football player, goes to France and falls in love with Stephanie, Minnie's assistant. His old girlfriend, Sophie, pursues him there, but he sticks with his new-found love, who turns out to be a Russian princess.

Robin Hood Comic opera (operetta) in three acts by Reginald **de Koven**; libretto by Harry B. **Smith**; Chicago Opera House, 1890.

The first New York performances were at the Standard Theatre in 1891 (40 perf.), by a touring company out of Boston, but the show proved so popular that it had dozens of revivals nationwide. Its most well known song is "Oh, Promise Me," lyrics by influential theater critic, dramatist, and writer of sentimental poetry Clement Scott (1841–1904). The rest of the score is full of lilting, rollicking solos and choruses, even if the "fal-la" and "singing tra la la" lyrics strike us today as mostly doggerel.

Sir Tristram Testy, the Sheriff of Nottingham (bar.), tries to force his ward, Maid Marian Fitzwalter (sop.), to wed his crony, Sir Guy of Gisborne (ten.), even though the king had commanded the sheriff to marry her to his other ward, Robert, Earl of Huntington (ten.), a prize-winning archer. She is saved from this dismal fate by Robert—turned out of his estates by Testy, unjustly outlawed, and calling himself Robin Hood—and his band of Merry Men. With Testy foiled and Robin restored to his earldom, Will Scarlet (bass), Little John (bar.), Friar Tuck (bass), and Allan-a-Dale (contr.) all attend the wedding of Robert and Marian.

Rock of Ages Broadway rock **jukebox musical** with music arranged, orchestrated, and supervised by Ethan Popp (b. 1977), featuring 1980s hits by such groups as Poison, Styx, and Journey; book by Chris D'Arienzo (b. 1972); three-month run Off-Broadway, 2008; transferred to Broadway, 2009 (still running as of this writing).

This lively, energetic show stars former *American Idol* contestant Constantine Maroulis (b. 1975), backed by a heavy metal band. Drew, a Los Angeles wannabe rocker, pursues the girl he loves, and a career, while German real estate developers threaten to destroy the Sunset Strip neighborhood.

rock opera; rock musical A musical theater piece with rock music, e.g., *Tommy*, the first of the genre to be so called; others are *Jesus Christ Superstar*, *Rent*, *The Toxic Avenger*, *The Rocky Horror Show* (London, 1973; New York, 1975; film, *The Rocky Horror Picture Show*, 1975), and *Rock of Ages*.

Rodgers and Hammerstein Writing partners, composer Richard **Rodgers** and librettist/lyricist Oscar Hammerstein II, known simply as Oscar **Hammerstein**: the team responsible for classic mid-20th c. Broadway musicals.

The musicals of Rodgers and Hammerstein:

1943 *Oklahoma!*
1945 *Carousel*
1945 (film; remade 1962; stage version 1996) *State Fair*
1947 *Allegro*
1949 *South Pacific*
1951 *The King and I*
1953 *Me and Juliet*
1955 *Pipe Dream*
1957 (television; remade for TV 1965, 1997; stage show 1958, 1961) *Cinderella*
1958 (revised, 2002) *Flower Drum Song*
1959 *The Sound of Music*

Rodgers and Hart Writing partners, composer Richard **Rodgers** and librettist/lyricist Lorenz **Hart**. They collaborated on thirty-four stage shows and films. Their most notable pieces include *The Garrick Gaieties*, a revue to which they contributed songs; their first book show, *Dearest Enemy* (1925), libretto by Herbert **Fields**, set during the American Revolution; *A Connecticut Yankee* (1927), book by Herbert Fields, based on *A Connecticut Yankee in King Arthur's Court* by Mark Twain; *Jumbo* (1935); *Babes in Arms*; *On Your Toes*; *I'd Rather Be Right*; *The Boys from Syracuse*; *I Married an Angel*; *Pal Joey*; and their last show, *By Jupiter*.

Rodgers, Mary (b. 1931) American composer of stage musicals and author of children's books; daughter of composer Richard Rodgers; mother of Adam **Guettel**; among her notable successes is *Once Upon a Mattress*.

Rodgers, Richard (1902–1979) One of the greatest and most beloved American Broadway musical composers, esp. famous for the Rodgers and Hammerstein and

Rodgers and Hart collaborations; also worked with other writers on such shows as *No Strings* (1962), the first Broadway show he had done since the death of Oscar Hammerstein two years before; *Two by Two*, and *Do I Hear a Waltz*; and composed many Hollywood musical film scores, notably with Hart. While still a preschooler, he had taught himself to play piano by ear. He began composing as a teenager, continuing during his college years at Columbia University. His professional career as a film and stage composer spanned sixty years.

Roi Carotte, Le (King Carrot) (luh *R*WAH kah *R*OT) **Opéra bouffe-féerie** in four acts (eighteen tableaux) by Jacques **Offenbach**; libretto by Victorien **Sardou**, suggested by the story "Klein Zaches, genannt Zinnober" (Little-Thing, Called Cinnabar) (1819) (KLIN ZAH khehs geh NAHNT TSIHN O: buh) by E. T. A. **Hoffmann**; Paris, Théâtre de la Gaité, 1872.

This sardonic political satire is set to one of Offenbach's most brilliant scores, full of lilting melody and entrancing airs. Fridolin was intended to be a portrait of Napoleon III, who had been dethroned after France lost the Franco-Prussian War in 1871, and King Carrot and his enchanted root-vegetable followers, who are terrible rulers, are supposed to be the radicals: the Latin word *radix* (RAH dih:ks) means "root." But the public misunderstood, and thought King Carrot was supposed to represent Napoleon III and that Fridolin had grown to understand democratic values by the end of the piece.

The dissolute King Fridolin XXIV (f*r*ih: do: LA*N*) (ten.) of Krokodyne (k*r*o ko: DEEN) is engaged to Cunégonde (kü né GO*N*D) (sop.), whom he is marrying for her money because the kingdom's finances are in a parlous state. Meanwhile, in a ruined tower of the castle, the sorceress Coloquinte (ko lo: KA*N*T) (mezz.) [bitter apple] bides her time with the princess Rosée-du-Soir (*r*o: zé dü SWAH*R*) (sop.) [evening dew], whom she has imprisoned for ten years with the intention of eventually making her queen of Krokodyne so that she, Coloquinte, can rule the kingdom from behind the throne. Rosée-du-Soir pines for the love of Fridolin, whom she has only seen at a distance through the tower window. The good genie Robin-Luron (*r*o ba*n* lü *R*O:*N*) (mezz.) appears, and helps her to escape. In the castle armory, Fridolin and a crowd of students whom he has invited back with him from the local brasserie are royally drunk and drinking out of helmets, which infuriates the ancestral armor. The ancient metal suits come clattering to life, accusing Fridolin of misrule. Everyone flees, but the enraged Coloquinte has brought all the garden vegetables to life, and the carrot has now become King Carrot (ten.). Led by the suits of armor, the vegetables revolt, and Fridolin flees for his life while his venal courtiers, self-serving advisers, and Cunégonde, who falls in love with King Carrot, betray him and join the "winning" side. Accompanied by Robin-Luron and Rosée-du-Soir, Fridolin goes through amazing adventures: He is advised by another sorcerer that he must find the Ring of Solomon in the ancient city of Pompeii, since it alone has the power to overcome the gnome, King Carrot. He does so, in an incredible **transformation scene** that brings ancient Pompeii to life. At one point, he finds himself in the kingdom of the insects, and learns about hard work from the ants. Eventually, all enchantments are broken, and Fridolin, having learned his lesson and led another revolution, becomes king once more. He now recognizes the true worth of Rosée-du-Soir, and all ends happily.

Romani, Felice (1788–1865) (feh LEE cheh: ro: MAH nee) Italian poet, scholar, and librettist who wrote the libretti for eight operas by Vincenzo **Bellini**, as well as libretti for Luigi **Ricci**, Gaetano **Donizetti**, and Gioachino **Rossini**.

Romberg, Sigmund (1887–1951) Prolific Austro-Hungarian-born American composer of more than sixty shows, and myriads of hit songs; among his most beloved masterpieces are *Maytime*, *Blossom Time*, *The Student Prince*, *The Desert Song* (1926), *The New Moon* (1928), and *Up in Central Park*. In 1954, Romberg was played by José Ferrer (1912–1992), whose performance is astonishing and brilliant, in the MGM biopic *Deep in My Heart*. The film features wonderful production numbers from the great shows Romberg wrote with Dorothy **Donnelly**, Otto **Harbach**, Oscar **Hammerstein**, and others, produced by the Shuberts.

Rome, Harold (1908–1993) American songwriter, lyricist, and film and Broadway musical composer; his works include *Pins and Needles*, *Call Me Mister*, *Fanny*, and *I Can Get It for You Wholesale*.

Rorem, Ned (b. 1923) American composer of instrumental and choral works, songs, and several operas, of which the only two full-length works are *Miss Julie* (1965), based on the play by August Strindberg (1849–1912), and the widely performed *Our Town* (2005), based on the play by Thornton Wilder (1897–1975). His diaries and letters are invaluable source material.

Rose-Marie Broadway operetta by Rudolf **Friml** and Herbert Stothart (1885–1949); book and lyrics by Otto **Harbach** and Oscar **Hammerstein**; Imperial Theatre, 1924 (557 perf.); Broadway revival, 1927, Century Theatre (48 perf.); international hit: London, Theatre Royal, Drury Lane (581 perf.), Paris (1250 perf.); many revivals; films: 1928 (silent; believed lost); 1936, with Jeannette MacDonald and Nelson Eddy: the "Indian Love Call" became their signature song; 1954, with Ann Blyth (b. 1928) and Howard Keel (1919–2004).

In Fond-du-Lac, Saskatchewan, Rose-Marie la Flamme, daughter of a French-Canadian trapper, is a singer at Lady Jane's Hotel, where Sergeant Malone of the Royal Canadian Mounted Police flirts with the owner. Despite the objections of her brother, Emile, Rose-Marie wants to marry Jim Kenyon, a fur trapper. Edward Hawley, a city slicker, is in love with her but is having an affair with Wanda, lover of the Indian Black Eagle. He frames Jim for the murder of Black Eagle, who was actually killed by Wanda, saving Hawley's life when Black Eagle caught them together and attacked him. Hard-Boiled Herman, Jim's friend, worms the truth from her in time to stop Rose-Marie's wedding to Hawley. She and Jim are reunited.

Rosenkavalier, Der (The Knight of the Rose) (deh *R*O: zehn KAH vah LEE uh) Opera in three acts by Richard **Strauss**; libretto by Hugo von **Hofmannsthal**; Dresden Hofoper, 1911.

The Marschallin (mah[r] shah LEEN) (sop.) has been making love to young Octavian (ok TAH vee ahn) (sop. or mezz.), and when they hear voices, Octavian quickly disguises himself as a maid. The Marschallin's portly, crude cousin, Baron Ochs (OKS) (bass), comes in with the request that she nominate a Knight of the Rose to present the traditional silver rose as a token of his fealty to his intended, the young and innocent Sophie (sop.); but when "Mariandel" (mah ree AHN dehl) appears, the Baron's eyes grow wide with desire. Octavian escapes, but returns later. She is pessimistic about their future, and their leave-taking is not a happy one. Later, Sophie, at home in her father's house, awaits the Knight of the Rose, and when Octavian arrives to present the silver rose on behalf of Ochs, they fall instantly in love. Ochs arrives shortly thereafter, and Octavian challenges him to a duel, wounding him slightly. Sophie's father, Faninal (FAH nee NAHL) (bar.), threatens to send her to a convent if she will not marry Ochs, who receives a billet-doux from "Mariandel" arranging a rendezvous at an inn. Faninal will be there as well, and will see his prospective son-in-law exposed for the coarse lecher he is. The eager Ochs appears for the rendezvous. There is further plotting, and in all the ensuing commotion, the police arrive. The Marschallin, having gotten wind of what is about to transpire, shows up and puts things right, sending everybody away, except for Sophie and Octavian, whom she sadly but discreetly leaves together.

Ross, Adrian (1859–1933) [b. Adrian Reed Ropes] Prolific English lyricist of more than eighty original musicals and translations. For Richard D'Oyly Carte, he did lyrics for the Savoy Theatre adaptations of Offenbach's *La Grande-Duchesse de Gérolstein*, under the title *The Grand Duchess*, and Chabrier's *L'étoile*, renamed *The Lucky Star*; and he did the English lyrics for Lehár's *Die lustige Witwe* and *Der Graf von Luxemburg*, as well as for operettas by André **Messager** (*Monsieur Beaucaire*), Leo **Fall**, and Paul **Abraham**. He is best remembered, however, for the **Gaiety musicals**, for which he did lyrics for Sidney **Jones**, Lionel **Monckton**, and Ivan **Caryll**.

Ross, Jerry (1926–1955) American composer and lyricist; collaborated with Richard **Adler** on the Broadway musicals *The Pajama Game* and *Damn Yankees*.

Rossi, Gaetano (1774–1855) (GAH eh TAH no: RO:S see) Prolific Italian librettist; wrote more than 100 libretti for **Mayr**, **Mercadante**, **Pacini**, **Donizetti**, the **Ricci brothers**, and Rossini, notably *Semiramide* and *Tancredi*. He was also the artistic director of the Teatro Filarmonico (fih:' lahr MO: nee ko:) in Verona.
See also FIDELIO; IVANHOE.

Rossini, Gioachino (1791–1868) (dgo:' ah KEE no: ro:s SEE nee) Brilliant, innovative Italian opera composer, whose works are filled with gorgeous melody and inventive coloratura ornamentation; he wrote thirty-nine operas, and revised versions of many of them. His full-length operas include *L'italiana in Algieri* (The Italian Woman in Algiers) (1813) (lih tahl YAH nah ihn ahl DGEH ree); *Tancredi*; *Il turco in Italia* (The Turk in Italy) (1814) (ihl TOOR ko: ihn ee TAHL yah); *Il* *barbiere di Siviglia (The Barber of Seville)*; *Otello, ossia Il moro di Venezia*; *La Cenerentola, ossia La bontà in trionfo*; *Armida*; *La gazza ladra* (The Thieving Magpie) (1817) (lah GAHD dzah LAH drah); *Mosè in Egitto* (Moses in Egypt) (1818) (mo: ZEH: ihn eh: DGIH:T to:); *La donna del lago* (The Lady of the Lake) (1819) (lah DO:N nah dehl LAH go:); *Maometto II* (Mahomet II) (1820) (mah' o: MEHT to: seh GO:N do:); *Semiramide*; and *Guillaume Tell (William Tell)*. After the triumph of *Guillaume Tell* in 1829, Rossini wrote no more operas. In 1855, he settled in Paris, where he became a great salon host to the artistic world, renowned as a raconteur and wit at his Saturday musical soirées, for which he composed hundreds of songs and piano pieces, and prepared gourmet feasts. His culinary skill was so admired that his name has been attached to a number of dishes he is said to have invented.

Rossinian (ro: SEE nee uhn) *adj.* Pertaining to and characteristic of the felicitous musical style, verve, and melodic fertility of the works of Gioachino Rossini; also, pertaining to the way in which he built rousing crescendos into his opera overtures, repeating them **da capo** to even greater effect; and to the crescendos themselves: *a Rossinian crescendo*. Also, *Rossini-esque*.

rotating rep [Rep: short for *repertory*] The system of alternating presentations of plays, comic operas, operas, or musicals in a company's repertoire. **Gilbert and Sullivan** was done in rotating rep by the D'Oyly Carte Opera Company: they might do *The Mikado* for two nights, *H. M. S. Pinafore* for the next two, and so on. And the practice is ubiquitous in **opera** seasons worldwide.

Rousseau, Jean-Jacques (1712–1778) (zhahn zhahk roo SOH) Swiss Enlightenment philosopher, whose ideas on equality and freedom influenced the French Revolution; composer; wrote articles on music; composed seven musical theater pieces, most to his own libretti, of which the most famous is the rather undistinguished, mildly tuneful *Le devin du village* (The Village Soothsayer) (1753) (luh duh van' dü vee LAHZH); available in a 1956 recording from EMI (5 756625 2; 2002); the CD includes *Richard Coeur de Lion* by **Grétry**. Rousseau also invented a practically unworkable system of musical notation using letters and numbers, even though the perfectly good system we now use was already in place.

rubato (roo BAH to:) *adj.* [Italian: robbed] Varied tempo, i.e., varied from the strict way in which it is written, so that when a note is slowed down or prolonged, it "robs" the time from another note; much used in opera, e.g., when holding a high note, for which the orchestra waits before continuing.

Rubens, Paul Alfred (1875–1917) English lyricist, songwriter and composer of musical comedies, including a number of very popular **Gaiety musicals**, e.g., *The Sunshine Girl* (1912); *San Toy* (1899); *A Country Girl* (1902); *The School Girl* (1903); and *The Cingalee* (1904). His greatest success was *Miss Hook of Holland*. In ill health all his life, the genial, well liked Rubens retired from the theater and went to live in Falmouth, Cornwall, where he died of tuberculosis at only forty-one years of age.

Ruddigore, or The Witch's Curse Comic opera in two acts by **Gilbert and Sullivan**; London, Savoy Theatre, 1887.

Gilbert's libretto spoofs transpontine (tranz PON tuhn; —tIn) melodrama in general, i.e., those melodramas that were done "across the bridge" over the Thames, in Southwark (SUTH uhrk) theaters; and *nautical melodrama*, its subgenre, which dealt with the lives and loves of sailors. Sullivan's gift for musical parody is also much in evidence: Among the gems in this brilliant score are a send-up of **Meyerbeer** in the act 2 Ghost Scene, and a spoof of **Donizetti** for Mad Margaret in act 1. The collaborators had difficulty in getting the show in shape, and made a number of cuts and revisions to the original **version** even after it had opened; further changes were made for its first revival in 1921 by the D'Oyly Carte conductor Sir Geoffrey Toye (1889–1942), who also wrote a new overture.

In the village of Rederring, Rose Maybud (sop.), the moralistic village maiden, is engaged to the shy farmer Robin Oakapple (bar.). The sailor Richard Dauntless (ten.) arrives fresh from the Napoleonic wars. He, too, is in love with Rose. He persuades Sir Despard Murgatroyd (bar.), baronet of Ruddigore, who jilted Mad Margaret (mezz.) and drove her insane, to reveal that Robin is really Sir Ruthven Murgatroyd (RIH vuhn), his older brother, who, to escape the curse that obliges each baronet of Ruddigore to commit a crime a day or perish, has renounced the baronetcy and gone to live on a farm. Despard insists that Robin resume his rightful place. When he does, Despard is free to redeem himself by marrying Mad Margaret and nursing her back to mental health, while Dauntless can wed Rose, who has renounced the now wicked Robin. Act 2 takes place in the picture gallery of the Murgatroyd castle. Robin is having a great deal of difficulty in committing a crime a day, and his ancestors, who come to life from their portraits, reproach him for it. The previous baronet, Robin's uncle, Sir Roderick Murgatroyd (bass-bar.), informs him that he had better commit a real crime (tax evasion simply won't do), or it will go hard with him. Despard and Mad Margaret have now reformed, as they tell us in a droll and decorous duet, "I Once Was a Very Abandoned Person." They want Robin to reform as well, even if it means he must die! Robin's faithful retainer, Old Adam Goodheart (bar.), arrives with Rose's aunt, Dame Hannah (contr.), whom he has abducted—just the sort of crime a day the ancestors have been hoping for. She was in love with Sir Roderick, and they are happy to see each other. Robin realizes that since a baronet can only die if he refuses to commit his daily crime, this refusal is tantamount to suicide. But suicide itself is a crime. The curse is therefore null and void! Robin and Rose are reunited, as are Dame Hannah and Sir Roderick—he seems to have come unexpectedly to life again, for he ought never to have died.

rumba *n.* A syncopated, lively South American dance of Cuban origin, very popular as a ballroom dance in the United States, esp. from the 1930s through the '50s.

Rusalka (ROO sahl' kah) **1.** In Slavonic mythology, a water sprite who lures unwary passers-by to their doom in the depths of the river where she lives, but who wants to be human, as she once was. The legend, similar to that of *Undine*, has been the subject and the title of several operas, including one written in 1921 by the Russian composer Alexander Dargomyzhsky (1813–1869) (dahr go: MIIIZII skee).

2. Opera in three acts by Antonín **Dvořák**; libretto by Czech composer and conductor Jaroslav Kvapil (1892–1959) (YAH ro: slahv KVAH pih:l), based on de la Motte Fouqué's poem *Undine* and the fairy tale, ***The Little Mermaid***, by Hans Christian **Andersen**; 1901.

Rusalka (sop.), a water sprite, begs the witch Ježibaba (YEH zhih: BAH bah) (mezz.) to help her become human, because she is in love with the Prince and wants to marry him. The witch obliges her, but Rusalka must remain silent, or the enchantment will be broken. The Prince is soon bored with her and, in despair, she breaks her vow. Disaster ensues, and both die.

S

Saidy, Fred (1907–1982) American film, television, and Broadway musical book writer; collaborated with E. Y. Harburg on *Bloomer Girl* and *Finian's Rainbow*.

Saint-Saëns, Camille (1835–1921) (ka mee' yuh sa*n* SAH*N*S) French composer, conductor, pianist, organist, author; composed ballets, symphonies, concertos, choral and chamber music; studied with **Halévy**; wrote twelve operas, the best known being *Samson et Dalila* (Samson and Delilah) (1872) (sah*n* SO:*N* eh: dah lee LAH).

Salieri, Antonio (1750–1825) (sah LYEH: ree) Influential Italian composer, resident at the Hapsburg court in Vienna; studied with **Gassmann**; music teacher to members of the royal family; taught **Beethoven**, Schubert, **Meyerbeer** and **Hérold**; wrote instrumental music and composed forty-four operas, including *Semiramide riconosciuta*; the highly successful **opera seria** *Axur, re d'Ormus* (Axur, King of Ormus) (1788) (ahk SOOR reh: DO:R m*oo*s), with a libretto by **Da Ponte**, who also wrote libretti for several of his **opera buffa** pieces; *Armida*; and *Falstaff*. Although he felt a certain rivalry with Mozart, he was also helpful to him quite often, and the stories about their enmity have been much exaggerated. The rumor that he poisoned Mozart is totally without foundation; Salieri had gone mad, and whispered that he had done so to a pupil of Beethoven's who was visiting him in the madhouse near the end of his life. But the rumor made for good drama, and was taken up first by Pushkin, whose dramatic poem *Mozart and Salieri* (1830) is the libretto of the opera by **Rimsky-Korsakov** and the basis for the play *Amadeus* (1980), by Peter Shaffer (b. 1926). A nice selection of opera arias is available on *The Salieri Album*, sung by Cecilia Bartoli (Decca; B0001097-02; 2003).

Sally Broadway musical by Jerome **Kern** and Victor **Herbert**; lyrics by P. G. **Wodehouse**, B. G. **De Sylva**, Clifford Gray (1887–1941), who also contributed to *Artists and Models*, and others; book by Guy **Bolton**; 1920 (561 perf.); Broadway revival, 1948, (38 perf.); film, 1929, with most of Kern's songs dropped, and new ones added by Joe Burke (1884–1950), who also wrote songs for the *Ziegfeld Follies*.

This Cinderella story was lavishly produced by Florenz Ziegfeld, with Herbert's music used for the "Butterfly Ballet" sequence. Among Kern's memorable songs for the show is "Look for the Silver Lining."

Sally Rhinelander, a poor orphan, is a dishwasher in a Greenwich Village restaurant. Blair Farquar goes there to hire people to work a party he is throwing. He is immediately attracted to Sally. When the dancer that Otis Hooper, an agent, has hired as the main entertainer for the gala fails to show up, Sally substitutes for her. Otis is so impressed that he gets her a job in the *Ziegfeld Follies*. She becomes famous, and Blair and she are united.

saltimbanques, Les (The Acrobats) Operetta by Louis **Ganne**.

Salvator Rosa (sahl' vah TO:R RO: zah) Opera in four acts by Carlos **Gomes**; libretto by Antonio **Ghislanzoni**, based on the life of the Italian painter Salvator Rosa (1615–1673); Genoa, Gran Teatro Carlo Felice, 1874.

Salvator Rosa (ten.) supports the Neapolitan revolt led by Masaniello (1622–1647) (mah zah NYEHL lo:) (bar.) in 1647 against the Spanish occupiers. Masaniello is assassinated. Rosa, in love with the Spanish governor's daughter, Isabella (sop.), is spared when she kills herself to save his life.

sanglot (sah*n* GLO:) *n.* [French: sob] In singing, esp. in the 18th c., an ornament consisting of a sob-like sound interpolated at an emotional point in the piece, and achieved by starting low in the chest and rising to an accentuated note. A similar sobbing ornamentation is sometimes heard in recordings by 20th-c. opera singers, e.g., in some arias sung by tenor Beniamino Gigli.

sarabande (SA rah band) *n.* [French] A 17th- and early 18th-c. court dance in 3/4 or 3/8 time; it apparently began as a lively dance, but by the time it had disappeared from French court balls, it had become a slow, solemn dance.

Sardou, Victorien (1831–1908) (vihk' to: *R*YEHN sah*r* DOO) Prolific, popular French playwright known for his melodramatic, well-made plays, including *La Tosca*, which he wrote as a vehicle for Sarah Bernhardt, and *Fedora*, both adapted for the operatic stage; author of *Les Noces de Fernande*, adapted for the operetta *Der Bettelstudent*; librettist of the brilliant political satire, Offenbach's little known masterpiece, *Le Roi Carotte*. George Bernard Shaw rather unfairly crowned the witty, astute playwright King of Sardoodledum, the fictitious kingdom where Sardou reigned supreme over his fellow writers of melodrama. According to Shaw, Sardou's works exemplified the false, the mindless, the facile, the nonsensical, and the overdone. But although his plays are seldom performed, posterity has been kinder than Shaw in its judgment of Sardou's legacy.

Sarti, Giuseppe (1729–1802) (SAHR tee) Italian music director, conductor, violinist, and composer of ca. seventy-five operas, including *Didone abbandonata* and *Semiramide* (both, 1762) to libretti by **Metastasio**. Mozart quotes his immensely popular comic opera, *Fra i due litiganti* (Between the Two Litigants) (1782) (frah ee DOO eh: lih: tee GAHN tee), in the last act of *Don Giovanni*.

Savoyard (sa VAW yuhrd), *n.* [Fr. London's Savoy Theater, built by producer Richard D'Oyly Carte in 1881 esp. for the production of **Gilbert and Sullivan** comic operas] **1.** A member of the company that performed in the original productions of G & S. **2.** A performer in G & S operas. **3.** A Gilbert and Sullivan fan.

Savoy operas 1. The fourteen comic operas by Sir. W. S. **Gilbert** (libretti) and Sir Arthur S. **Sullivan** (music), even though the first five were not produced at the Savoy Theater. **2.** Operas or musicals by Sullivan and other librettists, e.g., *The Rose of Persia* (libretto by Basil **Hood**; 1899) and *The Emerald Isle* (libretto by Hood; score completed by Edward **German**; posthumously produced, 1901), or by other composers and librettists, e.g., a new **version** of Offenbach's *La Grande-Duchesse* *de Gérolstein (The Grand Duchess of Gerolstein)* (lyrics by Adrian **Ross**, dialogue by actor, journalist, and playwright Charles H. E. Brookfield (1857–1913); 1897); produced by Richard D'Oyly Carte at the Savoy in the 1890s, during the times when Gilbert and Sullivan were not working together.

For a complete list of the G & S comic operas, see GILBERT AND SULLIVAN.

Scarlatti, Alessandro (1660–1725) (skahr LAHT tee) Italian composer from a family of musicians; wrote at least sixty-six operas, but claimed to have written eighty. Among his influential stylistic innovations is a greater differentiation between recitative and the melodic aria it introduces. His son, Domenico Scarlatti (1685–1757), is known for his keyboard sonatas.

scat singing Nonsense syllables and words used in **jazz** singing; often done improvisationally, so that the syllables may vary from performance to performance.

Schmidt, Harvey (b. 1929) American composer, best known for *The Fantasticks*, written with Tom **Jones**; other shows include *110 in the Shade* (1963), *I Do, I Do* (1966), and *Celebration* (1969), all with Jones.

Schönberg, Claude-Michel (b. 1944) (klo:d mee shehl' sh:ön BEH*R*G) French composer who usually works with Alain **Boublil**; the team created the international megahits *Les Misérables* and *Miss Saigon*. They have been working together since 1973. Their latest collaboration, in conjunction with prolific film composer Michel Legrand (b. 1932) (mee shehl' luh GRAH*N*) and others, is *Marguerite* (2008), based on the Alexandre Dumas, fils play that also was adapted for Verdi's *La traviata*.

Schreker, Franz (1878–1934) (SH*R*EH kuh) Austrian conductor and composer of instrumental, choral, and chamber works; head of the Berlin Musikhochschule (Music Academy) (moo ZEEK HO:KH SHOO leh) for more than a decade, until he was forced out as director in 1932 because of the rising power of the Nazis, who dismissed him in 1933 from his teaching duties and banned his music because he was Jewish. He composed nine operas in late-romantic style, including the exciting, emotional three-act *Der ferne Klang* (The Distant Sound) (1912) (deh FEH:[*R*] neh KLAHNG), which owes something stylistically to Richard **Strauss**; wonderful recording on Naxos CD (8.660074-75; 1989).

Schwartz, Arthur (1900–1984) Prolific American producer, composer, and songwriter, known for his collaborations with lyricist Howard **Dietz**, with whom he wrote revues and a number of book musicals, including *A Tree Grows in Brooklyn*; also wrote *By the Beautiful Sea* (1954), book by Herbert and Dorothy **Fields**.

Schwartz, Stephen (b. 1948) American composer, lyricist, and director; wrote *Godspell*, *Pippin*, *The Magic Show*, and *Wicked*, among other stage shows, as well as scores for Hollywood animated features.

scissors kick A scissors-like dance movement. See CISEAUX.

scoop *v. i.* [Also used as a n.] **1.** In singing, sliding smoothly from a lower note to a higher note, through all the pitches but without separating the slide into distinct pitches, in a kind of **portamento**, which is sometimes desirable. **2.** Sliding roughly from a lower note to a higher note, sometimes simply due to inept technique; i.e., an imprecise attack on a note, thus necessitating a slide up to it, so as to get on pitch; this can be a quite undesirable mannerism, or it can be an occasional, effective technique.

score *n., v.* —*n.* **1.** The music for a composition. **2.** The music of a composition written out on staffs, using musical **notation**. —*v. t.* **3.** To write out music for a composition. **4.** To orchestrate a musical composition.

Scotto, Vincent (1876–1952) (va*n* sah*n* sko TO:) French composer from Marseille; son of Neapolitan immigrants; an icon of French popular culture. He composed ca. sixty operettas, seven of them examples of the **Marseille operetta**, and ca. 4000 songs, often featured by such famous artists as Edith Piaf (1915–1963), Maurice Chevalier, and Josephine Baker (1906–1975), including her great hit, "J'ai deux amours" (I have two loves) (zheh: d*oo* zah MOO*R*); occasional movie actor; wrote ca. 200 film scores, among them those for most of his friend Marcel Pagnol's movies, including the ***Fanny*** trilogy.

Scribe, Eugène (1791–1861) (*oo* ZHEH*N* SK*R*EEB) Prolific French playwright and opera librettist whose works fill seventy-six volumes; practically invented the well-made play. Among Scribe's major works for the musical theater are the libretti for Auber's *Fra Diavolo*, and *La Muette de Portici*; Halévy's ***La Juive***; Meyerbeer's *Les Huguenots* and *Robert le Diable*; and Verdi's *I vespri siciliani (Les vêpres siciliennes)*. Several projects of his were adapted for the operatic stage, among them those that form the basis for Bellini's ***La sonnambula***, Donizetti's ***L'elisir d'amore***, and Cilea's ***Adriana Lecouvreur***.

second position In dance, the placement of the feet so that they form a line, but at a distance from each other, so that the heels are not touching, as they are in **first position**.

Secret Garden, The Broadway musical by Lucy Simon (b. 1943); book and lyrics by Marsha Norman (b. 1947), based on the novel by Frances Hodgson Burnett (1849–1924); St. James Theatre, 1991 (732 perf.).

The orphaned Mary Lennox goes to Yorkshire to live with her widowed Uncle Archibald and crippled cousin, Colin. When she brings her aunt's garden back to life, she also brings sunshine and a sense of hope into all their lives.

Secunda, Sholem (1894–1974) Prolific Ukrainian-born American **Yiddish musical theater** composer. One of his enduring popular songs, played by American bands and sung by many vocalists, is "Bei mir bist du shayn" (To me, you are beautiful) (bI mee*r* BIH:S doo SHEH:N), with lyrics by Jacob Jacobs (1890/91–1977), from their 1932 musical comedy *M'ken lebn nor m'lost nit* (You Can Live, But You're Not Allowed) (muh kehn LEH:BN no:*r* muh LO:ST niht)

[Official English title: *I Would If I Could*], book by Abraham Blum (1893–1960). It was first performed by the Yiddish theater musical star Aaron Lebedeff (1873–1960).

segreto di Susannah, Il Opera by Ermanno **Wolf-Ferrari**.

segue *n., v.* —*n.* **1.** A smooth transition from one musical piece or section to the next. —*v. i.* **2.** To move smoothly from one section of a piece into the next.
See also BRIDGE.

sell *v. t.* To perform in a committed, forceful way, putting an interpretation across so that the audience really "buys" it; esp. said of songs: *She really sold that number*.

Sellars, Peter (b. 1957) Innovative, sometimes controversial opera director; librettist of John Adams's ***Dr. Atomic*** (2005).

semi-opera Esp. in England from ca. the 1670s to the 1710s, a play with vocal music, **incidental music** to spoken scenes, and special **masque** scenes, with transformations and dancing; e.g., ***The Fairy Queen*** by Henry **Purcell**, who wrote several semi-operas.

Semiramide (Semiramis) (seh' mee RAH mee deh:) **1.** Opera in two acts by Gioachino **Rossini**; libretto by Gaetano **Rossi**, based on the play *Sémiramis* (sé mee' *r*ah MEES) by Voltaire; Venice, Teatro La Fenice, 1823.
   In ancient Babylon, Queen Semiramide (sop.) and Prince Assur (ah SOOR) (bass.) have murdered her husband, King Nino (NEE no:) (bass). They have tried to kill her son, Arsace (ahr SAH cheh:) (mezz.), but he has been saved, spirited away, and has grown up to become a great general on the kingdom's frontiers. Arsace, who has been raised without the knowledge of his true identity, arrives home, and Semiramide, not knowing who he is, falls in love with him and decides to marry him. But the terrifying ghost of Nino arises and announces that there are crimes that must be avenged. The marriage cannot take place. Oroe (o: RO: eh:) (bass), the High Priest, informs Arsace of the truth of what happened, and tells him he is the rightful heir to the throne. Arsace tells his mother that he now knows everything, but that he will spare her life. In the darkness of Nino's sanctuary, Arsace mistakenly murders her instead of his intended victim, Assur. He is crowned king as the opera ends.
2. Opera in two acts by Giacomo **Meyerbeer**: librettist(s) unknown, possibly the composer in collaboration with Count Lodovico Pacifico Piossasco de Feys (1773–1848) (lo: do: VEE ko: pah CHIH fee ko: pee o:s SAHS ko: deh: feh: EES), a poet, dramatist, and former Jacobin supporter of the French Revolution, who often worked with **Mercadante**; libretto based on Metastasio's *Semiramide riconosciuta* (ree' ko no SHOO tah); Turin, Teatro Regio, 1819. The music to this youthful masterpiece is magnificent, and heralds things to come in the great Paris grand operas. The story is very different from Rossini's opera.

Semiramide riconosciuta (Semiramis Recognized) Libretto by Pietro **Metastasio**; 1729; set by ca. forty composers, including **Gluck**, from whose opera some florid arias have been recorded by several singers, including Cecilia Bartoli, on the

Decca CD *Gluck Italian Arias* (289 467 248-2; 2001); **Hasse**, **Vivaldi**, **Sarti**, and **Salieri**: the overture to his opera is available from ASV (CD DCA 955; 1996).

The Egyptian princess Semiramide (raised in Bactria), having survived an attempt on her life by her lover, the Indian prince Scitalce (shee TAHL cheh:)—who had been led by Sibari (see BAH ree), who was also in love with her, to believe that she betrayed him—had escaped to Assyria, where the king, Nino, fell in love with her and married her. When he died, she disguised herself as their son, and now rules Babylon. Sibari arrives in Babylon as chief escort to Tamiri (tah MEE ree), Princess of Bactria. She is to select a husband from a group of three princes: Ircano (eer KAH no:), Prince of Scythia; Mirteo (meer TEH: o:), Prince of Egypt (brother of Semiramide, whom he believes long dead); and Scitalce. Semiramide and Scitalce recognize each other. When Tamiri chooses him, Semiramide is in despair. Knowing the past, Sibari intends to kill him by poisoning his drink at the betrothal banquet. But Scitalce refuses to accept Tamiri as his bride, and Ircano, whom she chooses next, is also reluctant. Eventually, after many plot complications, Semiramide's identity is publicly revealed, she and Scitalce are reunited, and Sibari is pardoned for all his machinations and evil plotting, while Tamiri is united with Mirteo, the one who truly loves her.

serenade *n.* Song or aria, usually in 6/8 time and with guitar accompaniment, addressed by one person to his (usually) or her lover, who is ordinarily inside or on a balcony, while the singer is outside or down below. The opening number, "Ecco ridente" (There laughing) (EHK ko: ree DEHN the:), sung by Almaviva in Rossini's *Il barbiere di Siviglia*; Ernesto's "Com'è gentil" (How nice it is) (ko: MEH: DGEHN teel) in *Don Pasquale*; and the Prince's "(Serenade) Overhead the Moon Is Shining" in Romberg's *The Student Prince* are only a few of many examples.

serva padrona, La (The Maid as Mistress) (lah SEHR vah pah DRO: nah) Comic opera in two acts by Giovanni Battista **Pergolesi**; libretto by lawyer, comedy writer, and librettist Gennaro Antonio Federico (?–1743/1744?) (dgehn NAH ro:; feh deh REE ko:); Naples, Teatro San Bartolomeo (bahr to: lo: MEH: o:), 1733.

This piece was first performed between the acts of Pergolesi's **opera seria** *Il prigionero superbo* (The Proud Prisoner) (eel prih dgo: NYEH ro: soo PEHR bo:).

The ambitious serving maid Serpina (sehr PEE nah) (sop.) pretends to leave the employ of Uberto (oo BEHR to:) (bass) by eloping with a soldier—in reality another servant, Vespone (vehs PO: neh:) (silent part)—so that she can lure Uberto into marrying her.

set *n., v.* —*n.* **1.** Scenery; décor for a theater piece. —*v. t.* **2.** To put words to music, i.e., the act of writing music to fit lyrics. **3.** To fix a musical tempo in rehearsal for a performance, so that it will remain more or less stable. **4.** To establish the more or less final, repeatable version of an interpretation or a performance, whether in music, e.g., in singing a particular number; or in acting, e.g., establishing the way or manner in which a scene is to be played.

set piece Any detachable number, aria, or ensemble section from a musical theater piece that is complete and self-contained, and can be sung by itself, e.g., in a concert.

setting *n.* **1.** The musical composition to which words or lyrics have been fitted: *the setting of the words.* **2.** Where and when a piece or the individual scenes in it take place: *The setting of Verdi's* **Aida** *is Pharaonic Egypt. The setting for act 1 of Gilbert and Sullivan's* The Gondoliers *is outside the ducal palace in Venice.*

1776 1. Broadway musical by Sherman Edwards (1919–1981) (music and lyrics); book by Peter **Stone**, based on a concept by Edwards; 46th Street Theater, 1969 (1222 perf.); Broadway revival: Criterion Center Stage Right, 1997 (367 perf.); film, 1972.

At Independence Hall in Philadelphia, the Continental Congress meets and decides to declare independence from Great Britain. With much travail, Benjamin Franklin (1706–1790), Thomas Jefferson (1743–1826), and John Adams (1735–1826) persuade the delegates to sign the Declaration of Independence.
2. Broadway musical by Ludwig **Englander**; libretto by Leo **Goldmark**; 1884.

The show was written in German and produced at New York's German-speaking theater, the Thalia; then translated into English and produced as *Adjutant James*; revived in 1895 as *The Daughter of the Revolution*, book and lyrics by J. Cheever **Goodwin**.

The story concerns events on the eve of the Battle of Trenton, when a young lady tries to rescue her lover, kept a prisoner by the Hessians.

According to the anonymous *New York Times* reviewer of the "romantic comic opera," in its original incarnation as *1776*, "A representation of Washington crossing the Delaware—following that given in the well-known picture—is one of the best of the scenic 'hits.' " But the reviewer dismissed the music as derivative and basically uninteresting, although the production was well mounted. Goldmark was quoted in an interview for the January, 1884 issue of the periodical *Folio: A Journal of Music, Drama, Art and Literature*: "The critics said I jumbled history. Did they want a history of the war of Independence, six years condensed into two hours and a half?" And he added, "I know him. Whom? Why, the critic who declared that the music was not original. He was a man, sir, who could not tell a fugue from a foghorn."

sextet *n.* A musical piece for six instrumentalists or singers, e.g., the sextet in the wedding scene of *Lucia di Lammermoor*.

Shakespeare, William (1564–1616) The greatest of English playwrights and poets has inspired composers over the centuries, and his works have been adapted for the musical theater more than 200 times. The most adapted play is *The Tempest*, with nearly fifty musical theater versions, including an 1850 opera by **Halévy**. **Sullivan**'s incidental music for *The Tempest*, composed in 1861, was a sensation, and immediately made his reputation as the most promising young English composer. *Hamlet* was adapted as an opera more than thirty times, including *Amleto*

(1715) (ahm LEH: to:) by Domenico **Scarlatti**; *Amleto* (1822) by Saverio **Mercadante**, with a libretto by Felice **Romani**; and *Amleto* (1871) by the Italian composer and conductor Franco Faccio (1840–1891) (FRAH*N* ko: FAHCH cho:), with a libretto by Arrigo **Boito**; but the most famous operatic version nowadays is *Hamlet* by Ambroise **Thomas**. Among the most celebrated, and performed Shakespearean operas are *Otello*, *Falstaff*, and *Macbeth* by Giuseppe **Verdi**; *Otello* by Gioachino **Rossini**; Nicolai's *Die lustigen Weiber von Windsor*; *I Capuleti ed i Montecchi* by Vincenzo **Bellini**; *Roméo et Juliette* by Charles **Gounod** (the play has been made into an opera twenty-five times); *Béatrice et Bénédict* by Hector **Berlioz**, based on Shakespeare's *Much Ado About Nothing* (in 1936, Reynaldo **Hahn** also adapted that play for the opera stage); and two operas based on *A Midsummer Night's Dream*: Henry **Purcell**'s *The Fairy Queen* and Benjamin **Britten**'s *A Midsummer Night's Dream*. In 1844, Franz von **Suppé** composed an operetta based on the same play, and Ruggiero **Leoncavallo** wrote a now obscure operatic version of it in 1899: it was privately performed. Among other less well known Shakespearean operas are *Antony and Cleopatra* by Samuel **Barber**; *Brutus* (1774) by J. C. F. Bach (1732–1795), based on *Julius Caesar*; *Coriolano* (1749) (ko:' ree o: LAH no:) by Johann Gottlieb Graun, based on *Coriolanus*; *La gioventù di Enrico V* (The Youth of Henry V) (1820) (lah dgo:' vehn TOO dee ehn REE ko: CHIH:N kweh:) by Giovanni **Pacini**, based on *Henry IV, Parts 1 and 2*; and *Le marchand de Venise* (The Merchant of Venice) (1935) (luh mah*r* shah*n*' duh vuh NEEZ) by Reynaldo Hahn. Arthur **Sullivan** had composed incidental music for an 1871 production of that play in Manchester, and for actor-manager Sir Henry Irving's (1838–1905) Lyceum Theatre production of *Macbeth* (1888), as well as incidental music for productions of *A Midsummer Night's Dream* (1874) and *King Henry VIII* (1877). Musical comedies based on Shakespeare include *The Boys from Syracuse*, *Kiss Me, Kate*, and *Two Gentlemen of Verona*.

Shamus O'Brien Opera in two acts by Sir Charles Villiers **Stanford**; libretto by Irish-born American journalist and playwright George H. Jessup, based on a poem by Joseph Sheridan Le Fanu (1814–1873); London, Opera Comique, 1896; New York, Broadway Theatre, 1897 (56 perf.).

In Ireland in 1798, after the suppression of the uprising, the patriot Shamus O'Brien (ten.) is pursued by the English Captain Trevor (ten.) and his soldiers. He is betrayed by Mike Murphy (ten.), rival for the love of Shamus's wife, Nora (sop.). As the soldiers prepare to hang him, he escapes. They fire, accidentally killing Murphy.

Shaw, George Bernard (1856–1950) Influential, witty, iconoclastic Irish playwright; novelist; Socialist polemicist; theater critic, and music critic; received Nobel Prize for Literature in 1925. Two of his plays were adapted for the musical theater: *Arms and the Man* for *Der tapfere Soldat* (The Chocolate Soldier) by Oscar **Straus**, and *Pygmalion* for Lerner and Loewe's Broadway megahit, *My Fair Lady*.

See also ALLUSION; PRINCESS THEATRE MUSICALS; SARDOU, VICTORIEN; UTOPIA LIMITED; WAGNER, RICHARD.

Shield, William (1748–1829) English librettist, composer, violinist; wrote ca. thirty-five operas, his second being an **afterpiece**, *The Flitch of Bacon* (1778), which made him famous. He particularly enjoyed fantasy and exoticism, and his operas include *The Mysteries of the Castle* (1795). He also wrote operas on historical and legendary subjects, e.g., *Richard, Coeur de Lion* (1786), freely adapted from the opera by **Grétry**, and *The Crusade* (1790). His most famous opera is *Rosina* (1782), a comic afterpiece **pasticcio** that incorporates Scots and Irish folk music; one of its tunes was used for "Auld Lang Syne," the poem by the Scottish poet Robert Burns (1759–1796).

Shostakovich, Dmitry (1906–1975) Russian composer of symphonies, concertos, other instrumental music, an operetta, and four operas: *Nos* (The Nose) (1927) (NO:S) and *Igroki* (1942) (ee GRO: kee), both based on stories by Ukrainian-born Russian author Nicolai Gogol (1809–1852); *Bol'shaya molniya* (The Big Lightning) (1931) (BOL shah yah MOL nyah); and ***Ledy Makbet Mtsentskovo uyezda (The Lady Macbeth of the Mtsensk District)***.

showboat *n.* A barge on which a long, low building was erected, housing an auditorium and stage for the presentation of plays, melodramas and/or variety entertainment; the barge was pushed along the waterway by a small, attached tugboat. In the 19th c., such craft plied the Mississippi and other rivers in the United States, docking at various landings along the way, and presenting spectacles for several evenings before moving on to the next venue, mostly during the summer months; hence, *boat show*: the entertainment presented on a showboat. The musical *Show Boat* inaccurately, if romantically depicts the craft as a majestic paddlewheel steamer.

Show Boat Broadway operetta by Jerome **Kern**; book and lyrics by Oscar **Hammerstein**, based on the novel *Show Boat* (1926) by Edna Ferber (1885–1968); Ziegfeld Theatre, 1927 (572 perf.). Broadway revivals: Casino Theatre, 1932 (180 perf.); Ziegfeld Theatre, 1946 (418 perf.); Uris Theatre, 1983 (78 perf.); George Gershwin Theatre, 1994 (959 perf.), Tony® Award–winning production, directed by Harold Prince; numerous revivals in many venues. Films: 1929, partially silent version (some spoken dialogue scenes; some soundtrack portions lost), with an eclectic background score partly taken from Kern; 1936; 1951.

The *Cotton Blossom*, captained by Andy Hawks, plies the Mississippi, bringing variety shows and melodrama to towns up and down the mighty river. Parthy, Captain Andy's stern wife, tries to keep their daughter, Magnolia, sheltered and protected from the show people, whom she considers mostly low class. Magnolia falls in love with a no-good gambler, Gaylord Ravenal, who comes on board. Julie La Verne, the leading lady, is married to the melodrama's leading man, Steve, but they are forced to leave when it is revealed that she has some black ancestry. Steve is white, and marriages between whites and blacks were illegal; nor is Julie allowed to work in a white entertainment venue. Magnolia and Gaylord take over the leading roles. With Captain Andy's help, they elope, and go to Chicago. Gaylord goes bankrupt and abandons Magnolia and their daughter, Kim. Magnolia gets a job singing in a nightclub, and her career is launched, thanks to Julie, who was the leading singer, but who generously quit after having heard Magnolia's audition, without ever revealing herself to Magnolia. Kim grows up to become a singing star herself, in the 1920s, and when Magnolia retires from the business and goes back to stay with her aging parents on the *Cotton Blossom*, she is reunited with the now elderly and much chastened Gaylord, who had seen their daughter's stage debut and was filled with remorse. On hand as well are the faithful African American, Joe, who has worked on the boat forever, and his wife, Queenie. As he well knows, the circumstances of life may change, but "Ol' Man River," "he just keeps rollin' along."

showgirl *n. Archaic.* A young lady member of the chorus in a musical comedy, esp. one dressed in a showy costume, as in the ***Ziegfeld Follies***.

Shrek the Musical Broadway musical by Jeanine Tesori (b. ca. 1961); book and lyrics by David Lindsay-Abaire (b. 1969), based on the film *Shrek* (2001), adapted from the children's book *Shrek!* (1990) by William Steig (1907–2003); Broadway Theatre, 2008 (441 perf.).

The embittered ogre Shrek, living alone in his swamp, finds it invaded by fairy tale characters exiled by the evil Lord Farquaad, who wants to become king, which he cannot do unless he marries a princess. Determining that Princess Fiona is the best candidate, Farquaad holds a lottery to find someone to rescue her from the castle where she has been imprisoned, under the guard of a ferocious dragon. When Shrek and his friend Donkey arrive to protest Farquaad's treatment of the fairy tale characters, Farquaad selects them to rescue her. Shrek and Donkey accept the mission, and, with the help of Puss in Boots, they free her from captivity. She turns out to be enchanted, and when the enchantment is lifted every night, Shrek sees that she is an ogre just like him. The two fall in love, are married, and become king and queen after they defeat Farquaad with the help of the fairy tale characters.

Siegfried The third opera in Wagner's **Ring cycle**.

sight-read; sight-sing *v. t.* To look at music for the first time, and play or sing it accurately without prior acquaintance with the score; esp. applied to vocal music sung without the help of an instrumental accompaniment; hence, *sight-reading*, *sight-singing*; useful and necessary in many situations, e.g., choral singing; jingle singing for commercials; rehearsing a new number for a show.

Silk Stockings Broadway musical by Cole **Porter**; book by George S. **Kaufman**, actress and writer Leueen McGrath (1914–1992) (muhk GRAW), and Abe **Burrows**, adapted from the film *Ninotchka* (1939); Imperial Theatre, 1955 (478 perf.); film, 1957. This was Porter's last, not terribly brilliant Broadway show.

Ninotchka, a cold, unapproachable Soviet official, goes to Paris on a mission to prevent the composer Boroff from defecting to Hollywood, and to take him back to Russia. She meets an American talent agent, Steve, and falls in love with him, and with Paris. She ends up defecting and going away with Steve.

sing *v. t.* To produce the voice in a controlled, sustained manner in order to perform music written or improvised for the voice; hence, *singing*: the art of doing this; *singer*: a performer of vocal music; a vocalist.

> See BELT; CHI PRONUNCIA BENE, CANTA BENE; LEGITIMATE SINGING; MUSICAL COMEDY; OPERA; OPERETTA; VOICE.

Singspiel (ZIHNG SHPEEL) *n.* [German: sing-play] *Hist.* In the 18th c. esp., a play with incidental music and songs; also, an opera with spoken dialogue, e.g., Mozart's *Die Zauberflöte*, *Die Entführung aus dem Serail*. A very popular genre in Hapsburg Vienna; the ancestor of Viennese operetta.

Sissle, Noble (1889–1975) American performer, writer, and lyricist; wrote *Shuffle Along* and five other shows with composer Eubie **Blake**.

Sitzprobe (ZIH:TS PRO: buh; —PROHB) *n.* [German: sit-rehearsal; sometimes called a *sitz*, for short] **1.** The first rehearsal of an opera with singers and orchestra, usually after the singers have memorized their parts; the piece is worked through with no stage movement or action. **2.** Any sit-down **rehearsal** of an opera without movement or action.

Slade, Julian (1930–2006) [b. Julian Penklvil Slade] English composer of ca. a dozen musical comedies, of which the most well known is the phenomenally successful *Salad Days* (1954), with 2283 perf. in the West End.

Smetana, Bedřich (1824–1884) (BEH dzhihkh SMEH tah nah) Czech composer of piano, chamber, and orchestral works; helped develop Czech national musical style, using folk motifs and songs; known for his majestic set of six symphonic poems, *Má Vlast* (My Country) (MAH VLAHST), (composed 1874–1879); wrote eight operas, including *Dalibor* (composed, 1865–1867) (DAH lee bo:r); *Libuše* (composed 1869–1872) (LIH: boo sheh); and *Prodaná Nevěsta (The Bartered Bride)*. Like Beethoven, Smetana lost his hearing; he resigned from his post as conductor at the Provisional Theatre in Prague in 1874, but continued to compose.

Smith, Harry B. (1860–1936) [Harry Bache Smith] American music and drama critic; phenomenally prolific writer of ca. 6000 song lyrics and 300 books for Broadway musicals, including those for *Robin Hood* by Reginald **de Koven**, Irving Berlin's *Watch Your Step*, and scripts for John Philip **Sousa**, Victor **Herbert** (including *Sweethearts*), Jerome **Kern**, Ivan **Caryll**, Ludwig **Englander**, and Sigmund **Romberg**. He also adapted for the Broadway stage works by Jacques **Offenbach**, and Viennese operettas by Oscar **Straus**, Emmerich **Kálmán**, and Franz **Lehár**. And he wrote numbers for the *Ziegfeld Follies*.

Smyth, Dame Ethel Mary (1858–1944) English composer; studied music in Germany; wrote six operas, including the highly regarded *Fantasio* (1895), and *The Wreckers* (1906), considered her greatest opera.

soft shoe A jazzy style of dancing in musical comedy or variety shows, using shoes that make a brushing sound during the dance. Cf. its opposite, **tap**.

solo *n., adj., adv.* [Italian: alone] —*n.* **1.** A number sung by one singer alone. **2.** A dance number for a single dancer. **3.** A piece, or a section of a piece, for one instrument: *an oboe solo*, e.g., in a symphony movement. —*adj.* **4.** Pertaining to music or dance performed by one person alone: *a solo song.* —*adv.* **5.** To sing, play, or dance alone by oneself: *to sing solo.*

Solomon, Edward (1855–1895) English composer of musical theater pieces; known also for his bigamous marriage to the American musical theater star Lillian Russell, which resulted in a scandalous divorce case. Of Solomon's forty musical comedies and comic operas, the notable successes were *Billee Taylor* (1880); and the highly successful *The Nautch Girl* (1891), produced by D'Oyly Carte at the Savoy Theatre, with a score that is pleasantly imitative of Sullivan.

See also ALLUSION.

Sondheim, Stephen (b. 1930) Innovative, award-winning American composer and lyricist; a phenomenon in the musical theater, known for his individuality and distinctive style of composition, which at times resembles the operatic. His lyrics for Jule Styne's ***Gypsy***, Bernstein's ***West Side Story***, and Richard Rodgers's *Do I Hear A Waltz* (1965) are masterpieces. He has also written film scores, and there have been several revues of his work, including *Side by Side by Sondheim* (1977).

Stephen Sondheim's major works as composer/lyricist:

1962 ***A Funny Thing Happened on the Way to the Forum***
1964 *Anyone Can Whistle*
1971 ***Company***
1971 ***Follies***
1973 ***A Little Night Music***
1976 ***Pacific Overtures***
1979 ***Sweeney Todd, The Demon Barber of Fleet Street***
1981 *Merrily We Roll Along*
1984 *Sunday in the Park with George*
1987 ***Into the Woods***
1990 *Assassins*
1994 *Passion*
2008 ***Road Show***

song *n.* A short, self-contained piece of vocal music that has a beginning, middle, and end, usually with several verses. There are many genres of song: the **art song**; folk songs, the composers of most of them being unknown; popular songs; and songs written as part of a musical comedy, some of which become popular out of context.

song and dance man *Archaic* **1.** A male musical comedy performer. **2.** A vaudeville performer with a musical act that included dance routines.

song and supper rooms *Hist.* In the 19th c., special rooms in pubs where variety entertainments were presented, for a small admission charge.

Song of Norway Broadway **pastiche** (def. 2) musical, with the music of Edvard Grieg (1843–1907) adapted by Robert Wright and George Forrest; book by Milton Lazarus, based on a play by producer-writer Homer Curran (1885–1952); Imperial Theatre, 1944 (860 perf.), after a successful run in CA; film, 1970.

The Norwegian composer Edvard Grieg is lured away from his wife Nina by sop. Louisa Giovanni. He goes to Italy with her, but his wife's love and the lure of his homeland prove stronger, and he returns to Norway.

song stylist A **vocalist** who sings in an intimate way; a nightclub singer who uses various techniques, esp. crooning and half talking, half singing to put across a number.

sonnambula, La (The Sleepwalking Maiden) (lah so:n' NAHM boo lah) Opera in two acts by Vincenzo **Bellini**; libretto by Felice **Romani**, based on a ballet-pantomime scenario by Eugène **Scribe**; Milan, Teatro Carcano, 1831.

Amina (ah MEE nah) (sop.), foster daughter of Teresa (teh REH: zah) (mezz.), the mill owner in a Swiss village, is engaged to the peasant Elvino (ehl VEE no:) (ten.). Lisa (LEE zah) (sop.), owner of the local inn, where the newly returned Count Rodolfo (ro: DO:L fo:) (bass) is temporarily lodging, is in love with Elvino. Amina is a sleepwalker—a fact unknown in the village—and one night she wanders into the Count's room, where she is found asleep in his bed. Lisa, although she has seen that nothing happened, implies that Amina and Rodolfo have been having an affair. Outraged and deeply upset, Elvino agrees to marry Lisa, despite the Count's explanations. Everyone suddenly sees Amina walking in her sleep on the roof of the mill. Realizing his error, Elvino forgives her, and she awakens in his arms.

soprano *n.* The highest-pitched female singing voice. There are also boy sopranos. A *lyric* or *spinto* soprano has a lighter voice than a *dramatic* soprano. A **coloratura** soprano is one who specializes in the technique of singing the florid ornamentations in the music found, for instance, in 19th-c. **bel canto** opera.

soubrette (soo BREHT), *n.* **1.** The light **ingénue** role in a play, opera, or operetta of a pert, perky, lively, clever, and sometimes impertinent young lady, esp. a lady's maid or serving girl. **2.** The actress or singer who plays such a role.

soul music Of African-American origin, this largely vocal music is a secular outgrowth of gospel music, combined with the rhythm and blues of popular songs. It is one of the idioms used in some Broadway musicals. Soul includes improvisational elements and, often, plastic body movements and handclapping during performance. It began particularly in the inner city ghetto areas of Chicago, Detroit, New York, and Memphis. One of its inventors and greatest practitioners was Ray Charles (1930–2004).

sound design In the theater, the strategic placement of microphones, amplifiers, and loudspeakers in order to create the desired audio effect, and to have the actors and musicians heard evenly all over the auditorium; the job of a *sound designer*, who is also responsible for checking the level and quality of the acoustics, dealing with actors' personal body or head mikes, and arranging such special effects as the rumbling of thunder in a storm scene.

Sound of Music, The Broadway musical by **Rodgers and Hammerstein**: music by Richard **Rodgers**; lyrics by Oscar **Hammerstein**; book by **Lindsay and Crouse**, based on the autobiography *The Story of the Trapp Family Singers* (1954) by Austrian-born American singer Maria von Trapp (1905–1987); Lunt-Fontanne Theatre, 1959 (1448 perf.); Broadway revival: Martin Beck Theatre, 1998 (571 perf.); many regional revivals; film, 1965; the original stage show starred Mary Martin, and the film starred Julie Andrews.

Maria Rainer, a postulant at the abbey at Nonnberg, Austria, is not considered the best candidate for the religious order, so she is sent away to be governess to the seven children of the widowed Captain von Trapp, who is engaged to Elsa Schrader. Maria teaches the children to sing, and they form a family singing group. Von Trapp, meanwhile, has fallen in love with her. When the Nazis occupy Austria in 1938, Elsa and the Captain disagree over how to respond, and break off their engagement. He marries Maria, and, finding himself ordered to report for naval duty under the Nazis, flees with her and the children from a music festival where they are performing. They escape over the mountains to Switzerland.

Sousa, John Philip (1854–1932) Popular American conductor, bandmaster, and composer; known as "The March King" for his many famous marches, including *The Stars and Stripes Forever* (1896). His nine musical theater pieces include *Désirée* (1884), produced in Washington, DC and set in the Paris of the Three Musketeers; *El Capitan* (1896), first produced in Boston, starring DeWolf Hopper; and ***Chris and the Wonderful Lamp*** (1899/1900), with a book by Glen **MacDonough**.

South Pacific Broadway musical by **Rodgers and Hammerstein**: music by Richard **Rodgers**; book by Oscar **Hammerstein** and Joshua Logan, who also directed, based on two stories from *Tales of the South Pacific* (1947) by James Michener (1907–1997); Majestic Theatre, 1949 (1925 perf.); Broadway revival: Vivian Beaumont Theatre, 2008 (still running as of this writing); film, 1958.

This is one of Rodgers and Hammerstein's masterpieces, and a landmark in the American musical theater. The theme of racism and its consequences is movingly dealt with. There were some cities in the South that would not book the show because of the song "You've Got to Be Taught," which makes the point that prejudice, always unnatural, is instilled at an early age. The show was notable also for the performances of Mary Martin as Nellie Forbush and celebrated opera basso Ezio Pinza, making his Broadway debut as Emile de Becque.

The Allies are stationed in the South Pacific islands during World War Two. Navy nurse Nellie Forbush falls in love with a French émigré gentleman planter, Emile, whose Polynesian wife has died, leaving him to raise their two children. Lieutenant Cable arrives to prepare for a dangerous mission to monitor Japanese fleet movements from a remote island, and he falls in love with the Polynesian girl

Liat, daughter of Bloody Mary. Emile proposes marriage, but Nellie rejects him, because of her prejudices. Cable leaves Liat, because he feels he cannot take her with him to America and his bigoted, upper-class family. In despair, Emile volunteers to accompany Joe on the mission. Cable is killed, but Emile manages to make his way back to the island. Nellie, who has overcome her prejudices and decided that she adores his children, is overjoyed to see him, and accepts his proposal.

Spamalot Broadway musical by absurdist comedy team Monty Python regular Eric Idle (b. 1943) and John Du Prez (b. 1946); book and lyrics by Idle, based on the film *Monty Python and the Holy Grail* (1975); Shubert Theatre, 2005 (1609 perf.).

This hilariously silly show is a parody of musicals, movies, movie musicals, and the story of King Arthur and the Knights of the Round Table. It might have been called "Spoofalot," were it not for the punning reminder of Camelot and Spam luncheon meat.

King Arthur, his well known knights, and his squire, Patsy, set off in quest of the Holy Grail. They get nowhere fast, until they are helped by the Lady of the Lake, who is unaccountably borrowed from the epic poem by Sir Walter Scott. They may not find the Grail, but Arthur and the Lady end up in each other's arms.

speaking role A character in an opera or other musical theater piece who does not sing, but whose role consists of spoken lines only; e.g., the jailer Frosch in *Die Fledermaus*.

Spewack, Samuel (1899–1971) and Bella (1890–1990) American husband and wife play- and screenwriting team, who also wrote the books for several musicals, among them *Leave It to Me!* and *Kiss Me Kate* by Cole **Porter**.

split *n.* In dance, to land with the legs as wide apart as possible, with one stretched full length forward of the body and the other stretched full length out behind it.

See also JUMP SPLIT.

Spohr, Ludwig (1784–1859) (SHPO:[*R*]) [also called Louis Spohr] German violinist and composer of ten operettas and operas, including *Faust*; *Zémire und Azor* (1819), on the same subject as the opera by **Grétry**; and his most famous opera, *Jessonda* (1823) (yehs SO:N dah). He was the first major composer to support **Wagner** artistically.

Spontini, Gaspare (1774–1851) (gah SPAH reh: spon TEE nee) Important, highly influential Italian composer of twenty-four operas, some of them revised several times. He moved from Italy to the Paris of Napoleon, where he taught singing, and produced his first operas at the Théâtre Italien. His masterpiece is *La vestale*, which was first performed due to the good offices of his patron, the Empress Josephine. After its triumphant reception, Napoleon commissioned him to write a propagandistic opera to popularize the Spanish Peninsula campaign, and in 1809 Spontini composed the stirring, melodramatic *Fernand Cortez* (fehr nahn' ko:*r* TEHZ), about the conquest of Mexico; recording of a live 1951 performance, in Italian, as *Fernando Cortez*, available from IDIS (6441/42; 2004).

spotting *n.* In dance, selecting a particular place or object a bit above eye level to focus on when doing a series of turns, so that balance is maintained and dizziness avoided. The dancer snaps the head forward at each turn, and refocuses on the chosen object.

Sprechstimme (SHP*REKH* SHTIH muh) *n.* [German: speak-voice] Half singing, half speaking, similar to **recitative**; used in opera, or in the delivery of a song by an actor who does not sing it fully but who half speaks it on pitch; e.g., Professor Higgins' "Why Can't the English?" in Lerner and Loewe's *My Fair Lady*. Also called *Sprechgesang* (SHP*REHKH* geh ZAHNG) [German: speak-sing].

Spring Awakening Broadway musical by Duncan Sheik (b. 1969); book and lyrics by Steven Sater, based on the expressionistic play *Frühlings Erwachen* (Spring's Awakening) (written 1890–1891; premiere 1906) (F*RÜ* lihngs ehr VAH khehn), by German dramatist Frank Wedekind (1864–1918) (VEH: duh KIHNT) [b. Benjamin Franklin Wedekind]; Eugene O'Neill Theatre, 2006 (887 perf.).

Among the sexually confused adolescents in a small German town is Moritz, who does badly in school and ends up committing suicide out of his sexual misery and frustration, while the iconoclastic Melchior and the naïve Wendla indulge their passions. She becomes pregnant, and she dies during an abortion procedure. The ghosts of Moritz and Wendla haunt Melchior as he grows to manhood.

square dance An American dance for couples, who face each other in groups of two couples; also, a dance event, originating in rural areas but also popular urban settings, in which such groups go through the moves announced by a "caller" while the music plays. The moves at such an event include other kinds of dance formations, e.g., reels, line dances, and circle dances. The square dance is featured in some American musicals, e.g., *Oklahoma!*

staccato (stahk KAH to:) *adj.* [Italian: detached] Disconnected; detached one from another; separate; hence, *staccato mark*: a performance mark consisting of dots over a series of notes, showing that they are to be played or sung disconnectedly, one after the other.

stage band A group of instrumentalists that performs in costume on stage, acting the role of musicians as part of a show, e.g., the uniformed martial band that precedes the entrance of the peers in act 1 of Gilbert and Sullivan's *Iolanthe*, or the military band in Offenbach's *La Grande-Duchesse de Gérolstein*.

stagione season (stah DGO: neh:) [Italian: season] An opera company's organization of its annual season, with productions succeeding each other, as opposed to being performed in **rotating rep**.

Stanford, Sir Charles Villiers (1852–1924) Irish composer resident in England; studied in Dublin, Leipzig, and Berlin; influential composition teacher at the

Royal College of Music in London; composed symphonies, piano and violin concertos, a series of six Irish Rhapsodies, chamber music, choral and sacred works, and ten operas, including *Shamus O'Brien*, his greatest success.

stanza *n.* A verse, i.e., a discreet division of a poem, hymn, or song.

Stein, Joseph (b. 1912) American playwright, film, and television writer; best known for his book for *Fiddler on the Roof*; also wrote the books for *Plain and Fancy* and several other musicals.

Stein, Leo (1861–1921) (LEH: o: SHTIN) [b. Leon Rosenstein (LEH: on *RO* zehn SHTIN)] Austrian librettist, known esp. for his texts to *Wiener Blut* (in collaboration with Viktor **Léon**) by Johann **Strauss**; *Csárdásfürstin (The Csárdás Princess)* (in collaboration with Béla Jenbach) by Emmerich **Kálmán**; *Die lustige Witwe, Die (The Merry Widow)* (in collaboration with Viktor Léon) and *Der Graf von Luxemburg (The Count of Luxembourg)* (in collaboration with A. M. **Willner** and Robert Bodanzky) by Franz **Lehár**; and *Polenblut* (Polish Blood) by Oscar **Nedbal**.

step *n., v.* —*n.* **1.** A single, completed move with the foot, consisting of lifting the foot and putting it down again in a different place. A dance step is one movement in a rhythmic, patterned series of such moves, perhaps accompanied by arm movement; hence, *in step*: doing the moves in the correct pattern and rhythm; *out of step*: not keeping in time to the rhythm of a dance; not moving in conformity to its established pattern. **2.** In music, the interval between two notes. —*v. i.* **3.** To move with the feet: *to step in time to the dance*.

Stewart, Michael (1924–1987) American playwright; wrote books for many musicals, including *Hello, Dolly!*, *Mack and Mabel*, and *The Grand Tour*, all with music by Jerry Herman, as well as *Barnum*, *42nd Street*, *Bye Bye Birdie*, and co-wrote the book for *George M.!*

step ball change In **dance**, an often used transitional **combination**, consisting of shifting the weight from one foot to the other; e.g., keeping the weight on the left foot, stepping out on the right foot, then shifting the weight to the right foot.

stock *n.* Usually, summer theater; short for *summer stock*, although winter stock also exists. In *one-week stock* theaters, a resident company is hired for the season and rehearses a musical comedy or play for a week while performing another in the evening or at matinees. Some summer stock theaters are star **package** houses.

Stolz, Robert (1880–1975) (SHTO:LTS) Austrian conductor and prolific stage and film composer, with ca. ninety Viennese operettas to his credit, some in collaboration with other composers; more than a dozen were filmed; studied with **Humperdinck**. He is known for his contributions to *Im weissen Rössl (The White Horse Inn)* and for a number of other operettas, among them *Venus in Seide* (Venus in Silk) (1932) (VEH: noos ihn ZI deh); and *Die Tanzgräfin* (The Dance Countess) (1921) (dee TAHNTS GREH fih:n). During the Nazi period, Stolz, a committed and courageous anti-Nazi, helped persecuted Jews escape over the border by driving them hidden in his car, and giving autographs to border guards who were dazzled by his fame. He left Vienna for Zurich and Paris, and then for the United States, where he composed film scores, returning to Europe after the war, in 1946. Stolz spent the rest of his life in Vienna, where he was much honored.

Stone, Peter (b.) Tony® Award–winning American writer, known for his books for such musicals as *1776* and *Two by Two*.

Straus, Oscar (1870–1954) (O:S kah*r* SHT*R*OWS; English pron.: STROWS) [b. Strauss; dropped second "s" to avoid confusion with Johann Strauss and family, to whom he was not related] Brilliant Austrian composer of some fifty operettas, as well as chamber music, songs, piano pieces, many film scores; noted conductor; studied with Max **Bruch**. His most famous work in the English-speaking world is *Der tapfere Soldat* (The Brave Solider) (1908) (deh[*r*] TAHP fuh *r*uh zo:l DAHT), adapted from George Bernard Shaw's comedy *Arms and the Man*. Its usual English title is *The Chocolate Soldier*; in German, it is also known as *Der Praliné-Soldat* (The Praline Soldier) (deh[*r*] prah' lee NÉ zo:l DAHT). His series of "waltz-operettas" include the masterpiece *Ein Walzertraum* (A Waltz Dream) (1907) (In VAHL tseh:[*r*] T*R*OWM), with a gorgeous, melodious score and a rather pedestrian if charming triangular love story by librettist Leopold Jacobson (1878–1943), who was murdered by the Nazis at Theresienstadt; *Der letzte Walzer* (The Last Waltz) (1922) (deh[*r*] LEHTS tuh VAHL tsuh[*r*]); and *Drei Walzer* (Three Waltzes) (1935) (D*R*I VAHL tseh[*r*]). *Die Perlen der Cleopatra* (Cleopatra's Pearls) (1923) (dee PEH[*R*] lehn deh[*r*] KLEH: o: PAH t*r*ah) is sentimental and hilarious, with its mixture of heady, romantic Viennese ballads, waltzes, and faux-Egyptian minor-key passages; there are also a couple of positively **Offenbachian** songs in this work. Straus's first operetta, *Die lustigen Nibelungen*, is a satiric and musical masterpiece. In 1939, he was able to escape the Nazi persecution of the Jews, and he spent the war years in Hollywood, returning to Europe afterwards.

Strauss family (SHT*R*OWS; English pron.: STROWS) Austrian musical family that produced several famous composers; known for waltzes, polkas, other dance music, and marches. Every New Year's Day in Vienna, where they lived and worked, there is a gala celebration using their music. The dynasty was begun by **Johann Strauss I (1804–1849)** [Also known as Johann Strauss the Elder, Johann Strauss, Sr.], famous for his waltzes and march music. His parents were innkeepers, and there was no doubt a lively musical atmosphere at the inn. Because he had a Jewish grandfather, **Johann Michael Strauss (1720–1800)**, a Catholic convert, the Nazis, in their delusional psychosis, considered banning all the music written by the Strauss family, but that would have created more complications than they wished to deal with. The son of Johann Strauss I, **Johann Strauss II (1825–1899)** [Also known as Johann Strauss the Younger, Johann Strauss, Jr.], became one of the most famous and beloved Austrian composers, known for his sparkling waltzes and his superbly crafted, melodious operettas, among them *Die Fledermaus*; *Der Zigeunerbaron*; his first operetta, the delightfully tuneful *Indigo* *und die vierzig Räuber* (Indigo and the Forty Thieves) (1871) (IHN dee go: *oo*nt dee FEE[*R*] tsih*kh R*OY buh); the romantic, gorgeously melodious *Das Spitzentuch der Königin* (The Queen's Lace Handkerchief) (1880) (dahs SHPIHT sehn T*OO*KH deh[*r*] KÖ nih gihn); *Wiener Blut* (Vienna Blood) (1899) (VEE nuh BLOOT), libretto by Viktor **Léon** and Leo **Stein**; and *Eine Nacht in Venedig* (One Night in Venice) (1883) (I nuh NAHKHT ihn veh NEH: di*kh*), libretto by Richard **Genée** and Friedrich **Zell**. His brother, **Josef Strauss (1827–1870)**, was a conductor and composer of many waltzes and other dance music. The third brother, **Eduard Strauss (1835–1916)**, was a major conductor with his own orchestra, the Strauss Orchestra, for which Victor **Herbert** played cello for a time, and a composer of dozens of waltzes, polkas, and other dance music. Eduard's son, **Johann Strauss III (1866–1939)**, continued the family tradition, composing a few operettas and instrumental music, but was known more as a conductor than as a composer.

See also GREAT WALTZ, THE.

Strauss, Richard (1864–1949) (*R*IH: *kh*a[*r*]t SHT*R*OWS) Highly influential, late-romantic German conductor and composer of orchestral, chamber, and vocal music; the leading German opera composer of the 20th c. Much influenced by Wagner's music, Strauss is known for his brilliantly textured, atmospheric orchestrations. His fifteen operas include *Arabella*, *Ariadne auf Naxos*, *Der Rosenkavalier*, *Salome* (1905), *Elektra* (1909), *Die Frau ohne Schatten* (The Woman without a Shadow) (1919) (dee F*R*OW O: neh SHAH tehn), *Intermezzo* (1924), *Die ägyptische Helena* (The Egyptian Helen) (1928) (dee eh: GÜP tih sheh heh LEH: nah), and *Daphne* (1938). Strauss was a controversial figure: Under the Nazi government, he was held up as one of the regime's cultural icons. He was not a very political person, certainly not a Nazi, and he was deliberately placed in an untenable, threatened position that was tantamount to blackmail, because he had to protect his Jewish daughter-in-law and his grandchildren. In the end, even they were placed under house arrest from early 1944 on, for the duration of the war. The Nazis would have preferred to place the overtly nationalist Hans Pfitzner (1869–1949) (PFIHTS nuh) at the head of the musical establishment, but even he had associations with Jewish musicians, esp. the conductor Bruno Walter (1876–1962)—who escaped to America—that the Nazis found unacceptable; and Pfitzner ultimately spoke out against the Nazis, and was dismissed from his posts. One must conclude that Strauss collaborated with the regime as little as he possibly could. He had even composed an opera, *Friedenstag* (Day of Peace) (1938) (F*R*EE dehns TAHK), that could be interpreted as pacifist.

Stravinsky, Igor (1882–1971) Innovative, influential, iconoclastic, sometimes controversial Russian-born American composer of instrumental works, ballets, and six operas; studied with **Rimsky-Korsakov**. His operas include *The Nightingale* (1908), his first; *The Rake's Progress*; and the opera-oratorio *Oedipus Rex*.

Street Scene Broadway opera by Kurt **Weill**; book by Elmer Rice (1892–1967), based on his 1929 Pulitzer Prize–winning play; lyrics by Harlem Renaissance poet Langston Hughes (1902–1967); Adelphi Theatre, 1947 (148 perf.).

308

Weill's score is eclectic and engrossing, and ranges from the operatic to jazzy Broadway musical styles, with some snazzy dances. There is also a great variety of characters, all beautifully written. The piece is quite effective on stage, and very moving, as director Jay Lesenger's riveting productions at the Manhattan School of Music and the Chautauqua Opera, both in 2008, amply showed. But the grim story did not appeal to audiences at its original production, and the score's operatic demands ultimately made it material for revival by opera companies, rather than summer stock.

On a terribly hot day, a group of New Yorkers—a cross-section of the 1930s population, including natives and immigrants from Germany, Sweden, Russia, and Italy—are out on the street in front of their building, where it is cooler than in their baking apartments. The bookish Sam Kaplan (ten.) is in love with Rose (sop.), a secretary, daughter of the jealous, angry stagehand Mr. Maurrant (bass-bar.), who keeps a strict eye on her and is abusive to his wife, Anna (sop.). She is having an affair with the milk bill collector (speaking role), and all the neighbors gossip about it, except Sam, who can't stand such behavior. His socialist immigrant father (ten.) gets into political arguments with his more conservative neighbors. Mr. Maurrant suspects Anna, but does not really know what is going on. One day, when he is supposed to leave for an unexpectedly postponed out of town tryout in New Haven, he comes home to find the two lovers in his apartment. He goes berserk and shoots them.

strike up To begin playing; hence, the instruction to *strike up the band*: let the musicians start playing.

Strike Up the Band Broadway musical by George **Gershwin**; lyrics by Ira Gershwin; book by George S. **Kaufman**, revised by Morrie Ryskind; Times Square Theatre, 1930 (191 perf.); film. 1940, much altered from the stage show.

This political satire concerns a potential war between the U.S. and Switzerland over tariffs on imported Swiss cheese. The war is desired by the American chocolate maker Horace J. Fletcher, to boost his sales, and he even wants to have the war named after him, since he proposes to underwrite it. By the time his daughter Joan's fiancé, Jim Townsend, blackmails him into turning pacifist, it is too late: America has already won the war, and is now contemplating going to war with the USSR over caviar.

strophic *adj.* Applies to a number or aria in which the same music is sung for each verse, e.g., many folk songs, serenades, patter songs in **Gilbert and Sullivan**.

Strouse, Charles American Broadway musical composer. See ADAMS, LEE AND CHARLES STROUSE.

Stuart, Leslie (1863–1928) English composer and lyricist of music hall songs and musical comedies, best known for the smash hit, *Florodora*. He contributed numbers to revues and later performed his own songs, accompanying himself on the piano. But, tragically, having become an alcoholic, Stuart went downhill and never achieved anything like the success of *Florodora* again. He went through the bankruptcy courts, although revivals of his hit did generate some income for him, and spent the remainder of his life unsuccessfully trying to have other works of his produced.

Student Prince, The Broadway "musical play" (operetta) by Sigmund **Romberg**; book and lyrics by Dorothy **Donnelly**, based on the play *Alt Heidelberg* (Old Heidelberg) (1903) (AHLT HI duhl beh[*r*]k) by Wilhelm Meyer Förster (1882–1934) (FÖ[*R*] stuh); Jolson's 59th Street Theatre, 1924 (608 perf.); Broadway revivals: Majestic Theatre, 1931 (42 perf.); Broadway Theatre, 1943 (153 perf.); numerous other revivals, tours, and summer productions; film, 1954.

This is one of Romberg's best and most cherished works. Among its famous numbers are the rousing drinking song, "Drink! Drink! Drink!" and the enthralling love song, "Serenade (Overhead the Moon Is Beaming)."

Prince Karl-Franz (ten.), his pompous valet, Lutz (ten.), and his tutor, Dr. Engel (bar.), are staying at The Three Apples, an inn in Heidelberg, while the prince pursues his studies in the last year before he is to ascend the throne. The inn is a gathering place for students, and everyone drinks and makes merry. Karl-Franz falls in love with the waitress Kathie (sop.), but their romance is cut short when the old king dies and the prince must return home to be crowned and to marry Princess Margaret (mezz.). He cannot forget the girl he truly loves, and he returns surreptitiously to Heidelberg, where he and Kathie bid each other a fond farewell, vowing to remember always what they have meant to each other.

style *n.* **1.** In musical performance, in musical theater presentation and performance, and in singing, a distinctive, characteristic way of dealing with the music of a particular kind of piece; also, with regard to the period in which it was written; e.g., 18th-c. opera, as opposed to the operas of **Puccini**; Broadway musical comedy, as opposed to Viennese operettas. See also AUTHENTICITY. **2.** In **dance**, the particular, distinctive approach to and manner of execution of the steps, combinations, and patterns; e.g., classical **ballet**, as opposed to modern, interpretive dance, or the kind of show dancing seen in Broadway musicals. **3.** In acting, a distinctive, characteristic way or mode of behaving or comporting oneself in accordance with the requirements of a particular play, such as a farce, as opposed to a drama; or a realistic modern prose play as opposed to an Elizabethan verse tragedy: *acting style*. **4.** The characteristic way of behaving in a particular historical epoch: *period style*, which includes how the actor wears costumes, makeup, and such special hairpieces as wigs, how one moves and gestures, etc. Acting and period styles are inextricably connected. For more on the subject, see my book *Using the Stanislavsky System: A Practical Guide to Character Creation and Period Styles* (Limelight, 2008).

Styne, Jule (1905–1994) [b. Jules Kerwin Stein] Prolific English-born American film and stage composer and producer; wrote scores to more than twenty Broadway musicals, including *High Button Shoes* (1948), *Gentlemen Prefer Blondes*, *Bells Are Ringing*, *Do Re Mi* (1960), *Fade Out-Fade In* (1964), *Hallelujah, Baby!* (1967), *Funny Girl*, *Peter Pan*, and *Gypsy*.

Sullivan, Sir Arthur Seymour (1842–1900) Anglo-Irish composer of hymns, oratorios, and other religious music and of musical theater pieces, best known for the **Gilbert and Sullivan** series of fourteen comic operas he composed to libretti by playwright W. S. **Gilbert**. He also wrote comic operas with other librettists, as well as instrumental music, ballets, and one opera, *Ivanhoe*, based on Sir Walter Scott's novel; one symphony, called the "Irish"; and **incidental music** for actor-manager Henry Irving's (1838–1905) productions of Shakespeare's *Macbeth* and *The Merchant of Venice*.

See also SAVOY OPERAS.

supernumerary *n.* A background player or extra, esp. in an opera company, where they sometimes supplement the chorus, particularly in large-scale spectacle operas. At the New York City Opera, they are called *character mimes.* Called *super*, for short.

Suppé, Franz von (1819–1895) (FRAHNTS fuhn zoo PÉ) Croatian-born Austrian conductor, opera singer, and composer of ca. forty tuneful operettas full of charm, elegance and fluidity, including his masterpiece, ***Boccaccio***; *Die schöne Galathée* (The Beautiful Galathea) (1865) (dee SHÖ neh gah' lah TÉ); and *Die leichte Kavallerie* (Light Cavalry) (1866) (dee LIKH teh kah' vahl uh REE). The overture to the latter, as well as to the operettas *Ein Morgen, ein Mittag, eine Nacht in Wien* (Morning, Noon and Night in Vienna) (1844) (In MAW[R] gehn In MIH tahk I neh NAKHT ihn VEEN) and *Dichter und Bauer* (Poet and Peasant) (1846) (DIH:*KH* tuh *oo*nt BOW uh), are extremely well known and often played at pops concerts.

support *n., v.* —*n.* **1.** The use of the diaphragmatic muscle in sending the breath from the lungs when singing or speaking on stage. **2.** Backup or background accompaniment to a lead vocalist in a popular singing group, or choral background accompaniment for a lead singer or singers in an oratorio or other piece of music. —*v. t.* **3.** To use the diaphragm in the way just described: *to support the voice.* **4.** To back up or accompany a lead singer or singers, in the performance of either a popular or classical piece: *The chorus supported the soprano for her aria.*

Sweeney Todd, The Demon Barber of Fleet Street Broadway musical by Stephen **Sondheim** (music and lyrics); book by Hugh **Wheeler**, based on the legendary character in 19th-c. penny dreadful serials, as adapted in 1973 by English playwright Christopher Bond; Uris Theater, 1979 (557 perf.); Broadway revivals: Circle in the Square Theatre, 1989 (235 perf.); Eugene O'Neill Theatre, scaled-down version, 2005 (384 perf.); film, 2007, brilliantly directed by Tim Burton (b. 1958).

The dark and brooding score that supports this creepy, eerie, Grand Guignol story has been considered operatic, and several opera companies have produced it. The original production was superbly directed by Harold Prince on a startlingly abstract, multi-level set with projections of grimy Victorian London in the background. Angela Lansbury was a wonderful Mrs. Lovett, and Len Cariou (b. 1939) created the role of the barber.

The vicious Judge Turpin, who lusts after barber Benjamin Barker's wife, Lucy, has Barker sent to prison on a trumped-up charge. Years later, Barker is released, and, vowing revenge, he returns to London under the name Sweeney Todd. He finds that Turpin has the guardianship of Johanna, Todd's daughter, who is in love with a handsome sailor, Anthony Hope, with whom she wants to elope. Todd meets Mrs. Lovett, who befriends him, and he sets up a barbershop on the floor above her pie shop, which is doing poorly because of the high cost of meat. He soon gains a reputation for being excellent at his work. When Turpin comes to his shop, Todd is working up the nerve to cut his throat, but he is interrupted. The now crazed barber cooks up a scheme to supply Mrs. Lovett with meat, to which she readily agrees, because she is madly in love with him: He will cut the throats of his unwary customers, and, by means of a mechanical barber chair, tip them down into the cellar. The plan works to perfection, and the pies are devoured by eager Londoners. Todd lures Turpin back into his chair under the pretense of helping him to prevent the elopement of Johanna and Hope, and finally cuts his throat. Among Todd's other victims is a beggar woman, whom he had not recognized as Lucy, his wife. The jealous Mrs. Lovett had known all along that the woman was Lucy, but had kept it a secret from Todd. When he discovers Lucy's body in the cellar, and realizes what has happened, the enraged barber throws Mrs. Lovett into the baking ovens. The poor distraught waif Toby, who has adored her ever since she had taken him in, emerges from the corner where he has been cowering, and cuts Todd's throat.

Sweet Adeline Broadway musical by Jerome **Kern**; book and lyrics by Oscar **Hammerstein**; Hammerstein's Theatre, 1929 (234 perf.); film, 1935.

The score contains two hit songs, the title number and "Why Was I Born?" which became the signature tune of the show's star, singer Helen Morgan (1900–1941), who had played Julie in *Show Boat*. Unfortunately, the show was forced to close when the stock market crashed two months into the run.

The year is 1898. Adeline, whom everyone calls Addie, works at her family's beer garden in Hoboken, NJ, and she is in love with Tom. But he jilts her for her sister, Nellie. She crosses the river to New York and pursues a show business career. She makes it big, thanks to the financial support of her wealthy friend, Jimmy, whom she marries. But does she really love him? She is not sure, and his family is horrible to her, so she ends up leaving him for the playwright Sid Barnett.

Sweet Bye and Bye, The Opera in two acts by Jack **Beeson**; libretto by poet, performer, editor, and writer, Kenward Elmslie (b. 1929); 1956. As the composer says in a note written in 1995 and appended to the libretto included in a re-release of the 1974 recording that he supervised (Citadel; CT-DOS-2000), this opera is "a serious piece about the misuse of belief, the fleecing of the gullible for private gain." He concludes, "Our Sister Rose Ora Easter is but a later version of the **Bellini/Romani** *Norma* and **Puccini**/Sforzano *Suor Angelica*."

The opera, a parody based on the life of 1920s and '30s evangelist Aimee Semple McPherson (1890–1944), is set in Atlantic City against a background of religious revivalism.

The inspiration behind the Lifeshine Mission League, Sister Rose Ora Easter (sop.), is mourned by the members, led by Mother Rainey (mezz.), for she has gone to her final rest, having drowned in the ocean. The scene changes to a luxurious suite in a New York hotel, where Billy Wilcox is having an affair with Sister Rose, who had faked her drowning. The guilty Sister Gladys, who knows Sister Rose's secret, betrays her, and she and Mother Rainey go to the hotel to take Rose away from her life of sin. Mother Rainey has also discovered that $30,000 is missing, and now realizes that Rose has taken it, but Rose says it is hers by right. She returns to her flock, who all adore her, and will never believe she has done any wrong. Rose gives sermons about how she was kidnapped and miraculously released. She carries on in secret with Billy while publicly curing the incurable. At the end, the money rolls in, and the members of the Lifeshine Mission continue to worship her.

Sweet Charity Broadway musical by Cy **Coleman**.

Sweethearts Broadway operetta by Victor **Herbert**; book by Harry B. **Smith** and French-born American journalist and librettist Fred de Grésac (1866–1943) [Frédérique Rosine de Grésac (freh dé reek' ro zeen' duh gré SAHK); wife of bar. Victor Maurel]; New Amsterdam Theatre, 1913 (136 perf.); Broadway revivals: Jolson's 59th Street Theatre, 1929 (17 perf.); Shubert Theatre, 1947 (288 perf.); film, 1938, with Jeannette MacDonald and Nelson Eddy.

The unintentionally silly story unfolds against the background of one of Herbert's most romantic scores: The baby princess Sylvia of Zilania, spirited away to Bruges in order to keep her safe while war rages, has been raised by the laundress Mother Goose. All grown up, she meets Prince Franz, heir to Zilania's throne, who is traveling incognito. They fall in love, and after a series of attempts by various villains to keep them apart, they discover each other's identities and go off to get married and rule Zilania together.

See also ARDITI, LUIGI.

Swift, Kay (1897–1993) American composer; protégée and friend of George **Gershwin**; contributed numbers to the *Garrick Gaieties*; first woman to compose a complete score for a Broadway musical (her only one), *Fine and Dandy* (1930).

swing *n.* **1.** A member of a musical comedy chorus who covers the dance tracks of different members and substitutes for any of them if someone is absent, often earning extra pay for each track. **2.** A kind of jazz with a smoothly rhythmic beat that admits of dancing, very popular in dance halls during the 1930s.

swing the beat 1. To vary the rhythm of a piece of music, departing from the exact beat in which it is written, i.e., making a long beat, such as a dotted quarter note, slightly longer, and other beats slightly shorter; a kind of **rubato**. Also called *leaning on the beat*. **2.** The direction to do this, given by the conductor to instrumentalists and singers. **3.** To bring out the dissonance in a piece before arriving at the resolution.

T

tableau *n. pl.* tableaux [Fr. French: picture] **1.** [short for *tableau vivant* (tah BLO: vee VAH:*N*): living picture] A silent stage picture, like a living, three-dimensional painting, formed by actors freezing in poses or attitudes, singly and in groups, indicating the opening or climactic action in a scene; often utilized in 19th- and early 20th-c. staging, esp. at the beginning or end of a scene or at the end of an act, esp. in opera. **2.** A long scene in a French opera, e.g., ***Pelléas et Mélisande***, ***Le Roi Carotte***.

Tales of Hoffmann, The Opera by Jacques **Offenbach**. See CONTES D'HOFFMANN, LES.

Tambo; Brudder [Brother] Tambo *Hist.* In a **minstrel show**, the performer who sat on the end of the semicircle opposite the end where the **Bones** sat, and played the tambourine. He and the Bones exchanged witty sallies and repartee with the **Interlocutor**.

tambourin (tah*n* boo *RAN*) *n.* [French] A Provençal dance in 2/4 time, done to the beat of a cylindrical, two-headed Provençal drum called a *tambourin*; esp. popular in the 18th c. The drum player is also called a *tambourin*.

Tancredi (tahn KREH: dee) Opera in two acts by Gioachino **Rossini**; libretto by Gaetano **Rossi**, based on Voltaire's play *Tancrède* (1760) (tah*n* K*R*EHD) and Torquato Tasso's epic poem *Gerusalemme Liberata*; Venice, Teatro La Fenice, 1813.

This work made Rossini famous world-wide, and the **cabaletta** "Di tanti palpiti" (From So Much Agitation) (dee TAHN tee PAHL pee tee) was so popular that it was said judges had to stop its being whistled in the Venetian law courts; Rossini called it his *aria dei risi* (AH ree ah deh:'ee REE zee), "rice aria," because he said he wrote it in the time it took him to boil a pot of rice—but he was probably not serious.

In the 11th c., the general Tancredi (mezz.) returns from enforced exile in time to prevent the marriage of his beloved Amenaide (ah mehn' ah EE deh) (sop.) to Obrazzano (o:' braht TSAH no:) (bass). She is accused of treasonous correspondence with the Saracens, and will be executed unless a champion fights for her. Although he believes her guilty, Tancredi becomes her champion, defeats her accusers, and is victorious over the Saracens. He learns that Amenaide is innocent, and they are happily reunited.

tango *n.* A slow, sensual, South American dance in 2/4 time; of African origin, esp. associated with Argentina; it originated in Buenos Aires in the 1860s, and by the 1920s was popular in dance halls worldwide; used in ballets and such musical theater pieces as Brecht and Weill's ***Die Dreigroschenoper (The Threepenny Opera)*** and ***The Pajama Game*** ("Hernando's Hideaway"); and popularized in Hollywood musical films of the 1930s and '40s. Its gliding moves include sensuous dips and embraces.

tap *n., v.* —*n.* **1.** [Short for *tap dance*] A jazzy style of dancing in shoes with metal attachments to heel and toe that make a rhythmic, clickety-click sound. Cf. its opposite, **soft shoe**. —*v. i.* **2.** To tap dance in a variety show, musical comedy, etc.

Tap-Dance Kid, The Broadway musical with music by Henry **Krieger**; book by actor, stage manager, and writer Charles Blackwell (?–1995), based on the novel *Nobody's Family Is Going to Chicago* (1974) by Louise Fitzhugh (1928–1974); lyrics by Robert Lorick; Broadhurst Theatre, 1983 (669 perf.). The show was notable for its social themes, for Danny Daniels's choreography, and for Krieger's vivacious, tuneful score.

Willie, a young African-American, wants to be a tap dancer, but his father, a lawyer, objects to the idea of his son's playing into one of the African-American stereotypes. Willie's uncle, a tap dancer himself, persuades Willie's mother, and then his father, to allow their son to pursue his dreams.

tarantella (tah' rahn TEHL lah) *n.* [From the city of Taranto (tah RAHN to:)] A swift-paced Italian folk dance of 14th c. origin, in 3/8 or 6/8 rhythm, with tunes alternating between major and minor keys; the dance speeds up and gains momentum as it goes along. It is used in ballets and operettas, e.g., Tchaikovsky's *Swan Lake*, Offenbach's *La fille du tambour-major*, Gilbert and Sullivan's ***Utopia Limited***.

Tauber, Richard (1891–1948) (TOW buhr) Renowned, highly popular Austrian stage and screen tenor; opera and operetta singer gifted with a gorgeous voice and wonderful technique, heard in his many recordings; composer. He starred as Schubert in the film ***Blossom Time***, and Franz **Lehár** wrote several roles for him, including the leads in *Paganini* and ***Das Land des Lächelns (The Land of Smiles)***, which he sang more than 700 times. In fact, Tauber became so identified with the soaring tenor ballads Lehár had written that they became known as *Tauberlieder* (Tauber songs) (TOW buh LEE duh), and each *Tauberlied* was eagerly awaited by the audience. When the Nazis came to power in 1933, he was forced to leave Germany, and then Austria, because of his Jewish ancestry. He settled in London, where he wrote three operettas, including the successful *Old Chelsea* (1943), additional numbers by Bernard Grun (1901–1972) and libretto by lyricist Fred S. Tysh and Walter Ellis (1874–1956); the music is imitative of Lehár. The story, which takes place in the 18th c. in London, concerns the struggles of a composer to gain recognition, and, of course, a love story is involved. It was broadcast on the BBC, with Tauber singing the lead, Jacob Bray, a professor of philosophy and a composer, and is available on CD (Eklipse Records, Ltd.; EKR CD22, 1993).

Taylor, Deems (1885–1966) American composer; he wrote four successful operas, now virtually unknown: *Peter Ibbetson* (1931), *Ramuntzko* (1942), *The Dragon* (1958), and the best known, ***The King's Henchman***.

Tchaikovsky, Pyotr Ilyich (1840–1893) Prolific Russian composer of symphonies, ballets, operas, and many other works. Among his most famous full-length ballets are *Swan Lake*, *Sleeping Beauty*, and the perennial Christmas favorite, *The Nut-cracker*. His operas include ***Yevgenyi Onegin (Eugene Onegin)*** and ***Pikovaya Dama (The Queen of Spades)***. Also notable are *Orleanskaya deva* (The Maid of Orleans) (1881) (awr' leh: AHN skah yah DYEHV ah); *Mazeppa* (1884) (mah ZEHP ah); and *Yolanta* (1892) (yo LAHN tah).

tempo *n.* **1.** The **pace**, or rate of speed, at which a piece of music is performed; its rhythm. The pace, indicated by the time signature and sometimes by metronome markings in the score, is interpreted, set, and indicated by a conductor in rehearsal and performance. In other words, tempo is fluid and is an aspect of interpretation. **2.** The pace at which a spoken play, scene, or dialogue is performed.

The Tender Land Opera in three acts by Aaron **Copland**; libretto by Horace Everett; New York City Opera, 1954. Most of the opera is a **music-drama** composed in a kind of **Sprechstimme**, or accompanied **recitative**; but there are also passages of great lyricism and some beautiful choral writing.

Laurie, the overly protected daughter of a domineering mother, has just graduated from her Midwestern high school and falls in love with a drifter, Martin. She plans to run away with him, but he abandons her, and she learns about pain and adulthood from the experience.

tenor *n.* The high-range male speaking and singing voice. A *lyric tenor* voice is one that is light in timbre and register, e.g., one suited to such roles as Nemorino in Donizetti's ***L'elisir d'amore***. A *dramatic tenor* has a more powerful voice, e.g., one suited to such roles as Verdi's ***Otello***.

tenore di forza (teh NO: reh: dee FO:R tsah) [Italian: tenor of force, strength] A tenor with a very strong voice; suitable for dramatic roles in romantic operas or French grand opera, but not as strong as the *tenore robusto*.

tenore di grazia (dee GRAH tsee ah) [Italian: tenor of grace, gracefulness] A lyric tenor with an agile, graceful technique suitable for 18th-c. operas such as those of **Mozart**, and for the romantic **bel canto** roles written by **Bellini**, **Donizetti**, and **Rossini**. Also called *tenore leggero* (ledg DGEH: ro:): light tenor.

tenore robusto (ro: BOOS to:) [Italian: robust tenor] A tenor with incredible lung power and a huge voice, who sings such dramatic roles as Manrico in Verdi's ***Il trovatore*** or the title role in ***Otello***. Cf. **Heldentenor**.

tessitura (teh:s' sih: TOO rah) *n.* [Italian: texture] The range, with its high and low notes, that constitutes the general area in which a melody or other sung passage lies for a particular voice category: *a high tessitura*.

text *n.* The words of a song, aria, or of an entire libretto; or of any piece of written material, whether a novel, poem, or play.

texture *n.* The nature of the depth of sound created by the arrangements or orchestration for whatever number of instruments are playing at any one time. Texture can be thin, e.g., that for guitar or piano and voice; or dense, e.g., that for

316

some symphonic orchestration. Hence, *texture music*: that for which a dense orchestration has been provided, making the depth of sound its salient or most prominent feature.

Thaïs (tah EES) Opera in three acts by Jules **Massenet**; libretto by novelist and librettist Louis Gallet (1835–1898) (gah LEH:), based on the novel by Nobel Prize–winning author Anatole France (1844–1924); Paris Opéra, 1894.

In a score noted for its melodic beauty and lush orchestral textures, the violin and harp act 2 **intermezzo**, the "Méditation religieuse" (mé' dee tah SYO:*N r*uh lih: ZHOOZ)—usually called simply the "Meditation"—is esp. outstanding.

In Alexandria in the 4th c., the Cenobite monk Athanaël (ah tah' nah EHL) (bar.) is attracted to the courtesan Thaïs (sop.), to whom he has been introduced at a banquet by her wealthy patron, Nicias (nee' see AHS) (ten.). He manages to convert her to his religious point of view, and persuades her to enter a convent. But he realizes that he has fallen hopelessly in love with her, and, in agony over his physical passion, he decides to reveal all, only to find that it is too late, because she is dying.

theme *n.* **1.** The principal melody in a musical composition, e.g., the melodies that will be developed in a symphony movement. **2.** The underlying and governing idea or ideas in a musical theater piece, play, or film, presenting the author's point of view about an aspect of life.

third position In dance, the placement of the feet so that one foot is in front of the other, with each heel touching the middle (arch) of the other foot.

third stream Music that has characteristics of classical harmonics and contemporary jazz performance practice, with its improvisational feel, e.g., that heard in many Broadway musicals.

This Is the Army Hit Broadway musical revue by Irving **Berlin**, following his World War I revue *Yip Yip Yahank* (1919); Broadway Theatre, 1942 (113 Performances); film, 1943, with Berlin himself reprising his role. This rousing, patriotic World War II fundraiser is full of famous songs, including "Oh, How I Hate to Get Up in the Morning" (from the 1919 revue) and "This Is the Army, Mr. Jones."

Thomas, Ambroise (1811–1896) (ahm br̄wahz' to: MAH) Prolific French composer of some twenty operas, best remembered nowadays for his *Hamlet* (1868), based on Shakespeare's tragedy; and for his seldom performed masterpiece, *Mignon*.

Thomson, Virgil (1896–1989) American composer and noted music critic. He wrote three operas: *Four Saints in Three Acts* and *The Mother of Us All*, both to libretti by his close friend, the avant-garde writer Gertrude Stein, who had a great influence on him; and *Lord Byron* (1972), with a libretto by actor, screenwriter, and actor-producer Jack Larson (b. 1928), best known for his portrayal of cub reporter Jimmy Olsen in the 1950s television series *Adventures of Superman*. His published works include *Virgil Thomson—An Autobiography* (A. A. Knopf, 1966) and *Music with Words: A Composer's View* (Yale University Press, 1989).

Thoroughly Modern Millie Broadway musical comedy by Jeanine Tesori (b. 1961); book by Richard Morris (1924–1996) and Dick Scanlan (b. 1960), who also did the lyrics—both were nominated for a Tony® Award in 2002; extra songs with music by James Van Heusen (1913–1990) and lyrics by Sammy Cahn; based on the 1967 film, screenplay by Morris; Marquis Theatre, 2002 (903 perf.).

In this spoof of fairy-tale romances, the naïve, eager, feisty Millie Dillmount arrives in jazz age New York City and looks for a job. Her main requirement is that her boss be a rich and eligible bachelor, but she falls in love with the apparently impoverished Jimmy, who turns out to be a millionaire.

Threepenny Opera, The English title of Brecht and Weill's *Die Dreigroschenoper*.

through-composed *adj.* Pertaining to an opera, music drama, or other full-length musical piece for voice and/or instruments, for which music is written all the way through, including that for sung operatic **recitative**, as opposed, for instance, to an opera that includes spoken dialogue between its musical numbers. Also pertains to a song or aria that is not broken into discreet verses, each followed by a refrain, but progresses from beginning to end in a continuous fashion.

Tiefland (Lowland) (TEEF LAHNT) [German: lowland] German **verismo** opera in a prologue and three acts by Eugen **d'Albert**; libretto by the prolific, Hungarian-born Austrian author Rudolf Lothar (ROO dolf LO: tahr) (1865–1943); Prague, German Theatre, 1903.

Sometime in the mid-19th-c. in the Pyrenees, the landowner Sebastiano (seh bahs' tee AH no:) (bar.), engaged to be married, forces the impoverished Marta (MAH[*R*] tah) (sop.) to become his mistress. In order to cover up the affair, he makes her marry Pedro (PEH: dro:) (ten.) and move to the lowlands, planning to retain her as his secret mistress. She confesses all to her husband, with whom she has fallen in love. His marriage plans having fallen through, Sebastiano tries to reclaim Marta, and Pedro kills him. The couple escape into the mountains.

timbre (TAM buhr; –bruh) *n.* [Fr. French] Particular quality of a sound, differentiating it in pitch and range from other sounds of the same nature; e.g., the **tone-color**, and high or deep qualities of a voice: *a high timbre*; *a low timbre*.

Tin Pan Alley; **tin-pan alley** *Archaic* **1.** A nickname for the then somewhat seedy district of New York City where most publishers of popular music had their offices from ca. 1885 to 1930, on West 28th Street between Sixth Avenue and Broadway; by extension, the music publishing district of any city. **2.** Collectively, the publishers and composers of popular music working in that era: *tin-pan alley musicians.* **3.** A 1940 musical film hit.

Tippett, Sir Michael (1905–1998) Prolific English composer who wrote five operas or music dramas, among them his first and most frequently heard opera, *The Midsummer Marriage*; *The Knot Garden* (1970); and *King Priam*.

Tip-Toes Broadway musical comedy by George **Gershwin**; lyrics by Ira Gershwin; book by Guy **Bolton** and English writer Fred Thompson (1884–1949); Liberty

Theatre, 1925 (194 perf.). The hit song "That Certain Feeling" is still remembered from this lively, jazzy score filled with good tunes—a delight worth rediscovering.

Tip-Tocs Kayc and hcr unclcs arc vaudcvillians who find thcmsclvcs brokc in Miami. As a way out of their dire predicament, Tip-Toes masquerades as a wealthy aristocrat in order to bag a rich husband. Her target is the glue magnate Steve Burton, but she actually falls in love with him, and then learns that he is also broke. She doesn't care; she wants him anyway. But he was only pretending to be broke, to test whether or not she really loved him.

Titanic Broadway musical by Maury **Yeston**; book by Peter **Stone**; Lunt-Fontanne Theatre, 1997 (864 perf.).

The show follows the stories of several characters of different social class, including that of Ida (1849–1912) and Isidor (1845–1912) Straus, the elderly married couple who owned Macy's department store in New York, and chose to give up their places in the lifeboats and go down with the sinking White Star liner *Titanic*. There were impressive special technical effects in the Broadway production, as the tilting ocean liner sank.

See also UNSINKABLE MOLLY BROWN, THE.

title song A short vocal piece that has the same name as the project in which it is sung; the song often includes in its lyrics the title of the project, e.g., the famous numbers in Lerner and Loewe's ***Brigadoon***, and Rodgers and Hammerstein's ***Oklahoma!***

Tom Jones 1. [Full title: *The History of Tom Jones, A Foundling* (1749)] Picaresque, bitingly satirical novel about the English class system by English magistrate and author Henry Fielding (1707–1754). Tom Jones is raised by the good Squire Alworthy on his estate in Somerset, in the west of England. He is the son of Alworthy's sister, although passed off as the son of a local girl, Jenny Jones. Tom falls in love with Sophia, daughter of the neighboring Squire Western, but she is destined for Master Blifil (Tom's half-brother, Alworthy's sister having married Captain Blifil). Master Blifil engineers Tom's downfall, and Tom is forced to leave the estate and make his way in the world. After a series of picaresque adventures, he arrives in London, where everyone eventually meets through the magnanimous but cynical Lady Bellaston, Sophia's kinswoman. Alworthy, having learned the truth of Tom's parentage, takes him back into the fold. Blifil is shown up as the villain he is, and Tom and Sophia are united. There have been two noteworthy adaptations for the musical theater.
2. Opéra comique in three acts by François-André Danican **Philidor**; libretto for acts 1 and 3 by Antoine-Alexandre-Henri Poinsinet (1735–1769) (ahn twahn' ah lehk sahn' druh ahn ree' pwan see NEH:), and for act 2 by painter and poet Bertin Davesne (behr tan dah VEHN); 1765; revised, 1766, with redone libretto by Michel-Jean Sedaine (1719–1797); Paris, Théâtre de la Bourgogne (duh lah boor GO: nyuh).

The simplified story eliminates most of the novel's characters (including Lady Bellaston), and concentrates on the love of Tom and Sophia, ending happily at an inn in Upton; there are no London episodes. There is a spirited recording by the Opéra de Lausanne (Dynamic, CDS 509/1-2; 2007).

3. Operetta in three acts by Edward **German**; libretto by Scottish theater manager, stage director, and playwright Robert Courtneidge (1859–1939) and the German-born, English writer and journalist Alexander M. Thompson (1861–1948); lyrics by Charles H. Taylor (1859–1907); Manchester, Prince's Theatre, 1907.

The operetta follows the basic storyline of the novel, while leaving out many of its colorful characters. With a nod to **Sullivan**, the melodious Edwardian score is very pleasant, and there are some nice pastiche folk songs and country dances. Tom's torrid but brief affair with Lady Bellaston, important in the novel, forms part of the plot, but is considerably toned down, in deference to the taste and prudishness of the times. A very fine complete recording is available from Naxos (8.660270-71; 2009).

Tommy (rock opera; film, 1975); The Who's Tommy (Broadway show) A Broadway rock musical called *The Who's Tommy*, based on Pete Townshend (b. 1945) [Peter Dennis Blandford Townshend] and The Who's [The Who: four-man rock band formed in 1964] recorded **rock opera** of the same name, opened at the St. James Theatre in 1993 (900 perf.).

Both the 1975 film (also based on the opera) and the stage show are pretentious and full of strange, bizarre touches; but the infectious score, with its verve and pounding rock rhythms, makes up for a certain lack of interest in the ineffectual plot.

Tommy, a young lad, is witness to a murder and, as a result, goes deaf, dumb, and blind. His uncle abuses him sexually, and he escapes into the world of pinball games, becoming the guru of a cult of pinball worshippers.

tonadilla (to:' nah DEE yah) *n.* [Spanish: a little musical piece, or little tune; diminutive of *tonada* (song) (to: NAH dah:)] A Spanish light musical comedy, opera, or operetta in one act of about twenty minutes' duration; burlesque or polit-ically satirical in nature, and placed in a Spanish, urban, working class setting, ending with a vivacious dance number. Often used as a filler between the acts of a play. *Tonadillas* were composed for two to four singers, or for female soloists, by a number of noted Spanish musicians, among them Manuel **García**. A more elaborate version, the *tonadilla generale* (general) (hehn' eh: RAH leh:), was composed for up to twelve singers. By the end of the 19th c., this type of piece was no longer used, and the **zarzuela** had largely replaced it. Also called a *tonadilla escénica* (for the stage; scenic) (ehs SEH: nee kah).

tonality *n.* In music, the relationship of pitches (tones) that are organized into a system of scales, each revolving around a particular musical note, for which the *scale* is named; e.g., the classical system of scales in western **harmonic** music, developed since the 16th c. Each eight-note scale—the eighth note being the same as the first note, but an octave higher—or *key* (the name of the scale) establishes the scale around its central *tonic* note: the key's particular main pitch, which begins the scale, and provides an aurally satisfying resolution at the end of a piece; there are two types of key: *major* and *minor*. Hence, the adj. *tonal*: characteristic of such music, which, in order to add coloration and interest to a melodic line, makes use of the full *chromatic scale*: one that includes all twelve semitone pitches in an octave, and that therefore moves up or down in half steps. The chromatic notes used in a piece are nonharmonic, i.e., not strictly part of the particular key of the composition in which they occur; e.g., a chromatic note sometimes occurs as a **grace note**. Cf. its opposite, **atonality**.

tone *n.* **1.** A musical note, i.e., a specific **pitch**. **2.** The general, overall acoustic quality of a sound, including its duration and timbre, and the richness of its harmonic vibrations, i.e., overtones and undertones. **3.** The specific or relative pitch and/or volume of an utterance during speech: *He spoke in low tones.* **4.** A particular pitch that gives a word or syllable its meaning in a *tonal language*, i.e., one where denotational meaning is determined by pitch, e.g., Mandarin, Vietnamese, Yoruba; as opposed to an *intonational language*, in which there are intonation patterns, i.e. pitch patterns specific to the language, and in which tone may imply an emotion or feeling but does not change the denotational meaning of a word, e.g., English, French, Hungarian. **5.** The manner or attitude of an utterance, as determined by a speaker's intentions: *a nasty tone*; *a sweet tone. Don't take that tone of voice with me!* **6.** The general effect or overall atmosphere created by a work of art: *Mozart's music often has an elegant tone. A piece in a minor key can have a depressing tone.* **7.** *Hist.* In 17th- and 18th-c. rhetorical terminology: affected speech, esp. declamatory emphasis on the rhythm of an utterance, e.g., in speaking verse.

tone-color *n.* **1.** The quality or **timbre** of a voice, such that a note sung by one singer can be differentiated from the same note sung by another. **2.** The timbre of a particular note or notes sung by a particular voice, e.g., the thinness or richness of a soprano's high notes, depending on natural anatomic construction as well on technique, muscular tension when singing them, and the amount of breath or air used to sing them.

torch singer A vocalist with a rich, full voice who performs in nightclubs and cabarets and croons sad songs, e.g., blues numbers that are full of misery, bemoaning the fate of unhappy lovers; the songs are called *torch songs.* Also sometimes called a *torcher.*

Tosca (TOS kah) Opera in three acts by Giacomo **Puccini**; libretto by Luigi **Illica**, based on *La Tosca* by Victorien **Sardou**; Rome, Teatro Costanzi, 1900.

The renowned singer Floria Tosca (sop.) is passionately in love with the painter Mario Cavaradossi (MAH ree o: kah' vah rah DO:S see) (ten.), who is arrested on suspicion of treason by Baron Scarpia (SKAHR pee ah) (bar.), the chief of police, and condemned to death. Tosca, who has come to plead for his release, is so distraught by having heard him scream under torture that she tells Scarpia she will do whatever he wants if he will rescind the sentence and let them leave Rome. He agrees to fake the execution, provided she give herself to him. Tosca acquiesces, but she cannot bear the idea, and she stabs him to death, takes the safe-conduct pass he has written, and flees. She arrives on the prison rooftop in time to witness the execution of Cavaradossi, which turns out to be real, to her surprise and horror. When she hears soldiers mounting the stairs, Tosca jumps to her death.

tote Stadt, Die (The Dead City) [dee TO: teh SHTAHT] Opera by Erich **Korngold**; libretto by the composer and his father, Julius Korngold (1860–1945), writing under the pen name Paul Schott (POWL SHO:T), based on the novel *Bruges-la-morte* (Bruges-the-Dead) (1892) (B*R*ÜZH lah MAW:*R*T) by the Belgian symbolist poet and writer Georges Rodenbach (1855–1898) (ZHAW*R*ZH *r*o:' dehn BAHK), and on his own adaptation of the novel for the stage, *Le mirage* (The Mirage) (1900) (luh mee *R*AZH); Hamburg, Opera,1920.

Near the end of the 19th c., in the beautiful museum city of Bruges, Paul (ten.) is sunk in deep mourning for his dead wife, Marie (sop.). His friend Frank (bar.) tries in vain to bring him out of his depression. Paul meets the dancer Marietta (sop.), and seems to find his dead wife embodied in her. But he has a nightmare in which he thinks she has betrayed him with Frank, and in a state of waking-sleeping, he strangles her. Waking completely, he is horrified to see what he has done.

tour jeté (too*r*' zhuh TÉ) [French: lit. turn thrown] In dance, esp. ballet, a smoothly executed spring and simultaneous turn; the movement begins with the dancer springing or leaping up and doing a turn in the air while scissor kicking with the legs, landing on the opposite leg from which the move began.

Toxic Avenger, The Off-Broadway **rock musical** by David Bryan (b. 1962), keyboardist and founding member of the Sayreville, NJ hard rock band Bon Jovi; lyrics by David Bryan and Joe DiPietro; book by DiPietro, based on the 1984 cult classic comedy horror film of the same name by Lloyd Kaufman (b. 1945); New World Stages, 2009 (300 perf.).

Melvin Ferd the Third, who lives in Tromaville, off exit 13-B of the New Jersey Turnpike, is in love with the blind librarian, Sarah, who tells him about the "Good Earth Company," which pollutes the environment. Melvin tries to get the town cleaned up, but he runs afoul of the do-nothing Mayor, who is in cahoots with the polluters. The Mayor's hoodlums dump Melvin into a vat of radioactive waste, from which he emerges, mutated into Toxie, the Toxic Avenger. He destroys the polluters, and Toxie and Sarah are married. Toxie becomes Governor of a pollution-free New Jersey.

track *n., v.* —*n.* **1.** In a musical comedy, the order of each chorus member's dance moves, the dance routine, and the positions on stage with each move, for each number: *dance track*. The **dance captain** is usually in charge of keeping these records. A **swing** has rehearsed and can perform more than one track. —*v. t.* **2.** To note the moves and positions of each dancer for each number.

tragédie-lyrique (t*r*ah' zhé dee' lih: *R*EEK) *n.* [French: lyric tragedy, musical tragedy] *Hist.* The staged musical works written and produced by composer Jean-Baptiste **Lully** and librettist Philippe **Quinault** at the court of Louis XIV; a term first used by them in 1673 to describe their mythological spectacle, *Cadmus et Hermione* (kahd müs' eh: eh*r* mee ON). Later used to mean any serious or tragic musical work, esp. opera for the late 17th- and early 18th-c. French stage.

transatlantic operetta The German-language musicals of the 1920s and '30s composed in Berlin and Vienna, imitative of Broadway shows of the period, and influenced by American jazz and dances such as the **Charleston** and **foxtrot**, e.g., *Die Herzogin von Chicago* by Emmerich **Kálmán**; works of Oscar **Straus**, Eduard **Künneke**.

transcribe *v. t.* **1.** To copy out music. **2.** To arrange or adapt music for instruments or voices other than those for which the piece was originally composed.

transcription *n.* An **arrangement** or adaptation of a musical composition that alters the original in some way, e.g., by adding ornamentations or changing instrumentation.

transformation scene The obligatory climactic scene in English **pantomime**, in which the set collapses in some way, to be replaced by another, even more marvelous decor. Such scenes were the centerpiece of the 1866 American musical *The Black Crook* and of the French **opéra-féerie**, e.g., Offenbach's *Le Roi Carotte*.

transition *n.* A musical **bridge**, often including a modulation from one key to another.

transpose *n.* To change the key in which a musical composition was written to a higher or lower one, and to write out the changes; sometimes necessary to accommodate the **range** of a particular singer.

transposition *n.* **1.** The act of changing the key of a musical composition to a higher or lower one. **2.** The **notation** of the changed composition.

traveling music Instrumental composition meant to accompany an actor, singer, or ensemble as they either leave the stage, or dance across it, perhaps in a **grapevine**, moving in time to its rhythms. Often used as a signature tune or theme music for a particular well known performer in vaudeville, or, later, in television. Cf. **exit music**.

travesti (trah veh: STEE) *adj.* [French: **drag**] Drag: pertaining to a role that requires cross-dressing; describes esp. an operatic **trousers role**, done *en travesti* (in drag).

traviata, La (She Who Has Strayed) (lah trah' vee AH tah) Opera in four acts by Giuseppe **Verdi**; libretto by Francesco Maria **Piave**, based on the play *La Dame aux camélias* (The Lady with the Camellias) (1852) (lah dahm' o: kah' mé LYAH) by Alexandre Dumas, fils (1824–1895), who adapted it from his own novel (1848); Venice, Teatro La Fenice, 1853.

At a grand Paris soirée, ca. 1850, Alfredo (ahl FREH: do:) (ten.), the wealthy, naive scion of an upper middle-class family from Provence, meets the beautiful courtesan Violetta (vee' o: LEHT tah) (sop.), and they fall instantly in love. Giving up her worldly life in Paris, she moves with him to a country house. During Alfredo's absence, his father, Germont (zhehr MO:*N*) (bar.), pleads with Violetta to leave his son for the sake of Alfredo's sister, who cannot marry her fiancé while Alfredo is living in sin. Distraught, and knowing that in any case she is dying of consumption, she tearfully agrees and departs. Alfredo returns to find her gone. Concealing the real reason for Violetta's departure, his father tries to comfort him. Alfredo returns to Paris and insults Violetta, whom he sees being escorted at a party by a rival. Germont, reproaching his son for his ungallant conduct, realizes what he himself has done, and finally tells Alfredo everything. Father and son go to see the desperately ill Violetta, and Alfredo begs her forgiveness. They dream of a new life together, but it is too late; she falls dead at his feet.

treble *n., adj.* —*n.* **1.** High voice; soprano, esp. a boy's unbroken soprano voice. **2.** A boy soprano. —*adj.* **3.** Pertaining to such a voice; **4.** The G-clef in a music score: *the treble clef.*

Tree Grows in Brooklyn, A Broadway musical by Arthur **Schwartz**; book by George **Abbott** (who also directed) and Betty Smith (1896–1972), based on her best-selling autobiographical novel of the same name; lyrics by Dorothy **Fields**; Alvin Theatre, 1951 (270 perf.).

It is obvious from the original cast recording that whatever success the show had was due to the excellent performers, esp. Shirley Booth (1898–1992), ebullient, romantic, cynical, and sassy as Cissie. The clever lyrics are enjoyable and cute, but the serviceable if unexciting score, although much acclaimed in some quarters, is often pedestrian and lacks sufficient variety.

At the beginning of the twentieth century, in a working-class Brooklyn neighborhood, the alcoholic Johnny Nolan can't seem to keep a job, despite the loving support of his wife Katie and their daughter, Francie. Aunt Cissie, Katie's sister, has her own problems coping with her romantic difficulties, but she is able to bring some comfort to her sister and niece when the unfortunate Johnny collapses and dies.

Treemonisha Opera in three acts by Scott **Joplin**; libretto by the composer; composed, 1907; first performed, Atlanta, Morehouse College, 1972.

The delightful score, melodic and appropriately melodramatic, reflects Joplin's fame as a legendary composer of **ragtime**, with its lively syncopated rhythms. There is an original cast recording available on a Deutsche Grammophon CD (435 709-2; 1992).

On an Arkansas plantation in 1884, the well educated Treemonisha (sop.) exposes soothsayers and conjurors to public excoriation for spreading superstitions among the people. The soothsayers, vowing revenge, kidnap her, but she is rescued by Remus (ten.), who has disguised himself as Satan and terrified her credulous captors. On returning to the plantation, she insists that they be let off, and the people proclaim her their leader.

tremolo *n.* **1.** In singing, a usually undesirable **vibrato**: an excessive shaking vibration of the voice; an unsteady, wobbly, quavering tone of voice, which causes flatting or sharping of the pitch and is usually the result of tension and poor technique, although it can also be deliberately used during an emotional moment in a dramatic piece. **2.** In instrumental playing, a very quick alternation of tones, or the rapid repetition of a single pitch, creating a tremulous effect.

trepak (TREH pahk) *n.* A Ukrainian folk dance; used in Tchaikovsky's *Nutcracker* ballet and by the Moiseyev Dance Company (moy SEH: yehf) that toured the world.

Trial by Jury Comic operetta in one act by **Gilbert and Sullivan**; London, New Royalty Theatre, 1875.

   The first successful collaboration by the famous pair took London by storm; it was originally presented as an **afterpiece** to Richard D'Oyly Carte's production of Offenbach's *La Périchole*. It starred the composer's brother, a singer-actor known for his **Offenbach** roles, Frederick Sullivan (1837–1877), as the Learned Judge; he had also created the role of Apollo in *Thespis; or The Gods Grown Old*. This is the only through-composed Gilbert and Sullivan operetta, and their only one-act piece.

   Edwin (ten.), a cad, is being sued by Angelina (sop.) for breach of promise of marriage. The jury, the Learned Judge (bar.), and everyone in the courtroom are entirely sympathetic to the lovely plaintiff, who behaves seductively but demurely, showing them her well-clad ankle. The defendant's hedonistic self-justification for his Casanova-like conduct fails to move anyone, even though the jury all admit, sotto voce, that they were like that when they were lads. Finally, tired of listening to wearisome discourses and disquisitions by the lawyers, the Judge orders them to put their "briefs upon the shelf": He will marry her himself! And they all go merrily dancing about in this affable, tuneful romp, with its mild, tongue-in-cheek satire of hypocrisy in the law courts, not to say in real life.

trill *n., v.* [Fr. Italian *trillo* (TRIH:L lo:)] —*n.* **1.** A musical ornament consisting of the rapid-fire, evenly sustained alternation of two neighboring pitches, the lower of which is the principal note, the upper, the actual ornament: one of the required techniques of **bel canto** singing; used in both singing and instrumental playing. In singing, also called a *shake*. —*v. i.* **2.** To alternate two notes at a minor or major second interval apart, producing a rapidly oscillating effect.

   See also BLEAT.

trio *n.* **1.** A group of three singers or instrumentalists. **2.** An ensemble piece written for three instrumentalists or singers; e.g., a number in an opera, where it is also called a *terzett*.

triplet *n.* **1.** In music, a group of three notes of equal value, played or sung in the same time as two notes of equal value would be in the particular rhythm established for the time signature. **2.** In dance, a series of three steps that can then be repeated in a combination.

triple threat A performer who acts (speaks), sings, and dances so well as to be serious competition for other performers; the term is sometimes used as a joke.

triple time A rhythm consisting of three equal notes or units, as in 3/4 or 3/8 time signatures, where there are either three quarter notes or three eighth notes to a bar.

Trip to Chinatown, A Broadway musical comedy **pasticcio** with music adapted from the works of various composers, e.g., Jacques Offenbach's *La vie parisienne*, and with original songs by Percy Gaunt (1852–1896), among them the famous numbers "The Bowery" and "Reuben and Cynthia," with its well known refrain, "Reuben, Reuben, I've been thinking"; book and lyrics by Charles Hoyt (1859–1900); Madison Square Theatre, 1891 (657 perf.).

    The plot is similar to that of the later megahit *Hello, Dolly!* Four friends go on a sightseeing tour in New York's Chinatown, telling Uncle Ben of the outing. They also request that Mrs. Guyer accompany them as chaperone. She replies that she will be happy to do so, but her reply is received by Uncle Ben, who takes it for a letter offering him an assignation at the restaurant where they are to meet. They all show up, and, in the manner of a French farce, they are in and out and roundabout, hiding from and spying on each other. Ben gets drunk, and the chaos is unrestrained. The next day, he takes the young people to task for having gone on a "racket" (spree), and they jocularly turn the tables and reveal that they know all about what he did!

Tristan und Isolde (T*R*IH: stahn *oo*nt ee ZOL deh) Opera in three acts by Richard **Wagner**; libretto by the composer, based on various versions of the medieval legend; Munich, Königliches Hof- und Nationaltheater, 1865.

    Tristan (ten.) is accompanying Isolde (sop.) from Ireland to Cornwall so that she can be married to King Mark (bass). In love with him, she decides that death is better than life without him. She orders her confidante, Brangäne (b*r*ahn GEH: neh) (mezz.), to prepare poison, but Brangäne substitutes a love potion, and now Tristan and Isolde are hopelessly in love. They meet during Mark's absence, and are betrayed by the king's loyal henchman, Melot (MEH lot) (bar.). Mark is prostrate with grief and unable to punish the betrayers, but Melot confronts Tristan, who allows himself to be mortally wounded. He is taken to his faraway castle in Brittany, and Isolde follows him there. He dies in her arms. Mark and Melot follow them, with the intention of pardoning them, but Kurwenal (koo[*r*]' veh NAHL) (bar.), Tristan's faithful steward, kills Melot. The grief-stricken Isolde is left lamenting.

trois débuts (t*r*wah' dé BÜ) [French: three debuts] *Hist.* In 19th-c. French theaters, a system of employing singers: they were obliged to perform three different roles, and to be voted on by the public, before being offered fulltime employment for a season.

troubadour *n.* An itinerant medieval minstrel and composer of his own material.

trousers role A male character played by a woman, e.g., Cherubino (keh' roo BEE no:) in Mozart's opera *The Marriage of Figaro*; or the **principal boy** in British **pantomime**. Also called a *breeches role*; *pants part*.

trovatore, Il (The Troubadour) (ih:l tro:' vah TO: reh) Opera in four acts by Giuseppe **Verdi**; libretto by Salvadore **Cammarano**, completed by poet Leone Emmanuele Bardare (1820–1874) (lch: O: neh: ehm mah' noo EII: leh: bahr DAH reh:), based on a Spanish melodrama, *El Trovador* (1836) (ehl tro:' vah THO:R) by romantic playwright Antonio Garcia Gutiérrez (1813–1884) (gahr SEE ah goo' TYEHR rehs); Rome, Teatro Apollo, 1853.

In the courtyard of his medieval Spanish castle, the Count di Luna (dee LOO nah) (bar.), general of the king's army, is skulking outside the residence of Leonora (leh:' o: NO: rah) (sop.), the woman he loves, and who lives under his protective custody, when he hears the **serenade** of the troubadour who sings to her nightly: Manrico (mahn REE ko:) (ten.), leader of the rebel army. When Manrico approaches and Leonora rushes out to meet her beloved, di Luna emerges from concealment, and the two fight a duel, from which Manrico manages to extricate himself. He returns to the gypsy camp to see his mother, Azucena (ah' dzoo CHE: nah) (mezz.). Meanwhile, Leonora, in despair, enters a convent, from which di Luna abducts her. Manrico rescues her and takes her to his stronghold. Di Luna captures Azucena, and holds her prisoner. His faithful retainer, Ferrando (fehr RAHN do:) (bass), recognizes her as the gypsy woman who had kidnapped di Luna's baby brother in revenge for the death of her mother, burned at the stake. When Manrico sallies forth to rescue her, he is captured, and the two are imprisoned. Leonora, who has disappeared and is nowhere to be found, appears at the prison and offers herself to di Luna provided he will free Manrico, which he agrees to do. But after a last visit with Manrico, who reproaches her for her evil bargain with di Luna, she reveals that she has taken a slow-acting poison, and falls dead at his feet. Di Luna has Manrico dragged off to be executed, and, as the axe falls, Azucena reveals that he is the Count's brother: She had killed her own baby and raised Manrico as hers.

Troyens, Les (The Trojans) (leh: t*r*wah YEH*N*) Opera in two parts (five acts) by Hector **Berlioz**; libretto by the composer, based on Virgil's (70 BCE–19 BCE) *Aeneid*; Paris, Théâtre Lyrique, 1890. Part One: *La Prise de Troie* (The Taking of Troy) (composed, 1862) (lah p*r*eez' duh T*R*WAH). Part Two: *Les Troyens à Carthage* (The Trojans at Carthage) (composed, 1863) (leh: t*r*wah ye*n*' ah kah*r* TAHZH).

When the Greeks overrun Troy, Aeneas's sister, Cassandra (sop.), leads the Trojan women in a mass suicide. Prince Aeneas (ten.) escapes out of the burning city with the surviving Trojans, and they are shipwrecked near the North African city of Carthage, where he and the Carthaginian princess Dido (mezz.) fall in love. But he realizes his destiny lies elsewhere, and abandons her to continue his voyage. She commits suicide.

Tsarskaya nevesta (The Tsar's Bride) (TSAHR skah yah nyeh VYIH stah) Opera in three acts by Nicolai **Rimsky-Korsakov**; libretto by the composer, in collaboration with **Wagner** translator, artist, and student of Rimsky-Korsakov, Ilya Fyodorovich Tyumenev (1855–1927) (eel YAH FYO: do: ro: vih:ch tyoo MEH:

nyehf), based on a drama by the playwright Lev Alexandrovich Mey (1822–1862) (LYEHF ah' lyiks AHN dro vihch MI); Moscow, Mamontov (mah MO:N to:f) Theatre, 1899.

In the Russia of Tsar Ivan IV, called Ivan the Terrible (1530–1584), the nobleman Gryaznoy (GRYAHZ NOY) (bar.) is in love with Marfa (MAHR fah) (sop.), who is betrothed to the boyar Lykov (lee KO:F) (ten.). Grigory's former love, Lyubasha (lyoo BAH shah) (mezz.), who dabbles in mystic arts, agrees to supply him with a love potion that he will give to Marfa. But the supposed love philter is in reality an excessively slow-acting poison. In any case, the unlucky Gryaznoy is forced to forego his love when the tsar chooses Marfa as his bride. She dies. Lyubasha confesses her crime, and is promptly killed by the infuriated Lykov.

tune *n., v.* —*n.* **1.** A melody. **2.** A whole song. **3.** The musical setting for words: *the tune for a hymn.* —*v. t.* **4.** To adjust a musical instrument to the standard pitch level: *to tune an instrument*; hence, *in tune*: correctly pitched; *in tune with*: in harmony with, e.g., with the other instruments in an orchestra; *tuned up*: brought to a harmony of pitches; *tuning*: the act of adjusting an instrument or an entire orchestra to make sure they are all in tune. The standard pitch level has changed over the centuries.

Turandot (too' rahn DO:; –DOT) **1.** Opera in three acts by Giacomo **Puccini**, with the score completed by Franco **Alfano** after Puccini's death; libretto by Renato Simoni (1875–1952) (reh NAH to: sih: MO: nee) and Giuseppe **Adami**, based on the play by the aristocrat Carlo Gozzi (1720–1806) (GO:T tsee), Venetian playwright of theatrical fairy tales; Milan, Teatro alla Scala, 1926.

In ancient China, the ice-cold but gorgeous Princess Turandot (sop.), misanthropic, cruel, and aloof, refuses to marry unless her suitor can solve three riddles. The penalty for failing to solve them is decapitation. As the opera opens, the Prince of Persia is being led to his untimely death. Prince Calaf (KAH lahf) (ten.), accompanied by his adoring slave girl, Liù (LYOO) (sop.), and his aged father, Timur (TEE moor') (bass), sees Turandot and falls in love with her. He strikes the gong and announces that he will solve the riddles. He does, and Turandot is horrified at the prospect of having to marry him. He gives her a day in which to discover his name. If she does, he will renounce her and sacrifice his life. She resolves to extract the name from Liù by torturing her, but the maiden loves Calaf so much that she commits suicide rather than betray him. The remorseful Calaf reveals his name to Turandot, and melts her heart with a kiss. She accepts him as her husband, and tells the world his name is Love.
2. Opera in two acts by Ferruccio **Busoni**; libretto by the composer, based on Gozzi's play, for which he had composed incidental music in 1905; Zurich, Stadttheater, 1917.

turn *n.* **1.** In vaudeville and other variety venues, the act put on by a performer; also, the individual performance of that act. **2.** In dance, a full or partial rotation of the body. **3.** In music, an ornament consisting of four or five notes gracing a main note.

Turn of the Screw, The Opera in a prologue and two acts by Benjamin **Britten**; libretto by Myfanwy Piper, based on the novella of the same name (1898) by Henry James (1843–1916); Venice, Teatro La Fenice, 1954.

In an isolated English country house in Victorian England, a Governess (sop.) has arrived to care for two young children, Miles (treble) and Flora (sop.). The house appears to be haunted by the ghosts of two former servants, Peter Quint (ten.) and his lover, Miss Jessel (sop.), who are attempting to lead the children into corruption. The strong-willed Governess is determined to save the children's souls, and has Flora leave in the company of the housekeeper, Mrs. Grose (sop.), but the highly strung Miles collapses and dies.

turnout; turn-out *n.* **1.** Dance position in which the feet form a ninety-degree angle with the legs, requiring the arms to be used for balance. **2.** Any dance position in which the feet form an angle with the body and are pointed to the right and left.

tutu *n.* A ballerina's costume consisting of a stiff short or long skirt made of many layers of netting.

twelve-tone scale The twelve chromatic notes of the **harmonic** scale, treated without regard to harmonics, thus giving an equal value to each tone; the scale is used in composing a twelve-note, or dodecaphonic composition, exemplified in the music of one of its innovators and chief practitioners, Arnold Schoenberg (1874–1951) (AH[R] nolt SHÖN beh[r]k). Twelve-tone operas were composed, including those by Schoenberg himself, e.g., *Von Heute auf Morgen* (From Today until Tomorrow) (1930) (fon HOY teh owf MAW[R] gehn), and notably by Schoenberg's student, Alban **Berg**.

25th Annual Putnam County Spelling Bee, The Broadway musical comedy by William **Finn** (music and lyrics); book by Rachel Sheinkin; transferred from Off-Broadway to Circle in the Square, 2005 (1136 perf.); many regional productions.

In this endearing, intimate show, the six adolescent finalists in a local spelling bee go through the closing rounds and reveal aspects of their personalities, conflicts, and desires.

Two by Two Broadway musical comedy by Richard **Rodgers**; lyrics by Martin Charnin; book by Peter **Stone**, based on Clifford Odets's (1906–1963) *The Flowering Peach* (1954); Imperial Theatre, 1970 (351 perf.). This uneven show, based on the Biblical story of Noah, was most notable as being a star **vehicle** for Hollywood legend Danny Kaye (1913–1987).

Two Gentlemen of Verona Broadway musical comedy (transferred from a summer run at the New York Shakespeare Festival's Delacorte Theater in Central Park) by Galt **MacDermot**; book and lyrics by noted playwright John Guare (b. 1938), based on Shakespeare's play; St. James Theatre, 1971 (627 performance); NYSF revival, limited engagement, Aug. 16–Sept. 11, 2005.

Shakespeare's comedy was reset in contemporary urban America in the Latino and African-American communities, with its plot otherwise unchanged, and with the dialogue considerably condensed to accommodate the music.

two-step A dance choreographed in the pattern step-close-step, esp. used in **soft-shoe** routines as an introduction leading into a more complicated dance, or for vamping, i.e., marking time, when used as a **bridge**.

tyrolienne (tee *r*o: lee YEHN; –LYEHN) *n.* [French: a song or dance from the Tirol] A Tyrolese song, often including a dance section, that features a yodeling refrain.

U

Ullmann, Viktor (1898–1944) (*OOL* mahn) Austrian-Czech composer; wrote several operas, including the bizarre, exciting, long one-act *Der Kaiser von Atlantis* (The Emperor of Atlantis) (composed, 1943–1944; premiere, 1975) (deh KI zuh fuhn aht LAHN tih:s); excellent recording on London CD (440 854-2; 1994). The Brechtian libretto was by poet and artist Peter Kien (1919–1944) (KEEN). The opera was written while both he and Ullmann were imprisoned in Theresienstadt concentration camp, the so-called "model ghetto" set up by the Nazis to mask genocide and demonstrate to the outside world how "well" they were treating Jews. The opera was in rehearsal, but performances were banned because of the obvious resemblance of the monstrously inhuman, warmongering Emperor Overall to Hitler. Ullman and Kien were shipped off to Auschwitz and gassed. So were their fellow inmates, composers Hans Kraša (1899–1944) (KRAH shah), who wrote the symbolic, anti-Nazi opera *Brundibár* (1938) (BROON dih: bah:r), recorded on Channel Classics (CCS 5168; 1993); Pavel Haas (1899–1944); and Gideon Klein (1919–1945).

Undine (*oo*n DEE neh:) The soulless female spirit of the waters in Central European folk legend: She can only gain a soul by marrying a mortal, with whom she must have a child. In order to accept a soul and the mortality that accompanies its possession, she must willingly renounce all the benefits of immortality. Some dozen operas and operettas based on the legend were written, among them *Undine*, an opera in three acts by composer E. T. A. **Hoffmann**, with a libretto by the German writer, Friedrich de la Motte Fouqué (1777–1843) (FREE d*r*ih*k*h duh lah mot' foo KÉ), based on his own 1811 fairytale novel that popularized the legend during the romantic era. Another opera titled *Undine* is one of the most important works by Albert **Lortzing**, in four acts, with a libretto by the composer, based on Fouqué's story; the score is superbly evocative and appropriately eerie. In 1865, Charles **Lecocq** wrote an operetta called *Les ondines au Champagne* (The Undines in Champagne [region]) (leh: zaw*n* deen' o: shah*n*' PAH nyuh). Pyotr Ilyich **Tchaikovsky** left an operatic version of the legend unfinished at his death. Serge **Prokofiev** wrote an unproduced opera, *Undina* (based on Fouqué's story), which he spent from 1904 to 1907 composing. And Hans Werner **Henze** composed a ballet, *Undine*, which premiered at the Royal Opera House at Covent Garden in London in 1958. Cf. *The Little Mermaid*; *Rusalka*.

See also CONTES D'HOFFMANN, LES.

unison *n.* **1.** Identity and simultaneity; in entire agreement or complete accord. **2.** Singing or playing all together as one voice or instrumental **ensemble**, observing the tempo set by a conductor or leader of the group; hence, *in unison*: singing or playing in accord or in **harmony**, with everyone observing the same rhythm; or singing the same note simultaneously, in octaves from high to low, depending on the voice part. **3.** Dancing the same step simultaneously, e.g., in the chorus dancing of a musical comedy.

Unsinkable Molly Brown, The Broadway musical comedy by Meredith **Willson** (music and lyrics); book by Richard Morris (1939–2003); Winter Garden Theatre, 1960 (532 perf.); film, 1964.

This show is based loosely on the true story of the uninhibited, spunky Margaret "Molly" Brown, née Tobin (1867–1932). A boisterous backwoods gal, she goes to Leadville, Colorado and tends bar in a saloon, where she meets and marries Johnny Brown, who makes and loses a fortune in mining, then makes another. They move to Denver, where she tries to break into high society, but nobody shows up for her grand gala. Disgusted, she goes to Europe, and befriends aristocrats and socialites. She then returns to Denver, and this time local society is duly impressed, until rowdy roisterers manage to turn her grand soirée into a disaster. Molly returns to Europe accompanied by the amorous Prince de Long, while Johnny stays home in Denver. The Prince begs her to divorce Johnny and marry him, but she loves her husband. She books passage for the much heralded maiden voyage of the *Titanic*, and survives the sinking of the ocean liner. On her return, Johnny is ecstatic to see his wife again, while Denver society acclaims its new-found heroine.

See also TITANIC.

upbeat *n.* **1.** In music, the unaccented note before the **downbeat**. **2.** In conducting, lifting the arm at the opening of a piece as the cue (signal) to the musicians to play on the downbeat.

Up in Central Park Broadway operetta by Sigmund **Romberg**; book by Herbert and Dorothy **Fields**; lyrics by Dorothy Fields; Century Theatre, 1945 (904 perf.); film, 1948.

This nostalgic romp is based on the true story of the corrupt Tammany Hall politician Boss William Marcy Tweed (1823-1878), who was involved in graft and scandals in the 1860s and '70s. The story is actually rather pedestrian, but the evocative score is Romberg at his lyrical and lilting best.

John Matthews, a *New York Times* reporter, decides to expose Tweed for his profiteering during the construction of Central Park in 1870. But Matthews is in love with Rosie Moore, the daughter of one of Tweed's hack cronies. Because of his integrity, he wins her affection, and at the same time, helps bring down her father's nefarious employer.

up-tempo *adj.* [Also used as a n.; also spelled "uptempo"] Pertaining to a number in a musical comedy that is fast-paced and ebullient.

Urinetown A hit Broadway musical by Mark Hollman, with book and lyrics by Greg Kotis (b. 1966); transferred from Off-Off-Broadway showcase run to Broadway; Henry Miller Theatre, 2001 (965 perf.).

The tuneful score includes elements of several types of music, including folk and country songs. The show's dark satire is reminiscent of **Brecht** and **Weill** collaborations, though with a much lighter tone.

In a blighted future urban landscape, Caldwell B. Cladwell, a corrupt capitalist, tyrannizes the population. When there is a water shortage, he obliges them to pay for the use of the public conveniences he owns. The political activist and reformer Bobby Strong leads a revolt, and Hope, Cladwell's daughter, falls in love with him. Cladwell has him killed, but Hope takes up the cause, and the revolt is successful.

Utopia Limited, or The Flowers of Progress Comic opera in two acts by **Gilbert and Sullivan**; London, Savoy Theatre, 1893.

The penultimate effort of Gilbert and Sullivan, after three years of their not working together, proved to be somewhat of a disaster, despite the excited anticipation of the public, and closed in a few months. This politically satiric work is rather unclear as to the targets of its satire, although Gilbert has supplied some clever, acerbic lyrics. The score contains some sparkling numbers and particularly ingenious orchestrations. George Bernard Shaw, reviewing the opening night performance for the newspaper *The World*, thought it wonderful, esp. Sullivan's contribution. There are allusions to previous successes, esp. *H.M.S. Pinafore*: Captain Corcoran is one of the flowers of progress. The original production was lavish: act 2 included a cabinet meeting in the form of a **minstrel show** number and an elaborate drawing room reception, showing off the ladies' gorgeous costumes, in imitation of those held by Queen Victoria.

Zara (sop.), daughter of the anglophile King Paramount (bar.) of the Pacific island nation of Utopia, has gone to England to be educated, leaving her two sisters, Nekaya (contr.) (sop.) and Kalyba (mezz.) to be raised by an English governess, Lady Sophie (contr.), with whom Paramount is in love. Zara returns home accompanied by a group of six Englishmen—the "flowers of progress"—who represent various aspects of English political and commercial life, and whose mission is to help reform Utopia and its institutions. Paramount decides to run his kingdom according to the English Joint Stock Company Act of 1862, thus threatening the power of Scaphio (bar.) and Phantis (bar.), the two Wise Men who have controlled the king, assisted by Tarara (bar.), the Public Exploder. [He is named for the refrain of a popular song of the day, "Ta-ra-ra-boom-dee-ay."] But the reforms don't work, and Scaphio and Phantis lead a revolt, which is effectively quelled when Zara remembers that she forgot to introduce the most essential reform of all, "government by party" along English lines. Adopt that, and all will be well! This is done, to the cheers of the Utopians. Eventually, all the romantic plot complications are resolved; Paramount is freed of the burden of being controlled by his two evil geniuses and ends up with Lady Sophie, and all the right couples get together as everyone sings a hymn in praise of England.

V

Vaccai, Nicola (1790–1848) (NEE ko: lah vah KAH-ee) [Also spelled "Vaccaj"] Italian opera singer; noted singing teacher who taught in Italy, France, and England; author of a now classic book on his singing technique, *Metodo pratico di canto italiano* (Practical Method of Italian Singing) (1832) (MEH: to: do: PRAH tee ko: dee KAHN to: ee tah' lee AH no:)—still in print, and an important source of information on the performance practice of the romantic era. A prolific composer of now largely forgotten operas, he wrote energetic, dramatic, and melodious music for his highly successful *Zadig ed Astartea* (1825) (zah DEEG ehd ahs tahr TEH: ah), based on Voltaire's novel *Zadig*. And he wrote some very charming, beguiling pages, e.g., in the two-act **opera buffa** (he called it a *dramma buffo*: a comic drama) *Pietro il grande, ossia un geloso alla tortura* (Peter the Great, or A Jealous Man in Torture) (1824) (PYEH tro: ih:l GRAHN deh: os SEE ah ih:l dgeh LO: zo: ahl' lah to:r TOO rah), in which he himself sang. His career was outshone by that of his rival, Vincenzo **Bellini**, whose *I Capuleti ed i Montecchi* (1830)—with a libretto by Felice **Romani**, with whom Vaccai had quarreled—eclipsed Vaccai's greatest success, *Giulietta e Romeo* (Juliet and Romeo) (1825) (dgoo LYEHT tah eh: ro: MEH: o:). But at the suggestion of Gioachino **Rossini**, the penultimate scene of Vaccai's opera, which is indeed very beautiful, was interpolated into the Bellini piece, and this became the usual practice during the romantic era.

Vagabond King, The Broadway operetta by Rudolf **Friml**; book and lyrics by poet and translator Brian Hooker (1880–1946) [William Brian Hooker] and William H. Post, based on the play *If I Were King* (1901) by Justin Huntly McCarthy (1860–1936); Casino Theatre, 1925 (511 perf.); films, 1930 and 1956, with new material by Friml.

The story of this masterful, tuneful operetta, one of Friml's greatest, is based loosely on the adventurous character of the French iconoclastic braggart-poet and thief François Villon (1431–1463) (frahn swah' vee YO:N; vee LO:N), known for his cynicism and for his starkly memorable, pessimistic poetry.

The Duke of Burgundy has besieged Paris, and the populace prefers him to the tyrannical French king, Louis XI, called Louis the Prudent (1423-1483). The king has unsuccessfully wooed Katherine de Vaucelles (duh vo: SEHL), to whom the hubristic Villon has dared to send love letters. Katherine decides to meet him at an inn, and she is followed by the king in disguise. He hears Villon mocking him and holding forth on what he would do if he were king. The monarch reveals himself and confronts Villon with a choice: Go immediately to the gallows, or become king for a day and be hanged in twenty-four hours. He must save Paris from the Duke of Burgundy, and he must stop courting Katherine. By this time, however, Villon and Katherine have fallen in love. He accepts the king's challenge, and, with the help of his friends, the Paris mob, defeats Burgundy. As a reward for his services, the king allows Villon to go into exile with Katherine.

vamp *n., v.* [Short for *vampire*] *Slang.* —*n.* **1.** A seductive young lady trying her wiles and ploys on a prospective lover. **2.** The role of such a seductress, a character type, esp. in the 1920s and 30s. **3.** A repeated, brief, introductory musical sequence. —*v. i.* **4.** In music, esp. in musical comedy, vaudeville, or burlesque, to play a brief introduction or musical figure repeatedly, e.g., while a strip-teaser makes a slow, seductive entrance; or while waiting for a performer to enter; or until a singer is ready to begin singing, e.g., the repeated notes in the rhythmic pattern tum-ta-ta, tum-ta-ta, played for a **Gilbert and Sullivan patter** song; hence, the direction to "vamp till ready."

Vampyr, Der (deh: VAHM pee'uh[*r*]) Opera in two acts by Heinrich **Marschner**; libretto by Wilhelm August Wöhlbruck (1796–1848) (VIHL hehlm OW g*oo*st VÖL br*oo*k'), based on the romantic horror classic *The Vampire* (1819), by Italian-English writer and doctor John William Polidori (1795–1821); Leipzig, Stadttheater, 1828.

Sir Ruthven (RUTH vehn; RIH vehn) (ten.), a Scottish noble, has become a vampire. He must sacrifice the lives of three virgins, or forfeit his soul to Satan. The first maiden to die is Janthe (YAHN teh) (sop.). In the struggle to kill her, Sir Ruthven himself falls as if dead, but he is revived in the moonlight, to the strains of eerily evocative music, by his faithful friend Aubry (AW bree) (bar.), to whom he has revealed his secret. Next to die is Emmy (sop.). Then Sir Ruthven makes a terrible mistake: In seeking desperately for a third victim, he lights upon Aubry's fiancée, Malvina (mahl VEE nah) (sop.), and tries to murder her, but Aubry intervenes just as the clock strikes the hour of midnight. Sir Ruthven's time is up, and the undead fiend descends into Hell.

Vanessa Opera in four acts by Samuel **Barber**; libretto by Gian-Carlo **Menotti**; New York, Metropolitan Opera, 1958.

Vanessa (sop.), has waited and yearned for twenty years for the return of the lover who had abandoned her. When his son, Anatol (ten.), arrives and informs her that her lover has died, she is in despair, but Anatol comforts her. She falls in love with him, and they are married. Anatol seduces Erika (mezz.), Vanessa's niece and companion. Vanessa and Anatol move to Paris, and Erika, in love with Anatol, will relive Vanessa's tragic fate.

Vanloo, Albert (1846–1920) (ahl BEH*R* vah*n* LO:) Belgian-born French librettist who, either on his own or together with writing partners, esp., his usual collaborator, Eugène Leterrier (1834–1884) (luh teh*r*' *r*ee EH:), wrote two dozen libretti, including those for **Offenbach**, among them *Le voyage dans la lune* (1875), which they wrote with A. Mortier (mo:*r* TYEH:); Charles **Lecocq**, including *Giroflé, Girofla*; *L'étoile* by **Chabrier**; and **Messager**. Vanloo's memoirs, *Sur le plateau* (On Stage) (sü*r* luh plah TO:), with a preface by Lecocq (Librairie Ollendorf, 1913), make fascinating reading.

See also VÉRONIQUE.

variety *n.* Entertainment that includes different kinds of acts, such as stand-up comedy, comic sketches, songs, specialty animal acts, and so forth.

Varney, Louis (1844–1908) (vah*r* NEH:) Prolific New Orleans-born French conductor, theater manager, composer; wrote thirty-nine operettas, of which three were huge hits: *Les Mousquetaires au couvent* (The Musketeers in the Convent) (1880) (leh: moos kuh TEH:*R* o: koo VAH*N*), *Coquelicot* (Poppy) (1882) (kok lee KO:), and *Fanfan la Tulipe* (Fanfan the Tulip) (1882) (fah*n* FAH*N* lah tü LEEP). He was known for the cheerful, melodious, and insouciant style of his music.

vaudeville *n.* **1.** Variety entertainment consisting of song and dance acts, comedy skits, juggling, acrobatics, magic, mind-reading acts, and other specialty performances. **2.** A comic, short theater piece, sketch, or farce. **3.** A satiric French **cabaret** song.

Vaughan Williams, Ralph (1872–1958) Prolific English composer of symphonies and symphonic poems, and of six operas, among them *Hugh the Drover* (1924); *Sir John in Love* (1929), based on Shakespeare's **Falstaff** character; *The Poisoned Kiss* (1936); and *Riders to the Sea* (1937), based on the play by John Millington Synge [1871–1909).

Věc Makropulos (The Makropulos Affair) Opera by Leoš **Janáček**.

vehicle *n.* A film, play, musical comedy, or other entertainment that showcases the talents of a particular performer; i.e., a *star vehicle*, such as Irving Berlin's ***Call Me Madam***, written for Ethel Merman.

vengeance aria In opera, a solo number expressing a character's vengeful desires. See ARIA DI VENDETTA.

Verdi, Giuseppe (1813–1901) (VEHR dee) One of Italy's favorite opera composers, deeply loved, respected, and honored, and one of the world's greatest; he almost constitutes his own school of romantic opera composition. Verdi wrote twenty-seven operas; instrumental pieces; and ecclesiastical works, of which the operatic *Requiem Mass* (1874), in honor of the great writer Alessandro Manzoni (1785–1873) (ah' lehs SAHN dro: mahn DZO: nee), is constantly performed. He was also revered for his great humanitarianism, patriotism, and political activism. The letters of his name, daubed on walls during the independence movement called the Risorgimento (resurgence) (ree so:r' dgih: MEHN to:), were an acronym for Vittorio Emmanuele, re d'Italia (Victor Emmanuel, King of Italy) (vee TO: ree o: eh mah' noo EH: leh: REH: dee TAH lyah): Viva V.E.R.D.I.
See also ARDITI, LUIGI.
Verdi's operas:
1839 *Oberto, Conte di San Bonifacio* (Oberto, Count of San Bonifacio) (o: BEHR to: KO:N te dee sahn bo:n' ee FAH cho:)
1840 *Un giorno di regno* (King for a Day; lit., One Day of Reign; The False Stanislaus) (*Il finto Stanislao*) (oon DGO:R no: dee REH nyo: / eel FEEN to: stahn' ee SLAH-o:)
1841 *Nabucco* (*Nabucodonosor*) (Nebuchadnezzar) (nah BOO ko:) (nah BOO ko: do:' no: SO:R)

1843 *I Lombardi alla prima crociata* (*Jérusalem*) (The Lombards at the First Crusade) (ee lom BAHR dee ahl' lah PREE mah kro: CHAH tah / zhé rü' zah LEHM)

1844 ***Ernani***

1844 *I due Foscari* (The Two Foscari) (ee DOO-eh: FO:S kah ree)

1845 *Giovanna d'Arco* (Joan of Arc) (dgo: VAHN nah DAHR ko:)

1845 *Alzira* (ahl DZEE rah)

1846 *Attila* (AH tee lah)

1847 *Macbeth*; revised for Paris Opéra, 1865

1847 *I masnadieri* (The Robbers) (ee mahz' nah DYEH: ree)

1848 *Il corsaro* (The Corsair) (eel ko:r SAH ro:)

1849 *La battaglia di Legnano* (The Battle of Legnano) (lah baht TAH [g]lyah dee leh: NYAH no:)

1849 *Luisa Miller* (loo EE zah MIH:L lehr)

1850 *Stiffelio* (later, *Aroldo*) (steef FEH: lee o: / ah RO:L do:)

1851 ***Rigoletto***

1853 ***Il trovatore (The Troubadour)***

1853 ***La traviata (She Who Has Strayed)***

1855 *I vespri siciliani (Les vêpres siciliennes)* (The Sicilian Vespers) (ee VEHS pree sih' chih LYAH nee) (leh: VEH pruh sih: sih: LYEHN)

1857 *Simon Boccanegra* (see MO:N bo:k' kah NEH: grah)

1857 *Aroldo* (originally, *Stiffelio*)

1859 *Un ballo in maschera* (A Masked Ball) (oon BAHL lo: een MAHS ke: rah)

1862 ***La forza del destino (The Force of Destiny)***

1867; 1884 ***Don Carlos (Don Carlo)***

1871 ***Aïda***

1887 ***Otello***

1893 ***Falstaff***

Verdian (VEHR dee uhn) *adj.* **1.** Pertaining to and characteristic of the rich melodic and orchestral gifts of composer Giuseppe Verdi. **2.** Dramatic, deeply felt emotion, expressed in passionate melody, as in Verdi's operas. **3.** Pertaining to singers who specialize in the Verdian **repertoire**, or to scholars and students of his work.

verismo (veh RIH:S mo), *n.* [Italian: realism; also used as an adjective] Late 19th- and early 20th-c. realism in Italian literature and opera; often dealing with domestic drama/tragedy, e.g., Giovanni Verga's (1840–1922) story ***Cavalleria Rusticana***, made into an opera by Pietro **Mascagni**. Among verismo composers are **Cilea**, **Giordano**, and **Leoncavallo**; the most famous exemplar of the school is undoubtedly **Puccini**. D'Albert's ***Tiefland*** and some operas of **Massenet** are also verismo works.

Véronique (vé ro NEEK) **Opéra comique** in three acts by André **Messager**; libretto by Albert **Vanloo**, based on an earlier libretto by Georges Duval (1777–1853); Paris, Théâtre des Bouffes-Parisiens, 1898.

The florist Coquenard (kok NAH*R*) (bar.) covets a position as Captain in the National Guard, which he hopes to obtain through Viscount Florestan de Valain-court (flo: *r*eh stah*n* duh vah la*n* KOO*R*) (ten.). He is encouraged because his wife, Agathe (ah GAHT) (mezz.), is having an affair with Florestan. The financially insolvent viscount has arranged a marriage, sight unseen, with a wealthy provincial heiress, Hélène de Solanges (é lehn' duh so LAH*N*ZH) (sop.). She comes to Paris with her aunt Emerance (eh muh *R*AH*N*S) (mezz.), and, entering the flower shop, discovers that he is having an affair with the florist's wife, and wants to marry her only for her money. She decides to teach him a lesson, and disguises herself as a working girl, Véronique, with her aunt masquerading as Estelle; both of the women get jobs at the flower shop. Florestan invites everyone to a gala picnic and falls in love with Véronique. She mocks him and leaves, and he is quite upset. As a surprise, she pays his debts. Astonished, he naturally wants to meet her. He is even more astonished to find that Véronique is really Hélène. Now thoroughly ashamed of himself, Florestan decides on the spot to marry her and give up Agathe, who is very proud to be in the company of her husband in his splendid new uniform as a Captain in the National Guard.

version *n.* **1.** A particular variant of a story, novel, opera or other musical theater piece; also, an adaptation of source material for the stage or the screen: *There are various versions of Gaston Leroux's story* **The Phantom of the Opera**. See also DEFINITIVE EDITION; FALSTAFF; FAUST; FIDELIO; IVANHOE. **2.** The particular form of adaptation: *the musical comedy version of a play*, e.g. **My Fair Lady**, adapted from Shaw's *Pygmalion*.

Very Good Eddie Broadway musical by Jerome **Kern**; book by Guy **Bolton** and Philip Bartholomae (1879–1947); lyrics by Schuyler Green, Herbert Reynolds, et al.; Princess Theatre, 1915 (341 perf.); Broadway revival: Goodspeed Opera production, with interpolated songs from other shows by Kern, Booth Theatre, 1975 (304 perf.). One of the first **Princess Theater musicals**.

Poor, put-upon, very good Eddie Kettle has no will of his own, and he has married one of the bossiest women in the world, Georgina. They go on a cruise up the Hudson River for their honeymoon and meet another newlywed couple, Percy and Elsie Darling. The boat makes a sightseeing stop, but when it starts off again, Eddie and Elsie have inadvertently been left ashore. That night, a storm rages, and the terrified Elsie seeks protection from Eddie in his room at the inn where they have been forced to lodge until the boat returns. When it does, and the proper couples are reunited, Eddie is no longer a spineless wimp; he has discovered that he is a man, and Georgina had better realize that fact! "Very good, Eddie," says she, as meekly as can be.

vestale, La (The Vestal Virgin) (Italian pron.: lah veh STAH leh:) (French pron.: lah veh: STAHL) **1.** This is the title of several operas using the same basic theme (love versus duty), including those by Antonio **Salieri** (1768; his first opera; score lost) and an opera in two acts by Giovanni **Pacini** (1823).

2. Opera in three acts by Gaspare **Spontini**; libretto in French by Victor-Joseph Étienne de **Jouy**; Paris Opéra, 1807.

A magnificent 1954 recording with Maria Callas is available on Membran CD (223253; 2005).

The vestal virgin Giulia (DGOO lyah) (sop.) is in love with the Roman general Licinio (lih: CHIH: nee o:) (ten.), one of the victors in the Gallic Wars. When he visits her secretly in the temple of the goddess Vesta, she inadvertently allows the sacred flame to go out. For this crime, and for refusing to name her lover, whom she had allowed to escape, she is to be buried alive. Licinio comes forward to confess his guilt, but she denies that he is the one. She is entombed, but by the intervention of the compassionate goddess, the flame is magically relit by a lightning bolt. Giulia is freed, released from her vestal vows, and reunited with her beloved.

3. Opera in three acts by Saverio **Mercadante**; libretto by Salvadore **Cammarano**; Naples, Teatro San Carlo, 1840.

Considered Mercadante's masterpiece, this opera has been superbly recorded on a Marco Polo CD (8.225310-11; 2005).

The story is very similar to that of Spontini's opera: The general Decio (DEH: cho:) (ten.) [Decius], believed killed in the Gallic Wars, returns in triumph. Meanwhile, believing him dead, the beautiful Emilia (mezz.), who had been in love with him, has taken her vows as a vestal. During his triumphal march, it is her duty to crown him with the laurel wreath of victory, and she does so in an agony of despair, without being able to acknowledge their love. Later, he hides in the temple, and when they meet, she inadvertently allows the sacred flame to go out. She must pay for her crime, but Decio has escaped in the mean time. He has raised an army, but he arrives too late to save her, and kills himself on her tomb.

Vetter aus Dingsda, Der (The Cousin from Wherever) (1921) (deh FEH tuh ows DIHNGZ DAH) Operetta in three acts by Eduard **Künneke**; libretto by theater director and librettist Hermann Haller (1871–1943) (HEH[R] mahn HAHL leh), and Dr. Fritz **Oliven**; Berlin, Theater am Nollendorfplatz (ahm NO: lehn daw[r]f PLAHTS), 1921.

This merry operetta is hilarious, what with its extremely silly story and the brilliance of Dr. Oliven's clever, deft lyrics. Musically, it is a rollicking, witty triumph, with catchy, lively, jaunty tunes and a bit of schmaltz thrown in for good measure.

The orphaned heiress Julia (YOO lee ah) (sop.) lives on her country estate with her officious guardians, Uncle Josse (YO:S seh) (bar.) and Aunt Wimpel (VIHM pehl) (mezz.), who are perpetually quarreling. Julia longs for the return of her cousin Roderich (*R*OH duh *r*ih:*kh*) (ten.), who left when she was seven, and went to live in Batavia. Uncle Josse wants her to marry her cousin Augustin (OW goo*s* TEEN) (ten.)—whom Julia has never met—before she comes of age and inherits the estate, so that Josse will still be in control. Word arrives that the court has declared her legally of age already, so she and her friend Hannchen (HAHN *kh*enn) (sop.) celebrate at the village inn. Meanwhile, Josse schemes to have Augustin, whom he has not seen since Augustin was a small boy, appear at the house pretending to be Roderich, so as to inveigle Julia into marriage; but he fails to keep their appointment to discuss matters. However, he has been at the inn and has learned a thing or two. He shows up, posing as Roderich, and Julia finds him attractive. Then the real Roderich shows up, and falls in love with Hannchen! Augustin reveals his true identity, and Julia realizes that she has fallen in love with him. Both couples are united and everyone is happy, including Josse, since, after all, Julia is marrying Augustin, her Vetter "aus Berlin."

vibrato (vee BRAH toh) *n.* [Fr. Italian] Shaking of the voice; **tremolo**.

Victor/Victoria Broadway musical based on the 1982 film produced, directed, and written by Blake Edwards (b. 1922), both starring Edwards's wife, Julie Andrews, in the title role, with Robert Preston as Toddy in the film; music by Henry **Mancini**; lyrics by Leslie **Bricusse**; book by Blake Edwards; extra songs for the stage show by Mancini, Bricusse, and Frank **Wildhorn**; Marquis Theatre, 1995 (734 perf.).

In the 1930s, the English singer Victoria Grant finds herself on the verge of starvation in Paris. A gay cabaret performer, Carroll "Toddy" Todd, is also on the way down, but, having seen Victoria in his borrowed clothes, he comes up with a scheme to save them both: She will become the male singer Victor, a female impersonator, and he will be her promoter. At the end of her act, "Victoria" will reveal herself to be a man! The scheme works, and Victor/Victoria becomes an overnight sensation—the greatest female impersonator in the business. But life is rarely simple, and an American gangster newly arrived in Paris, King Marchand, falls for Victoria, to the fury of his girlfriend, Norma Cassidy. He decides to investigate the situation—after all, how could he, a tough gangster, actually fall for another man? And Victoria has fallen for King. The complications accumulate, until everything is set right in the end, with the sex and sexuality of all the characters finally out in the open.

vie parisienne, La (Parisian Life) (lah vee' pah *r*ee' ZYEHN) **Opéra bouffe** in five acts by Jacques **Offenbach**; libretto by Henri **Meilhac** and Ludovic **Halévy**; Paris, Théâtre du Palais Royal, 1866; revised to four acts, 1873.

This is one of the few Offenbach pieces to be set in his own time, and it raises a cynical and knowing eyebrow at Parisian social and sexual life, with its courtesans, deceptions, and constant flirtations. The background: Baron Georges-Eugène Haussmann (1809–1891) (o:s MAHN), Napoleon the Third's urban planner, has overseen the rebuilding of Paris, with the broad boulevards and spacious squares we know today; and the railway has proved a sensation, as tourists arrive in droves from all over the world for the upcoming Exhibition of 1867.

The high society dandies Bobinet (bo bee NEH:) (bar.) and Raoul de Gardefeu (*r*ah OOL duh gah*r*' duh F*OO*) (ten.) are in a railway station awaiting the arrival of the woman they both adore, the courtesan Métella (mé tehl LAH) (mezz.). She arrives on the arm of another man and pretends she does not recognize them, whereupon they see themselves as brothers in misfortune and decide to give up courtesans and return to seeking the favors of young high society ladies. Raoul is happy to run into his former valet, Joseph (zho: ZEHF) (speaking role), who is now a tourist guide working for the Grand-Hôtel (grahn to: TEHL). He is waiting for the Swedish baron (bar.) and baroness (sop.) de Gondremarck (go:n druh MAHRK). As soon as Raoul sees her, he is madly in love, and he prevails on Joseph to let him take his place and pose as a guide. He takes them to his mansion, which he passes off as an annex of the Grand-Hôtel. The baron confides in his "guide" that he is out for a good time, and that he has heard of Métella, whom he is eager to meet and conquer. Raoul, hoping to seduce the baroness, promises him that Métella will be his. He then arranges with Bobinet to give a fantastic supper at the mansion, as if it were a hotel dinner, and Bobinet enlists his servants, as well as Gabrielle (gah bree EHL) (sop.), a glovemaker, and Frick (FRIH:K) (bar.), a bootmaker who lusts after her, to be their guests—all masquerading as the upper crust. In the end, though, Raoul does not succeed in seducing the baroness, nor does the baron have any luck in seducing Métella, who has the baroness keep their assignation in her place. Still, everyone has had a rollicking good time, including the Brazilian, a tourist who has gotten involved in the proceedings and who adores Parisian high life, as he tells us in one of Offenbach's liveliest tunes.

Village Romeo and Juliet, A Opera in a prologue and three acts by Frederick **Delius**; libretto by the composer, based on a short story by the Swiss writer Gottfried Keller (1819–1890) (GOT freet KEH luh); Berlin, Komische (KO: mih sheh) Oper, 1907. The opera, with its Wagnerian musical influence, is seldom done, but the famous "Walk to the Paradise Garden" is still played in concerts.

The story begins when Sali (treble; then ten.) and Vreli (girl sop., then sop.) are children, in love with each other. They are the son and daughter of two farmers, Marz (bass) and Marti (bar.), bitter enemies, both eventually ruined by the lawsuit they bring against each other. A character arrives as if out of nowhere: the lame Dark Fiddler (bar.), rightful heir to the woods that he cannot inherit because he cannot prove his claim. But he allows the children to play on the land, with the stipulation that it remain unplowed. As young adults, the pair arrange to meet at a country fair in the village's Paradise Gardens. The Dark Fiddler is there, and he encourages them to run away. They decide to cast off on a barge moored at the dock, while the Dark Fiddler plays madly. Sali pulls the plug from the bottom of the barge, and they drift off to their death.

Villati, Leopoldo de (1701–1752) (leh: o: PO:L do: deh: veel LAH tee) Italian poet and librettist; spent much of his life in Austria and Germany; wrote texts for oratorios and opera libretti, some for **Jommelli**, and many for **Graun**, including versions of the *Armida* (1751) and *Orfeo* (1752) stories, and *Coriolano* (1749) (ko:' ree o: LAH no:), a text based on Shakespeare's *Coriolanus*, and co-written with Frederick the Great and Italian poet and musicologist, Francesco Algarotti (1712–1764) (frahn CHEHS ko: ahl gah RO:T tee).

Vives, Amadeo (1871–1932) (ah' mah THEH: o: VEE veh:s) [Also known by his Catalan name, Amadeu Vives (ah' mah DEH: oo VEE vuhs)] Catalan composer of more than 100 works for the Spanish musical theater; esp. famous for his zarzuela *Doña Francisquita.*

See also BOHÈME, LA.

Vivaldi, Antonio (1678–1741) (vee VAHL dee) Italian violinist and composer known above all for his ca. 500 string compositions and concertos; composed more than forty-five operas—he claimed to have written ninety-four, but these probably included arrangements of operas by other composers. Only around twenty scores have been preserved, some intact, some incomplete. Although seldom performed, his operas have received renewed interest from both musicologists and those involved in production, and quite a few have been recorded. His typically baroque operatic music, sometimes reminiscent of his string compositions, can be very vibrant, dynamic, and exciting, as well as emotionally evocative and moving; e.g., as shown in excerpts recorded by mezz. Cecilia Bartoli (b. 1966) (che' CHEE lyah BAHR to: lee) on *The Vivaldi Album* (Decca 289 466 569-2, 1999), as well as in the complete, superb recordings (on various labels) of such operas as *La fida ninfa* (The Faithful Nymph) (1732) (lah FEE dah NIH:N fah), *Bajazet* (1735) (bah' yah ZEHT), *Griselda* (1735) (gree ZEHL dah), and *Il Teuzzone* (1718) (ihl teh:' oodz DZO: neh:)—the latter three named for their principal characters. Among the great virtues of these recordings is that they feature singers who all negotiate with gorgeous ease the ubiquitous, fiendishly difficult **coloratura** passages. The operas follow the standard compositional formula of solo and ensemble numbers with recitative in between them. But Vivaldi is an innovator with an individual style, quite distinct, for instance, from that of **Handel**: a master at varying not only tempo, depending on the dramatic demands of a situation, but also of constructing a melodic line in keeping with a character's emotional state; this in an age that had not yet seen the full flowering of operatic conventions and the soaring melodies of the romantic composers.

vocal *n., adj.* —*n.* [Fr. a shortening of *vocal music*] *Slang* **1.** A song, esp. in musical comedy, vaudeville, or revue. —*adj.* **2.** Pertaining to the voice.

vocal energy The force of the voice when projected using the muscles of the vocal apparatus and the diaphragm; and the amount of such force.

vocalist *n.* A singer, esp. in cabaret, nightclubs, or vaudeville.

vocalise (VOH kuh LEEZ), *n.* A singer's exercise using vowels or syllables, for developing agility, e.g., in opera singing.

vocalize (VOH kuh LIZ), *v. i.* **1.** To warm up the singing voice preparatory to performing. **2.** To practice vocal technique for singing, using exercises such as vocalises, scales, arpeggios, etc.

vocal line 1. The part of a **score** that shows what is to be sung; e.g., the melody on the upper staff, and the words that are in the space between the staffs of a **piano-vocal score**. **2.** In voice production technique, the smoothness and evenness or unevenness of tone (i.e., of the sounds produced by the voice), resulting from and dependent upon the singer's muscular tension, relaxation, **breathing technique**, **placement**, and negotiation of the different registers.

vocal score The music of the singers' parts, together with a **piano reduction** of the orchestral accompaniment, of an opera, operetta, musical comedy, or other musical theater piece.

vocal technique Method or way of producing and using the voice when performing.

Vogelhändler, Der (The Bird Seller) (deh: FO: guhl HEND luh) Operetta in three acts by Karl **Zeller**; libretto by Moritz West and Ludwig Held (1837–1900), based on a French comedy, *Ce que deviennent les roses* (What Becomes of Roses) (1857) (suh kuh duh VYEHN leh: RO:Z) by Victor Varin (1798–1869) (veek to:*r'* vah *RAN*) and Pierre de Bréville (1861–1949) (pee eh:*r'* duh bré VEEL); Vienna, Theater an der Wien, 1891.

The charming setting for this adorable operetta is a Rhineland village in the 18th c. But the villagers, who have hunted freely on the land of the Elector, are anything but charmed when they learn that he is arriving for a boar hunt. For one thing, there are no boar left: the villagers have poached them all. In addition, Baron Weps (VEHPS) (bar.), the gamekeeper, has a ne'er-do-well nephew, Count Stanislaus (STAH nih SLOWS) (ten.), whose debts he feels honor bound to pay. As a bribe, he accepts a couple of pigs offered by the villages to replace the decimated boar. Suddenly, he receives news that the Elector is not coming after all. What to do? He can't afford to return the bribes! He prevails upon Stanislaus to impersonate the Elector. Stanislaus regally holds an audience in the Elector's hunting lodge, where he receives the local postmistress, Christel (K*R*IH:S tehl) (sop.). She wants her lover, the Tyrolean bird seller Adam (ten.), to be given the post of zookeeper. Meanwhile, the Elector's wife, Princess Marie (sop.), is sure her husband is having an assignation in the hunting lodge. She flirts with Adam outside the lodge, and gives him a rose, in order to make the Elector jealous. Christel comes out, and Adam is shocked. So this is the woman the Elector has been seeing! But all complications are soon explained.

voice *n.* The sound produced by forcing air from the lungs through the larynx and vocal cords so that it creates **resonance** and sonority when it vibrates against the bones. Voices are characterized and categorized by their **range**; the name of the range is also used to mean the person having that range, e.g., **alto**, **bass**, **soprano**. The higher end of the range, where singers feel vibrations in the **mask**, is called the **head voice**. The lower end of the range, where singers feel vibrations in the chest, is called the **chest voice**. A **falsetto** is an artificial, high-pitched male voice, used in speaking and/or singing, sometimes to comic effect. Singers and actors both have a high, middle, and low voice, i.e., they have all three registers; it is the middle **register** of the speaking voice that, when properly supported, carries best in the theater. The human singing voice is capable of variations in tonal **coloration** (reflecting emotion), stress, and intensity, in accord with the harmonic and rhythmic content of the music being interpreted.

See also BARITONE; CASTRATO; COUNTERTENOR; MEZZO-SOPRANO; TENOR.

voice part 1. The music or melodic line for a particular category of singer in an ensemble piece: *the soprano voice in the "Hallelujah Chorus."* **2.** One of the melodic lines in a musical composition: *the bass voice of a piano sonata.*

voix humaine, La (The Human Voice) Opera by Francis **Poulenc**.

volta (VO:L tah) *n.* [Italian: turn] *Hist.* Rapid Italian dance in triple time for couples, popular at the court of the English queen Elizabeth I (1533–1603); similar to the **galliard**; includes a leaping step with the dancer simultaneously executing a turn while lifting his partner. The volta is featured in Benjamin Britten's three-act opera about Elizabeth and her court, *Gloriana* (1953).

Vorspiel (FO:[R] SHPEEL) *n.* [German: before-play] **1.** Prologue, spoken or sung; introductory scene. **2.** Brief musical prelude or introduction.

W

wagon stage A mechanized rolling platform the size of the performing area on a theater stage, on which an entire set can be mounted, and which can be wheeled from offstage onto the stage platform. At the Metropolitan Opera in New York, and in other large opera houses, a system of wagon stages is used to change the scenery during performances. Also called a *slip stage*.

Wagner, Richard (1813–1883) (*REE kh*ah[*r*]t VAHG nuh) Highly influential German composer, known for his innovative **through-composed** music dramas, for which he wrote his own libretti. The operas and music dramas of such composers as Franz **Schreker**, Werner Egk (1901–1983) (EHK), Hans Pfitzner, Hans Werner **Henze**, Paul **Hindemith**, Richard **Strauss**, Benjamin **Britten**, and many others would be unimaginable without Wagner. He is known, too, for his psychopathic, vitriolic anti-Semitism, which he ignored when he found a Jewish musician talented and useful to him; and his abject, vicious betrayal of his friends. Paradoxically, he wrote operas about love that many consider among the greatest ever composed. George Bernard **Shaw** wrote *The Perfect Wagnerite: A Commentary on the Ring* (1898), to show how universal Wagner's themes in the **Ring cycle** are. And listening to the old recordings of Wagner by Danish **Heldentenor** Lauritz Melchior (1890–1973) and Norwegian soprano Kirsten Flagstad (1895–1962) is thrilling—not so much because of Wagner as because of them: their incomparable, beautiful voices and their majestic singing are enthralling. But many people find Wagner pretentious, and his music turgid, hollow, and bombastic, full of empty, pseudo-heroic posturing—a true reflection of the man himself. Christopher Buck, who has played violin in the orchestra for many Wagner performances, says that for him Wagner's music is "like a big, fat steak … first couple of bites are quite breathtaking, then it just gets heavy, chewy, and cloying." Wagner designed the Bayreuth **Festspielhaus** to accommodate the large orchestras and innovative stage and stage machinery necessary for productions of his operas; it opened in 1876. And the town is still home to the annual, very popular Bayreuth Festival, devoted to presenting Wagner's works.

Richard Wagner's operas:

1832 *Die Hochzeit* (The Wedding; unfinished) (dee HOKH tsIt')

1833 *Die Feen* (The Fairies) (dee FEH: ehn)

1836 *Das Liebesverbot* (The Banning of Love) (dahs LEE behs feh[*r*]' BO:T

1837 *Rienzi, der Letzte der Tribunen* (Rienzi, Last of the Tribunes) (*r*ee EHN zee deh:[*r*] LEHTS teh deh:[r] t*r*ih:' BOO nehn)

1843 *Der fliegende Holländer* (The Flying Dutchman) (deh FLEE gehn duh HO: lehn duh)

1845 (revised for the Paris Opéra, 1861) *Tannhäuser und der Sängerkrieg auf Wartburg* (Tannhäuser and the Singing Contest on the Wartburg) (TAHN HOY zuh *oo*nt deh ZEHNG uh K*R*EEK owf VAH[*R*]T boo[*r*]k)

1850 *Lohengrin* (LO: ehn G*R*IH:N)

1865 *Tristan und Isolde*
1867 *Die Meistersinger von Nürnberg (The Mastersingers of Nuremberg)*
1876 **Ring cycle:** *Der Ring des Nibelungen (The Ring of the Nibelungs)*;
four-opera cycle (tetralogy):
1869 *Das Rheingold* (The Rhine Gold)
1870 *Die Walküre* (The Valkyrie)
1871 *Siegfried*
1874 *Götterdämmerung* (Twilight of the Gods)
1882 *Parsifal* (Percival) (PAH[*R*] see FAHL)

Wagnerian *n., adj. —n.* **1.** A singer known esp. for performing leading roles in Wagner's operas, or a conductor who is known for his or her interpretation of Wagner's operas. **2.** A scholar of Wagner's works. **3.** An adherent or fan of his operas. —*adj.* **4.** Pertaining to the kind of **through-composed** music dramas Wagner wrote, or to the kind of music he composed, with its densely textured orchestration and broad melodies.

Walküre, Die (The Valkyrie) The second opera in Wagner's **Ring cycle.**

Wallace, Vincent (1812–1865) [b. William Vincent Wallace] Irish opera composer, known for his one internationally successful work, *Maritana*. He led a very adventurous life, emigrating to Tasmania and Australia, and traveling in India and South America. In Mexico City, he conducted opera, then went to New York City, where he pursued his musical activities further. After traveling in Europe, Wallace settled in London. He wrote several more operas and some operettas, but none of them had the success of *Maritana*.

waltz *n.* Dance in 3/4 or 3/8 time; most associated with Vienna and the **Strauss** family; the dance consists of three steps, with a turn on every third step. It origins are to be found in the old folk dances, the **volta** and the **ländler**. Aside from the innumerable waltzes meant purely for dancing, there are superb waltzes written for musical theater; e.g., in the operettas of **Offenbach**, and ubiquitously of course in the Viennese operettas. Together with the **Strauss family** and Carl Michael **Ziehrer**, the Viennese composer Joseph Lanner (1801–1843) (LAH nuh) and the Alsatian-French composer Émile Waldteufel (1837–1915) (VAHLT TOY fuhl) were the Waltz Kings of Europe.

Wandelprobe *n.,* (VAHN duhl PROHB; P*R*OH buh) [German: wander-rehearsal] A rehearsal of an opera in which the singers on stage and the orchestra in the pit go through all the musical numbers of the piece while the on-stage performers go through some or all of their blocking, but without necessarily doing it fully, and sometimes by marking the music as well; hence, *wandeling* (VAHN duhl ihng): moving around during such a rehearsal. Sometimes, the performers simply sit, and sing as the spirit moves them. The term, used in America, is not used in Germany, where the usual phrase is *Bühnenorchesterprobe* (BÜ nuhn aw[*r*] KEHS tuh P*R*OH buh) [Stage-Orchestra Rehearsal]. Called a *wandel*, for short.

Wang Broadway musical comedy by Woolson Morse (1858–1897); book and lyrics by J. Cheever **Goodwin**; Broadway Theatre, 1891 (151 perf.).

Written as a **vehicle** for DeWolf Hopper (1858–1935), one of the greatest American musical comedy stars, known also for his playing of the leading comedian roles in **Gilbert and Sullivan**; the show proved very popular, silly as its plot was. The score is prettily tuneful and curiously forgettable.

Wang (played by Hopper), the Regent of Siam, is a conniver and a schemer, although not a terribly malicious one, but he does want to rule the country. This is of no account to Prince Mataya (a **trousers role**), who sees through him and finds his shenanigans amusing. In any case, the prince is too absorbed in his love for Gillette, daughter of a former French consul, but her widowed mother is convinced that the prince is only out for financial gain. She manages to get hold of the money in the treasury, and Wang, ever resourceful, ensures the marriage of the two lovers and marries the widow himself, thus securing both the fortune and the reins of power.

warhorse *n. Slang* A sturdy, tried-and-true, beloved play, opera, musical, or ballet that always works, and that is often revived with great success; the mainstay of an opera, repertory, ballet, or summer stock company, e.g., operas by **Puccini** or **Verdi**; musicals by **Rodgers and Hammerstein**; Tchaikovsky's ballets. But the term has a certain derogatory connotation as well, referring to a piece that is done so often that it seems hackneyed, and is therefore performed half-heartedly by a company that is tired of it.

Warren, Harry (1893–1981) [b. Salvtore Anthony Guaragna] Prolific American stage and film composer; known for his scores to such movies as the *Gold Diggers* series (1935, 1937, 1938) and *The Ziegfeld Follies* (1946), and esp. for the film and stage musical *42ⁿᵈ Street*; also wrote the scores for the film *The Belle of New York* and the unsuccessful Broadway musical *Shangri-la* (1956). Among his well known songs are "Lullaby of Broadway," "Shuffle Off to Buffalo," "Jeepers Creepers," and "On the Atchison, Topeka, and the Santa Fe."

Watch Your Step First complete Broadway musical score by Irving **Berlin**; book by Harry B. **Smith**; New Amsterdam Theatre, 1914 (175 perf.), followed by a three-year tour.

The score is altogether delicious; the opening night headline of the *New York Times* review called the show "festivity syncopated": "It is really vaudeville, done handsomely." Still remembered are the songs "A Simple Melody" and "The Syncopated Walk." The second act features a hilarious number called "Opera Melody," in which well known opera tunes are given a **ragtime** treatment. The show was also notable for its dance numbers, many performed by the celebrated husband and wife team of Vernon (1887–1918) and Irene (1893–1969) Castle, who did their famous **cakewalk**, **foxtrot**, and other ballroom dances.

In the opening number, the chorus, dancing its heart out, complains that it can't work all day if it has been dancing all night—and this inanity sets the tone for the whole silly show: In the program, Smith's credit reads "Book (if any)." The plot: The cantankerous millionaire Ebenezer Hardacre leaves his two million-dollar fortune to be divided among those of his relatives who have never been in love, engaged, or married. There are only two claimants, Ernesta and Joseph, and they are dragged around town by self-interested parties in an attempt to make them fall in love with anybody. They are even taken to the opera, so Ernestina can fall in love with Caruso and Joseph with some rich young lady. But they hold out against all temptations long enough to inherit the money. And, naturally, they fall in love and get married.

Weber, Carl Maria von (1786–1826) (fuhn VEH: buh) German conductor, pianist, music critic, and composer of instrumental works and ten operas, including *Der Freischütz*; *Abu Hassan* (1811), a **Singspiel** in one act; *Euryanthe* (OY *r*ee AHN teh:) (1823); and *Oberon* (1826), based on a medieval legend.

Weidman, Jerome (1913–1998) American novelist and musical book writer; author of the books for *Fiorello* (1959), based on the life of New York City mayor Fiorello LaGuardia (1882–1947); *Tenderloin* (1960), co-written with George **Abbott**; and of the book, based on his novel, for *I Can Get It for You Wholesale*.

Weidman, John (b. 1946) American writer of musical books, among them Stephen Sondheim's *Pacific Overtures* and *Road Show*; son of Jerome Weidman.

Weill, Kurt (1900–1950) (vIl') Prolific, German-born American composer who wrote the scores for a number of musical theater pieces with Berthold **Brecht**, as well as Broadway musicals; studied in Berlin with Ferruccio **Busoni**. He was brilliant at capturing in music the libertarian spirit of political protest that was part of the fabric of life in Weimar Germany in the 1920s, exemplified also by Brecht, with whom he collaborated on several projects; and, indeed, at capturing other styles, such as Broadway pop and jazz. His wife, the Austrian-born American Lotte Lenya (1898–1981), a brilliant actress and singer with a distinctive, unforgettably raw, but not unpleasant voice, was known for her haunting interpretations of his material, to which she brought a brash earthiness and a sense of abrasive, satiric irony. Weill's early career was spent in his native Germany, but, as a Jew, he was forced to flee the Nazis, even more so because of his left-wing leanings. In 1933, he and Lenya, who was not Jewish, went first to Paris and then to the United States. In 2007, *Lovemusik*, a Broadway musical based on their love letters, using Weill's music and the lyrics from many of his shows, with a book by playwright and librettist Alfred Uhry (b. 1936), had a brief run of 84 perf. There have been numerous concerts of his music, such as those done by Viennese-born American actor-singer Martha Schlamme (1923–1985) in the 1970s.

Kurt Weill's major works:

1928 *Die Dreigroschenoper (The Threepenny Opera)*
1929 *Happy End*, written with Berthold Brecht
1930 *Aufstieg und Fall der Stadt Mahagonny (Rise and Fall of the City of Mahagonny)*
1936 *Johnny Johnson*, his first Broadway show, an anti-war musical

1938 *Knickerbocker Holiday*
1941 *Lady in the Dark*
1943 *One Touch of Venus*
1947 *Street Scene*
1948 *Love Life*
1949 *Lost in the Stars*

Weinberger, Jaromir (1896–1967) (YAH ro: meer VIN behr gehr) Czech nationalist composer, later American citizen; wrote four operettas and five operas, of which one became famous: *Švanda dudák* (Shvanda the Bagpiper) (1927) (SHVAHN dah DOO dahk), based on a Czech children's story. As a Jew, Weinberger fled the Nazis in 1939 and eventually settled in Florida, where he committed suicide.

Werther (veh*r* TEH*R*) Opera in four acts by Jules **Massenet**; libretto by Edouard Blau (1836–1906) (eh dwah*r*' BLO:), Paul Milliet (1848–1924) (po:l mee LYEH:) and Massenet's friend, publisher, and librettist, Georges Hartmann (1843–1900) (zho:rzh' ah*r*t MAHN), based on Goethe's novel *Die Leiden des jungen Werthers* (The Sorrows of Young Werther) (1774) (dee LI dehn dehs Y*OO*NG ehn WEH*R* tuh[*r*]s); Vienna Staatsoper, 1892.

The role of Werther (ten.) was rewritten in 1902 by Massenet esp. for bar. Mattia Battistini (1856–1928) (MAH tyah baht tih:s TEE nee), known for his unusual high range, brilliant acting, and marvelous bel canto singing; he made more than 100 recordings, many available on CD. The bar. **version** is still sometimes performed.

In Wetzlar (VEHTS lah[*r*]), Germany, in 1772, the poet Werther is in love with Charlotte (mezz.), whom he hardly knows, but whom he perceives as his ideal of innocence and beauty. Although wary, and astonished at his declarations of love, she is attracted to him. But she is engaged to Albert (bar.), whom she had promised her dying mother to marry. Werther tells her she must keep her promise, and she marries Albert. Werther leaves for some time. Charlotte realizes she loves him, and rereads his love letters to her. He returns, and they fall into each other's arms, but Charlotte quickly breaks off the embrace. On the pretext that he is going on a long trip, Werther borrows Albert's pistols. Suspecting that Werther will use them to kill himself, Charlotte rushes to him through a December snowstorm, only to find him prostrate. He has shot himself in despair, and he dies in her arms.

West Side Story Internationally successful Broadway musical by Leonard **Bernstein**; lyrics by Stephen **Sondheim**; book by Arthur **Laurents**, based on *Romeo and Juliet* by William **Shakespeare**; Winter Garden Theatre, 1957 (732 perf.), followed by a national tour and a 1960 return to Broadway for 249 more perf.; Broadway revivals: Minskoff Theatre, 1980 (341 perf.); Palace Theatre, 2009 (still running as of this writing); many American summer productions; film, 1961, co-directed by Robert Wise (1914-2005) and Jerome Robbins, who had conceived the project.

The original production was directed and choreographed by Robbins, with Peter Gennaro (1919–2000) as co-choreographer. The 2009 revival was directed by Arthur Laurents, who rewrote the book with an authentically bilingual approach, partly in Spanish and partly in English for both the songs and the dialogue, unlike the original, which was all in English. The Spanish translations were by Lin-Manuel Miranda (*In the Heights*). The original choreography was retained as much as possible.

On the Upper West Side of New York City, the Jets, an Anglo gang, and the Sharks, a Puerto Rican gang, are at war. At a street dance where both gangs are present, native New Yorker Tony sees Maria, sister of the Sharks leader, Bernardo; she is engaged to the jealous Chino. But Tony and Maria instantly fall in love. The Jets and the Sharks are planning a rumble, and Maria makes Tony promise that he will try to stop it. But Bernardo kills Riff, the Jets leader, and Tony, in his fury, stabs and kills Bernardo. He is now on the run from the police. Maria sends him a message through her friend Anita, who is tormented unmercifully by the Jets when she tries to deliver it. Furious, she tells them that Chino has killed Maria, knowing that Tony will hear the news and surface. When Tony hears this misinformation, he goes looking for Chino, who shoots him. He dies in Maria's arms.

Wheeler, Hugh (1916–1987) British screenwriter and stage dramatist; wrote the books for several Broadway shows, including three by Stephen **Sondheim**: *A Little Night Music*, *Sweeney Todd: The Demon Barber of Fleet Street*, and *Pacific Overtures*.

Whiting, Richard A. (1891–1938) American film and stage composer; wrote songs for the 1919 and 1928 *George White's Scandals* and many hit songs, including "Louise," "Hooray for Hollywood," and "On the Good Ship Lollipop."

Wicked Broadway musical by Stephen **Schwartz**; book by poet and dramatist Winnie Holzman (b. 1954), based on Gregory Maguire's (b. 1954) *Wicked: The Life and Times of the Wicked Witch of the West*, itself based on characters from *The Wonderful Wizard of Oz* by L. Frank Baum (1856–1919); Gershwin Theatre, 2003 (still running as of this writing).

The good witch Glinda recalls how her childhood friend, Elphaba, became the villainous Wicked Witch of the West. Born green, Elphaba had wanted to be a good person, but she felt shy and was very much a loner. Despite Elphaba's awkwardness, Glinda's fiancé, Fiyero, falls in love with her. The two witches meet the Wizard of Oz, who is an evil sorcerer, and Elphaba defies him, earning the opprobrium of the entire establishment of Oz and the label "Wicked." She eventually fakes her death by melting, and escapes with Fiyero.

Wildcat Broadway musical by Cy **Coleman**.

Wildhorn, Frank (b. 1960) American composer of Broadway musicals, including *Jekyll and Hyde* (1990; lyrics by Leslie **Bricusse**), based on *The Strange Case of Dr. Jekyll and Mr. Hyde* by Robert Louis Stevenson (1850–1894) and *The Scarlet Pimpernel* (1997; three revised versions, the last in 2000, which toured nationally before returning to Broadway), based on the novel of the same name by the Hungarian-born English writer Baroness Emma Orczy (1865–1947) (O:R chee), about a British aristocrat who rescues victims destined for the guillotine during the French Revolution. He collaborated on the stage **version** of *Victor/Victoria* after the death of Henry **Mancini**.

Wild Party, The 1. A narrative poem published in 1928 by Joseph Moncure March (1899–1977); it was banned, first in Boston and then elsewhere. The story: A decadent party, replete with bathtub gin, is thrown for their friends and acolytes by two 1920s vaudevillians, Queenie and Burrs, who are lovers. Queenie has the hots for the gangster Black, who is being kept by her friend Kate. The jealous Burrs is enraged, and he shoots them. The poem served as the basis for a 1975 film, directed by James Ivory (b. 1928).
2. Broadway musical by Michael John **LaChiusa**; book, based on March's poem, by the composer and George C. Wolfe (b. 1954), who also directed; Virginia Theatre, 2000 (68 perf.).
3. Off-Broadway musical by English-born American composer, lyricist, and performer, Andrew Lippa (b. 1966); book by the composer, based on March's poem; Manhattan Theatre Club, limited engagement, 2000 (54 perf.).

Willemetz, Albert (1887–1964) (vih:l MEHS) Prolific French librettist and lyricist; wrote ca. fifty libretti for Henri **Christiné** (*Phi-Phi*; *Dédé*), Maurice **Yvain** (*Ta bouche*), Jacques **Ibert** (*Les petites cardinal*), and other composers, as well as adaptations for the Paris stage of American and Viennese musicals and operettas.

Willner, Dr. Alfred Maria (1859–1929) (VIH:L nuh) [usually, A. M. Willner] Austrian librettist; wrote ca. fifty-five libretti, including the pastiche operettas *Das Dreimädlerhaus* (adapted as **Blossom Time**) and *Walzer aus Wien* (adapted as **The Great Waltz**), both written in collaboration with Ernst Marischka and Heinz **Reichert**; and co-wrote the libretti for *Die Dollarprinzessin* (Willner's first big success) and other operettas by Leo **Fall**, and **Der Graf von Luxemburg** and *Zigeunerliebe* for Franz **Lehár**, as well as writing libretti for operas by Karl **Goldmark**.

Willson, Meredith (1902–1984) American composer, lyricist, flautist, and conductor; played flute for the New York Philharmonic under Arturo Toscanini; longtime music director for ABC radio; wrote many songs; did the score and lyrics and co-wrote the book for **The Music Man**; wrote music and lyrics for **The Unsinkable Molly Brown**.

wire flying The act of being suspended in the air by cables or wires attached to machinery controlled by technicians, so that the performer can seem to be flying, as in **Peter Pan**. The wires are concealed by being made of semitransparent material, and they are worn attached to a hidden harness.
    See also AIR DANCING.

Wiz, The Broadway musical by Charlie Smalls (1943–1987); book by playwright, novelist, and television writer William F. Brown (b. 1928), based on *The Wonderful Wizard of Oz* by L. Frank Baum; Majestic Theatre, 1975 (1672 perf.); film, 1978.

This show is a retelling of the famous story, with African-American characters and a funky, **Motown**-flavored score.

Dorothy is blown away by a lively jazz tornado to the land of the Munchkins, and wants to find her way back home. She is pointed down the Yellow Brick Road, peopled by jazz singers in yellow tuxedos, and manages to secure the help of the Tin Man (made out of garbage can covers and hubcaps), the Lion, and the Scarecrow in finding the Wiz, a fabulous rap talker, who will help her after they have defeated the Wicked Witch.

Wodehouse, P. G. (1881–1975) (W*OO*D hows) [Pelham Grenville] Brilliant, very popular British humorist who later emigrated to America; known for his more than ninety witty, hilarious, satiric short stories and novels, among them the Jeeves series and the Blandings Castle series. His forays into the theater as a collaborator with Guy **Bolton** on such hit **Princess Theatre musicals** as *Oh Boy!* had a great influence on musical book writing. He also contributed lyrics to *Sally*.

Wohl, Herman (1877–1936) Noted Austrian-born American conductor and composer in the **Yiddish musical theater**, which flourished at the turn of the 20th c. in New York City. He wrote hit songs and comic operas, some of them on biblical themes, both on his own, and with Arnold Perlmutter (1859–1953), who had been Abraham Goldfaden's orchestrator. His music is in the **Offenbachian** and **Gilbert and Sullivan** traditions of gorgeous melody and vivacious, effervescent rhythms, to which he added a rollicking minor-key lilt and use of chromatics that give it his individual stamp.

Wolf-Ferrari, Ermanno (1876–1948) (ehr MAHN no: VO:LF fehr RAH ree) Italian composer of some fifteen operas, of which the most well known are *Le donne curiose* (The Curious Women) (1903) (leh: DO:N neh: koo ree O: zeh:), *I quattro rusteghi* (The Four Rustics) (1906) (ee KWAHT tro: roo STEH: gee), both based on comedies by Carlo **Goldoni**; *I goielli della Madonna* (The Jewels of the Madonna) (1911) (ee dgo: YEHL lee dehl lah mah DO: nah); and *Il segreto di Susannna* (Susanna's Secret) (1909) (eel seh GREH: to: dee soo ZAHN nah), which is that she smokes cigarettes in an era when women were not supposed to, and hides the fact from her suspicious husband.

X, Y, Z

Xanadu Broadway musical with songs by Australian music producer and song-writer John Farrar (b. 1946) and English musician Jeff Lynne (b. 1947) and his Electric Light Orchestra group [usual abbrev., ELO]; libretto by Douglas Carter Beane (b. 1959), based on the 1980 film starring Olivia Newton-John (b. 1948) and Gene Kelly in his last musical; Helen Hayes Theatre, 2007 (577 perf.).

The muse Clio descends as Kira from Mt. Olympus and lands in Venice Beach, CA. She wishes to inspire an artist named Sonny to achieve his best, and to establish the first roller disco in history. Kira is in love with him, but since she is immortal, their love is forbidden. Eventually, Zeus is prevailed upon to make her mortal, so she and Sonny can be together.

xiqu; **hsi chü** (SHEE DGOO), *n.* [Chinese: song-theater] Traditional Chinese musical theater. It is a combination of mime, dance, instrumental and vocal music, and spoken lines, all in the service of telling a story, with characters played by individual actor-singers. There are more than three hundred forms of this music theater, sung in different Chinese languages and using different musical systems and structures. Female roles, and the people playing them, are called *dan* (DAHN); and the male roles as well as the actors playing them are called *sheng* (SHEHNG). Comic roles and the clown actors playing them are called *chou* (DGOW). The roles of gods, demons, villains, or aristocrats—"painted-face" roles—are called *jing* (CHIHNG). Also called *Chinese opera* or *music-drama*.

Yeomen of the Guard, The, or, The Merryman and His Maid "A New and Original Opera" in two acts by **Gilbert and Sullivan**; London, Savoy Theatre, 1888.

This is the most operatic of the G & S creations, with a romantic, melodious score that has touches of what the Victorians thought of as Elizabethan tonalities and a stirring theme that evokes the Tower of London, where the story takes place. Gilbert's plot uses a device similar to that of Wallace's *Maritana*.

Condemned to death for sorcery and imprisoned in the Tower, Colonel Fairfax (ten.) has been falsely accused by a greedy kinsman who hopes to inherit his estate, which he can only do if Fairfax dies unmarried. The Lieutenant of the Tower, Sir Richard Cholmondely (CHUHM lee) (bar.), has agreed to help Fairfax foil his kinsman's plans by finding him a wife. Two strolling players, jester Jack Point (bar.) and singer Elsie Maynard (sop.), arrive, and Sir Richard offers Elsie a hundred crowns if she will agree to marry an unnamed prisoner and accept immediate widowhood. She is led off, despite Point's misgivings, for he loves her. Fairfax and Elsie, both blindfolded, are married. Meanwhile, Fairfax's friends, Sergeant Merryl (bar.) and Merryl's daughter Phoebe (mezz.), in love with Fairfax, devise a ruse to save his life: they will spirit him out of his cell and disguise him as Merryl's son, the military hero Leonard (ten.), due to return this very day, and send Leonard into temporary hiding. The plan works, and the execution is about to take place, when the guards discover that Fairfax's cell is vacant. Wilfred Shadbolt (bar.), the jailer, is arrested, and Elsie faints in the arms of the supposed Leonard Merryl. In act 2, Point and Shadbolt concoct a plan whereby they pretend to shoot Fairfax as he is trying to swim the Thames to safety. The entire Tower is aroused, including the housekeeper, Dame Carruthers (contr.), in love with Sergeant Merryl. Elsie, meanwhile, has fallen in love with "Leonard," and he with her, not realizing that they are married to each other. The real Leonard arrives bearing Fairfax's reprieve. The price of everyone's silence is clear: Phoebe has to agree to marry Shadbolt, to whom she has inadvertently revealed everything, and Sergeant Merryl must wed the stern Dame Carruthers, who knows too much. When Elsie recognizes Fairfax, who comes to claim his bride, she is overjoyed. Jack Point collapses at her feet as the curtain falls.

Yeston, Maury (b. 1945) American composer, noted for the Broadway hit musicals *Nine* (1982) and *Titanic*; contributed songs to *Grand Hotel*. He also wrote *Phantom* (1991), a musical based on the *Phantom of the Opera* story, and his version is performed in stock and other venues.

Yevgenyi Onegin (Eugene Onegin) (yehv GYEHN yee o NYEH: gihn) Opera in three acts by Pyotr Ilyich **Tchaikovsky**; libretto by the composer and Konstantin Shilovsky (1849–1893) (shih LOF skee), based on Alexander Pushkin's dramatic poem; Moscow, Maly Theater, 1879.

Idyllic days pass on the country estate of the Larin family. Mme. Larina (LAH ree nah) (mezz.) and her two daughters, Olga (O:L gah) (contr.) and her young sister Tatyana (tah TYAH nah) (sop.), rejoice in the prospect of Olga's engagement to Count Lensky (LYEHN skee) (ten.). One day, Lensky brings his friend Yevgenyi Onegin (bar.) over to introduce him to the family. Tatyana falls in love with him, and, late one night, writes a letter expressing her feelings; but when they meet, he rejects her. At a party celebrating Tatyana's name-day feast, Onegin has the temerity to flirt with Olga. Lensky challenges him to a duel. Onegin accepts, and, the next morning, when they go through with it, he kills Lensky. He flees abroad, returning only after many years. In St. Petersburg, he goes to a ball given by Prince Gremin (GRYEH mih:n) (bass), who introduces Onegin to his wife. She is none other than Tatyana, now a beautiful, grown woman. Onegin decides he is in love with her, and, bursting in on her the next day, he throws himself at her feet, but although she remembers her passion for him, she will not be unfaithful to the husband who has been so good to her. She rushes out of the room, leaving him in despair.

Yiddish musical theater Originating in the 19th c. in Romania, and spreading to Russia and other parts of eastern Europe, a vibrant theater of plays and musical theater pieces performed in Yiddish flourished, esp. in major urban centers. Many of the pieces were original, and many were adaptations or translations. The Yiddish theater found a home in London, and also in New York City, centered on Second Avenue, at the end of the 19th c. and in the first few decades of the 20th, during the massive wave of Jewish immigration to America. Operas were performed in translation, there were songs composed for Yiddish vaudeville, and original operettas were written. The virtual founder of Yiddish theater, the Romanian Abraham Goldfaden (1840–1908), who emigrated to New York, wrote musical revues as well as spoken plays. One of the Yiddish theater's early composers was the Latvian David Meyerowitz (1867–1943), who wrote many songs and vaudeville pieces. Among the great American Yiddish composers are the Russian-born singer, actor, impresario, and songwriter Boris Tomashevsky (1865–1939); Herman **Wohl**; Abraham Ellstein (1907–1963), born in America; the German-born Ilia Trilling (1895–1947); Alexander Olshanetsky (1892–1946), born in Odessa; and Sholem **Secunda**. Yiddish musical theater pieces were often romantic and melodramatic, and their plots usually concerned unhappy marriages, unrequited love, or forbidden alliances. The music was influenced by the Hebrew liturgy, Viennese operetta, and Yiddish and gypsy folk song, and, later, by American jazz. The influence of Yiddish musical theater on the Broadway musical, and vice versa, is palpable, particularly as the two theaters existed side by side, and performers and writers often wrote or performed in both. An important set of recordings of Yiddish theater music has been released by Naxos in a series of albums from the Milken Archive of American Jewish Music.

Yip Yip Yahank Broadway musical revue by Irving **Berlin**; Century Theatre, 1919 (32 perf., limited run). Berlin himself performed his hit song, "Oh, How I Hate to Get Up in the Morning."

Yoruba opera (YO: roo bah) Nigerian musical plays, usually with moral lessons to teach; the orchestra is a combination of western and African instruments; often performed by traveling companies in the Yoruba language. The form developed in the 1930s, from religious plays and entertainments put on by churches; it was popular through the 1940s. Also called *native air opera*; *Yoruba folk opera.*

Youmans, Vincent (1898–1946) Highly gifted American songwriter; composer of musical films and several stage musical comedies, including *No, No, Nanette* and *Hit the Deck*; many of his stage shows were filmed.
   See also GERSHWIN, IRA.

Young Artists programs Many opera companies have programs for trained young opera singers who already have fine arts degrees in music that they have earned from such schools as the Eastman School of Music in Rochester, NY or the Manhattan School of Music in New York City. The programs offer more training, including on the job experience, **master classes**, and outreach programs in which the young artists perform for schools, getting children interested in the opera. These programs offer payment, living accommodations, and a warm, fostering, encouraging environment. Among the many excellent programs are those offered by the Chautauqua Opera in its summer season and the Seattle Opera in its fall through spring season; the Chicago Opera Theater's Young Artists Program; the Glimmerglass Opera's summer program for young artists, in upstate NY; and the Central City Opera's program in Central City, CO.

Young Frankenstein Broadway musical by Mel **Brooks**; libretto by Mel Brooks and Thomas **Meehan**, based on Brooks's 1974 hit comedy film, which is a parody of the horror film genre; Hilton Theatre, 2007 (514 perf.).

Although Brooks wrote the songs, one of the show's biggest hits was the Monster's debut number, "Puttin' on the Ritz" by Irving **Berlin**.

Frederick Frankenstein, the American descendant of the scientist Victor Frankenstein, arrives in Transylvania, and, with the help and support of Igor and Frau Blucher, two enthusiastic Transylvanians, recreates his ancestor's Monster. Frederick falls in love with a local girl, Inga, and his former fiancée Elizabeth, having arrived from America, happily ends up with the Monster.

You're a Good Man, Charlie Brown Off-Broadway musical by Clark Gesner (1938–2002); book and lyrics by the composer, based on the well known comic-strip characters created by Charles M. Schultz (1922–2000); Theatre 80 St. Marks, 1967 (1597 perf.); Broadway, John Golden Theatre, 1971 (47 perf.); Broadway revival, Ambassador Theatre, 1999 (163 perf.)

The show goes through a day in the life of the kid Charlie Brown and his friends, the philosopher, Linus; his sister, the self-confident, bossy Lucy; Schroeder, who loves Beethoven; and Charlie's dog, Snoopy.

Yvain, Maurice (1891–1965) (mo: *rees*' ee VA*N*) French composer of film scores, songs, and stage musicals, including his first big hit, the tongue-in-cheek *Ta bouche* (Your Mouth) (1922) (tah BOOSH), which is very funny, very cute, and musically very close to the most tuneful cabaret songs. The whole proceeding is sparkling and most enjoyable, to judge by the original cast recording. It was followed by the adorable *Pas sur la bouche* (Not on the Mouth!) (1925) (pah' sü*r* lah BOOSH) , film, 1931. Understandably, both were great popular hits in Paris. Original cast recordings, as for ***Ciboulette***, are available on CD in *L'Opérette Française 1921–1934 par ses Créateurs*. Yvain also wrote numbers for the ***Ziegfeld Follies***.

Zaïs: ballet héroique (Zaïs: A Heroic Ballet) (1748) (zah EES bah leh: é *r*o: EEK) An **opéra-ballet**, a **pastoral** in a prologue and four acts, by Jean-Philippe **Rameau**, with a libretto by Jean-Louis de Cahusac (1709–1759) (zhah*n* loo ee' duh ka ü ZAHK), who wrote many texts with supernatural stories; Paris Opéra, 1748. *Zaïs* is an astonishingly powerful and compelling example of the genre. There is an exciting recording of excerpts on Stil CD (2112 SAN 92; 1977).

The genie-spirit Zaïs (c-ten.) is in love with the shepherdess Zélide (zé LEED) (sop.). In order to win her, he sacrifices his powers, and the couple find themselves completely alone in a desert. But his powers are restored and the couple is united through the good offices of the ruler of the genies, Oromasès (bass) (o: *r*o:' mah ZEHS), who has been moved by their deep love.

Zampa [Full title: *Zampa ou La fiancée de marbre* (Zampa, or The Marble Fiancée) (zah*n* PAH oo lah fee ah*n* sé' duh MAH*R* b*r*uh)] A highly melodramatic

opéra comique in three acts by Ferdinand **Hérold**; libretto by **Mèlesville**; Paris, Théâtre de l'Opéra-Comique, 1831. The rousing, much recorded overture remains well known, but the opera itself is seldom if ever done.

Zampa (ten), a pirate chief and an outlawed nobleman, is the brother of Alphonse (ten.), the fiancé of Camille (sop.), whom Zampa tries to blackmail into marrying him by taking her father hostage. As a drunken joke, he slips her wedding ring onto the finger of a statue of Alice, a noblewoman Zampa had seduced and abandoned, and then he cannot get the ring off. The statue comes to life as Zampa and Camille are about to be married, and just as Mt. Etna erupts. The statue crushes the pirate chief in her arms, while Camille and Alphonse flee. Having escaped disaster, they are reunited with her father.

Zandonai, Riccardo (1883–1944) (reek KAHR do: DZAHN do: NI) Italian composer of thirteen operas, including a **verismo** version of *Giulietta e Romeo* (1922) (dgoo LYEHT tah eh ro: MEH: o:), based on Shakespeare's play; libretto by Arturo Rossato (1882–1942) (ro:s SAH to:), a novelist, political activist, and author of ca. thirty opera libretti. Zandonai's most famous opera is the problematic *Francesca da Rimini* (1914) (frahn CHEHS kah dah RIH: mee nee), in four acts, with a libretto by the quarrelsome music publisher and producer Tito Ricordi (1865–1933) (TEE to: ree KO:R dee), based on the story of the ill-fated lovers in Dante's (1265–1321) *Divine Comedy*, as retold in a tragedy by Gabriele D'Annunzio.

zarabanda (sah' rah BAHN dah) *n.* [Spanish: sarabande] In Renaissance Spanish theater, a slow, majestic dance, undulating and sensuous in nature, that was part of the musical entertainment.

Zar und Zimmermann (Czar and Carpenter) (TSAHR *oo*nt TSIH meh[*r*] MAHN) [full title: *Czaar und Zimmermann, oder Die zwei Peter* (—or The Two Peters) (—O: duh dee TSVI PEH: tuh[*r*])] Opera in three acts by Albert **Lortzing**; libretto by the composer, based on a German play, Georg Christian Römer's (1766–1829) (GEH: o:[*r*]k K*R*IHS tee (yahn *R*Ö meh[*r*]) *Der Bürgermeister von Saardam, oder Die zwei Peter* (deh BÜ[R] guh MI stuh fuhn ZAHR dahm—) (The Burgomaster of Saardam, or The Two Peters), which was based on a French comedy; Leipzig Stadttheater, 1837.

In the shipyards in Saardam, Holland in 1698, Czar Peter the Great (1672–1725) (bar.) is working incognito as Peter Michaelov (mee KHI lo:f), learning the trade of shipbuilding. He makes friends with another Russian, a fellow worker named Peter Ivanov (ee VAHN o:f) (ten.), who is in love with the Burgomaster's niece, Marie (sop.), and plagues her with his eternal jealousy, even though she assures him there is no cause. The English ambassador, Lord Syndham (bass), has paid Burgomaster van Bett (basso buffo) very handsomely to find out if a foreigner named Peter is working in the shipyard. Since there are only two foreigners by that name, van Bett, thinking himself very clever, identifies Ivanov as the one Lord Syndham would be interested in, and feels sure that he must be none other than the czar, who has been rumored to be in Holland. But finally, the real czar, in full uniform, is seen on a ship, about to sail away. He appoints Ivanov his Imperial Overseer, and asks van Bett to let Ivanov marry Marie, to everyone's rejoicing.

zarzuela (sahr SWEH: lah), *n.* [Spanish: from the name of a hunting lodge near Madrid, *Palacio de la Zarzuela* (pah LAH *th*ee o theh lah *th*ahr *TH*WEH: lah; *zarza* (SAHR sah; *TH*AHR *th*ah): bramble), where such pieces were first performed] The musically and dramatically sophisticated Spanish form of operetta or comic opera, often satiric in content; popular in Central and South America as well. The form evolved out of 17th-c. court entertainments called *fiestas de la zarzuela* (fee YEHS tahs), and the libretti were by famous playwrights, such as Lope de Vega and Pedro Calderón de la Barca (1600–1681) (PEH: thro: kahl theh: RO:N theh: lah BAHR kah), who wrote the first such piece to have been called a zarzuela: *El golfo de las sirenas* (The Gulf of the Sirens) (1657) (ehl GO:L fo: theh: lahs see REH: nahs). The form continued in the 18th c., with a host of outstanding zarzuela composers, including Antonio Rodriguez de Hita (1724–1787) (ahn TO: nyo: ro:th REE gehs theh: EE tah), and into the 19th and 20th centuries, with practitioners such as Jerónimo **Giménez** and Amadeo **Vives**.

See also DOÑA FRANCISQUITA.

Zauberflöte, Die (The Magic Flute) (dee TSOW buh FLÖ teh) **Singspiel** in two acts by Wolfgang Amadeus Mozart; libretto by Emmanuel Schikaneder (1751–1812) (SHIH:K ah NEH: duh[*r*]), based on various fairy tales; Vienna, Theater an der Wien, 1791.

In ancient Egypt, Prince Tamino (tah MEE no:) (ten.) is rescued from a deadly serpent by Three Ladies (sop., sop., mezz.), attendants of the Queen of the Night (sop.). When Tamino awakens from having fainted, the birdcatcher Papageno (PAH pah GEH: no:) (bar.) brags that it was he who killed the serpent, and the Ladies padlock his lying mouth. They give Tamino a portrait of Pamina (pah MEE nah) (sop.), daughter of the Queen of the Night, and he falls in love with her. She has been abducted by the evil Sarastro (zah *R*AHS tro:) (bass). The Queen of the Night tells Tamino that if only he can rescue her, he can marry her, which he undertakes to do with the help of the reluctant Papageno and with a magic glockenspiel and a magic flute given him by the Ladies, to be used in case of need. Three Boys (trebles) take him to Sarastro's stronghold. Pamina is being guarded by the lustful Moor Monostatos (mo:' NO: stah TO:S) (ten.), who is about to attack her when Papageno rushes in. Tamino soon learns that Sarastro is really the embodiment of good, and the Queen the embodiment of evil. Tamino leaves, and Pamina and Papageno go looking for him. In the Temple, all three are surprised by Monostatos and his Moors, but escape by bewitching them with the magic glockenspiel. Pamina falls asleep, and Monostatos, about to attack her again, is surprised by the arrival of the Queen of the Night, who gives Pamina a dagger and tells her that the only way for her to be free is to kill Sarastro. Pamina, in despair and not knowing what to do, is about to kill herself when the Three Boys appear and take her to Tamino. Sarastro sets them trials to go through, so that they can be initiated into the brotherhood of love. The couple meet the challenges successfully, going through fire and water with the help of the magic flute. Papageno also finds his helpmeet in Papagena (PAH pah GEH: nah) (sop.). The evil characters are all destroyed, and good has triumphed over evil, light over darkness.

Zeffirelli, Franco (b. 1923) (FRAH*N* co: dzehf fee REHL lee) Innovative, influential, prolific Italian film and opera director, designer, producer, and writer; wrote libretto for Barber's *Antony and Cleopatra*; known for his visually gorgeous, detailed, realistic staging of operas, e.g., *Tosca*, *Turandot*, and *La bohème* at the Metropolitan Opera; among his several opera films is an outstanding version of Verdi's *La traviata* (1983).

Zeitoper (TSIT O: puh) *n.* [German: time-opera; i.e., an opera of its time] German 20th-c. operas on timely, topical subjects, often with political themes, and with allusions to or music in the style of the popular music of the day.

See also JONNY SPIELT AUF.

Zell, Friedrich (1829–1895) (F*R*EE d*r*ih*kh* TSEHL) [pen name of Camillo Walzel (kah MIH:L o: VAHL tsehl)] German-born Austrian librettist, and frequent collaborator with Richard **Genée** on operetta texts, e.g., *Gräfin Dubarry*, *Gasparone*, and *Der Bettelstudent* by Karl **Millöcker**; *Boccaccio* by von **Suppé**; *Eine Nacht in Venedig* by Johann **Strauss**. Zell usually constructed the plots and wrote the dialogue, while Genée did the lyrics. From 1884 to 1889, Zell was also the Artistic Director of Vienna's Theater an der Wien, known for its presentation of operettas during the **Golden Age of Operetta**. The theater had been built by Emmanuel Schikaneder, librettist for Mozart's *Die Zauberflöte*. Zell also translated **Offenbach** and **Gilbert and Sullivan** for the Viennese stage.

Zeller, Carl (1842–1898) (KAH[*R*]L TSEHL uh[*r*]) [b. Carl Johann Adam Zeller] Austrian jurist, government official, and composer of seven Viennese operettas, his most famous being the brilliant, melodious masterpiece *Der Vogelhändler (The Bird Seller)*. He had another great success with *Der Obersteiger* (The Mine Foreman) (1894) (deh O: buh SHTI guh), which takes place in a mining community on the Austro-German border, where a certain Countess Fichtenau (FIH:*KH* teh NOW) (sop.) has fled, in order to avoid marrying a man she does not love. Zeller's later life was unfortunate: Although he had done well in his government work, he was involved in legal troubles, accused of perjury, and imprisoned. The sentence was repealed, but he died a broken man, the victim as well of mental disorder.

Zemlinsky, Alexander von (1971–1942) (tsehm LIH:N skee) [b. Alexander Zemlinsky; he added the particle to his name in order to sound more aristocratic] Austrian composer of instrumental and vocal music, much admired in his day; wrote eight operas, among them the astounding long one-act *Der Zwerg* (The Dwarf) (1922) (deh TSVEH[*R*]K), based on the story *The Birthday of the Infanta* (1892) by Oscar Wilde, which Franz **Schreker** had also adapted as a pantomime in 1908; superb EMI recording on CD (5 66247 2; 1996). Zemlinsky's entire family had converted from Roman Catholicism to Judaism before he was born. He fled the Nazis, but did not do well as a composer in the United States, and died in Larchmont, NY after a series of strokes.

Zhizn za tsarya (A Life for the Tsar) (ZHIHZN zah TSAHR yah) [Also called *Ivan Susanin* (ee VAN soo SAHN ihn), esp. under the Soviets] Opera in four acts and an epilogue by Mikhail **Glinka**; libretto by Baron Georgy Fyodorovich Rosen (1800–1860) (geh: O:R gee) [Yegor Fyodorovich Rozen (YEH go:r FYO: do:r o: vihch RO: zehn)], a translator, poet, critic, and secretary to the future Czar Alexander II (1818–1881); St. Petersburg, Bolshoy Teatr (bo:l' SHOY teh: AHTR), 1836.

In 1612, the powerful Ivan Susanin (bass), worried about the political future of Russia and a possible invasion by Poland, will not allow his daughter, Antonida (ahn' TO nee dah) (sop.), to marry her fiancé, Bogdan Sobinin (BO:G dahn so BEE neen) (ten.), until peace is secured and a new tsar elected, which is done. Mikhail Romanov (mih KHAYL ro MAH no:f) is chosen, and the wedding is being prepared when the Poles invade, capture Ivan Susanin, and compel him to take them to the new tsar. Instead, having told his stepson, Vanya (VAHN yah) (contr.), to go and warn the tsar of the plot against him, Susanin leads them deep into an enchanted forest, where they kill him. Tsar Mikhail wins the war. In the Kremlin, all mourn the courageous sacrifice of Ivan Susanin.

Ziegfeld Follies A series of twenty-one Broadway **extravaganza** revues, starting in 1907 at the rooftop space, the Jardin de Paris, and featuring choruses of beguiling, smiling dancing girls in lavish costumes that revealed their legs as they descended long staircases to lush music; comic skits and songs, as well as romantic numbers, were always part of the shows. The 1907 *Follies* (79 perf.) featured a book by Harry B. **Smith**, who also did the next three editions and contributed to others, and songs by Gus **Edwards**, who contributed to several editions. The music was often by well known composers, including Victor **Herbert**, whose first *Follies* was in 1919 (New Amsterdam Theatre; 171 perf.); Rudolf **Friml**, who first contributed in 1921 (Globe Theatre; 119 perf.); and Irving **Berlin**, who started composing for the *Follies* in 1910 (Jardin de Paris; 88 perf.), an edition also notable for the debut of Fanny Brice, who appeared in many of the revues. In 1911 (Jardin de Paris; 80 perf.), there were songs by Jerome **Kern**, who would also write songs for later editions. Among the show's perennial stalwarts was stage and screen actor Leon Erroll (1881–1951), who sometimes directed portions of the revues. They were produced by Florenz Ziegfeld, Jr. (1867–1932), who also produced many book musicals, among them ***Show Boat***. After his death, his widow, actress and singer Billie Burke (1884–1970), having inherited the rights to the shows, sold them to the Shuberts, who produced more *Follies* in the 1930s and '40s. There are two wonderful MGM musical films that show the *Follies* in action: the biopic *The Great Ziegfeld* (1936) and *Ziegfeld Follies* (1946), both with William Powell (1892–1984) as Ziegfeld.

See also IRENE; YVAIN, MAURICE.

Ziehrer, Carl Michael (1843–1922) (TSEE *r*uh[*r*]) Austrian bandmaster, conductor, and composer of 600 waltzes and other dance music, and twenty-three Viennese operettas, of which the most famous is the tuneful *Die Landstreicher* (The Tramps) (1899) (dee LAHNT SHT*R*I *kh*uh[*r*]), in a prologue and two acts; libretto by Leopold Krenn (1851–1930) (K*R*EHN) and Carl **Lindau**, about a pair of vagabonds, husband and wife, who find a pearl necklace and a thousand-mark bill on the highway, and the unexpected complications that ensue when they decide to masquerade as aristocrats. But the only complete recording available of any of his operettas is the enchanting, musically sparkling *Die drei Wünsche* (The Three Wishes) (1901) (dee D*R*I VÜN sheh), libretto by Krenn and Lindau, in which the ingenuous, ingenious Lotti (sop.) sees the fulfillment of her three wishes for happiness; CPO (777 404-2; 2009). A CD of some of Ziehrer's operetta overtures is available from Marco Polo (8.225332; 2006), as are four albums of his dance music.

Zigeunerbaron, Der (The Gypsy Baron) (deh[*r*] tsih: GOY nuh bah *R*O:N) Operetta in two acts by Johann **Strauss II**; libretto by Hungarian-born Austrian librettist Ignaz Schnitzer (1839–1921) (IH:G nahts SHNIH: tsuh), based on the novel *Sáffi* by Hungarian novelist and dramatist Mór Lókai (1825–1904) (MO:R LO: kI); Vienna, Theater an der Wien, 1885.

In the middle of the 18th c., after twenty years in exile for political reasons, Sandor Barinkay (SHAHN do:r BAH rihn kI) (ten.) returns to Temesvár (TEHM ehsh vah:r), Hungary, to reclaim his land and find the treasure his father has reportedly buried on the estate. The Royal Commissioner, Graf [Count] Carnero (GRAHF kahr NEH: ro:) (bar.), agrees to restore his rights to him, and asks the illiterate pig farmer Zsupán (TSHOO pahn) (ten. **buffo**) to witness the deed. Zsupán, hoping to become rich, encourages Barinkay to court his daughter, the snobby Arsena (ahr ZEH: nah) (sop.), but only a real live baron will do as a husband for her. Barinkay has heard the beautiful voice of the gypsy girl Sáffi (ZAH fee) (sop.) singing in the distance. He meets her and her band of gypsies, and they acclaim him as their leader, a position he is happy to accept. He tells Arsena that he is now a "gypsy baron!" But she finds this ridiculous and rejects him, whereupon he pledges himself to Sáffi. With her help and that of her mother, Czipra (TSIH: prah) (mezz.), he finds his father's buried treasure. Carnero is not sure that they will be allowed to keep it, because of the legal status of their marriage, if indeed they really are married, but they assure him in the lilting duet "Wer uns getraut?" (Who married us?) (VEH[*R*] OONTS geh T*R*OWT) that they have been married according to gypsy law, with a nightingale and two storks as witnesses. But now both Barinkay and Zsupán are drafted to go fight in a war against Spain. When they return in triumph, Barinkay is leading them. All ends happily as he rejoins Sáffi and the estates are restored to the "gypsy baron."

Selected Bibliography

Abrams, M. H. *A Glossary of Literary Terms*. 7th ed. Boston, MA: Heinle & Heinle, 1999.

Adler, Stella. *On the Technique of Acting*. Foreword by Marlon Brando. New York: Bantam Books, 1988.

Aristotle. *Poetics*. Edited and Translated by Stephen Halliwell. Longinus. *On the Sublime*. Translation by W. H. Fyfe. Revised by Donald Russell. Demetrius. *On Style*. Edited and translated by Doreen C. Innes, Based on W. Rhys Roberts. Cambridge, MA: Harvard University Press, 1999; reprinted, 2005.

Baily, Leslie. *The Gilbert and Sullivan Book*. New York: Coward-McCann, Inc., 1953.

Barba, Eugenio, and Nicola Savarese. *A Dictionary of Theatre Anthropology: The Secret Art of the Performer*. New York: Routledge, 2006.

Berlioz, Hector. *The Memoirs of Hector Berlioz*. Translated by David Cairns. New York: Everyman's Library, 2002.

Blumenfeld, Robert. *Accents: A Manual for Actors*. New York: Limelight Editions, 2002.

———. *Acting with the Voice: The Art of Recording Books*. New York: Limelight Editions, 2004.

———. *Blumenfeld's Dictionary of Acting and Show Business*. New York: Limelight Editions, 2009.

———. *Tools and Techniques for Character Interpretation: A Handbook of Psychology for Actors, Writers, and Directors*. New York: Limelight Editions, 2006.

———. *Using the Stanislavsky System: A Practical Guide to Character Creation and Period Styles*. New York: Limelight Editions, 2008.

Boleslavsky, Richard. *Acting: The First Six Lessons*. 29th printing. New York: Routledge, 1987.

Bordman, Gerald. *American Musical Theatre: A Chronicle*. 3rd edition. New York: Oxford University Press, 2001.

Bradley, Ian, ed. *The Complete Annotated Gilbert and Sullivan*. New York: Oxford University Press, 1996.

Carnovsky, Morris, with Peter Sander. *The Actor's Eye*. Foreword by John Houseman. New York: Performing Arts Journal Publications, 1984.

Chekhov, Michael. *Lessons for the Professional Actor*. From a collection of notes transcribed and arranged by Deirdre Hurst du Pray. Introduction by Mel Gordon. New York: Performing Arts Journal Publications, 1985.

———. *To the Actor on the Technique of Acting*. Revised and expanded edition. Foreword by Simon Callow. Preface by Yul Brynner. New York: Routledge, 2002.

Cole, Toby and Helen Krich Chinoy, eds. *Actors on Acting: The Theories, Techniques and Practices of the World's Great Actors Told in Their Own Words*. New York: Three Rivers Press, 1970.

Craine, Debra and Judith Mackrell. *Oxford Dictionary of the Dance*. New York: Oxford University Press, 2004.

Eaton, Quaintance. *Opera Production: A Handbook*. Minneapolis, MN: University of Minnesota Press, 1961.

————. *Opera in Production II: A Handbook*. With *Production Problems in Handel's Operas* by Randolph Mickelson. Minneapolis, MN: University of Minnesota Press, 1974.

Esper, William and Damon DiMarco. *The Actor's Art and Craft: William Esper Teaches the Meisner Technique*. Foreword by David Mamet. New York: Random House, 2008.

Everett, William A. and Paul R. Laird, eds. *The Cambridge Companion to the Musical*. New York: Cambridge University Press, 2002.

Franceschina, John. *David Braham: The American Offenbach*. New York: Routledge, 2003.

Gänzl, Kurt. *The Encyclopedia of the Musical Theatre*. 2 vols. Oxford, UK: Blackwell Publishers, 1994.

Garfield, David. *The Actors Studio: A Player's Place*. Preface by Ellen Burstyn. New York: Macmillan Collier Books, 1984.

Gossett, Philip. *Divas and Scholars: Performing Italian Opera*. Chicago: The University of Chicago Press, 2006.

Grant, Gail. *Technical Manual and Dictionary of Classical Ballet*. Illustrated by the author. 3rd revised edition. New York: Dover Publications, Inc., 1982.

Grotowski, Jerzy. *Towards a Poor Theatre*. First ed., 1968. New York: Routledge, 2002.

Hagen, Uta. *A Challenge for the Actor*. New York: Charles Scribner's Sons, 1991.

Hagen, Uta, with Haskell Frankel. *Respect for Acting*. New York: Macmillan, 1973.

Hindley, Geoffrey, ed. *The Larousse Encyclopedia of Music*. New York: Crown Publishers, Inc., 1971.

Hischak, Thomas. *The Oxford Companion to the American Musical: Theatre, Film, and Television*. New York: Oxford University Press, 2008.

Hull, S. Loraine. *Strasberg's Method as Taught by Lorrie Hull: A Practical Guide for Actors, Teachers and Directors*. Foreword by Susan Strasberg. Woodbridge, CT: Oxbow Publishing, Inc., 1985.

Kennedy, Dennis, ed. *The Oxford Encyclopedia of Theatre and Performance*. 2 vols. New York: Oxford University Press, 2003.

Kift, Dagmar and Roy Kift. *The Victorian Music Hall: Culture, Class and Conflict*. New York: Cambridge University Press, 1996.

Kracauer, Siegfried. *Orpheus in Paris: Offenbach and the Paris of His Time*. New York: Horizon Press, 1983.

Lewis, Robert. *Advice to the Players*. Introduction by Harold Clurman. New York: Theatre Communications Books, 1980.

Macy, Laura, ed. *The Grove Book of Opera Singers*. New York: Oxford University Press, 2008.

Meisner, Sanford, and Dennis Longwell. *On Acting*. New York: Random House Vintage Books, 1987.

Merriam-Webster's Encyclopedia of Literature. Springfield, MA: Merriam-Webster, Inc., 1995.

Miller, Richard. *Solutions for Singers: Tools for Performers and Teachers*. New York: Oxford University Press, 2004.

Moore, Sonia. *The Stanislavsky Method: The Professional Training of an Actor*. Preface by Sir John Gielgud. Foreword by Joshua Logan. New York: The Viking Press, 1960.

———. *Stanislavsky Revealed: The Actor's Guide to Spontaneity on Stage*. New York: Applause Theatre Books, 1968.

———. *Training an Actor: The Stanislavsky System in Class*. New York: Penguin Books, 1979.

Nagler, A. M. *A Source Book in Theatrical History (Sources of Theatrical History)*. New York: Dover Publications, Inc., 1952.

Nemirovich-Danchenko, Vladimir. *My Life in the Russian Theatre*. Translated by John Cournos. With an introduction by John Logan, a foreword by Oliver M. Saylor and a chronology by Elizabeth Reynolds Hapgood. New York: Theatre Arts Books, 1936.

Norman, Buford. *Touched by the Graces: The Libretti of Philippe Quinault in the Context of French Classicism*. Birmingham, AL: Summa Publications, 2001.

Pavis, Patrice. *Dictionary of the Theatre: Terms, Concepts, and Analysis*. Translated by Christine Shantz. Preface by Marvin Carlson. Toronto: University of Toronto Press, 1998.

Radice, Mark. *Opera in Context: Essays on Historical Staging from the Late Renaissance to the Time of Puccini*. New York: Amadeus Press, 1998.

Randel, Don Michael. *The Harvard Dictionary of Music*. 4th edition. Cambridge, MA: The Belknap Press of Harvard University Press, 2003.

Rudlin, John. *Commedia dell'Arte: An Actor's Handbook*. New York: Routledge, 1994.

Sadie, Stanley, ed. Revised by Laura Macy. *The Grove Book of Operas*. 2nd edition. New York: Oxford University Press, 2006.

Sadie, Stanley, ed. *The New Grove Dictionary of Opera*. 4 vols. New York: Grove, An Imprint of Oxford University Press, 1997.

Saint-Denis, Michel. *Theatre: The Rediscovery of Style*. Introduction by Sir Laurence Olivier. New York: Theatre Arts Books, 1960.

Sawyer, Gina. *The Performance Dictionary*. BackstageCoach.com, 2005.

Skinner, Edith. *Speak with Distinction*. Revised with new material added by Timothy Monich and Lilene Mansell. Edited by Lilene Mansell. New York: Applause Theatre Book Publishers, 1990.

Spivak, Alice, written in collaboration with Robert Blumenfeld. *How to Rehearse When There Is No Rehearsal: Acting and the Media*. New York: Limelight, 2007.

Stanislavski, Constantin and Pavel Rumantsev. *Stanislavski on Opera*. Translated and edited by Elizabeth Reynolds Hapgood. New York: Routledge, 1974.

Stanislavsky, Constantin. *An Actor Prepares*. Translated by Elizabeth Reynolds Hapgood. New York: Theatre Arts Books (1936; 23rd printing), 1969.

———. *Building a Character*. Translated by Elizabeth Reynolds Hapgood. New York: Theatre Arts Books (14th printing), 1949.

———. *Creating a Role*. Translated by Elizabeth Reynolds Hapgood. New York: Theatre Arts Books (6th printing), 1969.

———. *My Life in Art*. Translated by G. Ivanov-Mumjiev. Moscow: Foreign Languages Publishing House, n.d.

———. *My Life in Art*. Translated by J. J. Robbins. Orig. pub. Little, Brown and Company, 1924. New York: The World Publishing Co. Meridian Books, 1966.

———. *On the Art of the Stage*. Introduced and translated by David Magarshack. New York: Hill and Wang, 1961.

Strasberg, Lee. *A Dream of Passion*. New York: Penguin Plume Books, 1987.

Strasberg at the Actors Studio: Tape-Recorded Sessions. Edited and with an introduction by Robert H. Hethmon; preface by Burgess Meredith. New York: Theatre Communications Group, 1991; (5th Printing), 2000.

Suzuki, Tadashi. *The Way of Acting*. New York: Theatre Communications Group, 1986.

Thomson, Virgil. *Music with Words: A Composer's View*. New Haven, CT: Yale University Press, 1989.

———. *Virgil Thomson: An Autobiography*. New York: A. A. Knopf, 1996.

Traubner, Richard. *Operetta: A Theatrical History*. Revised ed. New York: Routledge, 2001.

Valgemae, Mardi. *Accelerated Grimace: Expressionism in the American Drama of the 1920s*. Preface by Harry T. Moore. Carbondale and Edwardsville, IL: Southern Illinois University Press, 1972.

Warrack, John and Ewan West. *The Oxford Dictionary of Opera*. New York: Oxford University Press, 1992.

Wood, Melusine. *Historical Dances, 12th to 19th Century: Their Manner of Performance and Their Place in the Social Life of the Time*. Princeton, NJ: Princeton Book Company Publishers, 1982.

Yon, Jean-Claude. *Jacques Offenbach*. Paris: Gallimard, 2000.

Index of People

Brooks, Mel, 5, 53, 219,
214, 233
The Producers
(musical), 53, 214
Young Frankenstein
(musical), 53, 214,
356
Brown, Clive, 21
*Classical and Romantic
Performing
Practice: 1750–1900*
(book), 21
Brown, Jason Robert, 53
Parade (musical), 53
Brown, Lew, 128
Brown, Margaret "Molly,"
332
Brown, William F., 351
Bruch, Max, 53, 153, 180,
307
Die Loreley (The
Loreley) (opera), 53
Bruckner, Anton, 276
Bruneau, Alfred, 11, 53
L'attaque du moulin
(The Attack on the
Mill) (opera), 53
Brunswick [pen name of
librettist Léon Lévy],
266
Bryan, David, 322
The Toxic Avenger (rock
musical), 322
Brynner, Yul, 175
as the King of Siam in
The King and I
(musical), 175
Bucchino, John, 64
A Catered Affair
(musical), 64
Büchner, Georg, 103
Woyzeck (play), 103
Buck, Christopher, 345
Bulwer-Lytton, Edward,
34
Bunn, Alfred, 44, 207
Burgess, Anthony, 82

Burke, Billie, 360
Burke, Joe, 290
Burnand, Sir Francis
Cowley, 54, 275
Burnett, Carol, 290
Burnett, Frances Hodgson,
293
Burns, Robert, 298
Burton, Montague
Maurice, 122
Burton, Richard, 59
in *Camelot* (musical), 59
Burton, Tim, 311
Busenello, Gian
Francesco, 160
Busenello, Giovanni, 65
Busoni, Ferruccio, 55,
109, 328, 348
Doktor Faust (opera),
55, 109
Turandot (opera), 328
Byron, H. J., 56

Caesar, Irving, 153, 235
Caesar, Sid, 191
Cagney, James, 73
Cahn, Sammy, 98, 318
Cahusac, Jean-Louis de,
356
Caldara, Antonio, 58
La clemenza di Tito
(Titus's Clemency)
(opera), 58, 72
Callas, Maria, 212, 213,
339
master classes at
Juilliard, 212, 213
Calloway III, Cabell
"Cab," 36, 168
Calvi, Gérard, 264
La Plume De Ma Tante
(revue), 264
Calzabigi, Ranieri de', 8,
247
Cammarano, Salvadore,
59, 195, 216, 327, 339
Campbell, Mark, 230

Cantor, Eddie, 36
Čapek, Karel, 166
Carmines, Reverend Al,
Jr., 63
Carr, Frank Osmond, 63
His Excellency (comic
opera), 63
Carré, Albert, 28
Carré, Michel, 26, 63, 76,
109, 135, 211, 219
Carroll, Earl, 98
Earl Carroll Vanities
(revues), 19, 98,
183
Caryll, Ivan, 64, 66, 102,
125, 286, 300
Caruso, Enrico, 170, 210,
252, 348
as Eléazar in *La Juive*
(The Jewess)
(opera), 170
as Canio in *Pagliacci*
(Clowns) (opera),
252
Casey, Warren, 138
Catherine the Great,
Czarina of Russia, 125
Catullus, 248
Cavalli, Pietro Francesco,
65, 89
La Calisto (opera), 65
Didone (Dido) (opera),
89
Cellier, Alfred, 65–66,
125, 275
Dorothy (comic opera),
65–66, 125
The Mountebanks
(comic opera), 66
Cellier, François, 66
Cervantes, Miguel de, 44,
205
Chabrier, Emmanuel, 66,
102
L'étoile (The Star)
(comic opera), 66,
102, 286, 335

About the Author

Robert Blumenfeld is the author of *Accents: A Manual for Actors* (Revised and Expanded Edition, 2002); *Acting with the Voice: The Art of Recording Books* (2004); *Tools and Techniques for Character Interpretation: A Handbook of Psychology for Actors, Writers, and Directors* (2006); *Using the Stanislavsky System: A Practical Guide to Character Creation and Period Styles* (2008); *Blumenfeld's Dictionary of Acting and Show Business* (2009); and the collaborator with noted teacher, acting coach, and actress Alice Spivak on the writing of her book *How to Rehearse When There Is No Rehearsal: Acting and the Media* (2007)—all published by Limelight Editions.

He lives and works as an actor, dialect coach, and writer in New York City, and is a longtime member of Equity, AFTRA, SAG, and the Dramatists Guild. He has worked in numerous regional and New York theaters as well as in television and independent films. He did an Off-Broadway season of six Gilbert and Sullivan comic operas for Dorothy Raedler's American Savoyards (under the name Robert Fields), for which he played the Lord Chancellor in Iolanthe and other patter-song roles. In 1994 he performed in Michael John LaChiusa's musical *The Petrified Prince*, directed by Harold Prince at the New York Shakespeare Festival's Public Theater. He created the roles of the Marquess of Queensberry and two prosecuting attorneys in Moisés Kaufman's Off-Broadway hit play *Gross Indecency: The Three Trials of Oscar Wilde*; he was the production's dialect coach, a job he also did for the Broadway musicals *Saturday Night Fever* and *The Scarlet Pimpernel* (third version and national tour) and for the New York workshop of David Henry Hwang's rewritten version of Rodgers and Hammerstein's *Flower Drum Song*. At the Manhattan School of Music, he was dialect coach for Dona D. Vaughn's production of Strauss's *Die Fledermaus* (2009), and for Jay Lesenger's production of Weill's *Street Scene* (2008), which he also coached for Mr. Lesenger at the Chautauqua Opera.

Mr. Blumenfeld has recorded more than 325 Talking Books for the American Foundation for the Blind, including the complete Sherlock Holmes canon and a bilingual edition of Samuel Beckett's *Waiting for Godot*. He received the 1997 Canadian National Institute for the Blind's Torgi Award for the Talking Book of the Year in the Fiction category, for his recording of Pat Conroy's *Beach Music*, and won the 1999 Alexander Scourby Talking Book Narrator of the Year Award in the Fiction category. He holds a B.A. in French from Rutgers University and an M.A. from Columbia University in French language and literature.